AQA Life and Enviro Sciences for Combined Science: Synergy

Message from AQA

This textbook has been approved by AQA for use with our qualification. This means that we have checked that it broadly covers the specification and we are satisfied with the overall quality. Full details of our approval process can be found on our website.

We approve textbooks because we know how important it is for teachers and students to have the right resources to support their teaching and learning. However, the publisher is ultimately responsible for the editorial control and quality of this book.

Please note that when teaching the *AQA GCSE Combined Science: Synergy* course, you must refer to AQA's specification as your definitive source of information. While this book has been written to match the specification, it cannot provide complete coverage of every aspect of the course.

A wide range of other useful resources can be found on the relevant subject pages of our website: www.aqa.org.uk.

Ann Fullick
Lawrie Ryan
Jim Breithaupt
Editor: Lawrie Ryan

OXFORD
UNIVERSITY PRESS

Great Clarendon Street, Oxford, OX2 6DP, United Kingdom

Oxford University Press is a department of the University of Oxford. It furthers the University's objective of excellence in research, scholarship, and education by publishing worldwide. Oxford is a registered trade mark of Oxford University Press in the UK and in certain other countries.

© Ann Fullick, Lawrie Ryan, Jim Breithaupt 2016

The moral rights of the authors have been asserted.

First published in 2016.

All rights reserved. No part of this publication may be reproduced, stored in a retrieval system, or transmitted, in any form or by any means, without the prior permission in writing of Oxford University Press, or as expressly permitted by law, by licence or under terms agreed with the appropriate reprographics rights organization. Enquiries concerning reproduction outside the scope of the above should be sent to the Rights Department, Oxford University Press, at the address above.

You must not circulate this work in any other form and you must impose this same condition on any acquirer.

British Library Cataloguing in Publication Data
Data available

978 0 19 839590 4

10 9 8 7 6 5 4 3 2

Paper used in the production of this book is a natural, recyclable product made from wood grown in sustainable forests. The manufacturing process conforms to the environmental regulations of the country of origin.

Printed in Great Britain by CPI Anthony Rowe

Ann would like to thank her husband Tony for his constant calm support and encouragement, his fantastic photos, and the wonderful distraction of their wedding. She would also like to thank their five sons, William, Thomas, James, Edward, and Chris for providing expert advice and a lot of fun throughout the project.

Lawrie would like to thank the following people for their help and support in producing this Student Book. Each one has added value to my initial efforts: Sally Jennings, Annie Hamblin, Sadie Garratt, Emma-Leigh Craig, Amie Hewish, Andy Chandler-Grevatt.

Jim would also like to thank Marie Breithaupt, Darren Forbes, and all the OUP editorial team named above for their help and support in producing this Student Book.

Practice questions prepared by Andy Austin, Liz Brennan, and Michelle Oldfield.

AQA examination questions are reproduced by permission of AQA.

Index compiled by Simon Yapp (through INDEXING SPECIALISTS (UK) Ltd.), 35 Old Shoreham Road, Brighton, BN1 5DQ United Kingdom.

COVER: Steve Gschmeissner/Science Photo Library
p2-3: Alfred Pasieka/Science Photo Library; **p4**: Wavebreakmedia/Shutterstock; **p12**: Andrew Lambert Photography/Science Photo Library; **p15**: Harvey Fitzhugh/Shutterstock; **p18**: Anne Gilbert/Alamy Stock Photo; **p22**: Science Photo Library; **p32**: Gerd Guenther/Science Photo Library; **p33**: Adrian T Sumner/Science Photo Library; **p34**: Jack Bostrack, Visuals Unlimited/Science Photo Library; **p35(L)**: Steve Gschmeissner/Science Photo Library; **p35(R)**: John Durham/Science Photo Library; **p39**: Dr R. Dourmashkin/Science Photo Library; **p42(L)**: Michael Abbey/Science Photo Library; **P42(R)**: Michael Abbey/Science Photo Library; **p45**: Anthony Short; **p46** CNRI/Science Photo Library; **p48(T)**: William Perugini/Shutterstock; **p48(B)**: Deva Studio/Shutterstock; **p51**: Eye of Science/Science Photo Library; **p54**: HighTide/Shutterstock; **p64(T)**: DeepGreen/Shutterstock; **p64(B)**: Christian Delbert/Shutterstock; **p66**: US Air Force/Micaiah Anthony/Science Photo Library; **p67**: Martyn F. Chillmaid/Science Photo Library; **p68(T)**: AJ Photo/Hop Americain/Science Photo Library; **p68(B)**: Wang Song/Shutterstock; **p69**: CNRI/Science Photo Library; **p73**: C.T.R. Wilson/Science Photo Library; **p74-75**: EcoPrint/Shutterstock; **p77**: Nancy Bauer/Shutterstock; **p78**: Liquorice Legs/Shutterstock; **p79(T)**: Anthony Short; **p79(B)**: Anthony Short; **p82**: St Bartholomew's Hospital/Science Photo Library; **p83**: National Cancer Institute/Science Photo Library; **p90(L)**: JPC-PROD/Shutterstock; **p90(R)**: Evgenia Sh./Shutterstock; **p91**: Africa Studio/Shutterstock; **p93**: ISM/Science Photo Library; **p94(T)**: Daxiao Productions/Shutterstock; **p94(B)**: Anthony Short; **p96**: Tony Wear/Shutterstock; **p98**: Rawpixel/Shutterstock; **p99**: Sarah2/Shutterstock; **p106**: Kansak Buranapreecha/Shutterstock; **p108**: Biodisc, Visuals Unlimited/Science Photo Library; **p109**: Anthony Short; **p110**: Welcomia/Shutterstock; **p112**: Anthony Short; **p114**: Mllevphoto/iStockphoto; **p115**: Dasha Petrenko/Shutterstock; **p118**: Lukasz Szwaj/Shutterstock; **p119**: Ngataringa/iStockphoto; **p120**: Norm Thomas/Science Photo Library; **p121(T)**: Anthony Short; **p121(B)**: Anthony Short; **p122**: Jamie Farrant/iStockphoto; **p124**: Martin Shields/Science Photo Library; **p129** Peter Jeffreys/Shutterstock; **p130-131**: Pavel Kubarkov/Shutterstock; **p142(L)**: Medical-on-Line/Alamy; **p142(R)**: Steve Allen/Science Photo Library; **p145(T)**: Science Photo Library; **p145(B)**: Sean Dempsey/PA Archive/Press Association Images; **p146(T)**: J. Helgason/Shutterstock; **p146(B)**: Marek Velechovsky/Shutterstock; **p147**: Manzrussali/Shutterstock; **p150**: Image Point Fr/Shutterstock; **p151**: Fotopool/Shutterstock; **p154**: Prof. P. Motta/ Dept. of Anatomy/University "La Sapienza", Rome/Science Photo Library; **p156**: JPC-PROD/Shutterstock; **p172**: Martyn F. Chillmaid/Science Photo Library; **p173**: SvedOliver/Shutterstock; **p175**: Anthony Short; **p176**: Simon Fraser/Royal Victoria Infirmary, Newcastle upon Tyne/Science Photo Library; **p178**: Nature's Geometry/Science Photo Library; **p179**: CDC/Science Photo Library; **p180**: Mark Thomas/Science Photo Library; **p181**: CDC/Science Photo Library; **p182**: Lowell Georgia/Science Photo Library; **p184**: Sergiy Zavgorodny/Shutterstock; **p186(T)**: Prof. P. Motta/Dept. of Anatomy/University "La Sapienza", Rome/Science Photo Library; **p186(B)**: Steve Gschmeissner/Science Photo Library; **p188**: Valeriya Anufriyeva/Shutterstock; **p190**: Paul Whitehill/Science Photo Library; **p191**: CC Studio/Science Photo Library; **p192(T)**: Sigrid Gombert/Cultura/ Science Photo Library; **p192(B)**: Anthony Short; **p194**: Sherry Yates Young/Shutterstock; **p195**: Ivan Nakonechnyy/Shutterstock; **p196**: Li Wa/Shutterstock; **p197**: Cordelia Molloy/Science Photo Library; **p199**: Julian Finney/Getty Images; **p202**: Africa Studio/Shutterstock; **p204-205**: Anthony Short; **p206(T)**: Rainer Albiez/Shutterstock; **p206(B)**: NASA/Science Photo Library; **p207**: David Seymour/123RF; **p208**: Martin Kunzel/123RF; **p210**: Anthony Short; **p211**: Anthony Short; **p212(T)**: Anthony Short; **p212(B)**: Gadag/Shutterstock; **p213**: Coxy58/Shutterstock; **p221**: Anthony Short; **p223(T)**: Gemphoto/Shutterstock; **p223(B)**: Kzenon/Shutterstock; **p225**: irabel8/Shutterstock; **p226**: Worker/Shutterstock; **p228**: Antikainen/iStockphoto; **p229**: Sigur/Shutterstock; **p232(L)**: Jamesdavidphoto/Shutterstock; **p232(R)**: Ikordela/Shutterstock; **p233(L)**: Fotos593/Shutterstock; **p233**: Anthony Short; **p234(T)**: Corbis; **p234(CT)**: Martin Fowler/Shutterstock; **p234(CB)**: Chris2766/Shutterstock; **p234(B)**: Peter Louwers/Shutterstock; **p236(T)**: Dennis W. Donohue/Shutterstock; **p236(B)**: Anthony Short; **p237(T)**: Anthony Short; **p237(B)**: Menno Schaefer/Shutterstock; **p238(T)**: Leungchopan/Shutterstock; **p238(B)**: Anthony Short; **p239(T)**: Anthony Short; **p239(B)**: Hintau Aliaksei/Shutterstock; **p240**: Anthony Short; **p241(T)**: Solarseven/Shutterstock; **p241(B)**: Smirnova Irina/Shutterstock; **p242**: Martyn F. Chillmaid/Science Photo Library; **p243**: Anthony Short; **p244(T)**: Anthony Short; **p244(B)**: Anthony Short; **p245**: Anthony Short; **p247**: Anthony Short; **p248(T)**: CNES, 2002 Distribution Spot Image/Science Photo Library; **p248(B)**: Kate Capture/Shutterstock; **p249**: Anthony Short; **p251**: Michael Marten/Science Photo Library; **p252(T)**: Anthony Short; **p252(B)**: Aleksander Bolbot/Shutterstock; **p256**: Lawrence Berkeley National Laboratory/Science Photo Library; **p258**: Floris Slooff/Shutterstock; **p262**: Erik Lam/Shutterstock; **p263**: Diplomedia/Shutterstock; **p264(L)**: 135pixels/Shutterstock; **p264(R)**: Anthony Short; **p266(T)**: Anthony Short; **p266(B)**: Hxdbzxy/Shutterstock; **p267**: Nattanan726/Shutterstock; **p268**: Ria Novosti/Science Photo Library; **p269**: John Reader/Science Photo Library; **p272(L)**: Bildagentur Zoonar GmbH/Shutterstock; **p272(R)**: Rasmus Holmboe Dahl/Shutterstock; **p273(T)**: Monkey Business Images/Shutterstock; **p273(C)**: Nicholas Lee/Shutterstock; **p273(B)**: Anthony Short; **p274(T)**: Bridgeman Images; **p274(C)**: Sally Jennings; **p274(B)**: Andyworks/iStockphoto; **p275**: Henk Bentlage/Shutterstock; **p277**: Panda3800/Shutterstock; **p279(L)**: Madlen/Shutterstock; **p279(R)**: Zcw/Shutterstock; **p282(T)**: Sebastian Kaulitzki/Shutterstock; **p282(B)**: isak55/Shutterstock; **p283**: Phattana Stock/Shutterstock; **p288(T)**: Roberto Piras/Shutterstock; **p288(B)**: Wacomka/Shutterstock; **p289**: Becris/Shutterstock; **p291**: Nomad_Soul/Shutterstock; **p294**: SpeedKingz/Shutterstock; **p296**: Richard Bowden/Shutterstock; **p297(T)**: Ozgurdonmaz/iStockphoto; **p297(B)**: Locrifa/Shutterstock; **p300**: Cavallini James/BSIP/Science Photo Library; **p304(T)**: Runi/Shutterstock; **p304(B)**: Michael J Thompson/Shutterstock; **p305**: Anntto/Shutterstock; **p306**: Kletr/Shutterstock; **p307**: Alexei Novikov/Shutterstock; **p308**: Hxdbzxy/Shutterstock; **p309**: Anthony Short

Contents

This book has been written for the *Life and Environmental Sciences* section of the *AQA GCSE Combined Science: Synergy* course.
Higher-Tier content is formatted in **bold** in the contents list below.

Required practicals	vi
How to use this book	vii
Kerboodle	ix
Introduction to *AQA GCSE Combined Science: Synergy*	x

1 Building blocks — 2

Chapter 1.1 States of matter — 4
- 1.1.1 Matter and particles — 4
- 1.1.2 Density — 6
- 1.1.3 Gas pressure and temperature — 8
- 1.1.4 Changes of state — 10
- 1.1.5 Internal energy — 12
- 1.1.6 Specific heat capacity — 14
- 1.1.7 Specific latent heat — 16
- 1.1.8 Pure substances and mixtures — 18
- 1.1 Summary questions — 20
- 1.1 Practice questions — 21

Chapter 1.2 Atomic structure — 22
- 1.2.1 Scientific models of the atom — 22
- 1.2.2 Sub-atomic particles — 24
- 1.2.3 Size of atoms, and isotopes — 26
- 1.2.4 Electronic structures — 28
- 1.2 Summary questions — 30
- 1.2 Practice questions — 31

Chapter 1.3 Cells in animals and plants — 32
- 1.3.1 The world of the microscope — 32
- 1.3.2 Animal and plant cells — 34
- 1.3.3 Eukaryotic and prokaryotic cells — 36
- 1.3.4 Diffusion — 38
- 1.3.5 Osmosis — 40
- 1.3.6 Osmosis in plants — 42
- 1.3.7 Active transport — 44
- 1.3.8 Cell division — 46
- 1.3.9 Differentiation and stem cells — 48
- 1.3.10 Cell division in sexual reproduction — 50
- 1.3 Summary questions — 52
- 1.3 Practice questions — 53

Chapter 1.4 Waves — 54
- 1.4.1 The nature of waves — 54
- 1.4.2 The properties of waves — 56
- 1.4.3 Electromagnetic waves — 58
- 1.4.4 **Reflection and refraction** — 60
- 1.4.5 Light, infrared, microwaves, and radio waves — 62
- 1.4.6 Communications — 64
- 1.4.7 Ultraviolet waves, X-rays, and gamma rays — 66
- 1.4.8 X-rays in medicine — 68
- 1.4 Summary questions — 70
- 1.4 Practice questions — 71
- Unit 1 in context: Development of the nuclear model of the atom — 72

2 Transport over larger distances — 74

Chapter 2.5 Systems in the human body — 76
- 2.5.1 Aerobic respiration — 76
- 2.5.2 Anaerobic respiration — 78
- 2.5.3 Exchanging materials — 80
- 2.5.4 The blood — 82
- 2.5.5 The blood vessels — 84
- 2.5.6 The heart — 86
- 2.5.7 Breathing and gas exchange — 88
- 2.5.8 The chemistry of food — 90
- 2.5.9 How the digestive system works — 92
- 2.5.10 The human nervous system — 94
- 2.5.11 Reflex actions — 96
- 2.5.12 Principles of hormonal control — 98
- 2.5.13 **The role of negative feedback** — 100
- 2.5 Summary questions — 102
- 2.5 Practice questions — 103

Chapter 2.6 Plants and photosynthesis — 104
- 2.6.1 Specialised plant cells — 104
- 2.6.2 Plant tissues and organs — 106
- 2.6.3 Meristems and plant cloning — 108
- 2.6.4 Evaporation and transpiration — 110
- 2.6.5 Factors affecting transpiration — 112
- 2.6.6 Photosynthesis — 114
- 2.6.7 The rate of photosynthesis — 116
- 2.6.8 **Making the most of photosynthesis** — 118
- 2.6.9 Plant diseases — 120
- 2.6.10 Chlorophyll and chromatography — 122
- 2.6.11 Analysing chromatograms — 124
- 2.6 Summary questions — 126
- 2.6 Practice questions — 127
- Unit 2 in context: Fighting fungi — 128

3 Interactions with the environment 130

Chapter 3.7 Lifestyle and health 132
3.7.1 Health and disease 132
3.7.2 Non-communicable diseases 134
3.7.3 Smoking and the risk of disease 136
3.7.4 Diet, exercise, and disease 138
3.7.5 Alcohol and other carcinogens 140
3.7.6 Helping the heart 142
3.7.7 Replacing the heart 144
3.7.8 Principles of homeostasis 146
3.7.9 The control of blood glucose levels 148
3.7.10 Treating diabetes 150
3.7.11 Human reproduction 152
3.7.12 **Hormones and the menstrual cycle** 154
3.7.13 Contraception 156
3.7.14 **Infertility treatments** 158
3.7 Summary questions 160
3.7 Practice questions 161

Chapter 3.8 Radiation and risk 162
3.8.1 Atoms and radiation 162
3.8.2 Radioactivity 164
3.8.3 Nuclear changes 166
3.8.4 Half-life 168
3.8.5 Properties of radiation 170
3.8.6 Radiation hazards 172
3.8.7 Cancer 174
3.8 Summary questions 176
3.8 Practice questions 177

Chapter 3.9 Preventing, treating, and curing diseases 178
3.9.1 Pathogens and disease 178
3.9.2 Preventing infections 180
3.9.3 Viral diseases 182
3.9.4 Bacterial diseases 184
3.9.5 Human defence responses 186
3.9.6 Vaccination 188
3.9.7 Antibiotics and painkillers 190
3.9.8 Testing new medical drugs 192
3.9.9 Genetic modification and medicine 194
3.9.10 Stem cells in medicine 196
3.9.11 Stem cell dilemmas 198
3.9 Summary questions 200
3.9 Practice questions 201
Unit 3 in context: Pig-to-human transplants – a step too far? 202

4 Explaining change 204

Chapter 4.10 The Earth's atmosphere 206
4.10.1 History of the Earth's atmosphere 206
4.10.2 The Earth's evolving atmosphere 208
4.10.3 Material recycling 210
4.10.4 The carbon cycle 212
4.10.5 The greenhouse effect 214
4.10.6 Analysing the evidence 216
4.10.7 The impacts of climate change 218
4.10.8 Mitigating climate change 220
4.10.9 Atmospheric pollutants 222
4.10.10 The water cycle 224
4.10.11 Potable water 226
4.10.12 Treating waste water 228
4.10 Summary questions 230
4.10 Practice questions 231

Chapter 4.11 Ecosystems and biodiversity 232
4.11.1 Organisation in ecosystems 232
4.11.2 Feeding relationships 234
4.11.3 Factors affecting communities 236
4.11.4 Competition in animals 238
4.11.5 Competition in plants 240
4.11.6 Field investigations 242
4.11.7 Biodiversity 244
4.11.8 Human factors affecting biodiversity 246
4.11.9 Deforestation and peat destruction 248
4.11.10 Land and water pollution 250
4.11.11 Positive human impacts on ecosystems 252
4.11 Summary questions 254
4.11 Practice questions 255

Chapter 4.12 Inheritance, variation, and evolution 256
4.12.1 DNA and the genome 256
4.12.2 Inheritance in action 258
4.12.3 More about genetics 260
4.12.4 Variation 262
4.12.5 Evolution by natural selection 264
4.12.6 Evolution in action 266
4.12.7 Fossil evidence for evolution 268
4.12.8 More evidence for evolution 270
4.12.9 Classification systems 272
4.12.10 Selective breeding 274
4.12.11 Genetic engineering 276
4.12.12 Ethics of genetic technologies 278
4.12 Summary questions 280
4.12 Practice questions 281
Unit 4 in context: Gene technologies 282

| Further practice questions | 284 |

Maths skills for Synergy — 288

MS 1	Arithmetic and numerical computation	288
MS 2	Handling data	293
MS 3	Algebra	300
MS 4	Data and graphs	301
MS 5	Geometry and trigonometry	303

Working scientifically for Synergy — 305

WS 1	Development of scientific thinking	305
WS 2	Experimental skills and strategies	305
WS 3	Analysis and evaluation	308

Glossary	312
Index	318
Appendix: Physics equations	323

Required practicals

Practical work is a vital part of science, helping to support and apply your scientific knowledge, and develop your investigative and practical skills. As part of the *Life and Environmental Sciences* section of your *GCSE Combined Science: Synergy* course, there are 12 Required practicals that you must carry out. Questions in your exams could draw on any of the knowledge and skills you have developed in carrying out these practicals.

A Required practical feature box has been included in this Student Book for each of your Required practicals. Further support is available on Kerboodle.

	Required practical	Topic
1	Measuring the density of a solid object Measuring the density of a liquid	1.1.2
2	Measuring specific heat capacity	1.1.6
3	Looking at cells	1.3.2
4	Investigating osmosis in plant cells	1.3.6
5	Measuring the speed of ripples Investigating waves on a stretched string	1.4.2
6	Testing absorption and emission of infrared radiation by different surfaces	1.4.5
7	Food tests	2.5.8
8	Measuring reaction times	2.5.10
9	Chromatography and finding R_f values	2.6.11
10	Light intensity and rate of photosynthesis	2.6.7
11	Analysis and purification of water samples	4.10.11
12	Measuring population size and using sampling techniques to investigate the effect of a factor on the distribution of a species	4.11.6

How to use this book

Learning objectives
- Learning objectives at the start of each spread tell you the content that you will cover.
- Any outcomes marked with the Higher Tier icon ⓗ are for students sitting the Higher Tier exams.

This book has been written by subject experts to match the new 2016 specifications. It is packed full of features to help you prepare for your course and achieve the very best you can.

Key words are highlighted in the text. You can look them up in the glossary at the back of the book if you are not sure what they mean.

Many diagrams are as important for your understanding as the text, so make sure you revise them carefully.

Synoptic link
Synoptic links show how the content of a topic links to other parts of the course. This will support you with the synoptic element of your assessment.

There are also links to the Maths skills for Synergy chapter, so that you can develop your maths skills whilst you study.

Practical
Practicals are a great way for you to see science in action for yourself. These boxes may be a simple introduction or reminder, or they may be the basis for a practical in the classroom. They will help your understanding of the course.

Required practical
These practicals have important skills that you will need to be confident with for part of your assessment. Your teacher will give you additional information about tackling these practicals.

Study tip
Hints giving you advice on things you need to know and remember, and what to watch out for.

Anything in the Higher Tier spreads and boxes must be learnt by those sitting the Higher Tier exam. If you will be sitting Foundation Tier, you will not be assessed on this content.

Go further
Go further boxes encourage you to think about the science you have learnt in a different context, and introduce you to science beyond the specification. You do not need to learn any of the content in a Go further box.

Using maths
This feature highlights and explains the key maths skills you need. There are also clear step-by-step worked examples.

Summary questions
Each topic has summary questions. These questions give you the chance to test whether you have learnt and understood everything in the topic. The questions start off easier and get harder, so that you can stretch yourself.

The literacy pen icon ✒ shows questions that help you to develop your literacy skills.

Any questions marked with the Higher Tier icon ⓗ are for students sitting the Higher Tier exams.

Key points
- Linking to the Learning objectives, the Key points boxes summarise what you should be able to do at the end of the topic. They can be used to help you with revision.
- Any Key points marked with the Higher Tier icon ⓗ are for students sitting the Higher Tier exams.

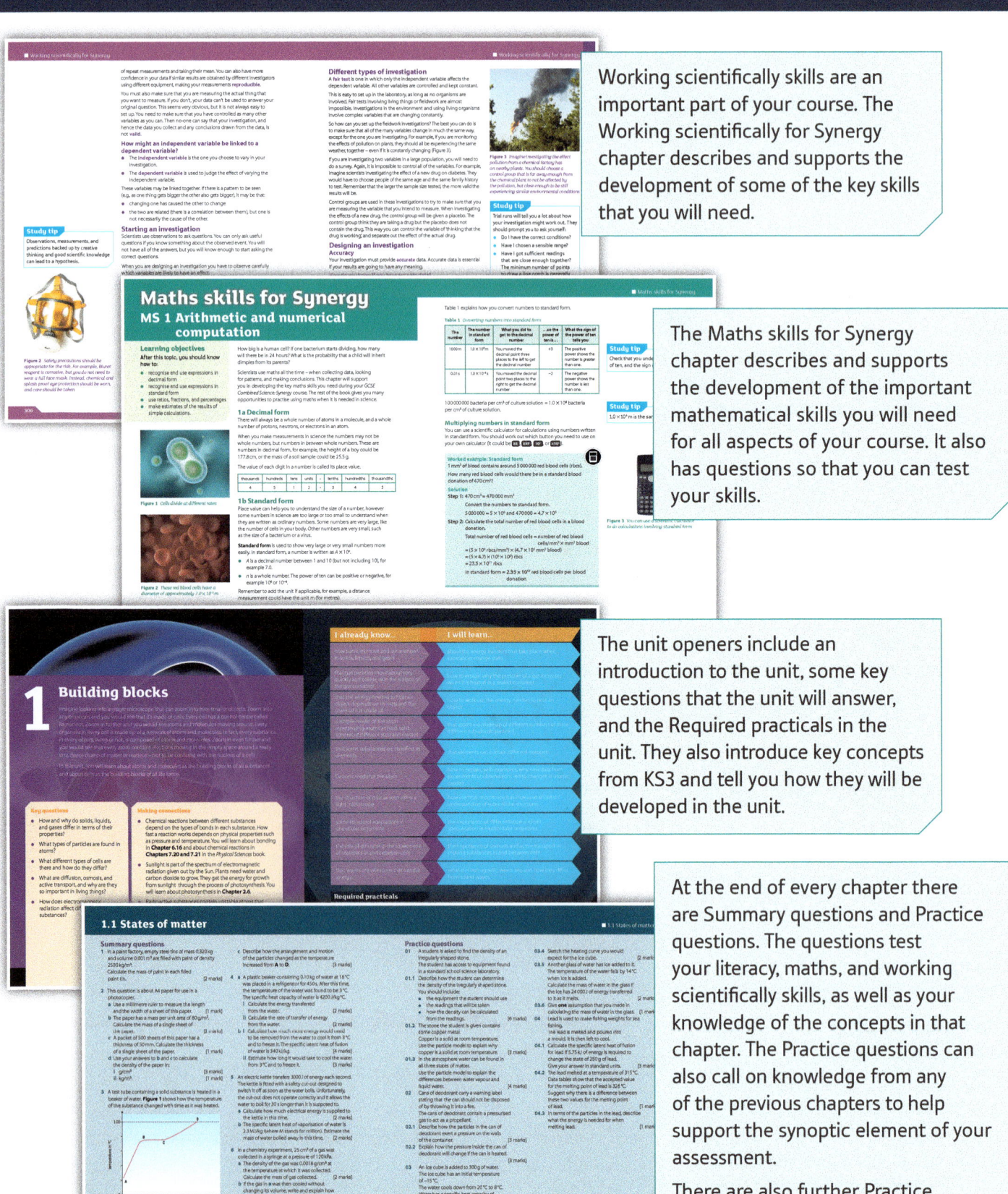

Kerboodle

This book is also supported by Kerboodle, offering unrivalled digital support for building your practical, maths, and literacy skills.

If your school subscribes to Kerboodle, you will find a wealth of additional resources to help you with your studies and revision:

- animations, videos, and revision podcasts
- WebQuests
- maths and literacy skills activities and worksheets
- 'on your marks' activities to help you achieve your best
- practicals and follow-up activities
- interactive quizzes that give question-by-question feedback
- self-assessment checklists.

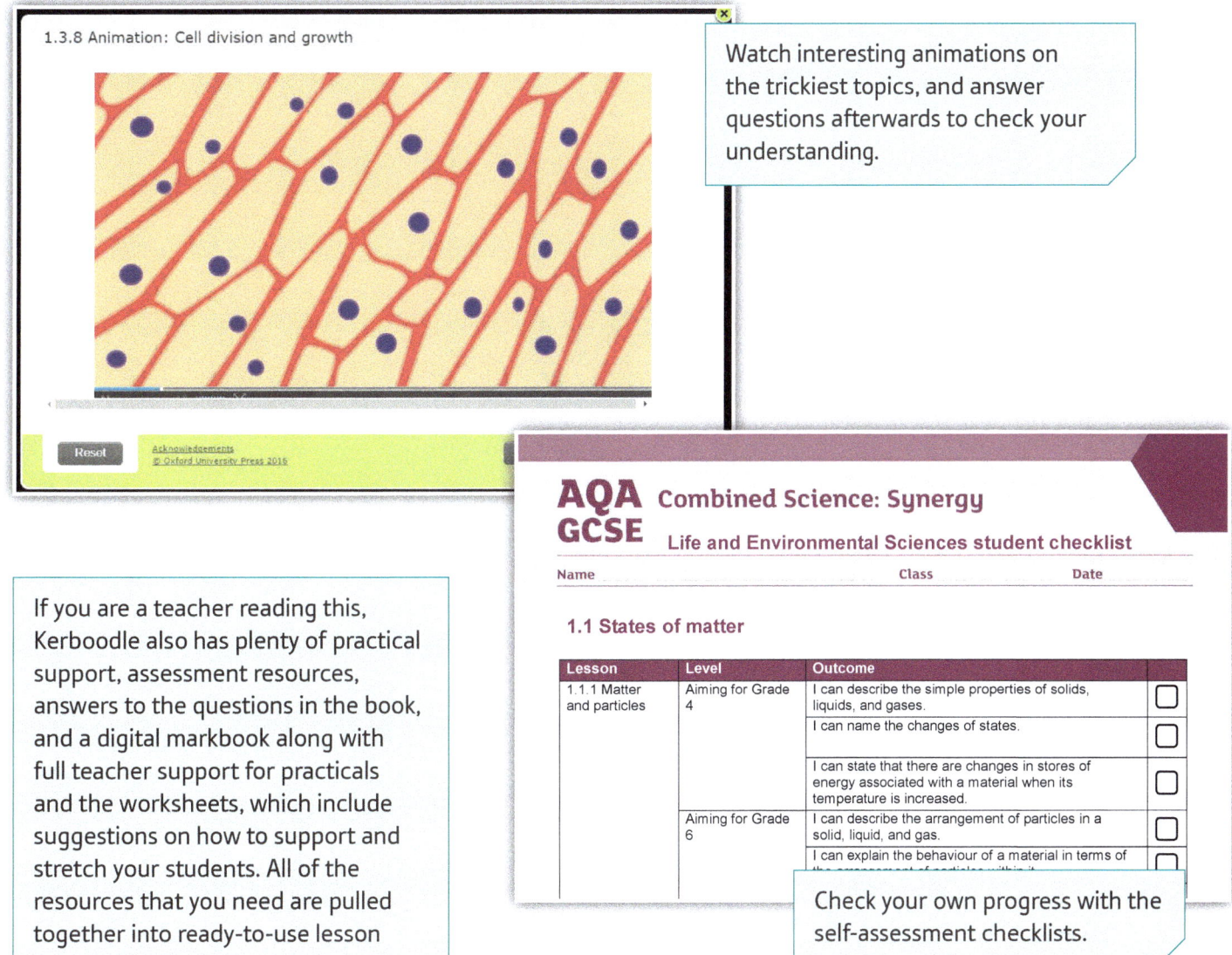

Watch interesting animations on the trickiest topics, and answer questions afterwards to check your understanding.

If you are a teacher reading this, Kerboodle also has plenty of practical support, assessment resources, answers to the questions in the book, and a digital markbook along with full teacher support for practicals and the worksheets, which include suggestions on how to support and stretch your students. All of the resources that you need are pulled together into ready-to-use lesson presentations.

Check your own progress with the self-assessment checklists.

Introduction to AQA GCSE Synergy

This new specification has been designed so that the key scientific concepts are introduced through eight units, split into two sections. The units provide the context for you to gain more experience of the skills needed to work scientifically and to develop your understanding. The two sections are *Life and Environmental Sciences* and *Physical Sciences*, which are covered in separate books. The first section draws its content mainly from biology and the second section from physics and chemistry. However, most of the eight units contain content from more than one area of science, representing an integrated approach.

Learning more about science in this integrated way will help you to make links between concepts across the traditional science subject boundaries of biology, chemistry, and physics. To help you see the links, there are Synoptic link boxes directing you to related topics. As well as this, in the introduction to each unit there is a Making connections feature that outlines the relevance of other parts of the specification to the unit you are about to study.

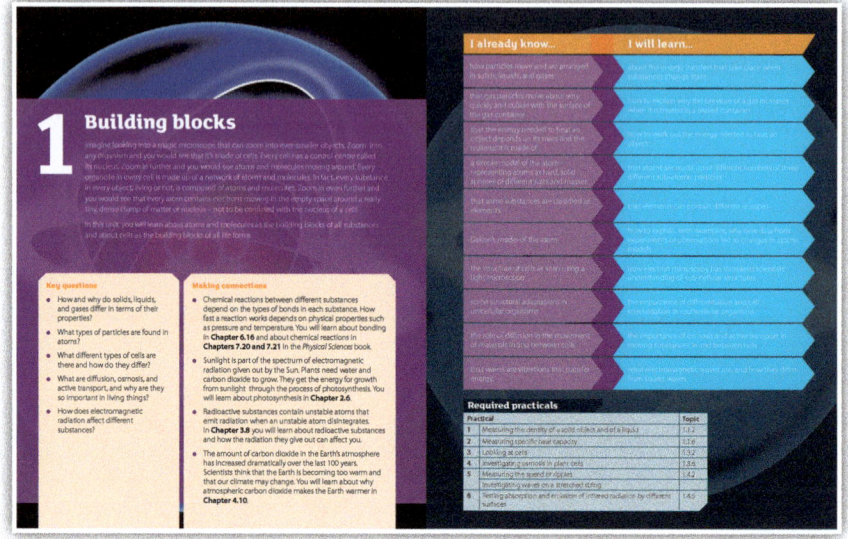

Here is a brief summary of the two *AQA GCSE Combined Science: Synergy* Student Books:

Life and Environmental Sciences (Units 1–4)

- **Unit 1 Building blocks** – explores content ranging from atoms to cells, behaviour, and transport on the small scale.
- **Unit 2 Transport over larger distances** – covers systems in animals and plants, and how these systems interact.
- **Unit 3 Interactions with the environment** – looks at the effects of factors in the environment on organisms, and at how your choices affect your health.
- **Unit 4 Explaining change** – reveals how organisms, species, living systems, and non-living systems change over time.

Physical Sciences (Units 5–8)

- **Unit 5 Building blocks for understanding** – deals with the periodic table of elements and chemical calculations.
- **Unit 6 Interactions over small and large distances** – explores strong and weak forces between atoms, molecules, and larger structures, and how they interact.
- **Unit 7 Movement and interactions** – introduces rates of change of motion and direction of large and small objects, and chemical changes.
- **Unit 8 Guiding Spaceship Earth towards a sustainable future** – focuses on the Earth's resources of materials and energy.

Both sections include topics that draw together and apply key concepts. These are the concepts needed to describe the natural and man-made world.

Examples in *Life and Environmental Sciences* include Chapter 3.8 *Radiation and risk* and Chapter 4.10 *The Earth's atmosphere*. The topics in these chapters use earlier work on atomic structure, waves, and electromagnetic radiation to explain the effects of different types of radiation on human tissues and on the climate.

An example in *Physical Sciences* is Chapter 8.24 *Resources of materials and energy*, which introduces life cycle assessment as a way of evaluating the impacts of using materials and energy to manufacture useful products.

Working scientifically

Working scientifically is the sum of all the activities that scientists do. This includes investigating, observing, experimenting or testing out ideas, and thinking about them. It involves talking, reading, and writing about science as well as actually doing it, and then representing scientific ideas both mathematically and visually through models. The *AQA GCSE Combined Science: Synergy* specification provides you with opportunities to work scientifically throughout the course. There are 21 Required practicals to complete. Questions in the written exams will include techniques used in these Required practicals, plus other 'Working scientifically' skills such as analysis and evaluation.

The unit in context

At the end of each of the eight units you will find a topic of interest that goes beyond the specification but is related to an important concept in that unit. Their titles are:

Development of the nuclear model of the atom

Fighting fungi

Pig-to-human transplants – a step too far?

Gene technologies

Interview with a chemical superhero

Polymer developments

Reaction times

Sustainable fuel

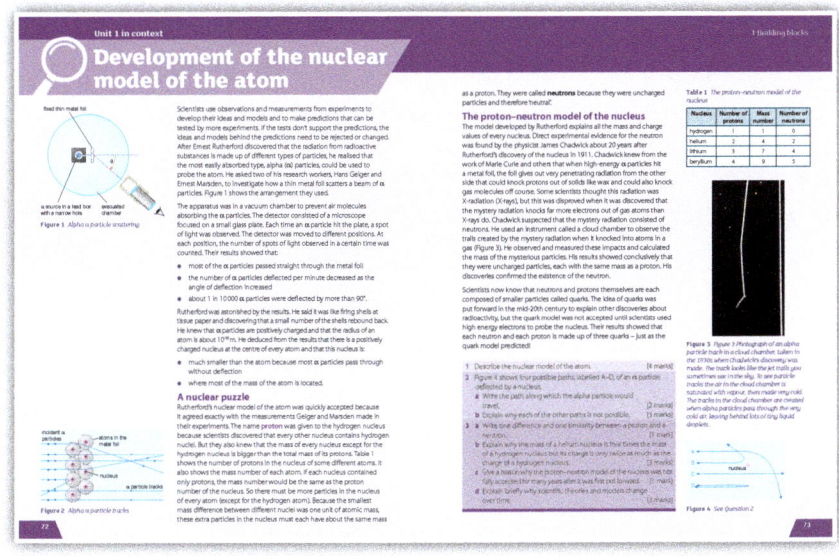

1 Building blocks

Imagine looking into a magic microscope that can zoom into ever-smaller objects. Zoom into any organism and you would see that it's made of cells. Every cell has a control centre called its nucleus. Zoom in further and you would see atoms and molecules moving around. Every organelle in every cell is made up of a network of atoms and molecules. In fact, every substance in every object, living or not, is composed of atoms and molecules. Zoom in even further and you would see that every atom contains electrons moving in the empty space around a really tiny, dense clump of matter or nucleus – not to be confused with the nucleus of a cell!

In this unit, you will learn about atoms and molecules as the building blocks of all substances and about cells as the building blocks of all life forms.

Key questions

- How and why do solids, liquids, and gases differ in terms of their properties?
- What types of particles are found in atoms?
- What different types of cells are there and how do they differ?
- What are diffusion, osmosis, and active transport, and why are they so important in living things?
- How does electromagnetic radiation affect different substances?

Making connections

- Chemical reactions between different substances depend on the types of bonds in each substance. How fast a reaction works depends on physical properties such as pressure and temperature. You will learn about bonding in **Chapter 6.16** and about chemical reactions in **Chapters 7.20 and 7.21** in the *Physical Sciences* book.
- Sunlight is part of the spectrum of electromagnetic radiation given out by the Sun. Plants need water and carbon dioxide to grow. They get the energy for growth from sunlight through the process of photosynthesis. You will learn about photosynthesis in **Chapter 2.6**.
- Radioactive substances contain unstable atoms that emit radiation when an unstable atom disintegrates. In **Chapter 3.8** you will learn about radioactive substances and how the radiation they give out can affect you.
- The amount of carbon dioxide in the Earth's atmosphere has increased dramatically over the last 100 years. Scientists think that the Earth is becoming too warm and that our climate may change. You will learn about why atmospheric carbon dioxide makes the Earth warmer in **Chapter 4.10**.

I already know...	I will learn...
how particles move and are arranged in solids, liquids, and gases	about the energy transfers that take place when substances change state
that gas particles move about very quickly and collide with the surface of the gas container	how to explain why the pressure of a gas increases when it is heated in a sealed container
that the energy needed to heat an object depends on its mass and the material it is made of	how to work out the energy needed to heat an object
a simple model of the atom representing atoms as hard, solid spheres of different sizes and masses	that atoms are made up of different numbers of three different sub-atomic particles
that some substances are classified as elements	that elements can contain different isotopes
Dalton's model of the atom	how to explain, with examples, why new data from experiments or observations led to changes in atomic models
the structure of cells as seen using a light microscope	how electron microscopy has increased scientists' understanding of sub-cellular structures
some structural adaptations in unicellular organisms	the importance of differentiation and cell specialisation in multicellular organisms
the role of diffusion in the movement of materials in and between cells	the importance of osmosis and active transport in moving substances in and between cells
that waves are vibrations that transfer energy.	what electromagnetic waves are, and how they differ from sound waves.

Required practicals

Practical		Topic
1	Measuring the density of a solid object and of a liquid	1.1.2
2	Measuring specific heat capacity	1.1.6
3	Looking at cells	1.3.2
4	Investigating osmosis in plant cells	1.3.6
5	Measuring the speed of ripples	1.4.2
	Investigating waves on a stretched string	
6	Testing absorption and emission of infrared radiation by different surfaces	1.4.5

1.1 States of matter
1.1.1 Matter and particles

Learning objectives
After this topic, you should know:
- the different properties of solids, liquids, and gases
- the arrangement and motion of particles in a solid, a liquid, and a gas
- the difference between a physical change and a chemical change
- Ⓗ the limitations of the simple particle model.

Everything around you is made up of matter and exists in one of three states – **solid**, **liquid**, or **gas** (Figure 1). Table 1 summarises the main differences between the three states of matter.

Table 1 *Differences between the three states of matter*

State	Flow	Shape	Volume	Density
solid	no	fixed	fixed	much higher than a gas
liquid	yes	fits container shape	fixed	much higher than a gas
gas	yes	fills container	can be changed	lower than a solid or a liquid

Change of state
A substance can change from one state to another. For example:

- when water in a kettle boils, the water turns into steam. Steam (also called water vapour) is water in its gaseous state
- when a beaker of water is placed in a freezer, the water cools down and then turns into ice when it freezes
- when solid carbon dioxide (also called dry ice) warms up, the solid turns into gas directly
- when steam touches a cold surface, the steam condenses and turns into water.

Changes of state are examples of physical changes because no new substances are produced. In a chemical change the substances react and form new substances.

Figure 1 *Spot the three states of matter*

Changing state
Heat some water in a beaker using a Bunsen burner (Figure 2).
- Steam (vapour) leaves the surface of the water before the water boils.
- When the water boils, bubbles of vapour form inside the water and rise to the surface to release steam.

Switch the Bunsen burner off and hold a cold beaker or cold metal object above the boiling water. Observe the condensation of steam from the boiling water on the cold object.

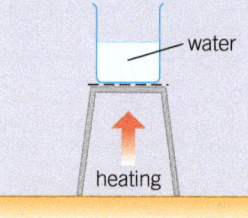

Figure 2 *Heating water to show a change of state*

Safety: Take care with boiling water. Wear eye protection.

1.1 States of matter

The kinetic theory of matter

Solids, liquids, and gases are made of particles. Figure 3 shows the arrangement of the particles of a substance in its solid, liquid, and gas states. When the temperature of the substance is increased, the particles move faster.

- The particles of a substance in its solid state are held next to each other in fixed positions. They vibrate about their fixed positions, so the solid keeps its own shape.
- The particles of a substance in its liquid state are in contact with each other. They move about at random. So a liquid doesn't have its own shape, and it can flow.
- The particles of a substance in its gas state move about at random much faster than they do in a liquid. They are, on average, much further apart from each other than the particles of a liquid. So the density of a gas is much less than that of a solid or a liquid.
- The particles of a substance in its solid, liquid, and gas states have different amounts of energy. For a given amount of a substance, its particles have more energy in the gas state than they have in the liquid state, and they have more energy in the liquid state than they have in the solid state.

Higher: Limitations of the simple particle model

A simple particle model in which the particles are considered as solid spheres with no forces between them can only be used to show how the particles are arranged in each state of matter. However, atoms are not solid spheres and they exert forces on each other that hold them together in solids and in liquids. In addition, atoms are elastic because they bounce off each other with no change in energy, whereas solid spheres are inelastic because some energy is transferred to the surroundings when they collide.

> **Study tip**
>
> It is important to understand how particles are arranged in solids, liquids, and gases.

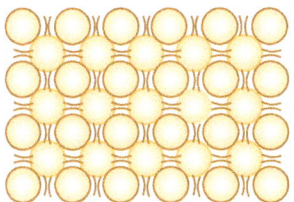
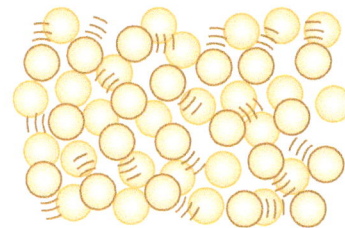

Figure 3 *The arrangement of particles of a substance in solid state, liquid state, and gas state*

1. Write the change of state that occurs when:
   a i wet clothing on a washing line dries out [1 mark]
   ii hailstones form [1 mark]
   iii snowflakes turn to liquid water. [1 mark]
   b When an ice cube in an empty beaker melts, the volume of water in the beaker just after the ice has melted is less than the volume of the ice cube. Explain what this tells you about the density of ice compared with the density of water. [2 marks]

2. Give the scientific word for each of the following changes:
   a The windows in a bus full of people mist up. [1 mark]
   b Steam is produced from the surface of the water in a pan when the water is heated before it boils. [1 mark]
   c Ice cubes taken from a freezer thaw out. [1 mark]
   d Water put into a freezer gradually turns to ice. [1 mark]

3. Describe the changes that take place in the movement and arrangement of the particles in:
   a an ice cube when the ice melts [2 marks]
   b water vapour when it condenses on a cold surface. [3 marks]

4. Explain, using the kinetic theory of matter, why liquids and solids are much denser than gases. [4 marks]

> **Key points**
>
> - The particles of a *solid* are held next to each other in fixed positions. They are the least energetic of the states of matter.
> - The particles of a *liquid* move about at random and are in contact with each other. They are more energetic than the particles in a solid.
> - The particles of a *gas* move about randomly and are far apart (so gases are much less dense than solids and liquids). They are the most energetic of the states of matter.
> - During a physical change, such as a change of state, no new substances are made.

1.1.2 Density

Learning objectives

After this topic, you should know:
- how density is defined and its unit
- how to measure the density of a solid object or a liquid
- how to use the density equation to calculate the mass or the volume of an object or a sample
- how to tell from its density if an object will float in water.

Converting units
1 kg = 1000 g = 10^3 g

1 m = 100 cm = 10^2 cm

1 m³ = 1 000 000 cm³ = 10^6 m³

So 1000 kg/m³ = $\dfrac{1\,000\,000 \text{ g}}{1\,000\,000 \text{ cm}^3}$

= 1 g/cm³

Synoptic link
For guidance on rearranging equations, see Maths skills 3b in the *Physical Sciences* book.

Study tip
The density of pure water is 1000 kg/m³. Objects that float in water have a density less than 1000 kg/m³.

Study tip
The instrument you choose to take a measurement is important – you should consider the resolution and range.

instrument	resolution	range
metre rule (mm scale)	±0.5 mm	1 m
vernier caliper	±0.05 mm	about 100 mm
micrometer	±0.005 mm	about 30 mm

Density comparisons

Any builder knows that a concrete post is much heavier than a wooden post of the same size. This is because the **density** of concrete is much greater than the density of wood. A volume of one cubic metre of wood has a mass of about 800 kg. But one cubic metre of concrete has a mass of about 2400 kg. So the density of concrete is about three times the density of wood.

The density of a substance is defined as its mass per unit volume.

You can use the equation below to calculate the density, ρ of a substance if you know the **mass**, m and the **volume**, V of a sample of it.

$$\text{density, } \rho \text{ (kilograms per cubic metre, kg/m}^3\text{)} = \dfrac{\text{mass, } m \text{ (kilograms, kg)}}{\text{volume, } V \text{ (metres cubed, m}^3\text{)}}$$

Rearranging the density equation
Rearranging the density equation gives:

$m = \rho V$ or $V = \dfrac{m}{\rho}$

Worked example
A wooden post has a volume of 0.025 m³ and a mass of 20 kg. Calculate its density in kg/m³.

Solution

$\text{density} = \dfrac{\text{mass}}{\text{volume}} = \dfrac{20 \text{ kg}}{0.025 \text{ m}^3} = 800 \text{ kg/m}^3$

Gases are much less dense than solids or liquids because the average spacing between the particles in a gas is much greater than in a solid or a liquid. For a given number of particles in a gas compared with the same number in a solid or a liquid, the mass of the particles is the same but the volume they occupy is very much greater in a gas. So the density of a gas is much less.

In general, a substance in its liquid state is less dense than in the solid state because particles in a liquid move about and are slightly further apart than in a solid. Water is an exception – ice is less dense than liquid water.

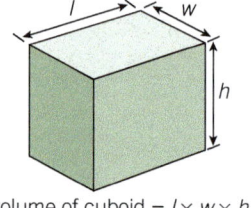

volume of cuboid = $l \times w \times h$

Figure 1 *The volume of a cuboid*

1.1 States of matter

Measuring the density of a solid object
To measure the mass of the object, use an electronic balance. Make sure the balance reads zero before you place the object on it.

To find the volume of a regular solid, such as a cube or a cuboid, measure its dimensions using a millimetre ruler, vernier caliper, or a micrometer – whichever is the most appropriate. Use the measurements and the equation shown in Figure 1 to calculate its volume.

For a small irregular solid, lower it on a thread into a measuring cylinder partly filled with water. You can work out the volume of the object by the rise in the water level.

Measuring the density of a liquid
Use a measuring cylinder to measure the volume of a particular amount of the liquid (Figure 2).

Measure the mass of an empty beaker using a balance. Remove the beaker from the balance and pour the liquid from the measuring cylinder into the beaker. Use the balance again to measure the total mass of the beaker and the liquid. You can work out the mass of the liquid by subtracting the mass of the empty beaker from the total mass of the beaker and the liquid. Then work out the density.

Safety: Take care not to spill any liquids. If liquids are spilt, let your teacher know immediately.

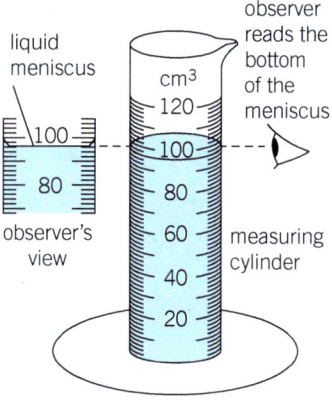

Figure 2 *Using a measuring cylinder*

Worked example
A measuring cylinder contained a volume of 120 cm³ of a particular liquid. The liquid was then poured into an empty beaker of mass 51 g. The total mass of the beaker and the liquid was found to be 145 g.
a Calculate the mass of the liquid in grams.
b Calculate the density of the liquid in kg/m³.

Solution
a mass of liquid = 145 g − 51 g = **94 g**
b density = $\dfrac{\text{mass}}{\text{volume}} = \dfrac{94\,\text{g}}{120\,\text{cm}^3} =$
$\dfrac{0.094\,\text{kg}}{0.000120\,\text{m}^3} =$ **780 kg/m³**

---

1 A rectangular concrete slab is 0.80 m long, 0.60 m wide, and 0.05 m thick.
   a Calculate its volume in m³. [1 mark]
   b The mass of the concrete slab is 60 kg. Calculate its density in kg/m³. [2 marks]

2 A measuring cylinder contains 80 cm³ of a particular liquid. The liquid is poured into an empty beaker of mass 48 g. The total mass of the beaker and the liquid was found to be 136 g.
   a Calculate the mass of the liquid in grams. [2 marks]
   b Calculate the density of the liquid in g/cm³. [2 marks]

3 A rectangular block of gold is 0.10 m in length, 0.08 m in width, and 0.05 m in thickness.
   a i Calculate its volume. [1 mark]
     ii The mass of the block is 0.76 kg. Calculate the density of gold. [2 marks]
   b A thin gold sheet has a length of 0.15 m and a width of 0.12 m. The mass of the sheet is 0.0015 kg. Use these measurements and the result of your density calculation in **a ii** to calculate the thickness of the sheet. [3 marks]

4 Describe how you would measure the density of a metal bolt. You may assume that the bolt will fit into a measuring cylinder of capacity 100 cm³. [4 marks]

Key points
- density = $\dfrac{\text{mass}}{\text{volume}}$ in kg/m³
- To measure the density of a solid object or a liquid, measure its mass and its volume, then use the density equation $\rho = \dfrac{m}{V}$
- Rearranging the density equation gives $m = \rho V$ or $V = \dfrac{m}{\rho}$
- Objects that are less dense than water (i.e., < 1000 kg/m³) float in water.

1.1.3 Gas pressure and temperature

Learning objectives

After this topic, you should know:

- how a gas exerts pressure on a surface
- how the pressure of a gas in a sealed container is affected by changing the temperature of the gas
- why raising the temperature of a gas in a sealed container increases the pressure of the gas
- how to see evidence of gas molecules moving around at random.

In the kitchen

Never heat food in a sealed can. The can will probably explode because the pressure of gas inside it increases as the temperature increases. This is because the molecules of gas in the can collide repeatedly with each other and with the surface inside their container, rebounding after each collision. Each impact with the surface exerts a tiny force on the surface. Millions of millions of these impacts happen every second, and together the total force causes a steady pressure on the surface inside the container. **The pressure of a gas on a surface is the total force exerted on a unit area of the surface.**

Increasing the temperature of any sealed container increases the pressure of the gas inside it. This is because:

- the energy transferred to the gas when it's heated increases the kinetic energy of its molecules. So the average kinetic energy of the gas molecules increases when the temperature of the gas is increased
- the average speed of the molecules increases when the kinetic energy increases, and the molecules on average hit the container surfaces with more force and more often. So the pressure of the gas increases.

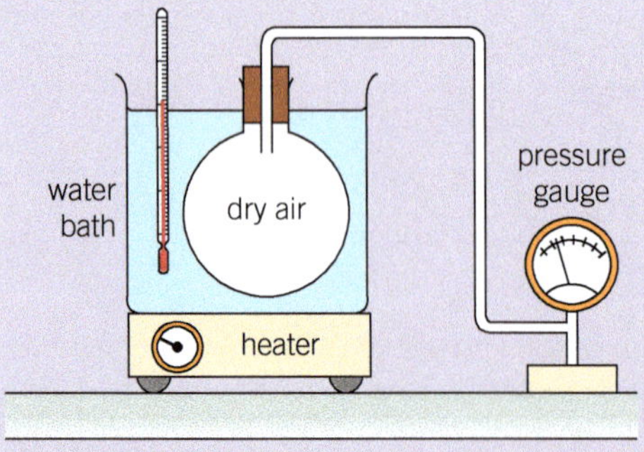

Investigating how the pressure of a gas varies with temperature

Figure 1 shows dry air in a sealed flask connected to a pressure gauge. The flask is in a big beaker of water, which is heated to raise the temperature of the gas. The water is heated in stages to raise the temperature in stages. At each stage, the water is stirred to make sure that its temperature is the same throughout the water. The temperature of the water is measured using the thermometer. The pressure is read off the pressure gauge.

If the measurements are plotted on a graph of pressure against temperature in °C, the results give you a straight-line graph as shown in Figure 2. This shows that the increase of pressure is the same for equal increases of temperature.

Safety: This is a demonstration and must be carried out by a teacher, behind a safety screen. Wear eye protection when watching this demonstration.

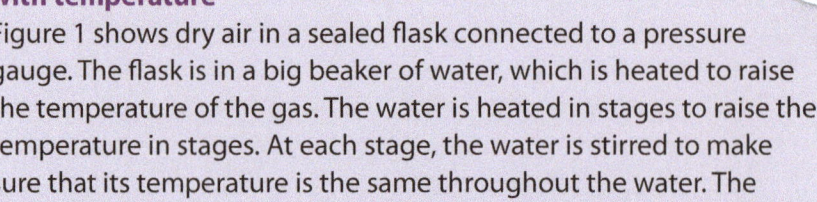

Figure 1 *Measuring gas pressure at different temperatures*

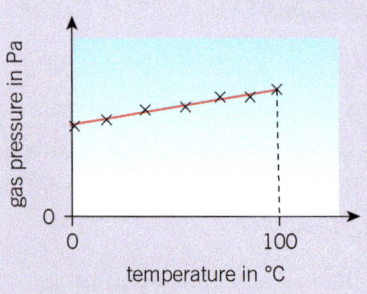

Figure 2 *Pressure versus temperature for a gas*

1.1 States of matter

Observing random motion

Individual molecules are too small for you to see directly. But you can see the effects of them by observing the motion of smoke particles in air. Figure 3 shows how you can do this using a smoke cell and a microscope. The smoke particles move about haphazardly and follow unpredictable paths.

1 A small glass cell is filled with smoke
2 Light is shone through the cell
3 The smoke is viewed through a microscope
4 You see the smoke particles constantly moving and changing direction. The path taken by one smoke particle will look something like this

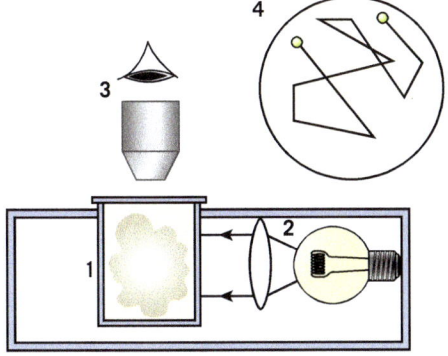

Figure 3 *A smoke cell*

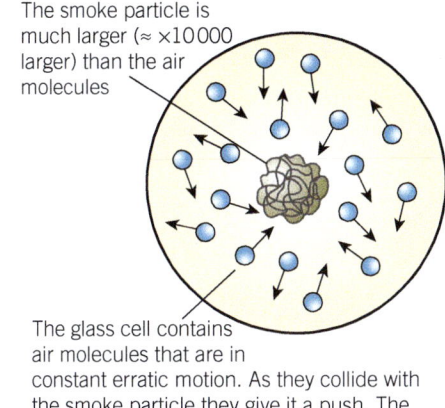

The smoke particle is much larger (≈ ×10 000 larger) than the air molecules

The glass cell contains air molecules that are in constant erratic motion. As they collide with the smoke particle they give it a push. The direction of the push changes at random

Figure 4 *The random motion of smoke particles*

Figure 4 shows how the random motion of smoke particles in air happens. Air molecules repeatedly collide at random with each smoke particle. The air molecules must be moving very fast to make this happen, because they are much too small to see, and the smoke particles are much, much bigger than the air molecules. What you see is the random motion of the smoke particles caused by the random impacts that the gas (air) molecules make on each smoke particle.

Go further

The random motion of tiny particles in a fluid is called **Brownian motion**, after the botanist Robert Brown, who first observed it in 1785. He used a microscope to observe pollen grains floating on water. He was amazed to see that the pollen grains were constantly moving about and changing direction haphazardly as if they had a life of their own. Brown couldn't explain what he saw. Brownian motion puzzled scientists until the kinetic theory of matter provided an explanation.

1 When a gas is heated in a sealed container, describe how, if at all, each of the following properties of the gas changes:
  a the pressure of the gas [1 mark]
  b the average separation of the molecules [1 mark]
  c the number of impacts each second the molecules make on the surface of the container each second. [1 mark]
2 Explain why smoke particles in air move about faster if the temperature of the air is increased. [3 marks]
3 A gas cylinder is fitted with a valve that opens and lets gas out if the gas becomes too hot. Explain how the gas pressure in the cylinder changes if the gas becomes too hot and the valve opens. [3 marks]
4 Look back at the Practical box opposite to investigate how the pressure of gas varies with temperature.
  a Explain why the water must be stirred before its temperature is measured. [2 marks]
  b Explain why the pressure gauge does not read zero before the water is heated. [2 marks]

Key points

- The pressure of a gas is caused by the random impacts of gas molecules on surfaces that are in contact with the gas.
- If the temperature of a gas in a sealed container is increased, the pressure of the gas increases because:
  - the molecules move faster so they hit the surfaces with more force
  - the number of impacts per second of gas molecules on the surfaces of a sealed container increases
  - the total force of the impacts increases.
- The unpredictable motion of smoke particles is evidence of the random motion of gas molecules.

1.1.4 Changes of state

Learning objectives

After this topic, you should know:

- what is meant by the melting point and the boiling point of a substance
- what is needed to melt a solid or to boil a liquid
- why the mass of a substance that changes state stays the same
- how to use a temperature–time graph to find the melting point or the boiling point of a substance.

Melting points and boiling points

You can change the state of any substance by heating or cooling it. A pure substance melts or freezes at the same fixed temperature – its **melting point** or its **freezing point** – and it boils at a higher fixed temperature – its **boiling point**. In chemistry, a pure substance is a single element or compound without any other substances present. A mixture is a combination of different substances in no fixed proportions.

Melting and boiling points are affected by impurities in the substance. For example, the melting point of water is lowered if you add salt to the water. This is why salt is added to the grit that is used for gritting roads in freezing weather – the water stays liquid at colder temperatures, helping prevent the roads becoming icy.

Melting and boiling point measurements can be used to distinguish a pure substance from a mixture. A pure substance has a sharp melting point and boiling point, characteristic of that particular substance. However, mixtures melt or boil over a range of temperatures, and not at one specific temperature.

Energy and change of state

Suppose a beaker of ice below 0 °C is heated steadily so that the ice melts and then the water boils. Figure 2 shows how the temperature changes with time. The temperature of the water:

1. increases until it reaches 0 °C when the ice starts to melt at 0 °C, then
2. stays constant at 0 °C until all the ice has melted, then
3. increases from 0 °C to 100 °C until the water in the beaker starts to boil at 100 °C.

The energy transferred to a substance when it changes its state is called **latent heat**. The energy transferred to the substance to melt or boil it is 'hidden' by the substance because its temperature does not change at the substance's melting point or at its boiling point.

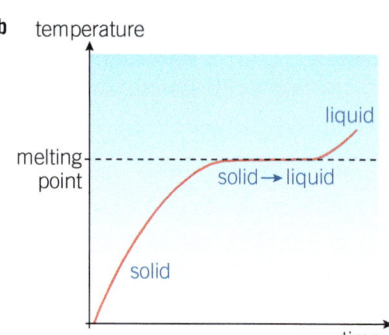

Figure 1a *Measuring the melting point of a substance* **b** *A temperature–time graph*

> **Measuring the melting point of a substance**
> Place a substance in its solid state in a suitable test tube in a beaker of water (Figure 1a). Heat the water, and measure the temperature of the substance when it melts. If its temperature is measured every minute, you can plot the measurements on a graph (Figure 1b). The melting point is the temperature of the flat section of the graph because this is when the temperature stays the same as the substance is melting. You can use the same arrangement without the beaker of water to find the boiling point of a liquid.
> **Safety:** Wear eye protection.

■ 1.1 States of matter

Most pure substances produce a temperature–time graph with similar features to Figure 2. Note that:
- Fusion is sometimes used to describe melting because different solids can be joined, or 'fused', together when they melt.
- Evaporation from a liquid happens at its surface when the liquid is at or below its boiling point. At its boiling point, a liquid boils because bubbles of vapour form inside the liquid and rise to the surface to release the gas.
- Some solid substances change directly into a vapour without melting. This process is called **sublimation**. For example, dry ice (solid carbon dioxide) turns directly into vapour (carbon dioxide gas) without melting.

Conservation of mass

When a substance changes state, the number of particles in the substance stays unchanged. So the mass of the substance after the change of state is the same as the mass of the substance before the change of state – the mass of the substance is conserved when it changes its state. For example:

- When a given mass of ice melts, the water it turns into has the same mass. So the mass of the substance stays unchanged.
- When water boils in a kettle, some of the water turns to steam. The mass of the steam produced is the same as the mass of water boiled away. So the mass of water is unchanged even though some of it (i.e., the steam) is no longer in the kettle.

> **Study tip**
> Don't forget that during the time a pure substance is changing its state, its temperature does *not* change.

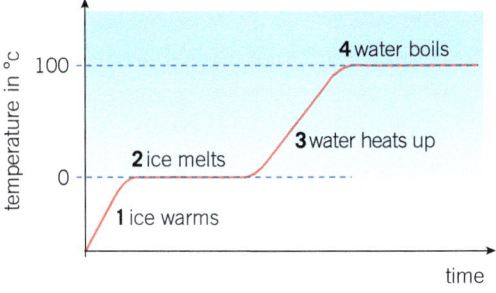

Figure 2 *Melting and boiling of water*

> **Study tip**
> Evaporation happens at any temperature – boiling happens only at the substance's boiling point.

---

1 **a** What is the difference between a pure substance and a mixture? [1 mark]
b State *three* differences between evaporation and boiling. [3 marks]

2 A pure solid substance X was heated in a tube and its temperature was measured every 30 s.
The measurements are given in the table below.

Time in s	0	30	60	90	120	150	180	210	240	270	300
Temperature in °C	20	35	49	61	71	79	79	79	79	86	92

a **i** Use the measurements in the table to plot a graph of temperature (*y*-axis) against time (*x*-axis). [3 marks]
ii Use your graph to find the melting point of X. [1 mark]
b Describe the physical state of the substance as it was heated from 60 °C to 90 °C. [3 marks]

3 A substance has a melting point of 75 °C. Describe how the arrangement and motion of the particles changes as the substance cools from 80 °C to 70 °C. [4 marks]

> **Key points**
> - For a pure substance:
>   - its melting point is the temperature at which it melts (which is the same temperature at which it solidifies)
>   - its boiling point is the temperature at which it boils (which is the same temperature at which it condenses).
> - Energy is needed to melt a solid or to boil a liquid.
> - When a substance changes state, its mass stays the same because the number of particles stays the same.
> - The flat section of a temperature against time graph gives the melting point or the boiling point of a substance.

1.1.5 Internal energy

Learning objectives

After this topic, you should know:

- how increasing the temperature of a substance affects its internal energy
- how to explain the different properties of a solid, a liquid, and a gas
- how the energy of the particles of a substance changes when the substance is heated
- how to explain in terms of particles why a gas exerts pressure.

When you switch a kettle on, the temperature of the water in the kettle increases until the water boils. The molecules in the water gain energy and move about faster as the temperature of the water increases. When the water boils, it means that the molecules have gained enough energy to move away from each other so that the water turns into vapour (steam).

The energy stored by the particles of a substance is called the substance's **internal energy**. This is the energy of the particles that is caused by their individual motion and positions. The internal energy of the particles is the sum of:

- the kinetic energy they have due to their individual motions relative to each other, and
- the potential energy they have due to their individual positions relative to each other.

So the internal energy of a substance is the total kinetic and potential energy of all the particles in the substance that is caused by their individual motions and positions.

Heating a substance changes the internal energy of the substance by increasing the energy of its particles. Because of this, the temperature of the substance increases or its physical state changes (i.e., it melts or boils).

- When the temperature of a substance increases (or decreases), the total kinetic energy of its particles increases (or decreases).
- When the physical state of a substance changes, the total potential energy of its particles changes.

Synoptic link

For more about energy transfers, see Topic 8.24.9 in the *Physical Sciences* book.

Synoptic link

You will learn more about different types of bonds in Chapter 6.16 in the *Physical Sciences* book.

Bonds between particles

The forces that hold particles together are called **bonds**. There are different types of bond and the type of bond in a substance affects its properties. The stronger the bonds between the particles of a substance are, the higher the melting point and the boiling point of the substance. For example, the melting point of common salt is about 800 °C compared with −114 °C for ethanol. This is because the type of bond between the particles in common salt is much stronger than the type of bond between the particles in ethanol.

Comparing the particles in solids, liquids, and gases

In a solid, the particles (i.e., atoms and molecules) are arranged in a three-dimensional (3D) structure (Figure 1).

- There are strong forces of attraction between these particles. These forces bond the particles in fixed positions.
- Each particle vibrates about an average position that is fixed.

Figure 1 *Molecular model of ice*

12

1.1 States of matter

- When a solid is heated, the particles' energy stores increase and they vibrate more. If the solid is heated up enough, the solid melts (or sublimates) because its particles have gained enough energy to break away from the structure.

In a liquid, forces of attraction still exist between the particles, but the particles have more kinetic energy than in a solid. The forces of attraction are not strong enough to hold the particles together in a rigid structure.

- The forces of attraction are strong enough to stop the particles moving away from each other completely at the surface.
- When a liquid is heated, some of the particles gain enough energy to break away from the other particles. The molecules that escape from the liquid are in a gas state above the liquid.

In a gas, the forces of attraction between the particles have no effect on the particles because they are moving so fast.

- The particles move about at high speed in random directions, colliding with each other and with the internal surface of their container. The pressure of a gas on a solid surface such as a container is caused by the force of impacts of the gas particles with the surface.
- When a gas is heated, its particles gain kinetic energy and on average move faster. This causes the pressure of the gas to increase because the particles collide with the container surface more often and with more force.

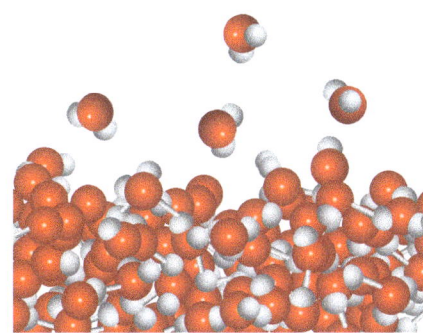

Figure 2 *Molecules in water*

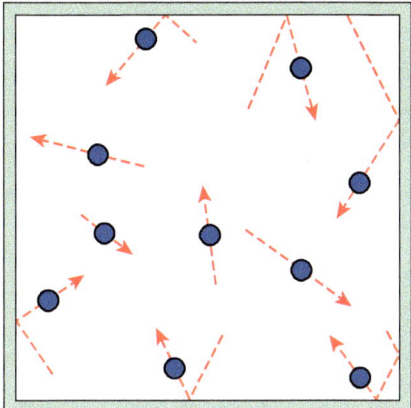

Figure 3 *Gas molecules in a box*

Study tip
Random means unpredictable or haphazard. The speed and direction of motion of a gas particle is unpredictable due to its random collisions with other particles.

Key points
- Increasing the temperature of a substance increases its internal energy.
- The strength of the forces of attraction between the particles of a substance explains why it is a solid, a liquid, or a gas at room temperature.
- When a substance is heated:
  - if its temperature rises, the kinetic energy of its particles increases
  - if it melts or it boils, the potential energy of its particles increases.
- The pressure of a gas on a surface is caused by the particles of the gas repeatedly hitting the surface.

---

1 Explain the following statements in terms of particles.
  a A gas exerts a pressure on any surface it is in contact with. [3 marks]
  b Heating a solid makes it melt. [3 marks]

2 The table below lists the properties of the molecules in four different substances. Write, with a reason, whether each substance is a solid, a liquid, or a gas, or doesn't exist.

	Distance between the molecules	Particle arrangement	Movement of the molecules	
a	close together	not fixed	move about	[1 mark]
b	far apart	not fixed	move about	[1 mark]
c	close together	fixed	vibrate	[1 mark]
d	far apart	fixed	vibrate	[1 mark]

3 a The boiling point of ethanol is 78 °C and that of common salt is over 1400 °C. Explain why common salt has a much higher boiling point than ethanol. [2 marks]
  b Explain why the internal energy of a solid increases when it is heated at its melting point. [2 marks]

4 An ice cube at 0 °C is placed in a beaker of water to cool the water down. Describe the energy changes of the particles in the ice and the water that take place. [4 marks]

1.1.6 Specific heat capacity

Learning objectives

After this topic, you should know:
- what is meant by the specific heat capacity of a substance
- how to calculate the energy changes that occur when an object changes temperature
- how the mass of a substance affects how quickly its temperature changes when it is heated
- how to measure the specific heat capacity of a substance.

A car that is parked in strong sunlight can become very hot. A concrete block of equal mass would not become as hot. Metal heats up more easily than concrete. Investigations show that when a substance is heated, its temperature rise depends on:
- the amount of energy supplied to it
- the mass of the substance
- what the substance is.

The following results were obtained using two different amounts of water. They show that:
- heating 0.1 kg of water by 4 °C required an energy transfer of 1600 J
- heating 0.2 kg of water by 4 °C required an energy transfer of 3200 J.

Using these results, you can say that:
- increasing the temperature of 1.0 kg of water by 4 °C requires a transfer of 16 000 J of energy
- increasing the temperature of 1.0 kg of water by 1 °C involves a transfer of 4000 J of energy.

More accurate measurements would give 4200 J per kg per °C for water. This is its **specific heat capacity**.

The specific heat capacity of a substance is the energy needed to raise the temperature of 1 kg of the substance by 1 °C.

The unit of specific heat capacity is the joule per kilogram degree Celsius (J/kg °C).

For a known change of temperature of a known mass of a substance:

energy transferred, ΔE = mass, m × specific heat capacity, c × temperature change, $\Delta\theta$
(joules, J)   (kilograms, kg)   (joule per kilogram degree Celsius, J/kg °C)   (degree Celsius, °C)

The energy transferred to the substance increases the internal energy store of the substance by an equal amount. To find the specific heat capacity of a substance, rearrange the above equation into the form:

$$c = \frac{\Delta E}{m\,\Delta\theta}$$

Note that the symbol Δ, pronounced 'delta', stands for 'change or transfer of'. The symbol θ, pronounced 'theta', stands for temperature.

Study tip

Water has a much higher specific heat capacity than most substances. For the same amount of energy transferred to or from a substance, the temperature change of water is much less than for the same mass of most other substances. This is why the temperature of water in the sea, in rivers, and elsewhere doesn't change as much from summer to winter as ground temperatures do. Creatures living in water experience much less variation in temperature than land creatures do.

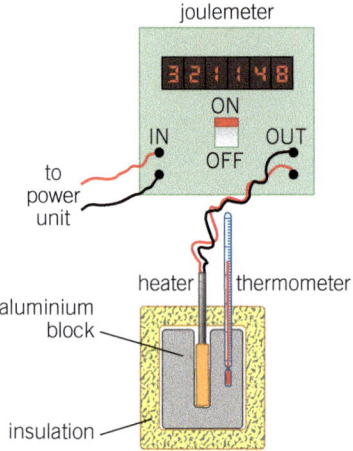

Figure 1 *Heating an aluminium block*

Measuring specific heat capacity
Use the arrangement shown in Figure 1 to heat a metal block of known mass.

Use the energy meter (or joulemeter) to measure the energy supplied to the block. Use the thermometer to measure its temperature rise.

■ 1.1 States of matter

To find the specific heat capacity of aluminium, insert your measurements into the equation:

$$c = \frac{\Delta E}{m \Delta \theta}$$

Replace the block with an equal mass of water in a suitable container. Measure the temperature rise of the water when the same amount of energy is supplied to it by the heater.

Your results should show that aluminium heats up more quickly than water.

Safety: Take care with hot objects. Wear eye protection.

Storage heaters

A storage heater (Figure 3) uses electricity at night (off-peak) to heat special bricks or concrete blocks in the heater. Energy transfer from the bricks keeps the room warm. The bricks have a high specific heat capacity, so they store lots of energy. They warm up slowly when the heater element is on, and cool down slowly when it is off.

Table 1 *The specific heat capacity for some substances*

Substance	water	oil	aluminium	iron	copper	lead	concrete
Specific heat capacity in J/kg °C	4200	2100	900	390	385	130	850

1 A small bucket of water and a large bucket of water are left in strong sunlight. Which one warms up faster? Give a reason for your answer. [2 marks]

2 Use the information in Table 1 above to answer this question.
  a Explain why a mass of lead heats up more quickly than an equal mass of aluminium. [2 marks]
  b Calculate the energy needed:
    i to raise the temperature of 0.20 kg of aluminium from 15 °C to 40 °C. [2 marks]
    ii to raise the temperature of 0.40 kg of water from 15 °C to 40 °C [2 marks]
    iii to raise the temperature of 0.40 kg of water in an aluminium container of mass 0.20 kg from 15 °C to 40 °C. [3 marks]
  c A copper water tank of mass 20 kg contains 150 kg of water at 15 °C. Calculate the energy needed to heat the water and the tank to 55 °C. [5 marks]

3 State *two* ways in which a storage heater differs from a radiant heater. [2 marks]

4 Design an experiment to measure the specific heat capacity of oil using the arrangement in Figure 1. [6 marks]

Synoptic link

You will see in Topic 7.19.9 in the *Physical Sciences* book that the electrical energy supplied E = heater potential difference, $V \times$ heater current, $I \times$ heating time, t.

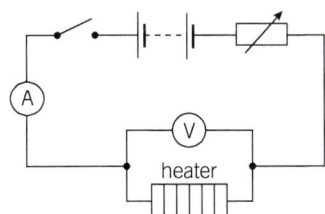

Figure 2 *Circuit diagram for measuring the heater current using an ammeter, and the heater potential difference using a voltmeter*

Figure 3 *A storage heater*

Key points

- The specific heat capacity of a substance is the amount of energy needed to change the temperature of 1 kg of the substance by 1 °C.
- The equation $\Delta E = m c \Delta \theta$ is used to calculate the energy needed to change the temperature of mass m by $\Delta \theta$.
- The greater the mass of an object, the more slowly its temperature increases when it is heated.
- To find the specific heat capacity c of a substance, use a joulemeter and a thermometer to measure ΔE and $\Delta \theta$ for a measured mass m, then use $c = \frac{\Delta E}{m \Delta \theta}$.

1.1.7 Specific latent heat

Learning objectives
After this topic, you should know:
- what is meant by latent heat as a substance changes its state
- what is meant by *specific* latent heat of fusion and of vaporisation
- how to use latent heat in calculations
- how to measure the specific latent heat of ice and of water.

Latent heat of fusion
When a solid substance is heated, at its melting point the substance melts and turns into liquid. Its temperature stays constant until all of the substance has melted. The energy supplied is called latent heat of fusion. It is the energy needed by the particles to break free from each other.

If the substance in its liquid state is cooled, it will solidify at the same temperature as its melting point. When this happens, the particles bond together into a rigid structure. Latent heat is released as the substance solidifies and the particles form stronger bonds.

The **specific latent heat of fusion**, L_F of a substance is the energy needed to change the state of 1 kg of the substance from solid to liquid at its melting point (i.e., without changing its temperature).

The unit of specific latent heat of fusion is the joule per kilogram (J/kg).

If energy, E is transferred to a solid at its melting point and mass, m of the substance melts without change in temperature:

$$\text{specific latent heat of fusion, } L_F \text{ (joules per kilogram, J/kg)} = \frac{\text{energy, } E \text{ (joules, J)}}{\text{mass, } m \text{ (kilograms, kg)}}$$

You can rearrange this equation to $E = m L_F$.

Study tip
Latent heat is the energy transferred when a substance changes its state.

Specific latent heat is the energy transferred per kilogram when a substance changes its state.

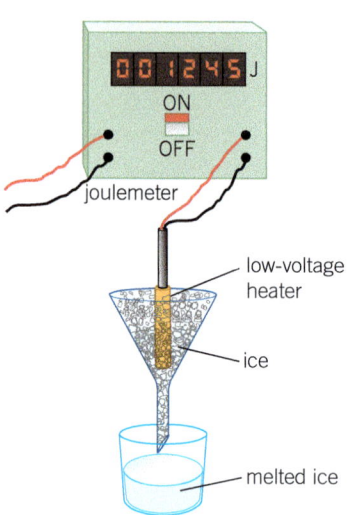

Figure 1 *Measuring the specific latent heat of fusion of ice*

Synoptic link
Instead of using a joulemeter, the energy supplied to the heater can be measured using the circuit and information in Topic 1.1.6.

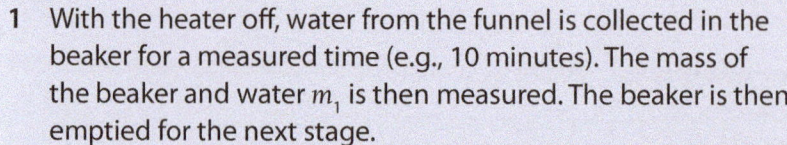

Specific latent heat of fusion of ice
In this experiment, a low-voltage heater is used to melt crushed ice in a funnel. The melted ice is collected using a beaker under the funnel (Figure 1). A joulemeter is used to measure the energy supplied to the heater.

1. With the heater off, water from the funnel is collected in the beaker for a measured time (e.g., 10 minutes). The mass of the beaker and water m_1 is then measured. The beaker is then emptied for the next stage.

2. With the heater on, the procedure is repeated for exactly the same time. The joulemeter readings before and after the heater is switched on are recorded. After the heater is switched off, the mass of the beaker and the water m_2 is measured once more.

To calculate the specific latent heat of fusion of ice, note that:
- the mass of ice melted because of the heater is $m = m_2 - m_1$
- the energy supplied E to the heater = the difference between the joulemeter readings
- the specific latent heat of fusion of ice is $L_F = \frac{E}{m} = \frac{E}{m_2 - m_1}$.

Safety: Take care with hot immersion heater. Wear eye protection.

1.1 States of matter

Latent heat of vaporisation

When a liquid substance is heated, at its boiling point the substance boils and turns into vapour. The energy supplied is called latent heat of vaporisation. It is the energy needed by the particles to break away from their neighbouring particles in the liquid.

If the substance in its gas state is cooled, it will condense at the same temperature as its boiling point. Latent heat is released as the substance condenses into a liquid and its particles form new bonds.

The **specific latent heat of vaporisation**, L_v of a substance is the energy needed to change the state of 1 kg of the substance from liquid to vapour at its boiling point (i.e., without changing its temperature).

The unit of specific latent heat of vaporisation is the joule per kilogram (J/kg).

If energy, E is transferred to a liquid at its boiling point and mass m of the substance boils away without change in temperature:

specific latent heat of vaporisation, L_v = $\dfrac{\text{energy, } E \text{ (joules, J)}}{\text{mass, } m \text{ (kilograms, kg)}}$
(joules per kilogram, J/Kg)

1 In the experiment shown in Figure 1, 0.024 kg of water was collected in the beaker in 300 s with the heater turned off. The beaker was then emptied and placed under the funnel again. With the heater on for exactly 300 s, the joulemeter reading increased from zero to 15 000 J, and 0.068 kg of water was collected in the beaker.
  a Calculate the mass of ice melted because of the heater being on. [1 mark]
  b Use the data to calculate the specific latent heat of fusion of water. [2 marks]

2 In the experiment shown in Figure 2, the balance reading decreased from 0.152 kg to 0.144 kg in the time taken to supply 18 400 J of energy to the boiling water. Use the data to calculate the specific latent heat of vaporisation of water. [2 marks]

3 An ice cube of mass 0.008 kg at 0 °C was placed in water at 15 °C in an insulated plastic beaker. The mass of water in the beaker was 0.120 kg. After the ice cube had melted, the water was stirred and its temperature was found to have fallen to 9 °C. The specific heat capacity of water is 4200 J/kg °C.
  a Calculate the energy transferred from the water. [2 marks]
  b Show that when the melted ice warmed from 0 °C to 9 °C, it gained 300 J of energy. [2 marks]
  c Use this data to calculate the specific latent heat of fusion of water. [3 marks]

4 Estimate how long an electric kettle that transfers 3000 J each second would take to boil away 100 g of water. The specific latent heat of vapourisation of water is 2.25 MJ/kg. [3 marks]

Specific latent heat of vaporisation of water

A low-voltage heater (Figure 2) is used to bring water in an insulated beaker to the boil. The joulemeter reading and the top pan balance reading are measured and then remeasured after a certain time (e.g., 5 minutes).

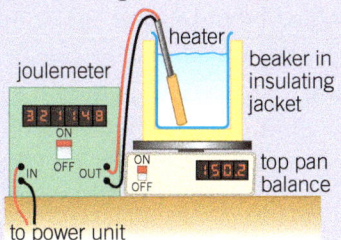

Figure 2 *Measuring the specific latent heat of vaporisation of water*

In this time:
- the mass of water boiled away m = the difference between the readings of the top pan balance
- the energy supplied E to the heater = the difference between the joulemeter readings
- the specific latent heat of vaporisation of water is $L_v = \dfrac{E}{m}$.

Safety: This is a demonstration and must be carried out by a teacher, who must take care with the hot immersion heater. Wear eye protection when watching this demonstration, and stand behind a safety screen.

Key points

- Latent heat is the energy needed for a substance to change its state without changing its temperature.
- *Specific* latent heat of fusion (or of vaporisation) is the energy needed to melt (or to boil) 1 kg of a substance without changing its temperature.
- In latent heat calculations, use the equation $E = m L$.
- The specific latent heat of fusion of ice (or of water) can be measured using a low-voltage heater to melt the ice.

1.1.8 Pure substances and mixtures

Learning objectives

After this topic, you should know:

- what is meant by the purity of a substance
- how the everyday and the scientific meanings of 'pure' differ
- how to use melting point data to distinguish pure from impure substances.

What is meant by purity?

When you talk about something being 'pure' in everyday life, often you are not referring to its chemical purity. For example, you often hear of orange juice or mineral water advertised as 'pure', but look at the label on a bottle of mineral water, such as the one in Figure 1.

When advertising a product, 'pure' is taken to mean that the product has had nothing added to it, and that it is in its natural state. For example, a drink advertised as 'pure orange juice' from 'freshly squeezed oranges' is unadulterated in that it contains no additives, but it is still a mixture of many different natural substances.

However, to a chemist:

A *pure substance* is one that is made up of just one substance. That substance can be either an element or a compound.

The everyday meaning of purity is not the same as its scientific meaning.

Analysing pure substances and mixtures

You can use boiling points and melting points to identify pure substances.

Do you remember a test for water? For example, it turns white anhydrous copper(II) sulfate blue. But that only tells you that water is present – it does not tell you if the water is pure or not. The test for *pure* water is that its melting point is exactly 0 °C, and its boiling point is exactly 100 °C.

You can use melting points or boiling points to identify substances because pure substances have characteristic temperatures at which they melt and boil. These melting and boiling points can be looked up in databooks or databases stored on computers. The melting and boiling points of pure bromine are shown in Figure 2 – its melting point is −7 °C and its boiling point is 59 °C. From a diagram like this, it is easy to see what state a substance is in at any given temperature.

- Above its boiling point, it will be a gas.
- Between its boiling point and its melting point, it will be a liquid.
- Below its melting point, it will be a solid.

You saw in Topic 1.1.4 that a pure substance, such as water (containing only H_2O molecules), stays at a constant temperature when it melts or boils. The flat sections of the heating or cooling curve of any pure substance can be used to measure melting and boiling points. However, the melting point and boiling point of a mixture will vary, depending on the composition of the mixture. A mixture does not have a sharp melting point or boiling point – it changes state over a range of temperatures. This difference between pure substances and mixtures can be used to determine whether an unknown sample is a pure substance or a mixture of substances. Doing an experiment to find a melting point (or melting range) is a quick and easy test of a compound's purity (Figure 3).

Figure 1 *This mineral water might be described as being 'as pure as a mountain stream', but it would not be called a pure substance by a chemist! Note that scientists now spell sulfate with an 'f', but in everyday use some still use sulphate with a 'ph'.*

Study tip

In everyday language, people often say that a substance such as milk is pure 'because nothing has been added to it', even though milk is not a pure substance – it is a mixture of lots of different substances.

1.1 States of matter

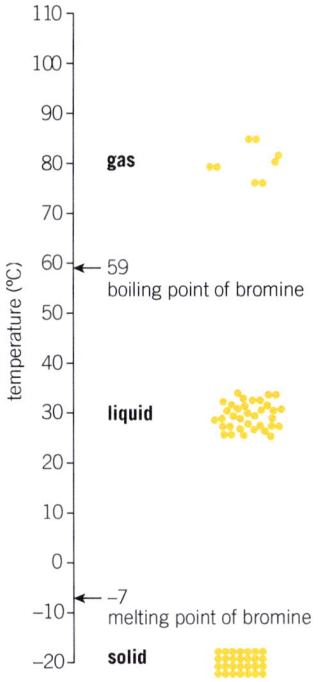

Figure 2 *The melting and boiling points of bromine will be sharp. If solid bromine is heated up, at −7 °C all the solid will melt before its temperature rises up to 59 °C when the liquid bromine starts to boil. The temperature remains at 59 °C until all the bromine has turned into a gas. In what state will bromine be at room temperature, taken as 20 °C?*

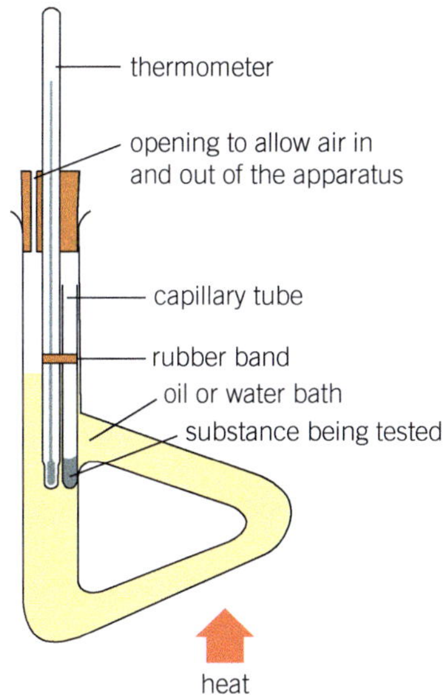

Figure 3 *This simple apparatus can be used to determine the melting point of a solid in powdered form*

The effect of impurities

Impurities tend to lower the melting point of a substance and raise its boiling point. The size of the difference from the melting or boiling point of a pure substance depends on the amount of any impurities mixed with it. The purer the compound is, the narrower the melting point range. For example, the melting point range of a largely purified sample of caffeine is 234–237 °C. However, the impure caffeine extracted from tea melts in the range 180–220 °C. This shows that the sample contains a high proportion of other substances mixed in with the caffeine.

1. Explain the difference between the use of the term 'pure' in advertising and its use in chemistry. [2 marks]
2. A white powder was placed in the melting point apparatus shown in Figure 3. The oil in the apparatus had a high boiling point. The chemist carrying out the test noted that the white powder started to melt at 158 °C and finished melting at 169 °C.
   a What was the melting range of the white powder? [1 mark]
   b What does this information tell us about the white powder? [1 mark]
   c Why was oil, and not water, used in the apparatus? [1 mark]
3. a The chemical element selenium has a melting point of 220 °C and its boiling point is 685 °C. In which state (solid, liquid, or gas) will selenium be found at the following temperatures?
   i 200 °C [1 mark]   ii 400 °C [1 mark]
   iii 600 °C [1 mark]   iv 800 °C [1 mark]
   b Krypton is another element. Its melting point is −157 °C and its boiling point is −153 °C. What state is krypton in at room temperature? [1 mark]
4. Pure water freezes (solidifies) at 0 °C. Explain why salty grit is spread on roads when low temperatures are forecast in winter. [5 marks]

Key points

- Pure substances can be compounds or elements, but they contain only one substance. An impure substance is a mixture of two or more different elements or compounds.
- Pure elements and compounds melt and boil at specific temperatures, and these melting and boiling points can be used to identify them.
- Melting point and boiling point data can be used to distinguish pure substances (specific temperatures) from mixtures (that melt or boil over a range of temperatures).

1.1 States of matter

Summary questions

1. In a paint factory, empty steel tins of mass 0.320 kg and volume 0.001 m³ are filled with paint of density 2500 kg/m³.
   Calculate the mass of paint in each filled paint tin. [2 marks]

2. This question is about A4 paper for use in a photocopier.
   a Use a millimetre ruler to measure the length and the width of a sheet of this paper. [1 mark]
   b The paper has a mass per unit area of 80 g/m². Calculate the mass of a single sheet of the paper. [2 marks]
   c A packet of 500 sheets of this paper has a thickness of 50 mm. Calculate the thickness of a single sheet of the paper. [1 mark]
   d Use your answers to **b** and **c** to calculate the density of the paper in:
     i g/cm³ [3 marks]
     ii kg/m³. [1 mark]

3. A test tube containing a solid substance is heated in a beaker of water. **Figure 1** shows how the temperature of the substance changed with time as it was heated.

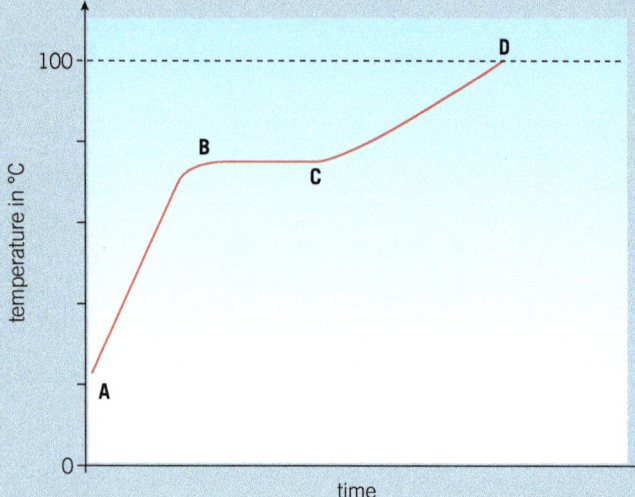

Figure 1

   a State why the temperature of the substance:
     i increased from **A** to **B** [1 mark]
     ii stayed the same from **B** to **C** [1 mark]
     iii increased from **C** to **D**. [1 mark]
   b Use **Figure 1** to estimate the melting point of the solid. [1 mark]
   c Describe how the arrangement and motion of the particles changed as the temperature increased from **A** to **D**. [3 marks]

4. a A plastic beaker containing 0.10 kg of water at 18 °C was placed in a refrigerator for 450 s. After this time, the temperature of the water was found to be 3 °C. The specific heat capacity of water is 4200 J/kg °C.
     i Calculate the energy transferred from the water. [2 marks]
     ii Calculate the rate of transfer of energy from the water. [2 marks]
   b i Calculate how much more energy would need to be removed from the water to cool it from 3 °C and to freeze it. The specific latent heat of fusion of water is 340 kJ/kg. [4 marks]
     ii Estimate how long it would take to cool the water from 3 °C and to freeze it. [3 marks]

5. An electric kettle transfers 3000 J of energy each second. The kettle is fitted with a safety cut-out designed to switch it off as soon as the water boils. Unfortunately, the cut-out does not operate correctly and it allows the water to boil for 30 s longer than it is supposed to.
   a Calculate how much electrical energy is supplied to the kettle in this time. [2 marks]
   b The specific latent heat of vaporisation of water is 2.3 MJ/kg (where M stands for million). Estimate the mass of water boiled away in this time. [2 marks]

6. In a chemistry experiment, 25 cm³ of a gas was collected in a syringe at a pressure of 120 kPa.
   a The density of the gas was 0.0018 g/cm³ at the temperature at which it was collected. Calculate the mass of gas collected. [2 marks]
   b If the gas in **a** was then cooled without changing its volume, write and explain how its pressure would change. [4 marks]
   c Explain why the pressure of a gas in a sealed container increases when the gas is heated. [4 marks]

7. a Explain in terms of particles why gases have a much lower density than solids and liquids. [3 marks]
   b Describe how the arrangement and motion of the particles of a substance change when the substance changes its state from liquid to solid. [4 marks]

1.1 States of matter

Practice questions

01 A student is asked to find the density of an irregularly shaped stone.
The student has access to equipment found in a standard school science laboratory.

01.1 Describe how the student can determine the density of the irregularly shaped stone.
You should include:
- the equipment the student should use
- the readings that will be taken
- how the density can be calculated from the readings. [6 marks]

01.2 The stone the student is given contains some copper metal.
Copper is a solid at room temperature.
Use the particle model to explain why copper is a solid at room temperature. [3 marks]

01.3 In the atmosphere water can be found in all three states of matter.
Use the particle model to explain the differences between water vapour and liquid water. [4 marks]

02 Cans of deodorant carry a warning label stating that the can should not be disposed of by throwing it into a fire.
The cans of deodorant contain a pressurised gas to act as a propellant.

02.1 Describe how the particles in the can of deodorant exert a pressure on the walls of the container. [3 marks]

02.2 Explain how the pressure inside the can of deodorant will change if the can is heated. [3 marks]

03 An ice cube is added to 300 g of water.
The ice cube has an initial temperature of −15 °C.
The water cools down from 20 °C to 8 °C.
Water has a specific heat capacity of 4200 J/kg°C.

03.1 Define specific heat capacity. [1 mark]

03.2 Calculate the energy transferred from the water. [3 marks]

03.3 Give the amount of energy gained by all the molecules from the ice cube as a result of the change in temperature from −15 °C to 8 °C. [1 mark]

03.4 Sketch the heating curve you would expect for the ice cube. [2 marks]

03.5 Another glass of water has ice added to it.
The temperature of the water falls by 14 °C when ice is added.
Calculate the mass of water in the glass if the ice has 24 000 J of energy transferred to it as it melts. [2 marks]

03.6 Give **one** assumption that you made in calculating the mass of water in the glass. [1 mark]

04 Lead is used to make fishing weights for sea fishing.
The lead is melted and poured into a mould. It is then left to cool.

04.1 Calculate the specific latent heat of fusion for lead if 5.75 kJ of energy is required to change the state of 250 g of lead.
Give your answer in standard units. [3 marks]

04.2 The lead melted at a temperature of 315 °C.
Data tables show that the accepted value for the melting point of lead is 328 °C.
Suggest why there is a difference between these two values for the melting point of lead. [1 mark]

04.3 In terms of the particles in the lead, describe what the energy is needed for when melting lead. [1 mark]

21

1.2 Atomic structure
1.2.1 Scientific models of the atom

Learning objectives
After this topic, you should know:
- how and why the atomic model has changed over time
- that scientific theories are revised or replaced by new ones in the light of new evidence.

Early ideas about atoms
The ancient Greeks were the first to have ideas about particles and atoms. However, it was not until 1804 that these ideas became linked to strong experimental evidence when John Dalton put forward his ideas about atoms. Based on his experiments on gases and chemical formulae, he suggested that substances were made up of atoms that were like tiny, hard spheres. He also suggested that each chemical element had its own atoms that differed from others in their mass. Dalton believed that these atoms could not be divided or split. They were the fundamental building blocks of nature.

In chemical reactions, he suggested that the atoms rearranged themselves and combined with other atoms in new ways. In many ways, Dalton's ideas are still useful today. For example, they help to visualise elements, compounds, and molecules, as well as the models still used to describe the different arrangement and movement of particles in solids, liquids, and gases.

Evidence for electrons in atoms
At the end of the 1800s, a scientist called J.J. Thomson discovered the **electron**. This is a tiny, negatively charged particle that was found to have a mass about 2000 times smaller than the lightest atom. Thomson was experimenting by applying high voltages to gases at low pressure (Figure 2).

Figure 1 *Dalton's list of 'elements'*

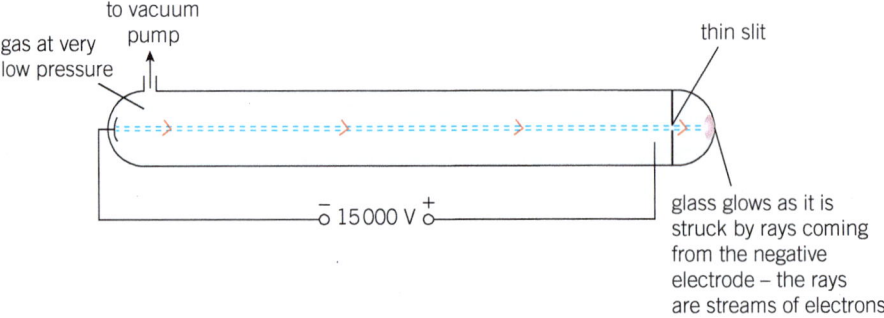

Figure 2 *Thomson's experimental evidence for the existence of electrons*

Thomson did experiments on the beams of the particles he discovered. They were attracted to a positive charge, showing they must be negatively charged themselves. He called the tiny, negatively charged particles electrons. These electrons must have come from inside atoms in the tube, as they were so much lighter than atoms themselves. So Dalton's idea that atoms could not be divided or split had to be revised. Thomson proposed a different model for the atom. He said that the tiny, negatively charged electrons must be embedded in a cloud of positive charge. He knew that atoms themselves carry no overall charge, so any charges in an atom must balance out. He imagined the electrons as the bits of plum in a plum pudding (Figure 3).

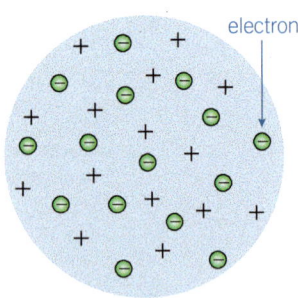

Figure 3 *Thomson's 'plum pudding' model of the atom*

1.2 Atomic structure

Evidence for the nuclear atom

The next breakthrough in understanding the atom came about 10 years later. Students Geiger and Marsden were doing an experiment with radioactive particles. They were firing dense, positively charged particles (called alpha particles) at the thinnest piece of gold foil they could make. They expected the particles to pass straight through the gold atoms with their diffuse cloud of positive charge (as in Thomson's 'plum pudding' model). However, their results shocked them (Figure 4).

Their results were used to suggest a new model for the atom (Figure 5). Their results suggested that Thomson's atomic model was not possible. The positive charge must be concentrated at a tiny spot in the centre of the atom. Otherwise the large, positive particles fired at the foil could never be repelled back towards their source. It was proposed that the electrons must be orbiting around this **nucleus** (centre of the atom), which contains very dense, positively charged **protons** (Figure 5).

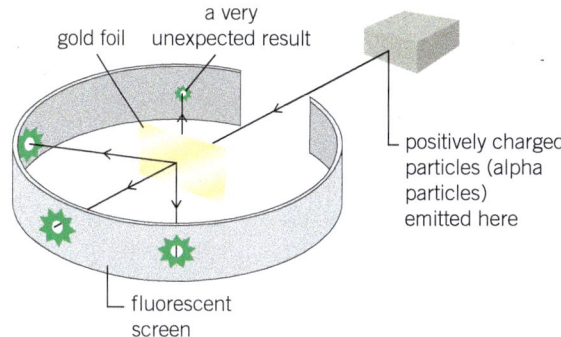

Figure 4 *The alpha particle scattering experiment carried out by Geiger and Marsden that changed the 'plum pudding' theory (see also page 72)*

Evidence for electrons in shells (energy levels)

The next important development came in 1914, when Niels Bohr revised the atomic model again. He noticed that the light given out when atoms were heated only had specific amounts of energy. He suggested that the electrons must be orbiting the nucleus at set distances, in certain fixed energy levels (or shells). The energy must be given out when excited electrons fall from a high to a low energy level. Bohr matched his model to the energy values observed (Figure 6).

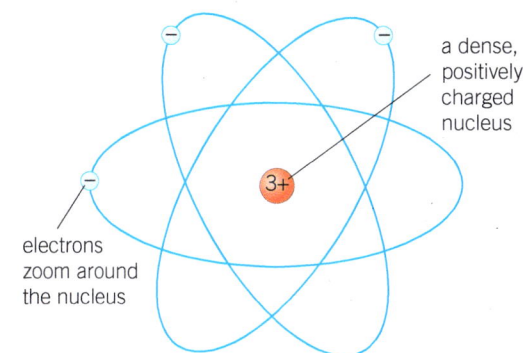

Figure 5 *Rutherford's nuclear model of the atom, proposed in 1911*

Evidence for neutrons in the nucleus

Scientists at the time speculated that there were two types of sub-atomic particles inside the nucleus. They had evidence of protons, but a second sub-atomic particle in the nucleus was also proposed to explain the missing mass that had been noticed in atoms. These **neutrons** must have no charge and have the same mass as a proton.

Because neutrons have no charge, it was very difficult to detect them in experiments. It was not until 1932 that James Chadwick did an experiment that could only be explained by the existence of neutrons (see page 73).

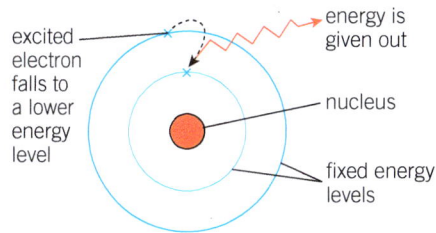

Figure 6 *Bohr's model of the atom. For more about energy levels in atoms, see Topic 3.8.1*

---

1 a Which sub-atomic particle did J.J. Thomson discover? [1 mark]
  b Describe J.J. Thomson's 'plum pudding' model of the atom. [2 marks]

2 a Which *one* of Dalton's ideas listed below about atoms do scientists no longer believe?
   A Elements cannot be broken down into simpler substances.
   B Atoms get rearranged in chemical reactions.
   C Atoms are solid spheres that cannot be split into simpler particles. [1 mark]
  b Which *two* of the following substances from Dalton's list of elements are not actually chemical elements?
   soda   oxygen   carbon   gold   lime [2 marks]

3 Describe *two* ways in which Rutherford changed Thomson's model of the atom. [2 marks]

Key points

- Ideas about atoms have changed over time.
- New evidence has been gathered from the experiments of scientists who have used their model of the atom to explain their observations and calculations.
- Key ideas were proposed successively by Dalton, Thomson, Rutherford, and Bohr, before arriving at the model of the atom you use at GCSE level today.

1.2.2 Sub-atomic particles

Learning objectives

After this topic, you should know:

- the location, relative charge, and relative mass of the protons, neutrons, and electrons in an atom
- what the atomic number and mass number of an atom represent
- why atoms have no overall charge
- that atoms of a particular element have the same number of protons.

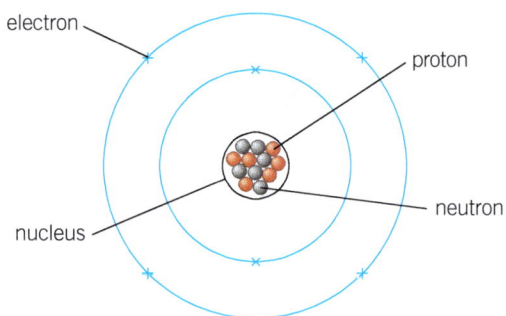

Figure 1 *Understanding the structure of an atom gives important clues to the way in which chemicals react together. This atom of carbon has six protons and six neutrons in its nucleus, and six electrons orbiting the nucleus. Although the number of protons and electrons are always equal in an atom, the number of neutrons can differ (but in this carbon atom they are the same). For example, an atom of beryllium (Be) has 4 protons, 4 electrons, and 5 neutrons*

You have now seen how ideas about atoms have developed over time. At GCSE level, you use the model in which a very small nucleus is in the centre of every atom. This nucleus contains two types of sub-atomic particles, called protons and neutrons. A third type of sub-atomic particle orbits the nucleus. These really tiny particles are called electrons.

Protons have a positive charge. Neutrons have no charge, that is, they are neutral. So the nucleus itself has an overall positive charge. The electrons orbiting the nucleus are negatively charged. The relative charge on a proton is +1 and the relative charge on an electron is −1.

The mass of an atom is concentrated in its nucleus. A proton and a neutron each have the same mass. The electrons are so light that their mass can be ignored when working out the relative mass of atoms (Table 1).

Table 1 *The relative charge and mass of sub-atomic particles*

Type of sub-atomic particle	Relative charge	Relative mass
proton	+1	1
neutron	0	1
electron	−1	very small (it would take almost 2000 electrons to have the same mass as one proton or neutron)

Because every atom contains equal numbers of protons and electrons, the positive and negative charges cancel out. So there is no overall charge on any atom. For example, a carbon atom is neutral. It has six protons, so you know it must have six electrons (Figure 1).

Atomic number

All the atoms of a particular element have the same number of protons. For example, hydrogen atoms all have one proton in their nucleus, carbon atoms have six protons in their nucleus, and sodium atoms have 11 protons in their nucleus.

The number of protons in each atom of an element is called its **atomic number**.

The elements in the periodic table are arranged in order of their atomic number (number of protons). If you are told that the atomic number of an element is eight, you can identify it using the periodic table. It will be the eighth element listed – oxygen. Knowing the atomic number of an element, you also know its number of electrons (as this will equal its number of protons). So oxygen atoms have eight protons and eight electrons.

Mass number

As you know, the protons and neutrons in an atom's nucleus make up the vast majority of the mass of the atom.

The number of protons plus neutrons in the nucleus of an atom is called its **mass number**. A beryllium atom, Be has four protons and five neutrons, so its mass number will be 4 + 5 = 9.

1.2 Atomic structure

Given the atomic number and mass number, you can work out how many protons, electrons, and neutrons are in an atom. For example, an argon atom has an atomic number of 18 and a mass number of 40.

- Its atomic number is 18, so it has 18 protons. Remember that atoms have an equal number of protons and electrons. So argon also has 18 electrons.
- Its mass number is 40, so you know that:
  18 (the number of protons) + the number of neutrons = 40
- Therefore, argon must have 22 neutrons (as 18 + 22 = 40).

You can summarise the last part of the calculation as:

number of neutrons = mass number − atomic number

Worked example
Lead has an atomic number of 82 and a mass number of 207.

How many protons, neutrons, and electrons does it contain?

Solution
atomic number = number of protons, p = number of electrons, e
$= 82$

mass number = number of protons, p + number of neutrons, n
$= 207$

So substituting in the value of p, you get $82 + n = 207$.

You can rearrange the equation so that its subject (i.e., the quantity you want to find out) is n, by subtracting 82 from both sides of the equation:

$n = 207 − 82$
$= 125$

So the lead atom has 82 protons, 125 neutrons, and 82 electrons.

---

1 Draw a table showing the location, relative charge, and relative mass of the three sub-atomic particles. [3 marks]
2 An atom has 27 protons and 32 neutrons. Give its atomic number and mass number. [2 marks]
3 Explain why all atoms are neutral. [2 marks]
4 How many protons, electrons, and neutrons do the following atoms contain?
   a A nitrogen atom, with atomic number 7 and mass number 14. [1 mark]
   b A chlorine atom, with atomic number 17 and mass number 35. [1 mark]
   c A silver atom, with atomic number 47 and mass number 108. [1 mark]
   d A uranium atom, with atomic number 92 and mass number 235. [1 mark]

Study tip
In an atom, the number of protons is always equal to the number of electrons. You can find out the number of protons and electrons in an atom by looking up its atomic number in the periodic table.

Key points
- Atoms are made of protons, neutrons, and electrons.
- Protons have a relative charge of +1, and electrons have a relative charge of −1. Neutrons have no electric charge. They are neutral.
- The relative masses of a proton and a neutron are both 1.
- Atoms contain an equal number of protons and electrons, so carry no overall charge.
- Atomic number = number of protons (= number of electrons).
- Mass number = number of protons + number of neutrons
- Atoms of the same element have the same number of protons (and hence electrons) in their atoms.

1.2.3 Size of atoms, and isotopes

Learning objectives

After this topic, you should know:

- how to work out the number of protons, neutrons, and electrons in an ion
- how to represent an atom's atomic number and mass number
- how to estimate the size and scale of atoms, using SI units and the prefix 'nano'
- the definition of isotopes.

The size of atoms

It has been estimated that a person has about 7 billion, billion, billion atoms in their body. That huge number is written as 7 followed by 27 zeros:

7 000 000 000 000 000 000 000 000 000

You cannot see the atoms because each individual atom is incredibly small. An atom is about a tenth of a billionth of a metre across.

Sizes of nuclei, atoms, and molecules

When dealing with very large or very small numbers, scientists use 'powers of ten' to express a number. For example, a distance of one million metres (1 000 000 m) is written as 1×10^6 m. One millionth of a metre is written as 1×10^{-6} m (see Maths skills MS1b).

Chemists use units called **nanometres** (nm) to quote distances on an atomic level, where 1 nm is 1×10^{-9} m. The radius of an atom is about 0.1 nm (or 1×10^{-10} m). Compare this to the approximate radius of its nucleus, which is about 1×10^{-14} m. This shows what a small space is occupied by the nucleus of an atom, as its radius is less than $\frac{1}{10\,000}$ the radius of a single atom. The radius of an atom is about four orders of magnitude (10^4) larger than its nucleus (see Maths skills MS2h). Therefore the vast majority of an atom is space, occupied by an atom's electrons. In comparison a small molecule such as methane, CH_4, has a radius of about 0.5 nm (5×10^{-10} m). So a methane molecule's radius is about five times bigger than an atom's radius.

Representing the atomic number and mass number

You can show the atomic number and mass number of an atom like this:

mass number $^{12}_{6}$C (carbon) $^{23}_{11}$Na (sodium)
atomic number

Given this information, you can work out the numbers of protons, neutrons, and electrons in an atom. The bottom number is its atomic number, giving you the number of protons (which equals the number of electrons). Then you can calculate the number of neutrons by subtracting its atomic number from its mass number.

Sodium, $^{23}_{11}$Na, has an atomic number of 11 and its mass number is 23.

So a sodium atom has 11 protons and 11 electrons, as well as (23 − 11) = 12 neutrons.

Synoptic link

For more about calculating the numbers of protons, neutrons, and electrons in an atom, look back at Topic 1.2.2.

1.2 Atomic structure

Isotopes

Atoms of the same element always have the same number of protons. However, they can have different numbers of neutrons.

Atoms of the same element with different numbers of neutrons are called **isotopes**.

Isotopes always have the same atomic number but different mass numbers. For example, two isotopes of carbon are $^{12}_{6}C$ (also written as carbon-12) and $^{13}_{6}C$ (carbon-13). The carbon-12 isotope has six protons and six neutrons in the nucleus (Figure 1). The carbon-13 isotope has six protons and seven neutrons, that is, one more neutron than carbon-12.

Sometimes extra neutrons make the nucleus unstable, so it is radioactive. However, not all isotopes are radioactive – they are simply atoms of the same element that have different masses.

Isotopes always have the same **chemical properties**, because their reactions depend on their electronic structures. As their atoms will have the same number of protons, and therefore electrons, the electronic structure will be same for all isotopes of an element.

For example, look at the three isotopes of hydrogen in Figure 2. The three isotopes are called hydrogen (hydrogen-1), deuterium (or hydrogen-2), and tritium (or hydrogen-3). Each has a different mass and tritium is radioactive. However, all have identical chemical properties, for example, they all react with oxygen to make water:

$$2H_2(g) + O_2(g) \rightarrow 2H_2O(l)$$

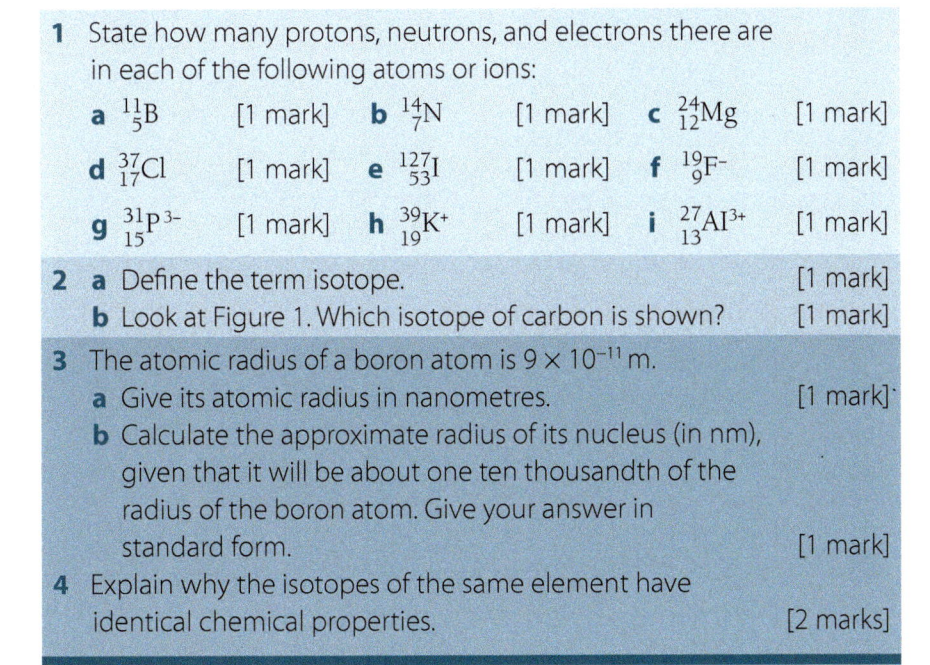

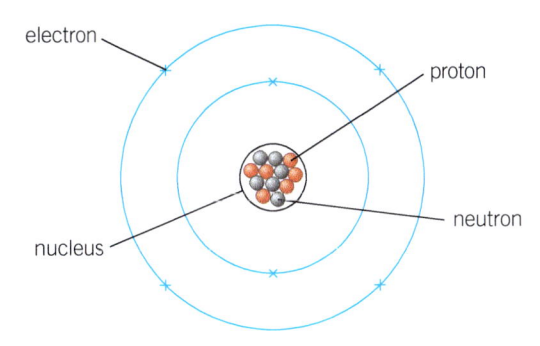

Figure 1 *An atom of carbon-12 (its atomic radius is 0.077 nm)*

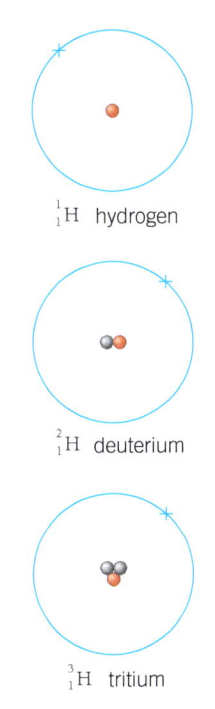

$^{1}_{1}H$ hydrogen

$^{2}_{1}H$ deuterium

$^{3}_{1}H$ tritium

Figure 2 *The isotopes of hydrogen – they have identical chemical properties. The radius of a hydrogen atom is about 0.05 nm*

Key points

- Atoms that gain electrons form negative ions. If atoms lose electrons they form positive ions.
- You can represent the atomic number and mass number of an atom using the notation: $^{24}_{12}Mg$, where magnesium's atomic number is 12 and its mass number is 24.
- Isotopes are atoms of the same element with different numbers of neutrons. They have identical chemical properties, but their physical properties, such as density, can differ.

---

1. State how many protons, neutrons, and electrons there are in each of the following atoms or ions:
   a $^{11}_{5}B$ [1 mark] b $^{14}_{7}N$ [1 mark] c $^{24}_{12}Mg$ [1 mark]
   d $^{37}_{17}Cl$ [1 mark] e $^{127}_{53}I$ [1 mark] f $^{19}_{9}F^-$ [1 mark]
   g $^{31}_{15}P^{3-}$ [1 mark] h $^{39}_{19}K^+$ [1 mark] i $^{27}_{13}Al^{3+}$ [1 mark]

2. a Define the term isotope. [1 mark]
   b Look at Figure 1. Which isotope of carbon is shown? [1 mark]

3. The atomic radius of a boron atom is 9×10^{-11} m.
   a Give its atomic radius in nanometres. [1 mark]
   b Calculate the approximate radius of its nucleus (in nm), given that it will be about one ten thousandth of the radius of the boron atom. Give your answer in standard form. [1 mark]

4. Explain why the isotopes of the same element have identical chemical properties. [2 marks]

1.2.4 Electronic structures

Learning objectives

After this topic, you should know:

- how the electrons are arranged in an atom
- the electronic structures of the first 20 elements in the periodic table
- how to represent electronic structures in diagrams and by using numbers.

The model of the atom that you use at GCSE level has electrons arranged around the nucleus in **shells**, rather like the layers of an onion. Each shell represents a different energy level.

The lowest energy level is shown by the shell that is nearest to the nucleus. The electrons in an atom occupy the lowest available energy level (the available shell closest to the nucleus).

Electron shell diagrams

An energy level (or shell) can only hold a certain number of electrons.

- The first, and lowest, energy level (nearest the nucleus) can hold up to two electrons.
- The second energy level can hold up to eight electrons.
- Once there are eight electrons in the third energy level, the fourth begins to fill up.

Beyond the first 20 elements in the periodic table, the situation gets more complex. You only need to know the full arrangement of electrons in atoms of the first 20 elements.

You can draw diagrams to show the arrangement of electrons in an atom. For example, a sodium atom has an atomic number of 11 so it has 11 protons, which means it also has 11 electrons. Figure 1 shows how you can represent an atom of sodium.

Study tip

You should be able to draw the electronic structure of the atoms for all of the first 20 elements when given their atomic number or their position in the periodic table (which tells you the number of electrons).

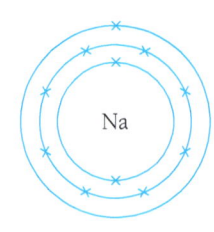

Figure 1 *A simple way of representing the arrangement of electrons in the energy levels (shells) of a sodium atom*

To save drawing atoms all the time, you can write down the numbers of electrons in each energy level. This is called an **electronic structure**. For example, the sodium atom in Figure 1 has an electronic structure of 2,8,1. You start at the lowest energy level (innermost or first shell), recording the numbers in each successive energy level or shell. The numbers of electrons in each shell are separated from each other by a comma.

Silicon, whose atoms have 14 electrons, is in Group 4 of the periodic table. It has the electronic structure 2,8,4. This represents two electrons in the lowest energy level (first shell), then eight in the next energy level, and four in its highest energy level (its outermost shell).

The best way to understand these electron arrangements is to look at the examples in Figure 2.

■ 1.2 Atomic structure

Examples from the first 20 elements

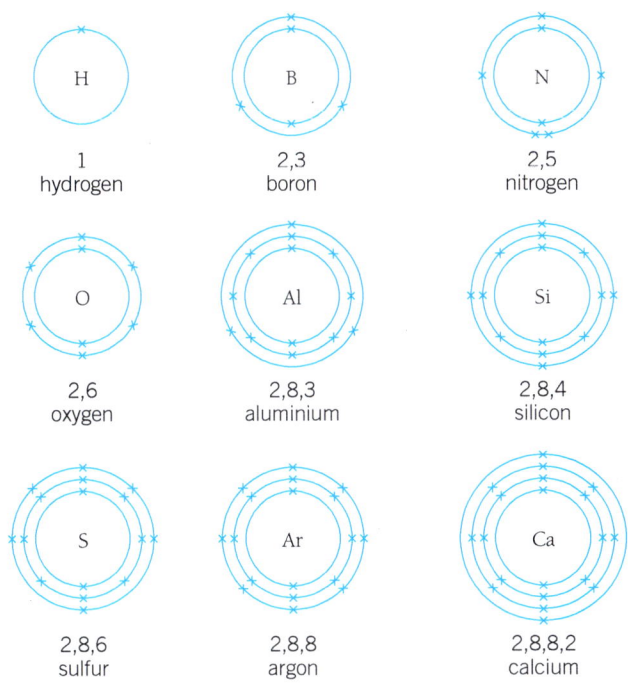

H
1
hydrogen

B
2,3
boron

N
2,5
nitrogen

O
2,6
oxygen

Al
2,8,3
aluminium

Si
2,8,4
silicon

S
2,8,6
sulfur

Ar
2,8,8
argon

Ca
2,8,8,2
calcium

Figure 2 *A selection of atoms from the first 20 elements in the periodic table, showing their electronic structures. Note that the chemical symbol of the atom is used in the centre of each diagram, to make it easier to distinguish between the different atoms at a glance*

Synoptic link

You will learn more about the reactions of elements and their electronic structures in Chapter 5.13 in the *Physical Sciences* book.

1 **a** Which shell represents the lowest energy level in an atom? [1 mark]
  b How many electrons can each of the lowest two energy levels hold? [1 mark]
2 Using the periodic table, draw the arrangement of electrons in the following atoms and label each one with its electronic structure.
  a He [1 mark]
  b Be [1 mark]
  c Cl [1 mark]
  d Ar [1 mark]
3 **a** Write the electronic structure of potassium (atomic number 19). [1 mark]
  b How many electrons does a potassium atom have in its highest energy level (outermost shell)? [1 mark]
4 Figure 3 shows an energy level diagram of an atom.
  a Give the name and symbol of the atom shown in Figure 3. [1 mark]
  b Write the electronic structure of the atom shown in Figure 3. [1 mark]
  c Suggest and explain the effect of adding three electrons into the outer shell (highest energy level) of the atom shown in Figure 3. [3 marks]

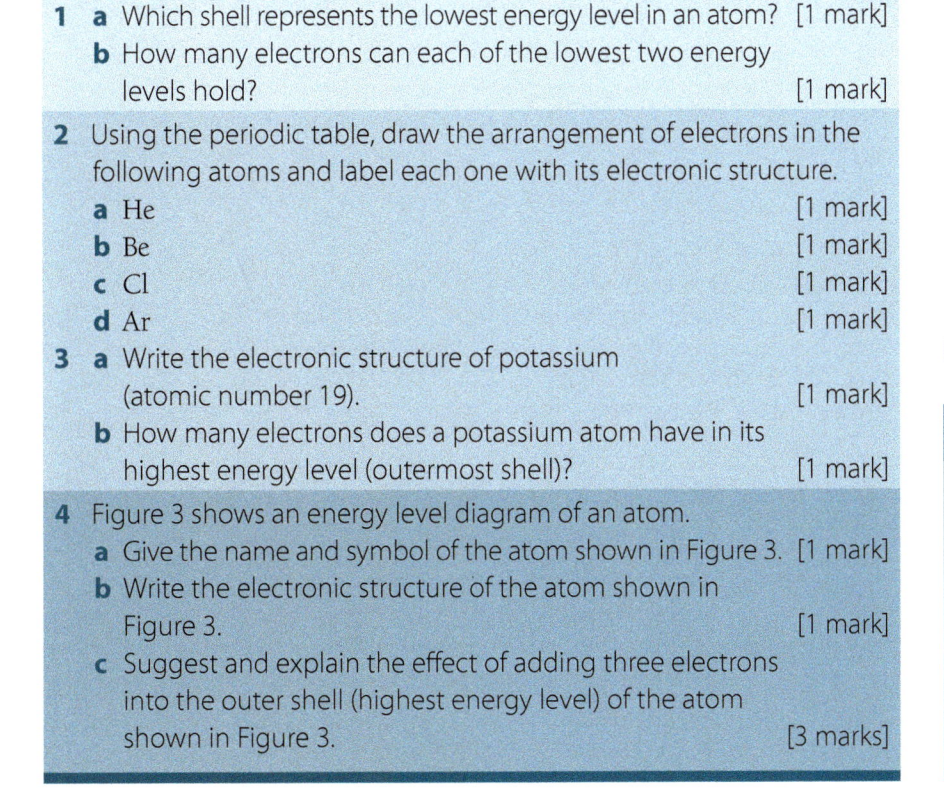

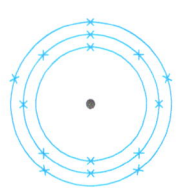

Figure 3 *See Question 4*

Key points

- The electrons in an atom are arranged in energy levels or shells.
- The lowest energy level (first shell) can hold up to 2 electrons and the next energy level (second shell) can hold up 8 electrons.
- The fourth shell starts to fill after 8 electrons occupy the third shell.

29

1.2 Atomic structure

Summary questions

1 a i Name the sub-atomic particles found in the nucleus of an atom. [1 mark]
      ii What is the maximum number of electrons that can occupy each of the first two energy levels or shells? [1 mark]
   b i Explain the overall charge on any atom. [3 marks]
      ii Define atomic number and mass number. [2 marks]

2 For each of the following atoms, give the numbers of protons, neutrons, and electrons:
   a $^{1}_{1}H$ [2 marks]
   b $^{4}_{2}He$ [2 marks]
   c $^{11}_{5}B$ [2 marks]
   d $^{19}_{9}F$ [2 marks]
   e $^{63}_{29}Cu$ [2 marks]
   f $^{238}_{92}U$ [2 marks]

3 **Figure 1** shows energy level diagrams of three atoms, **a–c**.

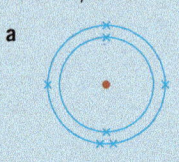

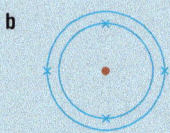

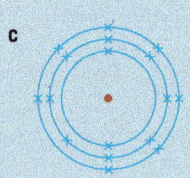

   a
   b
   c

   Figure 1

   For *each* atom **a–c**, write:
      i   the name [1 mark]
      ii the chemical symbol [1 mark]
      iii the electronic structure. [1 mark]

4 This question is about some of the elements in the periodic table.
   a Neon, Ne, is the tenth element in the periodic table, so its atomic number is 10.
      i   The mass number of a neon atom is 20. How many neutrons does it contain? [1 mark]
      ii Write the electronic structure of a neon atom. [1 mark]
   b The element radium, Ra, has 88 electrons.
      i   How many protons are in the nucleus of each radium atom? [1 mark]
      ii Radium's three most common isotopes are radium-224, radium-226, and radium-228. Describe the difference between the atomic structures of the three isotopes. [1 mark]
      iii Calcium is in the same group as radium. Its atomic number is 20. Write down its electronic structure. [1 mark]

5 a The atomic radius of an aluminium atom is 0.13 nm. Given that 1 nm = 1×10^9 m, write the atomic radius of an aluminium atom in metres, expressed in standard form (i.e., using 'powers of ten'). [1 mark]
   b The atomic radius of neon is 0.065 nm. Compare the size of the radius of a neon atom with that of an aluminium atom. [1 mark]
   c The nucleus of an aluminium atom is four orders of magnitude smaller than the atom itself. Give the appropximate radius of the aluminium nucleus in standard form, using nanometres (nm). [1 mark]

6 a Suggest *two* ways in which Dalton's original model of the atom is no longer accepted by scientists. [2 marks]
   b Thomson applied very high voltages to gases at low pressure in glass tubes. He observed the effects of negatively charged beams of particles. What evidence led Thomson to suggest that atoms contain sub-atomic particles? [2 marks]
   c i   In what way did the discovery of radioactivity, including alpha particles, help to overthrow Thomson's 'plum pudding' model of the atom? [2 marks]
      ii Describe how ideas about the location of electrons inside atoms changed going from the 'plum pudding' atomic model to the development of the 'nuclear model' in 1911. [3 marks]

1.2 Atomic structure

Practice questions

01 Atoms are so small that they cannot be seen with the naked eye.
The ancient Greeks thought that the atom was the smallest particle obtainable.

01.1 Give the typical size of an atom or small molecule. [1 mark]

01.2 In 1804 John Dalton proposed a model of the atom.
Give **two** key features of Dalton's ideas about atoms. [2 marks]

01.3 In 1897 J.J. Thomson discovered a particle that had a negative charge.
Name the particle discovered by J.J. Thomson. [1 mark]

01.4 Describe how J.J. Thomson showed that the particle had a negative charge. [1 mark]

02 Geiger and Marsden carried out an experiment using radioactive particles. The experiment supplied the evidence that disproved the 'plum pudding' model of the atom.

02.1 Describe the 'plum pudding' model of the atom. [2 marks]

02.2 Describe the experiment carried out by Geiger and Marsden.
You may use a labelled diagram to help answer this question. [2 marks]

02.3 Ernest Rutherford used the results of Geiger and Marsden's experiment to disprove the 'plum pudding' model of the atom.
Describe the conclusions drawn by Rutherford about the structure of the atom. [2 marks]

03 Gold is an element found in the Earth's crust. Atoms of one of the isotopes of gold are represented as $^{197}_{79}$Au.

03.1 Give the name and number of each type of particle present in a gold atom. [3 marks]

03.2 Carbon is another element in the periodic table. The common isotope of carbon is $^{12}_{6}$C. Another, much less common, isotope of carbon is $^{14}_{6}$C.
Compare the atoms of the two isotopes of carbon. [3 marks]

03.3 Different isotopes of the same element will have different densities.
Explain why the densities of the different isotopes of an element are not the same. [2 marks]

03.4 $^{12}_{6}$C and $^{14}_{6}$C both react in the same way with oxygen, producing carbon dioxide.
Explain why the two different isotopes of carbon react in the same way even though they have different physical properties. [2 marks]

04 Argon is in Group 0 of the periodic table. An argon atom is represented as $^{40}_{18}$Ar.

04.1 Give the atomic number of argon. [1 mark]

04.2 Atoms contain electrons. These electrons are arranged in energy levels in the atom.
Give the number of electrons that can occupy each of the first three energy levels in an atom before the next energy level starts to fill up. [2 marks]

04.3 Draw the electronic structure of an argon atom. [1 mark]

04.4 Oxygen is in Group 6 of the periodic table. Give the number of electrons in the outer shell of an atom of oxygen. [1 mark]

05 Scientists use models to understand complex systems. One such model is Dalton's model of the atom.
Describe fully the model that can be used to explain the position of elements in the periodic table.
You should include:
- the names of the particles present
- the location of the particles
- the properties of the particles.

You may use a labelled diagram to help answer this question. [5 marks]

1.3 Cells in animals and plants

1.3.1 The world of the microscope

Learning objectives

After this topic, you should know:
- how microscopy techniques have developed over time
- the differences in magnification and resolution between a light microscope and an electron microscope
- how to calculate the magnification, real size, and image size of a specimen.

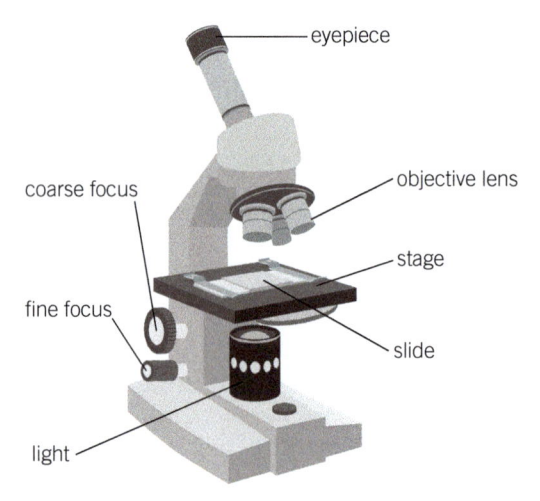

Living things are all made up of cells, but most cells are so small that you can only see them using a microscope. It is important to grasp the units used for such tiny specimens before you start to look at them.

Using units
1 kilometre (km) = 1000 metres (m)
1 m = 100 centimetres (cm)
1 cm = 10 millimetres (mm)
1 mm = 1000 micrometres (μm)
1 μm = 1000 nanometres (nm) – so a nanometre is 0.000 000 001 metres (written in standard form as 1×10^{-9} m).

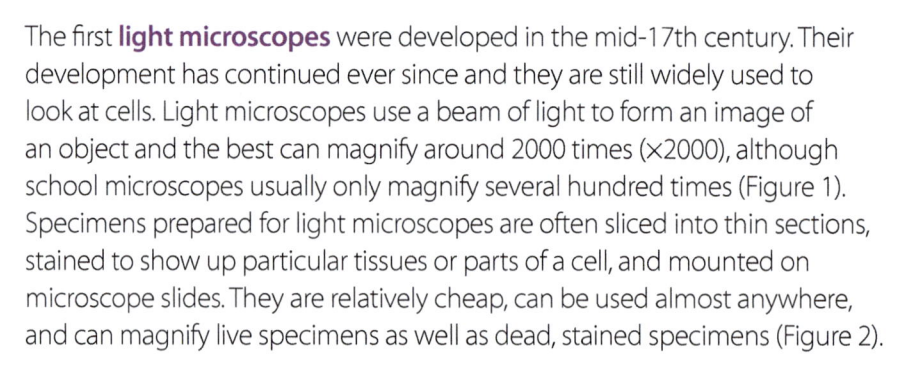

The first **light microscopes** were developed in the mid-17th century. Their development has continued ever since and they are still widely used to look at cells. Light microscopes use a beam of light to form an image of an object and the best can magnify around 2000 times (×2000), although school microscopes usually only magnify several hundred times (Figure 1). Specimens prepared for light microscopes are often sliced into thin sections, stained to show up particular tissues or parts of a cell, and mounted on microscope slides. They are relatively cheap, can be used almost anywhere, and can magnify live specimens as well as dead, stained specimens (Figure 2).

The invention of the **electron microscope** in the 1930s allowed biologists to see and understand more about the sub-cellular structures inside cells. These instruments use a beam of electrons to form an image and can magnify objects up to around 2 000 000 times. Transmission electron microscopes give 2D images with very high magnification and resolution. Scanning electron microscopes give dramatic 3D images but lower magnifications (Figure 3). Electron microscopes are large, very expensive, and have to be kept in special temperature, pressure, and humidity-controlled rooms. Only dead specimens can be used in an electron microscope.

Figure 1 *A light microscope*

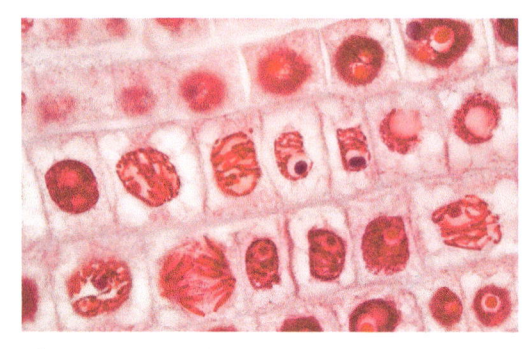

Figure 2 *Stained onion cells dividing as seen through a light microscope – magnification ×570*

Calculating magnification

You can calculate the magnification you are using with a light microscope very simply. You multiply the magnification of the eyepiece lens by the magnification of the objective lens. So if your eyepiece lens is ×4 and your objective lens is ×10, your overall magnification is:

$4 \times 10 = \times 40$

This is the magnification you should put on any drawings you make of what you can see under the microscope.

1.3 Cells in animals and plants

Calculating the size of an object
You will want to calculate the size of objects under the microscope. There is a simple formula for this, based on the magnification triangle.

As long as you know or can measure two of the factors, you can find the third.

$$\text{magnification} = \frac{\text{size of image}}{\text{size of real object}}$$

For example, if you know you are working at magnification ×40, and the image of the cell you are looking at measures 1 mm, you can work out the actual diameter of the cell. Rearranging the equation above gives:

$$\text{size of real object} = \frac{\text{size of image}}{\text{magnification}}$$

so

$$= \frac{1}{40}\,\text{mm} = 0.025\,\text{mm or } 25\,\mu m$$

Your cell has a diameter of **25 μm**.

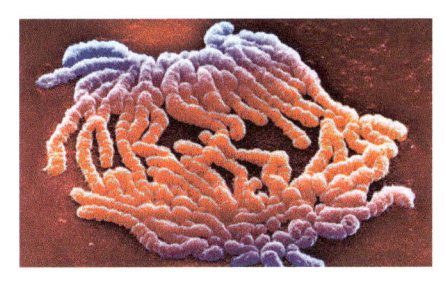

Figure 3 *Chromosomes during cell division seen with a scanning electron microscope – magnification ×4500. The chromosomes are specially treated so that they are visible under the electron microscope. False colours are often added – as shown here – to make different parts of the image easier to see*

Synoptic links
To learn more about writing very small or very large numbers in standard form, see Maths skills MS 1b.

For more information on the sizes of atoms, see Topic 1.2.3.

For more information on cell division, see Topic 1.3.8.

Study tip
You should be able to work out the magnification, the size of a cell, or the size of the image, depending on the information you are given.

Magnifying and resolving power
Microscopes are useful because they magnify things, making them look bigger. The height of an average person magnified by one of the best light microscopes would look about 3.5 km, and by an electron microscope about 3500 km.

There is, however, a minimum distance between two objects when you can see them clearly as two separate things. If they are closer together than this, they appear as one object. Resolution is the ability to distinguish between two separate points and it is the **resolving power** of a microscope that affects how much detail it can show. A light microscope has a resolving power of about 200 nm, a scanning electron microscope of about 10 nm, and a transmission electron microscope of about 0.2 nm – that is approximately the distance apart of two atoms in a solid substance! The high resolving power of an electron microscope allows us to study cells in much finer detail than is possible with a light microscope.

Key points
- Microscopes have developed over time, and as magnification and resolution have improved, our knowledge of sub-cellular structures has increased.
- Light microscopes magnify up to about ×2000, and have a resolving power of about 200 nm.
- Electron microscopes magnify up to about ×2 000 000, and have a resolving power of around 0.2 nm.
- Electron microscopes allow us to study sub-cellular structures at higher magnifications and in finer detail than light microscopes.
- $\text{magnification} = \dfrac{\text{size of image}}{\text{size of real object}}$

1. State *one* advantage and *one* disadvantage of using:
   a a light microscope [2 marks] b an electron microscope. [2 marks]
2. a A student measured the diameter of a human blood capillary on a micrograph. The image measures 5 mm and the student knows that the magnification is ×1000. How many micrometres is the diameter of the capillary? [4 marks]
   b A student is told that an image of a cell has a diameter of 800 μm. The actual cell has a diameter of 20 μm. At what magnification has the cell been observed? [3 marks]
3. Compare electron microscopes with light microscopes, giving one example where each type of microscope might be used. [6 marks]

1.3.2 Animal and plant cells

Learning objectives
After this topic, you should know:
- the main parts of animal cells
- the similarities and differences between plant and animal cells.

Synoptic links
You will find out more about classifying the living world in Topics 4.12.9 and 4.12.10.

You will learn more about how the structure of cells relates to their functions as you study specific animal and plant organ systems in Chapters 2.5 and 2.6.

Go further
The ultrastructure of a cell – the details you can see under an electron microscope – includes structures such as the cytoskeleton, the Golgi apparatus, and the rough and smooth endoplasmic reticulum. They support and move the cell, modify and package proteins and lipids, and produce the chemicals that control the way your body works.

Study tip
Learn the parts of the cells shown in Figures 1, 2, and 3, along with their functions.

Synoptic link
For more information on photosynthesis, look at Topic 2.6.6.

The cells that make up your body are typical animal cells. All cells have some features in common. You can see these features clearly in animal cells.

Animal cells – structure and functions
The structure and functions of the parts that make up a cell have been made clear by the electron microscope (Figure 1). An average animal cell is around 10–30 µm long (so it would take 33 333–100 000 cells to line up along the length of a metre ruler). Human beings are animals, so human cells are just like most other animal cells, and you will see exactly the same structures inside them:

- The **nucleus** – controls all the activities of the cell and is surrounded by the nuclear membrane. It contains **genes** on **chromosomes**, which carry instructions for making the proteins needed to build new cells or new organisms. The average diameter of a cell nucleus is around 10 µm.
- The **cytoplasm** – a liquid gel in which the organelles are suspended and where most of the chemical reactions needed for life take place.
- The **cell membrane** – controls the passage of substances such as glucose and mineral **ions** into the cell. It also controls the movement of substances such as urea or hormones out of the cell.
- The **mitochondria** – structures in the cytoplasm where aerobic respiration takes place, releasing energy for the cell. They are very small, 1–2 µm in length and only 0.2–0.7 µm in diameter.
- The **ribosomes** – where protein synthesis takes place, making all the proteins needed in the cell.

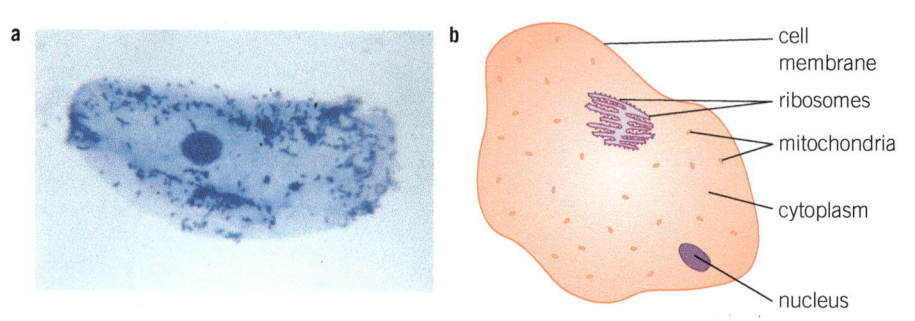

Figure 1 *Diagrams of cells are much easier to understand than the real thing seen under a microscope.* **a** *shows a simple animal cheek cell magnified ×1350 times under a light microscope.* **b** *is the way a model animal cell is drawn to show the main features common to most living cells*

Plant cells – structure and functions
Plants are very different organisms from animals. They make their own food by photosynthesis. They do not move their whole bodies about from one place to another. Plant cells are often rather bigger than animal cells – they range from 10 to 100 µm in length.

Plant cells have all the features of a typical animal cell, but they also contain features that are needed for their very different functions (Figures 2 and 3). **Algae** are simple aquatic organisms. They also make their own food by **photosynthesis** and have many similar features to plant cells. For centuries they were classified as plants, but now they are classified as part of a different kingdom – the protista.

All plant and algal cells have a **cell wall** made of **cellulose**, which strengthens the cell and gives it support.

Many (but not all) plant cells also have these other features:

- **Chloroplasts** are found in all the green parts of a plant. They are green because they contain the green substance **chlorophyll**. Chlorophyll absorbs light so that the plant can make food by photosynthesis. Each chloroplast is around 3–5 μm long. Root cells do not have chloroplasts because they are underground and do not photosynthesise.

- A **permanent vacuole** is a space in the cytoplasm filled with cell sap. This is important for keeping cells rigid to support the plant.

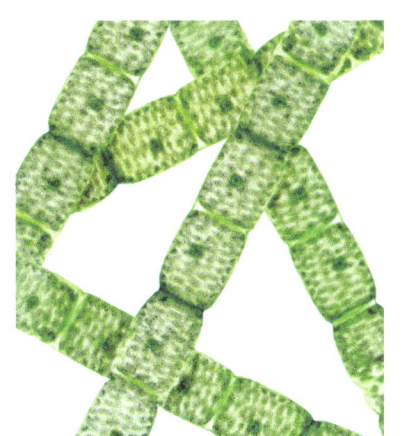

Figure 2 *Algal cells contain a nucleus and chloroplasts so that they can photosynthesise – magnification ~ ×10*

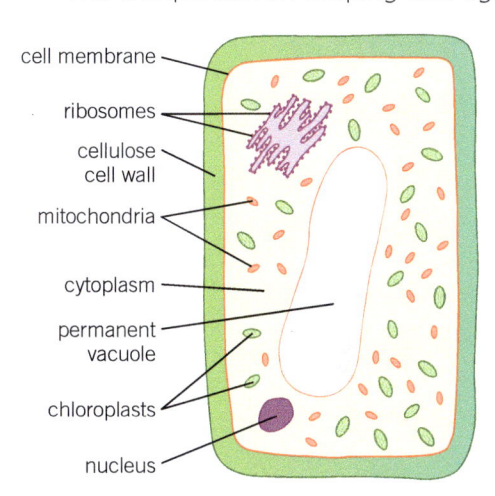

Figure 3 *A plant cell has many features in common with an animal cell, as well as other features that are unique to plants*

Looking at cells

Set up a microscope and observe, draw, and label examples of animal cells (e.g., cheek cells, Figure 1), algal cells (e.g., Figure 2) and plant cells (e.g., from onions or *Elodea*). In plant cells you should see the cell wall, the cytoplasm, and sometimes a vacuole. You will see chloroplasts in the *Elodea*, but not in the onion cells because they do not photosynthesise. Always show a scale magnification on your drawings.

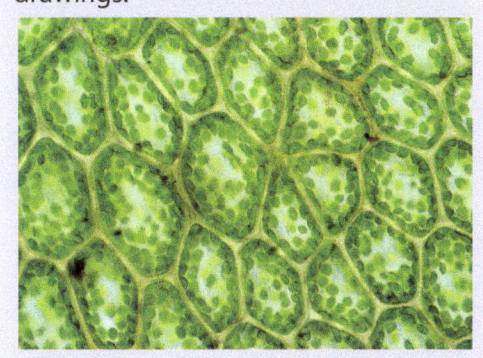

Figure 4 *Some of the common features of plant cells show up well under the light microscope. Here, the features are magnified ×40*

Study tip

Remember that not all plant cells have chloroplasts.

Do not confuse chloroplasts and chlorophyll.

1
  a List the main structures you would expect to find in a human cell. [5 marks]
  b State the *three* extra features that may be found in plant cells but not in animal cells. [3 marks]
  c Describe the main functions of these three extra structures. [1 mark]

2 Suggest why the nucleus and the mitochondria are so important in all cells. [4 marks]

3 Chloroplasts are found in many plant cells, but not all of them. Suggest *two* types of plant cells that are unlikely to have chloroplasts, and in each case explain why they have none. [4 marks]

Key points

- Animal cell features common to all cells are a nucleus, cytoplasm, a cell membrane, mitochondria, and ribosomes.
- Plant and algal cells contain all the structures seen in animal cells as well as a cellulose cell wall.
- Many plant cells also contain chloroplasts and a permanent vacuole filled with cell sap.

1.3.3 Eukaryotic and prokaryotic cells

Learning objectives

After this topic, you should know:
- the similarities and differences between eukaryotic cells and prokaryotic cells
- how bacteria compare to animal and plant cells
- the size and scale of cells including order of magnitude calculations.

Eukaryotic cells

Animal and plant cells are examples of **eukaryotic cells**. Eukaryotic cells all have a cell membrane, cytoplasm, and genetic material that is enclosed in a nucleus.

The genetic material is a chemical called DNA. This forms structures called chromosomes, which are contained within the nucleus. All animals (including human beings), plants, fungi, and protista are eukaryotes.

Prokaryotes

Bacteria are single-celled living organisms. They are examples of prokaryotes. At 0.2–2.0 µm in length, prokaryotes are 1–2 orders of magnitude smaller than eukaryotes. You could fit hundreds of thousands of bacteria on to the full stop at the end of this sentence, so you cannot see individual bacteria without a powerful microscope. When you grow bacteria in the laboratory, you get millions of bacteria together, so you can see them with the naked eye.

Bacteria have cytoplasm and a cell membrane surrounded by a cell wall, but the cell wall does not contain the cellulose you see in plant cells. In prokaryotic cells the genetic material is not enclosed in a nucleus. The bacterial chromosome is a single DNA loop found free in the cytoplasm.

Prokaryotic cells may also contain extra small rings of DNA called plasmids. Plasmids carry information about very specific features such as antibiotic resistance.

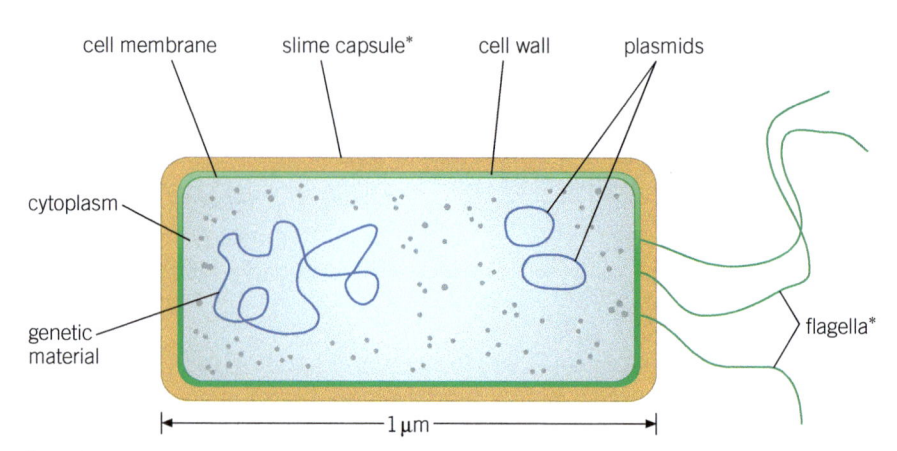

Synoptic link

You will learn more about about antibiotic resistance in bacteria in Topic 4.12.8.

Go further

The plasmids found in bacteria are used extensively in genetic engineering to carry new genes into the genetic material of other organisms ranging from bananas to sheep.

Study tip

Be clear about the similarities and differences between animal, plant, and bacterial cells and between eukaryotic cells and prokaryotic cells.

Synoptic links

You will learn more about bacteria that cause disease in Topic 3.9.4, and about bacteria that are important in the environment in Topic 4.10.3.

*not always present

Figure 1 *Bacteria come in a variety of shapes, but they all have the same basic structure*

Some bacteria have specialised features such as a protective slime capsule around the outside of the cell wall. Some types of bacteria have at least one flagellum (plural: flagella), that is, a long protein strand that lashes about (Figure 1). These bacteria use their flagella to move themselves around.

1.3 Cells in animals and plants

Many bacteria have little or no effect on other organisms and many are very useful.

Some bacteria are harmful. Bacteria can cause diseases in humans and other animals and also in plants. They can also decompose and destroy stored food.

Relative sizes

In cell biology it is easy to forget just how small everything is – and how much bigger some cells are than others. It is also important to remember just how large the organisms built up from individual cells can be. Figure 2 shows you some relative sizes.

Orders of magnitude

Orders of magnitude are used to make approximate comparisons between numbers or objects. If one number is about 10 times bigger than another, it is an order of magnitude bigger. You show orders of magnitude using powers of 10. If one cell or organelle is 10 times bigger than another, it is an order of magnitude or 10^1 bigger. If it is approximately 100 times bigger it is two orders of magnitude or 10^2 bigger.

If you have two numbers to compare, as a rule of thumb you can work out orders of magnitude as follows:

- If the bigger number divided by the smaller number is less than 10, then they are the same order of magnitude.
- If the bigger number divided by the smaller number is around 10, then it is an order of magnitude or 10^1 bigger.
- If the bigger number divided by the smaller number is around 100, then it is two orders of magnitude or 10^2 bigger.

Worked example

A small animal cell has a length of around 10 μm. A large plant cell has a length of around 100 μm.

$\frac{100}{10} = 10$

So, a large plant cell is an order of magnitude or 10^1 bigger than a small animal cell.

---

1 a Describe the difference between the genetic material in a prokaryotic cell and the genetic material in a eukaryotic cell. [2 marks]
 b i Describe what flagella are. [1 mark]
  ii State *one* use of flagella in a prokaryotes. [1 mark]
2 A cell nucleus has an average length of 6 μm. Calculate the order of magnitude comparison between the nucleus of a cell and:
 a a small animal cell [2 marks] **b** a large plant cell. [2 marks]
3 Describe the similarities and differences between the features found in prokaryotes and eukaryotic plant and animal cells. [6 marks]

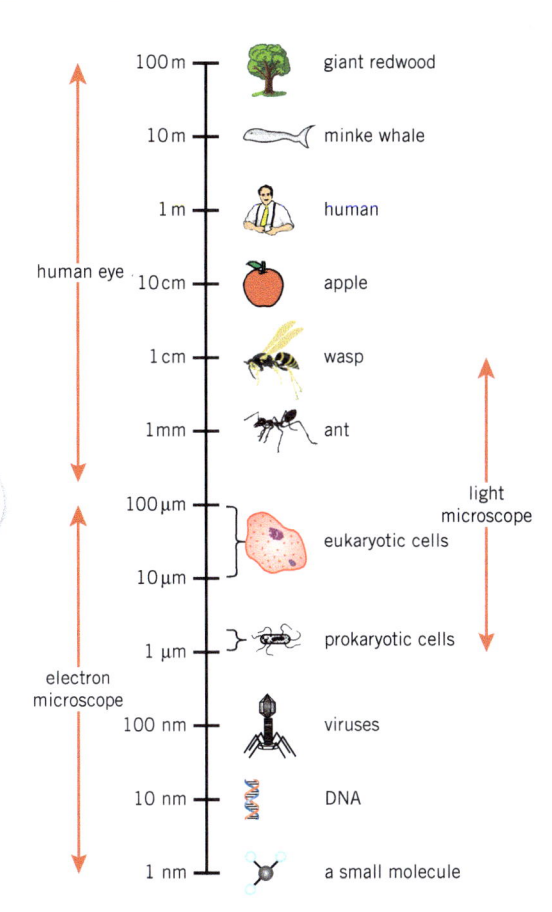

Figure 2 *The relative sizes of different cells and whole organisms and how they can be seen*

Key points

- Eukaryotic cells all have a cell membrane, cytoplasm, and genetic material enclosed in a nucleus.
- Prokaryotic cells consist of cytoplasm and a cell membrane surrounded by a cell wall. The genetic material is not in a distinct nucleus. It forms a single DNA loop. Prokaryotes may contain one or more extra small rings of DNA called plasmids. Prokaryotes are 1–2 orders of magnitude smaller than eukaryotes.
- Bacteria are all prokaryotes.
- Orders of magnitude are used to make approximate comparisons between numbers or objects. 1 order of magnitude = approximately 10 × bigger or smaller.

1.3.4 Diffusion

Learning objectives

After this topic, you should know:
- how diffusion takes place and why it is important in living organisms
- what affects the rate of diffusion.

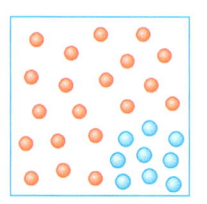

At the moment when the blue particles are added to the red particles they are not mixed at all

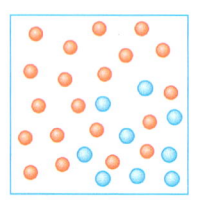

As the particles move randomly, the blue ones begin to mix with the red ones

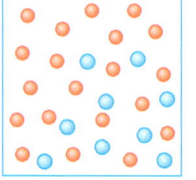

As the particles move and spread out, they bump into each other. This helps them to keep spreading randomly

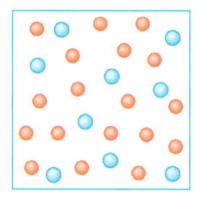

Eventually, the particles are completely mixed and diffusion is complete, although they do continue to move randomly

Figure 1 *The random movement of particles results in substances spreading out, or diffusing, from an area of higher concentration to an area of lower concentration*

Study tip

Particles move randomly, but the net movement is from a region of high concentration to a region of low concentration.

Synoptic link

Look back at Topics 1.1.1 and 1.1.3 to remind yourself about kinetic theory of matter and the random motion of particles in liquids and gases.

Your cells need to take in substances such as glucose and oxygen for respiration. They also need to get rid of waste products, and chemicals that are needed elsewhere in your body. Dissolved substances and gases can move into and out of your cells across the cell membrane. One of the main ways in which they move is by **diffusion**.

Diffusion

Diffusion is a spreading out and mixing process. This results in the net movement (overall movement) of particles of a gas, or of any substance in solution (a solute). The net movement is from an area of higher concentration to an area of lower concentration of the particle. It takes place because of the random movement of the particles (molecules or ions). The motion of the particles causes them to bump into each other, and this moves them all around. When substances diffuse across cell membranes:

net movement   =   particles moving   –   particles moving
                     into the cell   **out of the cell**

Imagine a room containing a group of boys on one side and a group of girls on the other. If everyone closes their eyes and moves around briskly but randomly, they will bump into each other. They will scatter until the room contains a mixture of boys and girls. This gives you a good model of diffusion (Figure 1).

Rates of diffusion

If there is a big difference in concentration between two areas, diffusion will take place quickly. Many particles will move randomly towards the area of low concentration. Only relatively few will move randomly in the other direction. There will be a large, relatively fast net movement of particles.

However, if there is only a small difference in concentration between two areas, the net movement by diffusion will be quite slow. The number of particles moving into the area of lower concentration by random movement will only be slightly more than the number of particles that are leaving the area.

In general, the greater the difference in concentration, the faster the rate of diffusion. This difference between two areas of concentration is called the **concentration gradient**. The bigger the difference, the steeper the concentration gradient and the faster the rate of diffusion. In other words, diffusion occurs *down* a concentration gradient.

Temperature also affects the rate of diffusion. An increase in temperature means the particles in a gas or a solution move around more quickly. When this happens, diffusion takes place more rapidly as the random movement of the particles speeds up.

Diffusion in living organisms

Dissolved substances move into and out of your cells by diffusion across the cell membrane. These include simple sugars, such as glucose, gases

■ 1.3 Cells in animals and plants

such as oxygen and carbon dioxide, and waste products, such as urea from the breakdown of amino acids in your liver. The urea passes from the liver cells into the blood plasma and will be excreted by the kidneys.

The oxygen you need for respiration passes from the air in your lungs into your red blood cells through the cell membranes by diffusion. The oxygen moves down a concentration gradient from a region of high oxygen concentration to a region of low oxygen concentration.

Oxygen then also moves by diffusion down a concentration gradient from the blood cells into the cells of the body where it is needed. Carbon dioxide moves by diffusion down a concentration gradient out from the body cells into the red blood cells and then into the air in the lungs in a similar way. The diffusion of oxygen and carbon dioxide in opposite directions in the lungs is known as **gas exchange**.

Individual cells may be adapted to make diffusion easier and more rapid. The most common adaptation is to increase the surface area of the cell membrane (Figure 2). By folding up the membrane of a cell or the tissue lining an organ, the area over which diffusion can take place is greatly increased. Therefore the rate of diffusion is also greatly increased, so that much more of a substance moves in a given time.

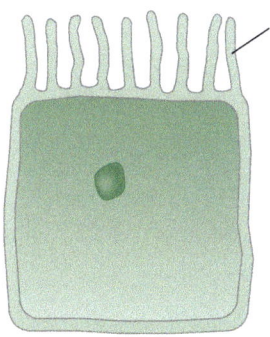

Synoptic links

You will learn more about gas exchange in Topic 2.5.7.

You will learn more about the impact of the surface area to volume ratio in Topic 2.5.3.

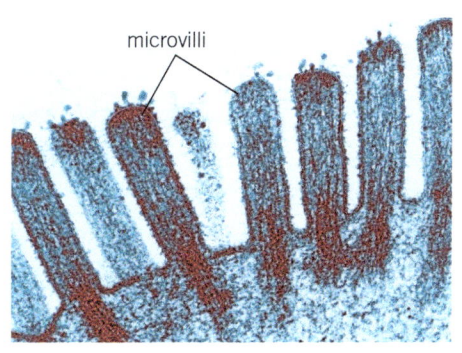

Figure 2 *An increase in the surface area of a cell membrane means diffusion can take place more quickly. The electron micrograph on the right shows the microvilli of an intestinal cell – magnification ~ ×30 000*

1. Define the process of diffusion in terms of the particles involved. [2 marks]

2. a Explain why diffusion takes place faster when there is an increase in temperature. [3 marks]
   b Explain why so many cells have folded membranes along at least one surface. [2 marks]

3. Describe the process of diffusion occurring in each of the following statements. Include any adaptations that are involved.
   a Digested food products move from your gut into the bloodstream. [3 marks]
   b Carbon dioxide moves from the blood in the capillaries of your lungs to the air in the lungs. [3 marks]
   c Male moths can track down a mate from up to three miles away because of the special chemicals produced by the female. [3 marks]

Key points

- Diffusion is the spreading out and mixing of particles of any substance, in solution or a gas, resulting in a net movement from a region of higher concentration to a region of lower concentration, down a concentration gradient.
- The rate of diffusion is affected by the difference in concentrations, the temperature, and the available surface area.

1.3.5 Osmosis

Learning objectives

After this topic, you should know:

- how osmosis differs from diffusion
- why osmosis is so important in animal cells.

Study tip

Remember, any particles can diffuse from an area of high concentration to an area of low concentration, provided that they are **soluble** and **small** enough to pass through the membrane.

Osmosis in organisms refers only to the diffusion of *water* molecules through the partially permeable cell membrane.

Modelling osmosis

You can make model cells using bags made of partially permeable membrane (Figure 1). You can find out what happens to the cells if the concentrations of the solutions inside or outside them change.

Diffusion takes place when particles can spread out freely from a higher to a lower concentration. However, the solutions inside cells are separated from those outside by the cell membrane. This membrane does not let all types of particles through. Membranes that only let some types of particles through are called **partially permeable membranes**.

How osmosis differs from diffusion

Partially permeable cell membranes let water move across them. Remember:

- A **dilute** solution of sugar contains a *high* concentration of water (the solvent). It has a *low* concentration of sugar (the solute).
- A **concentrated** sugar solution contains a relatively *low* concentration of water. It has a *high* concentration of sugar.

The cytoplasm of a cell is made up of chemicals dissolved in water inside a partially permeable cell membrane. The cytoplasm contains a fairly concentrated solution of salts and sugars. Water moves from a dilute solution (with a high concentration of water molecules) to a concentrated solution (with fewer water molecules in a given volume) across the membrane of the cell.

This special type of diffusion, where only water moves across a partially permeable membrane from a dilute solution to a concentrated solution is called **osmosis**.

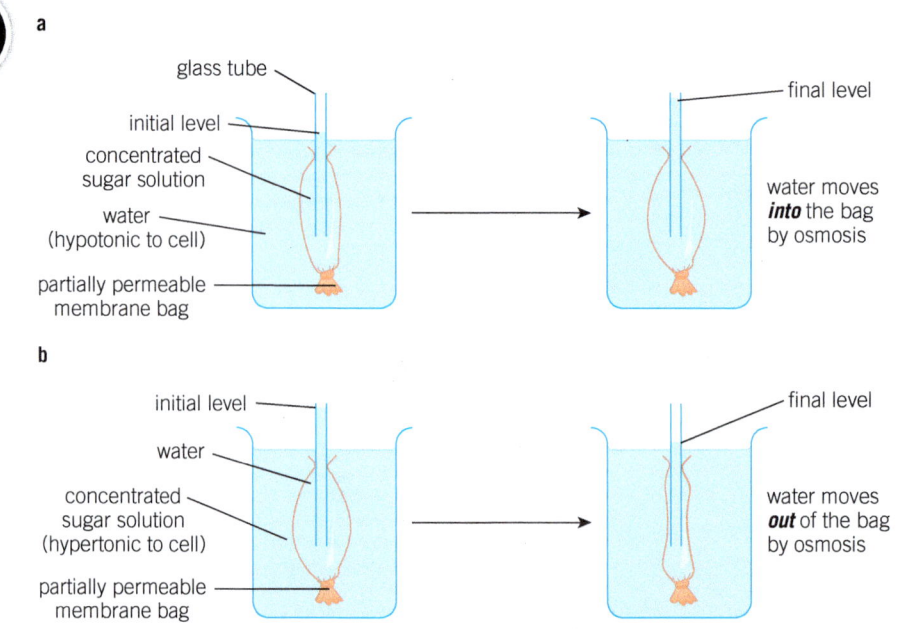

Figure 1 A model of osmosis in a cell. In **a** the model cell is in a hypotonic solution. In **b** the model cell is in a hypertonic solution

The concentration of solutes inside your body cells needs to stay at the same level for them to work properly. However, the concentration of the solutions outside your cells may be very different to the concentration

40

■ 1.3 Cells in animals and plants

inside them. This concentration gradient can cause water to move into or out of the cells by osmosis (Figure 1).

- If the concentration of solutes in the solution outside the cell is *lower* than the internal concentration, the solution is **hypotonic** to the cell.
- If the concentration of solutes in the solution outside the cell is *the same* as the internal concentration, the solution is **isotonic** to the cell.
- If the concentration of solutes in the solution outside the cell is *higher* than the internal concentration, the solution is **hypertonic** to the cell.

Osmosis in animals

If a cell uses up water in its chemical reactions, the cytoplasm becomes more concentrated. The surrounding fluid becomes hypotonic to the cell and more water immediately moves in by osmosis.

If the cytoplasm becomes too dilute because more water is made in chemical reactions, the surrounding fluid becomes hypertonic to the cell and water leaves the cell by osmosis. Osmosis restores the balance in both cases.

However, osmosis can also cause big problems. If the solution outside the cell becomes much more dilute (hypotonic) than the cell contents, water will move in by osmosis. The cell will swell and may burst. If the solution outside the cell becomes much more concentrated (hypertonic) than the cell contents, water will move out of the cell by osmosis. The cytoplasm will become too concentrated and the cell will shrivel up and can no longer survive. Once you understand the effect osmosis can have on cells, you can understand why it is so important for animals to keep the concentration of their body fluids as constant as possible.

> **Study tip**
>
> When writing about osmosis, be careful to specify whether it is the concentration of water or of solutes that you are referring to.
>
> Make sure you understand exactly what is meant by the terms isotonic, hypertonic, and hypotonic.

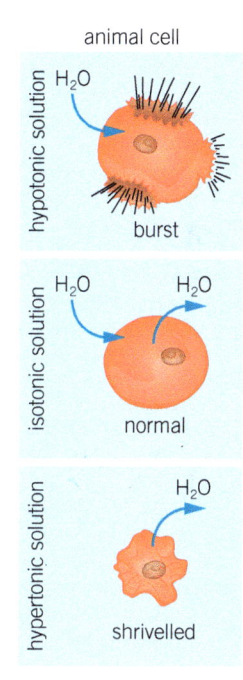

Figure 2 Osmosis can have a dramatic effect on animal cells

1 a State the difference between osmosis and diffusion. [2 marks]
  b Explain how osmosis helps to maintain the cytoplasm of plant and body cells at a specific concentration. [2 marks]
2 a Define the following terms:
   i isotonic solution [1 mark]
   ii hypotonic solution [1 mark]
   iii hypertonic solution. [1 mark]
  b Explain why it is so important for the cells of the human body that the solute concentration of the fluid surrounding the cells is kept as constant as possible. [4 marks]
3 Animals that live in fresh water have a constant problem with their water balance. The single-celled organism called *Amoeba* has a special vacuole in its cell. The vacuole fills with water and then moves to the outside of the cell and bursts. A new vacuole starts forming straight away. Explain in terms of osmosis why the *Amoeba* needs one of these vacuoles. [4 marks]

> **Key points**
>
> - Water may move across cell membranes by osmosis.
> - Cell membranes are partially permeable. They allow small molecules such as water through, but not larger molecules.
> - During osmosis water diffuses from where it is more concentrated (solute concentration is lower) through a partially permeable membrane to where it is less concentrated (solute concentration is higher).

1.3.6 Osmosis in plants

Learning objectives

After this topic, you should know:
- why osmosis is so important in plant cells
- how to investigate the effect of osmosis on plant tissues.

As you have seen, osmosis is the movement of water through a partially permeable membrane down a water concentration gradient. The effect of osmosis on animal cells can be dramatic. Animals have many complex ways of controlling the concentrations of their body solutions to prevent cell damage as a result of osmosis. In plants, osmosis is key to their whole way of life.

Osmosis for support

Plants rely on osmosis to support their stems and leaves. Water moves into plant cells by osmosis. This causes the vacuole to swell, which presses the cytoplasm against the plant cell wall. The pressure builds up until no more water can physically enter the cell – this pressure is known as **turgor**. Turgor pressure makes cells hard and rigid, which in turn keeps the leaves and stems of the plant rigid and firm.

Plants need the fluid surrounding the cells to always be hypotonic to the cytoplasm, with a lower concentration of solutes and a higher concentration of water than the plant cells themselves. This keeps water moving by osmosis in the right direction and the cells are turgid. If the solution surrounding the plant cells is hypertonic to (more concentrated than) the cell contents, water will leave the cells by osmosis. The cells will no longer be firm and swollen – they become flaccid (soft) as there is no pressure on the cell walls. At this point, the plant wilts as turgor no longer supports the plant tissues.

If more water is lost by osmosis, the vacuole and cytoplasm shrink, and eventually the cell membrane pulls away from the cell wall. This is **plasmolysis**. Plasmolysis is usually only seen in laboratory experiments. Plasmolysed cells die quickly unless the osmotic balance is restored.

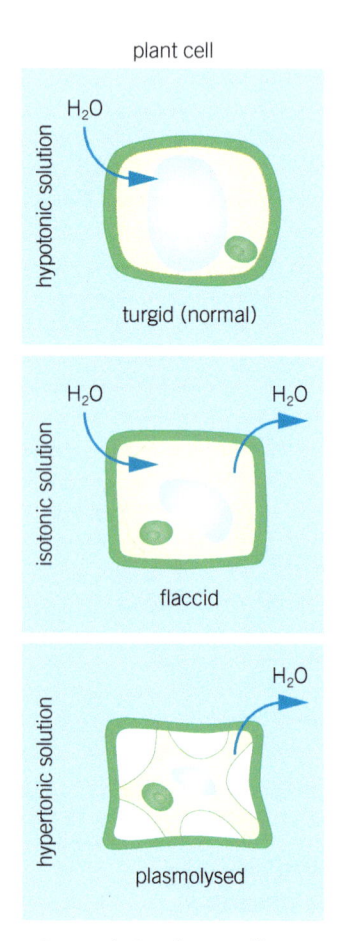

Figure 1 *Osmosis in plant cells*

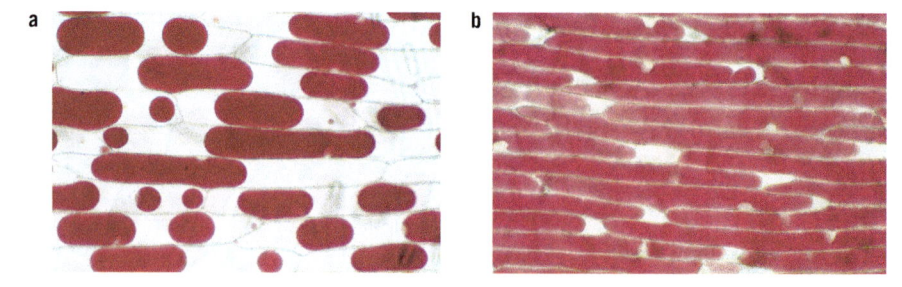

Figure 2 *Micrographs of red onion cells in* **a** *hypertonic and* **b** *hypotonic solutions show the effect of osmosis on the contents of the cell. It is easy to see the changes in these living cells because the cytoplasm is naturally red*

Investigating osmosis in plant cells
Plant tissue reacts so strongly to the concentration of the external solution that you can use it as an osmometer – a way of measuring osmosis. There are lots of ways you can investigate the effect of osmosis on plant tissue, each with advantages and disadvantages.

■ 1.3 Cells in animals and plants

The basis of many experiments is to put plant tissue into different concentrations of salt solutions or sugar solutions. You can even use squash to give you the sugar solution. If plant tissue is placed in a hypotonic solution, water will move in to the cells by osmosis. If it is placed in hypertonic solution, water will move out by osmosis. These changes can be measured by the effect they have on the tissue sample.

- Suggest why salt and sugar are used in osmosis experiments. How could you decide which gives the clearest results?
- Potato is commonly used as the experimental plant tissue. It can be cut into cylinders, rectangular 'chips' or smaller discs. Suggest why potato is so often used as a test plant tissue.
- Sweet potato and beetroot are other common sources of plant tissue for osmosis experiments – suggest possible advantages and disadvantages of using them. How could you determine which is the best experimental plant tissue?

Measuring changes in mass is a widely used method for investigating the uptake or loss of water from plant tissues by osmosis. You must take care not to include any liquid left on the outside of the plant tissue in your measurements, as this can have a big effect on your results.

- Discuss the possible advantages and disadvantages of using cylinders, chips, or discs for assessing the effect of osmosis on plant tissue. How would you determine which method is the most effective?
- Investigate the effect of surface area on osmosis.
- Explain how you think the surface area of the plant tissue samples might affect osmosis.
- Plan an investigation to see if your ideas are right.
- Show your plan to your teacher and then carry out your investigation.

Safety: Take care when using cutting instruments.

> **Go further**
>
> Scientists have discovered ways of measuring the turgor pressure inside individual cells using very tiny probes. The pressures inside the root or leaf cell of a plant are far higher than human blood pressure, or even the pressure in a car tyre.

1 Define the term osmosis. [1 mark]
2 Students carried out an investigation into the effects of osmosis on plant tissues, placing three sets of beetroot cylinders in three different sugar solutions for 30 min. One set gained mass, another lost mass, and the third set did not change. One student thought the last experiment hadn't worked. Another disagreed. Explain these results in terms of osmosis in plant cells. [6 marks]
3 Suggest and explain why osmosis is so important in the structural support systems of plants. [6 marks]

> **Key points**
>
> - Water may move across cell membranes by osmosis.
> - Cell membranes are partially permeable. They allow small molecules such as water through, but not larger molecules.
> - During osmosis water diffuses from where it is more concentrated (solute concentration is lower) through a partially permeable membrane to where it is less concentrated (solute concentration is higher).
> - The effect of different concentrations of salt or sugar solutions on plant tissue can be investigated by measuring changes in the mass of the plant tissue.

1.3.7 Active transport

Learning objectives

After this topic, you should know:
- how active transport works
- the importance of active transport in cells.

People with cystic fibrosis have thick, sticky mucus in their lungs, gut, and reproductive systems. This causes many different health problems and it happens because an active transport system in their mucus-producing cells does not work properly. Sometimes diffusion and osmosis are not enough.

All cells need to move substances in and out. Water often moves across the cell boundaries by osmosis. Dissolved substances also need to move in and out of cells. There are two main ways in which this happens:

- Substances move by diffusion, down a concentration gradient. This must be in the right direction to be useful to the cells.
- Sometimes the substances needed by a cell have to be moved against a concentration gradient, across a partially permeable membrane. This needs a special process called **active transport**.

Moving substances by active transport

Active transport allows cells to move substances from an area of low concentration to an area of high concentration. This movement is *against* the concentration gradient. As a result, cells can absorb ions from very dilute solutions. It also enables cells to move substances, such as molecules of sugars and mineral ions, from one place to another through the cell membrane.

Energy is needed for the active transport system to carry a molecule or a mineral ion across the membrane and then return to its original position. This energy is produced during cell respiration. Scientists have shown in a number of different cells that the rate of respiration and the rate of active transport are closely linked (Figure 1).

In other words, if a cell respires and releases a lot of energy, it can carry out lots of active transport. Examples include root hair cells in plants and the cells lining your gut. Cells involved in a lot of active transport usually have many mitochondria to release the energy they need.

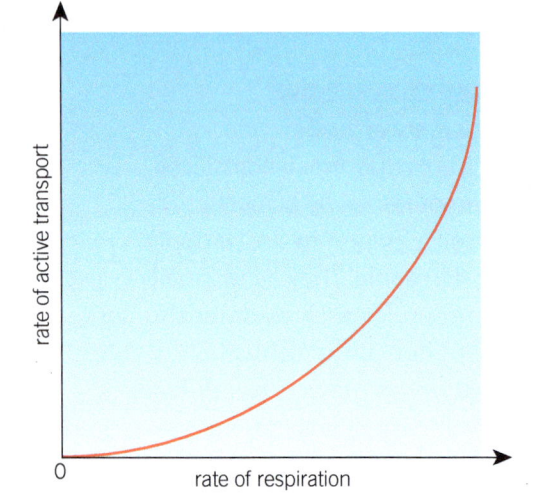

Figure 1 *The rate of active transport depends on the rate of respiration*

The importance of active transport

Active transport is widely used in cells. There are some situations in which it is particularly important. For example, mineral ions in the soil, such as nitrate ions, are usually found in very dilute solutions. These solutions are more dilute than the solution within the plant root hair cells. By using active transport, plants can absorb these mineral ions, even though it is against a concentration gradient (Figure 2).

Sugar, such as glucose, is always actively absorbed out of your gut and kidney tubules into your blood. This is often done against a large concentration gradient.

■ 1.3 Cells in animals and plants

For example, glucose is needed for cell respiration, so it is important to get as much as possible out of the gut. The concentration of glucose in your blood is kept steady, so sometimes it is higher than the concentration of glucose in your gut. When this happens, active transport is used to move the glucose from your gut into your blood against the concentration gradient.

Synoptic links

You can find out more about exchange systems in the human body in Chapter 2.5.

You will learn more about the chemistry of ions in Topic 6.16.1 in the *Physical Sciences* book.

Study tip

Do not refer to movement *along* a concentration gradient. Always refer to movement as *down* a concentration gradient (from higher to lower) for diffusion or osmosis and *against* a concentration gradient (from lower to higher) for active transport.

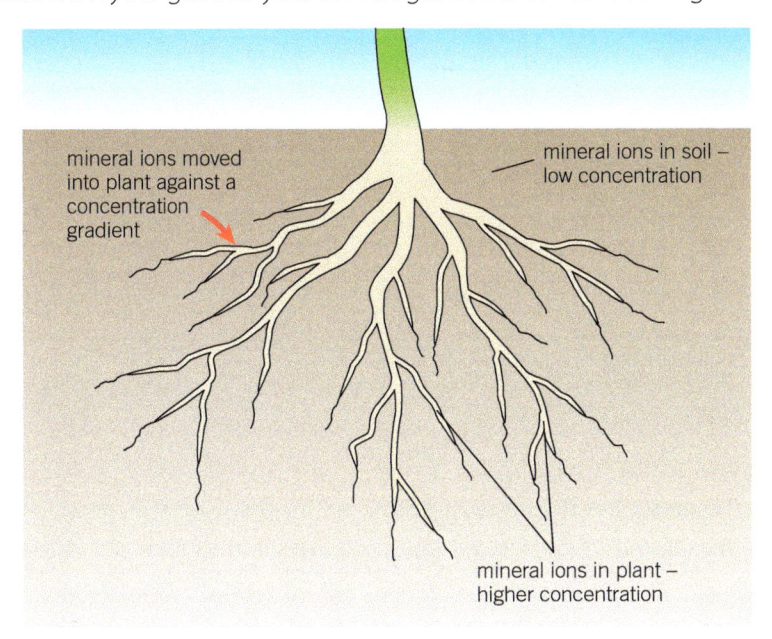

Figure 2 *Plants use active transport to move mineral ions from the soil into the roots against a concentration gradient*

Figure 3 *Some crocodiles have special salt glands in their tongues. These remove excess salt from the body against the concentration gradient by active transport. That's why members of the crocodile species* Crocodylus porosus *can live in estuaries and even the sea*

Key points

- Some substances move across cell membranes via active transport.
- Active transport involves the movement of a dissolved substance from a region where it is less concentrated to a region where it is more concentrated. This requires energy from respiration.
- Active transport allows plant root hairs to absorb mineral ions required for healthy growth from very dilute solutions in the soil against a concentration gradient.
- Active transport enables sugar molecules used for cell respiration to be absorbed from lower concentrations in the gut into the blood where the concentration of sugar is higher.

1 Describe how active transport works in a cell. [4 marks]

2 a Describe how active transport differs from diffusion and osmosis. [3 marks]
   b Explain why cells that carry out a lot of active transport also usually have many mitochondria. [2 marks]

3 Explain fully why active transport is so important to:
   a marine birds such as albatrosses, which have special salt glands producing very salty liquid [2 marks]
   b plants. [3 marks]

1.3.8 Cell division

Learning objectives

After this topic, you should know:
- the role of the chromosomes in cells
- the importance of the cell cycle
- how cells divide by mitosis.

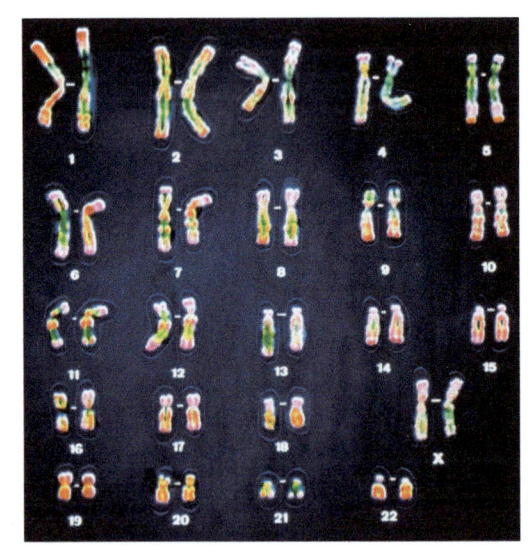

Figure 1 *This special image, a karyotype, shows the 23 pairs of chromosomes from a body cell of a female human being, coloured to make them easier to identify, and lined up in their pairs*

Synoptic link

For more information on genes, see Chapter 4.12.

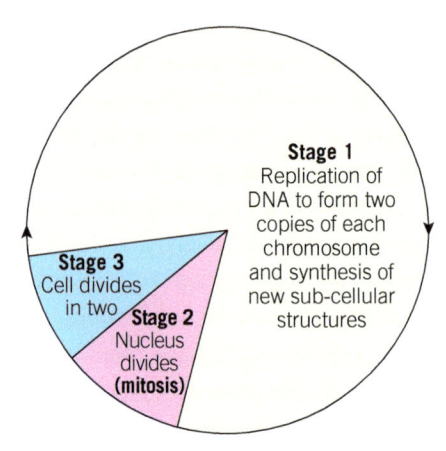

Figure 2 *The cell cycle. In rapidly growing tissue, stage 1 may only be a few hours, but in adult animals it can last for years*

New cells are needed for an organism, or part of an organism, to grow. They are also needed to replace cells that become worn out and to repair damaged tissue. However, the new cells must have the same genetic information as the originals, so that they can do the same job.

The information in the cells

Each of your cells has a nucleus, which contains chromosomes. Chromosomes carry the genes that contain the instructions for making both new cells and all the tissues and organs needed to make an entire new you.

A gene is a small packet of information that controls a characteristic, or part of a characteristic, of your body. It is a section of DNA, the unique molecule that makes up your chromosomes.

Most of your characteristics are the result of many different genes rather than a single gene. The genes are grouped together on chromosomes. A chromosome may carry several hundred or even thousands of genes.

You have 46 chromosomes in the nucleus of your body cells. They are arranged in 23 pairs (Figure 1). In each pair of chromosomes, one chromosome is inherited from your father and one from your mother. The sex cells (gametes) contain only half the number of chromosomes found in the normal body cells. Each gamete has one set of 23 chromosomes. When the gametes meet in sexual reproduction the new cell has 23 pairs of chromosomes, one set from each parent.

The cell cycle and mitosis

Body cells divide in a series of stages known as the **cell cycle** (Figure 2). Cell division in the cell cycle involves a process called **mitosis** and it produces two identical cells. As a result, all your normal body cells have the same chromosomes and so the same genetic information. Cell division by mitosis produces the additional cells needed for growth and development in multicellular organisms, and for the replacement of worn-out or damaged cells.

In asexual reproduction, the cells of the offspring are produced by mitosis from the cells of their parent. This is why they contain exactly the same genes as their parent with little or no genetic variation.

The cell cycle

The length of the cycle varies considerably. It can take less than 24 hours, or it can take several years, depending on the cells involved and the stage of life of the organism. The cell cycle is short as a baby develops before it is born, when new cells are being made all the time. It remains fairly rapid during childhood, but the cell cycle slows down once puberty is over and the body is adult. However, even in adults, there are regions where there is continued growth or regular replacement of cells. These regions include the hair follicles, the skin, the blood, and the lining of the digestive system.

1.3 Cells in animals and plants

The cell cycle in normal, healthy cells follows a regular pattern (Figure 2):

- **Stage 1** – The longest stage in the cell cycle. The cells grow bigger, increasing their mass, and carrying out normal cell activities. Most importantly they replicate their DNA to form two copies of each chromosome ready for cell division. They also increase the number of sub-cellular structures such as mitochondria, ribosomes, and chloroplasts ready for the cell to divide.
- **Stage 2** – Mitosis, during which one set of chromosomes is pulled to each end of the dividing cell and the nucleus divides.
- **Stage 3** – The stage during which the cytoplasm and the cell membranes also divide to form two identical daughter cells.

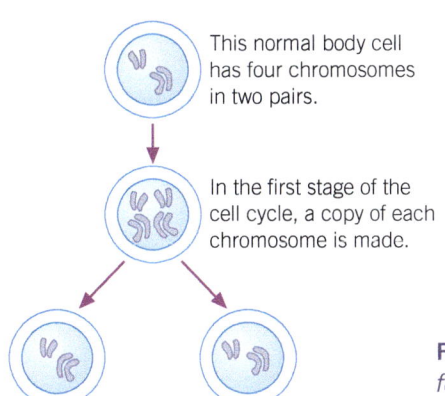

This normal body cell has four chromosomes in two pairs.

In the first stage of the cell cycle, a copy of each chromosome is made.

The cell divides in two to form two daughter cells, each with a nucleus containing four chromosomes identical to the ones in the original parent cell.

Figure 3 *Two identical cells are formed by mitotic division in the cell cycle. This cell is shown with only two pairs of chromosomes rather than 23, to make it easier to follow what happens*

In some parts of an animal or plant, mitotic cell division carries on rapidly all the time. For example, you constantly lose cells from the skin's surface and make new cells to replace them. In fact, about 300 million of your body cells die every minute, so cell division by mitosis is very important. In a child, mitotic divisions produce new cells faster than the old ones die. As an adult, cell death and mitosis keep more or less in balance. When you get very old, mitosis slows down and you show the typical signs of ageing.

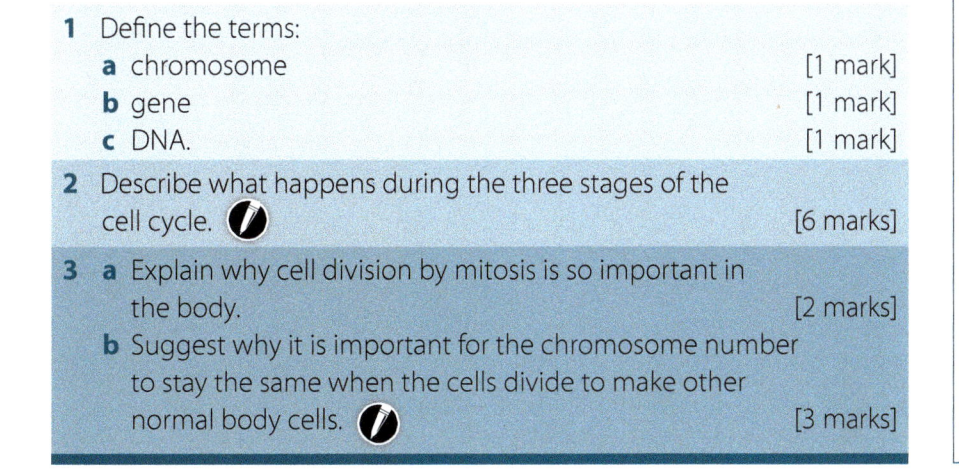

Observing cell division

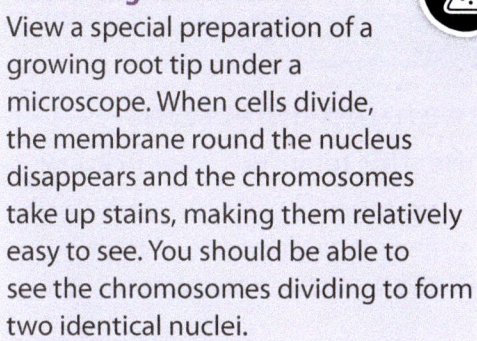

View a special preparation of a growing root tip under a microscope. When cells divide, the membrane round the nucleus disappears and the chromosomes take up stains, making them relatively easy to see. You should be able to see the chromosomes dividing to form two identical nuclei.

- Describe your observations of mitosis.

Key points

- In body cells, chromosomes are found in pairs. Chromosomes are made up of DNA and each chromosome carries a large number of genes.
- Body cells divide in a series of stages called the cell cycle.
- During the cell cycle the genetic material is doubled. It then divides into two identical nuclei in a process called mitosis.
- Before a cell can divide it needs to grow, replicate the DNA to form two copies of each chromosome, and increase the number of sub-cellular structures. In mitosis one of the two sets of chromosomes is pulled to each end of the cell and the nucleus divides. Finally, the cytoplasm and cell membranes divide to form two identical cells.
- Mitotic cell division is important in the growth, repair, and development of multicellular organisms.

---

1 Define the terms:
   a chromosome [1 mark]
   b gene [1 mark]
   c DNA. [1 mark]

2 Describe what happens during the three stages of the cell cycle. [6 marks]

3 a Explain why cell division by mitosis is so important in the body. [2 marks]
   b Suggest why it is important for the chromosome number to stay the same when the cells divide to make other normal body cells. [3 marks]

47

1.3.9 Differentiation and stem cells

Learning objectives

After this topic, you should know:

- the function of stem cells in embryonic and adult animals
- the importance of differentiation.

The smallest living organisms are remarkable. Although they are only single cells, they can carry out all of the functions of life. These range from feeding and respiration to excretion and reproduction. Most organisms are bigger and are made up of lots of cells. Some of these cells become **specialised** in order to carry out particular jobs.

Differentiation

The single cell formed when an egg and a sperm fuse has the potential to become a new human being. By the time you are an adult, scientists have estimated that your body will contain somewhere in the region of 37.2 trillion (written in standard form as 3.72×10^{13}) cells – although estimates vary from around 15 trillion to 100 trillion! Almost all of these cells are the result of mitosis. The growth that takes place is amazing. Growth is a permanent increase in size as a result of cell division or cell enlargement.

The cells of your body – or any complex multicellular organism – are not all the same. They are not the same as the original cell, either. This is because, as cells divide and grow, they also begin to **differentiate**.

In the early development of animal embryos, the cells are unspecialised. They are known as **stem cells**. The earliest stem cells in embryos, known as **embryonic stem cells**, can become any type of cell that is needed to make the embryo or the placenta. As the animal develops the embryonic stem cells become slightly less adaptable, but they can still differentiate to form the cells needed to produce a fully formed baby.

In many animals, the cells become specialised very early in life. By the time a human baby is born, most of its cells are specialised. They will all do a particular job, such as nerve cells, skin cells, or muscle cells. They have differentiated. Some of their genes have been switched on and others have been switched off.

When a cell becomes specialised, its structure is adapted to suit the particular job that it does. As a result, specialised cells often look very different to the typical plant or animal cell. Sometimes cells become so specialised that they only have one function within the body. Examples of this include sperm, eggs, red blood cells, muscle cells, and nerve cells. Some specialised cells, such as egg and sperm cells, work individually. Others are adapted to work as part of a tissue, an organ, or a whole organism.

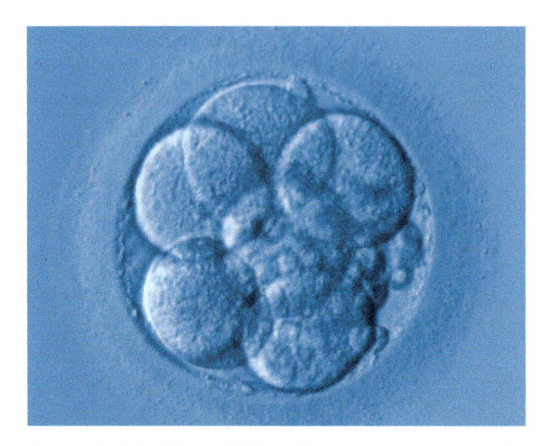

Figure 1 *This early embryo has only 8 cells, each of them an embyronic stem cell. A lot of mitosis and differentiation is needed before the embryo becomes a teenager!*

1.3 Cells in animals and plants

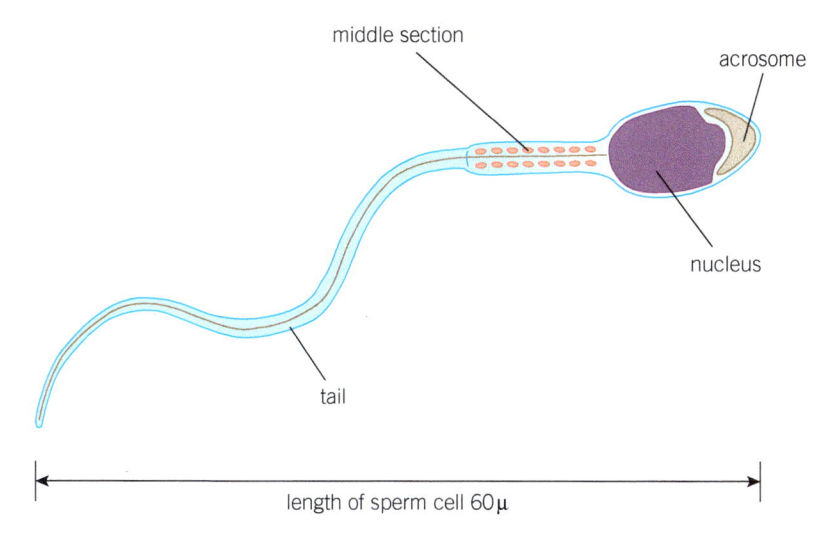

Figure 2 *Specialised cells, such as this sperm cell, often look very different from a generalised cell and from each other. Each type of specialised cell has adaptations to carry out specific functions in the body*

Replacing adult cells

When animal cells have differentiated and become specialised, they cannot later change into different types of cells. This means that when, for example, a muscle cell divides by mitosis, it can only form more muscle cells. So, in a mature (adult) animal, cell division is mainly restricted to the repair of damaged tissue and to replace worn out cells, because in most adult cells differentiation has already occurred. Specialised cells can divide by mitosis, but they only form the same sort of cell. Some differentiated cells, such as blood and skin cells, cannot divide at all.

In most adult tissues there are some relatively undifferentiated cells known as **adult stem cells**. These start dividing when they are needed to replace dead or damaged cells that cannot divide and replace themselves. Most tissues contain only a small number of adult stem cells and they are used only for replacement and repair, not for growth. Nerve cells do not divide once they have differentiated and they are not replaced by stem cells, so when nerve cells are damaged or lost they are not usually replaced.

Synoptic links
You will learn more about specialised cells in Topic 2.5.4 and more about stem cells in Topics 3.9.10 and 3.9.11.

Study tip
Remember – cells produced by mitosis are genetically identical.

Key points
- At first the cells in an embryo can grow and divide to form any type of cell. They are stem cells.
- As an animal develops, most of the cells differentiate and become specialised. Specialised cells carry out a particular function.
- Animal cells that have become specialised cannot later change into different kinds of cells. However, there are some stem cells in most adult tissues that are ready to start dividing to replace old cells or to repair damage in the tissues where they are found.

1	a Define differentiation.	[1 mark]
	b Explain why differentiation is important in living organisms.	[3 marks]
2	Describe the difference between embryonic stem cells and adult stem cells.	[5 marks]
3	Calculate by what order of magnitude an adult human is bigger than the original fertilised ovum (see Maths skills MS 2h).	[4 marks]

1.3.10 Cell division in sexual reproduction

Learning objectives

After this topic, you should know:
- how cells divide by meiosis to form gametes
- how meiosis halves the number of chromosomes in gametes and fertilisation restores the full number
- how sexual reproduction gives rise to variation.

Mitosis takes place all the time, in tissues all over your body and whenever organisms reproduce asexually. There is, however, another type of cell division, which takes place in the reproductive organs of animals and plants. In humans, these organs are the ovaries and the testes. **Meiosis** results in sex cells, called gametes, which have only half the original number of chromosomes.

Meiosis

In animals, the female gametes (egg cells or ova) are made in the ovaries. The male gametes (sperm) are made in the testes.

The gametes are formed by meiosis. In meiosis, the chromosome number is reduced by half. In a body cell there are two sets of each chromosomes, one inherited from the mother and one from the father. When a cell divides to form gametes:

- **The genetic information is copied so that there are four sets of each chromosome instead of the normal two sets. This is very similar to mitosis.**
- **The cell then divides twice in quick succession to form four gametes, each with a single set of chromosomes (Figure 1).**

Each gamete that is produced is genetically different from all the others. Gametes contain random mixtures of the original chromosomes. This introduces variation.

The testes can produce around 400 million sperm by meiosis every 24 hours. Only one sperm is needed to fertilise an egg, but each sperm needs to travel 100 000 times its own length to reach the egg. Fewer than one sperm in a million actually make it.

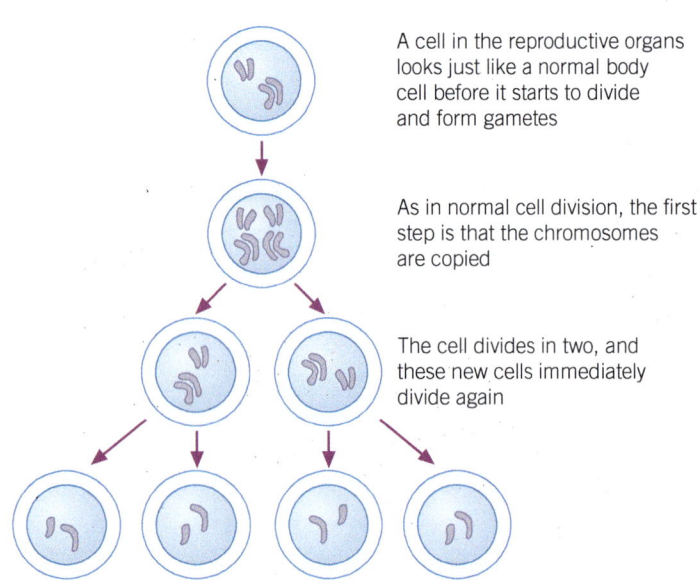

A cell in the reproductive organs looks just like a normal body cell before it starts to divide and form gametes

As in normal cell division, the first step is that the chromosomes are copied

The cell divides in two, and these new cells immediately divide again

This gives four sex cells, each with a single set of chromosomes – in this case two instead of the original four

Figure 1 *Meiosis halves the number of chromosomes in the gametes, and fertilisation restores the full number of chromosomes in the body cells*

Fertilisation

More variation is added when fertilisation takes place. Each sex cell has a single set of chromosomes. When two sex cells join during fertilisation, the single new cell formed has a full set of chromosomes. In humans, the egg cell has 23 chromosomes and so does the sperm. When they join together, they produce a single new body cell with 46 chromosomes in 23 pairs – the correct number of chromosomes for human body cells.

The combination of genes on the chromosomes of every newly fertilised egg is unique. Once fertilisation is complete, the unique new cell begins to divide by mitosis to form a new individual. The number of cells increases rapidly. As the embryo develops, the cells differentiate to form different tissues, organs, and organ systems.

1.3 Cells in animals and plants

Variation

The differences between asexual and sexual reproduction are reflected in the different types of cell division involved.

In asexual reproduction, offspring are produced as a result of mitosis from the parent cells. They contain exactly the same chromosomes and the same genes as their parents. There is no variation in the genetic material.

In sexual reproduction, gametes are produced by meiosis in the sex organs of the parents. This introduces variation as each gamete is different. Then, when the gametes fuse, one of each pair of chromosomes, and so one of each pair of genes, comes from each parent, adding more variation. The combination of genes in the new pair of chromosomes will contain different forms of the same genes (alleles) from each parent. This also helps to produce variation in the characteristics of the offspring.

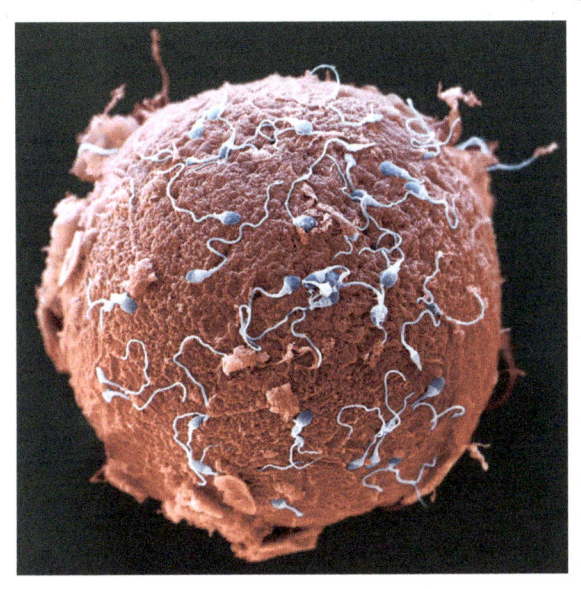

Figure 2 *This scanning electron micrograph of the moment of fertilisation has been coloured so that the egg and sperm can be identified more easily – magnification ~ ×500. The result of fertilisation is a new cell with a complete and unique set of chromosomes*

1 a State how many pairs of chromosomes there are in a normal human body cell. [1 mark]
   b State how many chromosomes there are in a human sperm cell. [1 mark]
   c State how many chromosomes there are in a fertilised human egg cell. [1 mark]
2 Sexual reproduction results in variation. Describe how this comes about. [5 marks]
3 a Name the special type of cell division that produces gametes from cells in the reproductive organs. Describe clearly what happens to the chromosomes in this process. [4 marks]
   b State where in your body this type of cell division would take place. [1 mark]
   c Explain why this type of cell division is so important in sexual reproduction. [5 marks]

Synoptic links

To remind yourself of the events of mitosis, look at Topic 1.3.8.

You will learn more about alleles and variation in Topics 4.12.2 and 4.12.4.

Study tip

Learn to spell mitosis and meiosis.
Remember their meanings:
Mitosis – **m**aking **i**dentical **t**wo.
Meiosis – **m**aking **e**ggs (and sperm).

Key points

- Cells in the reproductive organs divide by meiosis to form the gametes (sex cells – eggs and sperm).
- Body cells have two sets of chromosomes, gametes have only one set.
- In meiosis, the genetic material is copied and then the cell divides twice to form four gametes, each with a single set of chromosomes.
- All gametes are genetically different from each other.
- Gametes join at fertilisation to restore the normal number of chromosomes. The new cell divides by mitosis. The number of cells increases and as the embryo develops, the cells differentiate.

51

1.3 Cells in animals and plants

Summary questions

1 a Explain the importance of the light microscope in our understanding of cells. [4 marks]
  b Describe how the electron microscope has improved our knowledge of the fine structures inside cells. [6 marks]

2 **Figure 1** shows a bacterial cell.

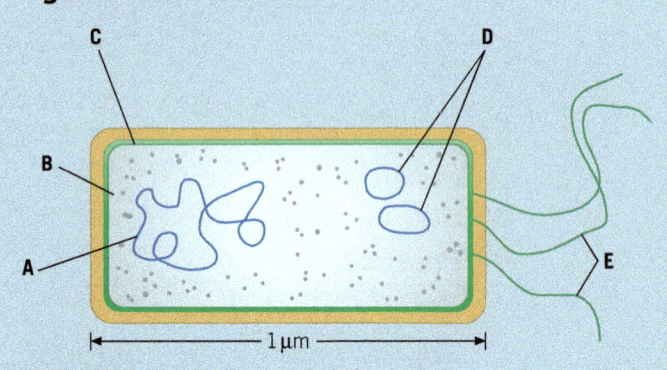

Figure 1

  a Name the structures labelled **A–E** in **Figure 1**. [5 marks]
  b Draw and label a typical eukaryotic cell to show its main characteristics, and give an indication of the expected size range. [6 marks]
  c Explain the similarities and differences between a bacterial cell and a plant cell. [6 marks]
  d Some people think that structures found in plant and animal cells, such as chloroplasts and mitochondria, may originally have been free-living bacteria. Discuss this possibility, using the relative sizes of prokaryotic cells, eukaryotic cells, and eukaryotic organelles to support the argument. [5 marks]

3 a Summarise the differences between diffusion, osmosis, and active transport. [6 marks]
  b Visking tubing is a partially permeable membrane. In an experiment to investigate osmosis, two Visking tubing bags were set up, with sugar solution inside the bags and water outside the bags. Bag **A** was kept at 20 °C and bag **B** was kept at 30 °C (**Figure 2**).

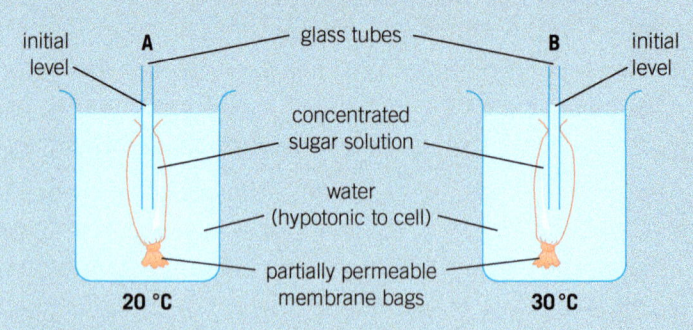

Figure 2

  Describe what you would expect to happen, and explain it in terms of osmosis and particle movement. [5 marks]
  c Evaluate the use of model cells such as those shown in **Figure 2** in practical investigations to demonstrate the importance of osmosis in:
    i animal cells [2 marks]
    ii plant cells. [2 marks]

4 a State what mitosis is, and explain its role in the cell cycle. [3 marks]
  b Explain, using diagrams, the stages of the cell cycle. [5 marks]
  c The cell cycle is very important during the development of a baby from a fertilised egg. It is also important all through life. Explain why. [5 marks]
  d The rate of the cell cycle can vary greatly.
    i Which stage of the cell cycle is variable? [1 mark]
    ii Discuss when the cell cycle is likely to be very rapid in a human, and when it is likely to be relatively slow. [5 marks]

5 a What is meiosis? [3 marks]
  b Explain why meiosis is so important for successful sexual reproduction. [3 marks]
  c Describe:
    i the main similarities between mitosis and meiosis [3 marks]
    ii the main differences between meiosis and mitosis. [3 marks]

1.3 Cells in animals and plants

Practice questions

01 Figure 1 shows an animal cell.

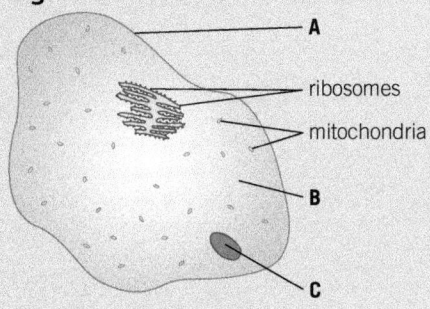

Figure 1

01.1 Which part (**A–C**) of the cell in **Figure 1** is the cytoplasm? [1 mark]

01.2 Describe the function of the mitochondrion. [1 mark]

01.3 **Figure 2** shows a cell seen under a powerful modern light microscope.

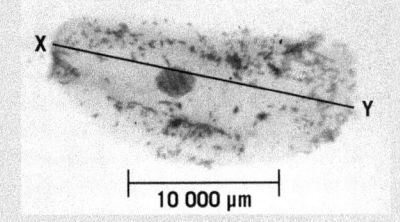

Figure 2

The size of the real cell is 16 μm. Calculate the magnification of the microscope. Use **Figure 2** to help your answer. [2 marks]

01.4 Give **two** advantages of using an electron microscope rather than a light microscope. [2 marks]

02 Substances move into and out of cells by different processes.
Table 1 shows the concentrations of different ions.

Table 1

Ion	Concentration inside cells in mmol/dm³	Concentration outside cells in mmol/dm³
chloride	10	50
magnesium	5	2
sodium	15	145
phosphate	40	2

All four ions in **Table 1** move in and out of cells.
Use the information in **Table 1** to answer the following questions.

02.1 Name the ions that will move into cells by diffusion.
Give a reason for your answer. [2 marks]

02.2 Name the ions that will move into cells by active transport.
Give a reason for your answer. [2 marks]

02.3 A student placed a 25 g slice of potato into a beaker of strong sugar solution and left it for 30 minutes. The mass of the potato after 30 minutes was 20 g.
Give **one** reason why the student dried the slice of potato with a paper towel before she measured its mass. [1 mark]

02.4 Explain why the mass of the slice of potato has changed. [3 marks]

03 **Figure 3** shows a cell with four chromosomes.

Figure 3

03.1 Cells **A**, **B**, and **C** in **Figure 4** show the stages of meiosis. They are **not** in the correct order.

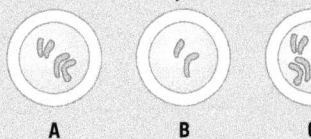

A   B   C

Figure 4

What is the correct order of cells **A**, **B**, and **C** to show the process of meiosis? [1 mark]

03.2 Compare the process of mitosis with meiosis. You should include similarities and differences in your answer. [4 marks]

03.3 The first cells in an embryo can grow and divide to form any type of cell.
Name this type of cell. [1 mark]

53

1.4 Waves

1.4.1 The nature of waves

Learning objectives

After this topic, you should know:

- what waves can be used for
- what transverse waves are
- what longitudinal waves are
- which types of waves are transverse and which are longitudinal.

Waves transfer energy and they can be used to transfer information. For example, they transfer energy to food when it is heated in a microwave oven, and they transfer information when you use a mobile phone or listen to the radio.

There are different types of waves. These include:

- sound waves, water waves, waves on springs and ropes, and seismic waves produced by earthquakes. These are all examples of **mechanical waves**, which are vibrations that travel through a **medium** (a substance).
- light waves, radio waves, and microwaves. These are all examples of **electromagnetic waves**, which can all travel through a vacuum at the same speed of 300 000 kilometres per second. No medium is needed.

Figure 1 *Waves in water are examples of mechanical waves*

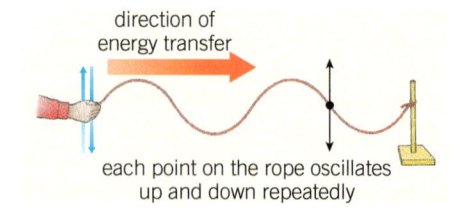

Figure 2 *Making transverse waves on a rope*

Observing mechanical waves

Figure 2 shows how you can make waves on a rope by moving one end up and down.

Tie a ribbon to the middle of the rope. Move one end of the rope up and down. You will see that the waves move along the rope but the ribbon doesn't move along the rope – it just moves up and down. This type of wave is known as a **transverse wave**. It is said that the ribbon vibrates or oscillates. This means that it moves repeatedly between two positions. When the ribbon is at the top of a wave, it is said to be at the peak (or crest) of the wave.

Repeat the test with a slinky spring. You should observe the same effects if you move one end of the slinky up and down.

However, if you push and pull the end of the slinky, as shown in Figure 3, you will see a different type of wave, known as a **longitudinal wave**. Notice that there are areas of **compression** (coils squashed together) and areas of **rarefaction** (coils spread further apart) moving along the slinky.

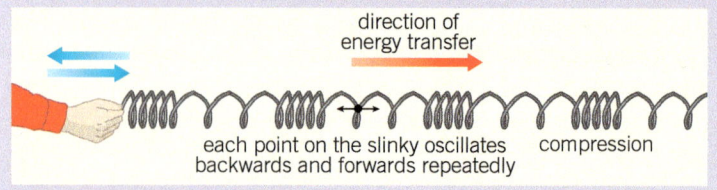

Figure 3 *Making longitudinal waves on a slinky*

- Describe how the ribbon moves when you send longitudinal waves along the slinky.

Safety: Handle the slinky spring carefully.

More wave tests

When waves travel through a substance, the substance itself doesn't travel. You can see this with waves on a rope and by observing:

- waves spreading out on water after a small object is dropped in the water. The waves travel across the surface but the water does not travel away from the object.

- a tuning fork vibrating so that it makes sound waves travel through the air away from the tuning fork. The air itself doesn't travel away from the vibrating object – if it did, a vacuum would be created.

Transverse waves

Imagine sending waves along a rope that has a white spot painted on it. You would see the spot move up and down without moving along the rope. In other words, the spot would oscillate perpendicular (at right angles) to the direction in which the waves are moving. The waves on a rope and the ripples on the surface of water are called transverse waves because the vibrations (called oscillations) move up and down or from side to side. All electromagnetic waves are transverse waves.

The oscillations of a transverse wave are perpendicular to the direction in which the waves transfer energy.

Longitudinal waves

The slinky spring in Figure 3 is useful to demonstrate how sound waves travel. When one end of the slinky is pushed in and out repeatedly, vibrations travel along the spring. These oscillations are parallel to the direction in which the waves transfer energy. Waves that travel in this way are called longitudinal waves.

Sound waves travelling through air are longitudinal waves. When an object vibrates in air, it makes the air around it vibrate as it pushes and pulls on the air. The oscillations (compressions and rarefactions) that travel through the air are sound waves. The oscillations are along the direction in which the wave travels.

The oscillations of a longitudinal wave are parallel to the direction in which the waves transfer energy.

Mechanical waves can be transverse or longitudinal.

> **Synoptic link**
>
> You will learn more about electromagnetic waves in Topic 1.4.3.

> **Study tips**
>
> - Make sure you know how to describe the difference between transverse waves and longitudinal waves.
> - Remember that electromagnetic waves are transverse, and sound waves are longitudinal.

> 1 a What is the difference between a longitudinal wave and
>   a transverse wave? [1 mark]
>   b Give *one* example of:
>   i a transverse wave [1 mark] ii a longitudinal wave. [1 mark]
>   c When a sound wave passes through air, describe what
>   happens to the air particles at a point of compression. [1 mark]
> 2 A long rope with a knot tied in the middle lies straight along
>   a smooth floor. A student picks up one end of the rope and
>   sends waves along the rope.
>   a State whether the waves on the rope are transverse or
>   longitudinal waves. [1 mark]
>   b Describe:
>   i the direction of energy transfer along the rope [1 mark]
>   ii the movement of the knot. [1 mark]
> 3 Describe how to use a slinky spring to demonstrate to a friend the
>   difference between longitudinal waves and transverse waves. [2 marks]
> 4 Describe and explain the motion of a small ball floating on a
>   pond when waves travel across the pond. [3 marks]

> **Key points**
>
> - Waves can be used to transfer energy and information.
> - Transverse waves oscillate perpendicular to the direction of energy transfer of the waves. Ripples on the surface of water are transverse waves. So are all electromagnetic waves.
> - Longitudinal waves oscillate parallel to the direction of energy transfer of the waves. Sound waves in air are longitudinal waves.
> - Mechanical waves need a medium (a substance) to travel through. They can be transverse or longitudinal waves.

1.4.2 The properties of waves

Learning objectives

After this topic, you should know:
- what is meant by the amplitude, frequency, and wavelength of a wave
- how the period of a wave is related to its frequency
- the relationship between the speed, wavelength, and frequency of a wave
- how to use the wave speed equation in calculations.

If you want to find out how much energy or information waves carry, you need to measure them. Figure 1 shows a snapshot of waves on a rope. The crests, or peaks, are at the top of the wave. The troughs are at the bottom. They are equally spaced.

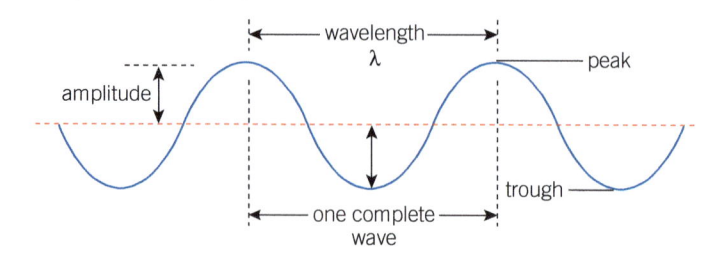

Figure 1 *Waves on a rope*

The **amplitude** of a wave is the maximum displacement of a point on the wave from its undisturbed position. For example, in Figure 1, this is the height of the wave crest (or the depth of the wave trough) from the middle.

The bigger the amplitude of the waves, the more energy the waves carry.

The **wavelength** of a wave is the distance from a point on the wave to the equivalent point on the adjacent wave. For example, in Figure 1, this is the distance from one wave crest to the next wave crest.

Frequency

If you made a video of the waves on the rope in Figure 1, you would see the waves moving steadily across the screen. The number of waves passing a fixed point every second is called the **frequency** of the waves.

The unit of frequency is the hertz (Hz). For the waves on the rope, one wave crest passing each second is equal to a frequency of 1 Hz.

The **period** of a wave is the time taken for each wave to pass a fixed point. For waves of frequency, f, the period, T is given by the equation:

$$\text{period, } T \text{ (seconds, s)} = \frac{1}{\text{frequency, } f \text{ (hertz, Hz)}}$$

Wave speed

Figure 2 shows a ripple tank, which is used to study water waves in controlled conditions. You can make straight waves by moving the long edge of a ruler up and down on the water surface in a ripple tank. Straight waves are called plane waves. The waves all move at the same speed and stay the same distance apart.

The **speed** of the waves is the distance travelled by each wave every second through a medium. Energy is transferred by the waves at this speed. For waves of constant frequency, the speed of the waves depends on the frequency and the wavelength as follows:

$$\text{wave speed, } v \text{ (metres per second, m/s)} = \text{frequency, } f \text{ (hertz, Hz)} \times \text{wavelength, } \lambda \text{ (metres, m)}$$

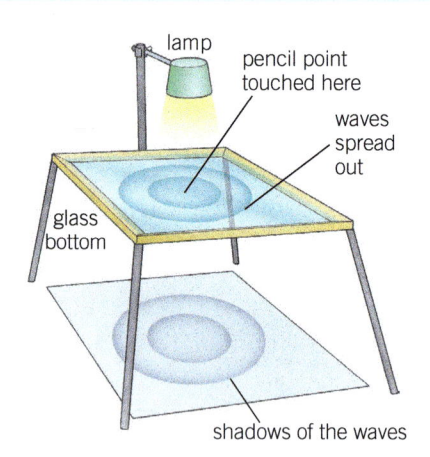

Figure 2 *A ripple tank*

Measuring the speed of ripples

Use a ruler to send plane waves towards one end of the ripple tank (Figure 2).
- Use a stopwatch to measure the time it takes for a wave to travel from one end of the ripple tank to the other.
- Measure the distance the waves travel in this time.
- Use the equation speed = distance ÷ time to calculate the speed of the waves.

Observe the effect on the waves of moving the ruler up and down faster.
- Determine whether the speed of the waves has changed.

Safety: Avoid spilling liquids. Advise your teacher of any spillages immediately.

1.4 Waves

To understand what the wave speed equation means, look at Figure 3. The surfer is riding on the crest of some unusually fast waves. Suppose the frequency of the waves is 3 Hz and the wavelength of the waves is 4.0 m.

- At this frequency, three wave crests pass a fixed point once every second (because the frequency is 3 Hz).
- The surfer therefore moves forward a distance of three wavelengths every second, which is 3 × 4.0 m = 12 m.

So the speed of the surfer is 12 m/s. This speed is equal to the frequency × the wavelength of the waves.

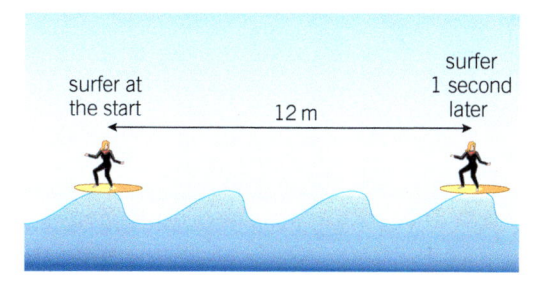

Figure 3 *Surfing*

Investigating waves on a stretched string

Use the apparatus shown in Figure 4. The oscillator sends waves along the string. You can adjust the frequency of the oscillator until there is a single loop on the string. Its length is half of one wavelength.

- Note the frequency of the oscillator
- Make suitable measurements to find the length, *L*, of a single loop and calculate the wavelength of the waves (= 2*L*).

Calculate the speed of the waves on the string using the equation:

wave speed = frequency × wavelength

- Increase the frequency to obtain more loops on the string. Make more measurements to see if the wave speed is the same.

Safety: Take care with hanging weights – clamp the stand to the bench. Wear eye protection.

Figure 4 *Investigating waves on a string*

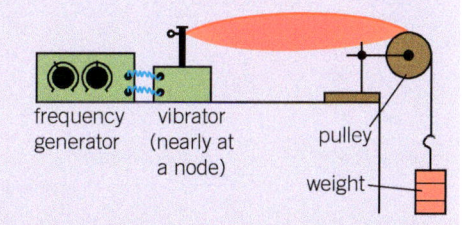

Measuring the speed of sound in air

You need two people for this. You and a friend need to stand on opposite sides of a field at a measured distance apart. You should be as far apart as possible but within sight of each other.

If your friend bangs two cymbals together, you will see them crash together straightaway, but you won't hear them straightaway. The crashing sound will be delayed because sound travels much more slowly than light. Use a stopwatch to time the interval between seeing the impact and hearing the sound. Repeat the test several times to get an average value of the time interval.

- Calculate the speed of sound in air using the equation:

$$\text{speed} = \frac{\text{distance}}{\text{time taken}}$$

Key points

- For any wave, its amplitude is the maximum displacement of a point on the wave from its undisturbed position.
- For any wave, its frequency is the number of waves passing a point per second.
- The period of a wave = $\frac{1}{\text{frequency}}$
- For any wave, its wavelength is the distance from a point on the wave to the equivalent point on the next wave (e.g., from one wave trough to the next wave trough).
- The speed of a wave is $v = f \times \lambda$.

---

1 State what is meant by the frequency of a wave. [1 mark]

2 Figure 5 shows a wave travelling from left to right along a rope.
   Figure 5
   a Copy the figure and mark on your diagram:
      i   one wavelength [1 mark]
      ii the amplitude of the waves. [1 mark]
   b Describe the motion of point **P** on the rope when the wave crest at **P** moves along by a distance of one wavelength. [2 marks]

3 a A speedboat on a lake sends waves travelling across a lake at a frequency of 2.0 Hz and a wavelength of 3.0 m. Calculate the speed of the waves. [2 marks]
   b If the waves had been produced at a frequency of 1.0 Hz and travelled at the speed calculated in **a**:
      i   calculate what their wavelength would be [2 marks]
      ii calculate the distance travelled by a wave crest in 60 s. [2 marks]

4 Sound waves in air travel at a speed of 340 m/s. Calculate their wavelength if their frequency is 3.0 kHz. [2 marks]

57

1.4.3 Electromagnetic waves

Learning objectives

After this topic, you should know:
- the parts of the electromagnetic spectrum
- the range of wavelengths within the electromagnetic spectrum that the human eye can detect
- how energy is transferred by electromagnetic waves
- how to calculate the frequency or wavelength of electromagnetic waves.

Electromagnetic waves are electric and magnetic disturbances that can be used to transfer energy from a source to an absorber. You use waves from different parts of the electromagnetic spectrum in everyday devices and gadgets, including:

- Microwave ovens – energy is transferred from a microwave source to the food in the oven, heating it.
- Radiant heaters – infrared radiation transfers energy from the heater to heat the surroundings.

Electromagnetic waves do not transfer matter. The energy they transfer each second depends on the wavelength of the waves as well as their amplitude. This is why waves of different wavelengths have different effects. Figure 1 shows some of the uses of each part of the electromagnetic spectrum.

radio waves | microwaves | infrared | visible light | ultraviolet radiation | X-rays and gamma radiation

1 kilometre   1 millimetre   1 nanometre   1 picometre

wavelength

(1 nanometre (1×10^{-9} m) = 0.000 001 millimetres, 1 picometre = 0.001 nanometres)

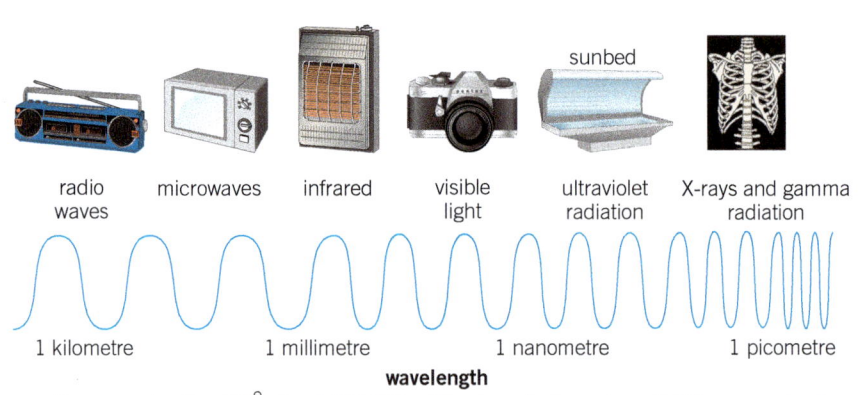

Figure 1 *The spectrum is continuous. The frequencies and wavelengths at the boundaries are approximate because the different parts of the spectrum are not precisely defined*

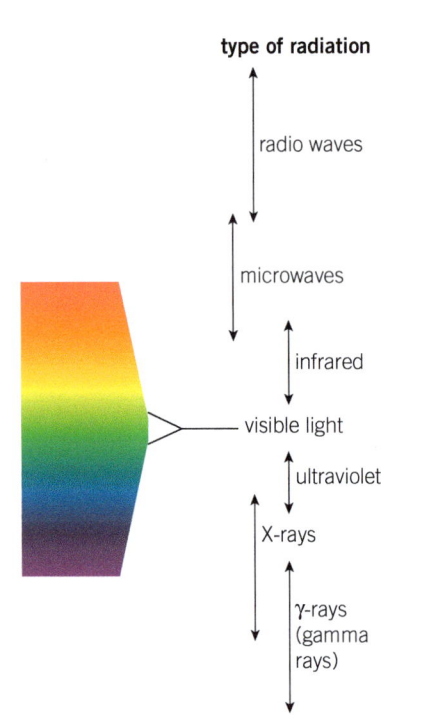

Waves from different parts of the electromagnetic spectrum have different wavelengths:

- Long-wave radio waves have wavelengths as long as 10 km (10^4 m).
- X-rays and gamma rays have wavelengths as short as a millionth of a millionth of a millimetre (= 0.000 000 000 001 mm or 10^{-15} m).
- Your eyes detect visible light, which is only a limited part of the electromagnetic spectrum (wavelengths of about 350 nm to about 650 nm). An expanded view of the visible range of light is shown in Figure 2.

Figure 2 *The electromagnetic spectrum with an expanded view of the visible range*

type of radiation: radio waves, microwaves, infrared, visible light, ultraviolet, X-rays, γ-rays (gamma rays)

The speed of electromagnetic waves

All electromagnetic waves travel at a speed of 300 million m/s (or 3.0×10^8 m/s in standard form) through space or in a vacuum. This is the distance that the waves travel each second. You can link the speed of the waves to their frequency and wavelength by using the **wave speed** equation:

wave speed, v =   frequency, f ×   wavelength, λ
(metres per second, m/s)   (hertz, Hz)   (metres, m)

Synoptic link

You learnt about the wave speed equation in Topic 1.4.2.

1.4 Waves

Rearranging the wave speed equation

You can work out the wavelength, λ or the frequency, f by rearranging the wave speed equation into:

$$\lambda = \frac{v}{f} \text{ or } f = \frac{v}{\lambda}$$

Worked example

A mobile phone gives out electromagnetic waves of frequency 900 million Hz. Calculate the wavelength of these waves.

The speed of electromagnetic waves in air = 300 million m/s.

Solution

$$\text{wavelength, } \lambda \text{ (m)} = \frac{\text{wave speed, } v \text{ (m/s)}}{\text{frequency, } f \text{ (Hz)}}$$

$$= \frac{300\,000\,000 \text{ m/s}}{900\,000\,000 \text{ Hz}} = 0.33 \text{ m}$$

Energy and frequency

The wave speed equation shows you that since electromagnetic waves all have a speed of 300 million m/s, the shorter the wavelength of the waves, the higher their frequency. The energy of the waves increases as the frequency increases. So as the wavelength decreases along the electromagnetic spectrum from radio waves to gamma rays, the energy and frequency of the waves increase.

1. **a** State which is greater – the wavelength of radio waves or the wavelength of visible light waves. [1 mark]
   b Describe the speed in a vacuum of different electromagnetic waves. [1 mark]
   c State which is greater – the frequency of X-rays or the frequency of infrared radiation. [1 mark]
   d Determine where in the electromagnetic spectrum you would find waves of wavelength 10 mm. [1 mark]

2. **a** Put the following parts of the electromagnetic spectrum in order of increasing frequency:
   infrared   radio   X-rays and gamma rays [1 mark]
   b Determine which parts of the electromagnetic spectrum are missing from the list in **a**. [1 mark]
   c Name the source, the absorber, and the part of the electromagnetic spectrum that transfers energy when someone uses a sunbed. [3 marks]

3. Electromagnetic waves travel through space at a speed of 300 million m/s. Calculate:
   a the wavelength of radio waves of frequency 600 million Hz
   b the frequency of microwaves of wavelength 0.30 m. [4 marks]

4. A distant star explodes and emits visible light and gamma rays simultaneously. Explain why the gamma rays and the visible light waves reach the Earth at the same time. [2 marks]

Synoptic links

Electromagnetic waves of different wavelengths interact with substances in different ways. For example, microwaves travel through cardboard but light waves do not – yet microwaves and light waves are both reflected by shiny metal plates. You will learn more about electromagnetic waves in later topics in this chapter and in other chapters in this GCSE course. For example, in Chapter 2.6 you will learn about the important light-absorbing properties of chlorophyll molecules, which enable photosynthesis in plants.

Study tip

The Worked example on this page is an example of where standard form can be useful. The large values for wave speed and frequency could have been written as 3×10^8 m/s and 9×10^8 Hz, respectively. It is worth learning how to do this on your calculator.

Key points

- The electromagnetic spectrum (in order of decreasing wavelength and increasing frequency and energy) is made up of:
  - radio waves
  - microwaves
  - infrared radiation
  - visible light (red to violet)
  - ultraviolet waves
  - X-rays and gamma rays.
- The human eye can only detect visible light. The wavelength of visible light ranges from about 350 nm to about 650 nm.
- Electromagnetic waves transfer energy from a source to an absorber.
- The wave speed equation $v = f\lambda$ is used to calculate the frequency or wavelength of electromagnetic waves.

Higher Tier

1.4.4 Reflection and refraction

Learning objectives

After this topic, you should know:

- the patterns of reflection and refraction of plane waves in a ripple tank
- what can happen to a wave when it reaches and crosses a boundary between two different materials
- how the behaviour of waves can be used to explain refraction.

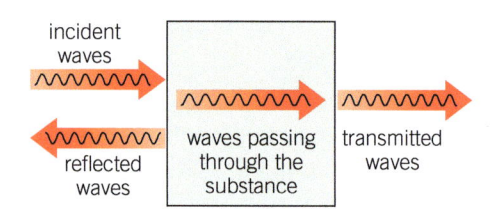

Figure 1 *Waves and substances*

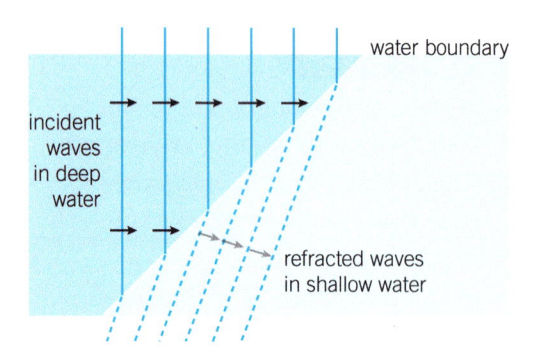

Figure 2 *Refraction. The arrows in this diagram show the direction in which the waves are moving*

Reflection and refraction
Materials and waves

When a wave is directed at a substance, some or all of the wave may be **reflected** at the surface (Figure 1). What happens is dependent on the wavelength of the wave and also on the substance (e.g., its surface). For example, microwaves are reflected by metal surfaces but they can pass through paper.

Of the waves that go into a substance, some or all of them may be absorbed by the substance. This would heat the substance because the energy from the waves would increase the thermal energy store of the substance. For example, food is heated in microwave ovens because the microwaves are absorbed by the food.

As waves travel through a substance, the amplitude of the waves gradually decreases because the waves transfer energy to the thermal energy store of the substance.

Waves that are not absorbed by the substance they are travelling through are transmitted by it. For example, light is mostly **transmitted** by ordinary glass, but is almost completely absorbed by darkened glass.

Refraction

When waves cross a boundary between two different materials, the waves may change direction when they cross the boundary. This change of direction is called **refraction** and is a property of all waves. You can see this in a ripple tank when water waves cross a boundary between deep and shallow water. The waves in Figure 2 are called **wavefronts** because they show where ripples are at a given time. Plane waves directed at a non-zero angle to the boundary change direction as they cross the boundary, as shown in Figure 2. Another example is light waves entering your eye from an object and forming an image on the retina, the layer of light-sensitive cells on the inside of the back of your eye. The light waves pass through different materials in your eye and they may change direction when they cross each boundary between two materials.

Partial **reflection** can occur at a boundary, as well as refraction. This is why you might see a faint mirror image of yourself when you look at a window. The waves that cross the boundary lose energy at the boundary and so have a smaller amplitude than that of the incident waves. This is because the reflected waves take away some energy from the incident waves.

> **Investigating waves using a ripple tank**
> Reflection and refraction of waves can be investigated using a ripple tank. Each ripple is called a wavefront because it represents the front of each wave as it travels across the water surface. Plane (i.e., straight) waves can be created continuously using a vibrating beam.

To observe reflection of waves – Place a smooth metal strip in the water in the path of the waves as a reflector. The reflected waves move away from the reflector at the same angle to the reflector as the waves moving towards the barrier (the incident waves). A reflector with an uneven, rough surface would break up each wave and scatter the waves in all directions. The light rays in Figure 3 represent the directions of the light waves before and after they reach a reflecting surface.

To observe refraction of waves – Place a transparent plastic plate under the water so that the waves cross a boundary between the deep and shallow water. The water over the plate needs to be very shallow.

At a non-zero angle to a boundary – The waves change their speed and direction when they cross the boundary.

- Find out if plane waves change direction towards or away from the boundary when they cross from deep to shallow water.

Perpendicular to a boundary (at normal incidence) – The waves cross the boundary without changing direction. However, their speed changes.

- Find out how wave speed changes when waves cross the boundary.

Safety: Avoid spilling liquids. Advise your teacher of any spillages immediately.

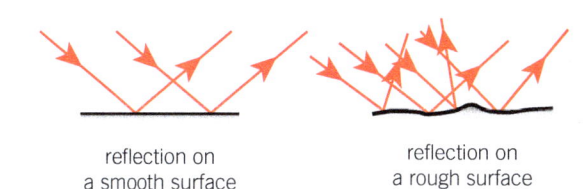

Figure 3 Reflection at a smooth and at a rough surface

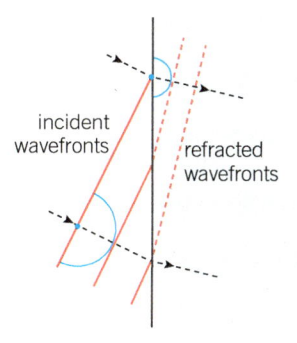

Figure 4 Explaining refraction

Explaining refraction

To explain how a wavefront moves forward, imagine that each tiny section creates a wavelet (a little wave) that travels forward (shown in blue in Figure 4). The wavelets move forward together to recreate the wavefront that created them.

In Figure 4, plane waves cross a boundary at a non-zero angle to the boundary. Each wavefront experiences a change in speed and direction. This is because the wavefronts move more slowly after they have crossed the boundary. So the refracted wavefronts are closer together and are at a smaller angle to the boundary than the incident wavefronts. The refracted waves and the incident waves have the same frequency, but they travel at different speeds, so they have different wavelengths.

1. When plane waves reflect from a straight barrier, describe the angle of each reflected wavefront to the barrier and the angle of each incident wavefront to the barrier. [1 mark]
2. Draw a diagram that shows plane waves passing from deep to shallow water at a non-zero angle to a straight boundary. Draw some refracted wavefronts, indicating their direction. [3 marks]
3. The speed of light in water is less than the speed of light in air. When light travels from air into water and is refracted, what happens to the direction of wave movement? [2 marks]
4. Sunglasses have lenses made of dark glass that reduce the amount of daylight entering your eyes. Design a test using a light meter and a lamp to find out whether the two lenses in a pair of sunglasses are equally effective. [4 marks]

Key points

- Plane waves in a ripple tank are reflected from a straight barrier at the same angle to the barrier as the incident waves because their speed and wavelength do not change on reflection.
- Plane waves crossing a boundary between two different materials are refracted unless they cross the boundary at normal incidence.
- Refraction occurs at a boundary between two different materials because the speed and wavelength of the waves change at the boundary.
- At a boundary between two different materials, waves can be reflected and refracted. When waves are transmitted through a substance, some of their energy may be absorbed by the substance as they travel through it.

1.4.5 Light, infrared, microwaves, and radio waves

Learning objectives

After this topic, you should know:
- the nature of white light
- what infrared radiation, microwaves, and radio waves are used for
- what mobile phone radiation is
- why these types of electromagnetic radiation are hazardous.

Light

Light from ordinary lamps and from the Sun is called **white light**. This is because it has all the colours of the visible spectrum in it. The wavelength increases across the spectrum as you go from violet to red. When you look at a rainbow, you see the colours of the spectrum. You can also see them if you use a glass prism to split a beam of white light.

Photographers need to know how shades and colours of light affect the photographs they take.

- In a film camera, the light is focused by the camera lens on to a light-sensitive film. The film then needs to be developed to see the image of the objects that were photographed.

- In a digital camera or a mobile phone camera, the light is focused by the lens on to a sensor. This is made up of thousands of tiny, light-sensitive cells called pixels. Each pixel gives a dot of the image. The image can be seen on a small screen at the back of the camera. When a photograph is taken, the image is stored electronically on a memory card.

Infrared radiation

All objects emit infrared radiation.

- The hotter an object is, the more infrared radiation it emits.
- Infrared radiation is absorbed by your skin. It can damage, burn, or kill skin cells because it heats up the cells.

Infrared devices

- Optical fibres in communications systems usually use infrared radiation instead of visible light. This is because infrared radiation is absorbed less than visible light in the glass fibres.

- Remote control handsets for TV and DVD equipment transmit signals carried by infrared radiation. When you press a button on the handset, it sends out a sequence of infrared pulses. Infrared radiation is used because suitable infrared pulses can easily be produced and detected electronically.

- Infrared scanners are used in medicine to detect infrared radiation emitted from hot spots on the body surface. These hot areas can mean that the tissue underneath is unhealthy.

- You can use infrared cameras to see people and animals in the dark.

- Infrared radiation is used to heat up objects quickly:
  - Electric heaters that emit infrared radiation warm rooms quickly.
  - Electric cookers that have halogen hobs heat food faster than ordinary hobs because halogen hobs are designed to emit much more infrared radiation than ordinary hobs.

Testing absorption and emission of infrared radiation by different surfaces

To compare emission from two different surfaces, measure how fast two cans of hot water cool. The surface of one can is light in colour and shiny, and the other has a dark, matt surface (Figure 1).

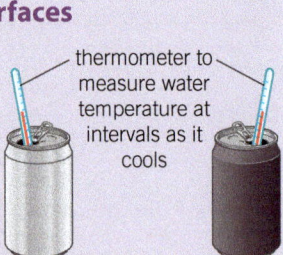

Figure 1 *Testing different surfaces*

To compare absorption by two different surfaces, measure how fast the two cans containing cold water heat up when placed in sunlight for the same time. Each can needs to contain the same amount of water.

At the start of each test, the volume and temperature of the water in each can must be the same.

- Write a report on your investigation and use your measurements to compare the two surfaces in terms of absorption and emission of infrared radiation.

Safety: Take care with hot water.

Microwaves

Microwaves have a shorter wavelength than radio waves.

- People use microwaves for communications (e.g., satellite TV) because they can pass through the atmosphere and reach satellites above the Earth. Microwaves can also carry mobile phone signals.
- Microwave ovens heat food faster than ordinary ovens. This is because microwaves can penetrate food and are absorbed by the water molecules in the food, heating it. The oven itself does not absorb microwaves as it does not contain any water molecules, so it does not become hot like the food it is cooking.

Radio waves

Radio wave frequencies range from about 300 000 Hz to 3000 million Hz (where microwave frequencies start). Radio waves are used to carry radio, TV, and mobile phone signals. Radio telescopes are used to detect radio waves from the Sun, from stars, and from other sources in space such as quasars, which are star-sized objects that each give out as much energy per second as a single galaxy.

You can also use radio waves instead of cables to connect a computer to other devices such as a printer or a computer mouse. For example, Bluetooth-enabled devices can communicate with each other over a range of about 10 metres without the need for cables.

Microwaves and radio waves can be hazardous because they penetrate people's bodies and can heat the internal parts of the body.

1. **a** When you watch a TV programme, name the type of electromagnetic wave that is:
    i detected by the aerial [1 mark]
    ii emitted by the screen. [1 mark]
   b Name the type of electromagnetic wave that is used:
    i to carry signals to and from a satellite [1 mark]
    ii to send signals to a printer from a computer without using a cable. [1 mark]

2. Mobile phones use electromagnetic waves in a wavelength range that includes short-wave radio waves and microwaves.
   a Describe the effect on mobile phone users if remote control handsets operated in this range as well. [1 mark]
   b Explain why the emergency services use radio waves in a wavelength range that no one else is allowed to use. [2 marks]

3. The speed of electromagnetic waves in air is 300 000 km/s. Calculate the wavelength in air of electromagnetic waves of frequency 2400 MHz. [2 marks]

4. Figure 2 shows a microwave receiver being used to detect microwaves from a transmitter. The reading on the receiver meter depends on how much radiation the receiver detects.
   a Describe what the metal plate does to the microwaves. [1 mark]
   b Design a test to find out whether microwaves can pass through:
    i a metal plate   ii a thick cardboard sheet. [4 marks]

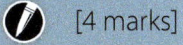

Synoptic link
You will learn more about infrared radiation in Topic 8.24.12 in the *Physical Sciences* book.

Demonstrating microwaves
Look at the demonstration in Figure 2. The receiver detects a signal.

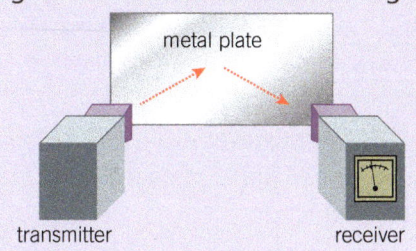

Figure 2 *Demonstrating microwaves*

- Describe what this shows.

Study tip
The spectrum of visible light covers only a very small part of the electromagnetic spectrum.

Key points
- White light contains all the colours of the visible spectrum.
- Infrared radiation is used for carrying signals from remote control handsets and inside optical fibres.
- Microwaves are used to carry satellite TV programmes and mobile phone calls. Radio waves are used for radio and TV broadcasting, radio communications, and mobile phone calls.
- Mobile phone radiation is microwave radiation, and is also radio waves at near-microwave frequencies.
- Different types of electromagnetic radiation are hazardous in different ways. Infrared radiation can cause skin burns. Microwaves and radio waves can heat the internal parts of people's bodies.

1.4.6 Communications

Learning objectives

After this topic, you should know:

- why radio waves of different frequencies are used for different purposes
- which waves are used for satellite TV
- how to decide whether or not mobile phones are safe to use
- what carrier waves are
- how optical fibres are used in communications.

Radio communications

When you use a mobile phone, radio waves carry signals between your mobile phone and the nearest mobile phone mast. The waves used to carry any type of signal are called **carrier waves**. They could be radio waves, microwaves, infrared radiation, or visible light. The type of wave used to carry a signal depends on how much information is in the signal and the distance the signal has to travel. For example, microwaves are used to carry signals via satellites to distant countries.

Radio wavelengths

The radio and microwave spectrum is divided into bands of different wavelength ranges. This is because the shorter the wavelength of the waves:

- the more information they can carry
- the shorter their range (due to increasing absorption by the atmosphere)
- the less they spread out.

Microwaves and radio waves of different wavelengths are used for different communications purposes. For example:

- Microwaves are used for satellite phone and TV links, and satellite TV broadcasting. This is because microwaves can travel between satellites in space and on the ground (Figure 1). Also, they spread out less than radio waves do, so the signal doesn't weaken as much.
- Radio waves of wavelengths less than about 1 metre are used for TV broadcasting from TV masts because they can carry more information than longer radio waves.
- Radio waves of wavelengths from about 1 metre up to about 100 metres are used by local radio stations (and for the emergency services) because their range is limited to the area round the transmitter.
- Radio waves of wavelengths greater than 100 metres are used by national and international radio stations because they have a much longer range than shorter-wavelength radio waves.

Figure 1 *Sending microwave signals to a satellite*

Figure 2 *A mobile phone mast*

Study tip

Remember that, in communications, electromagnetic waves carry the information.

Mobile phones and electromagnetic radiation

A mobile phone sends out a radio signal when you use it (Figure 2). If the phone is very close to your brain, some scientists think that the radiation might affect the brain. Because children have thinner skulls than adults, their brains might be more affected by mobile phone radiation. A UK Government report published in May 2000 and updated in 2005 recommended that the use of mobile phones by children should be limited. More research is being conducted to find out whether mobile phone users are affected.

1.4 Waves

Higher

More about signals and carrier waves

When you speak, you produce sound waves of different frequencies, so you vary the amplitude and the frequency of the sound waves you produce. In a radio station, a microphone produces an alternating current called an audio signal when sound waves reach it. Figure 3 shows how the signal is transmitted and detected.

- An oscillator supplies carrier waves to the transmitter in the form of an alternating current (a current that repeatedly reverses its direction).
- The audio signal is supplied to the transmitter where it is used to vary (i.e., modulate) the carrier waves.
- The modulated carrier waves from the transmitter are supplied to the transmitter aerial. The varying alternating current supplied to the aerial causes it to emit radio waves that carry the audio signal.
- When the radio waves are absorbed by a receiver aerial, they induce an alternating current in the receiver aerial, which causes oscillations in the receiver. The frequency of the oscillations is the same as the frequency of the radio waves.
- The receiver circuit separates the audio signal from the carrier waves. The audio signal is then supplied to a loudspeaker, which sends out sound waves similar to the sound waves received by the microphone in the radio station.

Optical fibre communications

Optical fibres are very thin glass fibres. They are used to transmit signals carried by light or infrared radiation. The light rays can't escape from the fibre. When they reach the surface of the fibre, they are reflected back into the fibre (Figure 4). Compared with radio waves and microwaves:

- optical fibres carry much more information as light has a much shorter wavelength than radio waves, so can carry more pulses of waves
- optical fibres are more secure because the signals stay in the fibre.

1 a Name the types of electromagnetic waves that are used to carry signals along a thin, transparent fibre. [1 mark]
   b Explain why signals in an optical fibre are more secure than radio signals. [2 marks]
2 a Explain why children could be more affected by mobile phone radiation than adults. [2 marks]
   b i Explain what is meant by a carrier wave. [2 marks]
      ii Explain why visible light waves can carry more information than radio waves. [2 marks]
3 Explain why microwaves are used for satellite TV and radio waves are used for terrestrial TV. [3 marks]
4 A local radio station broadcasts at a frequency of 105 MHz.
   a Calculate the wavelength of radio waves of this frequency. The speed of electromagnetic waves in air is 300 000 km/s. [2 marks]
   b Explain why national radio stations broadcast at much lower frequencies. [2 marks]

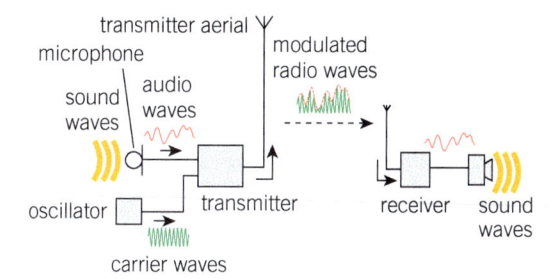

Figure 3 *Using radio waves*

Synoptic link
You will learn about alternating currents in Topic 7.19.6 in the *Physical Sciences* book.

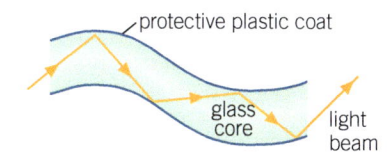

Figure 4 *The reflection of light inside an optical fibre. This is called total internal reflection, because all the light in the fibre is reflected when it reaches the surface of the fibre*

Key points
- Radio waves of different frequencies are used for different purposes because the wavelength (and so the frequency) of waves affects:
  - how far they can travel
  - how much they spread
  - how much information they can carry.
- Microwaves are used for satellite TV signals.
- Further research is needed to evaluate whether or not mobile phones are safe to use.
- Optical fibres are very thin transparent fibres that are used to transmit communication signals by light and infrared radiation.
- Carrier waves are waves that are used to carry information. They can do this by varying their amplitude.

65

1.4.7 Ultraviolet waves, X-rays, and gamma rays

Learning objectives

After this topic, you should know:

- the differences between ultraviolet and visible light
- what X-rays and gamma rays are used for
- what ionising radiation is
- why ultraviolet waves, X-rays, and gamma rays are dangerous.

Ultraviolet waves

Watch your teacher place different-coloured clothes under an ultraviolet lamp. Observe what happens.

- Describe what white clothes look like under a UV lamp.

Safety: Do not look directly into the UV light source.

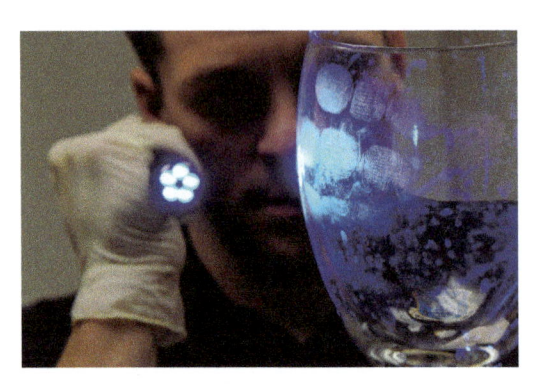

Figure 1 *Using an ultraviolet lamp to detect fingerprints*

Synoptic links

You will learn about radioactive substances in Topics 3.8.3 and 3.8.5.

You will learn more about the effect of ionising radiation on living cells in Topic 3.8.6.

Ultraviolet waves

Ultraviolet (UV) waves lie between violet light and X-rays in the electromagnetic spectrum. Some chemicals emit light as a result of absorbing ultraviolet waves (Figure 1). Posters and ink that glow in ultraviolet light contain these chemicals. Security marker pens containing this kind of ink are used to mark valuable objects. The chemicals absorb ultraviolet waves and then emit visible light.

Ultraviolet waves are harmful to human eyes and can cause blindness. UV wavelengths are smaller than visible light wavelengths. UV waves carry more energy than visible light waves.

Ultraviolet waves are harmful to your skin. For example, too much UV directly from the Sun or from a sunbed can cause sunburn and skin cancer. It can also age the skin prematurely.

- If you stay outdoors in summer, use skin creams to block UV waves and prevent them reaching your skin.
- Sunbed users must be aged 18 or over, and must not exceed the recommended time. They should wear special goggles to protect their eyes.

X-rays and gamma rays

X-rays and gamma rays both travel straight into substances and can pass through them if the substances are not too dense and not too thick. A thick plate made of lead will stop them.

X-rays and gamma rays have similar properties because they both:

- are at the short-wavelength end of the electromagnetic spectrum
- carry much more energy per second than longer-wavelength electromagnetic waves that have the same amplitude.

They differ from each other because:

- X-rays are produced when electrons or other particles moving at high speeds are stopped – X-ray tubes are used to produce X-rays
- gamma rays are produced by radioactive substances when unstable nuclei release energy
- gamma rays have shorter wavelengths than X-rays, so they can penetrate substances more than X-rays can.

X-rays are often used to detect internal cracks in metal objects. These kinds of application are usually possible because the more dense a substance is, the more X-rays it absorbs from an X-ray beam passing through it. X-rays are also used in medicine to create images of broken limbs. You will learn more about this in Topic 1.4.8.

1.4 Waves

Using gamma rays
High-energy gamma rays have several important uses.

Killing harmful bacteria
1 About 20% of the world's food is lost through spoilage, mostly due to bacteria. The waste products of bacteria cause food poisoning. Exposing food to gamma rays kills 99% of disease-carrying organisms, including *Salmonella* (found in poultry) and *Clostridium* (which causes botulism).

2 Exposing surgical instruments in sealed plastic wrappers to gamma rays kills any bacteria on the instruments. This helps to stop infection spreading in hospitals.

Killing cancer cells
Doctors and medical physicists use gamma-ray therapy to destroy cancerous tumours. A narrow beam of gamma rays from a radioactive source (cobalt-60) is directed at the tumour (Figure 2). The beam is aimed at it from different directions to kill the tumour but not the surrounding tissue.

Safety matters
X-rays and gamma rays passing through substances can knock electrons out of atoms in the substance. The atoms become charged because they lose electrons. This process is called **ionisation**, and so X-rays and gamma rays are examples of ionising radiation.

If ionisation happens to a living cell, it can damage or kill the cell. For this reason, exposure to too many X-rays or gamma rays is dangerous and can cause cancer. Because ultraviolet waves can cause skin cancer, they may also be considered as ionising radiation.

People who use equipment or substances that produce any form of ionising radiation (e.g., X-rays or gamma rays) must wear a film badge (Figure 3). If the badge shows that it is over-exposed to ionising radiation, its wearer is not allowed to continue working with the equipment for a period of time.

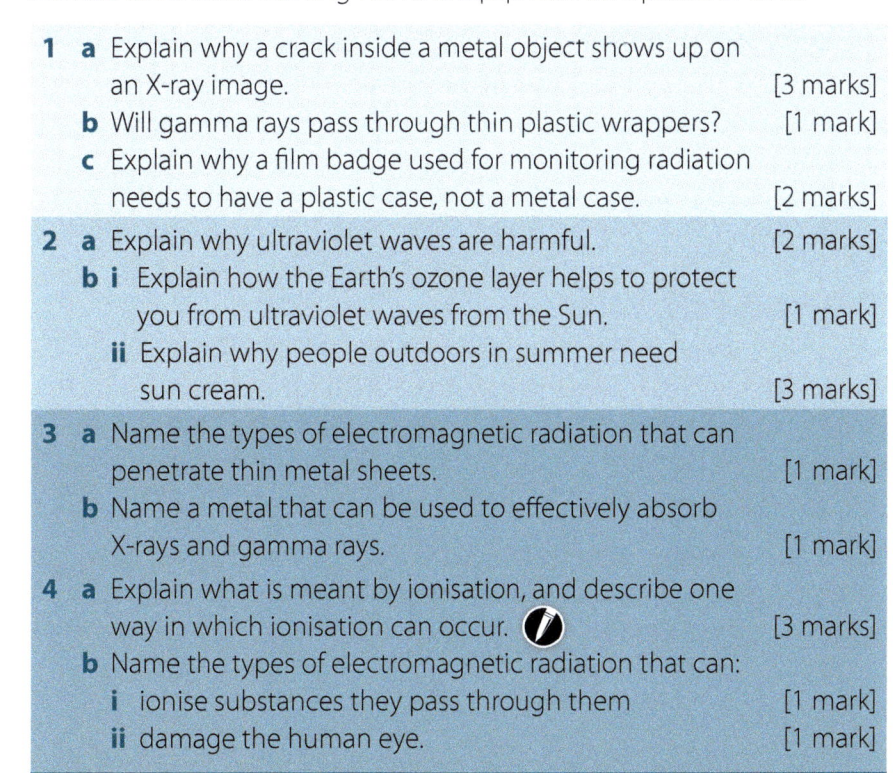

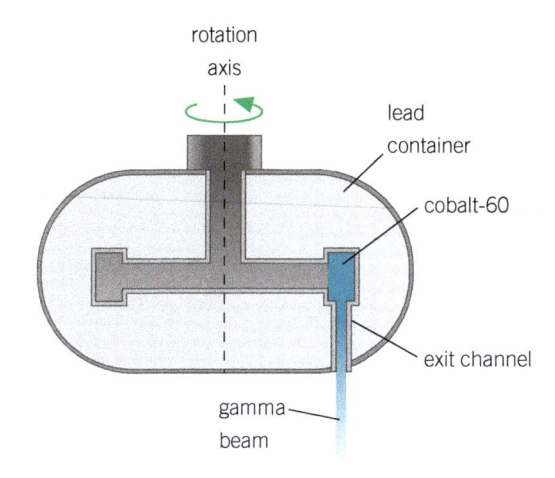

Figure 2 *Gamma treatment – the cobalt-60 source is in a thick lead container. When it is not in use, it is rotated away from the exit channel*

Figure 3 *A film badge tells you how much ionising radiation the wearer has received*

1 a Explain why a crack inside a metal object shows up on an X-ray image. [3 marks]
   b Will gamma rays pass through thin plastic wrappers? [1 mark]
   c Explain why a film badge used for monitoring radiation needs to have a plastic case, not a metal case. [2 marks]

2 a Explain why ultraviolet waves are harmful. [2 marks]
   b i Explain how the Earth's ozone layer helps to protect you from ultraviolet waves from the Sun. [1 mark]
      ii Explain why people outdoors in summer need sun cream. [3 marks]

3 a Name the types of electromagnetic radiation that can penetrate thin metal sheets. [1 mark]
   b Name a metal that can be used to effectively absorb X-rays and gamma rays. [1 mark]

4 a Explain what is meant by ionisation, and describe one way in which ionisation can occur. [3 marks]
   b Name the types of electromagnetic radiation that can:
      i ionise substances they pass through them [1 mark]
      ii damage the human eye. [1 mark]

Study tip
You should know the dangers, as well as the uses, of the different kinds of electromagnetic waves.

Key points
- Ultraviolet waves have a shorter wavelength than visible light and can harm the skin and the eyes.
- X-rays are used in hospitals to create X-ray images.
- Gamma rays are used to kill harmful bacteria in food, to sterilise surgical equipment, and to kill cancer cells.
- Ionising radiation makes uncharged atoms become charged.
- X-rays and gamma rays damage living tissue when they pass through it.

1.4.8 X-rays in medicine

Learning objectives

After this topic, you should know:
- what X-rays are used for in hospitals
- why X-rays are dangerous
- what absorbs X-rays when they pass through the body.

Have you ever broken one of your bones? If you have, you will have gone to your local hospital for an X-ray photograph. X-rays are electromagnetic waves at the short-wavelength end of the electromagnetic spectrum. They are produced in an X-ray tube when fast-moving electrons hit a target. Their wavelengths are about the same as the diameter of an atom.

To make an X-ray photograph or radiograph, X-rays from an X-ray tube are directed at the patient. A lightproof cassette containing a photographic film or a flat-panel detector is placed on the other side of the patient.

- When the X-ray tube is switched on, X-rays from the tube pass through the part of the patient's body under investigation (Figure 1).

- X-rays pass through soft tissue, but they are absorbed by bones, teeth, and metal objects that are not too thin. The parts of the film or the detector that the X-rays reach become darker than the other parts. So the bones appear lighter than the surrounding tissue, which appears dark (Figure 2). The radiograph shows a 'negative image' of the bones. A hole or a cavity in a tooth shows up as a dark area in the bright image of the tooth.

- An organ that consists of soft tissue can be filled with a substance called a **contrast medium** that absorbs X-rays easily. This enables the internal surfaces in the organ to be seen on the radiograph. For example, to obtain a radiograph of the stomach, the patient is given a barium meal before the X-ray machine is used (Figure 3). The barium compound is a good absorber of X-rays.

- Lead plates between the tube and the patient stop X-rays reaching other parts of the body. The X-rays reaching the patient pass through a gap between the plates. Lead is used because it is a good absorber of X-rays.

- A flat-panel detector is a small screen that contains a **charge-coupled device (CCD)**. The sensors in the CCD convert X-rays to light. The light rays then create electronic signals in the sensors that are sent to a computer, which displays a digital X-ray image.

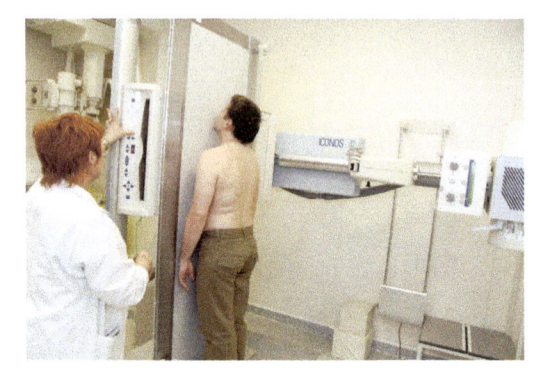

Figure 1 Taking a chest X-ray

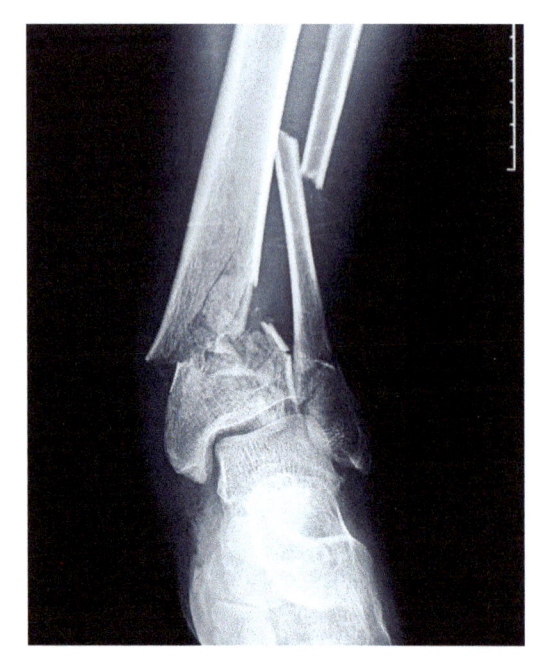

Figure 2 Spot the breaks

Radiation dose

X-rays, gamma rays, and the radiation from radioactive substances all ionise substances they pass through. There are three types of radiation from radioactive substances. You have already learnt about gamma rays, which are one of the three types. The other two types are called alpha and beta radiation.

All the different types of ionising radiation are dangerous. High doses of radiation kill living cells. Low doses can cause gene mutation and cancerous growth. There is no evidence of a safe limit below which living cells would not be damaged.

Everyone is exposed to low levels of ionising radiation from background sources such as cosmic radiation from space and radon gas which seeps through the earth from deep underground.

X-ray therapy

Doctors use X-ray therapy to destroy cancerous tumours in the body. X-rays for therapy are shorter in wavelength than those used for imaging. Thick lead plates between the X-ray tube and the body stop X-rays from reaching healthy body tissues. The plates need to be thicker than those used for X-ray imaging, otherwise the X-rays used for therapy would pass through them. A gap between the plates allows X-rays through to reach the tumour.

Higher

The X-rays used for therapy carry much more energy than X-rays used for imaging, and they are shorter in wavelength. Low-energy X-rays are suitable for imaging because they are absorbed by bones and teeth but they pass through soft tissue and gaps such as cracks in bones. Low-energy X-rays do not carry enough energy to destroy cancerous tumours.

Figure 3 *A coloured X-ray of a stomach ulcer*

Synoptic link

You will learn about radioactive substances and background radiation in Chapter 3.8.

1 a Explain what a contrast medium is used for when an X-ray photograph of the stomach is taken. [2 marks]
   b State *one* example of what X-ray therapy can be used for. [1 mark]
2 When an X-ray photograph is taken, explain why it is necessary:
   a to place the patient between the X-ray tube and the film cassette [3 marks]
   b to have the film in a lightproof cassette. [1 mark]
3 a Name *one* way in which X-rays used for X-ray therapy differ from X-rays used for X-ray imaging. [1 mark]
   b State why X-rays used for imaging cannot be used for X-ray therapy. [1 mark]
4 When an X-ray image is taken of a patient's limb or body organs, X-rays from an X-ray tube pass through a gap between lead plates before they reach the patient.
   a i Describe the purpose of the lead plates. [1 mark]
      ii Describe how the patient would be affected if the lead plates were not used. [2 marks]
   b Why is lead used rather than a different metal? [1 mark]

Key points

- X-rays are used in hospitals:
  - to make images of your internal body parts
  - to destroy tumours at or near the body surface.
- X-rays are ionising radiation, so can damage living tissue when they pass through it.
- X-rays are absorbed more by bones and teeth than by soft tissues.

1.4 Waves

Summary questions

1 **Figure 1** shows transverse waves on a string.

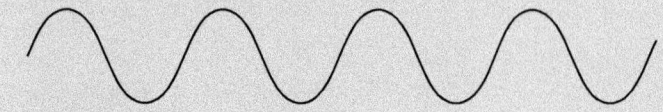

Figure 1

a Copy the diagram and label distances on it to show what is meant by:
  i the wavelength [1 mark]
  ii the amplitude of the waves. [1 mark]
b Describe the difference between a transverse wave and a longitudinal wave. [1 mark]
c Give *one* example of:
  i a transverse wave [1 mark]
  ii a longitudinal wave. [1 mark]

2 a When ripples travel across a water surface in a ripple tank, a small cork floating on the water surface bobs up and down without travelling across the tank. What does this tell you about the water in the ripple tank? [1 mark]
  b Copy and complete **Figure 2** to show the refraction of a straight wavefront at a straight boundary as the wavefront moves from deep to shallow water. [2 marks]

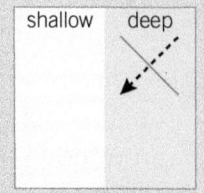

Figure 2

3 a Place the five types of electromagnetic wave listed below in order of increasing wavelength.
  A infrared waves
  B microwaves
  C radio waves
  D gamma rays
  E ultraviolet waves [1 mark]
  b Name the type(s) of electromagnetic radiation listed in **a** that:
    i can be used to send signals to and from a satellite [1 mark]
    ii ionise substances when they pass through them [1 mark]
    iii are used to carry signals in thin transparent fibres. [1 mark]

4 The radio waves from a local radio station have a wavelength of 2.9 m in air. The speed of electromagnetic waves in air is 300 000 km/s.
  a Write the equation that links frequency, wavelength, and wave speed. [1 mark]
  b Calculate the frequency of the radio waves. [2 marks]

5 **Figure 3** shows an X-ray source that is used to direct X-rays at a broken leg. A photographic film in a lightproof wrapper is placed under the leg. When the film is developed, an image of the broken bone is observed.

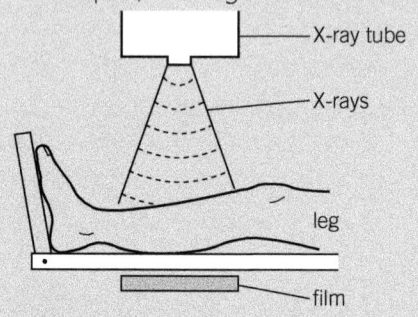

Figure 3

a i Explain why an image of the bone is seen on the film. [3 marks]
  ii Why is it possible to see the fracture on the image? [1 mark]
b When an X-ray photograph of the stomach is taken, the patient is given food containing barium before the photograph is taken.
  i Explain why it is necessary for the patient to be given this food before the photograph is taken. [3 marks]
  ii The exposure time for a stomach X-ray must be shorter than the X-ray time for a limb. Explain why. [2 marks]
  iii Very low-energy X-rays from the X-ray tube can be absorbed by placing a suitable metal plate between the patient and the X-ray tube. Such X-rays would otherwise be absorbed by the body. Describe the benefit of removing such low-energy X-rays in this way. [2 marks]

6 a Some chemicals can emit light as a result of absorbing ultraviolet waves. Describe and explain how these chemicals could be used as invisible ink. In your explanation, state the type of radiation that is absorbed and the type of radiation that is emitted. [3 marks]
  b Explain why a beam of infrared radiation cannot be used to carry signals to a detector that is more than a few metres from a transmitter. [2 marks]

1.4 Waves

Practice questions

01 Transverse waves and longitudinal waves are the two types of waves.

01.1 Describe how transverse waves and longitudinal waves differ in relation to the motion that produced them. [2 marks]

01.2 Waves on a pond are an example of a transverse wave.
Describe an experiment that will show that it is the wave that moves across the pond rather than the water. [3 marks]

01.3 Longitudinal waves are made up of regions of compression and regions of rarefaction. Describe how the arrangement of particles differs in the regions of compression and the regions of rarefaction. [2 marks]

02 Radio waves are an example of a transverse wave.
Figure 1 shows a transverse wave at a certain time.

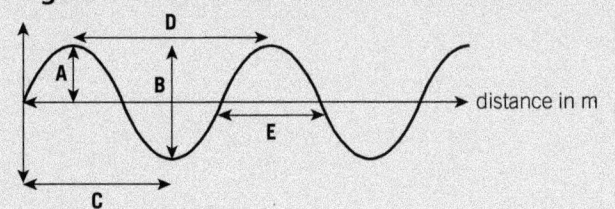

Figure 1

02.1 Which letter on the diagram in **Figure 1** shows the amplitude of the wave? [1 mark]

02.2 Give the number of complete waves shown in **Figure 1**. [1 mark]

02.3 Describe what is meant by the wavelength of a wave. [1 mark]

02.4 A radio station transmits signals at a frequency of 101.5 MHz.
Describe what is meant by 101.5 MHz. [1 mark]

02.5 Radio waves with a frequency of 101.5 MHz travel through a vacuum at a speed of 3×10^8 m/s.
Calculate the wavelength of the radio waves transmitted by the radio station.
Give your answer to 3 significant figures, with the correct unit. [3 marks]

02.6 A different radio station transmits signals at a higher frequency.
Describe how increasing the frequency of a wave affects the wave speed and the wavelength. [2 marks]

02.7 **H** Explain how radio waves can induce an alternating current of a given frequency in an electrical circuit. [3 marks]

03 Electromagnetic waves have many uses in the home. Visible light is used in lasers that are found in DVD players.

03.1 X-rays are used only under strict conditions, because they are harmful.
Explain why X-rays are harmful. [1 mark]

03.2 The colours that make up white light range in wavelength from 350 nm to 700 nm.
Light travels at 300 000 000 m/s in a vacuum.
Calculate the range of frequencies of the visible spectrum. [3 marks]

04 A ray of light can be refracted as it travels through a glass block.
Figure 2 shows a ray of light incident upon a rectangular glass block.

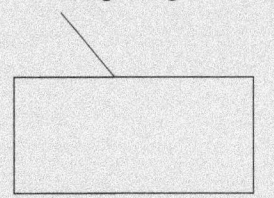

Figure 2

04.1 Light travels more slowly in glass than in air.
Compare the wavelength and the frequency of light in glass with the wavelength and the frequency of light in air. [2 marks]

04.2 Copy and complete **Figure 2** to show the path the light ray will take going through the rectangular glass prism. [3 marks]

04.3 **H** A mirror and a piece of paper both reflect the light incident upon them. The mirror produces an image of the object. The piece of paper does not. Explain, with the help of diagrams, why a mirror and a piece of paper look very different when light shines on them. [2 marks]

04.4 Sound also travels as a wave. The speed of sound is much lower than the speed of light.
Describe **one** method that could be used to measure the speed of sound in air.
In your answer you should describe the sources of error and the approximate size of the error that will occur in readings. [5 marks]

Unit 1 in context

Development of the nuclear model of the atom

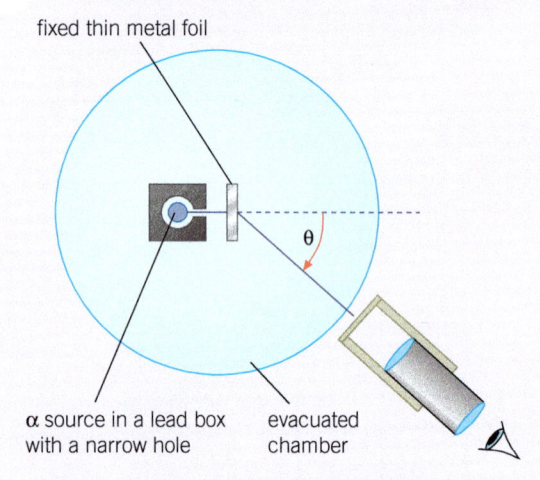

Figure 1 *Alpha α particle scattering*

Scientists use observations and measurements from experiments to develop their ideas and models and to make predictions that can be tested by more experiments. If the tests don't support the predictions, the ideas and models behind the predictions need to be rejected or changed. After Ernest Rutherford discovered that the radiation from radioactive substances is made up of different types of particles, he realised that the most easily absorbed type, alpha (α) particles, could be used to probe the atom. He asked two of his research workers, Hans Geiger and Ernest Marsden, to investigate how a thin metal foil scatters a beam of α particles. Figure 1 shows the arrangement they used.

The apparatus was in a vacuum chamber to prevent air molecules absorbing the α particles. The detector consisted of a microscope focused on a small glass plate. Each time an α particle hit the plate, a spot of light was observed. The detector was moved to different positions. At each position, the number of spots of light observed in a certain time was counted. Their results showed that:

- most of the α particles passed straight through the metal foil
- the number of α particles deflected per minute decreased as the angle of deflection increased
- about 1 in 10 000 α particles were deflected by more than 90°.

Rutherford was astonished by the results. He said it was like firing shells at tissue paper and discovering that a small number of the shells rebound back. He knew that α particles are positively charged and that the radius of an atom is about 10^{-10} m. He deduced from the results that there is a positively charged nucleus at the centre of every atom and that this nucleus is:

- much smaller than the atom because most α particles pass through without deflection
- where most of the mass of the atom is located.

A nuclear puzzle

Rutherford's nuclear model of the atom was quickly accepted because it agreed exactly with the measurements Geiger and Marsden made in their experiments. The name **proton** was given to the hydrogen nucleus because scientists discovered that every other nucleus contains hydrogen nuclei. But they also knew that the mass of every nucleus except for the hydrogen nucleus is bigger than the total mass of its protons. Table 1 shows the number of protons in the nucleus of some different atoms. It also shows the mass number of each atom. If each nucleus contained only protons, the mass number would be the same as the proton number of the nucleus. So there must be more particles in the nucleus of every atom (except for the hydrogen atom). Because the smallest mass difference between different nuclei was one unit of atomic mass, these extra particles in the nucleus must each have about the same mass

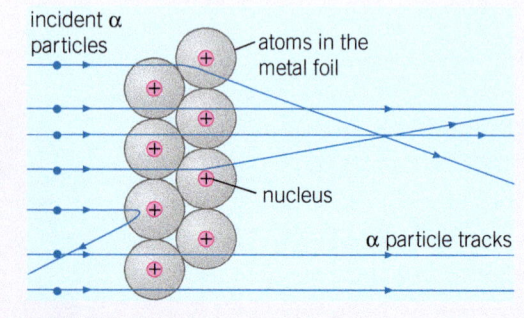

Figure 2 *Alpha α particle tracks*

as a proton. They were called **neutrons** because they were uncharged particles and therefore 'neutral'.

The proton–neutron model of the nucleus

The model developed by Rutherford explains all the mass and charge values of every nucleus. Direct experimental evidence for the neutron was found by the physicist James Chadwick about 20 years after Rutherford's discovery of the nucleus in 1911. Chadwick knew from the work of Marie Curie and others that when high-energy α particles hit a metal foil, the foil gives out very penetrating radiation from the other side that could knock protons out of solids like wax and could also knock gas molecules off course. Some scientists thought this radiation was X-radiation (X-rays), but this was disproved when it was discovered that the mystery radiation knocks far more electrons out of gas atoms than X-rays do. Chadwick suspected that the mystery radiation consisted of neutrons. He used an instrument called a cloud chamber to observe the trails created by the mystery radiation when it knocked into atoms in a gas (Figure 3). He observed and measured these impacts and calculated the mass of the mysterious particles. His results showed conclusively that they were uncharged particles, each with the same mass as a proton. His discoveries confirmed the existence of the neutron.

Scientists now know that neutrons and protons themselves are each composed of smaller particles called quarks. The idea of quarks was put forward in the mid-20th century to explain other discoveries about radioactivity, but the quark model was not accepted until scientists used high energy electrons to probe the nucleus. Their results showed that each neutron and each proton is made up of three quarks – just as the quark model predicted!

Table 1 *The proton–neutron model of the nucleus*

Nucleus	Number of protons	Mass number	Number of neutrons
hydrogen	1	1	0
helium	2	4	2
lithium	3	7	4
beryllium	4	9	5

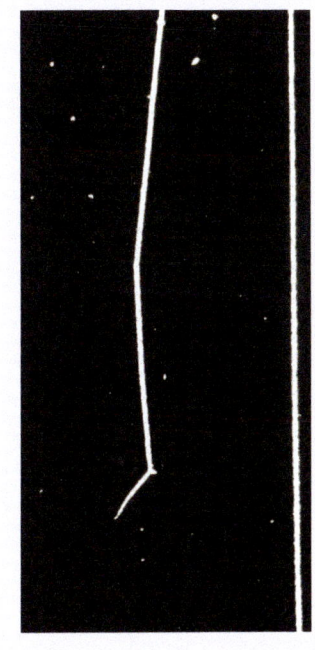

Figure 3 *Figure 3 Photograph of an alpha particle track in a cloud chamber, taken in the 1930s when Chadwick's discovery was made. The track looks like the jet trails you sometimes see in the sky. To see particle tracks the air in the cloud chamber is saturated with vapour, then made very cold. The tracks in the cloud chamber are created when alpha particles pass through the very cold air, leaving behind lots of tiny liquid droplets.*

1. Describe the nuclear model of the atom. [4 marks]
2. Figure 4 shows four possible paths, labelled **A–D**, of an α particle deflected by a single nucleus.
   a. Write the path along which the alpha particle would travel. [1 mark]
   b. Explain why each of the other paths is not possible. [3 marks]
3. a. Write one difference and one similarity between a proton and a neutron. [1 mark]
   b. Explain why the mass of a helium nucleus is four times the mass of a hydrogen nucleus but its charge is only twice as much as the charge of a hydrogen nucleus. [3 marks]
   c. Give a reason why the proton–neutron model of the nucleus was not fully accepted for many years after it was first put forward. [1 mark]
   d. Explain briefly why scientific theories and models change over time. [3 marks]

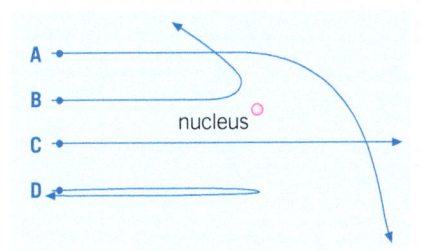

Figure 4 *See Question 2*

2 Transport over large distances

Every cell in the brain of a giraffe needs dissolved food molecules and oxygen for respiration to take place. The waste chemicals produced as the cells work need to be removed as well. Yet the head of a giraffe is up to six metres above the ground, and more than two metres above the digestive system and lungs. Respiration is the key reaction that transfers energy to be used in all the vital chemical processes that take place in every cell.

In the same way, the leaves of a giant redwood tree, towering over 100 metres above the forest floor, need water and minerals from the soil just as much as the grass and daisies in your local park. The cells in the roots of these magnificent trees also need to be supplied with the sugars made in the leaves so high above them.

In this unit you will look at ways in which living things transport materials over immense distances, often thousands of orders of magnitude greater than any individual cell. You will also look at the reactions of photosynthesis and respiration, which transfer the energy needed to maintain the processes of life that power these transport systems.

Key questions

- Why are transport systems needed in multicellular organisms?
- How are body systems in plants and animals adapted for their functions, including the exchange of materials?
- How are the systems of the body, including transport systems, coordinated and controlled?
- What are the links between photosynthesis and respiration?

Making connections

- Problems in the endocrine system can cause a range of non-communicable diseases. The lifestyle choices you make can also affect the health of your body systems and the way they work. You will look at some non-communicable diseases and how they can be caused in **Chapter 3.7**.
- Your nervous system plays a key role in coordinating your responses to the environment around you. The speed of your reactions can be a matter of life and death. You will learn more about reaction times and how they affect stopping distances in **Topic 7.18.9** in the *Physical Sciences* book.
- Hundreds of reactions take place in a living organism at the same time. The reactions of biological processes such as respiration, photosynthesis, or digestion could not take place without the catalytic effects of enzymes. You will learn more about enzymes and factors that affect the rate of biological reactions in **Topics 7.21.8 and 7.21.9** in the *Physical Sciences* book.

I already know...	I will learn...
the structural adaptations of some unicellular organisms	some structural adaptations of exchange surfaces in multicellular organisms
a word summary for respiration	about aerobic respiration as an endothermic reaction and why respiration is needed for chemical reactions to build larger molecules, for movement, and for keeping warm
the content of a healthy human diet	about the chemistry of carbohydrates, proteins, and lipids and how to test for their presence in food
the role of leaf stomata in gas exchange in plants	about the process of transpiration and how to investigate factors affecting the rate of water uptake in plants
the adaptations of leaves for photosynthesis	about the role of chlorophyll in photosynthesis and how to separate chlorophyll pigments using chromatography
how to observe and identify patterns in data.	how to carry out rate calculations for photosynthesis ⓗ to understand and use inverse proportion – the inverse square law – and light intensity in the context of factors affecting photosynthesis.

Required practicals

Practical		Topic
7	Food tests	2.5.8
8	Measuring reaction times	2.5.10
9	Chromatography and finding R_f values	2.6.11
10	Light intensity and rate of photosynthesis	2.6.7

2.5 Systems in the human body

2.5.1 Aerobic respiration

Learning objectives
After this topic, you should know:
- the chemistry of aerobic respiration
- why cellular respiration is so important.

One of the most important processes in living things is aerobic respiration. It takes place all the time in plant and animal cells.

Your digestive system, lungs, and circulation all work to provide your cells with the glucose and oxygen they need for respiration.

During **aerobic respiration**, glucose (a sugar) reacts with oxygen. This reaction transfers energy that your cells can use. This energy is vital for everything that goes on in your body.

Carbon dioxide and water are produced as waste products of the reaction. The process is called aerobic respiration because it uses oxygen from the air.

Aerobic respiration is an **exothermic reaction**. Exothermic reactions transfer energy to the environment – more energy is transferred to the environment when new bonds are formed in the products than is taken in to break the bonds in the reactants. Some of the energy transferred in respiration is used for all of the reactions that take place inside a cell. The rest of the energy is transferred to the environment, making it slightly warmer.

Aerobic respiration can be summarised as:

$$\text{glucose} + \text{oxygen} \rightarrow \text{carbon dioxide} + \text{water}$$

Aerobic respiration can be represented by the following balanced chemical equation:

$$C_6H_{12}O_6 + 6O_2 \rightarrow 6CO_2 + 6H_2O$$

The average energy needs of a teenage boy are around 11 510 kJ daily, but teenage girls only need 8830 kJ a day. This is partly because, on average, girls are smaller than boys, and also because boys have more muscle cells. More muscle cells mean more mitochondria requiring fuel for aerobic respiration.

Investigating respiration
Animals, plants, and microorganisms all respire. It is possible to show that cellular respiration is taking place. You can either deprive a living organism of the things it needs to respire, or show that waste products are produced from the reaction.

Depriving a living thing of food and/or oxygen would kill it. So you should concentrate on the products of respiration. Carbon dioxide is the easiest product to identify. You can also measure the energy transferred to the surroundings.

Limewater goes cloudy when carbon dioxide bubbles through it. The higher the concentration of carbon dioxide, the more quickly the limewater goes cloudy. This gives you an easy way of showing that carbon dioxide has been produced. You can also look for a rise in temperature to show that energy is being transferred to the environment during respiration.

- Plan an ethical investigation into aerobic respiration in living organisms.

cytoplasm – Where enzymes are made on the ribosomes. Location of reactions in anaerobic respiration.

mitochondrion – Contains the enzymes for aerobic respiration.

nucleus – Holds genetic code for enzymes involved in respiration.

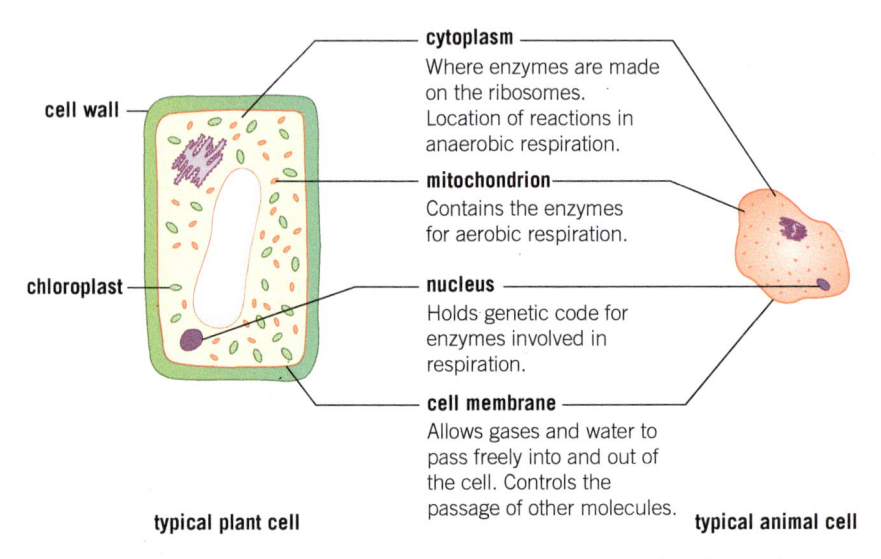

cell membrane – Allows gases and water to pass freely into and out of the cell. Controls the passage of other molecules.

cell wall

chloroplast

typical plant cell

typical animal cell

Figure 1 *Aerobic respiration takes place in the mitochondria, but other parts of the cell play vital roles*

Mitochondria – the site of respiration

Aerobic respiration involves lots of chemical reactions. Each reaction is controlled by a different enzyme. Most of these reactions take place in the mitochondria of your cells (Figure 1).

Mitochondria are tiny rod-shaped parts (organelles) that are found in almost all plant and animal cells as well as in fungal and algal cells. They have a folded inner membrane, which provides a large surface area for the enzymes involved in aerobic respiration. The number of mitochondria in a cell shows you how active the cell is.

The need for respiration

The energy transferred during respiration supplies all the energy needs for living processes in the cells.

- Living cells need energy to carry out the basic functions of life. They build up large molecules from smaller ones to make new cell material. Much of the energy transferred in respiration is used for these 'building' activities (synthesis reactions). Energy is also transferred to break down larger molecules to smaller ones, both during digestion and within the cells themselves.
- In animals, energy from respiration is transferred to make muscles contract. Muscles are working all the time in your body. Even when you sleep, your heart beats, you breathe, and your stomach churns. All muscular activities require energy.
- Mammals and birds maintain a constant internal body temperature almost regardless of the temperature of their surroundings (Figure 2). On cold days energy transferred from respiration helps you to stay warm, whilst on hot days you sweat and transfer energy to your surroundings to keep your body cool.
- In plants, energy from respiration is transferred to move mineral ions such as nitrates from the soil into root hair cells. It is also transferred to convert sugars, nitrates, and other nutrients into amino acids, which are then built up into proteins.

1 **a** Give the word equation for aerobic respiration. [2 marks]
   b Explain why muscle cells have many mitochondria whilst fat cells have very few. [4 marks]

2 You need a regular supply of food to provide the energy needed by your cells. If you don't get enough to eat, you become thin and stop growing. As a result, you don't want to move around and you start to feel cold.
   a State the *three* main uses of the energy transferred in your body during aerobic respiration. [3 marks]
   b Suggest how this explains the symptoms of starvation described above. [4 marks]

3 **(H)** Give the symbol equation for aerobic respiration. [2 marks]

4 Plan how you could demonstrate that oxygen is taken up and carbon dioxide is released during aerobic respiration. [6 marks]

Study tip

You should know the word equation for aerobic respiration.

Remember that aerobic respiration takes place in the mitochondria.

Synoptic links

You learnt about mitochondria in Topic 1.3.2, and about active transport and the movement of mineral ions into root hair cells in Topic 1.3.7.

Figure 2 *When the weather is cold, birds like this American robin need a lot of food for respiration just to keep warm. Giving them extra food supplies during the winter can therefore mean the difference between life and death*

Key points

- Aerobic respiration is an exothermic reaction. It can be represented as follows:
  glucose + oxygen → carbon dioxide + water
- **(H)** $C_6H_{12}O_6 + 6O_2 \rightarrow 6CO_2 + 6H_2O$
- An exothermic reaction is one that transfers energy to its surroundings.
- Organisms need energy for:
  - chemical reactions to build larger molecules
  - movement
  - keeping warm.

2.5.2 Anaerobic respiration

Learning objectives

After this topic, you should know:
- why less energy is transferred by anaerobic respiration than by aerobic respiration
- what is meant by an oxygen debt.

Your everyday muscle movements use energy transferred by aerobic respiration. However, when you exercise hard, your muscle cells may become short of oxygen. Although you increase your heart and breathing rates, sometimes the blood cannot supply oxygen to the muscles fast enough. When this happens, energy from the breakdown of glucose can still be transferred to the muscle cells. They use **anaerobic respiration**, which takes place without oxygen.

Anaerobic respiration

Anaerobic respiration is not as efficient as aerobic respiration because the glucose molecules are not broken down completely. In animal cells the end product of anaerobic respiration is **lactic acid** instead of carbon dioxide and water. Anaerobic respiration is also exothermic, but because the breakdown of glucose is incomplete, far less energy is transferred than during aerobic respiration.

Anaerobic respiration can be summarised as:

glucose → lactic acid (+ energy released)

Muscle fatigue

Using your muscle fibres vigorously for a long time can make them become fatigued and they stop contracting efficiently. One cause of this muscle fatigue is the build-up of lactic acid, produced by anaerobic respiration in the muscle cells. Blood flowing through the muscles eventually removes the lactic acid.

For example, repeated movements can soon lead to anaerobic respiration in your muscles – particularly if you're not used to the exercise. If you are fit, your heart and lungs will be able to keep a good supply of oxygen going to your muscles while you exercise for a relatively long time. If you are unfit, your muscles will run short of oxygen much sooner.

Figure 1 *When you are fit, you can get oxygen to your muscles and remove carbon dioxide more efficiently*

Oxygen debt

If you have been exercising hard, you often carry on puffing and panting for some time after you stop (Figure 2). The length of time you remain out of breath depends on how fit you are. Why do you carry on breathing fast and deeply when you have stopped using your muscles?

The waste lactic acid you produce during anaerobic respiration is a problem. You cannot simply get rid of lactic acid by breathing it out as you can with carbon dioxide. As a result, when the exercise is over, lactic acid has to be broken down to produce carbon dioxide and water. This needs oxygen.

The amount of oxygen needed to break down the lactic acid to carbon dioxide and water is known as the **oxygen debt**. After a race, your heart rate and breathing rate stay high to supply the extra oxygen needed to pay off the oxygen debt. The bigger the debt (the larger the amount of lactic acid), the longer you will puff and pant for.

Making lactic acid
Repeat a single action many times. For example, you could step up and down, lift a weight, or clench and unclench your fist. You will soon feel the effect of a build-up of lactic acid in your muscles as they begin to ache.

2.5 Systems in the human body

Oxygen debt repayment:

lactic acid + oxygen → carbon dioxide + water

In a 100 m sprint, some athletes do not breathe at all. This means that the muscles use the oxygen taken in before the start of the race and then don't get any more oxygen until the race is over. Although the race only takes a few seconds, a tremendous amount of energy is used up, so a big oxygen debt can develop, even if the athletes are very fit.

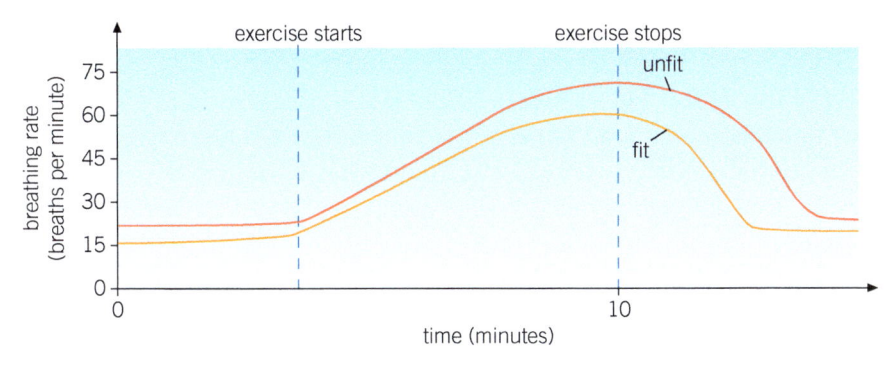

Figure 2 *Everyone gets an oxygen debt if they exercise hard, but if you are fit you can pay it off faster*

Testing fitness

A good way of telling how fit you are is to measure your resting heart rate and breathing rate. The fitter you are, the lower they will be. This is because the heart and lungs of fit people are bigger and have a better blood supply than those of people who are less fit. They are more efficient. Then see what happens when you exercise. The increase in your heart rate and breathing rate, along with how quickly they return to normal, are also ways of finding out how fit you are – or aren't!

Figure 3 *A runner at the start of an endurance race and during the race*

Key points

- If muscles don't get enough oxygen, they will respire anaerobically.
- Anaerobic respiration is respiration without oxygen. When this takes place in animal cells, glucose is incompletely broken down to form lactic acid.
- Anaerobic respiration in muscles can be represented as:
  glucose → lactic acid (+ energy released)
- The anaerobic breakdown of glucose transfers less energy than aerobic respiration.
- After exercise, oxygen is still needed to break down the lactic acid that has built up. The amount of oxygen needed is known as the oxygen debt.

1. If you exercise very hard or for a long time, your muscles begin to ache and do not work effectively. Explain why. [4 marks]
2. If you exercise vigorously, you often puff and pant for some time after you stop. Explain what is happening. [6 marks]
3. a Define anaerobic respiration. [1 mark]
   b Explain how anaerobic respiration differs from aerobic respiration. Give the word equations for what is happening in each case, and explain the benefits to an individual of being able to respire aerobically and anaerobically. [6 marks]

79

2.5.3 Exchanging materials

Learning objectives

After this topic, you should know:

- how the surface area to volume ratio varies depending on the size of an organism
- why large multicellular organisms need special systems for exchanging materials with the environment.

For many single-celled organisms, diffusion, osmosis, and active transport are all that is needed to exchange materials with their environment because they have a relatively large surface area compared to the volume of the cell. This allows sufficient transport of molecules into and out of the cell to meet the needs of the organism.

Surface area to volume ratio

The surface area to volume ratio is very important in biology. It makes a big difference to the way in which animals can exchange substances with the environment. Surface area to volume ratio is also important when you consider how energy is transferred by living organisms, and how water evaporates from the surfaces of plants and animals.

Surface area to volume ratio

The ratio of surface area to volume falls as objects get bigger. You can see this clearly in Figure 1. In a small object, the surface area to volume (SA:V) ratio is relatively large. This means that the diffusion distances are short and that simple diffusion is sufficient for the exchange of materials.

As organisms get bigger, the surface area to volume ratio falls. As the distances between the centre of the organism and the surface get bigger, simple diffusion is no longer enough to exchange materials between the cells and the environment.

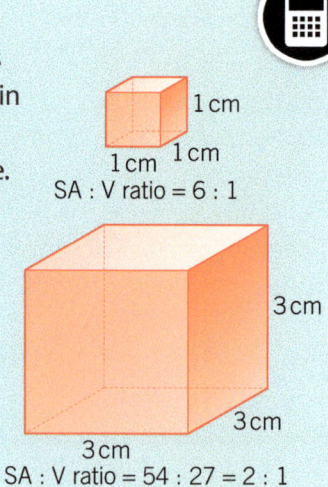

1 cm × 1 cm × 1 cm
SA : V ratio = 6 : 1

3 cm × 3 cm × 3 cm
SA : V ratio = 54 : 27 = 2 : 1

Figure 1 *Relationship of surface area to volume*

Getting bigger

As living organisms get bigger and more complex, their surface area to volume ratio gets smaller. This makes it increasingly difficult to exchange materials quickly enough with the outside world:

- Gases and food molecules can no longer reach every cell inside the organism by simple diffusion.
- Metabolic waste cannot be removed fast enough to avoid poisoning the cells.

In many larger organisms, there are special surfaces where the exchange of materials takes place. These surfaces are adapted to be as effective as possible. You can find them in humans, in other animals, and in plants.

Synoptic links

You will find out much more about gas exchange in the lungs in Topic 2.5.7.

You can find out more about the transpiration stream in Topic 2.6.4.

2.5 Systems in the human body

Adaptations for exchanging materials
There are various adaptations to make the process of exchange more efficient. The effectiveness of an exchange surface can be increased by:

- having a large surface area over which exchange can take place
- having a thin membrane or being thin to provide a short diffusion path
- in animals, having an efficient blood supply moves the diffusing substances away from the exchange surfaces and maintains a steep concentration (diffusion) gradient
- in animals, being **ventilated** makes gas exchange more efficient by maintaining steep concentration gradients.

Labels on figure: sacs for gas exchange; muscular opening pumps water in and out; finger-like folds on lining provide a large surface area and blood supply for gas exchange – magnification ≈ ×1000.

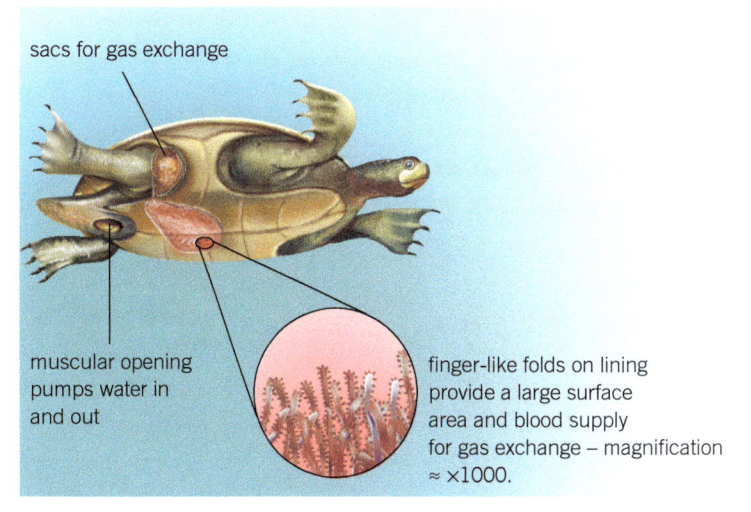

Figure 2 *Fitzroy river turtles obtain oxygen from the water through a specialised excretory opening*

Examples of adaptations
Different organisms have very different adaptations for the exchange of materials. For example, the human surface area to volume ratio is so low that the cells inside your body cannot possibly get the food and oxygen they need, or get rid of the waste they produce, by simple diffusion. Air is moved into and out of your lungs when you breathe, ventilating the millions of tiny air sacs called **alveoli**. The alveoli have an enormous surface area and a very rich blood supply, for effective gas exchange. The villi of the small intestine also provide a large surface area, short diffusion paths, and a rich blood supply to make exchange of materials more effective.

Fish need to exchange oxygen and carbon dioxide between their blood and the water in which they swim. This happens across the gills, which are made up of stacks of thin filaments, each with a rich blood supply. Fish need a constant flow of water over their gills to maintain the concentration gradients needed for gas exchange. They get this by pumping water over the gills using a flap that covers the gills, called the operculum.

Plant roots have a large surface area, made even bigger by the root hair cells, to make the uptake of water and mineral ions more efficient. Water constantly moves away from the roots in the transpiration stream, maintaining a steep concentration gradient in the cells.

Plant leaves are also modified to make gas and solute exchange as effective as possible. Flat, thin leaves, the presence of air spaces in the leaf tissues, and the **stomata** all help to provide a big surface area and maintain a steep concentration gradient for the diffusion of substances such as water, mineral ions, and carbon dioxide.

Key points
- Single-celled organisms have a relatively large surface area to volume ratio so all necessary exchanges with the environment take place over this surface.
- In multicellular organisms, many organs are specialised with effective exchange surfaces.
- Exchange surfaces usually have a large surface area and thin walls, which give short diffusion distances. In animals, exchange surfaces will have an efficient blood supply or, for gaseous exchange, be ventilated.

1. Describe *two* adaptations of an effective exchange surface. [2 marks]
2. Compare the gas exchange system of fish with that of the Fitzroy river turtle shown in Figure 2. [5 marks]
3. a. Explain how the surface area to volume ratio of an organism affects the way it exchanges materials with the environment. [3 marks]
   b. Summarise the adaptations you would expect to see in effective exchange surfaces and explain the importance of each adaptation. [3 marks]

81

2.5.4 The blood

Learning objectives

After this topic, you should know:

- how substances are transported to and from the cells
- that blood is made up of many different components
- the functions of each main component of blood.

Multicellular organisms with a small surface area to volume ratio often have specialised transport systems. The human circulatory system consists of the **blood**, the **blood vessels**, and the **heart**.

The components of the blood

Your blood is a unique tissue, based on a liquid called **plasma**. Plasma carries **red blood cells**, **white blood cells**, and **platelets** suspended in it (Figures 1 and 4). It also carries many dissolved substances around your body. The average person has between 4.7 and 5 litres of blood.

Blood plasma as a transport medium

Your blood plasma is a yellow liquid (Figure 2). The plasma transports all of your blood cells and some other substances around your body.

- Waste carbon dioxide produced by the cells is carried to the lungs.
- **Urea** formed in your liver from the breakdown of excess proteins is carried to your kidneys where it is removed from your blood to form **urine**.
- The small, soluble products of digestion pass into the plasma from your small intestine and are transported to individual cells.

Red blood cells

There are more red blood cells than any other type of blood cell in your body – about 5 million in each cubic millimetre of blood. These cells pick up oxygen from the air in your lungs and carry it to the cells where it is needed (Figure 3). Red blood cells have adaptations that make them very efficient at their job:

- They are biconcave discs. Being concave (pushed in) on both sides, gives them an increased surface area to volume ratio for diffusion.
- They are packed with a red pigment called **haemoglobin**, which binds to oxygen.
- They have no nucleus, making more space for haemoglobin.

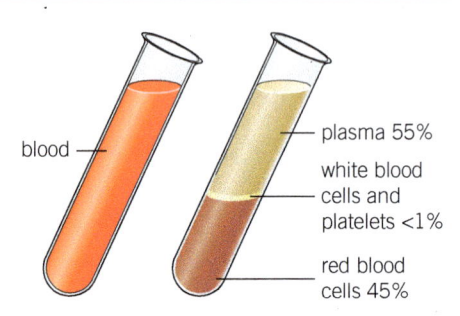

Figure 1 *The main components of the blood. The red colour of your blood comes from the red blood cells*

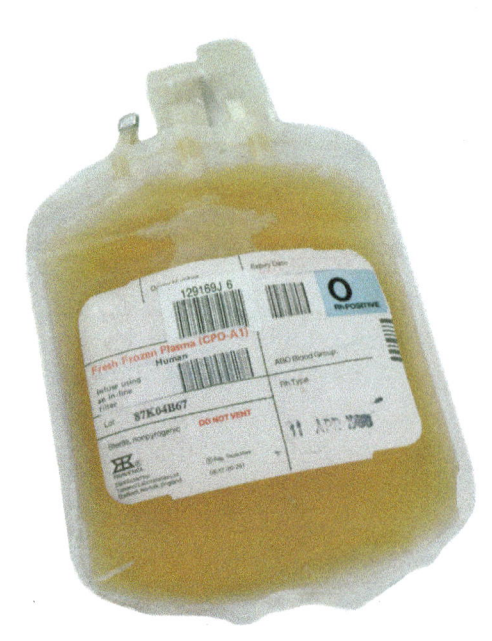

Figure 2 *Blood plasma is a yellow liquid that transports everything you need – and need to get rid of – around your body*

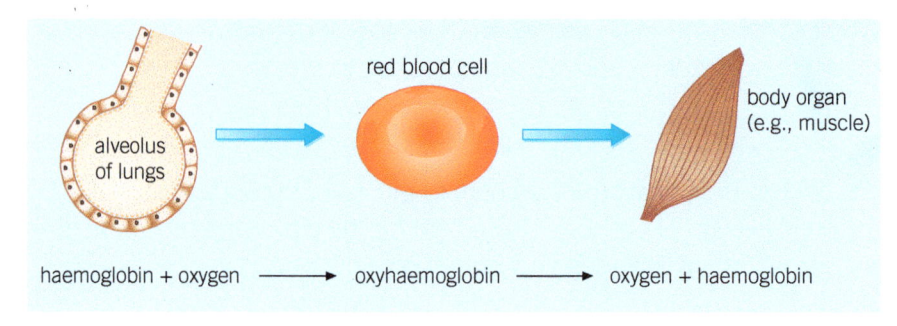

Figure 3 *The reversible reaction between oxygen and haemoglobin makes life as we know it possible by carrying oxygen to all the places where it is needed*

haemoglobin + oxygen ⟶ oxyhaemoglobin ⟶ oxygen + haemoglobin

82

2.5 Systems in the human body

White blood cells

White blood cells are often much bigger than red blood cells and there are fewer of them. They have a nucleus and form part of the body's defence system against harmful microorganisms. Some white blood cells (lymphocytes) form antibodies against microorganisms. Some form antitoxins against poisons made by microorganisms. Yet others (phagocytes) engulf and digest invading bacteria and viruses.

Platelets

Platelets are small fragments of cells. They have no nucleus. They are very important in helping the blood to clot at the site of a wound. Blood clotting is a series of enzyme-controlled reactions, which results in the conversion of fibrinogen in the plasma into fibrin. This produces a network of protein fibres. This captures lots of red blood cells and more platelets to form a jelly-like clot, which stops you from bleeding to death. The clot dries and hardens to form a scab. This protects the new skin as it grows and stops bacteria entering the body through the wound.

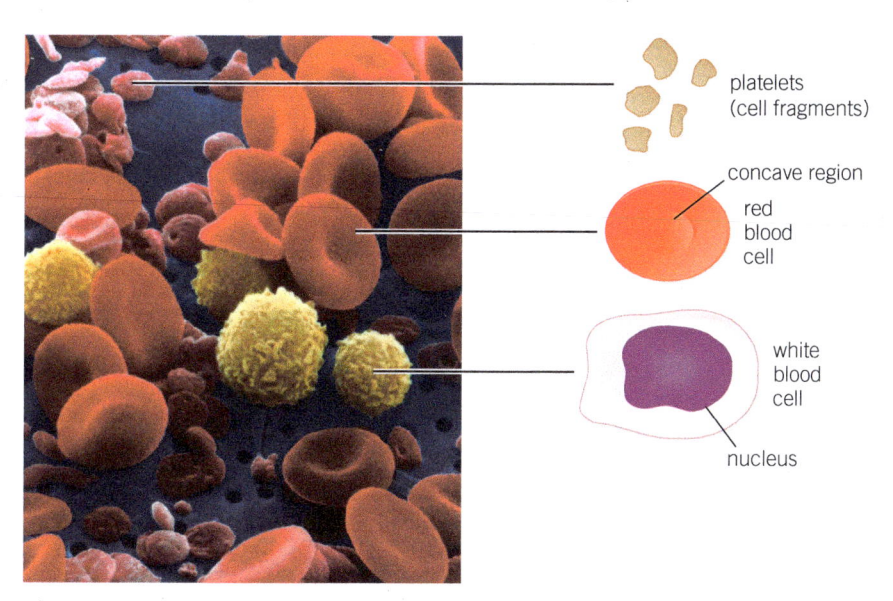

Figure 4 *This coloured scanning electron micrograph shows red blood cells, white blood cells, and platelets suspended in blood plasma – magnification ~×1000*

> **Synoptic links**
>
> For more about how digested food gets into the transport system, see Topic 2.5.9.
>
> For more about how oxygen and carbon dioxide enter or leave the blood, see Topic 2.5.7.

> **Key points**
>
> - Blood is a tissue made up of plasma in which red blood cells, white blood cells, and platelets are suspended. The different components of blood are adapted to their functions.
> - Plasma has blood cells suspended in it and transports proteins and other chemicals around the body.
> - Red blood cells contain haemoglobin that binds to oxygen to transport it from the lungs to the tissues.
> - White blood cells help to protect the body against infection.
> - Platelets are cell fragments that start the clotting process at wound sites.

1 State *three* functions of the blood. [3 marks]
2 **a** Explain why it is not accurate to describe the blood as a red liquid. [2 marks]
   b What actually makes the blood red? [1 mark]
   c Identify *three* important functions of blood plasma. [3 marks]
3 Discuss the main ways in which the blood helps you to avoid infection. Include a description of the parts of the blood involved. [6 marks]

2.5.5 The blood vessels

Learning objectives

After this topic, you should know:

- how the blood flows round the body
- that there are different types of blood vessels
- why valves are important
- the importance of a double circulatory system.

Blood flow

You can practise finding your pulse in the arteries that run close to the surface of the body in your wrist and in your neck.

You can find the valves in the veins in your hands, wrists, and forearms and see how the valves prevent the blood flowing backwards.

The substances transported in the blood need to reach the individual cells. Every cell in your body is within 0.05 mm of a capillary – the tiniest blood vessels in your circulatory system.

The blood vessels

Blood is carried around your body in three main types of blood vessels (Figure 1), each adapted for a different function:

- Your **arteries** carry blood away from your heart to the organs of your body. This blood is usually bright-red oxygenated blood. The arteries stretch as the blood is forced through them and go back into shape afterwards. You can feel this as a pulse where the arteries run close to the skin's surface (e.g., at your wrist). Arteries have thick walls containing muscle and elastic fibres. As the blood in the arteries is under pressure, it is very dangerous if an artery is cut, because the blood will spurt out rapidly every time the heart beats.

- The **veins** carry blood away from the organs of your body towards your heart. This blood is usually low in oxygen and is a deep purple-red colour. Veins do not have a pulse. They have much thinner walls than arteries and often have **valves** to prevent the backflow of blood. The valves open as the blood flows through them towards the heart, but if the blood starts to flow backwards the valves close and prevent a backflow of blood. The blood is squeezed back towards the heart by the action of the skeletal muscles (Figure 2).

- Throughout the body, **capillaries** form a huge network of tiny vessels linking the arteries and the veins. Capillaries are narrow with very thin walls. This enables substances, such as oxygen and glucose, to diffuse easily out of your blood and into your cells. The substances produced by your cells, such as carbon dioxide, pass easily into the blood through the walls of the capillaries.

artery — small lumen, thick walls, thick layer of muscle and elastic fibres — 4.0–25.0 mm

vein — large lumen, relatively thin walls, often have valves — 4.0–30.0 mm

capillary — tiny vessel with narrow lumen, walls a single cell thick — 5 μm

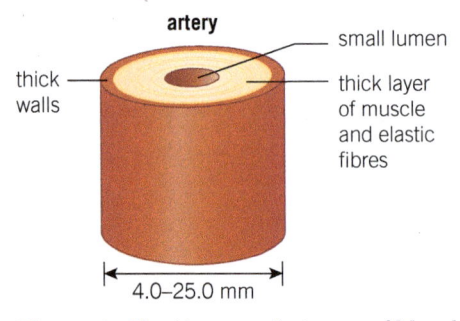

Figure 1 *The three main types of blood vessels*

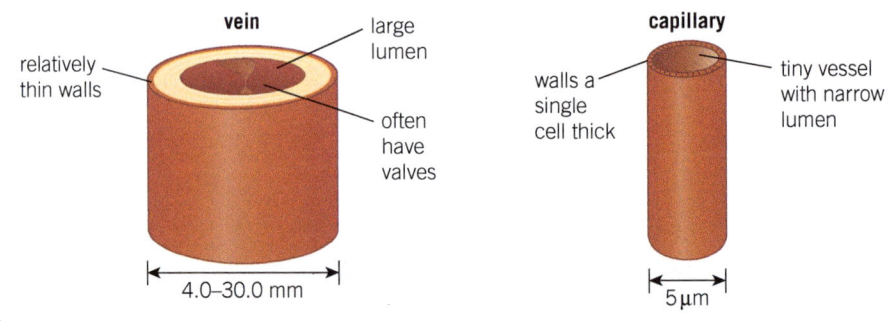

84

2.5 Systems in the human body

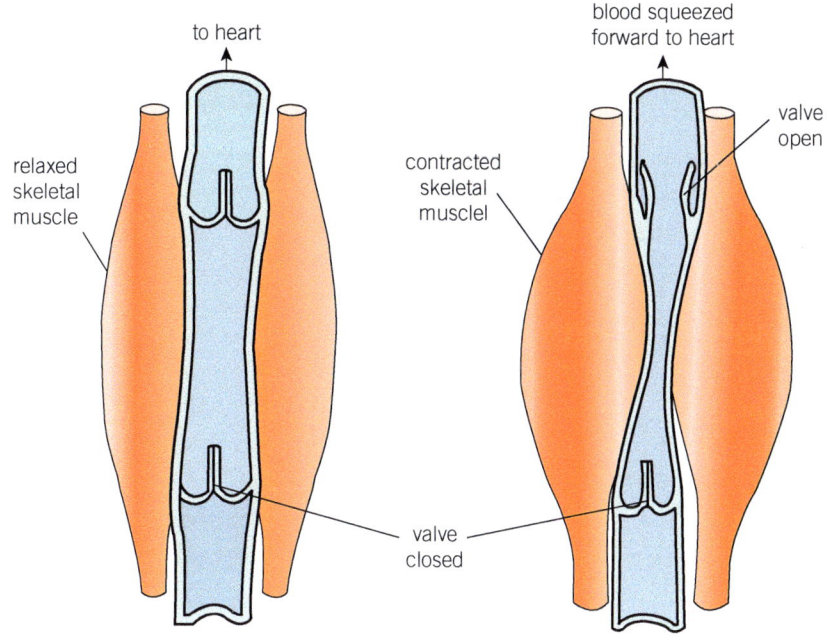

Figure 2 *How the valves and the muscles between them ensure that blood is moved from the body towards the heart*

In your circulatory system, arteries carry blood away from your heart to the organs of the body. Blood returns to your heart in the veins. The two are linked by the capillary network.

Double circulation

In humans and other mammals the blood vessels are arranged into a **dual circulatory system** (or double circulatory system).

- One transport system carries blood from your heart to your lungs and back again. This allows oxygen and carbon dioxide to be exchanged with the air in the lungs.
- The other transport system carries blood from your heart to all other organs of your body and back again.

A dual circulation like this is vital in warm-blooded, active animals such as humans. It makes our circulatory system very efficient. Fully oxygenated blood returns to the heart from the lungs. This blood can then be sent off to different parts of the body at high pressure, so more areas of your body can receive fully oxygenated blood quickly.

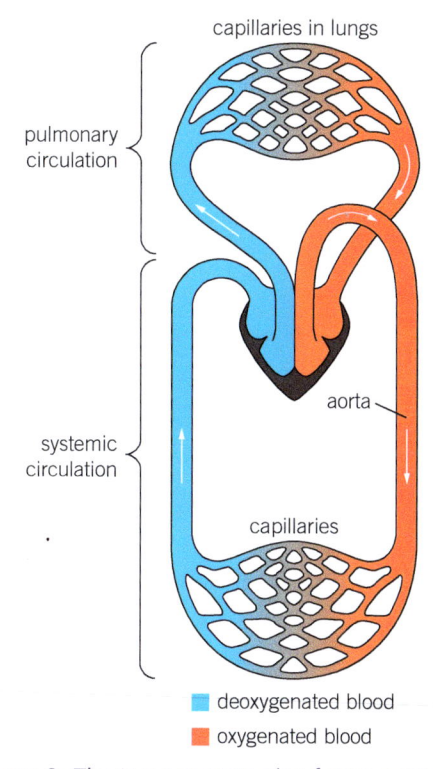

Figure 3 *The two separate circulatory systems supply the lungs and the rest of the body*

> **Study tip**
>
> Remember:
> Arteries carry blood away from the heart, and veins carry blood back to the heart – this applies to the circulation system of the lungs as well!

1 State the function of each of the following blood vessels. Describe how the structure of the blood vessel relates to its function:
   a arteries [3 marks]
   b veins [3 marks]
   c capillaries. [2 marks]

2 a Describe how the heart, arteries, veins, and capillaries are linked together in the circulatory system. [2 marks]
   b Describe what happens in the capillaries. [2 marks]

3 Fish have a single circulatory system. The blood goes from the heart, through the gills, around the body, and back to the heart. Describe the disadvantages of a single circulatory system like this for an active land mammal such as a human. [6 marks]

> **Key points**
>
> - Blood flows around the body in the blood vessels. The main types of blood vessels are arteries, veins, and capillaries.
> - Substances diffuse in and out of the blood in the capillaries.
> - Valves prevent backflow, ensuring that blood flows in the right direction.
> - Human beings have a dual (double) circulatory system.

2.5.6 The heart

Learning objectives

After this topic, you should know:

- the structure and functions of the heart
- how the heart keeps its natural rhythm
- how artificial pacemakers work.

Study tip

Remember:
- the heart has *four* chambers
- ventricles pump blood *out* of the heart
- blood comes from the veins into the atria, through valves to the ventricles, and then out via more valves into the arteries.

Your heart is the organ that pumps blood around your body. It is made up of two pumps (for the double circulation) that beat together about 70 times each minute. The walls of your heart are almost entirely muscle. This muscle is supplied with oxygen by the **coronary arteries**.

The heart as a pump

The structure of the human heart is perfectly adapted for pumping blood to your lungs and your body (Figure 1). The two sides of the heart fill and empty at the same time, giving a strong, coordinated heartbeat. Blood enters the top chambers of your heart, which are called the **atria**. The blood coming into the right atrium from the **vena cava** is deoxygenated blood from your body. The blood coming into the left atrium in the **pulmonary vein** is oxygenated blood from your lungs. The atria contract together and force blood down into the **ventricles**. Valves close to stop the blood flowing backwards out of the heart.

- **The ventricles contract and force blood out of the heart.**
- **The right ventricle forces deoxygenated blood to the lungs through the pulmonary artery.**
- **The left ventricle pumps oxygenated blood around the body through a big artery called the aorta.**

As the blood is pumped into the pulmonary artery and the aorta, valves close to make sure the blood flows in the right direction. The noise of the heartbeat heard through a stethoscope is the sound of the valves of the heart closing to prevent the blood flowing backwards.

The muscle wall of the left ventricle is noticeably thicker than the wall of the right ventricle. This allows the left ventricle to develop the pressure needed to force the blood through the arterial system all over your body. The blood leaving the right ventricle moves through the pulmonary arteries to your lungs, where high pressure would damage the delicate capillary network

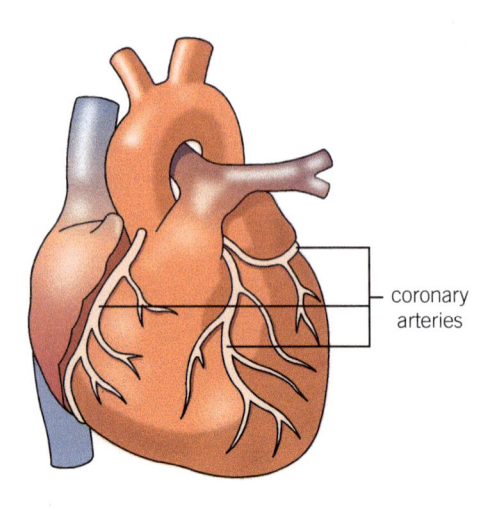

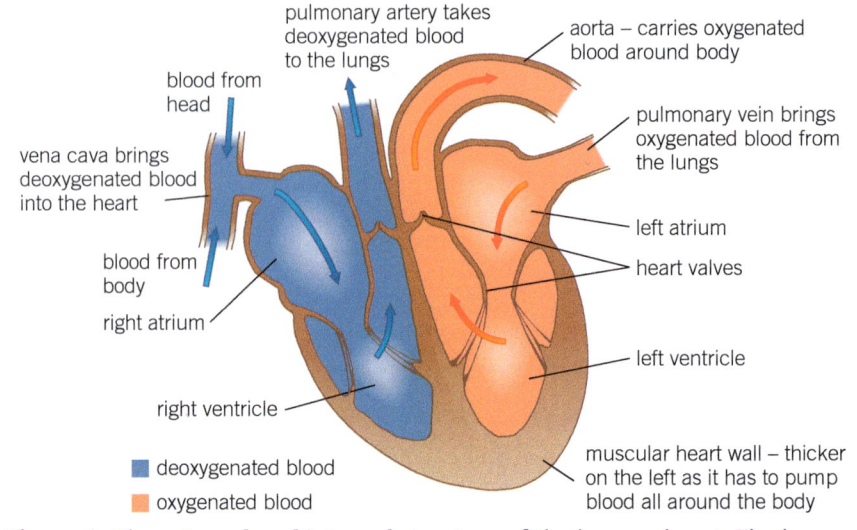

Figure 1 *The external and internal structure of the human heart. The human heart is about 12 cm long and 8–9 cm across at the widest part.*

2.5 Systems in the human body

where gas exchange takes place. The muscles of the heart are supplied with the oxygen and glucose they need by the coronary arteries.

Natural and artificial pacemakers

The resting rhythm of a healthy heart is around 70 beats per minute. It is controlled by a group of cells found in the right atrium of your heart, which acts as your natural pacemaker (Figure 2). If the natural pacemaker stops working properly, this can cause serious problems. If the heart beats too slowly, the person affected will not get enough oxygen. If the heart beats too fast, it cannot pump blood properly.

Problems with the rhythm of the heart can often be solved using an **artificial pacemaker** (Figure 3, below). This is an electrical device used to correct irregularities in the heart rate, which is implanted into your chest. Artificial pacemakers only weigh 20–50 g and they are attached to your heart by two wires. The artificial pacemaker sends strong, regular electrical signals to your heart, which stimulate it to beat properly. Modern pacemakers are often very sensitive to what your body needs and only work when the natural rhythm goes wrong. Some even stimulate the heart to beat faster when you exercise.

If you have a pacemaker fitted, you will need regular medical check-ups throughout your life. However, most people feel that this is a small price to pay for the increase in the quality and length of life that a pacemaker brings.

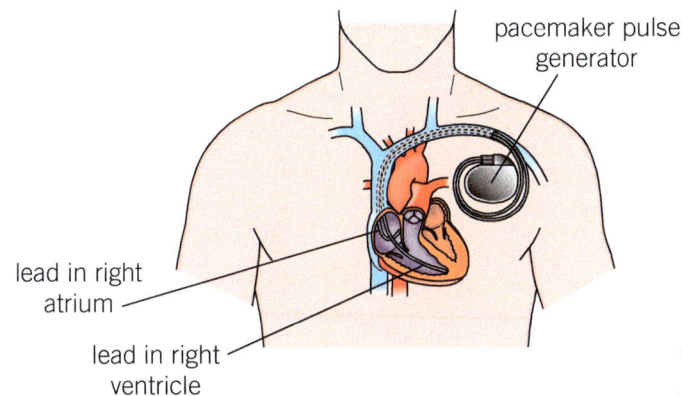

Figure 2 *The pacemaker region controls the basic rhythm of your heart using electrical impulses, which travel through the muscular walls. In this diagram the big blood vessels are not shown, as they are not involved in the action of the pacemaker region*

Go further

The natural pacemaker regions of the heart are very complex. Doctors and scientists are developing ever more complex pacemakers to try and mimic the natural responses of the heart as closely as possible. Modern pacemakers only act when they are needed. Many can respond to different activity levels and some of the latest pacemakers even respond to stress levels in the body so that the heart responds as naturally as possible.

Figure 3 *An artificial pacemaker is positioned under the skin of the chest with wires running to the heart itself*

1. Draw a flow chart to show how blood passes through the heart. [4 marks]
2. Describe how the heartbeat is controlled in a healthy adult. [3 marks]
3. Explain the importance of the following in making the heart an effective pump in the circulatory system of the body:
   a. heart valves [2 marks]
   b. coronary arteries [2 marks]
   c. the thickened muscular wall of the left ventricle. [3 marks]
4. Blood in the arteries is usually bright red because it is full of oxygen. This is not true of the blood in the pulmonary arteries. Explain this observation. [3 marks]
5. Explain how problems with the rhythm of the heart might be overcome using an artificial pacemaker. [5 marks]

Key points

- The heart is an organ that pumps blood around the body.
- Heart valves keep the blood flowing in the right direction.
- The resting heart rate is controlled by a group of cells in the right atrium, which forms a natural pacemaker.
- Artificial pacemakers are electrical devices used to correct irregularities in the heart rhythm.

2.5.7 Breathing and gas exchange

Learning objectives

After this topic, you should know:

- the structure of the human gas exchange system
- how gases are exchanged in the alveoli of the lungs.

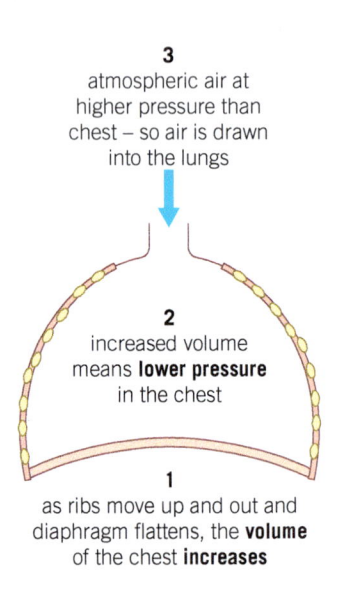

For a gas exchange system to work efficiently, you need a large difference in concentrations of the gas on different sides of the exchange membrane (a steep concentration gradient). Many large animals, including humans, move air in and out of their lungs regularly. By changing the composition of the air in the lungs, they maintain a steep concentration gradient for both oxygen diffusing into the blood and carbon dioxide diffusing out of the blood. This is known as ventilating the lungs or breathing. It takes place in a specially adapted gas exchange system.

The gas exchange system

Your lungs are found in your chest (or thorax) and are protected by your ribcage. They are separated from the digestive organs beneath (in your abdomen) by the diaphragm. The diaphragm is a strong sheet of muscle. The job of your ventilation system is to move air in and out of your lungs, which provide an efficient surface for gas exchange in the alveoli (Figure 1). Ventilating the lungs is brought about by the contraction and relaxation of the intercostal muscles between the ribs and the diaphragm, changing the pressure inside the chest cavity so air is forced in or out of the lungs as a result of differences in pressure (Figure 2).

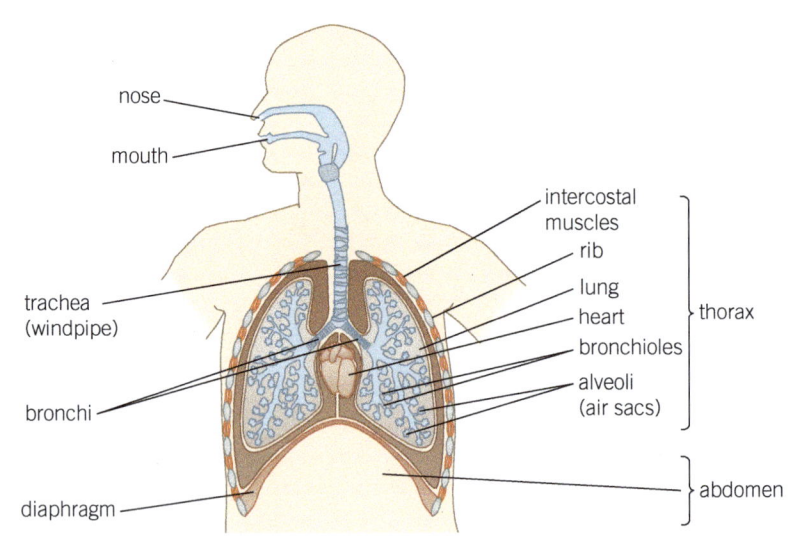

breathing in

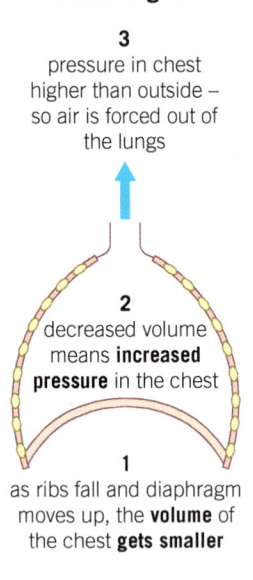

3. atmospheric air at higher pressure than chest – so air is drawn into the lungs
2. increased volume means **lower pressure** in the chest
1. as ribs move up and out and diaphragm flattens, the **volume** of the chest **increases**

breathing out

3. pressure in chest higher than outside – so air is forced out of the lungs
2. decreased volume means **increased pressure** in the chest
1. as ribs fall and diaphragm moves up, the **volume** of the chest **gets smaller**

Figure 2 *Ventilation of the lungs*

Figure 1 *The gas exchange system supplies your body with vital oxygen and removes waste carbon dioxide*

When you breathe in, oxygen-rich air moves into your lungs. This maintains a steep concentration gradient with the blood. As a result, oxygen continually diffuses into your bloodstream through the gas exchange surfaces of your alveoli. Breathing out removes carbon dioxide-rich air from the lungs. This maintains a concentration gradient so that carbon dioxide can continually diffuse out of the bloodstream into the air in the lungs.

2.5 Systems in the human body

Table 1 *The composition of inhaled and exhaled air (~ means approximately)*

Atmospheric gas	% of air breathed in	% of air breathed out
nitrogen	~80	~80
oxygen	~20	~16
carbon dioxide	~0.04	~4

Adaptations of the alveoli

Your lungs are specially adapted to make gas exchange more efficient. They are made up of clusters of alveoli, which provide a very large surface area (Figure 3). This is important for achieving the most effective diffusion of oxygen and carbon dioxide. The alveoli also have a rich supply of blood capillaries. This maintains a concentration gradient in both directions. The blood coming to the lungs is always relatively low in oxygen and high in carbon dioxide compared to the inhaled air.

As a result, gas exchange takes place down the steepest concentration gradients possible. This makes the exchange rapid and effective. The layer of cells between the air in the lungs and the blood in the capillaries is also very thin (only one cell wide). This allows diffusion to take place over the shortest possible distance. If all of the alveoli in your lungs were spread out flat, they would have a surface area equivalent to 10–15 table-tennis tables.

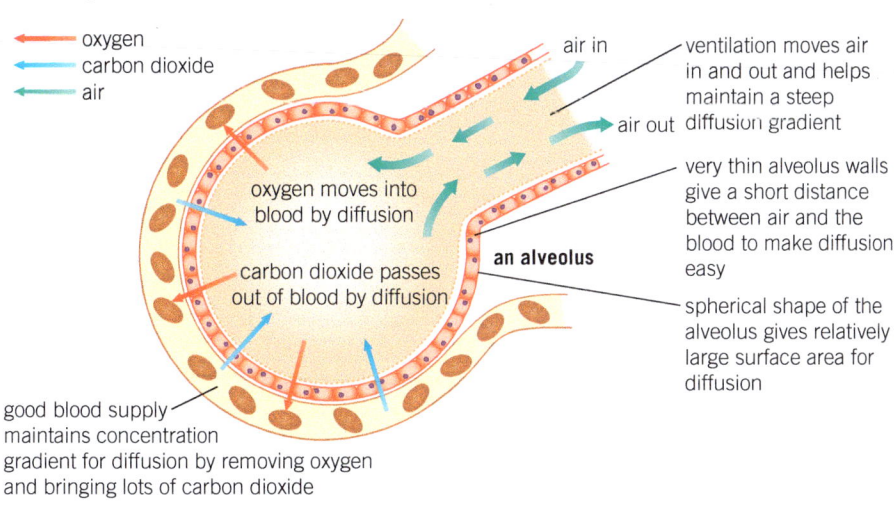

Synoptic links

For more about diffusion and concentration gradients, look back at Topic 1.3.4.

For more about exchange surfaces, look back at Topic 2.5.3.

Figure 3 *The alveoli are adapted so that gas exchange can take place as efficiently as possible in the lungs. There are around 500 million alveoli in a human lung, each one with a diameter of around 200 µm*

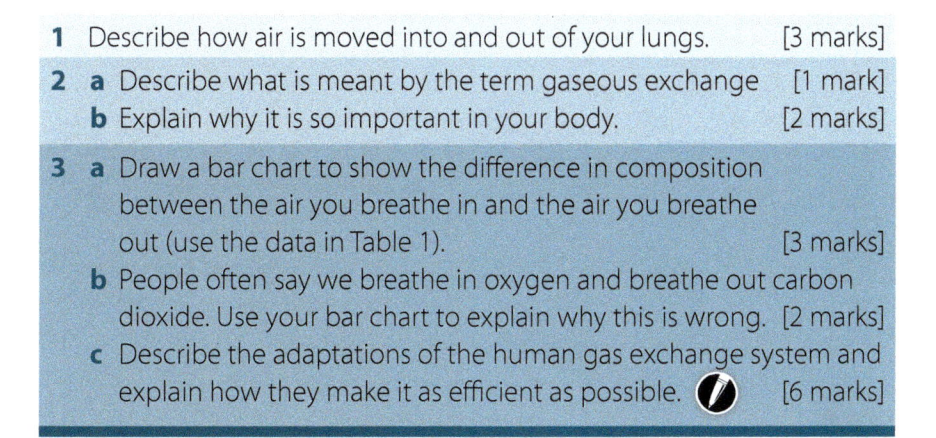

1. Describe how air is moved into and out of your lungs. [3 marks]
2. **a** Describe what is meant by the term gaseous exchange [1 mark]
   b Explain why it is so important in your body. [2 marks]
3. **a** Draw a bar chart to show the difference in composition between the air you breathe in and the air you breathe out (use the data in Table 1). [3 marks]
   b People often say we breathe in oxygen and breathe out carbon dioxide. Use your bar chart to explain why this is wrong. [2 marks]
   c Describe the adaptations of the human gas exchange system and explain how they make it as efficient as possible. [6 marks]

Key points

- The lungs are in your chest cavity, protected by your ribcage and separated from your abdomen by the diaphragm.
- The alveoli provide a very large surface area and a rich supply of blood capillaries. This means that gases can diffuse into and out of the blood as efficiently as possible.

89

2.5.8 The chemistry of food

Learning objectives
After this topic, you should know:
- the basic structures of carbohydrates, proteins, and lipids.

Synoptic links
You will learn much more about the structure of molecules, and how chemists develop models of compounds showing all the individual atoms, in Topics 6.16.5 and 8.23.2 in the *Physical Sciences* book.

Carbohydrates, lipids, and proteins are the main compounds that make up the structure of a cell. They are vital components in the balanced diet of any organism that cannot make its own food. Carbohydrates, lipids, and proteins are all large molecules that are often made up of smaller molecules joined together as part of the cell metabolism.

Carbohydrates
Carbohydrates provide us with the fuel that makes all of the other reactions of life possible. They contain the chemical elements carbon, hydrogen, and oxygen.

All carbohydrates are made up of units of sugars.

- Some carbohydrates contain only one sugar unit. The best-known of these single sugars is glucose, $C_6H_{12}O_6$. Other carbohydrates are made up of two sugar units joined together (e.g., sucrose, the compound we call 'sugar' in everyday life). These small carbohydrate units are referred to as **simple sugars**, and they are often soluble in water.
- Complex carbohydrates, such as starch and cellulose, are made up of long chains of simple sugar units bonded together (Figure 1). Many of them are insoluble in water.

Carbohydrate-rich foods include bread, potatoes, rice, and pasta. Most of the carbohydrates you eat will be broken down to glucose used in cellular respiration to provide energy for metabolic reactions in your cells. The carbohydrate cellulose is an important support material in plants.

Figure 1 *Carbohydrates are all based on simple sugar units*

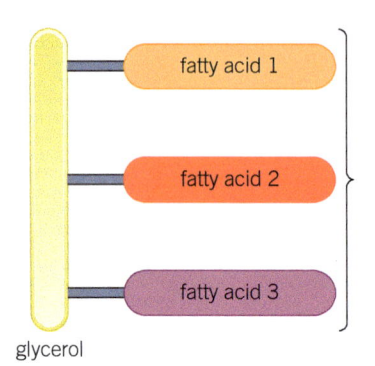

Figure 2 *Lipids are made of three molecules of fatty acids joined to a molecule of glycerol*

Lipids
Lipids are fats (solids) and oils (liquids). They are the most efficient energy store in your body and an important source of energy in your diet. Combined with other molecules, lipids are very important in your cell membranes, as hormones, and in your nervous system. Like carbohydrates, lipids are made up of carbon, hydrogen, and oxygen. All lipids are insoluble in water.

Lipids are made up of three molecules of **fatty acids** joined to a molecule of **glycerol** (Figure 2). The glycerol is always the same, but the fatty acids vary.

Lipid-rich foods include all the oils, such as olive oil and corn oil, as well as butter, margarine, cheese, and cream. The different combinations of fatty acids affect whether a lipid will be a liquid oil or a solid fat.

Proteins

Proteins are used for building up the cells and tissues of your body, and as the basis of all your enzymes. Between 15 and 16% of your body mass is protein. Protein is found in tissues ranging from your hair and nails to the muscles that move you around and the enzymes that control your body chemistry. Proteins are made up of the elements carbon, hydrogen, oxygen, and nitrogen. Protein-rich foods include meat, fish, pulses, and cheese.

A protein molecule is made up of long chains of small units called **amino acids** (Figure 3). There are around 20 different amino acids, and they are joined together into long chains by special bonds. Different arrangements of the various amino acids give you different proteins.

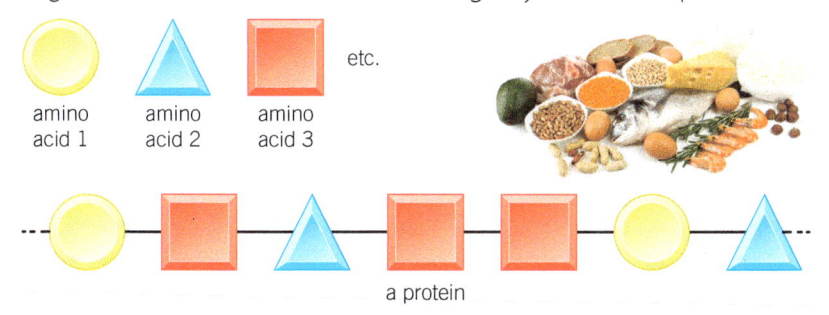

Figure 3 *Amino acids are the building blocks of proteins. They can join in an almost endless variety of ways to produce different proteins*

The long chains of amino acids that make up a protein are folded, coiled, and twisted to make specific 3D shapes. It is these specific shapes that enable other molecules to fit into the protein. The bonds that hold the proteins in these 3D shapes are very sensitive to temperature and pH, and can easily be broken. If this happens, the shape of the protein is lost and it may not function any more in your cells. The protein is **denatured**.

Proteins carry out many different functions in your body. They act as:
- structural components of tissues, such as muscles and tendons
- hormones, such as insulin
- antibodies, which destroy pathogens and are part of the immune system
- enzymes, which act as catalysts.

1 **a** State what a protein is. [1 mark]
   b Describe how proteins are used in the body. [4 marks]
2 Describe the main similarities and differences between the three main groups of chemicals (carbohydrates, proteins, and lipids) in the body. [6 marks]
3 Describe how you would test a food sample to see if it contained:
   a starch [2 marks]
   b lipids. [2 marks]
4 Explain why lipids can be either fats or oils. [3 marks]
5 Explain how simple sugars are related to complex carbohydrates. [3 marks]

Food tests

You can identify the main food groups using standard food tests.

- Carbohydrates:
  - iodine test for starch – yellow-red iodine solution turns blue-black if starch is present.
  - Benedict's test for sugars – blue Benedict's solution turns brick-red on heating if a sugar such as glucose is present.
- Protein: Biuret test – blue Biuret reagent turns purple if protein is present.
- Lipids: ethanol test – ethanol added to a solution gives a cloudy white layer if a lipid is present.

Safety: Biuret solution is corrosive. Ethanol is highly flammable and harmful. Wear chemical splash-proof eye protection.

Key points

- Carbohydrates are made up of units of sugars.
- Simple sugars are carbohydrates that contain only one or two sugar units (e.g. glucose).
- Some sugars, such as glucose, turn blue Benedict's solution brick-red on heating.
- Complex carbohydrates contain long chains of simple sugar units bonded together. Starch turns yellow-red iodine solution blue-black.
- Lipids consist of three molecules of fatty acids bonded to a molecule of glycerol. The ethanol test indicates the presence of lipids in solutions.
- Protein molecules are made up of long chains of amino acids. Biuret reagent turns from blue to purple in the presence of proteins.

2.5.9 How the digestive system works

Learning objectives

After this topic, you should know:
- how the food you eat is digested in your body
- the role played by the different parts of the digestive system
- the roles played by the different digestive enzymes.

The food you take in and eat is made up of large insoluble molecules, including starch (a carbohydrate), proteins, and lipids. Your body cannot absorb and use these molecules, so they need to be broken down or **digested** to form smaller, soluble molecules. These can then be absorbed in your small intestine and used by your cells. It is this chemical breakdown of your food that is controlled by the digestive enzymes in your digestive system.

The digestive system

The digestive system starts at one end with your mouth and finishes at the other end with your anus. It is made up of many different organs (Figure 1). There are also glands, such as the pancreas and the salivary glands, that make and release digestive juices containing enzymes to break down your food.

The stomach and the small intestine are the main organs where food is digested. Enzymes break down the large, insoluble food molecules into smaller, soluble ones.

Your small intestine is also where the soluble food molecules are absorbed into your blood. The digested food molecules are small enough to pass freely through the walls of the gut into the blood vessels by diffusion. They move in this direction because there is a very high concentration of food molecules in the small intestine and a much lower concentration of food molecules in the blood. They move into the blood down a steep concentration gradient. Some substances are also moved from the small intestine into your blood by active transport. The villi greatly increase the surface area of the small intestine so that the absorption of digested food is very efficient (Figure 2). Once in your blood, the digested food gets transported around your body in the bloodstream.

The muscular walls of the small intestine squeeze the undigested food onwards into your large intestine. This is where water is absorbed from the undigested food into your blood. The material that remains makes up the bulk of your faeces. Faeces are stored and then pass out of your body through the anus back into the environment.

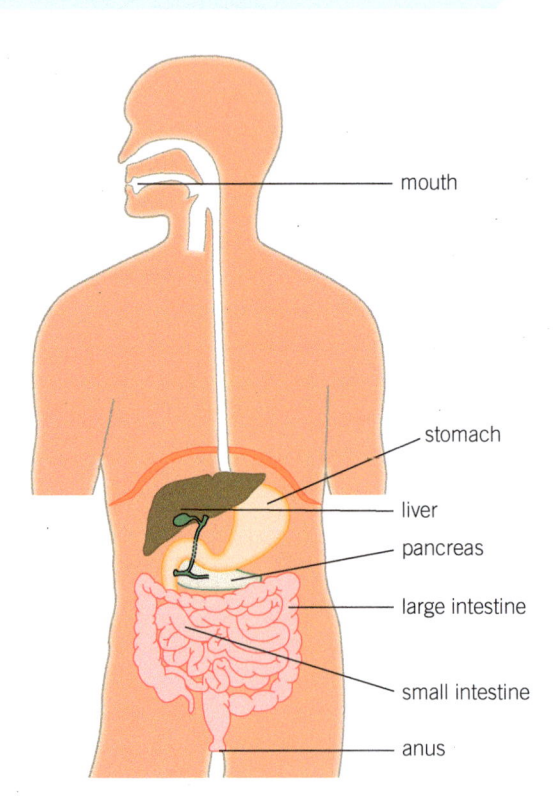

Figure 1 *The main organs of the human digestive system*

Digestive enzymes

Most of your enzymes work *inside* the cells of your body, controlling the rate of the chemical reactions. Your digestive enzymes are different. They work *outside* your cells. They are produced by specialised cells in glands (such as your salivary glands and your pancreas), and in the lining of your digestive system. The enzymes then pass out of these cells into the digestive system itself, where they come into contact with food molecules.

Your digestive system is a hollow, muscular tube that squeezes your food. It helps to break up your food into small pieces, which have a large surface area for your enzymes to work on. It mixes your food with your digestive juices so that the enzymes come into contact with as much of the food as possible. The muscles of the digestive system move your food

Synoptic links

For more on moving substances in and out of cells, look back at Topics 1.3.4 to 1.3.7, and for more on adaptations for effective absorption, look back at Topic 2.5.3.

along from one area to the next. Different areas of the digestive system have different pH levels which allow the enzymes in that region to work as efficiently as possible. For example, the mouth and small intestine are slightly alkaline, while the stomach has a low, acidic pH value.

Digesting carbohydrates

Enzymes that break down carbohydrates are called carbohydrases. Starch is one of the most common carbohydrates that you eat. It is broken down into sugars in your mouth and small intestine. This reaction is catalysed by an enzyme called **amylase**.

Amylase is produced in your salivary glands, so the digestion of starch starts in your mouth. Amylase is also made in the pancreas. No digestion takes place inside the pancreas. All the enzymes made there flow into your small intestine, where most of the starch you eat is digested.

Digesting proteins

The breakdown of protein foods such as meat, fish, and cheese into amino acids is catalysed by **protease** enzymes. Proteases are produced by your stomach, your pancreas, and your small intestine. The breakdown of proteins into amino acids takes place in your stomach and small intestine.

Digesting fats

The lipids (fats and oils) that you eat are broken down into fatty acids and glycerol in the small intestine. The reaction is catalysed by **lipase** enzymes, which are made in your pancreas and your small intestine. Again, the enzymes made in the pancreas are passed into the small intestine.

Once your food molecules have been completely digested into soluble glucose, amino acids, fatty acids, and glycerol, they leave your small intestine. They pass into your bloodstream to be carried around the body to the cells that need them. In the body cells the digested molecules can be used for respiration or to make the new, large molecules that the cells need as reserves of energy or for growth and repair.

All of the digested food from the gut passes through the liver in the blood. The liver breaks down unwanted amino acids to urea, which is then carried in the blood to the kidneys. The kidneys excrete urea in solution in the urine, along with excess water, excess salts, and other waste materials.

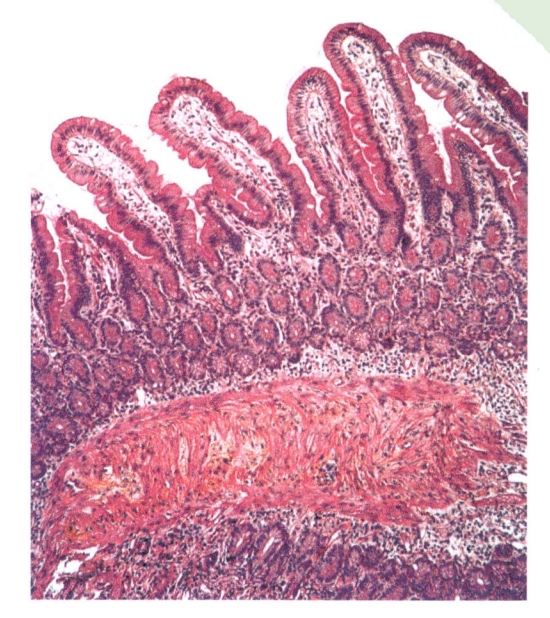

Figure 2 *This is a light micrograph of a thin section of the lining of the small intestine – magnification ×70. It shows the villi, which provide a large surface area for the efficient absorption of soluble food molecules into the blood*

1. Three types of enzymes found in the body are called amylase, protease, and lipase.
   a. State which reaction each enzyme catalyses. [3 marks]
   b. State where each reaction works in the digestive system. [3 marks]
2. a. Explain the importance in successful digestion and absorption of the following:
      i. the enzymes of the gut [3 marks]
      ii. the villi of the small intestine. [2 marks]
   b. What happens to soluble food molecules once they are absorbed into the blood? [4 marks]
3. Describe how the liver and kidneys are involved in removing excess protein. [4 marks]

Key points

- Digestion involves the breakdown of large insoluble molecules into soluble substances that can be absorbed into the blood across the wall of the small intestine.
- The blood carries the small molecules to the cells of the body where they can be used for respiration or to make new, larger molecules needed as energy reserves, or for growth or repair.
- Carbohydrases such as amylase catalyse the breakdown of carbohydrates to simple sugars.
- Proteases catalyse the breakdown of proteins to amino acids.
- Lipases catalyse the breakdown of lipids to fatty acids and glycerol.
- The liver breaks down unwanted amino acids to urea, which is then carried by the blood to the kidneys. The kidneys excrete urea in solution as urine.

The human nervous system

Learning objectives

After this topic, you should know:
- why you need a nervous system
- how the structure of the nervous system is adapted to its function
- how receptors enable you to respond to changes in your surroundings.

You need to know what is going on in the world around you. Your nervous system makes this possible. It enables you to react to your surroundings and coordinate your behaviour (Figure 1).

Your nervous system carries electrical signals (**impulses**) that travel fast – between 1 and 120 metres per second. This means you can react to changes in your surroundings very quickly.

The nervous system

As with most animals, you need to avoid danger, find food, and eventually find a mate! This is where your nervous system helps. Your body is particularly sensitive to changes in the world around you. Any changes (known as stimuli) are picked up by cells called **receptors**.

Receptor cells, such as the light receptor cells in your eyes, are similar to most animal cells. They have a nucleus, cytoplasm, and a cell membrane. These receptors are usually found clustered together in special sense organs, such as your eyes and your skin. You have many different types of sensory receptor (Figure 2). Some male moths have receptors so sensitive they can detect the scent of a female several kilometres away and follow the scent trail to find her!

How your nervous system works

Once a sensory receptor detects a stimulus, the information is sent as an electrical impulse that passes along special cells called **neurones**. These are usually found in bundles of hundreds or even thousands of neurones known as **nerves**.

The impulse travels along the neurone until it reaches the **central nervous system (CNS)**. The CNS is made up of the brain and the spinal cord. The cells that carry impulses from your sense organs to your CNS are called **sensory neurones**.

Your brain gets huge amounts of information from all the sensory receptors in your body. It coordinates the response to the information, and sends impulses out along special cells. These cells, called **motor neurones**, carry information from the CNS to the rest of your body. They carry impulses to make the right bits of your body – the **effectors** – respond (Figure 3).

Effectors may be muscles or glands. Your muscles respond to the arrival of impulses by contracting. Your glands respond by releasing (secreting) chemical substances. For example, your salivary glands produce and release extra saliva when you smell food cooking, and your pancreas releases the hormone insulin when your blood sugar levels go up after a meal.

Figure 1 *Your body is made up of millions of cells that have to work together. Whatever you do with your body, whether it's walking to school, learning to drive, or playing on the computer, your movements need to be coordinated*

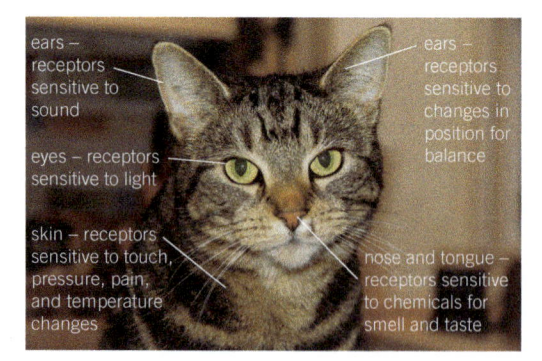

Figure 2 *This cat relies on its sensory receptors to detect changes in the external environment*

- ears – receptors sensitive to sound
- ears – receptors sensitive to changes in position for balance
- eyes – receptors sensitive to light
- skin – receptors sensitive to touch, pressure, pain, and temperature changes
- nose and tongue – receptors sensitive to chemicals for smell and taste

Synoptic link

You will learn about the impact of the nervous system on the lengths of stopping distances in Topic 7.18.9 in the *Physical Sciences* book.

■ 2.5 Systems in the human body

The way in which your nervous system works can be summed up as:

stimulus → receptor → coordinator (CNS) → effector → response

The receptor sends an impulse along a sensory neurone, carrying information about a change in the environment to the coordinator (CNS). Once all the incoming information has been processed, the coordinator sends impulses down motor neurones. These motor impulses stimulate the effectors to bring about the responses needed in any particular situation.

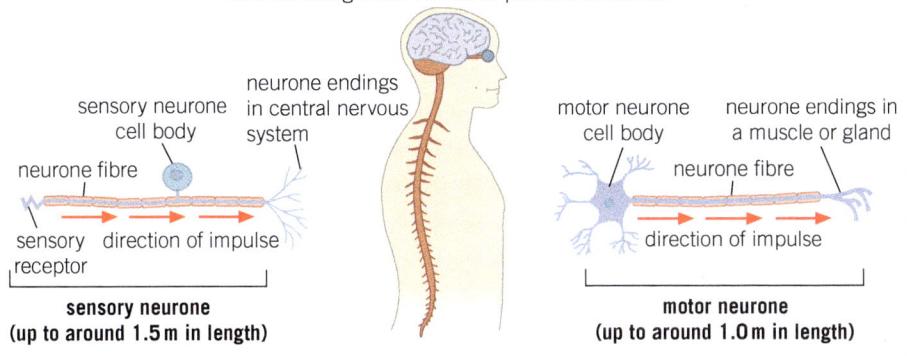

Figure 3 *The rapid responses of our nervous system allow us to respond to our surroundings quickly – and in the right way*

Reaction time

The time it takes you to respond to a stimulus is known as your **reaction time**. Reaction times vary from person to person. Typical values range from 0.3 s to 0.9 s. Reaction times are very important in everyday life, for example, when driving.

Factors that affect reaction time include your age, how tired you are (reaction times get slower with age and tiredness), your experience at a particular task (reaction times get faster with practice), and any drugs you may be taking. Legal drugs (e.g., caffeine), illegal drugs (e.g., cannabis), and some medicines (e.g., sleeping tablets) can all affect your reaction time. Distractions (e.g., loud noises, babies crying, or people talking) can also slow your reaction time.

Measuring reaction times

There are many ways to investigate how quickly nerve impulses travel in your body. Two simple methods are:

- use the ruler-drop test or digital sensors to measure how quickly you react to a visual stimulus
- stand in a circle holding hands with your eyes closed and measure how long it takes a hand-squeeze to pass around the circle.

People claim that activities such as drinking cola, talking on the phone, and listening to music affect our reaction times. Choose a factor that interests you and use the simple techniques outlined above to investigate the effect it has – or does not have – on human reaction times.

Safety: Do not drink or eat in the laboratory.

---

1 a State the main function of the nervous system. [2 marks]
  b Describe the difference between a neurone and a nerve. [2 marks]
  c Describe the difference between a sensory neurone and a motor neurone. [3 marks]
2 Explain why it is so important not to drive or use machinery when you are tired or when you have had several alcoholic drinks. [3 marks]
3 Explain what happens in your nervous system when you see a piece of fruit, pick it up, and eat it. [6 marks]

Key points

- The nervous system enables you to react quickly to your surroundings and coordinate your behaviour.
- Cells called receptors detect stimuli (changes in the environment).
- Impulses from receptors pass along sensory neurones to the brain or spinal cord (CNS). The CNS coordinates the response of effectors, which may be muscles contracting or glands secreting hormones or enzymes.
- stimulus → receptor → coordinator → effector → response
- Reaction times vary from person to person, but typical values range from 0.3 s to 0.9 s.

2.5.11 Reflex actions

Learning objectives

After this topic, you should know:

- what reflexes are
- how reflexes work
- why reflexes are important in your body
- how synapses work.

Your nervous system lets you take in information from your surroundings and respond in the right way. However, some of your responses are so fast that they happen without giving you time to think.

When you touch something hot, or sharp, you pull your hand back before you feel the pain. If something comes near your face, you blink. Automatic responses like these are known as **reflexes** (Figure 1).

What are reflexes for?

Reflexes are very important both for humans and other animals. They help you to avoid danger or harm because they happen so fast. There are also lots of reflexes that take care of your basic bodily functions. These functions include breathing and moving food through your digestive system.

Reflexes are automatic and rapid – they do not involve the conscious part of your brain. It would make life very difficult if you had to think consciously about those things all the time – and it would be fatal if you forgot to breathe!

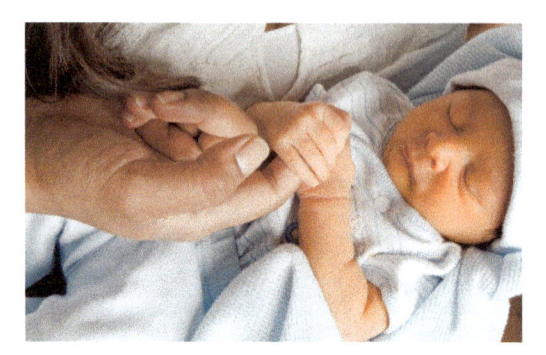

Figure 1 *Newborn babies have a number of special reflexes that disappear as they grow. This grasp reflex is one of them*

How do reflexes work?

Simple reflex actions such as the pain withdrawal reflex we are all familiar with often involve just three types of neurones. These are:

- **sensory neurones**
- **motor neurones**
- **relay neurones** – these connect a sensory neurone and a motor neurone, and are found in the CNS.

An electrical impulse passes from the receptor along the sensory neurone to the CNS. It then passes along a relay neurone within the CNS to a motor neurone. The impulse then travels along a motor neurone to the effector organ. The effector organ will be a muscle or a gland. We call this pathway a **reflex arc**.

The key point in a reflex arc is that the impulse bypasses the conscious areas of your brain. The result is that the time between the stimulus and the reflex action is as short as possible.

How do synapses work?

Your neurones are not joined up to each other directly. There are junctions between them called **synapses**, which form physical gaps between the neurones. The electrical impulses travelling along your neurones have to cross these synapses. They cannot leap the gap. The diffusion of the chemical across the synapse is slower than the electrical impulse in the neurones, but it makes it possible for the impulse to cross the gap between them. Figure 2 shows you how this happens.

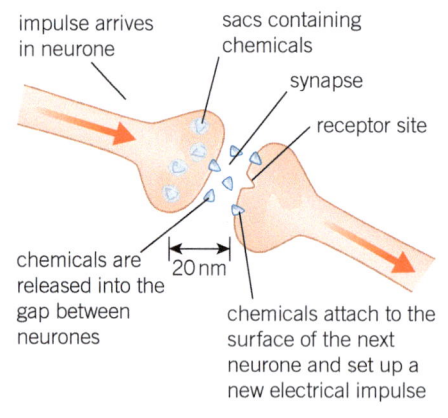

Figure 2 *When an impulse arrives at the junction between two neurones, chemicals are released. These chemicals cross the synapse and arrive at receptor sites on the next neurone. This starts up a new electrical impulse in the next neurone. In this model, the chemical molecules that carry the impulse across the gap between the neurones are shown several orders of magnitude larger than they really are*

■ 2.5 Systems in the human body

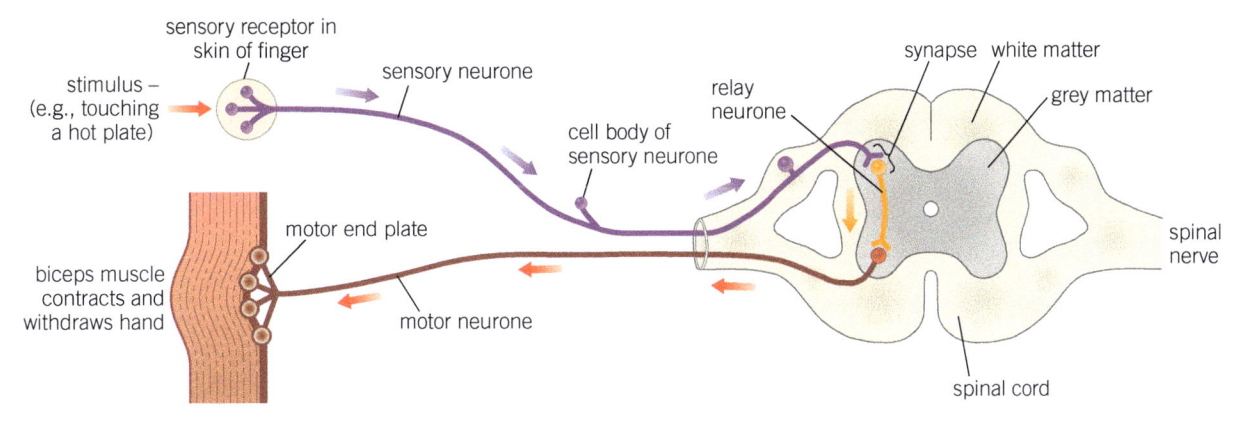

Figure 3 *The reflex action that moves your hand away from something hot can save you from being burnt. Reflex actions are quick and automatic – you do not think about them*

The reflex arc in detail

Look at Figure 3. It shows what would happen if you touched a hot object.

- When you touch the object, a receptor in your skin is stimulated. An electrical impulse from a receptor passes along a sensory neurone to the CNS – in this case, the spinal cord.
- When an impulse from the sensory neurone arrives at the synapse with a relay neurone, a chemical is released. The chemical diffuses across the synapse to the relay neurone where it sets off a new electrical impulse that travels along the relay neurone.
- When the impulse reaches the synapse between the relay neurone and a motor neurone returning to the arm, more chemical is released. Again, the chemical diffuses across the synapse and starts a new electrical impulse travelling down the motor neurone to the effector.
- When the impulse reaches the effector organ, it is stimulated to respond. In this example, the impulses arrive in the muscles of the arm, causing them to contract. This action moves the hand rapidly away from the source of pain. If the effector organ is a gland, it will respond by releasing (secreting) chemical substances.

The reflex pathway is not very different from a normal conscious action, which you think about before you do it. However, in a reflex action the coordinator is a relay neurone either in the spinal cord or in the unconscious areas of the brain. The whole reflex is very fast indeed.

An impulse also travels up the spinal cord to the conscious areas of your brain. You know about the reflex action, but only after it has happened.

1 a Why are reflexes important? [2 marks]
  b Why is it important that reflexes don't go to the conscious areas of your brain? [1 mark]
2 Explain why some actions such as breathing and swallowing are reflex actions, while others such as speaking and eating are under your conscious control. [4 marks]
3 Describe what happens when you step on a pin. Make sure you indicate when an electrical impulse or a chemical impulse is involved. [6 marks]

> **Study tip**
>
> Learn the reflex pathway off by heart.
>
> **stimulus → receptor → sensory neurone → relay neurone → motor neurone → effector → response.**

> **Key points**
>
> - Reflex actions are automatic and rapid and do not involve the conscious parts of the brain.
> - Sensory neurones carry impulses from receptors to the CNS. Relay neurones carry impulses within the CNS. Motor neurones carry impulses from the CNS to effectors.
> - Reflex actions control everyday bodily functions, such as breathing and digestion, and help you to avoid danger (e.g., the pain withdrawal reflex).
> - Where two neurones meet, there is a tiny gap called a synapse. Impulses cross this gap using chemicals.

2.5.12 Principles of hormonal control

Learning objectives

After this topic, you should know:

- what a hormone is
- the main organs of the endocrine system
- the role of the pituitary gland.

Figure 1 *Many aspects of the growth of children from birth to adulthood are controlled by hormones*

Go further

The effects of hormones on the body are the result of their interaction with DNA and the process of protein synthesis.

In Chapter 5.10 you discovered how the nervous system acts to coordinate and control your body, reacting in seconds to changes in your internal and external environments. However, it is very important that your body acts as a coordinated whole, not just from minute to minute but from day to day and year to year throughout your life. You have a second coordination and control system to help with this – the **endocrine system**.

The endocrine system

The endocrine system is made up of glands that secrete chemicals called **hormones** directly into the bloodstream. The blood carries the hormone to its target organ (or organs) where it produces an effect. The target organ has receptors on the cell membranes, which pick up the hormone molecules, triggering a response in the cell.

Many processes in your body are coordinated by these hormones. Hormones can act very rapidly but, compared to the nervous system, many hormonal effects are slower but longer-lasting. Hormones that give a rapid response include **insulin**, which controls your blood glucose, and adrenaline, which prepares your body for fight or flight. Slow-acting hormones with long-term effects include growth hormones and sex hormones (Figure 1).

The endocrine glands

Hormones provide chemical coordination and control for the body and are produced by the endocrine glands. Many endocrine glands around the body are themselves coordinated and controlled by one very small but powerful endocrine gland found in the brain – the **pituitary gland**. The pituitary gland acts as a master gland. It secretes a variety of different hormones into the blood in response to changes in body conditions. Some hormones produced by the pituitary gland in response to changes in the internal environment have a direct effect on the body. Examples include ADH, which affects the amount of urine produced by the kidney, and growth hormone, which controls the rate of growth in children.

Other hormones released by the pituitary gland affect specific endocrine glands, stimulating them to release hormones that bring about the required effects on the body. These include:

- **follicle stimulating hormone (FSH)**, which stimulates the **ovaries** to make the female sex hormone **oestrogen**
- thyroid stimulating hormone (TSH), which stimulates the thyroid gland to make thyroxine, a hormone that helps control the rate of your metabolism.

Each of the endocrine glands produces hormones that have a major effect on the way your body works (Figure 2). The levels of the hormones vary depending on changes in the internal environment of your body.

2.5 Systems in the human body

Table 1 *The main roles of hormones produced by the different endocrine glands*

Endocrine gland	Role of hormone
Pituitary	Controls growth in children
	Stimulates the thyroid gland to make thyroxine to control the rate of metabolism
	In women – stimulates the ovaries to produce and release eggs and make the female sex hormone oestrogen
	In men – stimulates the testes to make sperm and the male sex hormone testosterone
Thyroid	Controls the metabolic rate of the body
Pancreas	Controls the levels of glucose in the blood
Adrenal	Prepares the body for stressful situations – 'fight or flight' response
Ovaries	Controls the development of the female secondary sexual characteristics and is involved in the menstrual cycle
Testes	Controls the development of the male secondary sexual characteristics and is involved in the production of sperm

Figure 2 *It isn't just humans who need hormones – without the hormones from their thyroid glands, these tadpoles will never become frogs*

Synoptic link

You will learn more about the ovaries and the testes in Topic 3.7.11.

Study tip

Find a way to help you remember the main endocrine organs of the body – for example, learn them in the order in which they appear in your body from the head downwards.

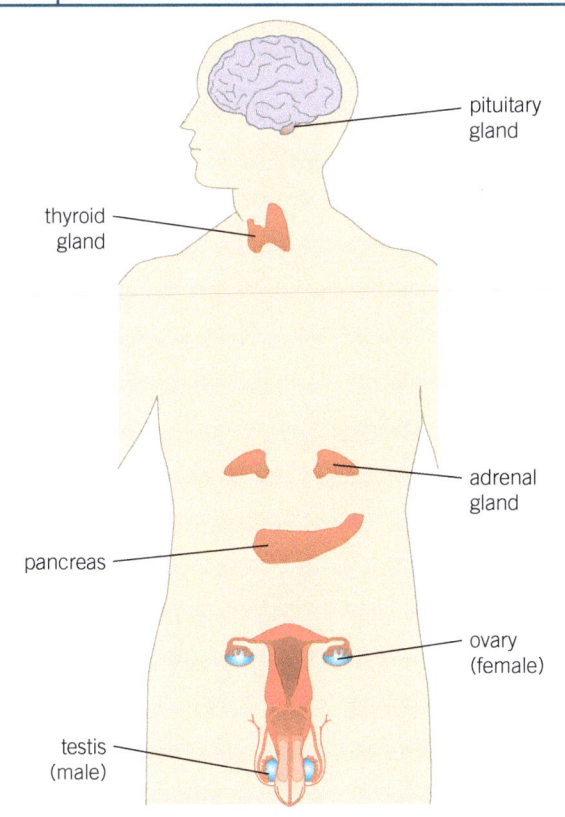

Figure 3 *The main endocrine glands of the human body*

1 a What is a hormone? [1 mark]
   b What is an endocrine gland? [1 mark]
2 Suggest why the pituitary gland is sometimes called the master gland of the endocrine system. [3 marks]
3 Explain how coordination and control by hormones differs from coordination and control by the nervous system. [6 marks]
4 Suggest what would happen if the pituitary gland:
   a did not produce enough growth hormone in a child [2 marks]
   b continued to produce lots of growth hormone in an adult. [2 marks]

Key points

- The endocrine system is composed of glands that secrete chemicals called hormones directly into the blood stream.
- Hormones are large molecules that are carried in the blood to a target organ where they produce an effect.
- Compared to the nervous system, the effects of hormones are often slower but longer lasting.
- The pituitary gland is the master gland and secretes several hormones that act on other glands and stimulate them to release other hormones.

Higher Tier

2.5.13 The role of negative feedback

Learning objectives

After this topic, you should know:

- what adrenaline and thyroxine do in the body
- the importance of negative feedback systems.

Many hormones in your body are controlled as part of negative feedback systems. These involve the coordination of changes in the internal environment of your body with the amounts of hormone produced.

Negative feedback

Put simply, negative feedback systems work to stabilise a system.

If a factor in the internal environment increases, changes take place to reduce it and restore the original level.

If a factor in the internal environment decreases, changes take place to increase it and restore the original level.

Whatever the initial change, in negative feedback the response tends to reverse the change (Figure 1). The principle is easier to understand when you see working examples. Many hormones are involved in negative feedback systems, including insulin and glucagon, most female sex hormones, and thyroxine (see below).

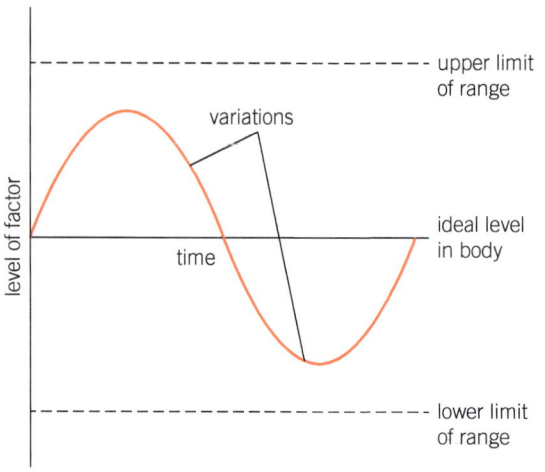

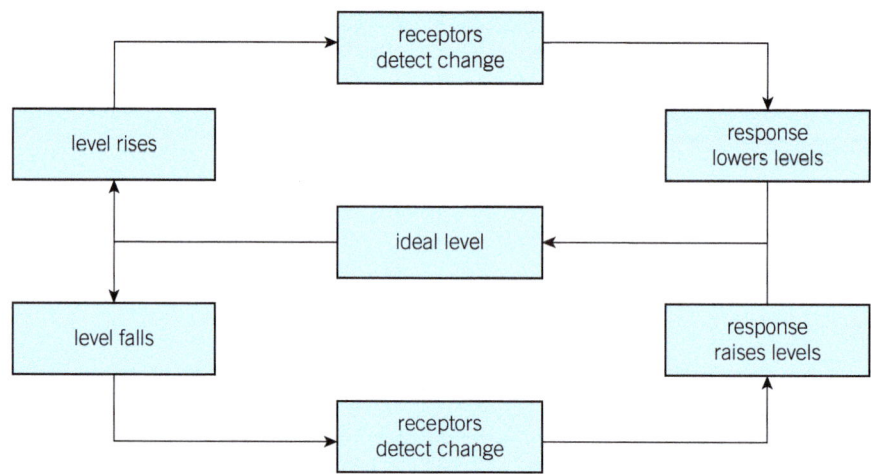

Figure 1 *A negative feedback loop means values will vary around a normal level within a limited range*

Thyroxine and negative feedback

The thyroid gland in your neck uses iodine from your diet to produce the hormone **thyroxine**. This controls the basal metabolic rate of your body – how quickly substances are broken down and built up, how much oxygen your tissues use, and how the brain of a growing child develops. Thyroxine plays an important part in growth and development. In adults the level of thyroxine in the blood usually remains relatively stable. This happens as a result of negative feedback control involving the pituitary gland and the hormone it produces – thyroid stimulating hormone (TSH).

100

2.5 Systems in the human body

If levels of thyroxine in the blood begin to fall, it is detected by sensors in the brain. As a result, the amount of TSH released from the pituitary gland increases. This is a negative feedback system. TSH stimulates the production of thryoxine by the thyroid gland. As the level of thyroxine goes up, it is detected by the sensors and in turn the level of TSH released falls.

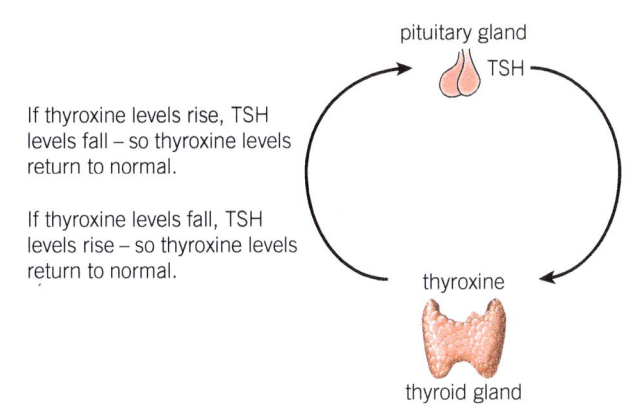

Figure 2 *The levels of thyroxine in your body are kept within narrow boundaries by a negative feedback loop*

Go further

The control of the hormones involved in homeostasis in your body is very complex. Simple feedback systems are rare. There are often interactions between the hypothalamus, the pituitary gland, and other endocrine glands, as well as the specific endocrine glands in the control of hormone levels in the body.

Adrenaline

Not all hormones are involved in such clear-cut negative feedback systems. If you are stressed, angry, excited, or frightened your body needs to be ready for action. Your adrenal glands, located at the top of your kidneys, secrete lots of **adrenaline**, which is carried rapidly around the body in your blood, affecting lots of organs. Adrenaline causes:

- your heart rate and breathing rate to increase
- stored glycogen in the liver to be converted to glucose for respiration
- the pupils of your eyes to dilate to let in more light
- your mental awareness to increase
- blood to be diverted away from your digestive system to the big muscles of the limbs.

Adrenaline boosts the delivery of oxygen and glucose to your brain and muscles, preparing your body for flight or fight. Once the danger is over, the raised levels of awareness are no longer needed. The adrenal glands stop releasing adrenaline and your systems return to their resting levels. This does not involve a negative feedback loop.

1. Describe how a negative feedback system works. [4 marks]
2. Compare the role of thyroxine in the body and the way it is controlled with the role of and control system for adrenaline. [4 marks]
3. In Ethiopia up to 40% of the population, both adults and children, are affected by iodine deficiency. Explain how a lack of iodine in the diet can affect thyroxine production and so affect health.
   Suggest a way of overcoming the problem. [6 marks]

Key points

- Thyroxine from the thyroid gland stimulates the basal metabolic rate. It plays an important role in growth and development.
- Adrenaline is produced by the adrenal glands in times of fear or stress. It increases the heart rate and boosts the delivery of oxygen and glucose to the brain and muscles, preparing the body for fight or flight.
- Thyroxine is controlled by negative feedback whereas adrenaline is not.

2.5 Systems in the human body

Summary questions

1 Some students investigated the process of cellular respiration. They set up three vacuum flasks. One contained live, soaked peas. One contained dry peas. One contained peas that had been soaked and then boiled. They took daily observations of the temperature in each flask for a week. The results are shown in the table below.

Table 1

Day	Room temperature in °C	Temperature in flask A (live, soaked peas) in °C	Temperature in flask B (dry peas) in °C	Temperature in flask C (soaked, boiled peas) in °C
1	20.0	20.0	20.0	20.0
2	20.0	20.5	20.0	20.0
3	20.0	21.0	20.0	20.0
4	20.0	21.5	20.0	20.0
5	20.0	22.0	20.0	20.0
6	20.0	22.2	20.0	20.5
7	20.0	22.5	20.0	21.0

a Plot a graph to show these results. [6 marks]
b Explain the results in flask **A**. [3 marks]
c Why were the results in flask **B** the same as the room temperature readings? [3 marks]
d Why was the room temperature in the laboratory recorded every day? [2 marks]
e Look at the results for flask **C**.
  i Why is the temperature at 20 °C for the first five days? [3 marks]
  ii After five days the temperature increases. Suggest *two* possible explanations for why the temperature increases. [4 marks]

2 Athletes want to be able to use their muscles aerobically for as long as possible when they compete. They train to develop their heart and lungs. Many athletes also train at altitude. There is less oxygen in the air at altitude so your body makes more red blood cells, which helps to avoid oxygen debt. Some athletes remove some of their own blood, store it, and then transfuse it back into their system just before a competition. This is called blood doping and it is illegal. Other athletes use hormones to stimulate the growth of extra red blood cells. This is also illegal.

a Why do athletes want to be able to use their muscles aerobically for as long as possible? [3 marks]
b How does developing more red blood cells by training at altitude help athletic performance? [3 marks]
c How does blood doping help performance? [2 marks]
d Explain in detail what happens to the muscles if the body cannot supply glucose and oxygen quickly enough when they are working hard. [4 marks]

3 Here are descriptions of three heart problems. In each case, use what you know about the heart and the circulatory system to explain the problems caused by the condition.
a The valve that stops blood flowing back into the left ventricle of the heart after it has been pumped into the aorta becomes weak and floppy and begins to leak. [4 marks]
b Some babies are born with a 'hole in the heart' – a gap in the central dividing wall of the heart. They may look blue in colour and be listless. [4 marks]
c The coronary arteries supplying blood to the heart muscle itself may become clogged with fatty material. The person affected may get chest pain when they exercise, or even have a heart attack. [4 marks]

4 a Describe how the lungs are adapted to allow the exchange of oxygen and carbon dioxide between the air and the blood. [3 marks]
b Describe how air is moved in and out of the lungs and explain how this ventilation of the lungs makes gas exchange more efficient. [4 marks]

5 **H** Many hormone systems in the body are controlled by negative feedback systems.
a Using the control of thyroxine levels in the body as an example, describe how a negative feedback system works. [5 marks]
b Explain why negative feedback control is so important in maintaining constant conditions in the body. [5 marks]
c Not all hormones are controlled by negative feedback systems. Explain the role of adrenaline in the response of your body to stress. [6 marks]
d Discuss the importance of the lack of a negative feedback control system for adrenaline. [5 marks]

2.5 Systems in the human body

Practice questions

01 Hormones are secreted from glands.

01.1 ⓗ Copy and complete **Table 1**.
Table 1

Hormone	Name of the gland that produces the hormone	Effect on the human body
adrenaline		
thyroxine		

[4 marks]

01.2 Name the master gland in the human body. [1 mark]

01.3 ⓗ Insulin is a hormone that reduces blood glucose levels. The control of blood glucose is by negative feedback. **Figure 1** shows a negative feedback graph.

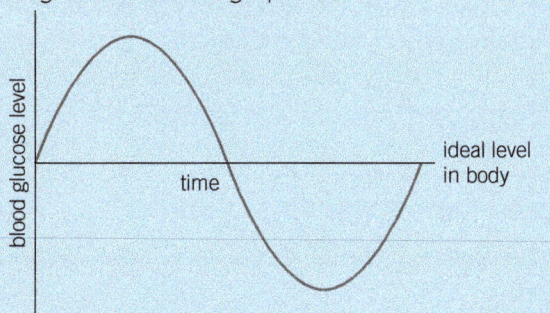

Figure 1

Use **Figure 1** to explain the negative feedback effect of insulin on blood glucose levels. [4 marks]

02 In multicellular organisms the effectiveness of exchange surfaces needs to be maximised. A large surface area to volume ratio is one way to increase the efficiency of an exchange surface. **Table 2** shows the surface area and volume of different animals.
Table 2

Animal	Surface area in m²	Volume in dm³	Surface area to volume ratio
human	1.6	75.0	1.47
X	4.0	3.0	
Y	10.5	2.1	

02.1 Use the data in **Table 2** to calculate the surface area to volume ratio for **X** and **Y**. [2 marks]

02.2 Suggest what type of environment animal **Y** lives in. [1 mark]

03 A student is given a ruler and a caffeine drink.

03.1 Describe how the ruler and caffeine drink could be used to investigate the effect of caffeine on human reaction time.

You should include:
- variables that you would need to keep the same
- measurements you would need to take
- how you would ensure that you would be able to draw a valid conclusion from your results. [6 marks]

03.2 A woman tested the effect of talking on a mobile phone on her reaction time, using a computer program.
At the start of the test a red box is shown on the screen. When the box turns green, the woman clicks the mouse as fast as possible.
Table 3 shows the results of the test.
Table 3

| | Reaction time in ms ||
	Not talking on mobile phone	Talking on mobile phone
1	353	395
2	320	408
3	297	528
4	313	432
5	380	683
6	335	452
Mean	333	

Calculate the mean reaction time when the woman was talking on her mobile phone. [1 mark]

03.3 The woman came to the following conclusion:
Talking on a mobile phone whilst driving means that you are more likely to crash your car.
Suggest **two** reasons why the woman's conclusion may **not** be valid. [2 marks]

03.4 What is the typical range of reaction time in humans?
A 0.1 s to 0.3 s
B 0.3 s to 0.9 s
C 0.7 s to 0.9 s
D 0.85 s to 1.0 s [1 mark]

04 A student is diagnosed with kidney disease. The student is advised to limit their intake of protein.

04.1 Describe a test that the student could use to find out if different foods contain protein. [2 marks]

04.2 The student also wants to avoid eating too much glucose.
Describe a test that the student could use to find out if different foods contain glucose. [3 marks]

103

2.6 Plants and photosynthesis

2.6.1 Specialised plant cells

Learning objectives

After this topic, you should know:
- how plant cells may be specialised to carry out a particular function
- how the structure of different types of plant cells relates to their function.

Plants contain specialised cells with clear adaptations for the job they carry out. Many of these specialised cells are involved in the transport of water, dissolved ions, or dissolved food over large distances around the plant. Here are four examples.

Root hair cells

You find **root hair cells** close to the tips of growing roots. Plants need to take in lots of water (and dissolved mineral ions). The root hair cells help them to take up water and dissolved ions more efficiently. Root hair cells are always relatively close to the xylem tissue, which carries water and dissolved ions up into the rest of the plant. Mineral ions are moved into the root hair cell by active transport. The dissolved ions include nitrate ions to make proteins and magnesium ions to make chlorophyll for **photosynthesis**.

Root hair cells (Figure 1) have three main adaptations:
- They greatly increase the surface area available for water and ions to move into the cell.
- They have a large permanent vacuole, which speeds up the movement of water by osmosis from the soil across the root hair cell.
- They have many mitochondria, which transfer the energy needed for the active transport of mineral ions into the root hair cells.

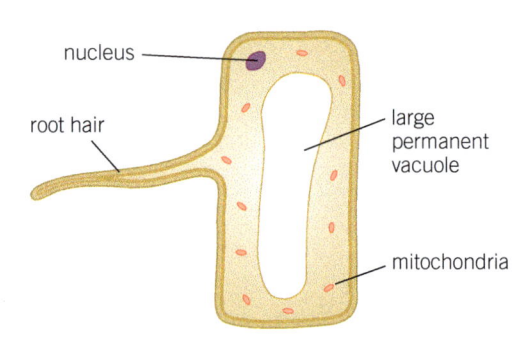

Figure 1 *A root hair cell – magnification ×50*

Synoptic links

For more about active transport, look back at Topic 1.3.7.

For more about osmosis, look back at Topics 1.3.5 and 1.3.6.

Photosynthetic cells

One of the ways in which plants differ from animals is that plants can make their own food by photosynthesis. There are lots of plant cells that can carry out photosynthesis – and lots that cannot. Photosynthetic cells (Figure 2) usually have a number of adaptations:
- They contain specialised green structures called chloroplasts containing chlorophyll, which trap the light needed for photosynthesis.
- They are usually positioned in continuous layers in the leaves and outer layers of the stem of a plant so they absorb as much light as possible.
- They have a large permanent vacuole, which helps keep the cell rigid as a result of osmosis. When lots of these rigid cells are arranged together to form photosynthetic tissue they help support the stem. They also keep the leaf spread out so that it can capture as much light as possible.

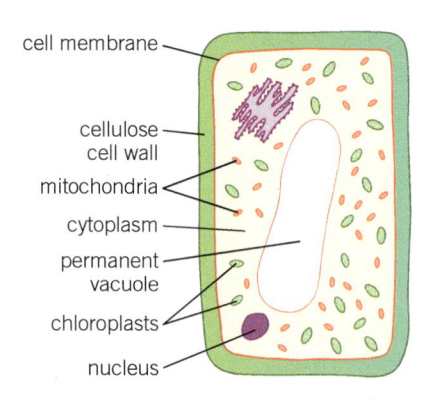

Figure 2 *A photosynthetic plant cell – magnification ×50*

Synoptic link

You will learn much more about photosynthesis in Topic 2.6.6.

Xylem cells

Xylem is the transport tissue in plants that carries water and mineral ions from the roots to the highest leaves and shoots. The xylem is also

2.6 Plants and photosynthesis

important in supporting the plant. The xylem is made up of xylem cells (Figure 3) that are adapted to their functions in two main ways:

- The xylem cells are alive when they are first formed but a special chemical called lignin builds up in spirals in the cell walls. The cells die and form long hollow tubes that allow water and mineral ions to move easily through them, from one end of the plant to the other.
- The spirals and rings of lignin in the xylem cells make them very strong and help them withstand the pressure of water moving up the plant. They also help support the plant stem.

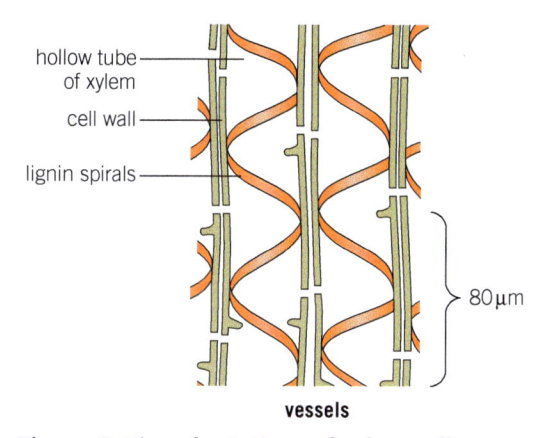

Phloem cells

Phloem tissue is made up of tubes of elongated, living phloem cells. These cells are adapted for **translocation** – the transport of sugars from where they are produced by photosynthesis in the leaves to other parts of the plant for immediate use or storage. The adaptations of the phloem cells (Figure 4, below) include:

- The cell walls between the cells break down to form special sieve plates full of pores. Cell sap containing dissolved sugars and other nutrients can move easily from one phloem cell to the next through these pores.

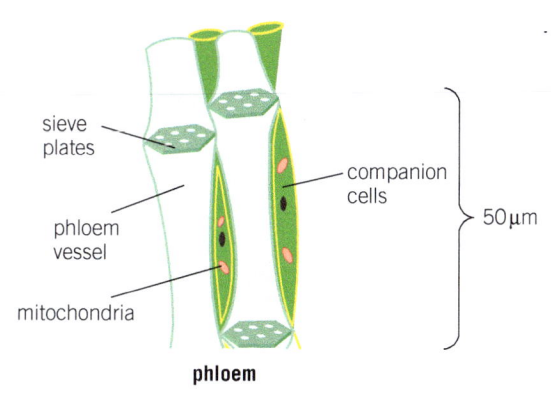

Figure 3 *The adaptations of xylem cells*

Go further

Plant cells communicate with each other. Plant cells that are under attack signal to nearby cells so that they can set up a defensive response. Sometimes a plant will signal both to neighbouring plants and to insects, bringing in defensive reinforcements.

Figure 4 *The adaptations of phloem cells*

- Phloem cells lose a lot of their internal structures but they are supported by companion cells, which help to keep them alive. The mitochondria of the companion cells transfer the energy needed to move dissolved food up and down the plant in phloem.

1. State *one* adaptation for each of the following specialised plant cells. Describe how this adaptation helps the cell carry out its function:
   a. root hair cell [2 marks]
   b. xylem cell [2 marks]
   c. phloem cell [2 marks]
   d. photosynthetic cell. [2 marks]
2. Suggest why a cell within the trunk of a tree cannot carry out photosynthesis. [2 marks]
3. Describe the features you would look for to decide on the function of an unknown specialised plant cell. [6 marks]

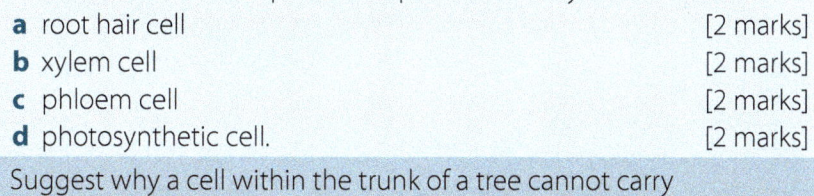

Key points

- Plant cells may be specialised to carry out a particular function.
- Examples of specialised plant cells are root hair cells, photosynthetic cells, xylem cells, and phloem cells.
- Plant cells may be specialised to function within tissues, organs, organ systems, or whole organisms.
- Xylem tissue is composed of hollow tubes made of dead cells strengthened by lignin for the transport of water.
- Phloem tissue is composed of elongated living cells with pores in the end walls which allow dissolved nutrients to move around the plant in translocation.
- Root hair cells have a large surface area for the movement of water into the cells by osmosis and dissolved ions by active transport.

2.6.2 Plant tissues and organs

Learning objectives

After this topic, you should know:

- the roots, stem, and leaves of a plant form a plant organ system for transport of substances around the plant.

Elephant yams are plants that produce a large flower (Figure 1), which releases a disgusting stench like rotting meat that attracts carrion beetles. The beetles become trapped in the flower – its slippery, waxy walls stop them escaping. Around 24 hours after the stench is released, the flower releases pollen that coats the trapped beetles. Then the walls of the flower change texture – they become rough so the beetles can crawl out, carrying the pollen to another flower, lured again by the powerful smell of dead meat. These flowers are one type of plant organ – they are temporary and for reproduction only. But as you will see, plants have other organs, made up of combinations of many different tissues.

Plant tissues

The specialised cells in multicellular plants are organised into tissues and organs. Protective tissues cover the surfaces and protect them. These cells often secrete a waxy substance that waterproofs the surface of the leaf. The photosynthetic tissue contains lots of chloroplasts, which carry out photosynthesis. Lower down in the leaf the cells contain some chloroplasts for photosynthesis but also have big air spaces and large surface areas to make the diffusion of gases easier. Xylem and phloem are the transport tissues in plants. Xylem carries water and dissolved mineral ions from the roots up to the leaves and phloem carries dissolved food from the leaves around the plant. The **meristem** tissue at the growing tips of roots and shoots is made up of rapidly dividing plant cells that grow and differentiate into all the other cell types needed.

Figure 1 *The flower of the elephant yam is a plant organ made up of a number of different tissues*

Synoptic links

For more about specialised plant cells, look back at Topic 2.6.1.

You will learn more about meristem tissue in Topic 2.6.3.

Plant organs

Within the body of a plant, specialised tissues such as palisade mesophyll, spongy mesophyll, xylem, and phloem are arranged to form organs. Each organ carries out its own particular functions. The leaves, stems, and roots are all plant organs, each of which has a very specific job to do (Figure 2).

- leaf carries out photosynthesis
- stem supports leaves and flowers
- roots take up water and mineral ions from the soil

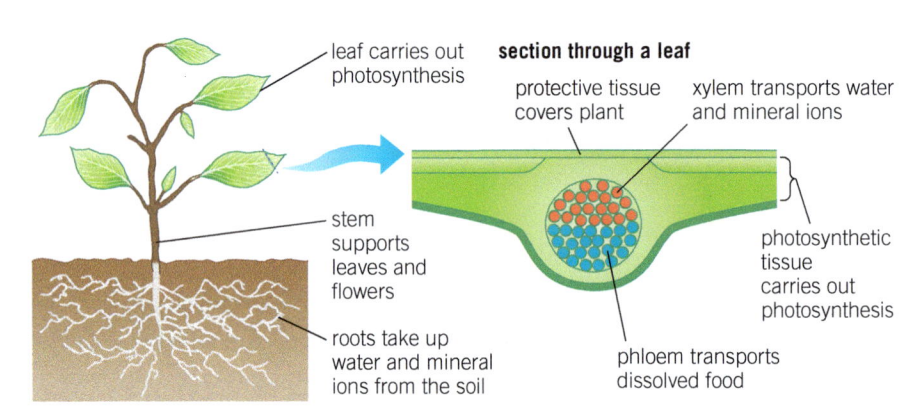

section through a leaf
- protective tissue covers plant
- xylem transports water and mineral ions
- phloem transports dissolved food
- photosynthetic tissue carries out photosynthesis

Figure 2 *Some of the main plant organs*

Within each plant organ there are collections of different tissues working together to perform specific functions for the organism.

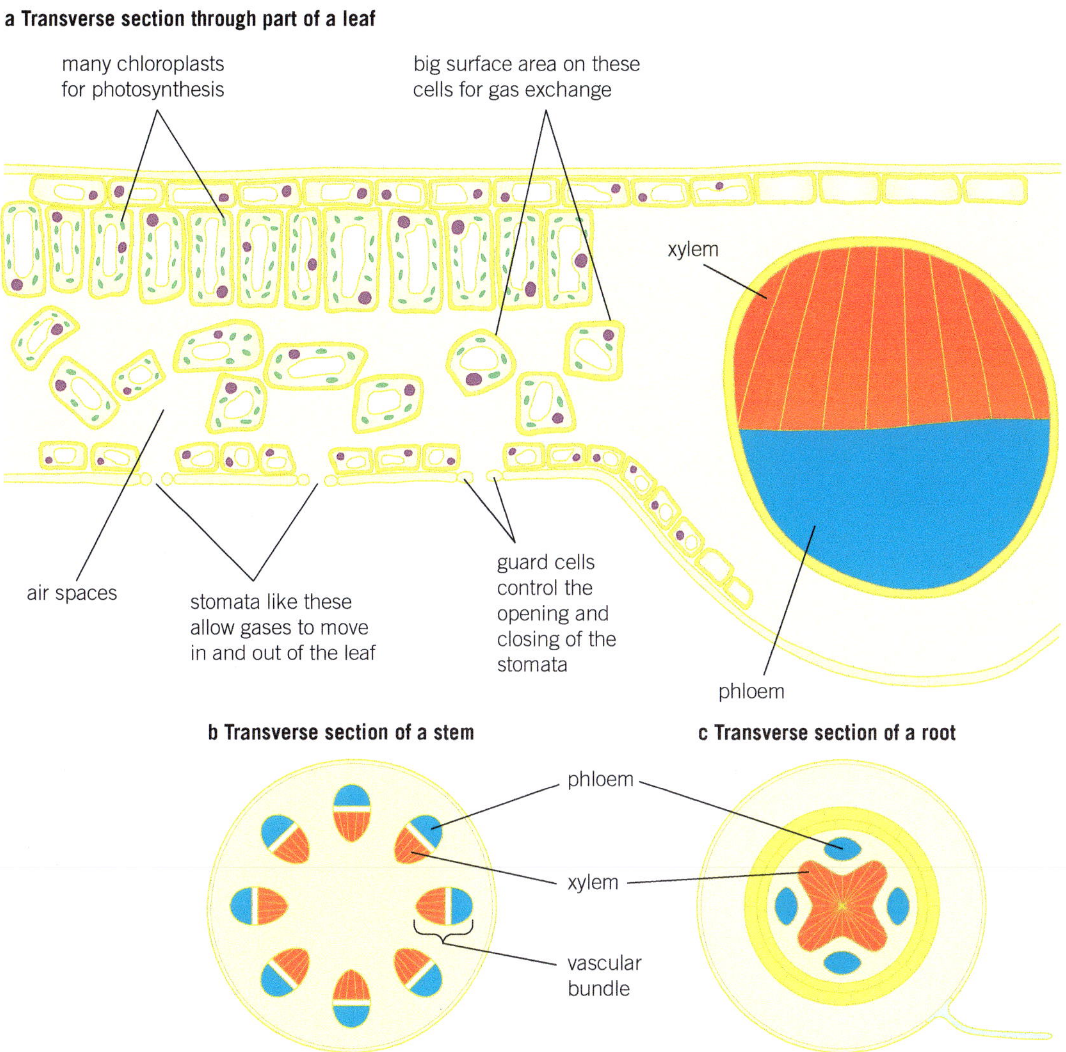

■ 2.6 Plants and photosynthesis

a Transverse section through part of a leaf

- many chloroplasts for photosynthesis
- big surface area on these cells for gas exchange
- xylem
- air spaces
- stomata like these allow gases to move in and out of the leaf
- guard cells control the opening and closing of the stomata
- phloem

b Transverse section of a stem
- phloem
- xylem
- vascular bundle

c Transverse section of a root

Figure 3 *Plants have specific tissues to carry out particular functions. They are arranged in organs such as* **a** *the leaf,* **b** *the stem, and* **c** *the roots. These diagrams are based on stained light micrographs of thin sections through plant organs – magnification ~ ×10*

Plant organs can be very large indeed. For example, some trees, such as the giant redwood, have trunks over 40 m tall. A plant cell is about 100 μm long. The plant stem is 400 000 times bigger than an individual cell.

Plant organ systems

The whole body of the plant – the roots, stem, and leaves – form an organ system for the transport of substances around the plant. Trees form the largest and oldest land organisms, so plant organ systems are also the biggest land-based organ systems in the living world.

1. Plants contain specialised tissues that are adapted to their functions. Describe how plant tissues are adapted:
   a. to protect the surface of the leaf [1 mark]
   b. for photosynthesis [1 mark]
2. Explain how the tissues in a leaf are arranged to form an effective organ for photosynthesis. [6 marks]

Go further
Many plants have specialised defence tissues and organs. For example, nettles have specialised hairs that act like hypodermic needles, injecting poison into any animal brushing past or attempting to eat them.

Key points
- Plant tissues are collections of cells specialised to carry out specific functions.
- The structure of the tissues in plant organs is related to their functions.
- The roots, stem, and leaves form a plant organ system for the transport of substances around the plant.

2.6.3 Meristems and plant cloning

Learning objectives

After this topic, you should know:
- the function of meristems in plants
- how plant clones can be produced quickly and economically.

Synoptic link

For more about cell differentiation and specialisation, look back at Topic 1.3.9.

As you have seen, plants are largely composed of very specialised cells, each adapted for specific functions within the tissues and organs of the plant. Once animal cells have differentiated and become specialised, most of them cannot change their function. Plant cells are rather different.

Differentiation in plant cells

In contrast with animal cells, most plant cells are able to **differentiate** throughout their lives. Undifferentiated cells are formed at active regions of the stems and roots, known as the meristems (Figure 1). In these areas, mitosis takes place almost continuously. The cells then elongate and grow before they finally differentiate. Plants keep growing at these 'growing points' throughout their lives. The plant cells produced do not differentiate until they are in their final position in the plant. Even then, the differentiation is not permanent. You can move a plant cell from one part of a plant to another. There, unless it is a xylem cell or a phloem sieve tube, it can redifferentiate and become a completely different type of cell. You cannot do this with animal cells – once a muscle cell, always a muscle cell.

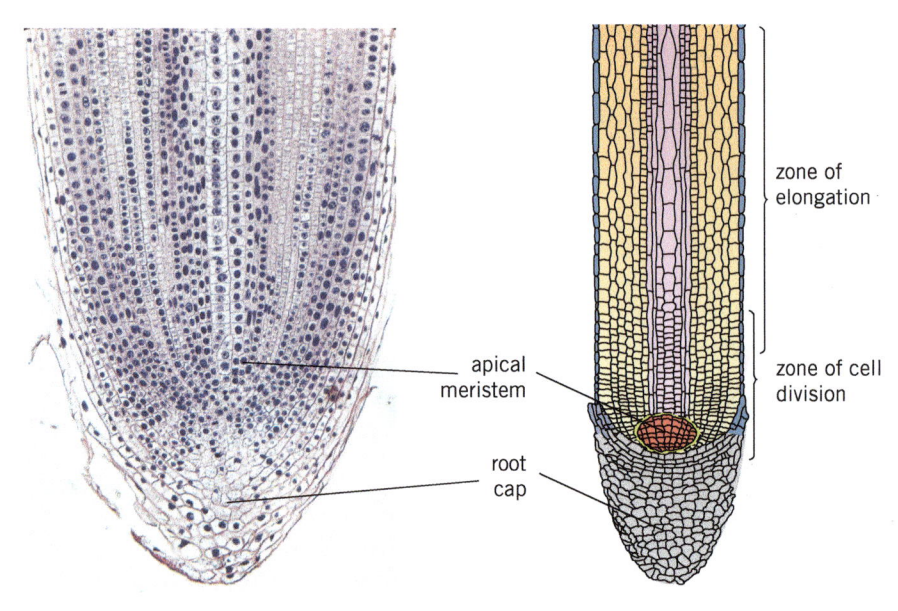

Figure 1 *The main zones of division, elongation, and differentiation in a plant root. The image on the left is a thin section of a stained plant root tip seen through a light microscope – magnification ×10. On the right is a diagram of the same area*

Cloning plants

Producing identical offspring is known as **cloning**. The stem cells from plant meristems can be used to make huge numbers of clones of the mature parent plant very quickly and economically. This is because, in the right conditions, each stem cell will undergo mitosis many times.

2.6 Plants and photosynthesis

Given different conditions, these will then differentiate to form tissues such as xylem, phloem, photosynthetic cells, and root hair cells that are needed to form a tiny new plant. The new plant will be identical to the original parent.

Plant cloning from meristems is important as it provides a way of producing large numbers of rare plants reliably and safely. Scientists may be able to save some rare plants from extinction in this way. Plant cloning also provides a way of producing large populations of identical plants for research. This is important as scientists can change variables and observe the effects on genetically identical individuals.

Cloning large numbers of identical plants from the stem cells in plant meristems is also widely used in horticulture, producing large numbers of plants such as orchids for sale (Figure 2). In agriculture cloning is used to produce large numbers of identical crop plants with special features such as disease resistance. For example, practically every banana you eat is produced from a cloned plant.

Figure 2 *Cloning exotic plants, like this orchid, from plant stem cells makes them relatively cheap and available for everyone to enjoy*

Study tips
Cloned cells produced by mitosis are genetically identical.

Cauliflower cloning
It is possible to clone plants in a school laboratory. For example, you can clone cauliflower plants from small sections of cauliflower. The procedure is not difficult, but it is very important to keep everything sterile. The tissue to be cloned is very vulnerable to going mouldy, for example!

Safety: Handle sterilant carefully and do not inhale its vapours. Take care with sharp instruments. Wear eye protection.

1. Describe the differences between a normal plant body cell and a cell from a plant meristem. [3 marks]
2. Describe how cloning plants can be used to save rare species of plants from extinction. [3 marks]
3. a Explain why the ability to produce large populations of clones of identical plants is such an advantage in plant research. [3 marks]
   b Suggest *two* advantages and *two* disadvantages of producing large numbers of cloned plants such as orchids or food crop plants. [4 marks]

Key points
- Meristem tissue in plants contains the cells that divide as the plant grows. It is found at the growing tips of shoots and roots.
- Plant cells differentiate into different types of plant cell depending on where they are in the plant.
- Stem cells from meristems can be used to produce clones of plants quickly and economically.

2.6.4 Evaporation and transpiration

Learning objectives

After this topic, you should know:
- what transpiration is
- the role of stomata and guard cells in controlling gas exchange and water loss.

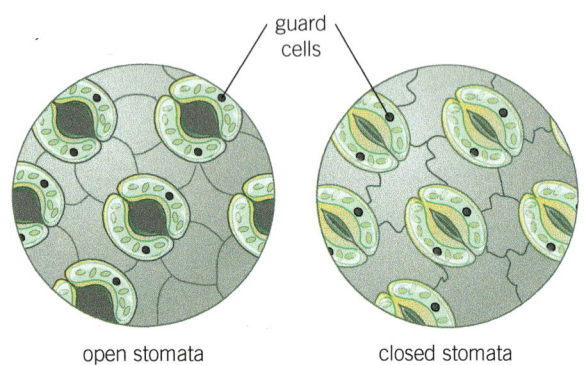

Figure 1 *The size of the opening of the stomata is controlled by the guard cells. This in turn controls the carbon dioxide going into the leaf and the water vapour and oxygen leaving it – magnification ~ ×40*

Figure 3 *The transpiration stream in trees can pull litres of water many metres above the ground*

The top of a tree may be many metres from the ground. Yet the leaves at the top need water just as much as those on the lower branches. So how do they get the water they need?

Water loss from the leaves

All over the leaf surface are small openings known as stomata. The stomata can be opened when the plant needs to allow air into the leaves. Carbon dioxide from the atmosphere diffuses into the air spaces and then into the cells down a concentration gradient. At the same time, oxygen produced by photosynthesis is removed from the leaf by diffusion into the surrounding air. This maintains a concentration gradient for oxygen to diffuse from the cells into the air spaces of the leaf. The size of the stomata and their opening and closing is controlled by the **guard cells** (Figure 1).

When the stomata are open, plants lose water vapour through them as well. The water vapour evaporates from the cells lining the air spaces and then passes out of the leaf through the stomata by diffusion. This loss of water vapour is known as **transpiration**.

As water is lost from the surface of the leaves, more water is pulled up through the xylem to take its place. This constant movement of water molecules through the xylem from the roots to the leaves is known as the **transpiration stream** (Figures 2 and 3). It is driven by the evaporation of water in the leaves and the loss of water vapour through the stomata. So, anything that affects the rate of evaporation will also affect transpiration.

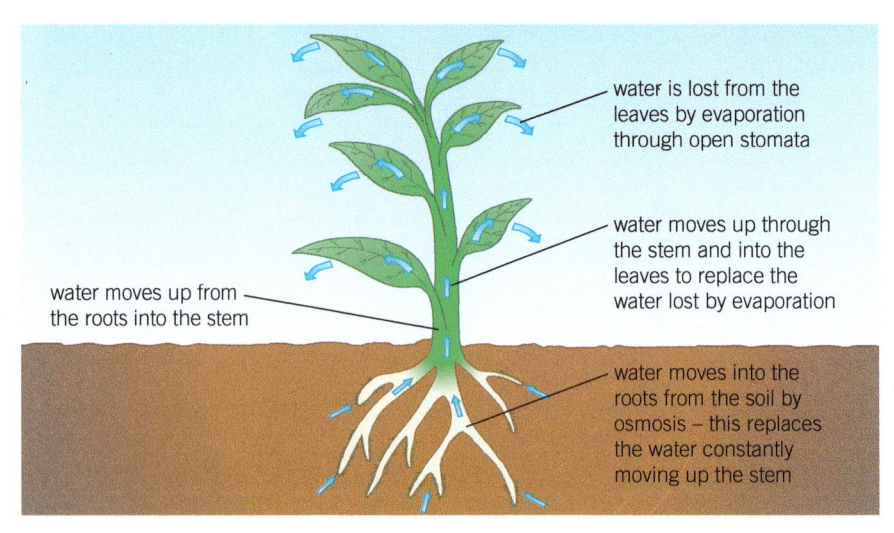

Figure 2 *The transpiration stream*

Most of the water vapour lost by plants is lost from the leaves. Most of this loss takes place by diffusion through the stomata when they are open. This is one of the main reasons why it is important that plants can close their stomata – to limit the loss of water vapour. The stomata can open or close as conditions change because the guard cells can gain or lose water by osmosis. This changes the shape of the guard cells and opens or closes the gap between them (Figure 1).

Finding the mean and estimating

When you carry out stomatal counts there are two bits of maths that will be useful – finding the mean and estimating.

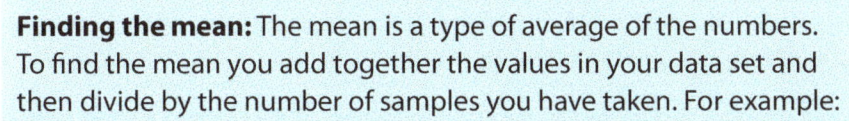

Finding the mean: The mean is a type of average of the numbers. To find the mean you add together the values in your data set and then divide by the number of samples you have taken. For example:

A student looked at the number of stomata on the underside of a leaf. They did five counts and the results per unit area were: 10, 12, 15, 8, 10.

The mean number of stomata per unit area of leaf surface (0.01 mm^2 where the graticule is divided into squares of side length 0.1 mm)

$$= \frac{10 + 12 + 15 + 8 + 10}{5}$$

$$= \frac{55}{5} = 11$$

Sampling: You can sample the surface area of a leaf by taking peels from randomly selected regions to make your counts (see Practical box).

Estimating: When you estimate, you are getting a 'ball-park' figure, not a precise measurement. For example, you might work out the mean number of stomata:

- per mm^2 of a leaf. If you know the size of the field of vision you were using, for example, 0.01 mm^2, you can get an estimated number of stomata per 1 mm^2. In this example this is 11 × 100 = **1100** stomata per mm^2 of leaf surface.
- per leaf. You can work out the approximate area of the entire leaf using graph paper. If, for example, the leaf has an area of 5 cm^2, the estimated number of stomata would be 110 × 500 = **55000** stomata per leaf.

You can find out more about finding the mean in Maths skills MS 2b, sampling in Maths skills MS 2d, and estimating numbers in Maths skills MS 2h.

---

1 **a** What are stomata? [1 mark]
  b Describe their role in the plant. [2 marks]
2 Describe the process of transpiration. [3 marks]
3 Explain how water moves up a plant in the transpiration stream. [3 marks]
4 A student measured the number of stomata per mm^2 of leaf surface. Their counts were: 250, 280, 265, 245, 270, 255, 290. Calculate the mean number of stomata (to 3 significant figures). [3 marks]

Investigating stomata

Stomata are key to the control of transpiration. There are a number of different ways you can investigate the numbers and distribution of stomata on a leaf. You can compare the upper and lower sides of a leaf, different areas of the same leaf surface, different leaves from the same plant, and different types of leaves. The main steps are:

1 Making a stomatal peel – use nail varnish or a water-based varnish to cover an area of the leaf and then peel it off.
2 Place the peel on a microscope slide.
3 With an eyepiece graticule, use a low magnification and count the number of stomata in a random sample of squares.
4 Without an eyepiece graticule, use a higher magnification and count the number of stomata in the field of vision and repeat this with a number of sample areas of the peel to collect your data.
5 You can *calculate* the mean number of stomata on a given area of a leaf.
6 You can use this to *estimate* the number of stomata on the whole leaf.

Key points

- The loss of water vapour from the surface of plant leaves is known as transpiration.
- Water evaporates in the leaves and the water vapour escapes through the stomata by diffusion.
- The stomata can open or close as conditions change because the guard cells can gain or lose water by osmosis.

■ 2.6 Plants and photosynthesis

111

2.6.5 Factors affecting transpiration

Learning objectives

After this topic, you should know:

- the factors that affect the rate of transpiration
- ways of investigating the effect of environmental factors on rate of water uptake.

The effect of the environment on transpiration

Different conditions affect the rate of transpiration. As a result, some environments are much tougher for plants to survive in than others (Figure 1). Factors that affect the rate of transpiration include temperature, air movements, and light intensity.

Anything that increases the rate of photosynthesis will increase the rate of transpiration, because more stomata open up to let in carbon dioxide. When stomata are open, the rate at which water is lost by evaporation and diffusion increases. Therefore, an increase in light intensity will increase the rate of transpiration because it increases the rate of photosynthesis.

Conditions that increase the rate of evaporation inside leaf cells and diffusion of water from open stomata will also make transpiration happen more rapidly. Hot, dry, windy conditions increase the rate of transpiration because more water evaporates from the cells and diffusion happens more quickly. Water vapour diffuses more rapidly into dry air than into humid air because the concentration gradient is steeper. Air movements both increase the rate of evaporation and maintain a steep concentration gradient from the inside of the leaf to the outside by removing water vapour as it diffuses out.

Temperature affects the rate of transpiration in several ways. Molecules move faster as the temperature increases, so diffusion occurs more rapidly. The rate of photosynthesis also increases as the temperature goes up, so more stomata will be open for gas exchange to take place. Each of these conditions individually increases the rate of transpiration and, when combined, a plant will lose a lot of water in this way.

Figure 1 *Dry air and high temperatures make it very hard for leafy plants to survive in a desert as they lose so much water through transpiration*

2.6 Plants and photosynthesis

Measuring water uptake

There are many ways in which to investigate the effect of different environmental factors on the rate of transpiration in plants. Many of them involve a piece of apparatus known as a potometer (Figure 2).

A potometer can be used to show how the uptake of water by a plant changes in different conditions. This gives you a good idea of the amount of water lost by the plant in transpiration. Almost all of the water taken up by a plant is lost in transpiration, but a small amount is used in the metabolism, for example, in photosynthesis. This is why we measure water uptake, and factors that affect water uptake in a plant. We do not usually measure actual transpiration in a school laboratory.

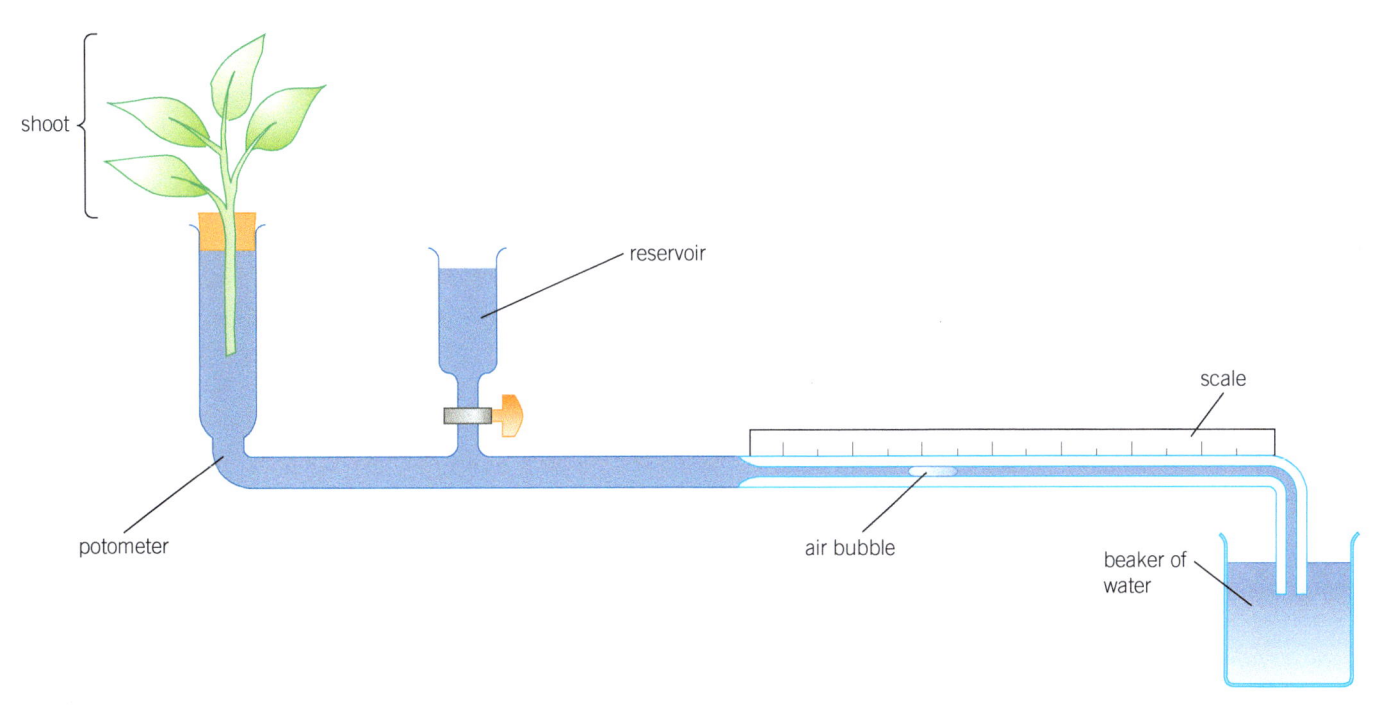

Figure 2 *A potometer is used to show the water uptake of a plant under different conditions*

1 Name the parts of the leaf that help the plant to reduce water loss under normal conditions. [2 marks]
2 a Explain the effect on transpiration of a fan blowing onto the leaves of a plant. [3 marks]
  b A potometer does not actually measure transpiration. Explain this statement. [3 marks]
3 Water lilies have their stomata on the tops of their leaves.
  a Suggest why this is an important adaptation for water lilies [2 marks]
  b Controlling transpiration is not very important to water lilies. Suggest reasons for this. [2 marks]

Key points

- Factors that increase the rate of photosynthesis or increase stomatal opening will increase the rate of transpiration.
- We measure water uptake, not transpiration. The rate of transpiration varies with:
  - light intensity, which affects the opening of the stomata
  - air movements, which affect the concentration of water vapour in the air around the leaves
  - temperature, which affects the rate at which water evaporates.

2.6.6 Photosynthesis

Learning objectives

After this topic, you should know:

- the raw materials and energy source for photosynthesis
- that photosynthesis is an endothermic reaction
- the equations that summarise photosynthesis.

Study tip

Learn the equation for photosynthesis.

Remember that photosynthesis is endothermic – energy is transferred from the environment to the chlorophyll by light.

All organisms, including plants and algae, need food for respiration, growth, and reproduction. However, plants don't need to eat – they can make their own food by photosynthesis. This takes place in the green parts of plants (especially the leaves) when it is light. Algae can also carry out photosynthesis.

The process of photosynthesis

The cells in algae and plant leaves are full of small green parts called chloroplasts, which contain a green substance called chlorophyll. During photosynthesis, energy is transferred from the environment to the chlorophyll by light. This energy is then transferred to convert carbon dioxide (CO_2) from the air, plus water (H_2O) from the soil into a simple sugar called **glucose** ($C_6H_{12}O_6$). The chemical reaction also produces oxygen gas (O_2) as a by-product. The oxygen is released into the air, which you can then use when you breathe it in. Every year plants produce about 368 000 000 000 tonnes of oxygen.

Photosynthesis is an **endothermic reaction** – it needs an input of energy from the environment. The energy transferred from the environment when the bonds in carbon dioxide and water are broken is more than the energy transferred back to the environment with the formation of the new bonds in glucose and oxygen. The extra energy required for the reaction to take place is transferred from the environment to the plant cells by light.

Photosynthesis can be summarised as:

$$\text{carbon dioxide} + \text{water} \xrightarrow{\text{light}} \text{glucose} + \text{oxygen}$$

Higher

$$6CO_2 + 6H_2O \xrightarrow{\text{light}} C_6H_{12}O_6 + 6O_2$$

Some of the glucose produced during photosynthesis is used immediately by the cells of the plant for respiration. However, a lot of the glucose is converted into insoluble starch and stored.

Figure 1 *The oxygen produced during photosynthesis is vital for life on Earth. You can demonstrate that it is produced using water plants*

Producing oxygen

You can show that a plant is photosynthesising by the oxygen gas it gives off as a by-product. Oxygen is a colourless gas, so in land plants it isn't easy to show that it is being produced. However, if you use water plants such as *Elodea*, you can see and collect the bubbles of gas they give off when they are photosynthesising. The gas will relight a glowing splint, showing that it is rich in oxygen.

■ 2.6 Plants and photosynthesis

Uses of glucose in plants
How do plants use the glucose they produce during photosynthesis?

- **In respiration:** Plant cells break down glucose with oxygen in respiration, transferring energy to be used by the cells. Chemically, respiration is the reverse of photosynthesis.
- **For storage:** Glucose is soluble in water, so it can affect the way in which water moves in to and out of the cells by osmosis. Starch is insoluble in water. It has no effect on the water balance of the plant, so plants can store large amounts of starch in their cells. Glucose is converted into starch, which acts as the main energy store in plants and is found in cells all over a plant.
- **To produce cellulose:** Plants use glucose to produce cellulose, a complex carbohydrate, which they use to strengthen their cell walls.
- **To produce amino acids for proteins:** Plants combine glucose with nitrate ions and other ions absorbed in solution from the soil to produce amino acids. These amino acids are then built up into proteins to be used in the plant cells in many ways, including as enzymes.
- **To produce lipids:** Fats and oils are produced for storage. Plants often use fats or oils as an energy store in their seeds. The lipids in the seeds provide lots of energy for the new plant as it germinates.

Synoptic link
For more on the structure and function of plant cells, look back at Topic 2.6.1.

Figure 2 *Plant oils, such as this olive oil, are important in human diets around the world*

Key points
- Photosynthesis is an endothermic reaction.
- Photosynthesis takes place in the chloroplasts in the cells of the leaves of plants. The chloroplasts contain chlorophyll, which absorbs sunlight.
- Photosynthesis can be represented as follows:

carbon dioxide + water $\xrightarrow{\text{light}}$ glucose + oxygen

(H) $6CO_2 + 6H_2O \xrightarrow{\text{light}} C_6H_{12}O_6 + 6O_2$

- Energy is transferred to plant cells by light. The glucose produced in photosynthesis may be used by the plant for respiration; to produce starch, fats, or oils for storage; to produce cellulose; or, combined with nitrate ions, to produce amino acids to build proteins.

---

1. State where a plant gets the carbon dioxide and water that it needs for photosynthesis. [2 marks]
2. Describe the path taken by a carbon atom as it moves from being part of the carbon dioxide in the air to being part of a starch molecule in a plant. [5 marks]
3. **a** Some of the glucose made in photosynthesis is converted into starch. State *three* other ways in which it may be used in the plant. [3 marks]
   b Explain why some of the glucose is converted into starch. [3 marks]
4. **a** Give the word equation used to summarise the process of photosynthesis. [2 marks]
   b (H) Give the balanced symbol equation for photosynthesis. [2 marks]
   c Explain why photosynthesis is an endothermic reaction. [3 marks]

115

2.6.7 The rate of photosynthesis

Learning objectives

After this topic, you should know:
- how temperature, light intensity, and carbon dioxide concentration affect the rate of photosynthesis.

You may have noticed that plants grow quickly in the summer, yet they hardly grow at all in the winter. Plants need light, warmth, and carbon dioxide if they are going to photosynthesise and grow as fast as they can. Sometimes any one or more of these things can be in short supply and can limit the amount of photosynthesis a plant can manage. This is why they are known as **limiting factors**.

Light intensity

The most obvious factor affecting the rate of photosynthesis is light intensity. If there is plenty of light, lots of photosynthesis can take place. If there is very little or no light, photosynthesis will stop, whatever the other conditions are around the plant. For most plants, the greater the light intensity, the more energy is available to the plant and the faster the rate of photosynthesis (Figure 1).

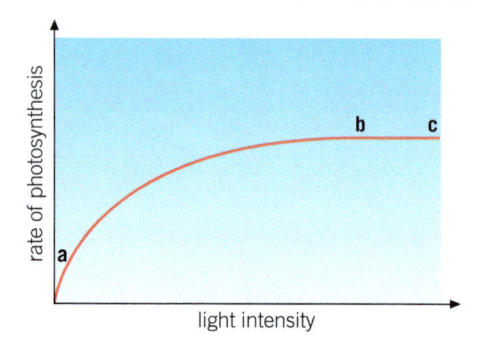

Figure 1 *Investigating the effect of light intensity on the rate of photosynthesis*

Temperature

Temperature affects all chemical reactions, including photosynthesis. As the temperature rises, the rate of photosynthesis increases as the reaction speeds up. However, photosynthesis is controlled by enzymes. Most enzymes are denatured once the temperature rises to around 40–50 °C. If the temperature gets too high, the enzymes controlling photosynthesis are denatured and the rate of photosynthesis will fall (Figure 2).

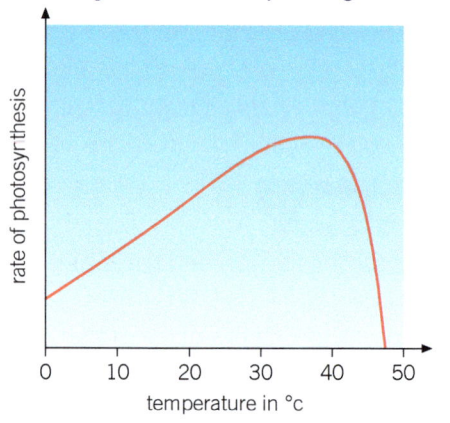

Figure 2 *The effect of increasing temperature on the rate of photosynthesis*

Carbon dioxide concentration

Plants need carbon dioxide to make glucose. The atmosphere is only about 0.04% carbon dioxide. This means carbon dioxide often limits the rate of photosynthesis. Increasing the carbon dioxide concentration will increase the rate of photosynthesis (Figure 3).

On a sunny day, carbon dioxide concentration is the most common limiting factor for plants. The carbon dioxide concentrations around a plant tend to rise at night, because in the dark a plant respires but doesn't photosynthesise. As light intensity and temperature increase in the morning, most of the carbon dioxide around the plant gets used up.

In a science laboratory or a greenhouse the levels of carbon dioxide can be increased artificially. This means that carbon dioxide is no longer the limiting factor. Then the rate of photosynthesis increases with the rise in carbon dioxide concentration.

In a garden, woodland, or field (rather than a laboratory or greenhouse, where conditions can be controlled), light intensity, temperature, and carbon dioxide concentrations interact, and any one of them might be the factor that limits photosynthesis.

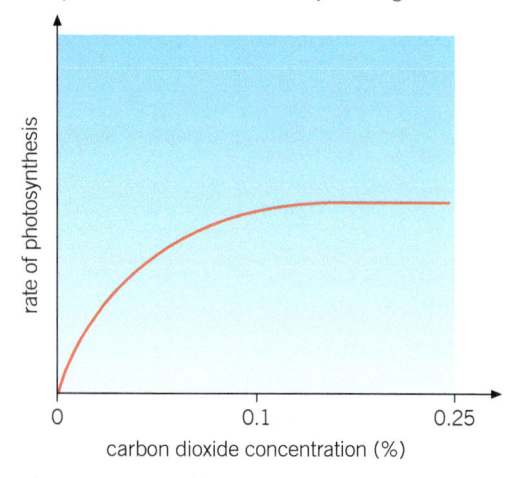

Figure 3 *The effect of increasing carbon dioxide concentration on the rate of photosynthesis*

2.6 Plants and photosynthesis

Light intensity and rate of photosynthesis

You can investigate the effect of light intensity on the rate of photosynthesis (Figure 4).

At the beginning of the investigation, the rate of photosynthesis in the water plant increases as the light is moved closer to the plant, which increases the light intensity. This tells us that light is acting as a limiting factor. When the light is moved further away from the water plant, the rate of photosynthesis falls, shown by a slowing down in the stream of bubbles produced. If the light is moved closer again the stream of bubbles becomes faster, showing an increased rate of photosynthesis. We often add a heat shield to the apparatus in Figure 4. This helps keep the temperature of the water around the plant constant regardless of the position of the light source.

Eventually, no matter how close the light, the rate of photosynthesis stays the same. At this point, light is no longer limiting the rate of photosynthesis. Something else has become the limiting factor.

The results can be plotted on a graph showing the effect of light intensity on the rate of photosynthesis (Figure 1).

Safety: Keep electrical equipment dry and do not handle if your hands are wet.

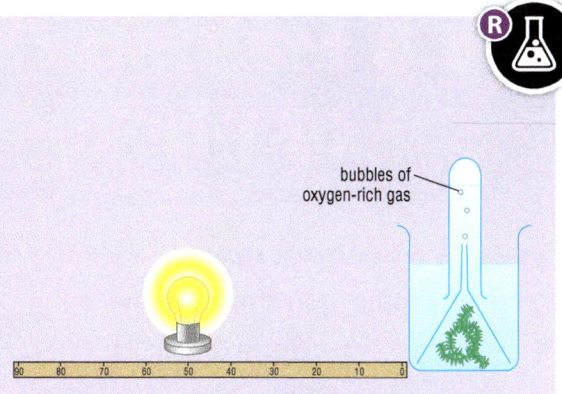

Figure 4 Simple apparatus for investigating the effect of light intensity on the rate of photosynthesis

Chlorophyll levels in the leaf

Chlorophyll does not affect the rate of photosynthesis in the same way as light intensity, temperature, and carbon dioxide concentration. However, if the amount of chlorophyll in a leaf is limited in any way, less photosynthesis will take place. The leaves of some ornamental plants have white, chlorophyll-free areas. These plants grow less vigorously than plants with all-green leaves. If they are permanently in dim light, variegated leaves often turn completely green. If a plant does not have enough minerals, especially magnesium, it cannot make chlorophyll. The rate of photosynthesis drops and eventually the plant may die.

1. State the *three* main factors that affect the rate of photosynthesis in a plant. [3 marks]
2. Look at the graph in Figure 1.
   a. Explain what is happening between points **a** and **b** on the graph. [2 marks]
   b. Explain what is happening between points **b** and **c** on the graph. [2 marks]
   c. Now look at Figure 2. Explain why it is a different shape than the graphs in Figures 1 and 3. [4 marks]
3. **(H)** Explain in terms of factors limiting the rate of photosynthesis why the plants growing in a tropical rainforest are so much bigger than the plants that grow in a UK woodland, and why both are bigger than the plants on the Arctic tundra. [6 marks]

Light intensity and the inverse square law

The relationship between light intensity and the rate of photosynthesis is not a simple one. This is because light intensity involves the inverse square law.

As the distance of the light from the plant increases, the light intensity decreases. This is an inverse relationship – as one goes up, the other goes down. However, the relationship between distance and light intensity is not linear. The light intensity decreases or increases in inverse proportion to the square of the distance.

$$\text{light intensity} \propto \frac{1}{\text{distance}^2}$$

For example, if you double the distance between the light and your plant, light intensity falls by a quarter:

$$\text{light intensity} \propto \frac{1}{2^2} = \frac{1}{4}$$

Key points

- The rate of photosynthesis may be affected by light intensity, temperature and carbon dioxide concentration.

Higher Tier

2.6.8 Making the most of photosynthesis

Learning objectives

After this topic, you should know:

- how the different factors affecting the rate of photosynthesis interact
- how humans can manipulate the environment in which plants grow.

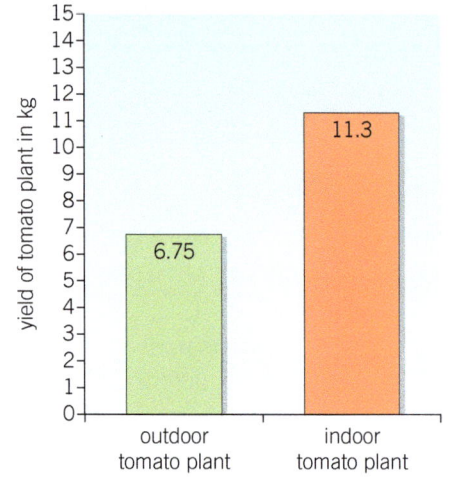

Figure 1 *One piece of American research showed that the crop yield for tomatoes was almost doubled in a greenhouse*

> **Synoptic link**
>
> To remind yourself of the effects of limiting factors on the rate of photosynthesis, look back at Topic 2.6.7.

The more a plant photosynthesises, the more biomass it makes and the faster it grows. It's not surprising that farmers want their plants to grow as fast and as big as possible. It makes more food for people to eat and helps them to make a profit (Figure 1).

In theory, if you give plants a warm environment with plenty of light, carbon dioxide, and water, they should grow as fast as possible. Out in the fields it is almost impossible to manipulate any of these factors. However, people have found a number of ways in which they can artificially manipulate the environment of their plants – and obtain a number of benefits from doing so.

The garden greenhouse

Lots of people have a greenhouse in their garden. The first recorded greenhouse was built in about AD 30 for Tiberius Caesar, a Roman emperor who wanted to eat cucumbers out of season. Glass hadn't been invented so they used sheets of the mineral mica to build it. Now farmers use huge plastic polytunnels as giant greenhouses for growing crops from tomatoes to strawberries and potatoes.

How does a greenhouse affect the rate of photosynthesis? The environment inside the glass or plastic building is much more controllable than that in an ordinary garden or field. Most importantly, the atmosphere is warmer inside than out. This affects the rate of photosynthesis, speeding it up so that plants grow faster, flower and fruit earlier, and crop better. In the UK, greenhouses can be used to grow fruit like peaches, lemons, and oranges that don't grow well outside.

Controlling everything

More and more farmers are taking the idea of the greenhouse a bit further. In the laboratory you can isolate different factors and see how they limit the rate of photosynthesis. However, for most plants it is usually a mixture of these factors that affects them. Early in the morning, light levels and temperature probably limit the rate of photosynthesis. Then as the levels of light and temperature rise, carbon dioxide levels become limiting. On a bright, cold winter day, temperature probably limits the rate of the process. There is a constant interaction between the different factors.

Big commercial greenhouses now take advantage of what is known about limiting factors. They control not only the temperature but also the levels of light and carbon dioxide in order to obtain the fastest possible rate of photosynthesis. As a result the plants grow as quickly as possible.

2.6 Plants and photosynthesis

These greenhouses are enormous and conditions are controlled using computer software. All this costs a lot of money but manipulating the environment has many benefits. You can change the carbon dioxide levels in the greenhouses during the day as well as the temperature and light levels.

Turnover is fast, which means profits can be high. There is no need to plough or prepare the land in these systems, and crops can be grown where the land is poor.

Greenhouse economics

It takes a lot of planning to keep conditions in greenhouses just right. Electricity and gas are used to maintain the lighting and temperature and to control the carbon dioxide levels. Expensive monitoring equipment and computers are needed to maintain conditions inside the greenhouse within narrow boundaries, and alarms are vital if things go wrong. On the other hand, fewer staff are needed, the time from seed to harvest is much shorter, and the final crop is larger and cleaner. All of these factors, along with the size of the business, have to be considered when deciding whether an enclosed system will increase or reduce profits (Figure 3). The increased income from a larger crop and the ability to grow more crops each year has to be balanced against the cost of setting up and maintaining the system.

There are many decisions for growers to make, but for plants grown in an enclosed system, limiting factors are a thing of the past.

Figure 2 *By controlling the temperature, light, and carbon dioxide levels in a greenhouse like this you can produce the biggest possible crops*

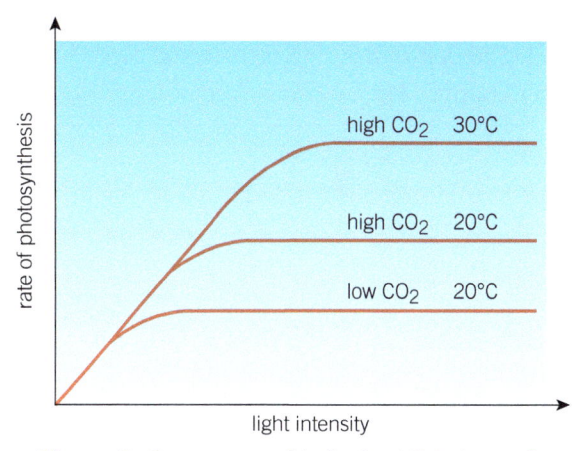

Figure 3 *Growers need to look at this type of data to help them decide the best economic conditions for growing their plants. The cost of providing the conditions that give the very highest yields may be too expensive and may wipe out the profits from the bigger, cleaner crop*

1. **a** State the main differences between a garden greenhouse and a large commercial greenhouse. [3 marks]
   b State the main benefits of artificially manipulating the environment in which food plants are grown. [3 marks]
2. **a** In each of these situations, identify the *one* factor that is most likely to be limiting photosynthesis. In *each* case explain why the rate of photosynthesis is limited.
   i A wheat field first thing in the morning [3 marks]
   ii The same field later on in the day [3 marks]
   iii Plants growing on a woodland floor in winter [3 marks]
   iv Plants growing on a woodland floor in summer. [3 marks]
   b Explain why is it impossible to be certain which factor is involved in each of these cases. [3 marks]
3. Use Figure 3 to answer this question.
   The cost of running a large greenhouse is particularly affected by the levels of light and temperature. If plants are provided with plenty of carbon dioxide the grower can get two crops a year at 20 °C and three crops a year at 30 °C. Explain why many growers use 20 °C rather than 30 °C in their greenhouses. In your explanation, suggest why many growers are investing in computer-controlled thermal insulation systems that can add or remove thermal insulation automatically. [6 marks]

Key points

- The factors that limit the rate of photosynthesis interact and any one of them may limit photosynthesis.
- Increasing any one of the limiting factors speeds up the rate of photosynthesis until the rate is limited by the factor that is in shortest supply.
- Limiting factors are important in the economics of enhancing the conditions in greenhouses to gain the maximum rate of photosynthesis, while still maintaining profit.

2.6.9 Plant diseases

Learning objectives

After this topic, you should know:
- how plant diseases are spread
- examples of viral and fungal diseases in plants.

Synoptic link
You will learn more about pathogens and communicable diseases in Chapter 3.9.

Communicable (infectious) diseases are found all over the world. Microorganisms that cause disease are called pathogens. The pathogens that affect plants are mainly viruses and fungi, and they cause a wide range of diseases. Plant diseases are very important to people, because plants are such an important source of food. If we could prevent plant diseases, millions of people who are currently starving might have enough food to eat.

How are plant diseases spread?

There are three main ways in which plant diseases are commonly spread:

- By air (including droplet infection) – Many pathogens, including the viruses and fungal spores that often cause plant diseases, are carried and spread from one organism to another in the air.

- Direct contact – The spread of a disease by direct contact of an infected organism with a healthy one is common in plants. A tiny piece of infected plant material left in a field can infect an entire new crop. Animals such as aphids that feed on plants can also carry pathogens between infected and uninfected individuals.

- By water – Fungal spores and viruses carried in splashes of water often spread plant diseases.

Viral diseases in plants

When viruses infect a plant, they destroy its cells as part of their life cycle. This causes damage to the plant tissues. In the worst cases this may lead to the death of the plant. Often the viral infections do not kill the plant but weaken it, reducing the crop or fruit yield. For gardeners, viral diseases can make plants look misshapen and can spoil the flowers and leaves. There are many different types of viral plant diseases. Those caused by the mosaic viruses are some of the most widely studied.

Tobacco mosaic virus

Tobacco mosaic virus (TMV) was the first virus ever to be isolated. It is a widespread plant pathogen that affects around 150 species of plants, including tomatoes and tobacco plants. It causes a distinctive 'mosaic' pattern of discolouration on the leaves as the viruses destroy the cells. This affects the growth of the plant because the affected areas of the leaf do not photosynthesise. TMV can seriously reduce the yield of a crop.

It is spread by contact between diseased plant material and healthy plants, and insects can act as vectors. The virus can remain infectious for years in ideal conditions. There is no treatment and farmers now grow TMV resistant strains of many crop plants. Methods used to help prevent the spread of the tobacco mosaic virus include good field hygiene. This involves removing and destroying infected plants, and also washing hands and tools after handling infected plants. Farmers can also use crop rotation to avoid planting vulnerable plants in soil that has been infected for at least two years.

Figure 1 *Mosaic viruses, including tobacco mosaic virus, cause a typical pattern of damage in many different types of plants*

2.6 Plants and photosynthesis

Fungal diseases in plants
There are relatively few fungal diseases that affect people. In plants, however, fungal diseases are common and can be devastating. Huge areas of crops, from cereals to bananas, are lost every year as a result of fungal infections, including stem rust and various rotting diseases. Fungal diseases also affect plants grown to look nice or to provide flowers for sale, an important part of the economy for many countries.

Rose black spot
Rose black spot is a fungal disease of rose leaves. It causes purple or black spots to develop on the leaves and it is a nuisance in gardens and for commercial flower growers. The leaves often turn yellow and drop early. This affects the growth of the plant because it reduces the area of leaves available for photosynthesis. As a result the plant does not flower well – and the main reason people grow roses is for the lovely flowers!

The disease is spread by spores of the fungus, produced in the black spots on the leaves. The spores are carried by the wind. They are then spread over the plant after it rains in drips of water that splash from one leaf or plant to another. The spores stay dormant over winter on dead leaves and on the stems of rose plants. There are a number of ways to control black spot. Not planting roses too close together allows air to flow freely around them and keeps them dry. Watering the roots without wetting the leaves reduces the spread of spores in water drips. Removing and burning affected leaves and stems can reduce spore spread.

Chemical fungicides can also help to treat the disease and prevent it spreading, especially when sprayed on the leaves before warm, wet weather. Horticulturists have bred types of roses that are relatively resistant to black spot, but the disease still cannot be entirely prevented or cured.

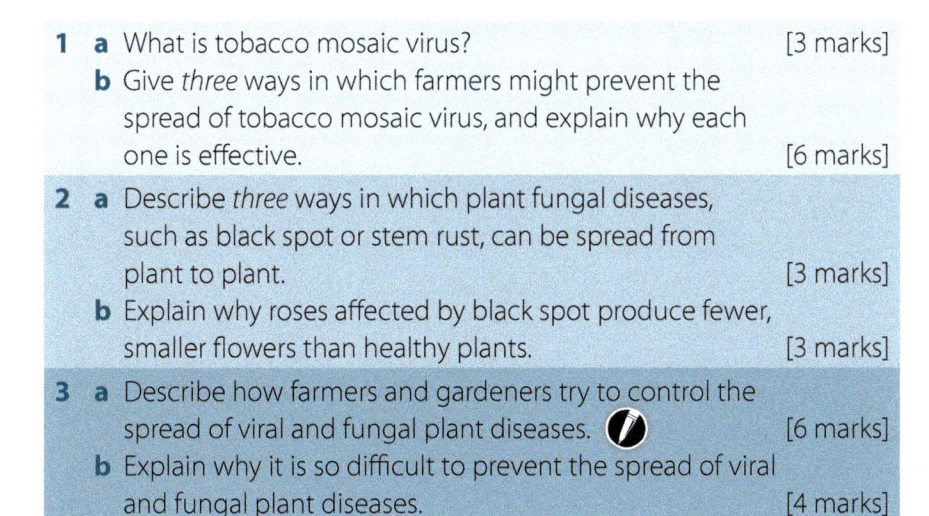

Figure 2 *Roses are beautiful flowers, but fungal black spot infections weaken the plant and reduce the number of flowers. Similar fungal diseases weaken and destroy crop plants around the world*

Key points
- Communicable diseases in plants such as tobacco mosaic virus or rose black spot can be spread by viruses or spores in the air, in water, or by direct contact between diseased tissue and healthy plants.
- Communicable diseases in plants can be reduced or prevented by methods including:
  - removing and destroying infected plants or parts of plants
  - washing hands and tools after handling infected plants
  - planting plants a good distance apart to avoid contact and to increase air flow between them
  - watering roots, not leaves, to avoid spreading pathogens and because fungal spores only germinate when wet
  - using a fungicide to prevent fungal diseases, applied in advance of the warm, wet conditions that encourage fungal growth.

1 a What is tobacco mosaic virus? [3 marks]
  b Give *three* ways in which farmers might prevent the spread of tobacco mosaic virus, and explain why each one is effective. [6 marks]
2 a Describe *three* ways in which plant fungal diseases, such as black spot or stem rust, can be spread from plant to plant. [3 marks]
  b Explain why roses affected by black spot produce fewer, smaller flowers than healthy plants. [3 marks]
3 a Describe how farmers and gardeners try to control the spread of viral and fungal plant diseases. [6 marks]
  b Explain why it is so difficult to prevent the spread of viral and fungal plant diseases. [4 marks]

2.6.10 Chlorophyll and chromatography

Learning objectives

After this topic, you should know:
- about chlorophyll and other plant pigments
- how chromatography works.

Synoptic links
You learnt about photosynthesis in Topics 2.6.6, 2.6.7, and 2.6.8.

Chlorophyll is the name given to the green substance found in chloroplasts in the cells of the leaves and stems of plants. It has been described as a miracle molecule. This green chemical transfers energy from the light of the Sun to the bonds of glucose and oxygen molecules during the process of photosynthesis. But what *is* chlorophyll, and how have scientists found out about this amazing molecule?

Plant pigments

Scientists have discovered that the green substance we call chlorophyll is often made up of several different pigments, each absorbing a different wavelength of light. What's more, not all of the pigments found in plant leaves are green. Some leaves appear red or yellow all year round, but they can still photosynthesise. Many deciduous plants have leaves that turn beautiful shades of red, orange, yellow, or brown in the autumn before they fall off the tree.

The discovery of the existence of these different plant pigments has been made possible using **chromatography**. This is a widely used technique for separating mixtures. It can be used to show whether a substance is pure or not – in other words, whether it contains one single substance.

Carrying out paper chromatography

One technique that is used to separate (and identify) substances from mixtures in solution is paper chromatography. It works because some compounds in a mixture will dissolve better than others in the solvent chosen (Figure 2).

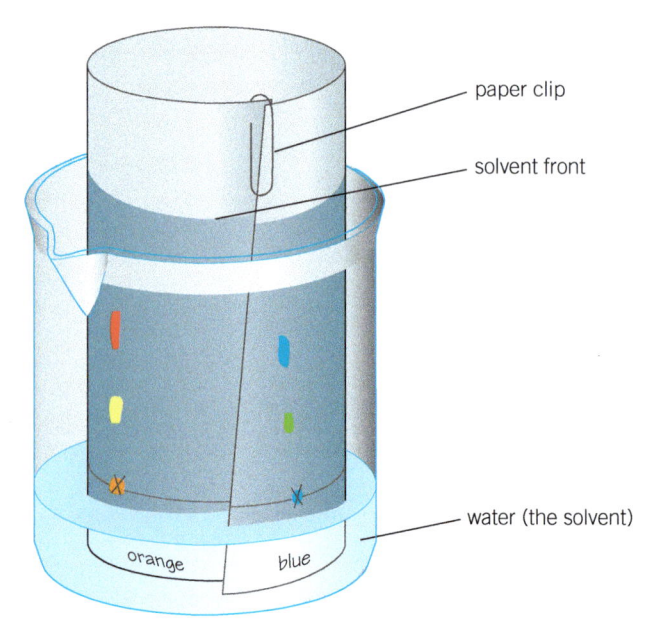

Figure 1 *The green colour of these leaves comes from chlorophyll*

Synoptic link
You will learn more about the use of chromatography to help identify unknown substances in Topic 2.6.11.

Figure 2 *A chromatogram is a paper record of the separation of a mixture. If the components of the mixture are not coloured, you can sometimes spray the chromatogram with a detecting agent that colours the components to reveal their positions on the paper*

■ 2.6 Plants and photosynthesis

A capillary tube is used to dab a spot of the solution on a pencil line near the bottom of a sheet of absorbent chromatography paper. The paper is then placed in a solvent at the bottom of a beaker or tank. The solvent (called the **mobile phase**) is allowed to soak up the paper (called the **stationary phase**), running past the spot of mixture. Different solvents can be used to maximise separation.

Detecting dyes in food colourings
In this experiment you can make a chromatogram to analyse various food colourings.

Set up the experiment, as shown in Figures 2 and 3.

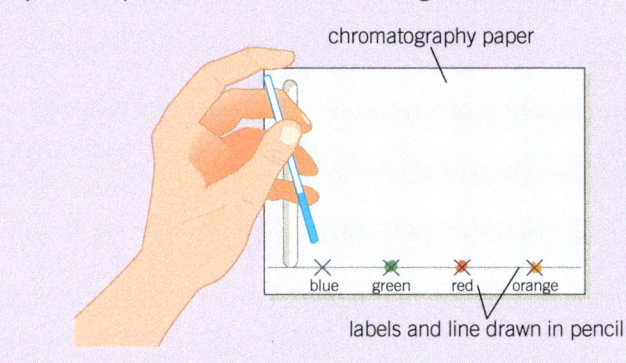

Figure 3 *Setting up a chromatogram*

- What can you deduce from your chromatography experiment?

Separating the components of chlorophyll
Collect some green plant matter in a mortar and add a spatula of washed sand. This will help to extract the coloured substances from the plant matter as you grind it up. Add a little ethanol and grind the mixture using a pestle. The more concentrated you can make the coloured solution, the better the results on your chromatogram will be.

Use a capillary tube to transfer a spot of the coloured solution to a strip of chromatography paper.

Run your chromatogram in a solvent of ethanol, dry it, and record your results.

Safety: Ethanol is highly flammable and harmful. Keep away from naked flames.

1 Describe a method to separate the dyes in coloured inks. [4 marks]
2 *Chlorophyll is a green pigment used in photosynthesis in plants.* Explain why this statement is not scientifically accurate. [3 marks]
3 A paper chromatogram from a mixture of two substances, **A** and **B**, was obtained using a solvent of propanone. Substance **B** was found to travel further up the paper than substance **A**. Suggest an explanation for the chromatogram. [3 marks]

Go further
There are other ways to analyse mixtures by chromatography. In thin-layer chromatography (TLC) the solvent runs up a solid pasted onto a microscope slide. In gas chromatography (GC) the substances in the mixture are vaporised and carried by a gas through a long, coiled tube packed with a solid.

Key points
- Leaves contain chlorophyll and a number of other pigments that can be separated and identified by chromatography.
- Chromatography can be used to separate mixtures and can give information to help identify substances.
- Paper chromatography separates mixtures of substances dissolved in a solvent as they move up a piece of chromatography paper. The different substances are separated because of their different relative attraction for the solvent used and for the paper.

2.6.11 Analysing chromatograms

Learning objectives

After this topic, you should know:

- how chromatography can be used for distinguishing pure substances from impure substances
- how to interpret chromatograms
- how to determine R_f values from chromatograms.

Scientists have many instruments that they can use to identify unknown compounds. Many of these are more sensitive, automated versions of techniques we use in school laboratories, such as paper chromatography. For example, chromatography can be used to separate and identify mixtures of amino acids. The amino acids are colourless but appear as purple spots on the paper when sprayed with a locating agent and dried. Chromatography can also be used to separate the different pigments in a plant leaf, as shown in Figure 1.

How does chromatography work?

Chromatography always involves a mobile phase and a stationary phase. The mobile phase moves through the stationary phase, carrying the components of the mixture under investigation with it. Each component in the mixture will have a different attraction for the mobile phase and the stationary phase. A substance with stronger forces of attraction between itself and the mobile phase than between itself and the stationary phase will be carried a greater distance in a given time. Substances with a stronger force of attraction for the stationary phase will not travel as far in the same time.

In paper chromatography the mobile phase is the solvent chosen and the stationary phase is the paper. In Figure 1, the yellow pigment from the chlorophyll has the strongest attraction to the solvent, and the green pigment has the strongest attraction to the paper.

Given an unknown organic solution, chromatography can usually tell you if it is a single compound or a mixture. If the unknown sample is a mixture of compounds, there will probably be more than one spot formed on the chromatogram. On the other hand, a single spot indicates the possibility of a pure substance.

Figure 1 *Chromatograms like this can be used to separate the different pigments in a plant leaf. As you can see, they are not all green!*

Synoptic link

To remind yourself about how to set up a paper chromatogram, look back at Topic 2.6.10.

Identifying unknown substances using chromatography

Once the compounds in a mixture have been separated using chromatography, they can be identified. You can compare spots on the chromatogram with others obtained from known substances:

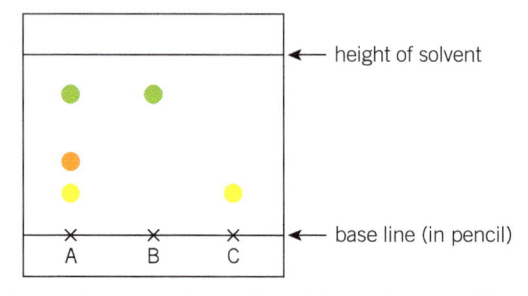

Figure 2 *This chromatogram shows that A is a mixture of three substances, B and C plus one other unknown substance*

2.6 Plants and photosynthesis

Following the chromatography in Figure 2, mixture A still has one substance left unknown. A scientist making the chromatogram often does not know which pure compounds to include in their experiment to make a positive identification. It is also not practical to store actual chromatograms or their images, even on computer. Matching these would mean every variable that affects a chromatogram would need to be exactly the same to make valid comparisons.

It is far more effective to measure data taken from any chromatogram of the unknown sample that can be matched against a database. So the data from a chromatogram is presented as an R_f (**retention factor**) value. This is a ratio, calculated by dividing the distance a spot travels up the paper (measured to the centre of the spot) by the distance the solvent front travels:

$$R_f = \frac{\text{distance moved by substance}}{\text{distance moved by solvent}}$$

As the number generated in the calculation is a ratio, it does not matter how long you run your chromatography experiment or what quantities you use. For comparisons against an R_f database to be valid, you just have to ensure that the solvent, stationary phase, and temperature used are the same as those quoted in the database or book of data. Look at Figure 3 to see how to get the measurements to calculate R_f values.

Chromatography and finding R_f values

Using a capillary tube, a pencil, a pipette, a solvent, boiling tubes, and narrow strips of chromatography paper, find out the R_f values of the different compounds in the leaves provided.

- Present your evidence clearly. Include your chromatogram, calculations, and an evaluation.

Worked example

Find the R_f value of compounds **A** and **B**, extracted from a plant, using the chromatogram in Figure 3, below.

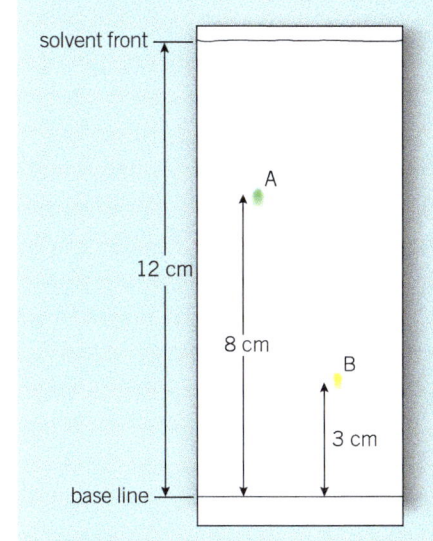

Figure 3 *The R_f value of an unknown substance, in a particular solvent at a given temperature, can be compared with values in a database to identify the substance*

Solution

The R_f value of **A** = $\frac{8}{12}$ = 0.67

The R_f value of **B** = $\frac{3}{12}$ = 0.25

---

1 Describe in detail how we can positively identify the dyes mixed to make a food colouring from its chromatogram. [5 marks]

2 What is the R_f value of substance **X** (one of the substances extracted from chlorophyll) in Figure 4?

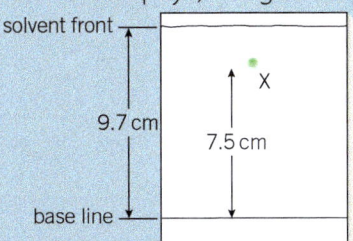

Figure 4 [1 mark]

3 The R_f values of two substances, **Y** and **Z**, were taken from a chromatogram run in a 50% water, 50% ethanol solvent at 20 °C. The R_f value of **Y** was 0.54 and that of **Z** was 0.79. What can you deduce about **Y** and **Z** from these values, and how could you use them to identify **Y** and **Z**? [3 marks]

4 In order to positively identify a compound from a chromatogram, explain why the solvent, stationary phase, and temperature must be the same as those used to generate the R_f values in a database. [4 marks]

Key points

- Chromatography can be used to distinguish pure from impure substances.
- Scientists can analyse unknown substances in solution using paper chromatography.
- R_f values can be measured and matched against databases to identify specific substances.
- $R_f = \dfrac{\text{distance moved by substance}}{\text{distance moved by solvent}}$

2.6 Plants and photosynthesis

Summary questions

1. **a** Complete the word equation for photosynthesis.

   _____ + water $\xrightarrow{light}$ glucose + _____ [2 marks]

   b Geraniums are green plants that grow in gardens.
   - **i** Where does the light for photosynthesis in the geranium come from? [1 mark]
   - **ii** How does the geranium absorb this light? [2 marks]

   c On a cold morning, the rate of photosynthesis in the geranium plant is very slow. Suggest which factors may be limiting and why. [2 marks]

   d Some of the glucose produced by the geranium plant is used for respiration. Give *three* other ways in which the plant uses the glucose produced in photosynthesis. [3 marks]

   e Plants grown in pure water will die, even if they are supplied with light, carbon dioxide, and a growing temperature of around 20 °C. Explain why this happens. [4 marks]

2. The figures in the table below show the mean growth of two sets of oak seedlings. One set was grown in 85% full sunlight and the other set in only 35% full sunlight.

Year	Mean height of seedlings grown in 85% full sunlight in cm	Mean height of seedlings grown in 35% full sunlight in cm
2000	12	10
2001	16	12.5
2002	18	14
2003	21	17
2004	28	20
2005	35	21
2006	36	23

   a Plot a graph to show the growth of both sets of oak seedlings. [4 marks]

   b Using what you know about photosynthesis and limiting factors, explain the difference in the growth of the two sets of seedlings. [4 marks]

3. Plants make food in one organ and take up water from the soil in another organ. But both the food and the water are needed all over the plant.

   a Where do plants make their food? [2 marks]

   b Where do plants take in water? [1 mark]

   c Describe how you would demonstrate that photosynthesis had taken place in the leaves of a plant. [6 marks]

4. Palm oil is made from the fruit of oil palms. Large areas of tropical rainforest have been destroyed to make space to plant these oil palms, which grow rapidly.

   a Explain why you think that oil palms can grow rapidly in the conditions that support a tropical rainforest. [3 marks]

   b Where does the oil in the oil palm fruit come from? [1 mark]

   c What is it used for in the plant? [2 marks]

5. **H** The table below shows the yields of some different plants grown in Bengal. The yields per acre when grown hydroponically (in water with a balance of minerals supplied) and when grown normally in the field are compared.

Name of crop	Hydroponic crop per acre in kg	Ordinary soil crop per acre in kg
wheat	3629	2540
rice	5443	408
potatoes	70760	8164
cabbage	8164	5896
peas	63503	11340
tomatoes	181437	9072
lettuce	9525	4080
cucumber	12700	3175

   a Explain why yields are always higher when crops are grown hydroponically. [2 marks]

   b Which crops would it be most economically sensible to grow hydroponically? Explain your choice. [4 marks]

   c Which crops would it be least sensible to grow hydroponically? Explain your choice. [3 marks]

   d State the benefits and problems associated with growing crops in:
   - **i** the natural environment [3 marks]
   - **ii** an artificially manipulated environment. [3 marks]

6. What is the R_f value of plant compound **A** in **Figure 1**? [1 mark]

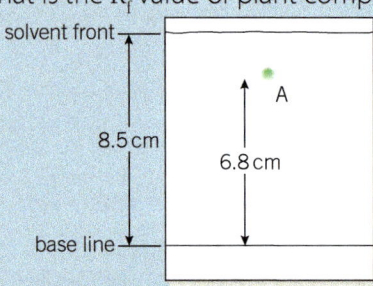

   Figure 1 (solvent front to A: 6.8 cm; solvent front to base line: 8.5 cm)

2.6 Plants and photosynthesis

Practice questions

01 A student used paper chromatography to study the pigments in a plant leaf.
Figure 1 shows the student's results with some of the measurements labelled.

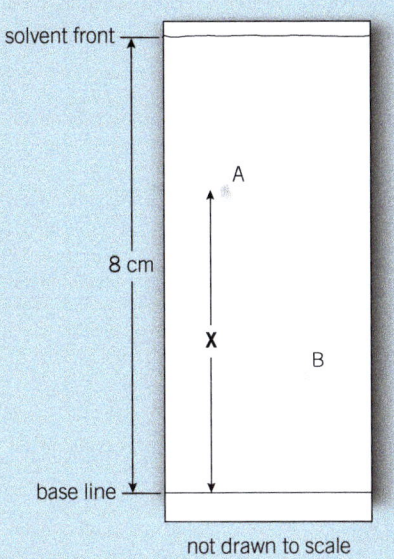

Figure 1

The R_f value for pigment **A** is 0.60.
Use the following equation to calculate the value of **X** (distance moved by pigment **A**) in **Figure 1**.

$$R_f = \frac{\text{distance moved by substance}}{\text{distance moved by solvent}}$$
[3 marks]

02 Meristem tissue is a specific tissue found in plants.

02.1 Where would you find meristem tissue in a plant? [1 mark]

02.2 Meristem cells can be cloned to produce plants such as strawberries.
Give **two** advantages of cloning strawberry plants using meristem cells. [2 marks]

03 A student investigated transpiration to find out the mean rate of water uptake in one type of plant. The student used a potometer to measure the rate of water uptake.
In the investigation the student measured the distance moved by an air bubble to give a measure of the volume of water taken up by the plant.
Figure 2 shows the three different plant shoots and the apparatus used.
The student measured the rate of water uptake by plant shoots **A**, **B**, and **C** and calculated a mean. Each test was carried out in the same environmental conditions.

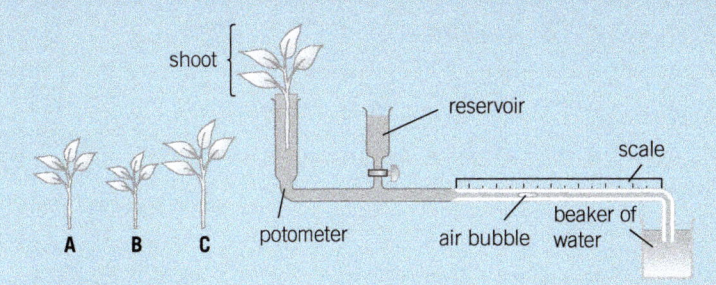

Figure 2

03.1 Give **one** way in which the student could improve their investigation to give valid results. [1 mark]

03.2 Another student investigated how the rate of water uptake changed when a fan was blowing on the plant.
Table 1 shows the student's results.

Table 1

Fan speed	Distance of the air bubble in mm — At the start	Distance of the air bubble in mm — After 10 minutes	Distance moved during 10 minutes in mm	Rate of transpiration in mm/h
no fan	0.0	2.0	2.0	12.0
slow	2.0	5.0	3.0	18.0
medium	1.0	6.0	5.0	30.0
high	3.0	12.0		

Calculate the rate of water uptake in mm per hour for the high fan speed result in **Table 1**. [2 marks]

03.3 Using the data in **Table 1**, write a conclusion showing how the rate of water uptake is affected. [1 mark]

03.4 **Figure 3** shows the transpiration rate of the same species of plant in two different environments.

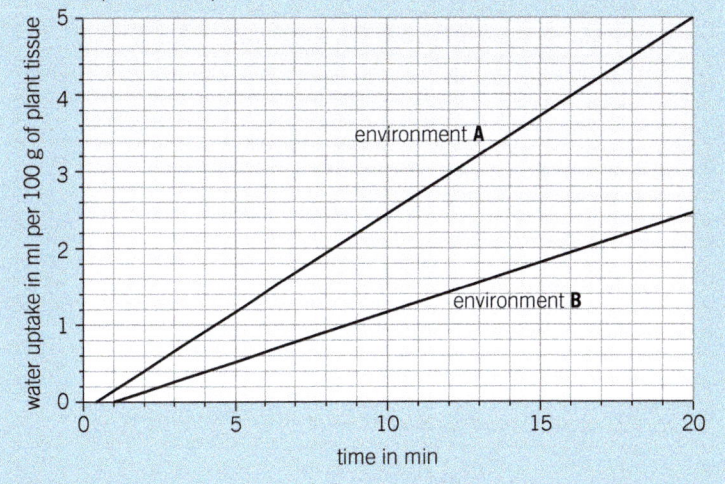

Figure 3

The water uptake in environment **A** is higher than in environment **B**.
Other than differences in wind speed, suggest **two** reasons why. [2 marks]

127

Unit 2 in context
Fighting fungi

Apart from the inconvenience of athlete's foot or thrush, most of the time human fungal diseases do not cause serious problems for most people. But fungi cause devastating diseases in plants, and this can have an enormous impact on people. Biologists are very aware of the massive impact of fungal diseases and lots of research is going on to try to tackle some of the biggest problems.

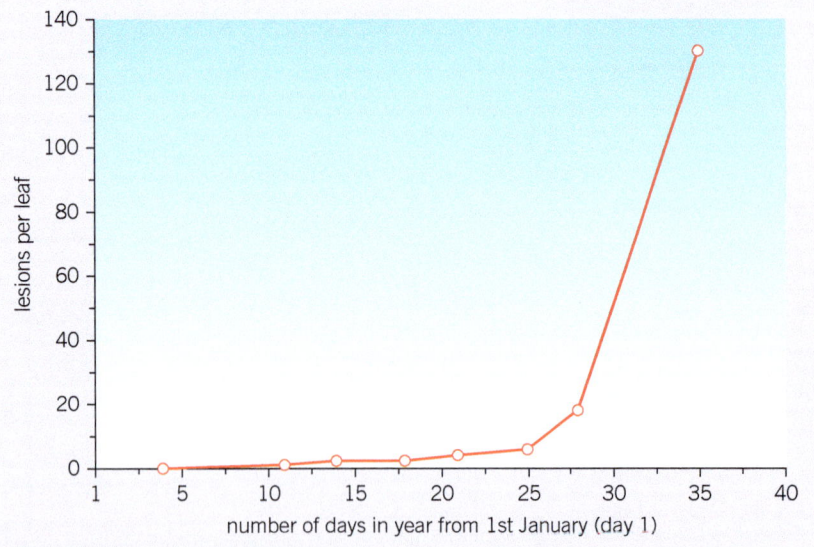

Figure 1 *The development of fungal disease grey leaf spot in maize*

Fungi vs. crops

Research published in the journal *Nature* suggests that 600 million more people could be fed each year if we could stop the spread of fungal diseases in the world's five most important food crops. These are rice, wheat, maize, potatoes, and soybeans. The research, carried out by teams at Imperial College London, the University of Oxford, and some US institutions, highlighted a number of problems:

- Fungal infections currently destroy at least 125 million tonnes of these food crops each year. This food could mean the difference between life and death for people on the edge of starvation.
- The damage caused by fungi to rice, wheat, and maize alone costs global agriculture around $60 billion per year – so fungal diseases affect the global economy as well as food security and global health.
- The incidence of fungal diseases in plants has been increasing since the mid-20th century, probably due to increased ease of global travel and trade.

Scientists have estimated that if the five main food crops were all hit by fungal diseases in the same year, 900 million tonnes of food crops would be destroyed and over 4.2 billion people would be at risk of starvation.

Fungi vs. trees

Even trees, the biggest land organisms, are not immune to attack by fungi. Dutch elm disease is a fungus spread by beetles that has almost wiped out elm trees in the UK. It has killed over 60 million British elm trees in the last hundred years. The fungus blocks the xylem vessels of the tree, so water cannot be transported up from the soil to the branches and the leaves, which die.

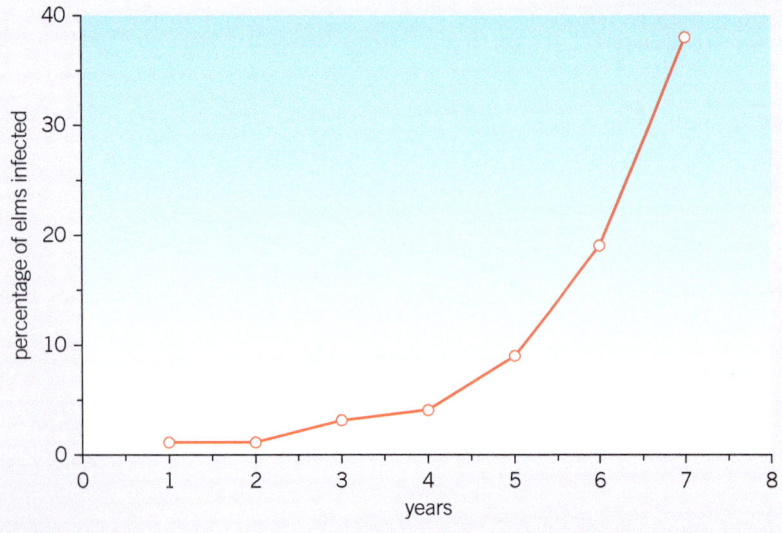

Figure 2 *The spread of Dutch elm disease through an elm population after initial infection*

Now it is feared that another plant fungal disease called ash dieback will destroy ash trees all over Europe. Some ash trees seem to be immune to the fungus that causes ash dieback, but sadly another killer, a beetle called the emerald ash borer, is likely to kill any ash trees that escape the fungus. The fungus blocks the transport vessels of the tree, whilst the beetle cuts through them. The beetle larvae eat their way around the trees under the bark, breaking the xylem columns and destroying the layer of living phloem vessels. Tree death is swift and the beetles are spreading fast throughout Europe, although they haven't reached the UK yet.

Fighting back

Plant scientists are fighting back against the fungi that threaten our future. Professor Sarah Gurr at Exeter University is one of many scientists who are aware of the potential effects of climate change and apathy on food security. They are looking for ways to meet the fungal challenge to our plants, through:

- more research into pathogen biology
- development of new antifungal chemicals
- development of mechanisms that can be used in developing countries as well as in countries like the UK to detect and monitor the spread of fungal pathogens
- breeding strains of plants that are more resistant to fungal diseases, or genetically modifying plants to be resistant to fungal attack
- increased awareness of the threat plant diseases pose to global food security
- the training of a new generation of scientists in epidemiology, climate forecasting, global pathogen surveillance, host–pathogen biology, genetic modification, and the development of antifungals.

Figure 3 *Even large trees like this elm can be destroyed by plant fungal diseases*

1 **a** What are the *five* main global food crops? [1 mark]
   b What is the predicted increase between the current level of crop loss due to fungal infections and the estimated loss if all five main global food crops were affected by fungal infections at once? [4 marks]
2 **a** What do Dutch elm disease and ash dieback have in common? [1 mark]
   b What is the common factor in the death of trees as a result of attack by Dutch elm disease, ash dieback, and the emerald ash borer beetle? [2 marks]
   c Why is it so difficult to stop these diseases spreading? [3 marks]
3 State *three* ways in which scientists suggest that fungal diseases may be prevented from causing major food shortages in future. For each, give a reason why it might help. [6 marks]

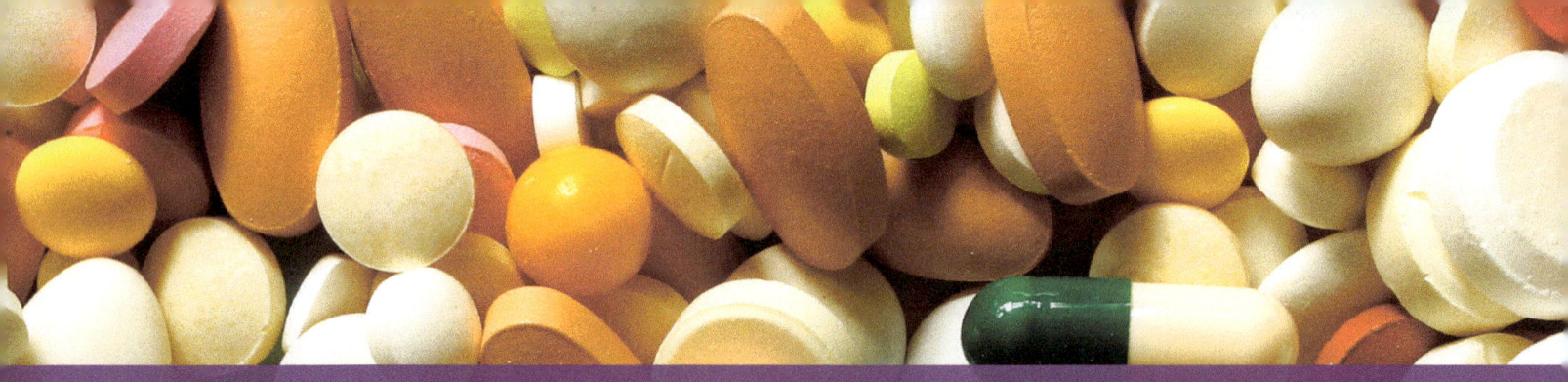

3 Interactions with the environment

Organisms live in a changing environment. They are constantly bombarded with different stimuli. Factors such as the levels of ionising radiation reaching the surface of the Earth from the Sun, the amount of food available, and the number and type of disease-causing organisms in the environment change from day–to–day. Humans, like all other living things, find themselves in an ever changing world. They have to interact with their changing environment to survive.

In this unit, you will look at how environmental factors cause a range of non-communicable diseases in people. You will look at the ways in which the body interacts with both the internal and external environment through the nervous system and the hormonal system, detecting changes and responding to them. You will learn about the properties and effects of different types of radiation and the associated risks to living things. Finally, you will discover how pathogenic microorganisms cause diseases and investigate some of the ways in which people prevent, treat, and cure both communicable and non-communicable diseases.

Key questions
- What are communicable and non-communicable diseases?
- How does the human body detect and respond to changes in the internal and external environment?
- What is radiation?
- How does exposure to ionising radiation increase the risk of developing cancer?
- How do pathogens cause disease?
- Why is it so important to develop new medicines and test them thoroughly?

Making connections
- A range of environmental factors affects the health of your heart and lungs. Look back to **Chapter 2.5** to remind yourself of how these body systems work when they are healthy.
- Your risk of getting many diseases is affected by the genetic information you inherited from your parents. You will discover more about inheritance in **Chapter 4.12**.
- You will learn more about the interaction of radiation with matter when you learn about the greenhouse effect in **Chapter 4.10**.
- Your knowledge of how pathogens cause disease, of how antibiotics affect bacteria, and of the challenges of developing new drugs will help you to understand the significance of the evolution of antibiotic-resistant bacteria, explored in **Chapter 4.12**.

I already know...	I will learn...
the consequences of imbalances in the diet	how obesity increases the risk of non-communicable diseases including heart disease and Type 2 diabetes
the importance of bacteria in the human digestive system	the role of bacteria in communicable diseases and how the bacteria and viruses that cause gut diseases can be spread through contaminated water and food
the impact of exercise and smoking on the human gas exchange system	the impact of lifestyle factors including exercise, diet, alcohol, and smoking on the incidence of non-communicable diseases at local, national, and global levels
the process of reproduction in humans	the roles of hormones in human reproduction, including the menstrual cycle, and their roles in both contraception and infertility treatment
about light waves and the transmission of light through materials.	the absorption and emission of radiation, including radioactive decay, the penetration of different types of radiation, contamination, ionising radiation, and how exposure to ionising radiation increases the risk of mutation and cancer in organisms, including people.

3.7 Lifestyle and health
3.7.1 Health and disease

Learning objectives

After this topic, you should know:
- what health is
- the different causes of ill health
- how different types of disease interact.

Synoptic links

You will learn more about diseases in Chapter 3.9.

You will learn more about cancer in Topic 3.8.7.

You will learn more about scatter graphs in Maths skills MS 2g.

Your health is a state of physical, mental, and social well-being, not just an absence of disease. Disease occurs when the body doesn't work normally for whatever reason. This causes **symptoms** that are experienced by the person affected by the disease. Symptoms are at least partly based on individual perceptions. A cold or headache that might make you feel ill enough to stay in bed on a school day might be less likely to be a problem if you are on holiday.

What makes us ill?

Communicable (infectious) diseases (e.g., tuberculosis and flu) are caused by **pathogens** such as bacteria and viruses that can be passed from one person to another. **Non-communicable diseases** (e.g., heart disease and arthritis) cannot be transmitted from one person to another. A variety of factors can affect both physical and mental health. They include:

- Diet – if you do not get enough to eat, or the right nutrients, you may suffer from diseases ranging from starvation to anaemia or rickets. Too much food, or the wrong type of food, can lead to problems such as obesity, some cancers, or Type 2 diabetes.

- Stress – a certain level of stress is inevitable in everyone's life and is probably needed for our bodies to function properly. However, scientists are increasingly linking too much stress to an increased risk of developing a wide range of health problems. These include heart disease, certain cancers, and mental health problems (Figure 1).

- Life situations – these include:
    - the part of the world where you live
    - your gender
    - your financial status
    - your ethnic group
    - the levels of free healthcare provided where you live
    - how many children you have
    - local sewage and rubbish disposal.

People often have little or no control over their life situation, especially as children or young people. Yet such factors have a big effect on health and well-being and are responsible for many causes of ill health around the world. These include communicable diseases such as diarrhoeal diseases and malaria, through to non-communicable diseases such as heart disease and cancer.

The causes of diseases are not always easy to establish. For example, the data shown in Figure 1 are based on a reasonably large sample size, but the points are quite widely scattered. Whilst a line showing a possible **correlation** between stress and depression can be drawn, data like this suggests that a lot more research is needed if a causal link is to be established.

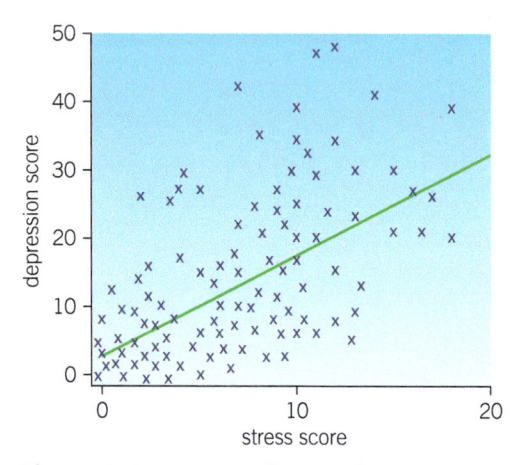

Figure 1 *Scatter graphs can show a correlation between stress and depression*

3.7 Lifestyle and health

How health problems interact

In this unit you will be looking at different types of diseases in isolation. It is important to remember that, in the real world, different diseases and health conditions happen at the same time. They interact and often one problem makes another worse. Here are a number of examples – you will learn more about the details of many of these conditions in later chapters.

- Viruses living in cells can trigger changes that lead to cancers – for example, the human papilloma virus can cause cervical cancer.
- The immune system of your body helps you destroy pathogens and get better. If there are defects in your immune system, it may not work effectively. This may be a result of your genetic makeup, poor nutrition, or infections such as HIV/AIDS. This means you will be more likely to suffer from other communicable diseases (Figure 2).
- Immune reactions initially caused by a pathogen, even something like the common cold, can trigger allergies to factors in the environment. These allergies may cause skin rashes, hives, or asthma.
- Physical and mental health are often closely linked. Severe physical ill health can lead to depression and other mental illness.
- Malnutrition is often linked to health problems including deficiency diseases, a weakened immune system, obesity, cardiovascular diseases, Type 2 diabetes, and cancer.

The interaction between different factors, including lifestyle, environment, and pathogens, is an important principle to remember as you look at different types of disease. It is not easy to find clear links between lifestyle factors and disease. People are complex organisms and their lives are very varied. To obtain meaningful results, scientists must carry out studies on thousands of people. This maximises the chances of identifying a causal effect for a particular factor, and minimises the effect of the many variations in people's lifestyles. Longitudinal studies, carried out over many years with the same large group of people, give particularly useful results.

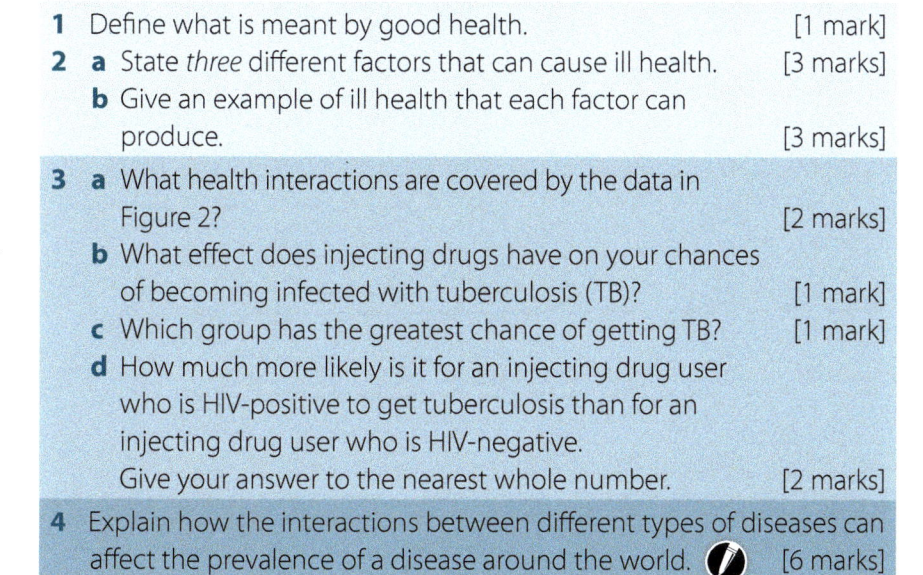

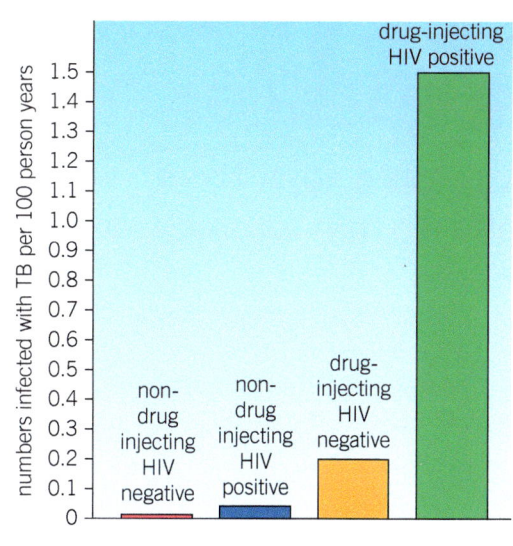

Figure 2 *Data collected in the Netherlands looks at the interaction between a number of health problems including HIV status and drug use in the incidence of tuberculosis (TB) in Amsterdam*

1. Define what is meant by good health. [1 mark]
2. **a** State *three* different factors that can cause ill health. [3 marks]
   b Give an example of ill health that each factor can produce. [3 marks]
3. **a** What health interactions are covered by the data in Figure 2? [2 marks]
   b What effect does injecting drugs have on your chances of becoming infected with tuberculosis (TB)? [1 mark]
   c Which group has the greatest chance of getting TB? [1 mark]
   d How much more likely is it for an injecting drug user who is HIV-positive to get tuberculosis than for an injecting drug user who is HIV-negative. Give your answer to the nearest whole number. [2 marks]
4. Explain how the interactions between different types of diseases can affect the prevalence of a disease around the world. [6 marks]

Key points

- Health is a state of physical, mental, and social well-being.
- Diseases, both communicable and non-communicable, are major causes of ill health.
- Other factors including diet, stress, and life situations may have a profound effect on both mental and physical health.
- Different types of diseases may and often do interact.

3.7.2 Non-communicable diseases

Learning objectives

After this topic, you should know:
- what is meant by a non-communicable disease
- what a lifestyle factor is
- how scientists consider risk
- the human and financial costs involved
- what a causal mechanism is.

Only 3 of the top 10 killer diseases in the world in 2012 were communicable diseases – lower respiratory tract infections such as pneumonia, HIV/AIDS, and diarrhoeal diseases. The other seven were non-communicable diseases. These are diseases that are not infectious and affect people as a result of their genetic make-up, their lifestyle, and factors in their environment.

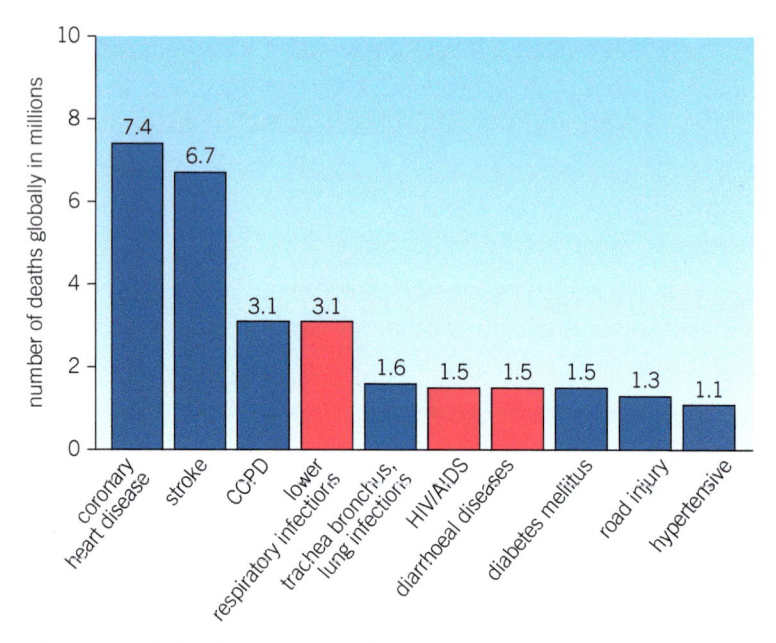

Figure 1 *The leading causes of death globally in 2012 (WHO). Non-communicable diseases (blue bars) contribute to more deaths than communicable diseases (pink bars)*

Risk factors for disease

A **risk** factor makes it more likely that you will be affected by a disease. There are many risk factors for disease, including the genes you inherit from your parents and your age, which you cannot change. Risk factors for disease also include:

- aspects of your lifestyle such as smoking, lack of exercise, or overeating
- substances that are present in the environment or in your body such as **ionising radiation**, UV light from the sun, or second-hand tobacco smoke.

Certain lifestyle factors, or environmental substances, have been shown to increase your risk of developing particular diseases. Risk factors for non-communicable diseases vary from one disease to another and some may affect more than one disease. Examples of risk factors for a number of non-communicable diseases include diet, obesity, fitness levels, smoking, drinking alcohol, and exposure to **carcinogens** in the environment such as ionising radiation. We have the power to influence, change, or remove many of these risk factors.

Synoptic links

You will learn more about the concept of risk and risk estimates in Topic 3.8.6.

For more help in interpreting correlations, see Maths skills MS 2g.

3.7 Lifestyle and health

Causal mechanisms

Scientists often see similarities in the patterns between non-communicable diseases such as cardiovascular disease or lung cancer with lifestyle factors such as lack of exercise or smoking. These similarities may suggest a link or relationship between the two, known as a **correlation**. However, a correlation does not prove that one thing is the cause of another (Figure 2).

It is useful to find correlations between lifestyle factors and particular diseases, but this is only the first step. Doctors and scientists then need to do lots of research to discover if there is a **causal mechanism**. A causal mechanism explains how one factor influences another through a biological process. If a causal mechanism can be demonstrated between two factors, there is a link between the two. For example, there is a clear causal link between smoking tobacco and lung cancer. Anyone can get lung cancer, but smoking increases that risk because you take carcinogens into your lungs.

The impact of non-communicable disease

Non-communicable diseases are the leading cause of death in the world. Even when they do not kill, every non-communicable disease has a human impact on the individual affected and their family. It will often have a financial cost as well if a wage-earner becomes ill and cannot work. Local communities often bear the cost of supporting people who are ill, whether formally through taxes or informally by taking care of affected families.

Diseases cost nations huge sums of money both in the expense of treating ill people and in the loss of money earned when large numbers of the population are ill. The global economy suffers, too, especially when diseases affect younger populations of working age. Non-communicable diseases affect far more people than communicable diseases, so they have the greatest effect at both human and economic levels.

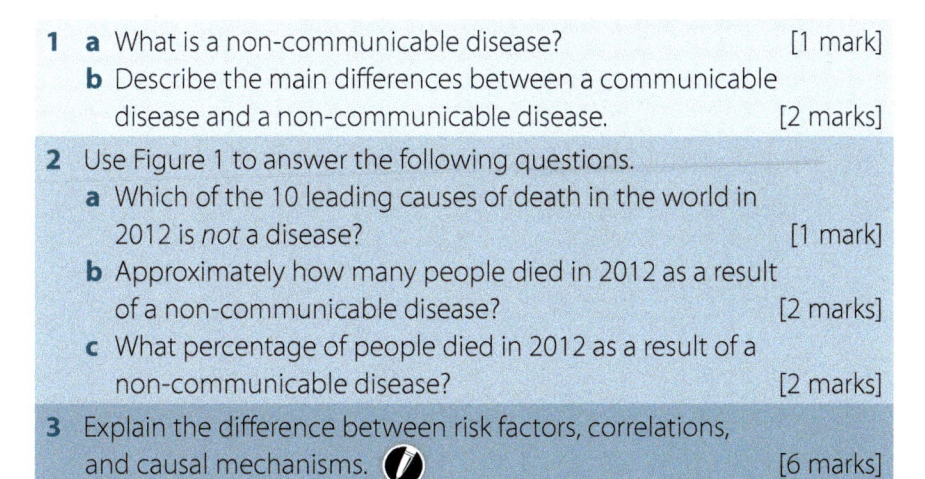

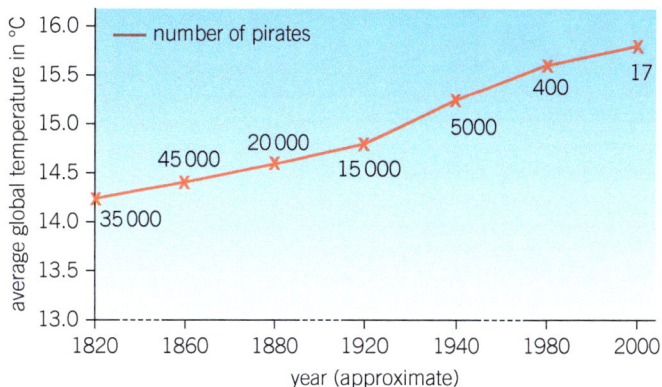

Figure 2 *Falling levels of piracy and rising global temperatures between the years 1820 and 2000 look to be closely linked on this very unscientific graph, but the apparent correlation does not mean that one causes the other*

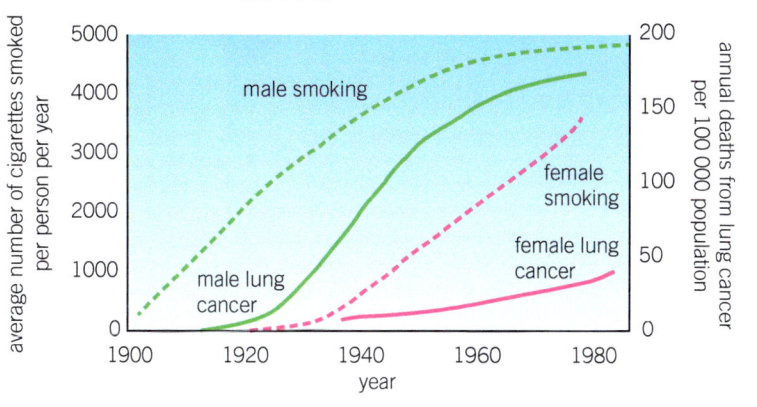

Figure 3 *This graph shows the number of deaths from lung cancer and the average number of cigarettes smoked. The solid lines relate to the right-hand scale, and the dotted lines relate to the left-hand scale. In the UK, 86% of lung cancer cases are linked to smoking*

1. **a** What is a non-communicable disease? [1 mark]
   b Describe the main differences between a communicable disease and a non-communicable disease. [2 marks]
2. Use Figure 1 to answer the following questions.
   a Which of the 10 leading causes of death in the world in 2012 is *not* a disease? [1 mark]
   b Approximately how many people died in 2012 as a result of a non-communicable disease? [2 marks]
   c What percentage of people died in 2012 as a result of a non-communicable disease? [2 marks]
3. Explain the difference between risk factors, correlations, and causal mechanisms. [6 marks]

Key points

- A non-communicable disease cannot be passed from one individual to another.
- Non-communicable diseases are the leading cause of death in the world.
- Risk factors are aspects of a person's lifestyle, or substances present in a person's body or environment, that have been shown to be linked to an increased rate of a disease.
- For some non-communicable diseases, a causal mechanism for some risk factors has been proven, but not others.

3.7.3 Smoking and the risk of disease

Learning objectives

After this topic, you should know:
- how smoking affects the risk of developing cardiovascular disease
- how smoking affects the risk of developing lung disease and lung cancer
- the effect of smoking on unborn babies.

Synoptic links

You can remind yourself of the structure of the breathing system in Topic 2.5.7 and of the way in which oxygen is carried around the body in Topic 2.5.4.

There are around 1.1 billion smokers worldwide, smoking around 6000 billion cigarettes each year, so smoking is big business. Every cigarette smoked contains tobacco leaves which, as they burn, produce around 4000 different chemicals that are inhaled into the throat, trachea, and lungs. At least 150 of these are linked to disease. Some of these chemicals are absorbed into the bloodstream to be carried around the body to the brain.

Nicotine and carbon monoxide

Nicotine is the addictive but relatively harmless drug found in tobacco smoke. It produces a sensation of calm, well-being, and 'being able to cope', which is why people like smoking. Unfortunately some of the other chemicals in tobacco smoke can cause lasting and often fatal damage to the body cells. Carbon monoxide is a poisonous gas found in tobacco smoke, which takes up some of the oxygen-carrying capacity of the blood. After smoking a cigarette, up to 10% of the smoker's red blood cells will be carrying carbon monoxide rather than oxygen. This can lead to a shortage of oxygen, one reason why many smokers get more breathless when they exercise than non-smokers.

Smoking during pregnancy

Oxygen shortage is a particular problem in pregnant women who smoke. During pregnancy a woman is carrying oxygen for her developing fetus as well as for herself. If the mother's blood is carrying carbon monoxide, the fetus may not get enough oxygen to grow properly. This can lead to premature births, low birthweight babies, and even stillbirths, where the baby is born dead (Figure 1). There are around 3500 stillbirths in the UK each year. Scientists estimate that around 20% result from the mother smoking during her pregnancy. In other words, 700 babies a year are born dead due to smoking.

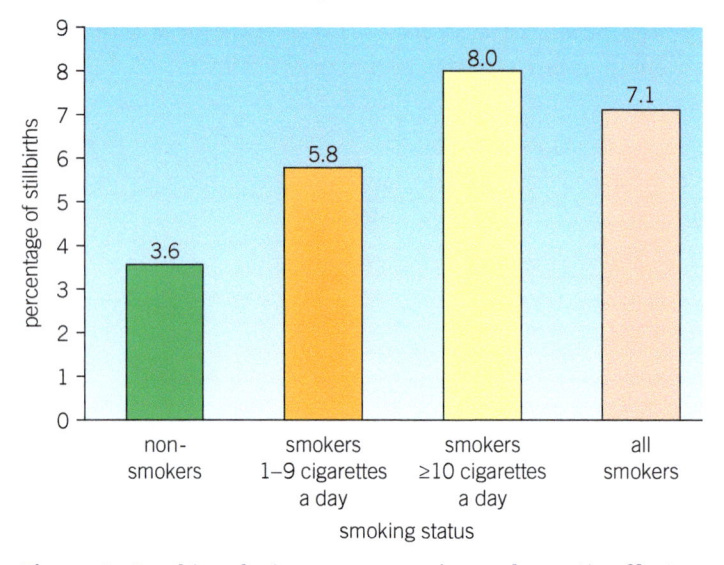

Figure 1 *Smoking during pregnancy has a dramatic effect on the risk of stillbirth*

3.7 Lifestyle and health

Carcinogens

The cilia in the trachea and bronchi that move mucus, bacteria, and dirt away from the lungs are anaesthetised by some of the chemicals in tobacco smoke. They stop working for a time, allowing dirt and pathogens down into the lungs and increasing the risk of infection. Mucus also builds up over time, causing coughing.

Other toxic compounds in tobacco smoke include tar. This is a sticky, black chemical that accumulates in the lungs, turning them from pink to grey. Along with other chemicals in the smoke, tar makes smokers much more likely to develop bronchitis (inflammation and infection of the bronchi). The build-up of tar in the delicate lung tissue can lead to a breakdown in the structure of the alveoli, causing chronic obstructive pulmonary disease (COPD). This reduces the surface area to volume ratio of the lungs, leading to severe breathlessness and eventual death.

Tar is also a carcinogen. It acts on the delicate cells of the lungs and greatly increases the risk of lung cancer developing. Tar also causes other cancers of the breathing system, for example, the throat, larynx, and trachea.

Smoking and the heart

The chemicals in tobacco smoke also affect the heart and blood vessels. Scientists have data showing that smokers are more likely to suffer from cardiovascular problems than non-smokers (Table 1). They have also worked out the mechanisms that show that this is a causal link, not just a correlation.

Smoking narrows the blood vessels in your skin, ageing it. Nicotine makes the heart rate increase, whilst other chemicals damage the lining of the arteries. This makes coronary heart disease more likely, and it increases the risk of clot formation. The mixture of chemicals in cigarette smoke also leads to an increase in blood pressure. This combination of effects increases the risk of suffering cardiovascular disease, including heart attacks and strokes.

> ### Synoptic links
> You will learn more about what happens when cancer develops in Topic 3.8.7.
>
> You can find out more about atherosclerosis and coronary heart disease and how it can be treated in Topics 3.7.6 and 3.7.7.

Table 1 *The number of deaths by cardiovascular disease (CVD) by average number of cigarettes smoked a day*

Cigarettes smoked per day	CVD deaths per 100 000 men per year
0	572
10 (range 1–14)	802
20 (range 15–24)	892
30 (range >24)	1025

1. **a** State *three* components of tobacco smoke. [3 marks]
   b State what effect the three components you gave in part **a** have on the human body. [3 marks]
2. **a** Display the data from Table 1 as a bar chart. [4 marks]
   b Summarise what this data shows. [1 mark]
   c Describe possible causal mechanisms to explain the trend shown in the data. [3 marks]
3. Summarise the information given on cigarette smoking increasing the risk of developing lung cancer, and explain how scientists think this effect is caused. [4 marks]
4. Many women continue to smoke when they are pregnant. Explain why smoking during pregnancy is so harmful. [5 marks]
5. Discuss the human and financial cost of smoking to individuals and to nations around the world. [6 marks]

> ### Key points
> - Smoking increases the risk of developing cardiovascular disease, lung cancer, and lung diseases such as bronchitis and COPD.
> - A fetus exposed to tobacco smoke has restricted oxygen, which can lead to premature birth, low birthweight, and even stillbirth.

3.7.4 Diet, exercise, and disease

Learning objectives

After this topic, you should know:
- the effect of diet and exercise on the development of obesity
- how diet and exercise affect the risk of developing cardiovascular disease
- that obesity is a risk factor for Type 2 diabetes.

Synoptic link

You will learn more about atherosclerosis and cardiovascular disease in Topics 3.7.6 and 3.7.7.

The evidence is building that your weight and the amount of exercise you take affects your risk of developing various diseases. These diseases can be life-changing and even life-threatening.

Diet, exercise, and obesity

If you eat more food than you need, the excess is stored as fat. You need some body fat to cushion your internal organs and to act as an energy store. However, over time, regularly eating too much food will make you overweight and then obese.

Carrying too much weight is often inconvenient and uncomfortable. Far worse, **obesity** can lead to serious health problems. These include high blood pressure and heart disease. They also include Type 2 diabetes, in which blood sugar levels cannot be controlled properly.

Exercise and health

The food you eat transfers energy from respiration to your muscles as they work, so the amount of exercise you do affects the amount of respiration in your muscles and the amount of food you need. People who exercise regularly are usually much fitter than people who take little exercise. People who take regular exercise make bigger muscles, up to 40% of their body mass, and muscle tissue needs much more energy to be transferred from food than body fat. People who exercise regularly have fitter hearts and bigger lungs than people who don't exercise. But exercise doesn't always mean time spent training or 'working out' in the gym. Walking to school, running around the house looking after small children, or doing a physically active job all count as exercise, too. Between 60% and 75% of your daily food intake is needed for the basic reactions that keep you alive. A further 10% is needed to digest your food, so only the final 15–30% is affected by your physical activity!

Scientists and doctors have collected lots of evidence that people who exercise regularly are less likely to develop cardiovascular disease than people who do not exercise (Figure 2). They are less likely to suffer from many other health problems too, including Type 2 diabetes (see later).

Here are some of the causal mechanisms that explain why exercise helps to keep you healthy:

- You will have more muscle tissue, increasing your metabolic rate, so you are less likely to be overweight. This reduces the risk of developing arthritis, diabetes, and high blood pressure, for example.
- Your heart will be fitter and will develop a better blood supply.

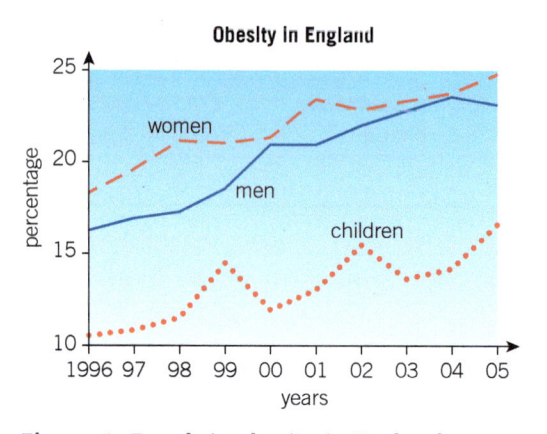

Figure 1 Trends in obesity in England between 1996 and 2005

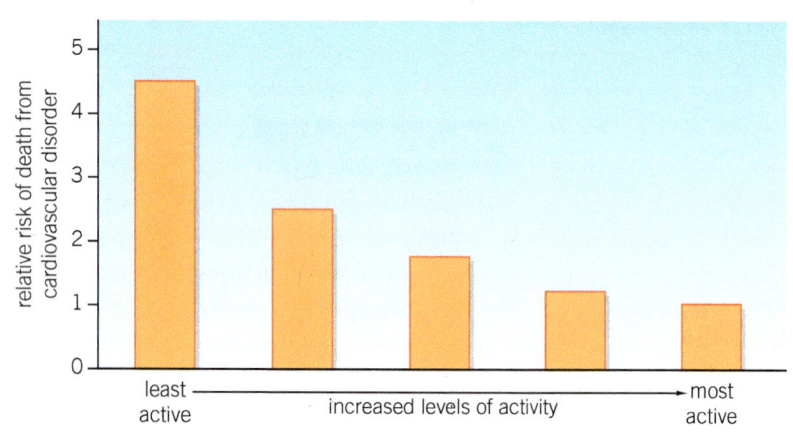

Figure 2 The effect of exercise on the risk of death associated with cardiovascular disease in men and women

■ 3.7 Lifestyle and health

- Regular exercise lowers your blood cholesterol levels and helps the balance of the different types of cholesterol. This reduces your risk of fatty deposits building up in your coronary arteries, so lowering your risk of heart disease and other health problems.

Obesity and Type 2 diabetes

In Type 2 diabetes, either your body doesn't make enough insulin to control your blood sugar levels or your cells stop responding to insulin. This can lead to problems with circulation, kidney function, and eyesight, which may eventually lead to death. Type 2 diabetes gets more common with age and some people have a genetic tendency to develop it. The evidence is now overwhelming that being overweight or obese and not doing much exercise are risk factors for Type 2 diabetes at any age (Figure 3). Type 2 diabetes is becoming increasingly common in young people. In 2016 over 4 million people in the UK had diabetes and 90% of those cases were Type 2. Fortunately most people can restore their normal blood glucose balance simply by eating a balanced diet with controlled amounts of carbohydrate, losing weight, and doing regular exercise.

Synoptic link

You will learn more about both Type 1 and Type 2 diabetes in Topics 3.7.9 and 3.7.10.

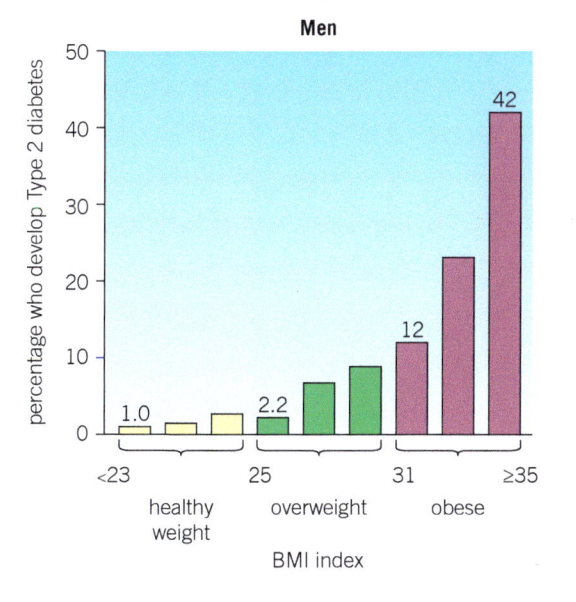

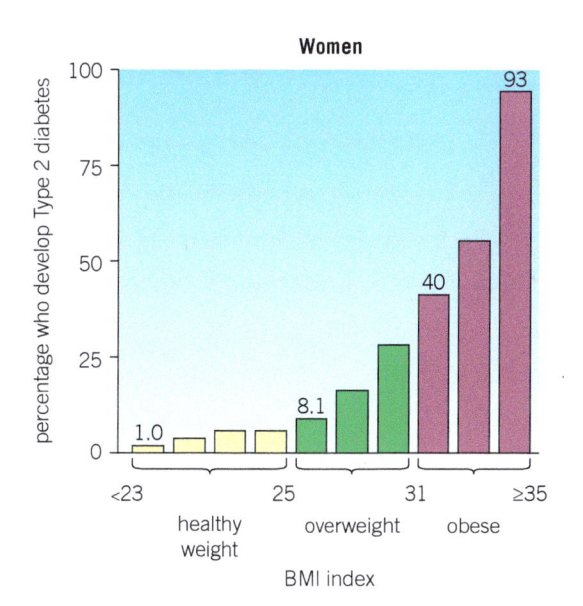

Figure 3 The effect of obesity on the risk of developing Type 2 diabetes in men and women

1 Explain why people who exercise regularly are usually healthier than people who take little exercise. [5 marks]

2 Exercise levels and obesity levels are often linked. Suggest reasons for this. [4 marks]

3 Based on the data in Figure 2, what is the relative risk of suffering cardiovascular disease in men who exercise least compared to men who exercise most? [2 marks]

4 Type 2 diabetes has been described as an epidemic. It was observed that if it is an epidemic, it is an epidemic that particularly affects women. Look at the data in Figures 1 and 3 and discuss these statements, taking into account the scientific evidence. Suggest both the reasons for the observations and how the 'epidemic' might be controlled. [6 marks]

Key points

- Diet affects your risk of developing cardiovascular and other diseases directly through cholesterol levels and indirectly through obesity.
- Exercise levels affect the likelihood of developing cardiovascular disease.
- Obesity is a strong risk factor for Type 2 diabetes.

3.7.5 Alcohol and other carcinogens

Learning objectives

After this topic, you should know:
- that alcohol affects liver and brain function
- that alcohol can affect unborn babies
- that alcohol is a carcinogen
- that many other agents act as carcinogens.

Study tip

Be clear that both ionising radiation and chemicals, such as the tar in tobacco smoke and alcohol, can act as carcinogens.

There are many different agents that increase your risk of developing non-communicable diseases. Some of these you may take into your body willingly, and some you may be unaware of.

Alcohol and health

Alcohol (ethanol) is a commonly used social drug in many parts of the world. It is poisonous but the liver can usually remove it before permanent damage or death results. Alcohol is also very addictive.

After an alcoholic drink, the ethanol is absorbed into the blood from the gut and passes easily into the body tissues, including the brain. It affects the nervous system, making thought processes, reflexes, and many reactions slower than normal. In small amounts alcohol makes people feel relaxed, cheerful, and reduces inhibitions. Larger amounts lead to lack of self-control and lack of judgement. If the dose of alcohol is too high, it can sometimes lead to unconsciousness, coma, and death.

Brain and liver damage

People can easily become addicted to alcohol, needing the drug to function, and they may drink heavily for many years. Their liver and brain may suffer long-term damage and eventually the alcohol can kill them (Figure 1):

- They may develop cirrhosis of the liver, a disease that destroys the liver tissue. The active liver cells are replaced with scar tissue that cannot carry out vital functions.
- Alcohol is a carcinogen so heavy drinkers are at increased risk of developing liver cancer. This usually spreads rapidly and is difficult to treat.
- Long-term heavy alcohol use also causes damage to the brain. In some alcoholics the brain becomes so soft and pulpy that the normal brain structures are lost and it can no longer function properly. This too can cause death.

The damage to the liver and brain associated with heavy drinking usually develops over years, but short bouts of very heavy drinking risk the same symptoms appearing relatively fast, even in young people.

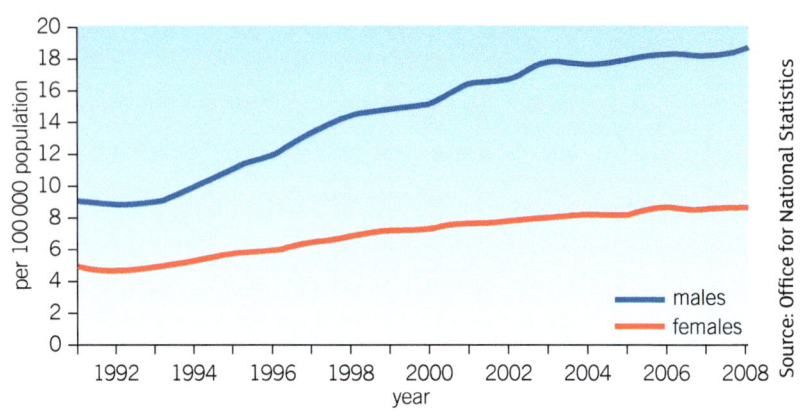

Figure 1 *This graph shows the increase in alcohol-related deaths in the UK between 1990 and 2008*

3.7 Lifestyle and health

Alcohol and pregnancy

If a pregnant woman drinks alcohol, it passes across the placenta into the developing baby. Miscarriage, stillbirths, premature births, and low birthweight are all risks linked to drinking alcohol during pregnancy. The developing liver cannot cope with alcohol, so the development of the brain and body of an unborn baby can be badly affected by it, especially in the early stages of pregnancy.

The baby may have facial deformities; problems with its teeth, jaw, or hearing; kidney, liver, and heart problems, and learning and other developmental problems. This is known as fetal alcohol syndrome (FAS). Doctors are not sure how much alcohol is safe during pregnancy. The best advice to avoid fetal alcohol syndrome is not to drink at all. The more you drink, the higher the risk to the unborn baby.

Ionising radiation

Ionising radiation in the form of different types of electromagnetic waves is a well-known carcinogen (risk factor for cancer). Radioactive materials are a source of ionising radiation. The radiation penetrates the cells and damages the chromosomes, causing mutations in the DNA. The more you are exposed to ionising radiation, the more likely it is that mutations will occur and that cancer will develop.

It is particularly dangerous when a source of ionising radiation is taken directly into your body. For example, breathing radioactive materials into the lungs enables the ionising radiation to penetrate directly into the cells. Well-known sources of ionising radiation include:

- Ultraviolet light from the sun – this increases the risk of skin cancers such as melanoma (protection includes sunscreen and sensible clothing).
- Radioactive materials found in the soil, water, and air (including radon gas in granite-rich areas such as Cornwall and the Pennines).
- Medical and dental X-rays.
- Accidents in nuclear power generation, especially accidents such as the one in Chernobyl, Ukraine in 1986, can spread ionising radiation over wide areas.

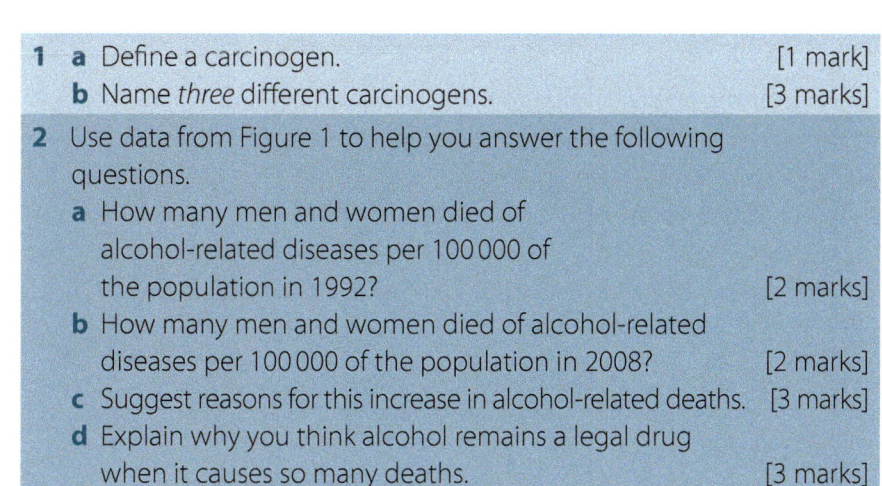

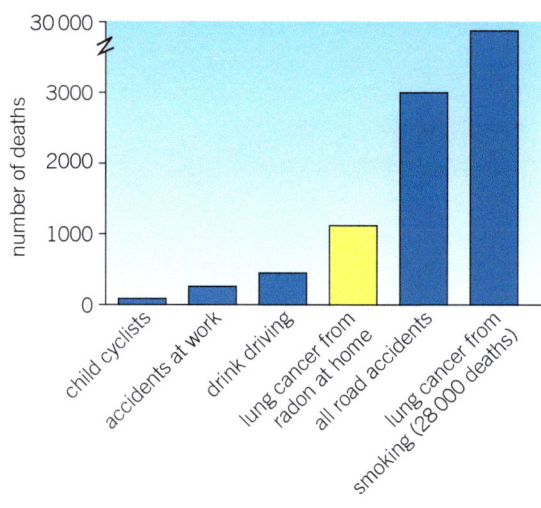

Figure 2 *In some areas of the country there are naturally high levels of a radioactive gas called radon in the environment. Living in a home contaminated by radon gas can increase your risk of dying from lung cancer, especially if you are also a smoker. This sounds dangerous, but, the number of people directly affected is small compared to the number who die each year as a result of smoking tobacco, or from road accidents*

1   a   Define a carcinogen. [1 mark]
    b   Name *three* different carcinogens. [3 marks]
2   Use data from Figure 1 to help you answer the following questions.
    a   How many men and women died of alcohol-related diseases per 100 000 of the population in 1992? [2 marks]
    b   How many men and women died of alcohol-related diseases per 100 000 of the population in 2008? [2 marks]
    c   Suggest reasons for this increase in alcohol-related deaths. [3 marks]
    d   Explain why you think alcohol remains a legal drug when it causes so many deaths. [3 marks]

Synoptic link

You will learn more about ionising radiation and its effect on human health in Chapter 3.8.

Key points

- Alcohol can damage the liver and cause cirrhosis and liver cancer.
- Alcohol can cause brain damage and death.
- Alcohol taken in by a pregnant woman can affect the development of her unborn baby.

3.7.6 Helping the heart

Learning objectives

After this topic, you should know:

- how leaky heart valves can be replaced
- how bypass surgery and stents can be used to treat cardiovascular disease
- what statins are used for.

Synoptic link

To remind yourself about the structure of the heart and how it works, look back at Topic 2.5.6.

The heart can be affected by a number of problems. Doctors, scientists, and engineers have worked out some amazing ways to help solve them.

Leaky valves

Heart valves have to withstand a lot of pressure. Over time they may start to leak or become stiff and not open fully, making the heart less efficient. People affected may become breathless and without treatment, will eventually die.

Doctors can operate and replace faulty heart valves. Mechanical valves are made of materials such as titanium and polymers. They last a very long time. However, with a mechanical valve you have to take medicine for the rest of your life to prevent your blood from clotting around it. Biological valves are based on valves taken from animals such as pigs or cattle, or even human donors. These work extremely well and the patient does not need any medication. However, they only last about 12–15 years.

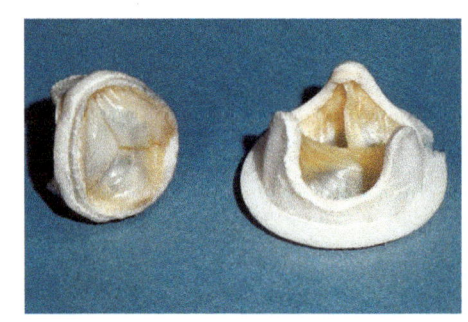

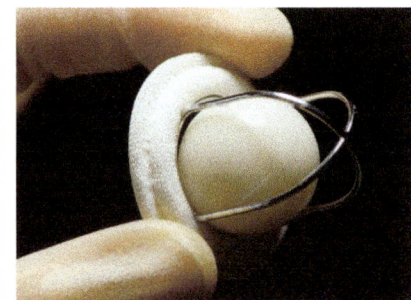

Figure 1 *Both biological (left) and mechanical (right) heart valves work very well. They each have advantages and disadvantages for the patient.*

Problems with blood flow through the heart

In coronary heart disease the coronary arteries that supply blood to the heart muscle become narrow. A common cause is a build-up of fatty material on the lining of the vessels. If the blood flow through the coronary arteries is reduced, the supply of oxygen to the heart muscle is also reduced. This can cause pain, a heart attack, and even death.

Doctors often solve the problem of coronary heart disease with a **stent** (Figure 2). A stent is a metal mesh that is placed in the artery. A tiny balloon is inflated to open up the blood vessel and the stent at the same time. The balloon is deflated and removed but the stent remains in place, holding the blood vessel open. As soon as this is done, the blood in the coronary artery flows freely. Doctors can put a stent in place without a general anaesthetic.

3.7 Lifestyle and health

Stents can be used to open up a blocked artery almost anywhere in the body. Many stents also release drugs to prevent the blood clotting, although some studies suggest that the benefits do not justify the additional expense.

Doctors can also carry out bypass surgery, replacing the narrow or blocked coronary arteries with bits of veins from other parts of the body. This works for badly blocked arteries where stents cannot help. The surgery is expensive and involves the risk associated with a general anaesthetic.

Increasingly doctors prescribe **statins** to anyone at risk from cardiovascular disease. They reduce blood cholesterol levels and this slows down the rate at which fatty material is deposited in the coronary arteries.

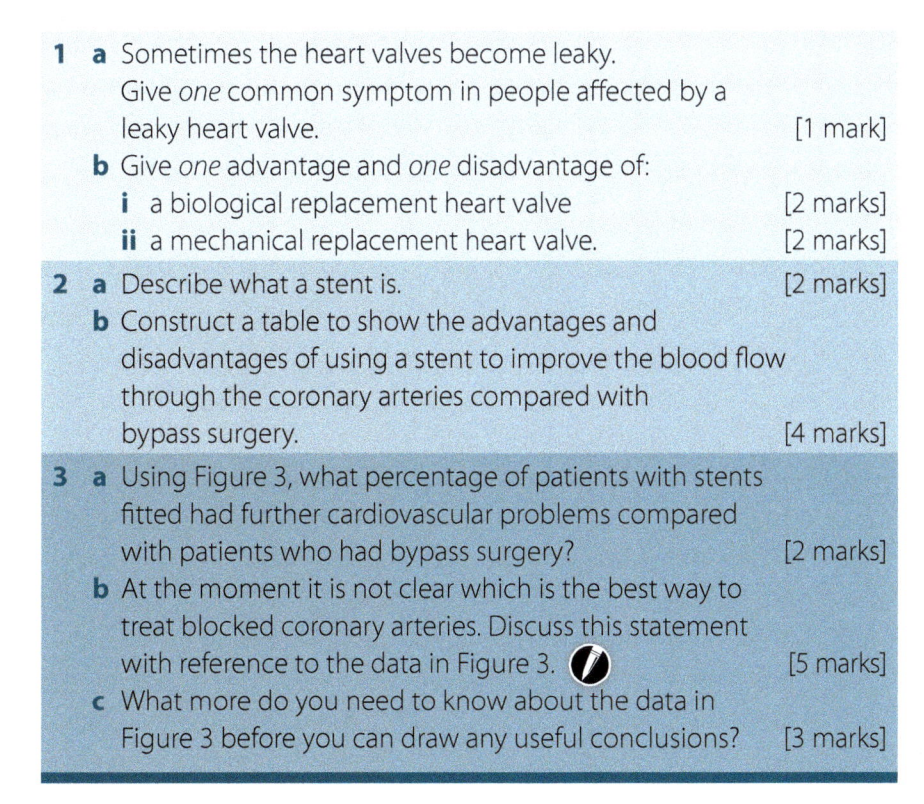

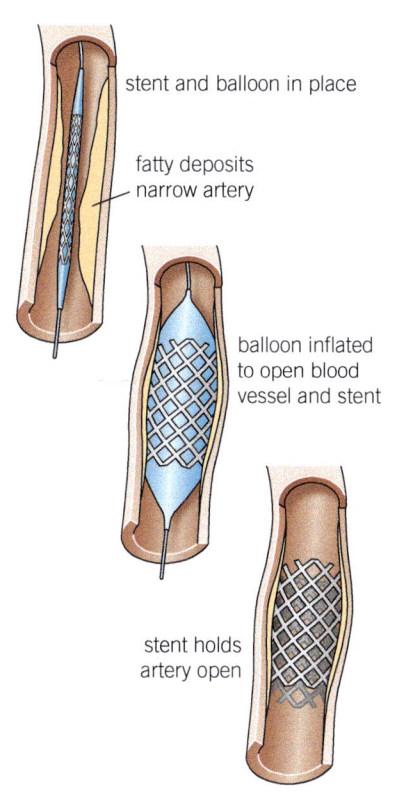

Figure 2 *A stent being positioned in an artery*

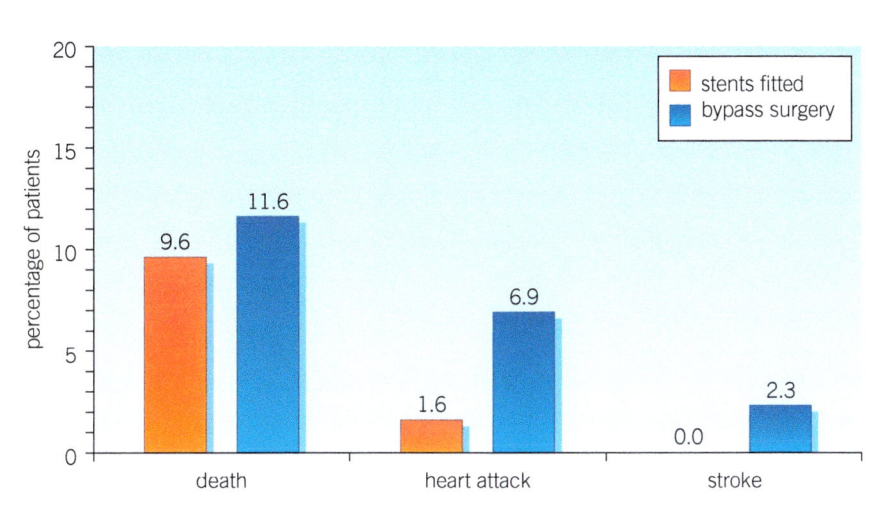

Figure 3 *Results after one year following treatment of blocked blood vessels with stents or bypass procedures*

1 a Sometimes the heart valves become leaky. Give *one* common symptom in people affected by a leaky heart valve. [1 mark]
  b Give *one* advantage and *one* disadvantage of:
    i a biological replacement heart valve [2 marks]
    ii a mechanical replacement heart valve. [2 marks]
2 a Describe what a stent is. [2 marks]
  b Construct a table to show the advantages and disadvantages of using a stent to improve the blood flow through the coronary arteries compared with bypass surgery. [4 marks]
3 a Using Figure 3, what percentage of patients with stents fitted had further cardiovascular problems compared with patients who had bypass surgery? [2 marks]
  b At the moment it is not clear which is the best way to treat blocked coronary arteries. Discuss this statement with reference to the data in Figure 3. [5 marks]
  c What more do you need to know about the data in Figure 3 before you can draw any useful conclusions? [3 marks]

Key points

- Damaged heart valves can be replaced using biological or mechanical valves.
- Stents can be used to keep narrowed or blocked arteries open.
- Statins reduce cholesterol levels in the blood, reducing the risk of coronary heart disease.

3.7.7 Replacing the heart

Learning objectives

After this topic, you should know:
- some of the risks and benefits of heart transplants
- the ways in which artificial hearts can be used.

Heart failure is a relatively common condition in which the heart does not pump the blood very effectively around the body. It sounds dramatic but many people live for years with heart failure, which can be managed and improved using different drugs. In some cases, however, heart failure becomes so severe that the person affected has a very limited lifespan. Even then, doctors can sometimes overcome the problems through a heart **transplant** or the use of an artificial heart.

Heart transplants

In extreme cases a diseased heart may be replaced by a healthy heart from a **donor**. The problems that cause heart disease can often damage the lungs as well, so in some cases a complete heart and lungs will be transplanted. When this takes place, the donor pulmonary circulation is left intact. The donor is often someone who has died suddenly in an accident, or following a stroke. Successful organ transplants can restore the **recipient** to health and allow them to lead an almost completely normal life. In England organs can be taken from people if they carry an organ donor card or are on the online donor register. Alternatively, a relative of someone who has died suddenly can give their consent for organ donation. In Wales it is assumed that people will be organ donors unless they opt out of the scheme.

There are two big problems with heart transplants, which also apply to all other organ transplants. There are never enough donor organs to go round. Many people in England do not register as donors. What's more, as cars become safer, fewer people die in traffic accidents. This is very good news, but it means that there are fewer potential organ donors. In 2015 there were 267 people waiting for a heart transplant but only about 150 operations were performed. Fewer than 60% of the people who need a transplant get one.

Figure 1 shows the approximate survival rates for patients with severe heart failure managed with the best drug treatment compared to the outlook for patients with the same condition who were given a heart transplant.

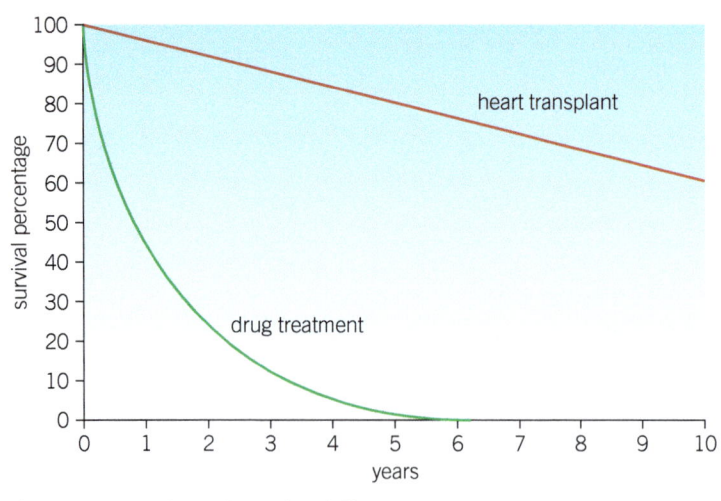

Figure 1 *Graph to show the difference in long term survival rate between patients with severe heart failure who receive heart transplants and those who do not. This data is from studies carried out in the US and Spain on hundreds of patients*

The other major problem with organ transplants is that the antigens on the surface of the cells of the donor organ are different to those of the recipient. The recipient makes antibodies that will attack the antigens on the donor organ. This may result in the rejection and destruction of the new organ. There are a number of ways of reducing the risk of a transplanted organ being rejected.

- Make the match between the donor and recipient organs as close as possible.

Synoptic link

You will learn more about the immune system in Topic 3.9.5.

3.7 Lifestyle and health

- Treat the recipient with **immunosuppressant drugs** to suppress their immune system for the rest of their life. This helps to prevent the rejection of the new organ. Immunosuppressant drugs are improving all the time, so the need for a really close tissue match is becoming less important, although it still makes a transplant more likely to succeed.

The disadvantage of taking immunosuppressant drugs is they prevent the immune system from dealing effectively with infectious diseases. Patients have to take great care if they become ill in any way, although this is a small price to pay for a working donor organ. Also, transplanted organs don't last forever. Eventually the donor organ will fail and another transplant is needed. Survival times are increasing as immunosuppressant drugs get better. In 2016 the record for survival after a heart transplant stood at 33 years!

Artificial hearts

When people need a heart transplant, they have to wait for a donor heart that is a tissue match. As a result of this wait, many people die before they get a chance to have a new heart. Scientists have developed temporary artificial hearts that can support your natural heart until it can be replaced (Figure 2). Replacing your heart permanently with a machine is still a long way off, but by 2015 almost 1500 people worldwide had been fitted with a completely artificial heart. These artificial hearts need a lot of machinery to keep them working, with most patients having to stay in hospital until they have their transplant. However, this new technology gives people a chance to live a relatively normal life while they wait for a heart transplant.

In 2011, 40-year-old Matthew Green became the first UK patient to leave hospital and go home with a completely artificial heart carried in a backpack (Figure 3). This kept him alive for two years until he had a heart transplant and no longer needed this life-saving machine. One disadvantage of an artificial heart is that there is always a risk of the blood clotting in them, which can kill the patient.

Artificial hearts can also be used to give diseased hearts a rest, so that they can recover. Patients have a part or whole artificial heart implanted that removes the strain of keeping the blood circulating for a few weeks or months. In some cases, the heart will recover and can then work normally again. However, the resources needed to develop artificial hearts and the cost of each one mean that they are not yet widely used in patients. This is likely to change in future.

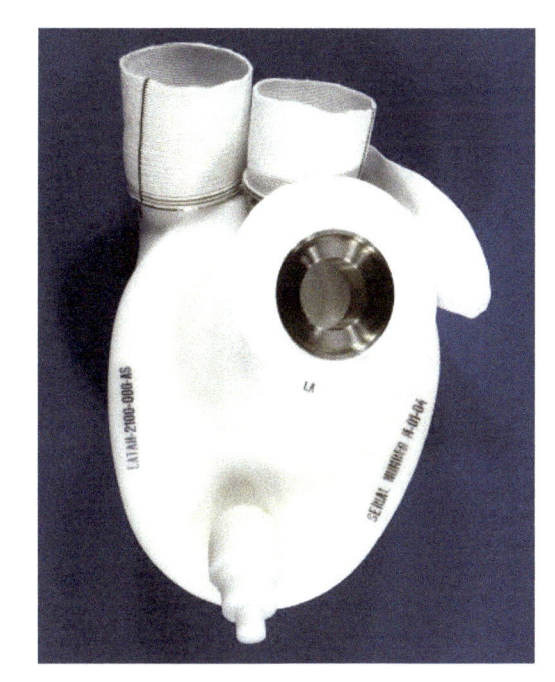

Figure 2 *This amazing artificial heart uses air pressure to pump blood around the body*

Figure 3 *Matthew Green out for a walk with his family before his heart transplant surgery in 2013. His artificial heart is being carried by his wife*

1	What are the main uses and limitations of artificial hearts? [4 marks]
2	Compare the advantages and disadvantages of treating severe heart failure with a heart transplant, with an artificial heart, or with drugs. [6 marks]
3	Discuss some of the issues that arise with using a voluntary register to provide the organs needed for organ donation. [6 marks]

Key points

- In the case of severe heart failure, a donor heart, or heart and lungs, can be transplanted.
- Artificial hearts are occasionally used to keep patients alive whilst waiting for a heart transplant, or to allow the heart to rest as an aid to recovery.

3.7.8 Principles of homeostasis

Learning objectives

After this topic, you should know:
- why it is important to control your internal environment
- the key elements of control systems.

Synoptic link

You learnt about the role of the hormonal system in Topic 2.5.12.

Go further

Scientists are investigating homeostasis in organisms from whales to plants. More and more astonishing mechanisms are being discovered. They range from colour changes to regulate body temperature in invertebrates, to protecting the immune system from responding at the wrong time in plants.

Humans live everywhere, from the equator to the Antarctic. People survive wearing no clothes or many clothes, running a marathon, or never moving from the computer screen. Conditions can change dramatically around people and even inside them and yet they survive. How do they do it?

Figure 1 *Humans are not the only organisms that can survive in extremes of temperature. Animals such as the Icelandic ponies and the desert lizard shown here all have complex coordination and control mechanisms. These enable them to cope with extreme conditions and dramatic changes in the external environment*

Homeostasis in action

The conditions inside your body are known as its internal environment. Your organs cannot work properly if this keeps changing. Many of the processes that go on inside your body aim to keep everything as constant as possible. As well as the body as a whole, this includes the regulation of the internal conditions of cells to maintain optimum conditions for functioning, in response to internal and external changes. This balancing act is called **homeostasis** (Figure 2).

3.7 Lifestyle and health

You know that enzymes only work at their best in specific conditions of temperature and pH. Enzymes control all the functions of a cell. The functioning of individual cells is vital for the way tissues, organs, and whole organisms work. It is important to respond to changes in the internal or external environment to maintain optimum conditions for the cellular enzymes.

Internal conditions that are controlled include:
- body temperature
- the water content of the body
- blood glucose concentration.

Working together
Homeostasis involves coordination and control. Organisms need to be aware of changes in the world around them, such as changes in temperature or levels of sunlight. They also need to respond to changes in the internal environment. For example, when you exercise your muscles get hotter, when you have eaten a meal your blood sugar levels go up, and in hot weather you lose water and salt through sweating.

Detecting changes and responding to them involves automatic control systems. These automatic systems include nervous responses in your nervous system and chemical responses in your hormone system. They also involve many of your body organs.

The demands of a control system
All control systems in the body need certain key features in order to function:

- **Receptors** – cells that detect changes in the internal or external environment. These changes are known as **stimuli**. Receptors may be part of the nervous or the hormonal control systems of the body.
- **Coordination centres** – areas that receive and process information from the receptors. They send out signals and coordinate the body's response. They include the brain (which acts as a coordination centre for both the nervous system and parts of the hormonal system), the spinal cord, and some organs such as the pancreas.
- **Effectors** – muscles or glands that bring about responses to the stimulus that has been received. These responses restore conditions in the body to the optimum levels.

> **Synoptic links**
>
> You will learn more about the effect of temperature and pH changes on enzyme activity in Topic 7.21.9 in the *Physical Sciences* book.
>
> Ⓗ You learnt about negative feedback systems in Topic 2.5.13.

Figure 2 *During the month of Ramadan, Muslims fast from dawn to sunset. Homeostatic mechanisms maintain blood sugar levels and the ion and water balance of the body during the hours of fasting*

> **Key points**
>
> - Homeostasis is the regulation of the internal conditions of a cell or organism to maintain optimum conditions for function, in response to internal and external changes.
> - Homeostasis is important for maintaining optimal conditions for enzyme action and all cell functions.
> - In the human body homeostasis includes control of blood glucose concentration, body temperature, and water levels.
> - The automatic control systems may involve nervous or chemical responses.

1. Describe homeostasis. [3 marks]
2. Explain why homeostasis is so important in the human body. [3 marks]
3. Describe *three* ways in which your external environment might vary and explain how each of them affects your body. [6 marks]

147

3.7.9 The control of blood glucose levels

Learning objectives

After this topic, you should know:

- the role of the pancreas in monitoring and controlling blood glucose concentration
- how insulin controls blood glucose levels in the body
- **H** how glucagon and insulin interact to control blood glucose levels
- what causes diabetes.

Study tip

Know the difference between:

- glucose – the sugar used in respiration
- glycogen – a storage carbohydrate found in the liver and muscles
- **H** glucagon – a hormone that stimulates the liver to break down glycogen to glucose.

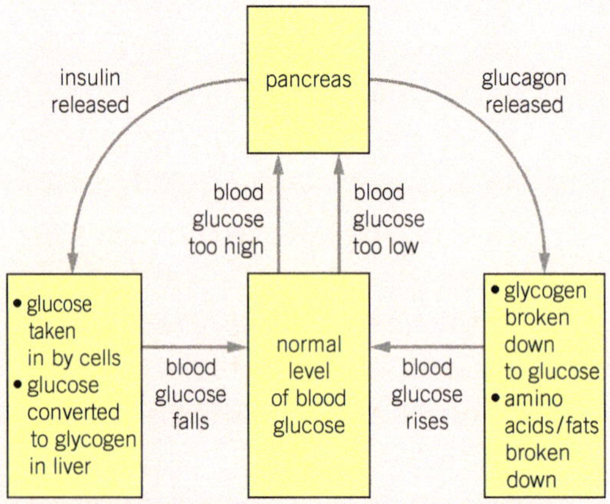

It is essential that your cells have a constant supply of the glucose they need for respiration. To achieve this, one of your body systems responds to changes in your blood glucose levels and controls it to within very narrow limits. This is an example of homeostasis in action.

Insulin and the control of blood glucose levels

When you digest a meal, large amounts of glucose pass into your blood. Without a control mechanism, your blood glucose levels would vary significantly. They would range from very high after a meal to very low several hours later – so low that cells would not have enough glucose to respire.

This situation is prevented by your pancreas. The pancreas is a small, pink organ found under your stomach. It constantly monitors and controls your blood glucose concentration using two hormones. The better-known of these is insulin.

When your blood glucose concentration rises after you have eaten a meal, the pancreas produces insulin. Insulin allows glucose to move from the blood into your cells where it is used. Soluble glucose is also converted to an insoluble carbohydrate called glycogen. Insulin controls the storage of glycogen in your liver and muscles. Stored glycogen can be converted back into glucose when it is needed. As a result, your blood glucose stays stable within a narrow concentration range.

When the glycogen stores in the liver and muscles are full, any excess glucose is converted into lipids and stored. If you regularly take in food that results in having more glucose than the liver and muscles can store as glycogen, you will gradually store more and more of it as lipids. Eventually you may become obese.

Glucagon and control of blood glucose levels

The control of your blood glucose doesn't just involve insulin. When your blood glucose concentration falls below the ideal range, the pancreas secretes another hormone called **glucagon**. Glucagon makes your liver break down glycogen, converting it back into glucose. In this way, the stored glucose is released back into the blood.

By using two hormones and the glycogen store in your liver, your pancreas keeps your blood glucose concentration fairly constant. It does this using negative feedback control, which involves switching between the two hormones (Figure 1).

Figure 2 shows a model of your blood glucose control system where the blood glucose is a tank. It has both controlled and uncontrolled inlets and outlets. In every case, any control is given by the hormones insulin and glucagon.

Figure 1 *Negative feedback control of blood glucose levels using insulin and glucagon*

148

3.7 Lifestyle and health

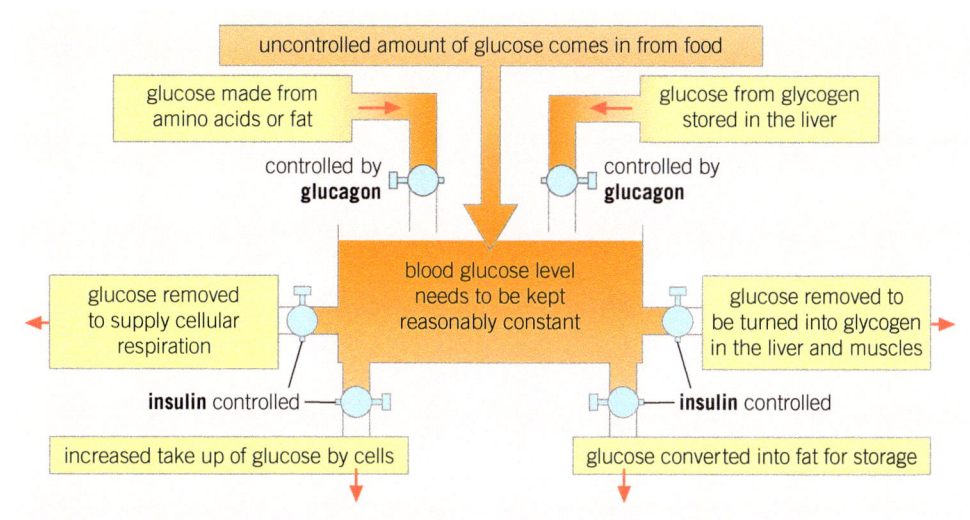

Figure 2 *A model of your blood glucose control system*

What causes diabetes?

If your pancreas does not make enough (or any) insulin, your blood glucose concentration is not controlled. You have **Type 1 diabetes**.

Without insulin your blood glucose levels get very high after you eat. Eventually your kidneys excrete glucose in your urine. You produce lots of urine and feel thirsty all the time. Without insulin, glucose cannot get into the cells of your body, so you lack energy and feel tired. You break down fat and protein to use as fuel instead, so you lose weight. Type 1 diabetes is a disorder that usually starts in young children and teenagers. There seems to be a genetic element to the development of the disease.

Type 2 diabetes is another, very common type of diabetes. Risk factors for Type 2 diabetes include age (it gets more common as people get older), obesity, and lack of exercise. There is also a strong genetic tendency to develop Type 2 diabetes. In Type 2 diabetes, the pancreas still makes insulin, although it may make less than your body needs. Most importantly, your body cells stop responding properly to the insulin you make. In countries such as the UK and the USA, levels of Type 2 diabetes are rising rapidly as obesity becomes more common.

> 1 Define the terms:
>   a insulin [1 mark]   b diabetes [1 mark]   c glycogen. [1 mark]
> 2 Explain the difference between Type 1 and Type 2 diabetes. [6 marks]
> 3 a Why is it so important to control the level of glucose in your blood? [3 marks]
>   b Explain how the pancreas responds when blood glucose levels go above the ideal range. [3 marks]
>   c **H** Explain how the pancreas responds when blood glucose levels go below the ideal range. [3 marks]
> 4 **H** Compare and contrast the roles of insulin and glucagon in controlling the body's blood glucose levels. [6 marks]

Synoptic link

H You learnt about negative feedback systems in Topic 2.5.13.

Key points

- Your blood glucose concentration is monitored and controlled by your pancreas.
- The pancreas produces the hormone insulin, which allows glucose to move from the blood into the cells and to be stored as glycogen in the liver and muscles.
- **H** The pancreas also produces glucagon, which allows glycogen to be converted back into glucose and released into the blood.
- **H** Glucagon interacts with insulin in a negative feedback cycle to control glucose levels.
- In Type 1 diabetes, blood glucose levels rise because the pancreas does not secrete enough insulin.
- In Type 2 diabetes, the body stops responding to its own insulin.

149

3.7.10 Treating diabetes

Learning objective

After this topic, you should know:

- the differences in the way in which Type 1 and Type 2 diabetes are treated.

Before there was any treatment for diabetes, people would waste away. Eventually they would fall into a coma and die.

The treatment of diabetes has developed over the years and continues to improve today. There are now some very effective ways of treating people with diabetes. However, over the long term, even well-managed diabetes may cause problems with the circulatory system, kidneys, or eyesight.

Treating Type 1 diabetes

If you have Type 1 diabetes, you need replacement insulin before meals. Insulin is a protein that would be digested in your stomach, so it is usually given as an injection to get it into your blood (Figure 1).

This injected insulin allows glucose to be taken into your body cells and converted into glycogen in the liver. This stops the concentration of glucose in your blood from getting too high. Then, as the blood glucose levels fall, the glycogen is converted back to glucose. As a result, your blood glucose levels are kept as stable as possible.

If you have Type 1 diabetes, you also need to be careful about the levels of carbohydrate that you eat. You need to have regular meals. Like everyone else, you need to exercise to keep your heart and blood vessels healthy. However, taking exercise needs careful planning to keep your blood glucose levels steady (Figure 2). Your cells need enough glucose to respire more rapidly to produce the energy required for your muscles to work.

Figure 1 *The treatment of Type 1 diabetes involves regular blood glucose tests and insulin injections to keep the blood glucose levels constant*

Insulin injections treat diabetes successfully but they do not cure it. Until a cure is developed, someone with Type 1 diabetes has to inject insulin every day of their life.

Curing Type 1 diabetes

Scientists and doctors want to find a treatment that means people with diabetes never have to take insulin again.

- Doctors can transplant a pancreas successfully. However, the operations are difficult and risky. Only a few hundred pancreas transplants take place each year in the UK. There are 250 000 people in the UK with Type 1 diabetes, but not enough pancreas donors are available. In addition, the patient exchanges one medicine (insulin) for another (immunosuppressants).

- Transplanting the pancreatic cells that make insulin from both dead and living donors has been tried, with limited success so far.

In 2005, scientists produced insulin-secreting cells from embryonic stem cells and used them to cure diabetes in mice. In 2008, UK scientists discovered a completely new technique. Using genetic engineering, they turned mouse pancreas cells that normally make enzymes into

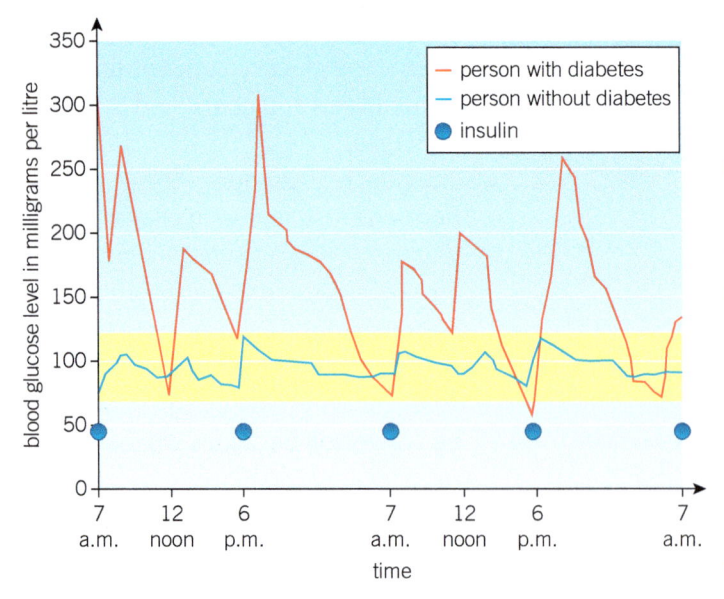

Figure 2 *The blood glucose levels of people with and without diabetes over two days. The yellow band shows normal blood glucose levels and the peaks show the effect of food intake. Insulin injections cannot mimic natural control, but enable people with diabetes to live active lives*

150

insulin-producing cells. Other groups are using adult stem cells from patients with diabetes to try the same technique.

Scientists hope that eventually they will be able to genetically engineer faulty human pancreatic cells so that they work properly. Then they will be able to return them to the patient with no rejection issues. It still seems likely that the easiest cure will be to use stem cells from human embryos that have been specially created for the process. However, for some people, this is not ethically acceptable.

Much more research is needed. However, scientists hope that Type 1 diabetes will soon be an illness they can cure rather than just manage.

Treating Type 2 diabetes

Type 2 diabetes is linked to obesity, lack of exercise, and old age. If you develop the disease, your body cells no longer respond to any insulin made by the pancreas. This can often be treated without needing to inject insulin. Many people can restore their normal blood glucose balance by:

- eating a balanced diet with carefully controlled amounts of carbohydrates
- losing weight
- doing regular exercise.

If this doesn't work, there are drugs that:

- help insulin work better on the body cells
- help your pancreas make more insulin
- reduce the amount of glucose you absorb from your gut.

If none of these treatments work, you will probably need insulin injections.

Type 2 diabetes usually affects older people. However, it is becoming more and more common in young people who are very overweight.

1 State *three* differences between Type 1 diabetes and Type 2 diabetes. [3 marks]

2 It is a common misconception that diabetes is treated only by using insulin injections.
   a Explain why this is not always true for people with Type 1 diabetes. [3 marks]
   b Explain why treatment with insulin injections is relatively uncommon for people with Type 2 diabetes. [3 marks]

3 Transplanting a pancreas to replace natural insulin production seems to be the ideal treatment for Type 1 diabetes. Compare this treatment with insulin injections and explain why it is not more widely used. [4 marks]

4 Explain the different methods used to treat Type 1 and Type 2 diabetes, linking these methods to how the types of diabetes are caused. [6 marks]

Synoptic link

You will learn about stem cells and some of the issues surrounding their use in Topics 3.9.10 and 3.9.11.

Figure 3 *Losing weight and taking exercise are simple ways to help overcome Type 2 diabetes*

Synoptic link

For more on the links between obesity and diseases such as Type 2 diabetes, look back to Topic 3.7.4.

Key points

- Type 1 diabetes is normally controlled by injecting insulin to replace the hormone that is not made in the body.
- Type 2 diabetes is often treated using a carbohydrate-controlled diet and by taking more exercise. If this doesn't work, drugs may be needed.
- Obesity is often a risk factor for Type 2 diabetes.

3.7.11 Human reproduction

Learning objectives

After this topic, you should know:
- the main human reproductive hormones
- how hormones control the changes at puberty.

The big physical changes that make boys and girls look very different take place at the time of puberty. This is when the reproductive organs become active and the body takes on its adult form. Hormones play an important part in human reproduction at every stage.

Hormones and puberty

During puberty, the reproductive hormones control the development of the secondary sexual characteristics. The primary sexual characteristics are the ones you are born with – the ovaries in girls and the testes in boys. These reproductive organs produce the female and male sex hormones and the special sex cells or gametes that join together in reproduction. To understand the changes that take place in puberty it helps to understand the basic female and male anatomy (Figures 1 and 2).

The timing of puberty and the order and rate of the changes that take place varies but the basic changes are the same for everyone.

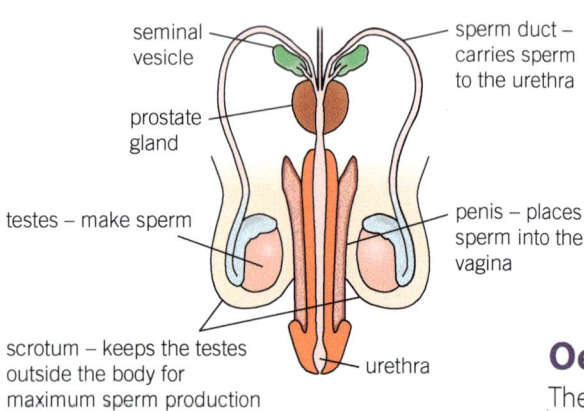

Figure 1 *Male reproductive organs*

Oestrogen and puberty in females

The main female reproductive hormone is oestrogen, produced by the ovaries. Rising oestrogen levels trigger the development of the female secondary sexual characteristics, usually between the ages of 8 and 14 years. The main changes include a growth spurt; the growth of hair under the arms and pubic hair; the breasts develop; the external genitals grow and the skin darkens; a female pattern of fat is deposited on the hips, buttocks and thighs; the brain changes and matures; mature ova start to form every month in the ovaries; the uterus grows and becomes active; and menstruation begins.

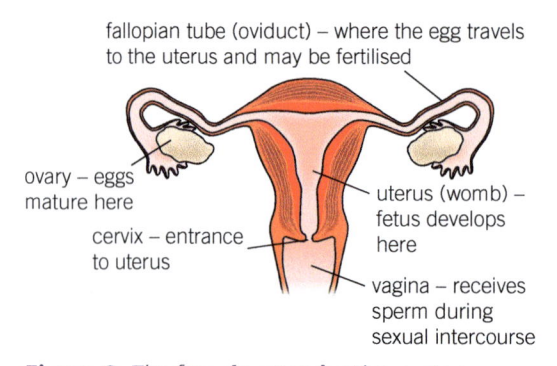

Figure 2 *The female reproductive system*

The menstrual cycle

Once a girl has gone through puberty she will have a monthly menstrual cycle. Each month, eggs begin to mature in the ovary. At the same time the uterus produces a thickened lining ready for a pregnancy. Every 28 days a mature egg is released. This is called **ovulation**. If the egg is not fertilised, around 14 days later the lining of the uterus is shed along with the egg. This is the monthly period and this also takes place at approximately 28-day intervals.

> **Synoptic link**
>
> To remind yourself about the cell division that takes place as gametes are formed, halving the number of chromosomes in each sex cell, look back at Topic 1.3.10.

3.7 Lifestyle and health

Several hormones are involved in controlling the menstrual cycle (Figure 3):

- Follicle stimulating hormone (FSH) causes the eggs in the ovary to mature (the eggs grow surrounded by cells called the follicle).
- Luteinising hormone (LH) stimulates the release of the egg at ovulation.
- Oestrogen and progesterone stimulate the build-up and maintenance of the uterus lining.

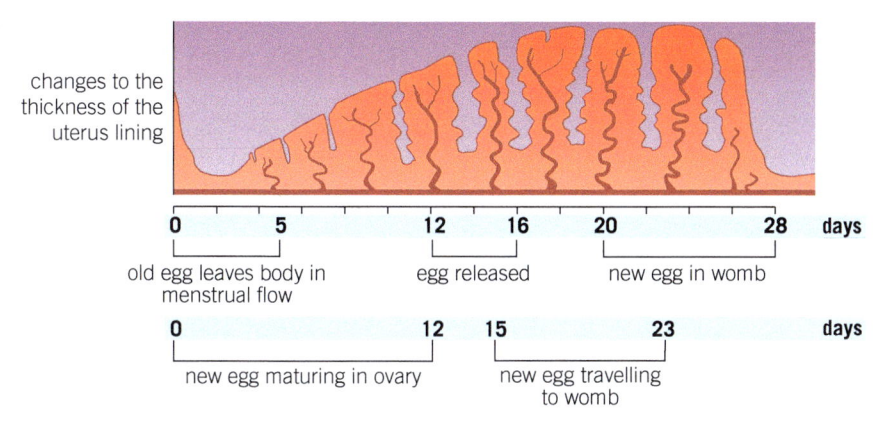

Figure 3 *The menstrual cycle*

Female fertility
The ovaries of a baby girl contain all the eggs she will ever have. After puberty, eggs mature and are released every month, for an average of 35–40 years, except if she is pregnant. Eventually the supply of eggs runs out and the woman goes through the menopause – she can no longer have children. Approaching the menopause, a woman is less fertile and has a higher risk of having a baby with genetic problems.

Testosterone and puberty in males
The main male reproductive hormone is **testosterone**, produced by the testes. As levels of testosterone rise, all kinds of changes are triggered and the male secondary sexual characteristics develop. Boys usually go into the first stages of puberty slightly later than girls, between the ages of 9 and 15. The main changes include a growth spurt; the growth of pubic hair, underarm hair, and facial hair; the larynx gets bigger and the voice breaks; the external genitalia grow and the skin darkens; the testes grow and become active, producing sperm throughout life; the shoulders and chest broaden as muscle develops; and the brain matures.

1. State *three* reasons why hormones are important in human reproduction. [3 marks]
2. Describe *three* similarities and three differences in puberty between boys and girls. [6 marks]
3. a State the differences between the production of mature eggs in women and mature sperm in men. [6 marks]
   b Describe the role of hormones in the menstrual cycle. [4 marks]

Key points
- During puberty reproductive hormones cause secondary sexual characteristics to develop.
- Oestrogen is the main female reproductive hormone produced by the ovary. At puberty eggs begin to mature in the ovary and one is released approximately every 28 days in ovulation.
- Testosterone is the main male reproductive hormone produced by the testes. It stimulates sperm production.
- Hormones involved in the menstrual cycle of a woman include follicle stimulating hormone (FSH), luteinising hormone (LH), oestrogen, and progesterone.

Higher Tier

3.7.12 Hormones and the menstrual cycle

Learning objectives

After this topic, you should know:
- the roles of hormones in human reproduction
- how hormones interact to control the menstrual cycle.

The levels of testosterone in a man's body remain relatively constant after puberty, and sperm are made continuously in the testes. In contrast, a baby girl is born with all of the immature eggs she will ever have already in place in her ovaries. After puberty, a small number of eggs mature each month until one (or occasionally two) is released into the oviduct (Figure 1). A woman's menstrual cycle is a good example of control by hormones. The levels of different hormones made in the pituitary gland and the ovaries rise and fall in a regular pattern, affecting the way the body of the woman works.

The menstrual cycle

The average length of the menstrual cycle is about 28 days. Each month the lining of the uterus (womb) thickens ready to support a developing baby. At the same time, eggs start maturing in the follicles of the ovary.

About 14 days after the eggs start maturing, one is released from the ovary in ovulation. The lining of the uterus stays thick for several days after the egg has been released.

If the egg is fertilised by a sperm, a pregnancy may take place. The lining of the uterus provides protection and food for the developing embryo. If the egg is not fertilised, about 14 days after ovulation the lining of the uterus and the egg are shed from the body in the monthly period.

Control of the menstrual cycle

The complex events of the menstrual cycle (Figure 2) are coordinated by the interactions of the four different hormones outlined in Topic 3.7.11. Once a month, a surge of hormones from the pituitary gland in the brain starts egg maturation in the ovaries. The hormones also stimulate the ovaries to produce the female sex hormone oestrogen.

Follicle stimulating hormone (FSH) is secreted by the pituitary gland. It makes eggs mature in their follicles in the ovaries. It also stimulates the ovaries to produce hormones including oestrogen.

Oestrogen is made and secreted by the ovaries in response to FSH. It stimulates the lining of the uterus to grow again after menstruation in preparation for pregnancy. High levels of oestrogen inhibit the production of more FSH and stimulate the release of luteinising hormone (LH).

LH from the pituitary gland stimulates the release of a mature egg from the ovary. Once ovulation has taken place, LH levels fall again.

Progesterone is secreted by the empty egg follicle in the ovary after ovulation. It is one of the hormones that helps to maintain a pregnancy if the egg is fertilised. Progesterone inhibits both FSH and LH and it maintains the lining of the uterus in the second half of the cycle, so that it is ready to receive a developing embryo if the egg is fertilised.

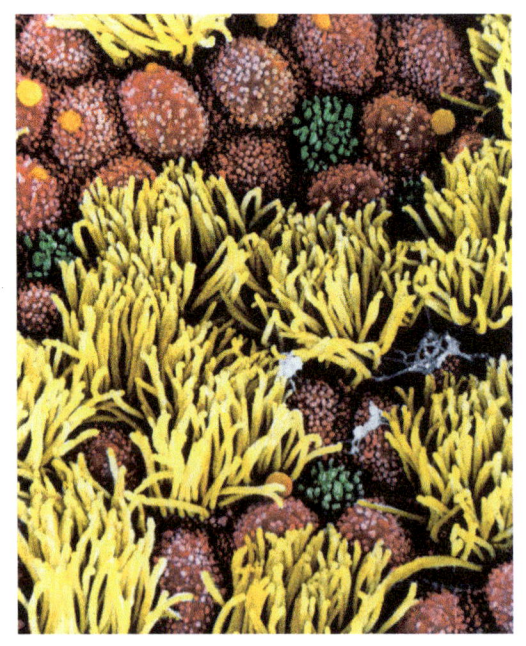

Figure 1 *The egg cannot move itself, but the cilia of the fallopian tubes, shown here in yellow in a false colour scanning electron micrograph, beat to move it along to the uterus – magnification ~ ×2000*

■ 3.7 Lifestyle and health

The hormones produced by the pituitary gland and the ovary act together to control what happens in the menstrual cycle. As oestrogen levels rise, they inhibit the production of FSH and encourage the production of LH by the pituitary gland. When LH levels reach a peak in the middle of the cycle, they stimulate the release of a mature egg.

FSH and LH are then suppressed and the body is kept ready for pregnancy until it becomes clear that the egg is not fertilised.

The levels of all the hormones then drop and the lining of the uterus pulls away and is lost from the body. At this stage a new cycle begins and the levels of FSH and oestrogen start to build up again.

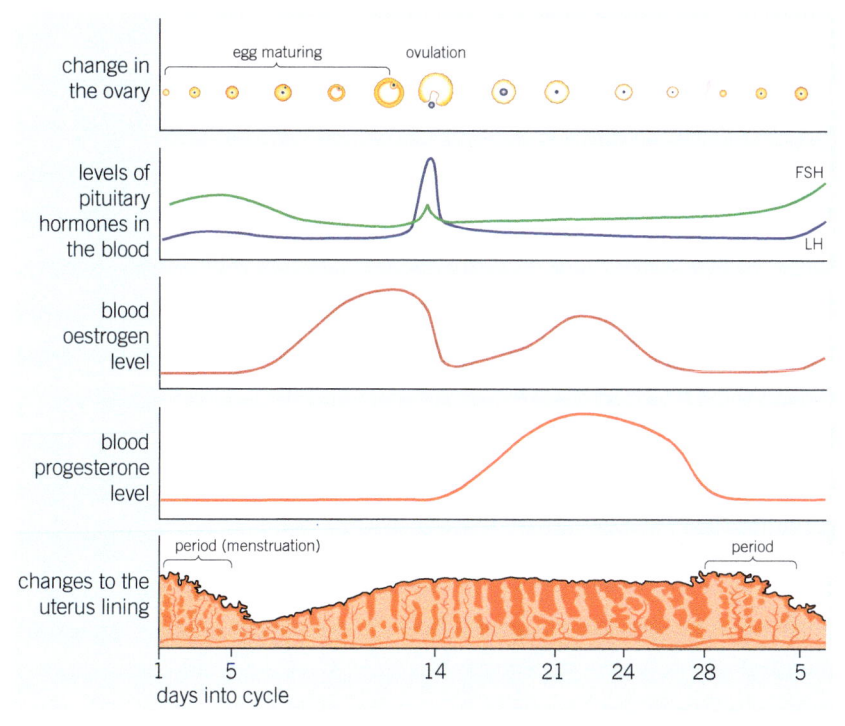

Figure 2 *The main events of the menstrual cycle*

Study tip

Be clear on the difference between the female reproductive hormones:

FSH
- causes eggs to mature
- stimulates the ovary to produce oestrogen.

LH
- triggers ovulation.

Oestrogen
- causes the lining of the uterus to develop
- inhibits the release of FSH
- stimulates the release of LH.

Progesterone
- maintains the lining of the uterus
- inhibits the release of both FSH and LH.

Key points

- The interactions of four hormones control the maturation and release of an egg from the ovary and the build-up of the lining of the uterus in the menstrual cycle.
- FSH from the pituitary gland stimulates eggs to mature in the follicles of the ovary and stimulates the ovary to produce oestrogen.
- Oestrogen secreted by the ovaries stimulates the growth of the lining of the uterus and the release of LH and inhibits FSH.
- LH stimulates ovulation.
- Progesterone is produced by the empty follicle after ovulation. It maintains the lining of the uterus for around 10 days and inhibits FSH and LH.

1 a State the *four* hormones that control the menstrual cycle. [2 marks]
   b State why the lining of the uterus builds up each month. [1 mark]
2 Look at Figure 2 and answer the following questions.
   a On which days is the woman having a menstrual period? [1 mark]
   b Explain what happens to the levels of FSH and LH during the cycle. [4 marks]
   c Name the hormone that controls the build-up of the lining of the uterus. [1 mark]
3 Explain the main events of the menstrual cycle, identifying the stage at which a woman is most likely to become pregnant. [6 marks]

155

3.7.13 Contraception

Learning objectives

After this topic, you should know:

- a number of different methods of hormonal and non-hormonal contraception.

To prevent pregnancy, you need to prevent the egg and sperm meeting or a fertilised egg implanting in the uterus. This is known as **contraception**. The different methods all have advantages and disadvantages.

Hormone-based contraception

Scientists have worked out a number of different ways to use the hormones of the menstrual cycle, or synthetic versions of them, to prevent pregnancy.

Oral contraceptives, often referred to as the contraceptive pill, use female hormones to prevent pregnancy. The mixed pill contains low doses of oestrogen along with some progesterone. The hormones inhibit the production and release of FSH by the pituitary gland, affecting the ovaries so that no eggs mature, preventing pregnancy. The pill hormones also stop the uterus lining developing, preventing implantation. They also make the mucus in the cervix thick to prevent sperm getting through. The contraceptive pill is easy to use but there is a slight risk of side effects, including raised blood pressure, thrombosis, and breast cancer.

Some contraceptive pills contain only progesterone. They have fewer side effects than the mixed pill. Women must take the pill very regularly, especially the progesterone-only pill. If they don't, the artificial hormone levels drop and their body's own hormones can take over very quickly. This can lead to the unexpected release of an egg – and an unexpected baby!

There are alternative ways of delivering hormones to prevent pregnancy. A contraceptive implant can last for up to three years. A tiny tube is inserted under your skin by a doctor and slowly releases progesterone. This is 99.95% effective! Contraceptive injections also use progesterone but they only last for about 12 weeks.

The contraceptive patch, like the mixed pill, contains a mixture of oestrogen and progesterone. You stick the patch to your skin, replacing it every seven days, and the hormones are absorbed directly into your bloodstream. All of these methods prevent an egg maturing and being released, as well as affecting the uterus lining and the mucus in the cervix.

Chemical methods

Chemicals that kill or disable sperm are known as spermicides. They are readily available but are not very effective at preventing pregnancy.

Barrier methods

Barrier methods of contraception prevent the sperm reaching the egg. A condom is a thin latex sheath placed over the penis during intercourse to collect the semen and prevent the egg and sperm meeting. Condoms have no side effects and no medical advice is required. Condoms offer some protection against sexually transmitted diseases such as syphilis and HIV/AIDS. They can, however, get damaged and let sperm through.

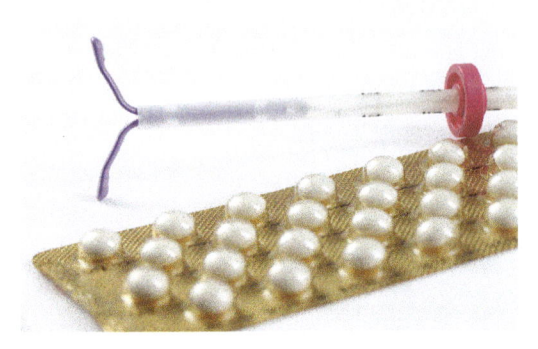

Figure 1 *Contraceptive pills and an intrauterine device (IUD)*

3.7 Lifestyle and health

A diaphragm or cap is a thin rubber diaphragm placed over the cervix before sex to prevent the entry of sperm. Like condoms, they have no side effects but must be fitted by a doctor initially. If the cap is not positioned correctly, sperm may get past and reach the egg. Barrier methods work better when combined with spermicide.

Intrauterine devices

Intrauterine devices (IUDs) are small structures inserted into the uterus by a doctor (one is shown in Figure 1). They last for 3–5 years, although they can be removed at any time if you want to get pregnant. Some intrauterine devices contain copper and prevent any early embryos implanting in the lining of the uterus. Others contain progesterone, releasing it slowly to prevent the build-up of the uterus lining and to thicken the mucus of the cervix. These devices are very effective but they may cause period problems or infections.

Abstinence

If people do not have sex they will not get pregnant. Some religious groups do not accept the use of artificial methods of contraception. Abstaining from intercourse around ovulation or when an egg is in the oviduct means sperm cannot fertilise the egg – this is known as the rhythm method. This method has no side effects but it is very unreliable. Ovulation indicators make it more effective.

Surgical methods

If people do not want any more children, they can be surgically sterilised. In men the sperm ducts are cut and tied, preventing sperm getting into the semen. This is called a vasectomy.

In women the oviducts are cut or tied to prevent the egg reaching the uterus and the sperm reaching the egg. Although this gives effective, permanent contraception with no risk of human error, women need a general anaesthetic for the surgery.

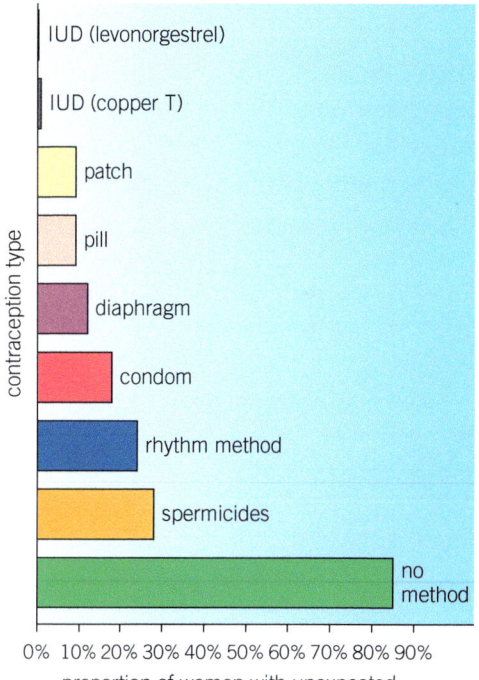

Figure 2 *Failure rates for different methods of birth control based on data from the American Academy of Pediatrics*

1. Define the term contraception. [1 mark]
2. The progesterone-only pill, the contraceptive implant, and the contraceptive patch are all forms of contraceptive.
   a. State *one* similarity between each contraceptive. [1 mark]
   b. For each contraceptive, state *one* way in which it is different. [3 marks]
   c. Explain which of these three methods is likely to be the most effective contraceptive and why. [3 marks]
3. Compare the effectiveness of the three main types of contraception – hormone-based contraception, barrier methods, and surgical methods. [3 marks]

Key points

- Fertility can be controlled by a number of hormonal and non-hormonal methods of contraception.
- Contraceptive methods include oral contraceptives, hormonal injections, implants and patches, barrier methods such as condoms and diaphragms, intrauterine devices, spermicidal agents, abstinence, and surgical sterilisation.

3.7.14 Infertility treatments

Learning objectives

After this topic, you should know:

- how hormones can be used to treat infertility.

> **Study tip**
>
> A combination of FSH and LH can be used in fertility treatments to cause eggs to mature in the ovary and to trigger ovulation.

In the UK as many as one couple in six have problems having a family when they want one. There are many possible reasons for this infertility. It may be linked to a lack of female hormones, to damaged oviducts, or to a lack of sperm in the semen. About a third of cases of infertility are due to problems with the female reproductive system, about a third due to the male system, and about a third are hard to explain, with both partners being a bit less fertile than normal. Common causes of infertility are obesity and eating disorders such as anorexia nervosa, but one of the most common causes of infertility is age. Increasingly, couples wait until they are in their late thirties to have children, and then find that they cannot conceive naturally.

Lack of ovulation

Some women want children but do not make enough FSH to stimulate the maturation of the eggs in their ovaries. Fortunately, artificial FSH can be used as a fertility drug. It stimulates the eggs in the ovary to mature and also triggers oestrogen production. An artificial form of LH can then be used to trigger ovulation. If a woman who is not ovulating as a result of a lack of her own FSH is treated in this way, she may be able to get pregnant naturally. In the early days of using fertility drugs there were big problems with the doses used. In 1971, an Italian doctor removed 15 four-month-old foetuses (ten girls and five boys) from the womb of a 35-year-old woman after treatment with fertility drugs. Not one of them survived. Now the doses are much more carefully controlled and most people using fertility drugs end up with just one or two babies.

In vitro fertilisation

Fertility drugs are also used in *in vitro* fertilisation (IVF). IVF is a form of fertility treatment used if the oviducts have been damaged or blocked by infection, if a donor egg has to be used, or if there is no obvious cause for long-term infertility.

In some cases a man produces very few sperm or the sperm do not mature properly. Individual sperm may be injected into an egg during the IVF process.

In all these cases it would not be possible to get pregnant naturally.

Fortunately, doctors can now help.

- They give the mother synthetic FSH to stimulate the maturation of a number of eggs at the same time, followed by LH to bring the eggs to the point of ovulation.
- They collect the eggs from the ovary of the mother and fertilise them with sperm from the father outside the body in the laboratory.
- The fertilised eggs are kept in special solutions in a warm environment to develop into tiny embryos.
- At the stage when they are minute balls of cells, one or two of the embryos are inserted back into the uterus of the mother. In this way they bypass the faulty tubes.

Table 1 *Data from 2010 showing the decreasing success rate of IVF as the mother gets older*

Age of mother	IVF % success rate
Under 35	32.2
35–37	27.7
38–39	20.8
40–42	13.6
43–44	5
Over 44	1.9

3.7 Lifestyle and health

Modern infertility treatments such as these rely on advanced microscopy techniques (Figure 1). It takes a high level of manipulative skill and a high magnification to work on single eggs and sperm, or early embryos, without damaging them.

The advantages and disadvantages of fertility treatment

The use of hormones to help overcome infertility has been a major scientific breakthrough. It gives women and men who would otherwise be infertile the chance to have a baby of their own. But like most things there are advantages and disadvantages.

IVF is expensive both for society, if it is provided by the National Health Service (NHS), and for individuals – many people end up paying thousands of pounds for repeated cycles of treatment.

It is not always successful. The older the parents, the less likely it is that they will have a baby (Table 1). Using donor eggs from younger women or donor sperm from younger men can help the success rate but then the baby is not biologically the parents' child.

The use of fertility drugs can have some health risks for the mother. The process of IVF is very emotionally and physically stressful.

IVF increases the chances of a multiple pregnancy. On average, 1 in 5 IVF pregnancies is a multiple pregnancy. The figure for natural pregnancies is 1 in 80. Multiple births increase the risks for both mothers and babies, and are more likely to lead to stillbirths and other problems including very premature births. It costs hospitals a lot of money to keep very small premature babies alive and if they survive many will have permanent and often severe disabilities.

The mature eggs produced by a woman using fertility drugs may be collected and stored, or fertilised and stored, until she wants to get pregnant later. But this raises ethical problems if the woman dies, the relationship breaks up, or one of the parents no longer wants the eggs or embryos.

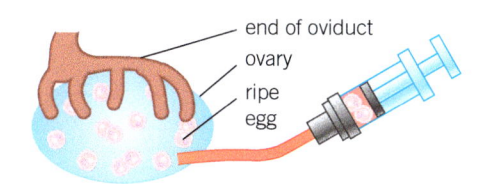

1 Fertility drugs are used to make lots of eggs mature at the same time for collection.

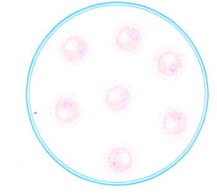

2 The eggs are collected and placed in a special solution in a Petri dish.

3 A sample of semen is collected and the sperm and eggs are mixed in the Petri dish.

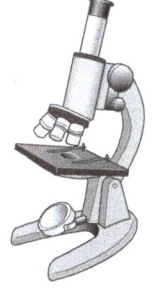

4 The eggs are checked to make sure they have been fertilised and the early embryos are developing properly.

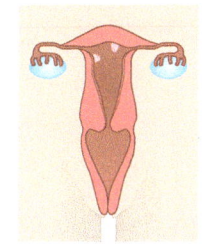

5 When the fertilised eggs have formed tiny balls of cells, 1 or 2 of the tiny embryos are placed in the womb of the mother. Then, if all goes well, at least one baby will grow and develop successfully.

Figure 1 *New reproductive technology using hormones and IVF helps thousands of otherwise infertile couples to have babies each year. Note that the ovary, eggs, syringe, sperm, and microscope are not drawn to scale*

1 What is IVF? [2 marks]
2 Explain how artificial female hormones can be used to:
   a help people overcome infertility and conceive naturally [3 marks]
   b help people overcome infertility and conceive through IVF. [3 marks]
3 a Draw a graph to show the effect of age on the chances of a woman having a baby successfully using IVF. [4 marks]
   b Some people think that IVF treatment should not be offered to people over the age of 40. Suggest arguments for and against this idea. [6 marks]
4 Suggest and explain some advantages and disadvantages of using artificial hormones to control female fertility. [6 marks]

Key points

- FSH and LH can be used as a fertility drug to stimulate ovulation in women with low FSH levels.
- *In vitro* fertilisation (IVF) uses FSH and LH to stimulate the maturation of ova that are collected, fertilised, allowed to start development, and replaced in the uterus.
- IVF is emotionally and physically stressful, often unsuccessful, and can lead to risky multiple births.

3.7 Lifestyle and health

Summary questions

1. **a** What is a non-communicable disease? [1 mark]
   b Define a lifestyle factor and give *three* examples. [3 marks]
   c Explain what is meant by:
      i a correlation between a lifestyle factor and a non-communicable disease [2 marks]
      ii a causal link between a lifestyle factor and a particular disease. [3 marks]

2. **a** What are the main symptoms of COPD? [2 marks]
   b Explain how smoking causes COPD and the reason for the symptoms. [5 marks]
   c Name *two* more of these smoking-related diseases. [2 marks]
   d Explain how both the number of cigarettes smoked and the time someone has been a smoker affects their risk of developing a smoking-related disease. [4 marks]

3. **a** Which *two* body organs are most affected by a large amount of alcohol over a long period of time? [2 marks]
   b Explain why it is unsafe for someone to drive when they have been drinking alcohol. [4 marks]
   c Alcohol is closely linked to violence and crime. Suggest why alcohol has this effect. [3 marks]
   d Pregnant women are advised not to drink alcohol, even though scientists do not have clear evidence of exactly what level of alcohol consumption is safe for the unborn baby. Discuss why this is sensible advice. [6 marks]

4. **Figure 1** shows the blood glucose levels of a person without diabetes and someone with Type 1 diabetes managed with regular insulin injections. They both eat at the same times.

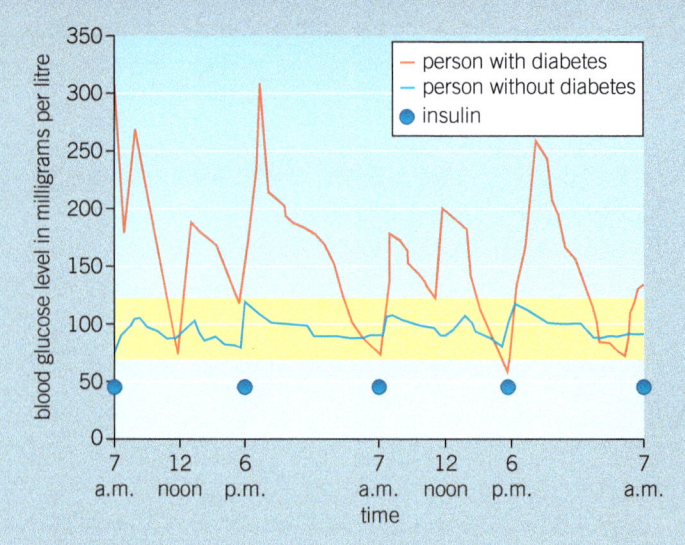

Figure 1

Use **Figure 1** to help you answer these questions:
   a What happens to the blood glucose levels of both individuals after eating? [1 mark]
   b What is the range of blood glucose concentration of the person without diabetes? [1 mark]
   c What is the range of blood glucose concentration of the person with diabetes? [1 mark]
   d Figure 1 shows the effect of regular insulin injections on the blood glucose level of someone with diabetes. Why are the insulin injections important to their health and well-being? What limitations are suggested by the data? [4 marks]
   e People with diabetes have to monitor the amount of carbohydrate in their diet. Explain why. [4 marks]

5. **a** Describe the main events of the menstrual cycle. [6 marks]
   b Explain the role of the following hormones in the menstrual cycle:
      i FSH [2 marks]
      ii oestrogen [3 marks]
      iii LH [2 marks]
      iv progesterone. [2 marks]

6. **a** Explain how artificial hormones can be used in pills to prevent people getting pregnant. [4 marks]
   b Describe *three* other ways in which contraceptive hormones can be given and give *one* advantage for each method. [6 marks]
   c Explain how artificial hormones can be used to help treat infertility. [4 marks]
   d Compare the way in which artificial hormones are used in contraception and infertility treatment. [4 marks]

3.7 Lifestyle and health

Practice questions

01 **Figure 1** shows how smoking and the prevalence of lung cancer has changed since 1900.

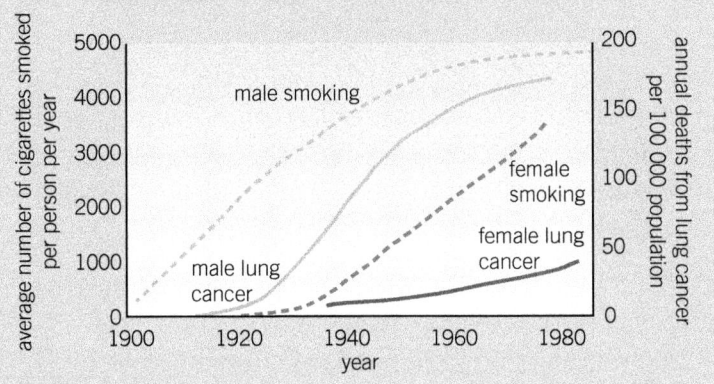

Figure 1

01.1 Use **Figure 1** to describe the patterns in smoking amongst males and females. [3 marks]

01.2 A student states:

If people stopped smoking they would not get lung cancer.

Use information in **Figure 1** and your own knowledge to give **two** reasons why this conclusion may not be correct. [2 marks]

02 Several hormones are involved in the menstrual cycle of a woman.

02.1 Match each hormone to its function.

Hormone: FSH, LH

Function:
- maintains uterus lining
- stimulates maturation of an egg in the ovary
- stimulates the release of an egg from the ovary

[2 marks]

02.2 Explain how the female reproductive hormones in the contraceptive pill interact with other female reproductive hormones to prevent pregnancy. [4 marks]

02.3 Testosterone is a male reproductive hormone.
Give the role of testosterone in males. [1 mark]

03 Every year, many patients need to have heart valve replacements.
Table 1 gives information about two types of heart valve.

Table 1

Living human heart valve	Cow-tissue heart valve
• It has been used for transplants for more than 12 years.	• It has only been used since 2010.
• It can take many years to find a suitable human donor.	• It is made from the artery tissue of a cow.
• It is transplanted during an operation after a donor has been found.	• It is attached to a stent and inserted inside the existing faulty valve.
• During the operation, the patient's chest is opened and the old valve is removed before the new valve is transplanted.	• A doctor inserts the stent into a blood vessel in the leg and pushes it through the blood vessel to the heart.

A patient needs a heart valve replacement. A doctor recommends the use of a cow-tissue heart valve.
Give the advantages and disadvantages of using a cow-tissue heart valve compared with those of using a living human heart valve.
Use information from **Table 1** and your own knowledge in your answer. [6 marks]
[AQA, 2016]

3.8 Radiation and risk

3.8.1 Atoms and radiation

Learning objectives

After this topic, you should know:
- how atoms can gain energy
- what changes take place in an atom when it emits or absorbs electromagnetic radiation
- why the energy of the radiation emitted by an atom depends on the energy levels of the electrons in the atom
- what determines the frequency of the radiation given out by an atom.

Synoptic link

In Chapter 1.2 you learnt that the nucleus is composed of protons and neutrons. You will find out much more about neutrons and protons in this chapter.

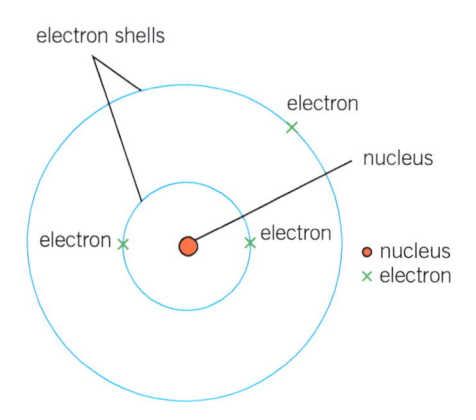

Figure 1 *The lowest energy state of a lithium atom*

Every atom contains one or more electrons that move about in the space around the nucleus of the atom. The nucleus exerts an attractive force on each electron in the atom. This force is an example of an **electrostatic force**. This is because the nucleus is positively charged and each electron is negatively charged – oppositely charged objects always attract each other. The nucleus is about 10 000 times smaller in size than the atom. However, its mass is much greater than the mass of its electrons so it is hardly affected by its electrons moving around.

The force on each electron due to the nucleus keeps the electron in the atom unless the atom gains energy. As explained in Topic 1.2.4, the electrons in an atom are arranged around the nucleus in shells. The energy of each electron depends on which shell it is in, so shells are also referred to **energy levels**. Each shell can hold no more than a certain number of electrons that depends on the shell. For example, the innermost shell of an atom can only hold two electrons, whereas the next shell can hold eight electrons.

- The shell nearest the nucleus has the lowest energy level.
- The further away a shell is from the nucleus, the higher its energy level is compared with the shell nearest the nucleus.

The electrons in an atom usually occupy the lowest available energy levels (the available shell closest to the nucleus). When atoms gain energy, their electrons jump to energy levels further from the nucleus that are empty or not completely filled. For example, a lithium atom has three electrons. In its lowest energy state (sometimes called its 'ground state'), two of its electrons are in the lowest energy level nearest to the nucleus and the third electron is in the next-highest energy level. If the atom gains enough energy, one of its electrons can 'jump' to a higher energy level further from the nucleus.

How atoms gain and lose energy

1 **Atoms can gain energy in different ways:**
   - **When a substance is heated either directly or by electricity**, the internal energy of the substance is increased. Its atoms move about faster so they shake each other up more when they bump into each other. As a result, electrons in the atoms may jump to higher energy levels further from the nucleus of 'their' atom.
   - **When electromagnetic radiation is absorbed by a substance**, electrons in the atoms of the substance absorb electromagnetic waves passing through the substance. An electron jumps to a higher energy level further from the nucleus of 'their' atom if it gains the necessary amount of energy from the radiation.

■ 3.8 Radiation and risk

2 An atom can lose energy by giving out **electromagnetic radiation** when it is not in its lowest energy state. This happens when an electron in one of its energy levels moves to a lower energy level that is not full. The electromagnetic radiation is emitted as a 'burst' of electromagnetic waves that transfers energy to the surroundings equal to the difference between the energy level the electron moved from and the energy level it moved to (Figure 2).

Energy and frequency

The electromagnetic spectrum covers a continuous range of frequencies, from radio waves at the low-frequency end of the spectrum to gamma rays at the highest frequency end. This is because the frequency of the electromagnetic waves emitted by an electron in an atom when it moves to a lower energy level is proportional to the size of the energy jump. Gamma rays, which are at the high-frequency end of the electromagnetic spectrum, are caused by much bigger energy jumps than radio waves, which are at the low-frequency end of the electromagnetic spectrum. Energy jumps that cause light waves are smaller than the jumps that cause ultraviolet radiation, but larger than the jumps that cause infrared radiation.

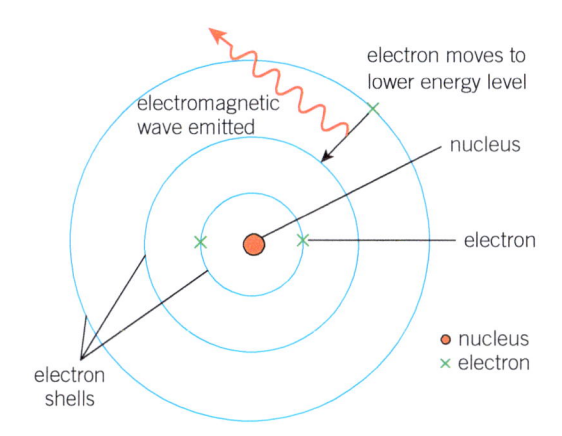

Figure 2 *Electromagnetic radiation from a lithium atom*

> **Synoptic link**
>
> You learnt about the different parts of the electromagnetic spectrum in Topic 1.4.3.

1 What is meant by the energy levels of an atom? [2 marks]
2 State *two* ways in which the atoms of a substance can gain energy. [2 marks]
3 Describe the changes that take place in an atom when it emits electromagnetic waves. [3 marks]
4 **a** An electron in a certain energy level **A** of an atom emits electromagnetic radiation of a certain frequency when it jumps to a lower energy level **B**. The electron then jumps to an energy level **C** and gives out electromagnetic radiation of greater frequency than before.
   Compare the two energy jumps **AB** and **BC** and write down which one is bigger. Give a reason for your answer. [2 marks]
   b An electron in energy level **A** of an identical atom jumps straight to energy level **C**. State how the frequency of the radiation emitted in this jump compares with the frequency of each energy jump described in part **a**. Give a reason for your answer. [3 marks]

> **Key points**
>
> - Atoms can gain energy when a substance is heated, when an electric current is passed through it, or when it absorbs electromagnetic radiation.
> - An atom emits (or absorbs) electromagnetic radiation when electrons jump from one energy level to a lower (or higher) energy level.
> - The energy of the radiation emitted by an atom is equal to the energy difference between the energy levels the electron moves to and from.
> - The frequency of the radiation given out by an atom is proportional to the energy of the radiation given out by an atom.

163

3.8.2 Radioactivity

Learning objectives

After this topic, you should know:

- what a radioactive substance is
- the types of radiation given out from a radioactive substance
- why a radioactive source emits radiation (radioactive decay)
- that there are different types of radiation emitted by radioactive sources.

Figure 1 *Becquerel's key*

Synoptic link

For more about X-rays, look back at Topic 1.4.7.

A key discovery

If your photos showed a mysterious image, what would you think? In 1896 a French physicist, Henri Becquerel, discovered the image of a key on a photographic film he developed. He remembered the film had been in a drawer under a key. On top of that there had been a packet of uranium salts (Figure 1). The uranium salts must have sent out some form of radiation that passed through paper (the film wrapper) but not through metal (the key).

Becquerel asked a young physicist, Marie Curie, to investigate. She knew that substances could be made to emit infrared, visible, and ultraviolet radiation by heating them or by passing a current through them. However, she found that the uranium salts emitted radiation all the time. She used the word radioactivity to describe this strange new property of uranium.

She and her husband, Pierre, did more research into this new branch of science. They discovered new radioactive elements. They named one of the elements polonium, after Marie's native country, Poland.

Investigating radioactivity

You can use a Geiger counter to detect radioactivity. This is made up of a detector called a Geiger–Müller tube (or Geiger tube) connected to an electronic counter (Figure 2). The counter clicks each time a particle of radiation from a radioactive substance enters the Geiger tube.

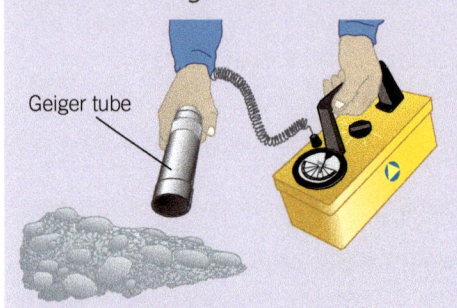

Figure 2 *Using a Geiger counter*

Safety: Avoid touching and inhaling radioactive material.

Inside the atom

What stops the radiation from radioactive substances? The physicist Ernest Rutherford carried out tests to answer this question about a century ago. He put different materials between the radioactive substance and a detector.

He discovered two types of radiation:

- One type (**alpha radiation** α) was stopped by paper.
- The other type (**beta radiation** β) went through the paper.

Scientists later discovered a third type, **gamma radiation** γ, which is even more penetrating than beta radiation.

Rutherford carried out more investigations and discovered that alpha radiation is made up of positively charged particles. He realised that these particles could be used to probe the atom, as explained in Topic 1.2.1. His research students included Hans Geiger, who invented what was later called the Geiger counter (Figure 2). They carried out investigations in which a narrow beam of alpha particles was directed at a thin metal foil. Rutherford was astonished to find that some of the alpha particles rebounded from the foil. He proved that this happens because every atom has at its centre a positively charged nucleus containing most of the mass of the atom. He went on to propose that the nucleus contains two types of particle – protons and neutrons.

A radioactive puzzle

Why are some substances radioactive? Every atom has a nucleus made up of protons and neutrons. Electrons move about in energy levels (or shells) surrounding the nucleus.

Most atoms each have a stable nucleus that doesn't change. But the atoms of a radioactive substance each have a nucleus that is unstable. An unstable nucleus becomes stable or less unstable by emitting alpha, beta, or gamma radiation. An unstable nucleus is described as decaying when it emits radiation. No one can tell exactly when an unstable nucleus will decay. It is a **random** event that happens without anything being done to the nucleus.

The radiation emitted by a radioactive substance is due to a change in its nucleus. Don't confuse this high-energy radiation with the radiation emitted when electrons moving around the nucleus inside the atom jump to a lower energy level. The energy released when an unstable nucleus emits radiation is about a million times greater than that released when an atom gives out light waves.

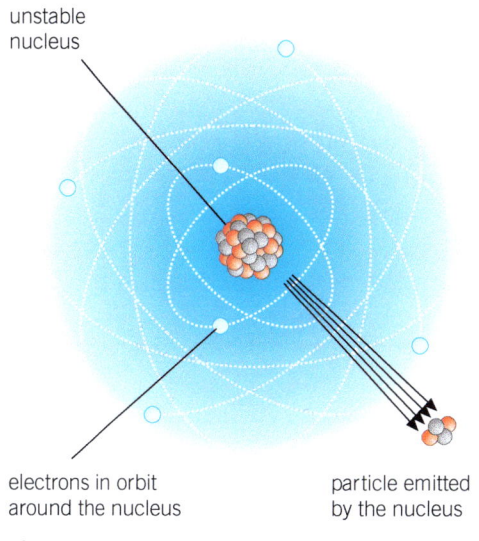

Figure 3 *Radioactive decay. An alpha particle is emitted by the nucleus in this example*

Synoptic link

To remind yourself about how scientists discovered that the nucleus of an atom is made up of protons and neutrons, look back at *Unit 1 in context – Development of the nuclear model of the atom.*

Key points

- A radioactive substance contains unstable nuclei that become stable by emitting radiation.
- There are three main types of radiation from radioactive substances – α, β, and γ.
- Radioactive decay is a random event – you can't predict or influence when it will happen.
- Radioactive sources emit α, β, and γ radiation.

1 a Write *two* differences between the radiation from uranium and the radiation from a lamp. [2 marks]
  b Write *two* differences between radioactive atoms compared with the atoms that emit light from a lamp. [2 marks]
2 a i The radiation from a radioactive source is stopped by paper. Name the type of radiation that this source emits. [1 mark]
    ii The radiation from a different source goes through paper. Name *one* type of radiation that this source might emit. [1 mark]
  b Name the type of radiation from radioactive sources that is the most penetrating. [1 mark]
3 Explain, in terms of the stability of their atoms, why some substances are radioactive. [2 marks]
4 A Geiger counter clicks very rapidly when a certain substance is brought near it.
  a Describe what causes the Geiger counter to click. [2 marks]
  b When the Geiger tube was near the substance, the counter clicked much less when a sheet of paper was placed between the substance and the tube. Explain why the counter clicked much less. [3 marks]

3.8.3 Nuclear changes

Learning objectives

After this topic, you should know:
- what an isotope is
- how the nucleus of an atom changes when it emits an alpha particle or a beta particle
- how to represent the emission of an alpha particle from a nucleus
- how to represent the emission of a beta particle from a nucleus.

Table 1 *Relative mass and charge of subatomic particles*

	Relative mass	Relative charge
proton	1	+1
neutron	1	0
electron	$\cong \frac{1}{2000}$	−1

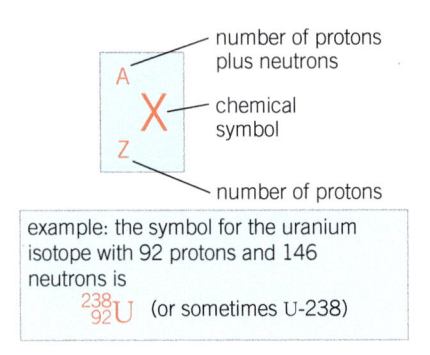

example: the symbol for the uranium isotope with 92 protons and 146 neutrons is $^{238}_{92}U$ (or sometimes U-238)

Figure 1 *Representing an isotope*

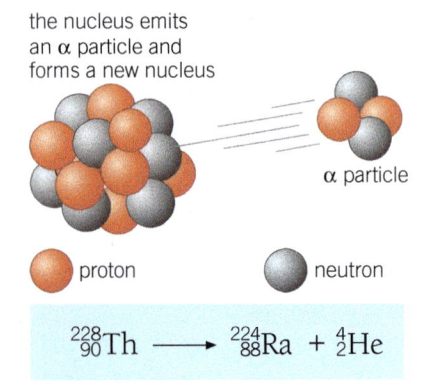

the nucleus emits an α particle and forms a new nucleus

$^{228}_{90}Th \longrightarrow {}^{224}_{88}Ra + {}^{4}_{2}He$

Figure 2 *α emission*

In alpha (α) or beta (β) decay, the number of protons in a nucleus changes. In α decay, the number of neutrons also changes. How do the changes happen in α and β decay, and how can you represent these changes? Table 1 gives the relative masses and the relative electric charges of a proton, a neutron, and an electron.

The **atomic number** (or proton number) of a nucleus is the number of protons in it. It has the symbol Z. Atoms of the same element each have the same number of protons.

The **mass number** of a nucleus is the number of protons plus neutrons in it. It has the symbol A.

Isotopes are atoms of the same element with different numbers of neutrons. You met isotopes in Topic 1.2.3. The isotopes of an element have nuclei with the same number of protons but a different number of neutrons. Figure 1 shows how to represent an isotope of an element X, which has Z protons and A protons plus neutrons.

Radioactive decay

An unstable nucleus becomes more stable by emitting an α (alpha) or a β (beta) particle or by emitting a γ (gamma) ray.

α emission

An α particle is made up of two protons plus two neutrons. Its relative mass is 4, and its relative charge is +2, so it is usually represented by the symbol $^{4}_{2}\alpha$. It is identical to a helium nucleus, so in nuclear equations you might see it represented by the symbol $^{4}_{2}He$.

When an unstable nucleus emits an α particle:
- its atomic number goes down by 2, and its mass number goes down by 4
- the mass and the charge of the nucleus are both reduced.

For example, the thorium isotope $^{228}_{90}Th$ decays by emitting an α particle. It forms the radium isotope $^{224}_{88}Ra$.

Figure 2 shows an equation to represent this decay.

- The numbers along the top show that the total number of protons and neutrons after the change (= 224 + 4) is equal to the total number of protons and neutrons before the change (= 228).
- The numbers along the bottom show that the total number of protons after the change (= 88 + 2) is equal to the total number of protons before the change (= 90).

β emission

A β particle is an electron created and emitted by a nucleus that has too many neutrons compared with its protons. A neutron in the nucleus changes into a proton and a β particle (i.e., an electron), which is instantly emitted. The relative mass of a β particle is effectively zero, and its relative charge is −1, so a β particle can be represented by the symbol $^{0}_{-1}\beta$ or $^{0}_{-1}e$.

3.8 Radiation and risk

When an unstable nucleus emits a β particle:
- the atomic number of the nucleus goes up by 1, and its mass number is unchanged (because a neutron changes into a proton)
- the charge of the nucleus is increased, and the mass of the nucleus is unchanged.

For example, the potassium isotope $^{40}_{19}K$ decays by emitting a β particle. It forms a nucleus of the calcium isotope $^{40}_{20}Ca$. Figure 3 shows an equation to represent this decay.

- The numbers along the top show that the total number of protons and neutrons after the change (= 40 + 0) is equal to the total number of protons and neutrons before the change (= 40).
- The numbers along the bottom show that the total charge (in relative units) after the change (= 20 − 1) is equal to the total charge before the change (= 19).

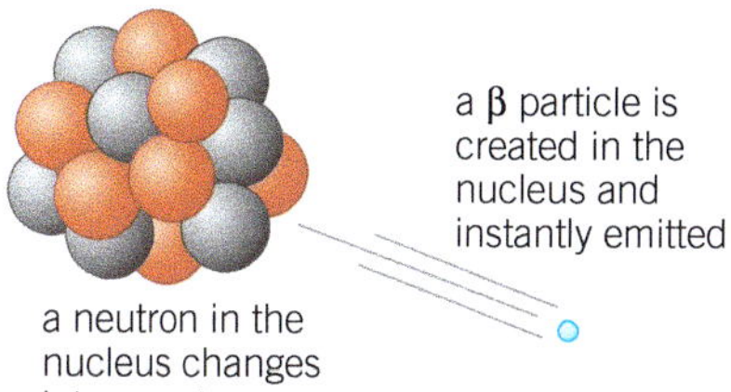

γ emission

A γ-ray is electromagnetic radiation from the nucleus of an atom. It is uncharged and has no mass. Its emission does not change the number of protons or neutrons in a nucleus, so the mass and the charge of the nucleus are both unchanged.

Neutron emission

Neutrons are emitted by some radioactive substances as a result of α particles colliding with unstable nuclei in the substance. Such a collision causes the unstable nuclei to become even more unstable and emit a neutron. Because the emitted neutrons are uncharged, they can pass through substances more easily than an α particle or a β particle can.

a β particle is created in the nucleus and instantly emitted

a neutron in the nucleus changes into a proton

$$^{40}_{19}K \longrightarrow {}^{40}_{20}Ca + {}^{0}_{-1}e$$

Figure 3 β emission

Go further

Most nuclei are stable because the protons and neutrons inside a nucleus are held together by a strong attractive force called the strong nuclear force. This force is strong enough in stable nuclei to overcome the electrostatic repulsion between protons, and to stop the neutrons moving away from the nucleus.

Study tip

Make sure you know the changes to mass number and to atomic number in α decay and in β decay.

1. How many protons and how many neutrons are there in the nucleus of each of the following isotopes:
   a $^{12}_{6}C$ [1 mark] b $^{60}_{27}Co$ [1 mark] c $^{235}_{92}U$? [1 mark]
   d How many more protons and how many more neutrons are in $^{238}_{92}U$ compared with $^{224}_{88}Ra$? [2 marks]

2. A substance contains the radioactive isotope $^{238}_{92}U$, which emits α radiation. The product nucleus **X** emits β radiation and forms a nucleus **Y**. Determine how many protons and how many neutrons are present in:
   a a nucleus of $^{238}_{92}U$ [1 mark]
   b a nucleus of **X** [2 marks]
   c a nucleus of **Y**. [2 marks]

3. Copy and complete the following equations for α and β decay.
   a $^{238}_{92}U \rightarrow {}^{?}_{?}Th + {}^{4}_{2}He$ b $^{64}_{29}Cu \rightarrow {}^{?}_{?}Zn + {}^{0}_{-1}e$ [4 marks]

4. A radioactive isotope of polonium (Po) has 84 protons and 126 neutrons. The isotope is formed from the decay of a radioactive isotope of bismuth (Bi), which emits a β particle in the process. Copy and complete the following equation to represent this decay. Bi → Po + β [3 marks]

Key points

- Isotopes of an element are atoms with the same number of protons but different numbers of neutrons. So they have the same atomic number but different mass numbers.

α decay	β decay
Change in the nucleus	
Nucleus loses 2 protons and 2 neutrons	A neutron in the nucleus changes into a proton
Particle emitted	
2 protons and 2 neutrons emitted as an α particle	An electron is created in the nucleus and instantly emitted
Equation	
$^{A}_{Z}X \rightarrow {}^{A-4}_{Z-2}Y + {}^{4}_{2}He$	$^{A}_{Z}X \rightarrow {}^{A}_{Z+1}Y + {}^{0}_{-1}e$

167

3.8.4 Half-life

Learning objectives

After this topic, you should know:

- what is meant by the half-life of a radioactive source
- what is meant by the count rate from a radioactive source
- what happens to the count rate from a radioactive isotope as it decays
- **H** how to calculate count rates after a given number of half-lives.

Higher

Half-life calculations

Figure 1 shows that the count rate from a sample of a radioactive isotope decreases from 600 to 300 to 150 to 75 after three successive half-life intervals. In general, you can work out the count rate or the number of unstable nuclei left after n half-lives by dividing the initial value by 2 to the power n (i.e., 2 multiplied by itself n times). You can write this as an equation:

$$\text{count rate (number of unstable nuclei) after } n \text{ half-lives} = \frac{\text{initial count rate (number of unstable nuclei)}}{2^n}$$

Worked example

A particular radioactive isotope has a half-life of 6.0 hours. A sample of this isotope contains 60 000 radioactive nuclei. Calculate the number of radioactive nuclei of this isotope remaining after 24 hours.

Solution

$n = 4$ because 24 hours equals 4 half-lives for this isotope.

$2^4 = 16$, so the number of radioactive nuclei of the isotope remaining after 24 hours $= \dfrac{60\,000}{2^4} = \dfrac{60\,000}{16} = \textbf{3750}$

Every atom of an element always has the same number of protons in its nucleus. But the number of neutrons in the nucleus can differ. An atom of a specific element with a certain number of neutrons is called an isotope of that element.

The **activity** of a radioactive source is the number of unstable atoms in the source that decay per second. The unit of activity is the Becquerel, Bq, which is one decay per second. As the nucleus of each unstable atom (the parent atom) decays, the number of parent atoms decreases. So the activity of the sample decreases.

You can use a Geiger counter to monitor the activity of a radioactive sample. To do this, you need to measure the **count rate** from the sample. The count rate is the number of counts per second. This is proportional to the activity of the source, as long as the distance between the tube and the source stays the same. The graph in Figure 1 shows that the count rate of a sample decreases with time.

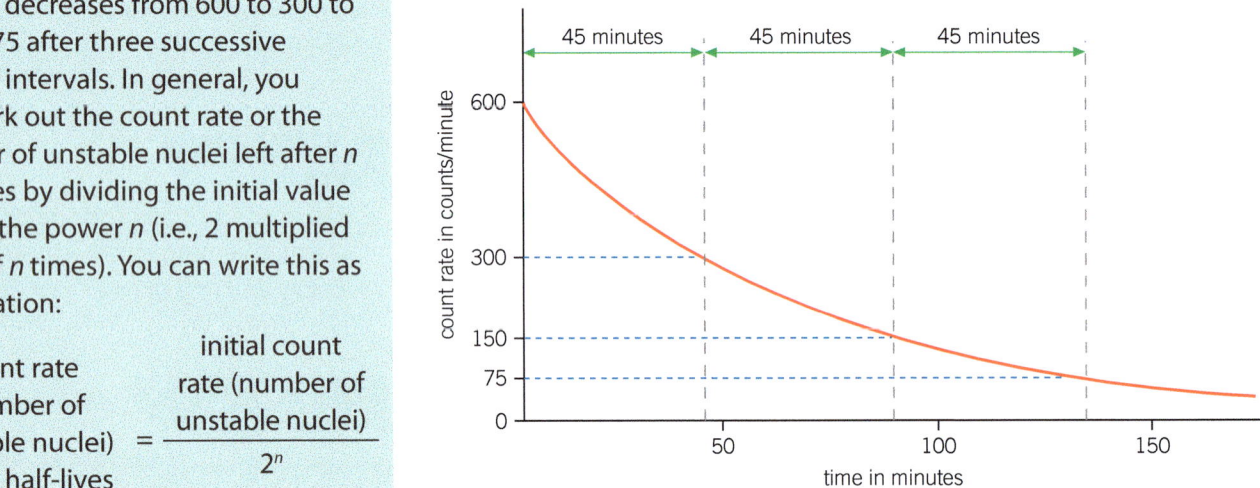

Figure 1 *A graph of count rate against time. The count rate here is measured in counts per minute*

The average time taken for the count rate (and so the number of parent atoms) to fall by half is always the same. This time is called the **half-life**. The half-life shown on the graph is 45 minutes.

The half-life of a radioactive isotope is the average time it takes:

- for the number of nuclei of the isotope in a sample (and so the mass of parent atoms) to halve
- for the count rate from the isotope in a sample to fall to half its initial value.

3.8 Radiation and risk

The random nature of radioactive decay

Radioactive decay is a random process. This means that no one can predict exactly *when* an individual atom will suddenly decay. But you *can* predict how many atoms will decay in a given time – because there are so many of them. This is a bit like throwing dice. You can't predict what number you will get with a single throw. But if you threw 1000 dice, you would expect one-sixth of the throws to come up with a particular number.

Suppose you start with 1000 unstable atoms. Look at the graph in Figure 2.

If 10% decay every hour:

- 100 atoms will decay in the first hour, leaving 900 atoms
- 90 atoms (= 10% of 900) will decay in the second hour, leaving 810 atoms.

Table 1 shows what you get if you continue the above calculations. The results are plotted as a graph in Figure 2. The graph is like Figure 1, except that the half life is just over six hours. The similarity is because radioactive decay, like throwing dice, is a random process.

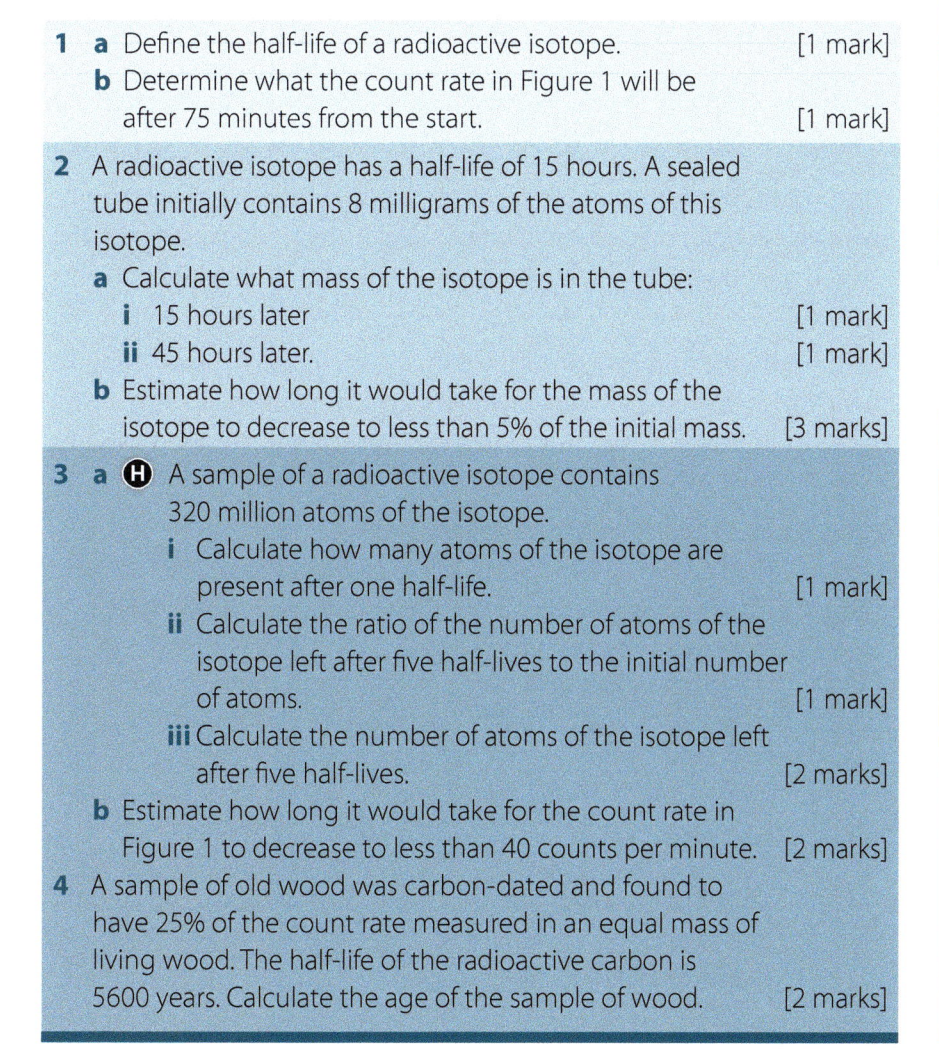

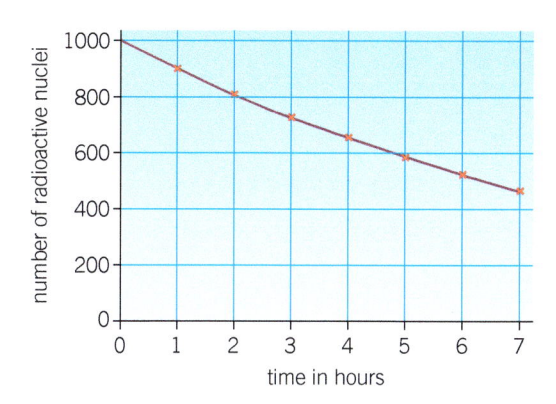

Figure 2 *Half-life*

Table 1 *What you get if you continue the calculations. The results are plotted as a graph in Figure 2*

Time from start (in hours)	No. of unstable atoms present	No. of unstable atoms that decay in the next hour
0	1000	100
1	900	90
2	810	81
3	729	73
4	656	66
5	590	59
6	531	53
7	478	48

1 a Define the half-life of a radioactive isotope. [1 mark]
   b Determine what the count rate in Figure 1 will be after 75 minutes from the start. [1 mark]

2 A radioactive isotope has a half-life of 15 hours. A sealed tube initially contains 8 milligrams of the atoms of this isotope.
   a Calculate what mass of the isotope is in the tube:
      i   15 hours later [1 mark]
      ii 45 hours later. [1 mark]
   b Estimate how long it would take for the mass of the isotope to decrease to less than 5% of the initial mass. [3 marks]

3 a Ⓗ A sample of a radioactive isotope contains 320 million atoms of the isotope.
      i   Calculate how many atoms of the isotope are present after one half-life. [1 mark]
      ii Calculate the ratio of the number of atoms of the isotope left after five half-lives to the initial number of atoms. [1 mark]
      iii Calculate the number of atoms of the isotope left after five half-lives. [2 marks]
   b Estimate how long it would take for the count rate in Figure 1 to decrease to less than 40 counts per minute. [2 marks]

4 A sample of old wood was carbon-dated and found to have 25% of the count rate measured in an equal mass of living wood. The half-life of the radioactive carbon is 5600 years. Calculate the age of the sample of wood. [2 marks]

Key points

- The half-life of a radioactive isotope is the average time it takes for the number of nuclei of the isotope in a sample to halve.
- The count rate of a Geiger counter caused by a radioactive source decreases as the activity of the source decreases.
- The number of atoms of a radioactive isotope and the count rate both decrease by half every half-life.
- Ⓗ The count rate after n half-lives $= \dfrac{\text{the initial count rate}}{2^n}$

169

3.8.5 Properties of radiation

Learning objectives

After this topic, you should know:
- how far each type of radiation can travel in air
- how different materials absorb alpha, beta, and gamma radiation
- how to find out what types of radiation a radioactive source emits
- what is meant by ionisation

Penetrating power

Alpha radiation can't penetrate paper. But what stops beta and gamma radiation? And how far can each type of radiation travel through air? You can use a Geiger counter to find out, but you must take account of **background radiation**, which is radiation from unstable nuclei in materials around us and in the atmosphere. To do this you need to:

1. Measure the count rate (which is the number of counts per second) without the radioactive source present. This is the background count rate.
2. Measure the count rate with the source in place. Subtracting the background count rate from this gives you the count rate from the source alone.

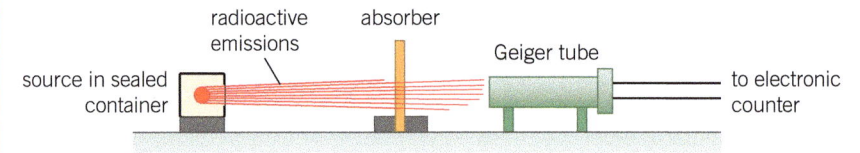

Figure 1 Absorption tests

You can then test absorber materials and the range that each type of radiation travels in air.

To test different materials, you need to place each material between the tube and the radioactive source (Figure 1). Then you measure the count rate. You can add more layers of material until the count rate from the source is zero. The radiation from the source has then been stopped by the absorber material.

To test the range that each type of radiation travels in air, you need to move the tube away from the source. When the tube is beyond the range of the radiation, the count rate from the source is zero.

Automatic thickness monitoring

Automatic thickness monitoring is used when making metal foil. Look at Figure 3. The radioactive source emits β radiation. The amount of β radiation passing through the foil depends on the thickness of the foil. A detector on the other side of the foil measures the amount of radiation passing through it. If the thickness of the foil increases too much, the detector reading drops. The detector then sends a signal to increase the pressure of the rollers on the metal sheet. This makes the foil thinner again.

- γ radiation isn't used because it would all pass through the foil unaffected.
- α radiation isn't used as it would all be stopped by the foil.

Table 1 The results of the two tests

Radiation	Absorber materials	Range in air
alpha α	Thin sheet of paper	about 5 cm
beta β	Aluminium sheet (about 5 mm thick) Lead sheet (2–3 mm thick)	about 1 m
gamma γ	Thick lead sheet (several cm thick) Concrete (more than 1 m thick)	unlimited – spreads out in air without being absorbed

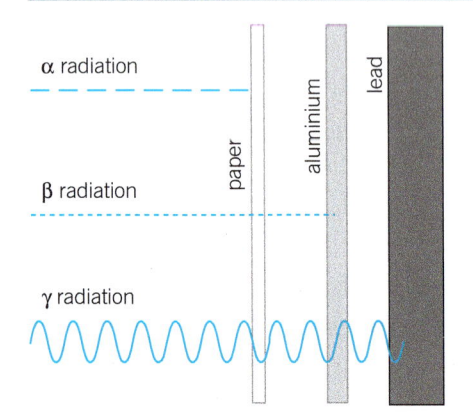

Figure 2 The penetrating power of alpha, beta, and gamma radiation

Synoptic link

Automatic thickness monitoring is an example of negative feedback in a system. A signal from a detector makes the system automatically correct any change in its output so that the thickness of the foil stays the same. To remind yourself about the role of negative feedback in the body, look back at Topic 2.5.13.

170

3.8 Radiation and risk

Ionisation

The radiation from a radioactive substance can knock electrons out of atoms when it travels through any substance. The atoms become charged becaused they lose electrons. The process is called ionisation – remember that a charged atom is called an ion. X-rays, fast-moving protons and neutrons, and ultraviolet radiation also cause ionisation. Radiation that causes ionisation is referred to as **ionising radiation**.

Ionising radiation in a living cell can damage or kill the cell by breaking up molecules within it. The fragments can then take part in chemical reactions that can damage living cells. Damage to a cell can change its DNA, causing gene mutation that can lead to cancer, or can be passed on if the cell generates more cells. High-energy gamma radiation targeted at cancer cells can be used to destroy these cells in tumours (see Topic 1.4.8).

Strict safety rules must always be followed when radioactive substances and other sources of radiation are used. For example, people who use ionising radiation in their jobs reduce their exposure by:

- reducing the length of time for which they are exposed to the radiation
- keeping as far away as possible from radioactive sources by using remote-handling devices or long-handled tools to move the sources
- storing radioactive sources in secure containers lined with thick lead plates
- ensuring that thick lead plates are between the source and themselves to absorb as much radiation as possible.

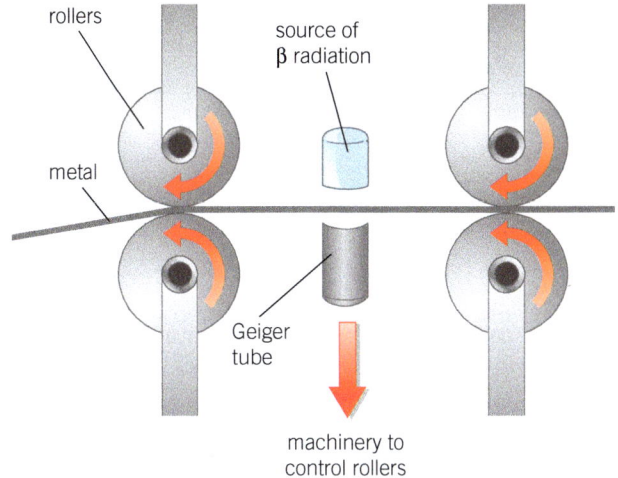

Figure 3 *Thickness monitoring using a radioactive source*

Synoptic links

For more about the ionising effects of these electromagnetic waves on living cells, look back at Topic 1.4.7.

You will learn about why the atoms of some elements form negative ions by gaining electrons and other atoms lose electrons and form positive ions in Topic 6.16.1 in the *Physical Sciences* book.

---

1. **a** State why a radioactive source is stored in a lead-lined box. [1 mark]
   b Name the type of ionising radiation from radioactive substances that is most easily absorbed. [1 mark]
2. **a** Name the type of radiation that is:
      i uncharged [1 mark]   **ii** positively charged [1 mark]
   b Name the type of radiation from a radioactive source that:
      i has the longest range in air [1 mark]
      ii has the greatest ionising power. [1 mark]
3. **a** Explain why ionising radiation is dangerous. [2 marks]
   b Explain how you would use a Geiger counter to find the range of the radiation from a source of α radiation. [3 marks]
4. An investigation was carried out to find out what type of particles a radioactive source emits. The apparatus shown in Figure 1 was used. When a thin piece of paper or a 3 mm aluminium plate was placed between the source and the Geiger tube, the count rate scarcely changed. When a lead plate 20 mm thick was used, the count rate was significantly reduced. Deduce what type of particles the radioactive source emits. Explain your reasoning. [4 marks]

Key points

- α radiation is stopped by paper and has a range of a few centimetres in air. It consists of particles, each composed of two protons and two neutrons.
- β radiation is stopped by a thin sheet of metal and has a range of about one metre in air. It consists of fast-moving electrons emitted from the nucleus.
- γ radiation is stopped by thick lead and has an unlimited range in air. It consists of electromagnetic radiation.
- Ionisation is the process of creating ions by knocking electrons out of atoms

3.8.6 Radiation hazards

Learning objectives

After this topic, you should know:

- what is meant by irradiation and contamination
- how the effects of ionising radiation on people can be compared
- what radon gas is and why it is dangerous.

Table 1 *Hazards of α, β, and γ radiation*

	α radiation	β and γ radiation
inside body	**very dangerous** – affects all the surrounding tissue	**dangerous** – reaches cells throughout the body
outside body	**some danger** – absorbed by skin, damages skin cells, retinal cells	

Figure 1 *A film badge tells you how much ionising radiation the wearer has received*

Table 2 *Sources of background radiation in the UK. 1 μSv = 1 millionth of 1 Sv*

Source	Radiation dose in μSv
cosmic rays	238
ground & buildings	332
food & drink	274
natural radioactivity in the air	1190
medical applications	332
nuclear weapons tests	5
air travel	5
nuclear power	2

Irradiation and contamination

When an object is exposed to ionising radiation it is said to be **irradiated** but it does not become radioactive. Irradiation can be reduced by moving the object away from the source of radiation or by placing suitable absorbers (e.g., thick lead plates) as a screen between the object and the source. For example, lead plates are used by radiographers to screen themselves from X-rays when they are using an X-ray machine.

Radioactive substances can contaminate other materials with which they come into contact. **Radioactive contamination** is the unwanted presence of materials containing radioactive atoms on or in other materials or living organisms. The hazard or danger from contamination is due to the radiation emitted by the decay of the nuclei of the contaminating atoms. When radioactive contamination occurs, the affected area needs to be evacuated until the contaminated material has either been removed by specially-trained workers and stored safely, or until its activity has decreased to a very low level.

The **level of hazard** from ionising radiation depends on the effect of each type of radiation on living cells:

- α radiation ionises substances much more than β, γ, or X-radiation.
- β radiation is more ionising than gamma radiation and X-radiation.

The risk from a hazard is the chance of it causing harm to people. The risk from radiation also depends on how long the cells are exposed to the radiation for and, in the case of radiation from a radioactive source, whether or not the source is inside or outside the body. Even a tiny amount of a radioactive substance in the body can be dangerous (Table 1).

Radioactivity all around you

When you use a Geiger counter, it clicks even without a radioactive source near it. This is because of background radiation. Traces of radioactive substances are in many natural substances. Table 2 shows the sources of background radiation. The numbers in Table 2 are the **radiation dose** measured in **sieverts (Sv)**. This tells you the risk of harm resulting from exposure of the body to the radiation from each source. These measurements can be used to compare the risk from different sources of background radiation.

The bigger the dose of radiation someone gets, the bigger the risk of cancer. High doses kill living cells. The smaller the dose, the less the risk – but it is never zero. There is a very low level of risk to every person because of background radiation.

- Background radiation in the air is caused mostly by radon gas that seeps through the ground from radioactive substances in rocks deep underground. Radon gas emits α particles, so radon is a health hazard if it is breathed in. It can seep into homes and other buildings in some locations. In affected homes, pipes can be installed under

3.8 Radiation and risk

the building and fitted to a suction pump to draw the gas out of the ground before it seeps into the building.

- Medical sources include X-rays as well as radioactive substances, because X-rays have an ionising effect. People who work in jobs that involve the use of ionising radiation have to wear personal radiation monitors to make sure they aren't exposed to too much ionising radiation (Figure 1).

Risk estimates

The risk from a hazard can be estimated by measuring its effect on large groups of people exposed to it, or by comparing its effect with similar groups of people not exposed to the hazard. For the average person, the risk of death from background radiation is about the same as the risk of death from road traffic. Scientists have estimated that the risk from radiation is about 30 deaths per million people each year for each millisievert (mSv) of radiation.

Most people are prepared to accept the risk from road traffic when they travel, yet many people perceive nuclear reactors as unsafe, even though they cause far fewer deaths than road traffic does. This is an example of public perception of risk differing from the measured risk. This is often the case where a risk is unfamiliar, invisible, or involuntary (e.g., natural causes) – see Table 3.

Note that, for each source of background radiation, the risk = 30 deaths per million people per millisievert (mSv) multiplied by the radiation dose in mSv.

Peer review

Scientists know the effects of ionising radiation on humans from the health records of people exposed to ionising radiation from atomic bomb explosions or from nuclear accidents. Their findings have been checked by other scientists in a process called **peer review**. In this process, after scientists finish an investigation, they send a written paper on their methods and results to the editor of a scientific journal, who asks other scientists (the investigators' 'peers') to decide if the methods and results are appropriate, valid, and original, if due credit has been given if other work has been used in the investigation, and to recommend if the paper should be published.

---

1. Explain why radioactive waste from nuclear reactors needs to be stored securely for many years. [2 marks]

2. In some locations, the biggest radiation hazard comes from radon gas that seeps up through the ground and into buildings. Explain why radon gas is dangerous in a house. [3 marks]

3. a The average radiation dose a person receives from ionising radiation is about 2000 μSv per year. Medical X-rays account for about 14% of this. Estimate the average radiation dose that a person receives in one year due to medical X-rays. [1 mark]

   b The risk to the average person in the UK from background radiation is about the same as the risk from road traffic. Use Table 2 to evaluate whether measures such as avoiding air travel would reduce the risk from background radiation. [5 marks]

Chernobyl and Fukushima

In 1986, a nuclear reactor in Ukraine exploded. More than 100 000 people were evacuated from Chernobyl and the surrounding area. Over 30 people died in the accident. More have developed cancer since then.

Lessons learnt from Chernobyl were put into practice at Fukushima in Japan after three reactors were crippled in 2011 by an earthquake and a tsunami. Everyone within 20 km was evacuated, and cannot return for many years. Radiation levels and health effects, as well as food and milk production over a much wider area, will need to be monitored for many years.

Nearby reactors with greater protection from tsunamis were far less seriously affected than the crippled reactors. Major lessons will need to be learnt about how to minimise the impact of natural disasters on nuclear reactors.

Table 3 *Measured and perceived risks*

Source of risk	Type of risk	Risk / UK deaths per million people (measured)	Risk / UK deaths per million people (perceived)
radiation from food and drink	familiar, invisible, involuntary	8	lower
road traffic	familiar, visible, involuntary	28	lower
nuclear power	unfamiliar, invisible, voluntary	<0.1	higher

Key points

- Irradiation occurs when an object is exposed to ionising radiation. Radioactive contamination is the presence of unwanted radioactive atoms on or in other materials or living organisms.
- α radiation is more ionising than β radiation, which is more ionising than γ radiation.
- Radon gas is an α-emitting isotope that seeps into houses in some areas through the ground.

173

3.8.7 Cancer

Learning objectives

After this topic, you should know:
- what a tumour is
- the difference between benign and malignant tumours
- how cancer spreads.

Cancer is a disease that affects people in many families. The cells in your body divide on a regular basis in a set sequence known as the cell cycle that involves several stages. A **tumour** forms when control of this sequence is lost and the cells grow in an abnormal, uncontrolled way.

Tumour formation

Tumour cells do not respond to the normal mechanisms that control the cell cycle. They divide rapidly with very little non-dividing time for growth in between each division. This results in a mass of abnormally growing cells called a tumour (Figure 1). Some tumours are caused by communicable diseases. For example, the bacteria *agrobacterium tumefaciens* can cause crown galls in plants, and the human papilloma virus (HPV) can cause cervical cancer in humans.

Benign tumours are growths of abnormal cells contained in one place, usually within a membrane. They do not invade other parts of the body but a benign tumour can grow very large, very quickly. If it causes pressure or damage to an organ, this can be life-threatening. For example, benign tumours on the brain can be very dangerous because there is no extra space for them to grow into.

Malignant tumour cells can spread around the body, invading neighbouring healthy tissues. A malignant tumour is often referred to as cancer. The initial tumour may split up, releasing small clumps of cells into the bloodstream. They circulate and are carried to different parts of the body where they may lodge in another organ. Then they continue their uncontrolled division and form secondary tumours. Cancer cells not only divide more rapidly than normal cells, they also live longer. The growing tumour often completely disrupts normal tissues and, if left untreated, will often kill the person. Because of the way malignant tumours spread around the body, it can be very difficult to treat them.

Synoptic link

You learnt about mitosis and the cell cycle in Topic 1.3.8.

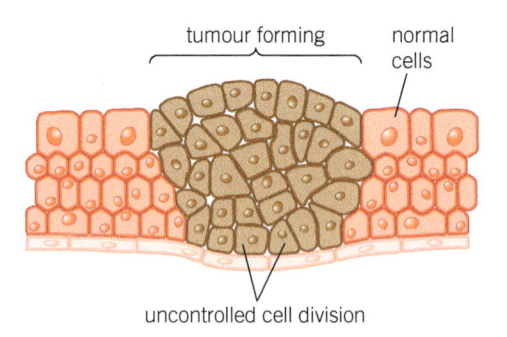

Figure 1 *A tumour forms when there is uncontrolled cell division. The tumour cells in a melanoma often contain a lot of dark pigment – magnification ~ ×1000*

Synoptic link

To remind yourself about risk factors for non-communicable diseases, including cancer, look back at Chapter 3.7.

The causes of cancer

Scientists still do not understand what triggers the formation of many cancers, but some of the causes are well known.

- There are clear genetic risk factors for some cancers, including early breast cancer and ovarian cancer.
- Most cancers are the result of mutations – changes in the genetic material. Chemicals such as asbestos and the tar found in tobacco smoke can cause mutations that trigger the formation of tumours. These cancer-causing agents are called carcinogens.
- Ionising radiation, such as ultraviolet light and X-rays, can also interrupt the normal cell cycle and cause tumours to form. For example, melanomas (Figure 2) appear when there is uncontrolled growth of pigment-forming cells in the skin as a result of exposure to ultraviolet light from the Sun.

3.8 Radiation and risk

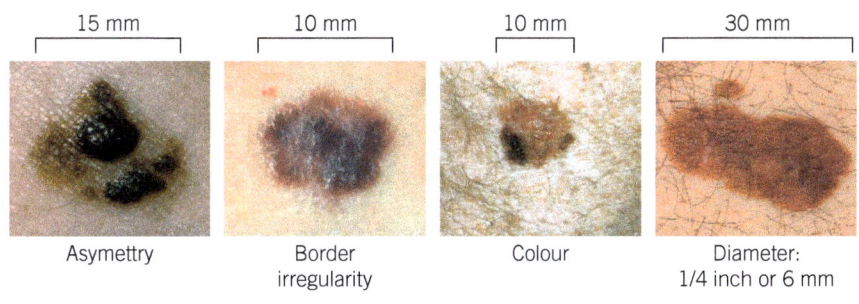

15 mm	10 mm	10 mm	30 mm
Asymmetry	Border irregularity	Colour	Diameter: 1/4 inch or 6 mm

Figure 2 *Melanomas are malignant tumours often triggered by exposure to UV radiation. Over 2000 people a year die from melanomas in the UK alone, so it is important to know the signs to look out for*

- About 15% of human cancers are caused by viral infections. For example, cervical cancer is almost always the result of infection by HPV. Teenagers in the UK are now routinely vaccinated against the virus.

Treating cancer

Because of the way in which cancer can spread through the body it can be difficult to treat. In recent years treatments have become increasingly successful. Scientists are working hard to develop new treatments, and are also finding that combining some older treatments makes them more successful. There are two main ways in which cancer is treated at the moment:

- Radiotherapy, through which the cancer cells are destroyed by targeted doses of radiation. This stops mitosis in the cancer cells but can also damage healthy cells. Methods of delivering different types of radiation in very targeted ways are improving cure rates.
- Chemotherapy, through which chemicals are used to either stop the cancer cells dividing or to make them 'self-destruct'. There are many different types of chemotherapy, and most chemotherapy drugs specifically target cells that are dividing rapidly. Scientists are working to make them as specific to cancer cells as possible, reducing the damage to normal, healthy cells. This will help to reduce the side effects of chemotherapy for patients..

---

1 a What is a tumour? [3 marks]
  b Describe the difference between a benign tumour and a malignant tumour. [3 marks]
  c Suggest ways in which both types of tumour can cause serious health problems. [4 marks]

2 One of the most common methods of treating cancers is chemotherapy. Chemotherapy drugs often affect other parts of the body, particularly hair follicles, skin cells, cells lining the stomach, and blood cells as well as the cancer cells.
  a Explain how the drugs used in chemotherapy might work. [2 marks]
  b Suggest reasons why healthy hair, skin, blood, and stomach lining cells are particularly badly affected by the drugs used to treat cancer. [4 marks]

3 Describe and explain the different treatments that are used to treat cancer. [4 marks]

Go further

There is more to the cancer story than mitosis out of control. Programmed cell death (known as apoptosis) normally gets rid of damaged or mutated cells but in tumours, apoptosis is sometimes suppressed. Signals from the cancer cells trigger the formation of blood vessels to feed the growing tumour. Scientists are now using DNA analysis of tumour cells to help them to develop new cures and to use the treatments they have as effectively as possible.

Key points

- Benign and malignant tumours result from abnormal, uncontrolled cell division.
- Benign tumours form in one place and do not spread to other tissues.
- Malignant tumour cells are cancers. They invade neighbouring tissues and may spread in the blood to different parts of the body, where they form secondary tumours.
- Lifestyle risk factors for various types of cancer include smoking, obesity, common viruses, and exposure to ultraviolet light. There are also genetic risk factors for some cancers.
- Ionising radiation can also cause cancer.

175

3.8 Radiation and risk

Summary questions

1 a Calculate how many protons and how many neutrons are in a nucleus of each of the following isotopes:
   i $^{14}_{6}C$ ii $^{228}_{90}Th$.   [2 marks]
   b $^{14}_{6}C$ emits a β particle and becomes an isotope of nitrogen (N).
   i Write how many protons and how many neutrons are in this nitrogen isotope. [2 marks]
   ii Write the symbol for this isotope.   [1 mark]
   c $^{228}_{90}Th$ emits an α particle and becomes an isotope of radium (Ra).
   i Write how many protons and how many neutrons are in this isotope of radium.   [2 marks]
   ii Write the symbol for this isotope.   [1 mark]

2 Copy and complete the following table about the properties of alpha, beta, and gamma radiation.   [4 marks]

		α	β	γ
a	Identity		electrons	
b	Stopped by			thick lead
c	Range in air		about 1 m	
d	Relative ionisation			weak

3 The following measurements were made of the count rate from a radioactive source.

Time in hours	0	0.5	1.0	1.5	2.0	2.5
Count rate due to the source in counts per minute	510	414	337	276	227	188

   a Plot a graph of the count rate (on the vertical axis) against time.   [3 marks]
   b Use your graph to find the half-life of the source.   [1 mark]

4 In a radioactive carbon dating experiment of ancient wood, a sample of the wood had an activity of 40 Bq. The same mass of living wood had an activity of 320 Bq.
   a i State what is meant by the activity of a radioactive source.   [1 mark]
     H ii Calculate how many half-lives the activity took to decrease from 320 to 40 Bq.   [2 marks]
   H b The half-life of the radioactive carbon in the wood is 5600 years. Calculate the age of the sample.   [1 mark]

5 In an investigation to find out what type of radiation was emitted from a given source, the following measurements were made with a Geiger counter.

Source S at 20 mm from tube T of the Geiger counter	Average count rate in counts per minute
no source S present	29
no absorber present	385
sheet of metal foil between S and T	384
thick aluminium plate between S and T	32

   a Write what caused the count rate when no source was present.   [1 mark]
   b Write the count rate from the source with no absorbers present.   [1 mark]
   c Write what type of radiation was emitted by the source. Explain how you arrived at your answer.   [4 marks]

6 a Explain what is meant by ionisation.   [1 mark]
   b Name the two types of electromagnetic radiation that can ionise substances.   [1 mark]
   c Give two reasons why ionising radiation is harmful.   [2 marks]

7 Figure 1 is a brain scan that clearly shows a brain tumour.

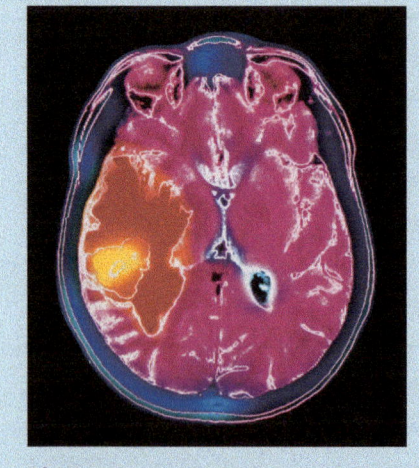

Figure 1

   a What is a tumour?   [2 marks]
   b This could be a benign or a malignant tumour. Explain the similarities and differences in the effect of the diagnosis on the situation for the patient.   [4 marks]

3.8 Radiation and risk

Practice questions

01 Unstable atoms may emit nuclear radiation. Alpha and beta particles are two types of nuclear radiation.

01.1 Name **one** other type of nuclear radiation. [1 mark]

01.2 Describe the changes that take place in an atom when it emits an alpha particle. [2 marks]

01.3 An alpha particle has the same constituent particles as the nucleus of which atom? [1 mark]

01.4 Alpha particles are strongly ionising. An alpha particle will produce positive ions as it travels through a gas. Describe how the alpha particle produces positive ions in the gas. [2 marks]

01.5 Suggest **two** reasons why alpha particles are strongly ionising. [2 marks]

02 A radioactive sample that emits only one type of radiation is brought into a science laboratory.

02.1 Describe how the type of nuclear radiation emitted by the radioactive source can be determined safely. You should include:
- how the nuclear radiation is detected
- how the radioactive source can be tested safely. [6 marks]

03 Uranium-235 ($^{235}_{92}U$) is an element that decays via alpha decay into the element thorium (Th).

03.1 Write a balanced nuclear decay equation for the emission of an alpha particle by uranium-235. [2 marks]

03.2 Carbon-14 is a radioactive isotope of carbon. Define isotope. [2 marks]

03.3 The half-life of carbon-14 is 6000 years. Define half-life. [1 mark]

03.4 A sample of carbon-14 has an activity of 1200 Bq. Calculate the activity of the sample after 18 000 years. [2 marks]

03.5 Medical tracers can be injected into a patient to monitor the movement of the radioactive source through the patient's body. The radioactive source is not removed from a patient after treatment. Technetium (Tc-99m) is a radioactive isotope that is used as a medical tracer.
Uranium (U-238) is not used as a medical tracer.
Figure 1 shows the decay curves for technetium and uranium.

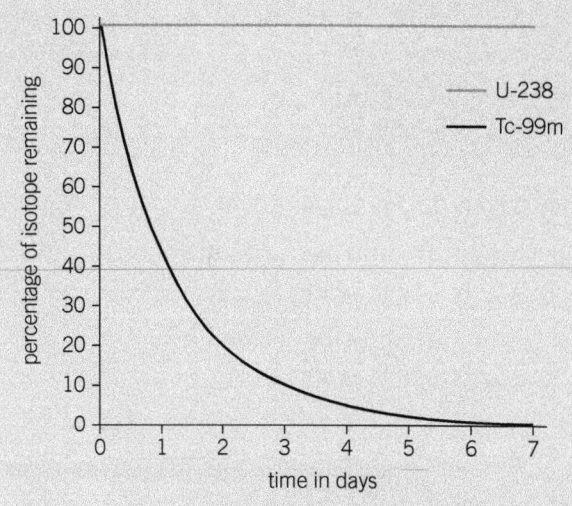

Figure 1

Explain why uranium is unsuitable for use as a radioactive tracer. [2 marks]

04 Radioactive waste from nuclear power stations has to be stored carefully to avoid contamination of ground water supplies. Ground water supplies are used as drinking water in large parts of the UK.

04.1 Explain what is meant by contamination of ground water. [1 mark]

04.2 Describe the consequences of contaminated ground water being consumed. [2 marks]

05 X-rays are used in hospitals to obtain images of broken bones and internal organs. Some patients feel worried about being exposed to X-rays. The measured risk of harm from X-rays is about the same as the measured risk from traces of radioactive substances in food and drink.

05.1 Give **one** effect that X-rays can have on living cells. [1 mark]

05.2 Define perceived risk. [1 mark]

05.3 Compare the perceived risk of harm with the measured risk of harm from:
A X-rays
B food and drink. [2 marks]

05.4 Radiographers who use X-ray machines have the potential to be exposed to a much higher level of radiation than patients. Give **two** ways in which radiographers reduce their exposure to radiation. [2 marks]

3.9 Preventing, treating, and curing diseases

3.9.1 Pathogens and disease

Learning objectives
After this topic, you should know:
- what pathogens are
- how pathogens cause disease
- how pathogens are spread.

Communicable (infectious) diseases are found all o... **Microorganisms** that cause disease are called path... ns may be bacteria, **viruses**, **protists**, or fungi, and ... and plants, causing a wide range of diseases.

Communicable diseases are caused either directly ... toxin made by a pathogen. The pathogen can be passe... individual to another individual who does not have the dis... communicable diseases are fairly mild, such as the commo... tonsillitis. Others are known killers, such as tetanus, influenza...

Sometimes communicable diseases can be passed betwee... species of organisms. For example, infected animals such as ... can pass rabies on to people. Tuberculosis can be passed fro... cows, and from cows to people.

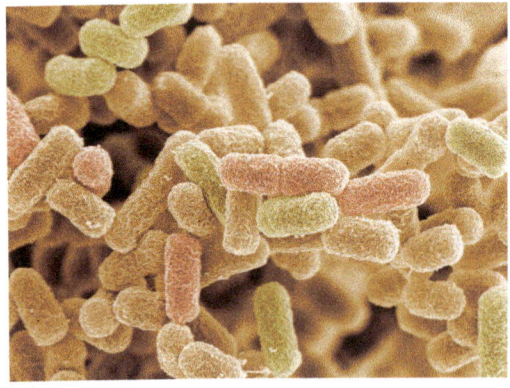

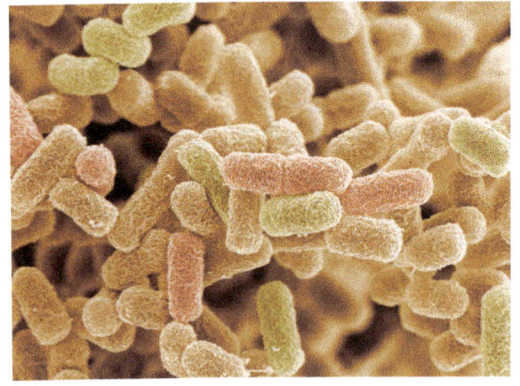

What are the differences between bacteria and viruses?
Bacteria and viruses cause the majority of communicable diseases in people. In plants, viruses and fungi are the most common pathogens. Bacteria are single-celled living organisms that are much smaller than animal and plant cells (Figure 1). Bacteria are used to make food such as yogurt and cheese, to treat sewage, and to make medicines. Bacteria are important both in the environment, as decomposers, and in your body. Scientists estimate that most people have between 1 and 2 kg of bacteria in their guts, and they are rapidly discovering that these bacteria have a major effect on our health and well-being.

Pathogenic bacteria are the minority – but they are significant because of the major effects they can have on individuals and on society.

Viruses are even smaller than bacteria. They usually have regular shapes. Viruses cause diseases in every type of living organism.

How pathogens cause disease
Once bacteria and viruses are inside your body, they may reproduce rapidly.

- Bacteria divide rapidly by splitting in two (called binary fission). They may produce toxins (poisons) that affect your body and make you feel ill. Sometimes they directly damage your cells.
- Viruses take over the cells of your body. They live and reproduce inside the cells, damaging and destroying them.

Figure 1 *Many bacteria are very useful to humans but some are pathogens that cause disease, such as the strain of E. coli shown in this false colour scanning electron micrograph – magnification ~ ×2500*

Synoptic link
Remind yourself about the structure of bacteria by looking back to Topic 1.3.3.

■ 3.9 Preventing, treating, and curing diseases

Common disease symptoms are a high temperature, headaches, and rashes. These are caused by the way in which your body responds to the cell damage and toxins produced by the pathogens.

How pathogens are spread

The more pathogens that get into your body, the more likely it is that you will develop an infectious disease. There are a number of ways in which pathogens spread from one individual to another:

- By air (including droplet infection). Many pathogens including bacteria, viruses, and fungal spores (that cause plant diseases) are carried and spread from one organism to another in the air. In human diseases, droplet infection is common. When you are ill, you expel tiny droplets full of pathogens from your breathing system when you cough, sneeze, or talk (Figure 2). Other people breathe in the droplets, along with the pathogens they contain, so they pick up the infection. Examples include influenza (flu), tuberculosis, and the common cold.
- Through food that is contaminated with bacteria or other pathogens. Eating raw or undercooked meat, or uncooked food such as salad that is contaminated by pathogens such as *Campylobacter*, can cause gut diseases in people.
- Through drinking water that is contaminated, often by sewage. This can spread diseases such as diarrhoea, cholera, or salmonellosis. The pathogen enters your body through your digestive system.
- Through contact with infected people, or surfaces that infected people have touched (e.g., fungal diseases such as athlete's foot can be passed on by walking barefoot over the same floor as an infected person). Sexually transmitted diseases are passed on through intimate contact with infected people.
- By animals carrying human pathogens that scratch, bite, or draw blood. Examples include malaria – passed on by the bite of a mosquito – and rabies – passed on by the bite of an infected dog or other mammal.

Lifestyle factors often affect the spread of disease. For example, when people live in crowded conditions with no sewage system, infectious diseases can spread very rapidly. If an individual has a defect in their immune system, or is taking immunosuppressant drugs, they are more likely to suffer from infectious diseases.

1 a What causes infectious diseases? [1 mark]
   b How do pathogens make you ill? [2 marks]
2 a Describe how pathogens can be passed from one person to another through the air. [3 marks]
   b Explain how animals can spread diseases between people. [5 marks]
3 Contaminated food and water spread diseases that affect millions of people globally. Suggest ways in which this can take place. [5 marks]

Figure 2 *Droplets carrying millions of pathogens fly out of your mouth and nose at up to 100 miles an hour when you sneeze*

Go further

Mutations in the genetic material of bacteria can result in changes to the bacterial cell walls or biochemistry. In turn this may mean that they are no longer affected by antibiotics. This leads to antibiotic resistance in a population of bacteria and bacterial diseases that cannot be cured.

Synoptic link

For more information on bacteria that are resistant to antibiotics, see Topic 4.12.8.

Key points

- Communicable diseases are caused by microorganisms called pathogens, which include bacteria, viruses, fungi, and protists.
- Bacteria and viruses reproduce rapidly inside your body. Bacteria can produce toxins that make you feel ill. Viruses destroy your cells as they reproduce.
- Pathogens can be spread through the air; by contaminated food or water; through contact with other people or contaminated surfaces; and by animals that scratch, bite, or draw blood.

3.9.2 Preventing infections

Learning objectives
After this topic, you should know:
- how the spread of disease can be reduced or prevented.

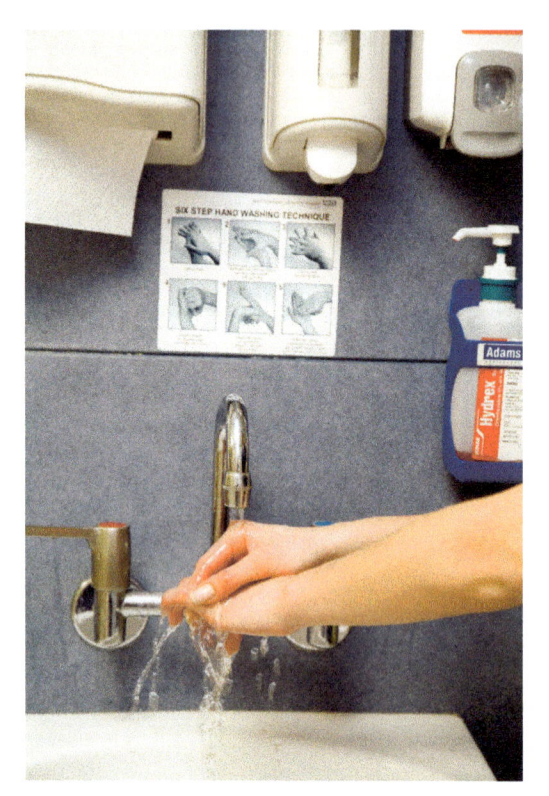

Figure 1 *In hospitals today, simply reminding doctors, nurses, and visitors to wash their hands more often is still an important way to prevent the spread of disease*

People have recognised the symptoms of disease for many centuries. There are records of illnesses people recognise today from the ancient Egyptians and ancient Greeks. However, it is only in the past 150–200 years that people have really understood the causes of these diseases and how they are spread. The work of pioneering doctors and scientists such as Ignaz Semmelweis, Louis Pasteur, and Joseph Lister has helped to develop the modern understanding of pathogens. Their work enabled people to prevent the spread of pathogens, and in some cases cure the diseases they cause.

The work of Ignaz Semmelweis

Semmelweis was a doctor in the mid-1850s. At the time, many women in hospital died from childbed fever a few days after giving birth. However, no one knew what caused it.

Semmelweis noticed that his medical students went straight from dissecting a dead body to delivering a baby without washing their hands. The women delivered by medical students and doctors rather than midwives were much more likely to die. Semmelweis wondered if they were carrying the cause of disease from the corpses to their patients.

He noticed that another doctor died from symptoms identical to childbed fever after cutting himself while working on a body. This convinced Semmelweis that the fever was caused by some kind of infectious agent. He therefore insisted that his medical students wash their hands before delivering babies. Immediately, fewer mothers died from the fever. However, other doctors were very resistant to Semmelweis's ideas.

Other discoveries
Also in the mid- to late-19th century:
- Louis Pasteur showed that microorganisms caused disease. He developed **vaccines** against diseases such as anthrax and rabies.
- Joseph Lister started to use antiseptic chemicals to destroy pathogens before they caused infection in operating theatres.
- As microscopes improved, it became possible to see pathogens more clearly. This helped to convince people that they were really there.

Understanding how communicable diseases are spread from one person to another helps us to prevent it happening.

Preventing the spread of communicable diseases
There are a number of key ways in which to help prevent the spread of communicable diseases between people and between animals and people.

Hygiene
Simple hygiene measures are one of the most effective ways of preventing the spread of pathogens. These include:
- Handwashing, especially after using the toilet, before cooking, or after contact with an animal or someone who has an infectious illness.

■ 3.9 Preventing, treating, and curing diseases

- Using disinfectants on kitchen work surfaces, toilets, etc. to reduce the number of pathogens.
- Keeping raw meat away from food that is eaten uncooked to prevent the spread of pathogens.
- Coughing or sneezing into a handkerchief, a tissue, or your hands (and then washing your hands).

Isolating infected individuals

If someone has an infectious disease, especially a serious disease such as Ebola or cholera, they need to be kept in isolation. The fewer healthy people who come into contact with the infected person, the less likely it is that the pathogens will be passed on. Children with infectious diseases should be kept away from school in order to avoid spreading the pathogens to others. These infectious diseases include impetigo, chickenpox, diarrhoea and vomiting, measles, and scarlet fever.

Destroying or controlling vectors

Some communicable diseases are passed on by vectors. For example, mosquitoes carry a range of diseases, such as malaria and dengue fever. Houseflies can carry over 100 human diseases, while rats also act as vectors of disease. The fleas on rats famously carried the Black Death, a bacterial disease that wiped out up to 50% of the population of Europe in the 14th century. If the vectors are destroyed, the spread of the disease can be prevented. By controlling the number of vectors, the spread of disease can be greatly reduced.

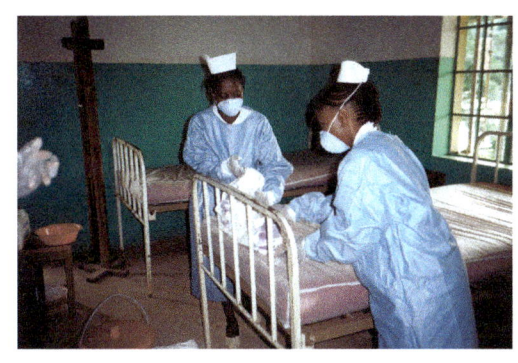

Figure 2 *Isolation of infected patients played a major role in the control of the deadly disease Ebola in West Africa during the 2014 outbreak*

Treatment and vaccination

One way in which to prevent the spread of an infectious disease is to treat and cure any patients affected as quickly as possible. This reduces the chance of the pathogens reaching other people.

Another approach is to use **vaccination** to protect entire populations against a particular disease. During vaccination, doctors introduce a small amount of a harmless form of a specific pathogen into your body. As a result, if you come into contact with the live pathogen, you will not become ill as your immune system will be prepared. Vaccination is a very successful way of protecting large numbers of humans and animals against serious diseases.

Synoptic link

You will learn more about preventing communicable diseases in Topics 3.9.6 and 3.9.7.

---

1. Give *three* examples of things people can do to reduce the spread of pathogens to lower the risk of disease. [3 marks]
2. Explain how each example given in your answer to Question 1 helps to prevent the spread of disease. [6 marks]
3. It is still necessary to remind doctors and nurses to wash their hands when moving from one patient to another, more than 150 years on from the work of Semmelweis. Visitors to hospitals need reminding, too. Suggest reasons for this. [6 marks]

Key points

- The spread of disease can be prevented by simple hygiene measures, isolation of infected individuals, destruction of vectors, treatment of disease, and vaccination.

3.9.3 Viral diseases

Learning objectives

After this topic, you should know:

- some examples of diseases caused by viruses including measles and HIV/AIDS in humans.

Viruses can infect and damage all types of cells. The diseases they cause can be mild or potentially deadly. Scientists have not developed medicines to cure viral diseases, so it is important to stop them spreading. In people, viral diseases often start relatively suddenly. The symptoms are the result of the way in which the body reacts to the viruses damaging and destroying cells as they reproduce. See below for examples of viral diseases.

Measles

The main symptoms of measles are a fever and a red skin rash. The virus is spread by the inhalation of droplets from coughs and sneezes and is very infectious. Measles is a serious disease that can cause blindness and brain damage and may be fatal if complications arise. In 2013, 145 700 people globally died of measles. There is no treatment for measles, so if someone becomes infected they need to be isolated to stop the spread of the virus. Measles is now rare in the UK as a result of improved living conditions and a vaccination programme for young children. The challenge now is to vaccinate children globally and make deaths from measles a thing of the past (Figure 2).

HIV/AIDS

Around 35 million people globally are infected with HIV, a virus that can eventually lead to AIDS. In 2013, around 1.5 million people died of HIV-related illnesses. Many people do not realise they are infected with HIV, because the virus only causes a mild, flu-like illness to begin with. HIV is a type of virus called a retrovirus. It attacks the immune cells and after the initial mild illness it remains hidden inside the immune system until the immune system is so badly damaged that it can no longer deal with infections or certain cancers. At this point the patient has developed AIDS.

The time between infection with HIV and the onset of the final stages of AIDS is affected by many factors. These include the level of nutrition and overall health of the person, as well as access to antiretroviral drugs, which help to control retroviruses.

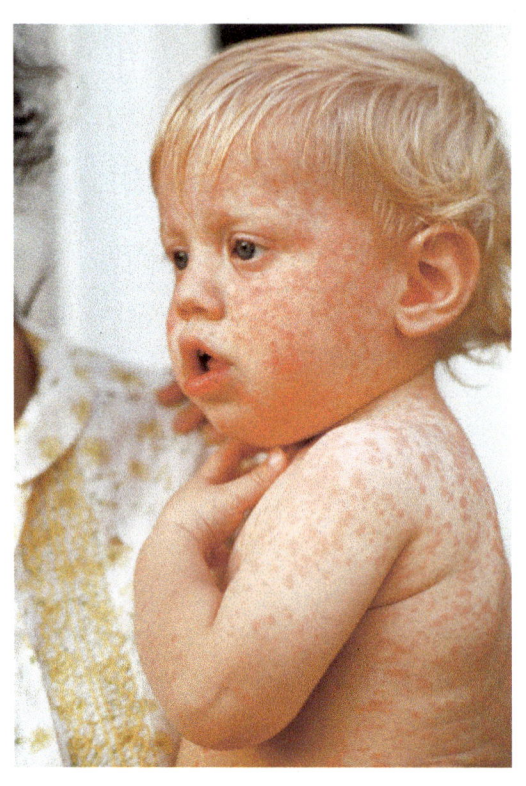

Figure 1 *A measles rash is now a rare sight in the UK*

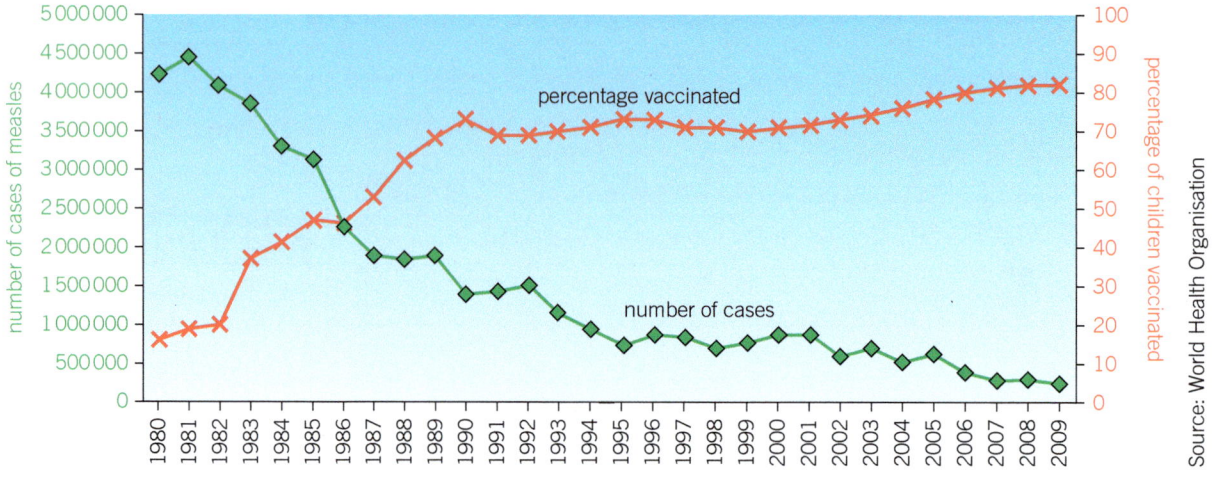

Figure 2 *Trends in global vaccination against measles and the numbers of reported measles cases*

Source: World Health Organisation

■ 3.9 Preventing, treating, and curing diseases

HIV is spread by direct sexual contact and the exchange of body fluids such as blood, which occurs when drug users share needles or when unscreened blood is used for transfusions. HIV can also be passed from mother to child in breast milk.

There is no cure for HIV/AIDS and no vaccine against it. The spread of the disease can be prevented by using condoms, not sharing needles, screening blood used for transfusions, and HIV-positive mothers bottle-feeding their children.

The regular use of antiretroviral drugs can prevent the development of AIDS for many years and give HIV positive people an almost normal life expectancy. Unfortunately, the majority of people infected with HIV live in areas such as sub-Saharan Africa, where it is hard to get antiretroviral drugs (Figure 3). In these areas the life expectancy for people with HIV/AIDs is still very low. To have the best chance of long-term survival, antiretroviral drugs must be started as soon as possible after infection.

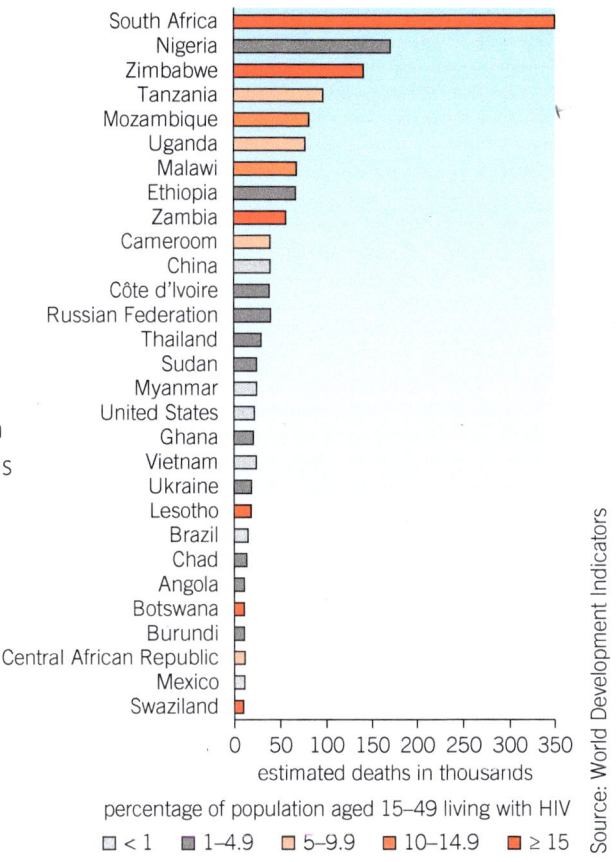

Figure 3 HIV infection rates and estimated deaths from AIDS in African countries

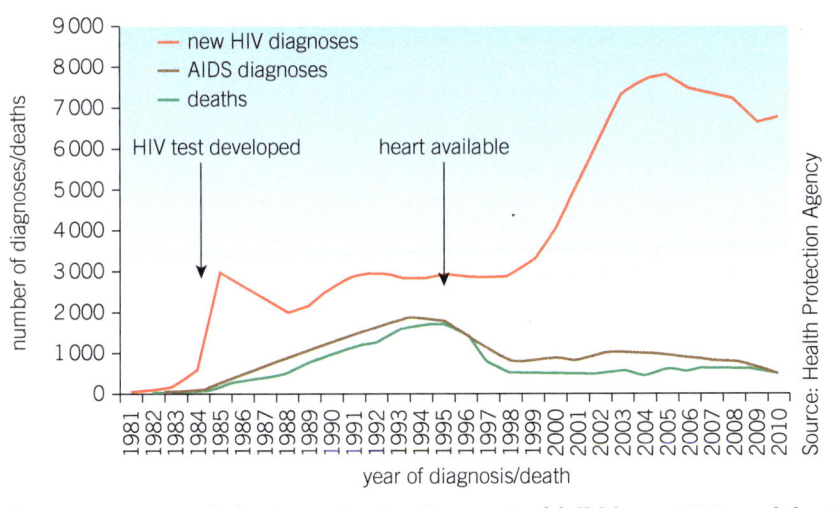

Figure 4 New HIV infections, the development of full-blown AIDS, and deaths from AIDS in the UK per year between 1981 and 2010

1 a State the main symptoms of measles. [2 marks]
   b Suggest why measles is now rare in the UK. [2 marks]
2 a Describe the link between HIV and AIDS. [1 mark]
   b Explain why untreated HIV is usually fatal. [4 marks]
3 Using Figure 2, estimate the following.
   a The number of cases of measles globally between:
      i   1980 and 1985 [3 marks]
      ii 2000 and 2005. [3 marks]
   b Assuming that 5% of patients (cases) will die, calculate how many people died of measles in each time period. [4 marks]
   c Discuss the apparent link between vaccination rates and cases of measles globally. [4 marks]
4 Using the data in Figures 3 and 4, discuss the pattern of HIV infection and numbers of people dying from AIDS in the UK and South Africa. [6 marks]

Key points

- Measles virus is spread by droplet infection. It causes fever and a rash and can be fatal. There is no cure. Isolation of patients and vaccination prevents spread.
- HIV initially causes flu-like illness. Unless it is successfully controlled with antiretroviral drugs the virus attacks the body's immune cells. Late-stage HIV infection, or AIDS, occurs when the body's immune system becomes so badly damaged that it can no longer deal with other infections or cancers. HIV is spread by sexual contact or by the exchange of body fluids, such as blood, which occurs when drug users share needles.

183

3.9.4 Bacterial diseases

Learning objectives

After this topic, you should know:
- some examples of diseases caused by bacteria, including *Salmonella* food poisoning and gonorrhoea in humans.

Synoptic links

To remind yourself about orders of magnitude, look back at Topic 1.3.1 and see Maths skills MS 2h.

You will learn more about antibiotics in Topic 3.9.7, and more about antibiotic resistance in Topic 4.12.8.

Figure 1 *Raw poultry, undercooked food, or salads contaminated with raw meat through poor kitchen hygiene are all common sources of the Salmonella bacteria that can cause food poisoning.*

Go further

Humans (and other animals) are not the only organisms to suffer from bacterial diseases. The bacterium *Agrobacterium tumefaciens* causes disease in plants. It creates galls, big masses of tissue that form on the roots and stems. This same bacterium is widely used in the genetic modification of plants, which could help to provide enough food for the whole world population.

Bacterial diseases affect animals and plants. In the early 20th century, more than 30% of all deaths in the USA were due to infectious diseases. That is now an order of magnitude lower, and most of the infectious diseases that cause death are viral. Improved living standards and vaccinations have had a major effect on the incidence and death rate of communicable diseases in countries such as the USA and the UK.

The development of antibiotics is the other key factor in combating bacterial diseases. Antibiotics kill bacteria or stop them growing, curing bacterial diseases. Unfortunately, bacteria are becoming resistant to many antibiotics and more people are dying from bacterial diseases again.

Salmonella food poisoning

Salmonella are bacteria that live in the guts of many different animals. They can be found in raw meat, poultry, eggs, and egg products such as mayonnaise. If these bacteria get into our bodies, they disrupt the balance of the natural gut bacteria and can cause *Salmonella* food poisoning. One common cause of infection is eating undercooked food, when the bacteria have not been killed by heating. Another is eating food prepared in unhygienic conditions where food is contaminated with *Salmonella* bacteria from raw meat.

Symptoms of *Salmonella* food poisoning develop within 8–72 hours of eating infected food. Fever, abdominal cramps, vomiting, and diarrhoea are caused by the bacteria and the toxins they secrete. For many people *Salmonella* infections are unpleasant but don't last many days and no antibiotics are given. In very young children and the elderly it can be fatal, usually because of dehydration. In countries where there is malnutrition, *Salmonella* is more serious. The World Health Organisation estimates that globally around 2.2 million people, mainly children under 5 years old, are killed by sickness and diarrhoea (including *Salmonella* food poisoning) each year.

Salmonella bacteria are killed by cooking, so if chicken products are thoroughly cooked there is no risk of disease. The bacteria are also killed by **pasteurisation**, when food is heated to a high temperature briefly and then cooled for storage. *Salmonella* infections are easily transmitted by raw eggs (e.g., in mayonnaise or soft-boiled eggs). In the food industry eggs are now always pasteurised to destroy any *Salmonella* bacteria before they are used to make products such as mayonnaise.

In the UK, poultry are vaccinated against *Salmonella* to control the spread of the disease. *Campylobacter*, another bacterium found in chickens, still causes around 280 000 cases of food poisoning each year. To prevent food poisoning, keep raw chicken away from food that is eaten uncooked, avoid washing raw chicken (washing sprays bacteria around the kitchen), wash hands and surfaces well after handling raw chicken, and cook chicken thoroughly.

3.9 Preventing, treating, and curing diseases

Gonorrhoea

Gonorrhoea is an example of a **sexually transmitted disease (STD)**. A disease like this is also known as a sexually transmitted infection (STI). It is spread by unprotected sexual contact with an infected person. Like many STDs, gonorrhoea has symptoms in the early stages but then becomes relatively symptomless. The early symptoms include a thick, yellow or green discharge from the vagina or penis and pain on urination. However, about 10% of infected men and 50% of infected women get no symptoms at all. Untreated gonorrhoea can cause long-term pelvic pain, infertility, and unsuccessful pregnancies. Babies born to infected mothers may have severe eye infections and may even become blind.

Gonorrhoea is bacterial, so it can be treated with antibiotics. Originally it was easily cured using penicillin, but now many antibiotic-resistant strains of gonorrhoea have evolved so it is increasingly difficult to treat. All sexual partners of an infected individual must be treated with antibiotics to prevent the disease spreading in the community. The spread of gonorrhoea can also be prevented by using a barrier method of contraception such as a condom and by reducing the number of sexual partners.

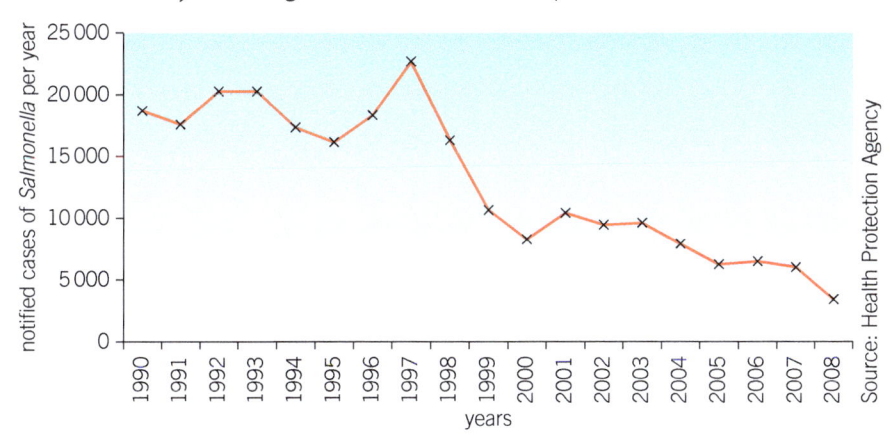

Figure 2 *Impact of* Salmonella *control measures, introduced in the late 1990s, on cases of* Salmonella *food poisoning in the UK*

1. State *one* way in which antibiotics work to cure bacterial infections. [1 mark]
2. a. Describe how people become infected with food poisoning caused by *Salmonella*. [2 marks]
   b. Doctors in the UK rarely treat *Salmonella* food poisoning with antibiotics. Suggest reasons for this. [3 marks]
3. a. Gonorrhoea is an STD. Explain what this means. [2 marks]
   b. Until recently gonorrhoea was relatively easy to treat. Explain this statement. [2 marks]
   c. Suggest *three* ways of preventing the spread of gonorrhoea. [3 marks]
   d. Discuss the implications of increased antibiotic resistance in the bacteria causing gonorrhoea for the 106 million people worldwide who are infected with the disease each year. [4 marks]
4. Write a paragraph for your local newspaper on food preparation for summer barbeques to help people avoid *Salmonella* and other forms of food poisoning. [6 marks]

Key points

- *Salmonella* is spread through bacteria ingested in undercooked food or on food prepared in unhygienic conditions. Symptoms include fever, abdominal cramps, diarrhoea, and vomiting caused by the toxins produced by the bacteria. *Salmonella* are killed by cooking and by pasteurisation. In the UK, poultry are vaccinated against *Salmonella* to control the spread of disease.
- Gonorrhoea is a sexually transmitted disease caused by a bacterium. Early symptoms include discharge from the penis or vagina and pain on urination. Treatment is by antibiotics, although many strains are now resistant. The spread of gonorrhoea is controlled by antibiotic treatment, using condoms, and limiting sexual partners.

3.9.5 Human defence responses

Learning objectives

After this topic, you should know:

- how your body stops pathogens getting in
- how your white blood cells protect you from disease.

The mucus produced from your nose turns green when you have a cold. Why does this happen? It is all part of the way in which your body defends itself against disease.

Preventing microorganisms getting into your body

Each day, you meet millions of disease-causing microorganisms. Every body opening, as well as any breaks in the skin, gives pathogens a way in. The more pathogens that get into your body, the more likely it is that you will develop an infectious disease. Fortunately, your body has many defence mechanisms that work together to keep the pathogens out.

Skin defences

- Your skin covers your body and acts as a barrier. It prevents bacteria and viruses from reaching the tissues beneath. If you damage or cut your skin, the barrier is broken but your body restores it. You bleed, and the platelets in your blood set up a chain of events to form a clot that dries into a scab (Figure 1). This forms a seal over the cut, stopping pathogens getting in. It also stops you from bleeding to death.
- Your skin produces antimicrobial secretions to destroy pathogenic bacteria.
- Healthy skin is covered with microorganisms that help keep you healthy and act as an extra barrier to the entry of pathogens.

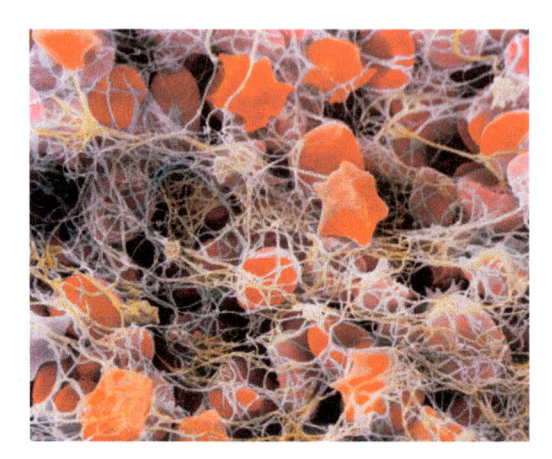

Figure 1 *This false colour scanning electron micrograph shows a scab that restores the protective barrier of the skin and prevents pathogens getting in. It is made of red blood cells tangled in a network of fibrin strands – magnification ~ ×2000*

Defences of the respiratory and digestive systems

Your respiratory system is a weak link in your body defences. Every time you breathe in, you draw air full of pathogens into the airways of the lungs. In the same way, you take food and drink, as well as air, into your digestive system through your mouth. Both systems have good defences to help prevent pathogens constantly causing infections.

- Your nose is full of hairs and produces a sticky liquid, called mucus. The hairs and mucus trap particles in the air that may contain pathogens or irritate your lungs. If you spend time in an environment with lots of air pollution, the mucus you produce when you blow your nose is blackened, showing that the system works.
- The trachea and bronchi also secrete mucus that traps pathogens from the air. The lining of the tubes is covered in cilia – tiny hair-like projections from the cells. The cilia beat to waft the mucus up to the back of the throat where it is swallowed.
- The stomach produces acid and this destroys the microorganisms in the mucus you swallow, as well as the majority of the pathogens you take in through your mouth in your food and drink.

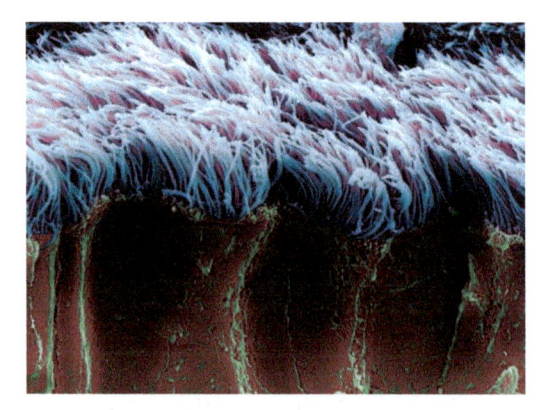

Figure 2 *The cilia of the airways, shown here magnified thousands of times in a false colour scanning electron micrgraph, beat together to move mucus containing trapped pathogens away from the lungs*

3.9 Preventing, treating, and curing diseases

The immune system – internal defences

In spite of your body's defence mechanisms, some pathogens still get inside your body. Once there, they will meet your second line of defence – the white blood cells, which are an important part of your immune system. The white blood cells will try to destroy any pathogens that enter the body in several ways.

Table 1 *Ways in which your white blood cells destroy pathogens and protect you against disease. Note that the cells, bacteria, antigens, and antitoxins are not drawn to scale and are represented schematically*

Role of white blood cell	How it protects you against disease
Phagocytosis (diagram: bacterium, white blood cell)	Some white blood cells ingest (take in) pathogens, digesting and destroying them so they cannot make you ill. Ingesting microorganisms in this way is called **phagocytosis**.
Producing antibodies (diagram: antibody, antigen, bacterium, white blood cell, antibody attached to antigen)	Some white blood cells produce special chemicals called antibodies. These target particular bacteria or viruses and destroy them. You need a unique antibody for each type of pathogen. When your white blood cells have produced antibodies once against a particular pathogen, they can be made very quickly if that pathogen gets into the body again. This stops you getting the disease twice.
Producing antitoxins (diagram: white blood cell, antitoxin molecule, toxin and antitoxin joined together, toxin molecule, bacterium)	Some white blood cells produce antitoxins. These counteract (cancel out) the toxins released by pathogens.

The different body systems work together to help protect you from disease. For example, some white blood cells contain green-coloured enzymes. These white blood cells destroy the cold viruses and any bacteria trapped in the mucus of your nose when you have a cold. The dead white blood cells, along with the dead bacteria and viruses, are removed in the mucus, making it look green.

1. Describe *three* ways in which your skin helps to prevent pathogens from entering your body. [3 marks]
2. Explain why the following symptoms of certain diseases increase your risk of getting infections.
   a. Your blood won't clot properly. [2 marks]
   b. The number of white cells in your blood falls. [3 marks]
3. Describe how your white blood cells help to prevent you from suffering from communicable diseases. [6 marks]

Go further

Very rarely, a baby is born without an immune system. This leaves the infant vulnerable to infections and is fatal if it is not treated. In autoimmune diseases, your immune system starts to destroy your own tissues. This can lead to many problems, from hives to arthritis.

Synoptic links

Remind yourself about the production of acid in the stomach by looking back at Topic 2.5.9, about the blood and clotting by looking back at Topic 2.5.4, and about the structure of the breathing system by looking back at Topic 2.5.7.

You will find out about antigens in Topic 3.9.6.

Key points

- Your body has several lines of defence against the entry of pathogens. These include the skin (which acts as a barrier and produces antimicrobial secretions), the nose, trachea, and bronchi (which trap microorganisms and move them out of the body), and the stomach (which produces acid).
- Your white blood cells help to defend you against pathogens through phagocytosis and by making antibodies and antitoxins.

3.9.6 Vaccination

Learning objectives

After this topic, you should know:
- how vaccination works
- how vaccination can protect a whole population from disease.

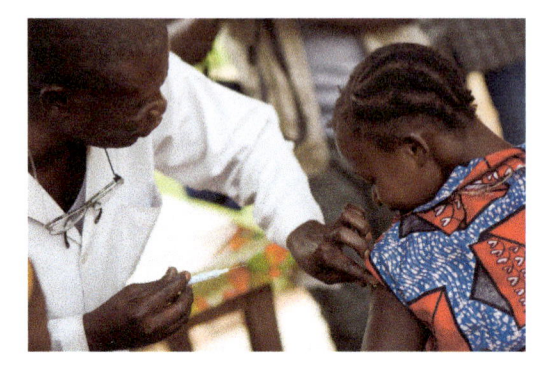

Figure 1 *No one likes having a vaccination very much – but they save millions of lives around the world every year!*

Study tip

High levels of antibodies do not stay in your blood forever. Immunity is *not* a constantly high level of antibodies to a disease. It is the ability of your white blood cells to produce the right antibodies quickly, as a result of memory cells, if you are re-infected by a disease.

Every cell has unique proteins on its surface called antigens. The antigens on the microorganisms that get into your body are different to the ones on your own cells. Your immune system recognises that they are different.

Your white blood cells then make specific antibodies, which join up with the antigens and inactivate or destroy that particular pathogen.

Some of your white blood cells (the memory cells) 'remember' the right antibody needed to destroy a particular pathogen. If you meet that pathogen again, these memory cells can make the same antibody very quickly to kill the pathogen, so you become immune to the disease.

The first time you meet a new pathogen you get ill because there is a delay while your body sorts out the right antibody needed. The next time, your immune system destroys the invaders before they can make you feel unwell.

Vaccination

Some pathogens, such as meningitis, can make you seriously ill very quickly. In fact, you can die before your body manages to make the right antibodies. Fortunately, you can be protected against many of these serious diseases by vaccination (also known as immunisation).

Vaccination involves giving you a vaccine made of a dead or inactivated form of a disease-causing microorganism. It stimulates your body's natural immune response to invading pathogens (Figure 2).

A small amount of a dead or inactive form of a pathogen is introduced into your body. This stimulates the white blood cells to produce the antibodies needed to fight the pathogen and prevent you from getting ill. Then, if you meet the same, live pathogen, your white blood cells can respond rapidly. They can make the right antibodies just as if you had already had the disease, so that you are protected against it.

Doctors use vaccines to protect us both against bacterial diseases (e.g., tetanus and diphtheria), and viral diseases (e.g., polio, measles, and mumps). For example, the MMR vaccine protects against measles, mumps, and rubella. Vaccines have saved millions of lives around the world. One disease – smallpox – has been completely wiped out by vaccinations. Doctors hope that polio will also disappear in the next few years.

■ 3.9 Preventing, treating, and curing diseases

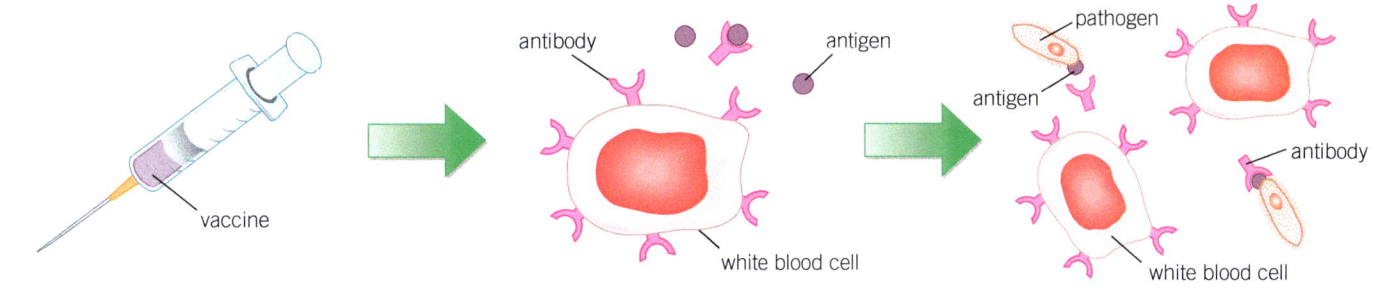

Small amounts of dead or inactive pathogen are put into your body, often by injection.

The antigens in the vaccine stimulate your white blood cells into making antibodies. The antibodies destroy the antigens without any risk of you getting the disease.

You are immune to future infections by the pathogen. That's because your body can respond rapidly and make the correct antibody as if you had already had the disease.

Figure 2 *This is how vaccination protects you against dangerous infectious diseases. Note that the syringe, cells, bacteria, and antigens are not drawn to scale and are represented schematically*

Herd immunity

If a large proportion of the population is immune to a disease, the spread of the pathogen in the population is very much reduced and the disease may even disappear. This is known as herd immunity. If for any reason the number of people taking up a vaccine falls, the herd immunity is lost and the disease can reappear. This is what happened in the UK in the 1970s when there was a scare about the safety of the whooping cough vaccine. Vaccination rates fell from over 80% to around 30% (Figure 3). In the following years, thousands of children got whooping cough again and a substantial number died. Yet the vaccine was as safe as any medicine. Eventually people realised this and enough children were vaccinated for herd immunity to be effective again. There are global vaccination programmes to control a number of diseases, including tetanus in mothers and newborn babies, polio, and measles. The World Health Organisation want 95% of children to have two doses of measles vaccine to give global herd immunity. Current global figures show that 85% of children get the first dose and 56% get the second. It will take money and determination to achieve global herd immunity against a range of different diseases, but the advantages both to individuals and to global economies are huge.

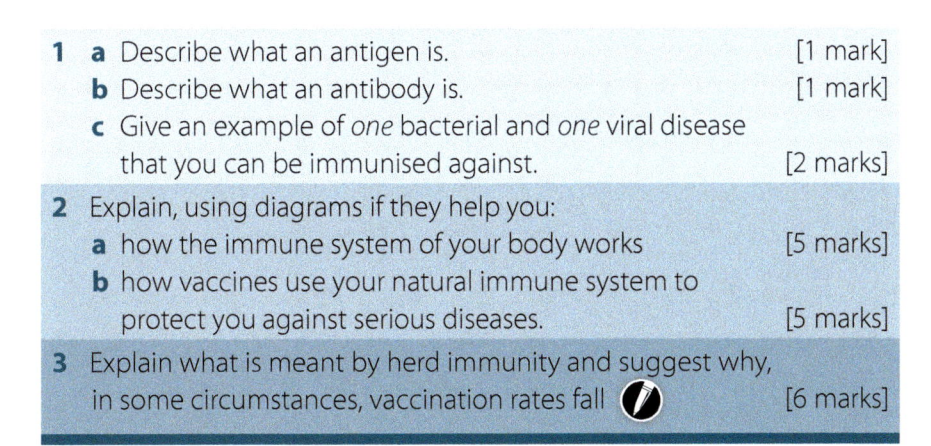

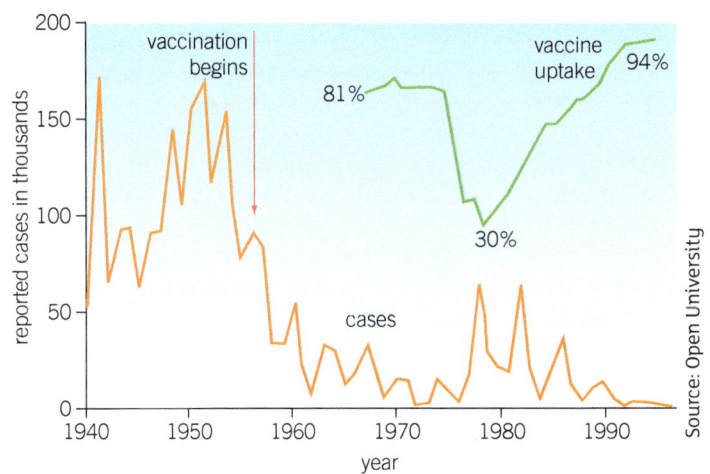

Figure 3 *Graph showing the effect of the whooping cough scare on both uptake of the vaccine and the number of cases of the disease in the UK*

1   a   Describe what an antigen is. [1 mark]
    b   Describe what an antibody is. [1 mark]
    c   Give an example of *one* bacterial and *one* viral disease that you can be immunised against. [2 marks]

2   Explain, using diagrams if they help you:
    a   how the immune system of your body works [5 marks]
    b   how vaccines use your natural immune system to protect you against serious diseases. [5 marks]

3   Explain what is meant by herd immunity and suggest why, in some circumstances, vaccination rates fall [6 marks]

Key points

- If a pathogen enters the body the immune system tries to destroy the pathogen.
- Vaccination involves introducing small amounts of a dead or inactive form of a pathogen into your body to stimulate the white blood cells to produce antibodies. If the same live pathogen re-enters the body, the white blood cells respond quickly to produce the correct antibodies, preventing infection.
- If a large proportion of the population is immune to a pathogen, the spread of the pathogen is much reduced.

3.9.7 Antibiotics and painkillers

Learning objectives

After this topic, you should know:

- what medicines are and how some of them work
- that painkillers and other medicines treat disease symptoms but do not kill pathogens
- the ways in which antibiotics can and cannot be used.

When you have an infectious disease, you generally take medicines that contain useful **drugs**. Often the medicine doesn't affect the pathogen – it just eases the symptoms and makes you feel better.

Treating the symptoms

Drugs such as aspirin and paracetamol are very useful painkillers. When you have a cold, they will help relieve your headache and sore throat. On the other hand, they will have no effect on the viruses that have entered your tissues and made you feel ill.

Many of the medicines you can buy at a pharmacy or supermarket relieve your symptoms but do not kill the pathogens, so they do not cure you any faster. You have to wait for your immune system to overcome the pathogens before you actually get well again.

Medicines as mixtures

Most medicines are not a single substance. They are **formulations** made by mixing the ingredients in carefully measured quantities to make sure that the medicine has the required properties. One or more of the ingredients will be the active drug, such as aspirin or penicillin. The other ingredients make it easier or more pleasant to take the drug either in solution or as a capsule or tablet.

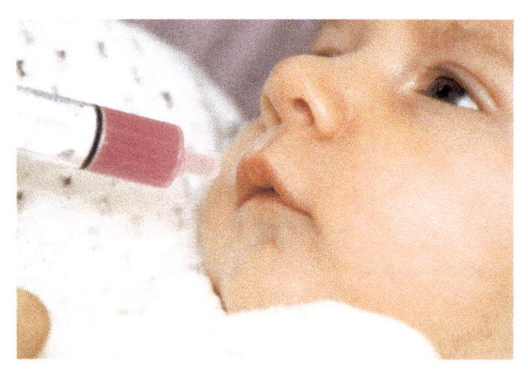

Figure 1 *Giving this baby a painkiller will make him feel better, but he will not actually get better any faster as a result*

Antibiotics – drugs to cure bacterial diseases

The drugs that have really changed the treatment of communicable diseases are antibiotics. These are medicines that can work inside your body to kill bacterial pathogens. The impact of antibiotics on deaths from communicable diseases has been enormous. Antibiotics first became widely available in the 1940s. They were regarded as wonder drugs because they saved so many lives (Figure 2).

Synoptic link

You learnt about pure substances and mixtures in Topic 1.1.8.

Go further

Don't confuse antiseptics, antibiotics, and antibodies.

- Antiseptics kill microorganisms in the environment.
- Antibiotics kill bacteria (*not* viruses) in the body.
- Antibodies are made by white blood cells to destroy pathogens (both bacteria *and* viruses).

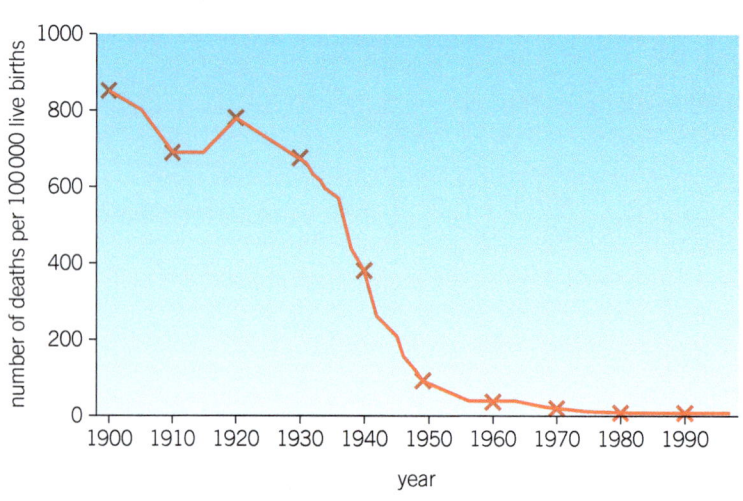

Figure 2 *The introduction of antibiotics in the 1940s had a huge impact on the numbers of women dying from infections after childbirth, as these data from the US show*

3.9 Preventing, treating, and curing diseases

How antibiotics work

Antibiotics such as penicillin (Figure 3) work by killing the bacteria that cause disease whilst they are inside your body. They damage the bacterial cells without harming your own cells. Bacterial diseases that killed millions of people in the past can now be cured using antibiotics. Antibiotics have had an enormous effect on our society.

If you need antibiotics, you usually take a pill or syrup, but if you are very ill antibiotics may be put straight into your bloodstream. This makes sure that they reach the pathogens in your cells as quickly as possible. Some antibiotics kill a wide range of bacteria. Others are very specific and only work against particular bacteria. It is important that the right antibiotic is chosen and used. Specific bacteria should be treated with the specific antibiotic that is effective against them.

Unfortunately, antibiotics are not the complete answer to the problem of infectious diseases.

- Antibiotics cannot kill viral pathogens so they have no effect on diseases caused by viruses. Viruses reproduce inside the cells of your body. It is extremely difficult to develop drugs that will kill the viruses without damaging the cells and tissues of your body at the same time.

- Strains of bacteria that are resistant to antibiotics are evolving. This means that antibiotics that used to kill a particular type of bacteria no longer have an effect, so they cannot cure the disease. There are some types of bacteria that are resistant to all known antibiotics. The emergence of antibiotic-resistant strains of bacteria is a matter of great concern. Unless scientists can discover new antibiotics soon, we may no longer be able to cure bacterial diseases. This means that many millions of people in the future will die of bacterial diseases that we can currently cure.

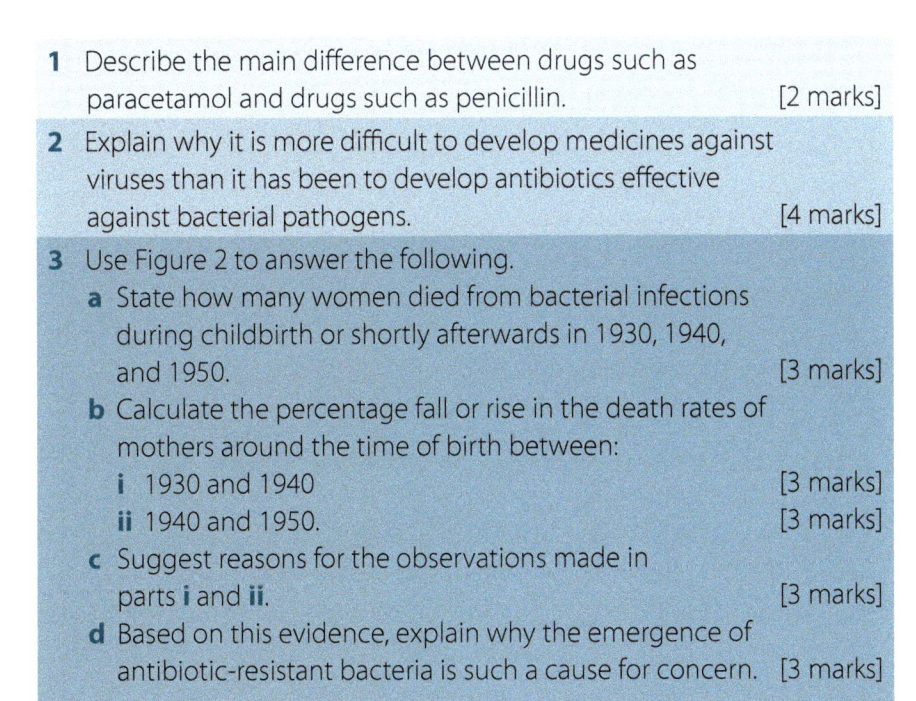

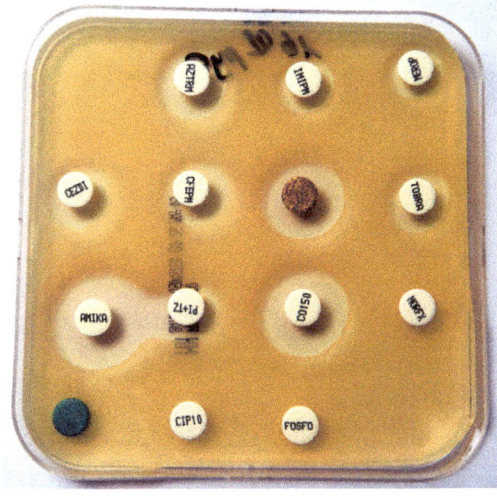

Figure 3 *Penicillin was the first antibiotic. Now there are many different ones that kill different types of bacterium. Here, several different antibiotics are being tested on an agar plate. Clear areas around the antibiotic patches appear when the bacteria are killed or cannot grow. They show how effectively each antibiotic has controlled the bacteria*

Synoptic link

You will learn more about the development of antibiotic resistance in bacteria in Topic 4.12.8.

---

1 Describe the main difference between drugs such as paracetamol and drugs such as penicillin. [2 marks]

2 Explain why it is more difficult to develop medicines against viruses than it has been to develop antibiotics effective against bacterial pathogens. [4 marks]

3 Use Figure 2 to answer the following.
   a State how many women died from bacterial infections during childbirth or shortly afterwards in 1930, 1940, and 1950. [3 marks]
   b Calculate the percentage fall or rise in the death rates of mothers around the time of birth between:
      i   1930 and 1940 [3 marks]
      ii 1940 and 1950. [3 marks]
   c Suggest reasons for the observations made in parts i and ii. [3 marks]
   d Based on this evidence, explain why the emergence of antibiotic-resistant bacteria is such a cause for concern. [3 marks]

Key points

- Many useful materials, including all medicines, are specific mixtures of substances called formulations.
- Painkillers and other medicines treat the symptoms of disease but do not kill the pathogens that cause it.
- Antibiotics cure bacterial diseases by killing the bacterial pathogens inside your body.
- The use of antibiotics has greatly reduced deaths from infectious diseases.
- The emergence of strains of bacteria resistant to antibiotics is a matter of great concern.
- Antibiotics cannot kill viral pathogens.

3.9.8 Testing new medical drugs

Learning objectives
After this topic, you should know:
- the stages involved in discovering, developing, and testing new medical drugs
- why testing new medical drugs is so important
- the importance of peer review in the process of publishing scientific results.

New medicines are being developed all the time, as scientists and doctors try to find ways of curing more diseases. Every new medical treatment has to be extensively tested and trialled in a series of stages before it is used. This process makes sure that the treatment works well and is as safe as possible.

A good medicine is:
- Effective – it must prevent or cure a disease or at least make you feel better.
- Safe – the drug must not be too toxic (poisonous) or have unacceptable side effects for the patient.
- Stable – you must be able to use the medicine under normal conditions and store it for some time.
- Successfully taken into and removed from your body – it must reach its target and be cleared from your system once it has done its work.

Developing and testing a new drug

It can take up to 12 years to bring a new medicine into your doctor's surgery and costs around £1800 million, including failures and capital costs (Figure 1).

Researchers target a disease and make lots of possible new drugs. Traditionally drugs were extracted from plants or microorganisms such as moulds (e.g., penicillin). Now most potential new drugs are designed using computer modelling of possible target molecules. However, scientists still discover some new medicines in the natural world (Figure 2). Thousands of these potential drugs are tested in the laboratory to find out if they are toxic (toxicity) and if they seem to do their job (efficacy). In the laboratory they are tested on cells, tissues, and even whole organs. Many chemicals fail at this stage.

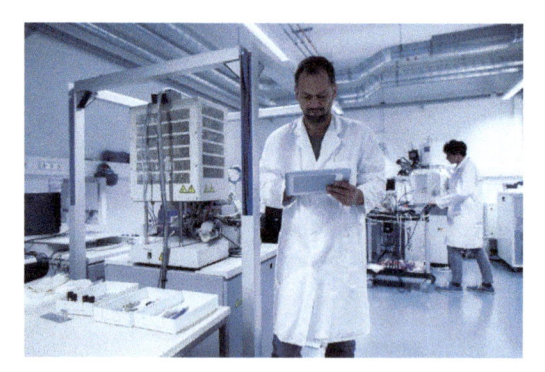

Figure 1 *The development of a new medicine costs millions of pounds and involves many people and lots of equipment*

The small numbers of chemicals that pass the earlier tests are then laboratory-tested on animals to find out how they work in a whole living organism. This also gives information about possible doses and side effects. The tissues and animals are used as models to predict how the drugs may behave in humans. Up to this point the chemicals are undergoing **preclinical testing**. This always takes place in the laboratory using cells, tissues, and live animals.

Drugs that pass animal testing move on to **clinical trials**. Clinical trials use healthy volunteers and patients. First, very low doses are given to healthy people to check for side effects. If the drug is found to be safe, it is tried on a small number of patients to see if it treats the disease. If it seems to be safe and effective, bigger clinical trials take place to find the optimum dose for the drug. If the medicine passes all the legal tests, it is licenced so that your doctor can prescribe it. Its safety will be monitored for as long as it is used.

Figure 2 *Scientists are investigating the noni fruit, used to treat a wide range of conditions in Polynesia and Costa Rica for centuries. It seems to contain many biologically active chemicals. Some may become the basis of modern synthetic medicines*

192

3.9 Preventing, treating, and curing diseases

Double-blind trials

In human trials, scientists use a double-blind trial to see just how effective the new medicine is. A group of patients with the target disease agree to take part in the trials. Some are given a **placebo** that does not contain the drug and some are given the new medicine. Patients are randomly allocated to the different groups. Then neither the doctor nor the patients know who has received the real drug or the placebo until the trial is complete. The patients' health is monitored carefully.

Often the placebo will contain a different drug that is already used to treat the disease. This means that the patient is not deprived of treatment whilst taking part in the trial.

Study tips

Make sure you are clear that new drugs are extensively tested for:
- efficacy
- toxicity
- dosage.

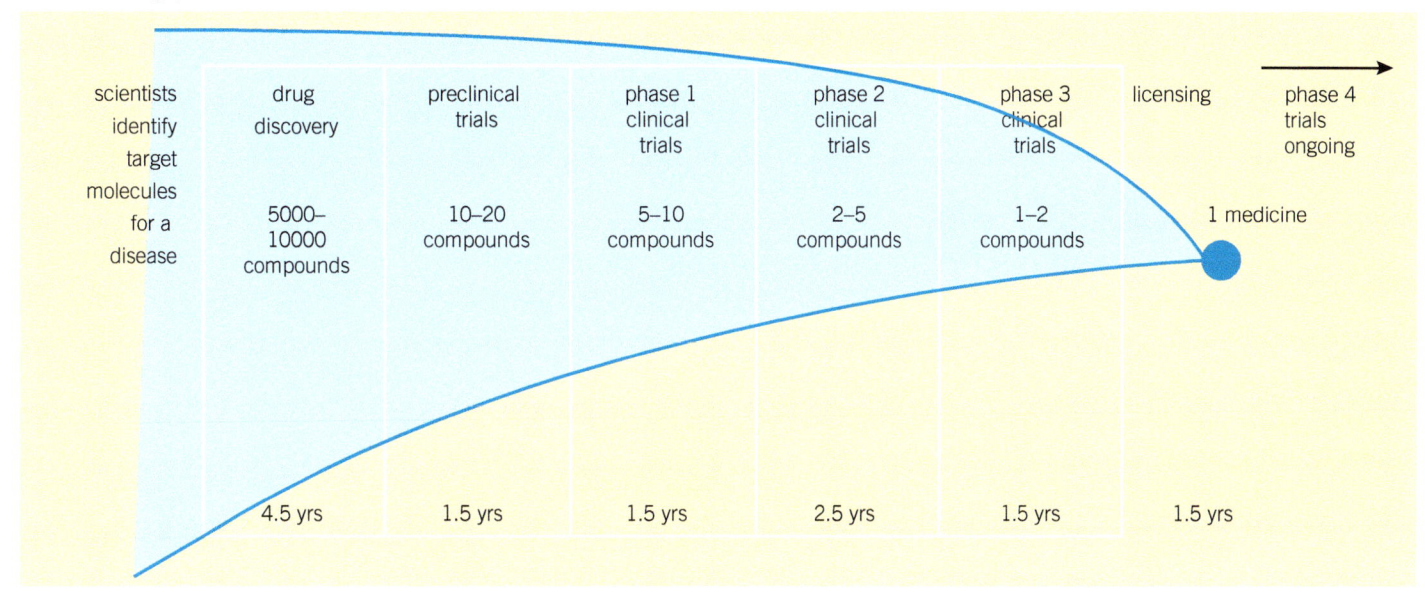

scientists identify target molecules for a disease	drug discovery	preclinical trials	phase 1 clinical trials	phase 2 clinical trials	phase 3 clinical trials	licensing	phase 4 trials ongoing
	5000–10000 compounds	10–20 compounds	5–10 compounds	2–5 compounds	1–2 compounds	1 medicine	
	4.5 yrs	1.5 yrs	1.5 yrs	2.5 yrs	1.5 yrs	1.5 yrs	

Figure 3 *An enormous number of chemicals start the selection process but few actually become a new, useful medicine. The shaded area highlights the reduction in the number of chemicals under consideration as drug trials progress*

Publishing results

The results of drug tests and trials, like all scientific research, are published in journals after they have been scrutinised in a process of **peer review**. This means that other scientists working in the same area can check the results over, helping to prevent false claims. National bodies such the National Institute for Clinical Excellence (NICE) look at the published results of drug trials and decide which drugs give good value for money and should be prescribed by the NHS.

Key points

- When new medical drugs are devised they have to be extensively tested for efficacy, toxicity, and dosage.
- New drugs are tested in the laboratory using cells, tissues, and live animals.
- Then they are tested in clinical trials on healthy volunteers and patients. Low doses are used to test for safety, followed by higher doses to test for optimum dose.
- In double-blind trials, some patients are given a placebo.
- Before results are published in scientific journals, they must be checked by other scientists in a process called peer review.

1 All new drugs are extensively tested for efficacy, toxicity, and dosage. Define these three terms. [3 marks]

2 Testing a new medicine costs a lot of money and can take up to 12 years. Draw a flow chart to show the main stages in testing new drugs. [6 marks]

3 Explain why an active drug is often used as the placebo in a clinical trial instead of a sugar pill that has no effect. [3 marks]

3.9.9 Genetic modification and medicine

Learning objectives

After this topic, you should know:
- some of the risks and benefits of using gene technology in modern medicine
- one of the most fast-moving areas of biology in the 21st century is gene technology. Scientists are looking more and more towards using gene technology in human medicine.

Synoptic links

To remind yourself about bacterial cells and plasmids, look back at Topic 1.3.3.

You will learn more about the techniques of genetic engineering and how it is used in agriculture in Topics 4.12.11 and 4.12.12.

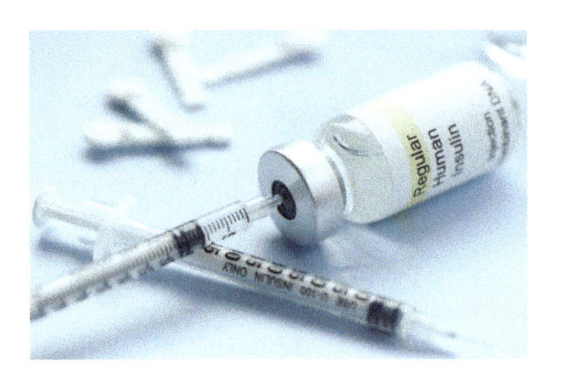

Figure 1 *Genetically modified (GM) bacteria have revolutionised the treatment of Type 1 diabetes worldwide by producing all of the human insulin we need*

What is genetic modification?

Genetic modification, also known as genetic engineering, involves changing the genetic material of an organism. It changes the code of life. Genes from one organism are removed and transferred to the genetic material of another organism. The second organism may be of the same type, a closely related species, or a completely different organism. The most modern technology is known as gene editing. It enables scientists to remove, add, or exchange genes relatively simply and with great accuracy.

Medicines from genetically modified bacteria

If people cannot make a chemical needed by their body it can cause major health problems. For example, lack of insulin causes Type 1 diabetes and lack of growth hormone can cause reduced growth in children. In the past, the hormones were replaced with difficulty. Insulin for people with diabetes was extracted from the pancreases of animals such as pigs or cattle slaughtered for meat. Human growth hormone was extracted from the bodies of people who died and left their bodies to be used in this way. The supply of insulin and growth hormone was limited, and some diabetics reacted badly to the animal hormones they were given. There was also a risk of the spread of disease when human tissues where used to produce growth hormone.

Now scientists can genetically modify bacteria to make these hormones. The genes for the production of growth hormone or insulin are cut out from the genetic material of healthy human cells. The genes are then transferred to plasmids, which are inserted into bacterial cells. The bacterial cells then make human growth hormone or insulin, depending on which gene they have been given. If genetically modified bacteria are cultured on a large scale they will make huge quantities of human proteins. We now use this technology to make a number of drugs and hormones to be used as medicines. Almost everyone affected by Type 1 diabetes now uses human insulin produced by bacteria. Children who lack growth hormone are given the hormone they need to grow normally, produced by bacteria.

Using genetically modified mammals

There is a limit to the types of proteins that bacteria have the enzymes to make. This means that some of the larger, more complex human proteins can never be produced by GM bacteria. Scientists have found ways in which to genetically modify sheep and goats so that they produce human chemicals in their milk that can be used to treat disease. For example, genetically modified sheep have been produced that make milk containing a protein needed to treat patients with cystic fibrosis and another similar disease that affects the lungs and the liver.

3.9 Preventing, treating, and curing diseases

Pushing the boundaries

As you saw in Topic 3.7.7, many people who need an organ transplant die before they get one because of the shortage of suitable donors. Some scientists are exploring the possibility of solving this problem in their research by genetically modifying animals to provide the tissues needed for human transplants. These genetic modifications change the antigens on the animal tissues so that they are not rejected by the human immune system. Progress is slow, but new techniques such as gene editing are enabling scientists to move faster as they can change many genes accurately at the same time.

Figure 2 *Pigs are often used in research into producing tissues for human transplants as their organs are very similar to ours in size and function*

There are many practical difficulties with these gene technologies. For example, it is very difficult to produce tissue that is not recognised by the human immune system. Scientists also need to ensure that there is no risk of animal diseases passing to people with the transplanted organs. There are ethical issues for some people about the use of animals in medical research. Some feel that animals should not be used in medical research at all, however much human suffering will be relieved. Others have ethical objections to genetic modification in particular, feeling that it is unnatural and concerned (unrealistically) with the formation of animal–human hybrids. Some people have religious objections to the use of pig organs in humans. There are few, if any, ethical objections to the use of genetically modified microorganisms in human medicine, even though it involves adding human genes to bacteria.

1 List *three* types of GM organism used in human medicine or medical research. [3 marks]
2 a State why some drugs can be produced by GM microorganisms and others cannot. [2 marks]
   b Explain how scientists are trying to use gene technology to increase the supply of organs for human transplants. [4 marks]
3 Discuss some of the practical and ethical issues that arise from using genetically modified animals in medical research. [6 marks]

Study tip

Consider the difference between a scientific or technical issue and an ethical issue with genetic modification.

Key points

- New medical products (e.g., insulin) have been produced by genetically modifying bacteria.
- Sheep and goats have been genetically modified to produce chemicals needed to treat people (e.g., for cystic fibrosis) in their milk.
- Research is exploring the possibility of providing tissues and organs for human transplants from genetically modified animals.

3.9.10 Stem cells in medicine

Learning objectives

After this topic, you should know:
- how stem cells are different from other body cells
- how stem cells work in bone marrow transplants
- some of the possible medical uses of embryonic stem cells

The function of stem cells

An egg and a sperm cell fuse to form a **zygote**, a single new cell. That cell divides and becomes a hollow ball of cells – the embryo. The inner cells of this ball are the embryonic stem cells that differentiate to form all of the specialised cells of your body. Even when you are an adult, some of your stem cells remain. An adult stem cell is an undifferentiated cell of an organism that can give rise to many more cells of the same type. Certain other types of cell can also arise from stem cells by differentiation. Your bone marrow is a good source of adult stem cells. Scientists now think there may be a tiny number of stem cells in most of the different tissues in your body including your blood, brain, muscle, and liver.

Many of your differentiated cells can divide to replace themselves. However, some tissues cannot do this and stem cells can stay in these tissues for years, only needed if the cells are injured or affected by disease. Then they start dividing to replace the different types of damaged cell.

Medical uses of stem cells

Many people suffer and even die because parts of their body stop working properly. For example, spinal injuries can cause paralysis, because the spinal nerves cannot repair themselves. People with Type 1 diabetes have to inject themselves with insulin every day because specialised cells in their pancreas do not work. Millions of people would benefit if we could replace damaged or diseased body parts.

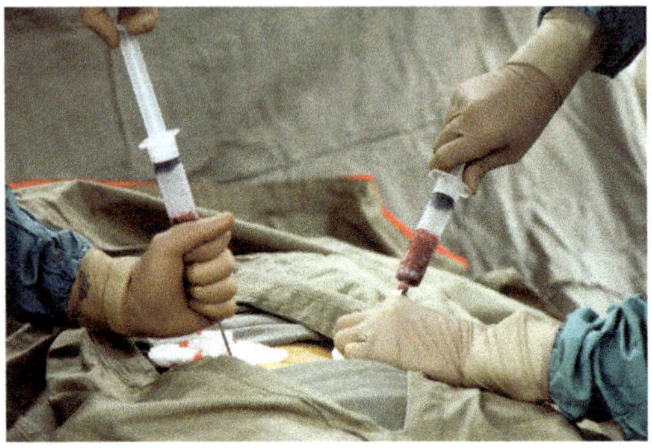

It seems obvious to use stem cells to replace damaged or diseased cells and tissues in the body, but this has proved to be very difficult. There is, however, one well established way in which we can use stem cells to cure people. The bone marrow contains many stem cells, white blood cells, and platelets. If someone is affected by a disease such as **leukaemia**, the bone marrow no longer functions normally. For years doctors have been able to transplant the bone marrow from a healthy person into the body of someone affected by leukaemia. The stem cells in the new bone marrow will make new blood cells for the transplant recipient. Sometimes blood cells circulating in the blood are harvested and used for the transplant, rather than the bone marrow itself.

Figure 1 *Bone marrow being harvested from the pelvis of a donor to be transplanted into a seriously ill patient*

Stem cell research

For years scientists tried to find ways of growing and using stem cells in medicine. In 1998, there was a breakthrough. Two American scientists managed to culture human embryonic stem cells capable of forming other types of cell. Scientists hope that the embryonic stem cells can be encouraged to grow into almost any different type of cell needed in the body. Already scientists have used nerve cells grown from embryonic stem cells to restore some movement to the legs of paralysed rats. In 2010, the first trials testing the safety of injecting nerve cells grown from

3.9 Preventing, treating, and curing diseases

embryonic stem cells into the spinal cords of paralysed human patients were carried out. The scientists and doctors hope it will not be long before they can use stem cells to help people who have been paralysed to walk again.

In 2014, doctors transplanted embryonic stem cells into the eyes of people going blind as a result of macular degeneration (Figure 2). It was only a small study to check the safety of the technique, but all of the patients found they could see better. Larger trials are now taking place. Scientists are also using different types of stem cells to try to grow cells that are sensitive to blood sugar levels and can produce the hormone insulin to help treat people with Type 1 diabetes.

We might also be able to grow whole new organs from embryonic stem cells. These could then be used in transplant surgery (Topic 3.9.11). Conditions from infertility to dementia could eventually be treated using stem cells.

Synoptic links

You will learn more about the spinal nerves in Topics 2.5.10 and 2.5.11.

For more about insulin and the control of blood glucose levels, look back at Topics 3.7.9 and 3.7.10.

Synoptic link

You learnt about stem cells and differentiation in Topic 1.3.9.

Figure 2 *This is what the world looks like to someone with macular degeneration. The light-sensitive cells in the middle of their retina stop working. Soon stem cell therapy might be able to restore the lost vision*

Key points

- Embryonic stem cells (from human embryos) and adult stem cells (from adult bone marrow) can be cloned and made to differentiate into many different types of cell.
- The use of stem cells in bone marrow transplants is well established. The stem cells provide a supply of new blood cells for the person receiving the transplant.
- Treatment with embryonic stem cells may be able to help people with conditions such as Type 1 diabetes and paralysis.

1   a   List the differences between a stem cell and a normal body cell. [4 marks]
    b   Give *three* sources of stem cells. [3 marks]
2   Describe the use of bone marrow transplants to treat leukaemia. [4 marks]
3   When American scientists managed to culture embryonic stem cells there was great excitement in the scientific community. Explain why this breakthrough was so important. [5 marks]

197

3.9.11 Stem cell dilemmas

Learning objectives

After this topic, you should know:

- some possible uses of stem cells in medicine
- some of the potential benefits, risks, and social and ethical issues associated with the use of stem cells in medical research and treatments.

As you saw in Topic 3.9.10, there are many potential benefits of using stem cells in human medicine and they are gradually being used to treat real patients. However, the technology is still very new, so there are still practical risks as well as social and ethical issues raised by the use of stem cells in both medical research and in treatments.

The potential of stem cell research

Scientists have found embryonic (fetal) stem cells in the umbilical cord blood of newborn babies and even in the amniotic fluid that surrounds the fetus as it grows. Using these instead of cells from spare embryos may help to overcome some of the ethical concerns about their use.

Scientists are also finding ways of growing adult stem cells, although so far they have only managed to develop them into a limited range of cell types. Adult stem cells avoid the controversial use of embryonic tissue. They have been used successfully to grow some new organs such as tracheas (windpipes). There are a number of ongoing research programmes looking into the use of adult stem cells from bone marrow to repair hearts damaged by heart disease. Early results are promising.

The area of stem cell research known as therapeutic cloning (Figure 1) has much potential but is proving very difficult. It involves using cells from an adult to produce a cloned early embryo of themselves. This would provide a source of perfectly matched embryonic stem cells. In theory, these could then be used for medical treatments such as growing new organs for the original donor. The new organs would not be rejected by the body because they have been made from the body's own cells and have the same genes.

Scientists have discovered stem cells in some of the tubes that connect the liver and the pancreas to the small intestine. They have managed to make these cells turn into the special insulin-producing cells in the pancreas that are so important for controlling blood sugar. These are the cells that are missing or destroyed in people with type 1 diabetes. Scientists have transplanted these modified stem cells into diabetic mice, which worked to control the blood sugar levels. The next stage is to work towards the same success in humans. Other scientists are using embryonic stem cells to produce functioning insulin-producing cells. One of the big obstacles to overcome is to prevent the immune system of the body destroying new insulin-producing cells in the same way that it destroyed the original ones in the body.

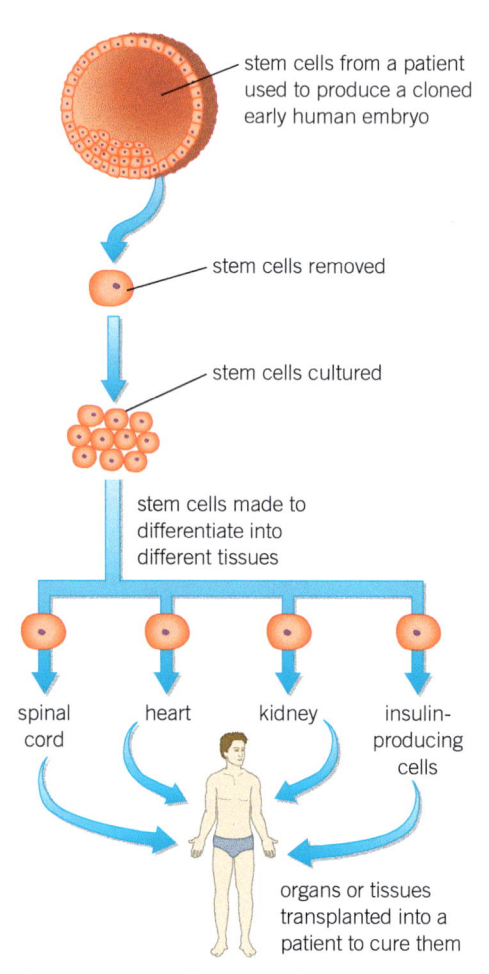

Figure 1 *This diagram illustrates therapeutic cloning, one way in which scientists hope that embryonic stem cells might be formed into adult cells and used as human treatments in the future*

Problems with using stem cells

Many embryonic stem cells come from aborted embryos. Others come from spare embryos from fertility treatment, donated because they will not otherwise be used. Some people question the use of a potential human being as a source of cells, even to cure others. Some people feel that, as the embryo cannot give permission, using it is a violation of its human rights. Other people hold religious beliefs that mean they cannot accept any interference with the process of human reproduction.

3.9 Preventing, treating, and curing diseases

In addition, progress in developing therapies using embryonic stem cells has been relatively slow, difficult, expensive, and hard to control. However, it is easy to forget that scientists have only been working with them for around 20 years. The signals that control cell differentiation are still not completely understood. Not surprisingly, it is proving difficult to persuade embryonic stem cells to differentiate into the type of cells needed to treat patients.

Embryonic stem cells divide and grow rapidly. This is partly why they are potentially so useful, but there is some concern that embryonic stem cells might cause cancer if they are used to treat people. This has sometimes been a problem when they have been used to treat mice and in early human treatments for autoimmune diseases.

There is a risk that adult stem cells might be infected with viruses, and could transfer the infections to patients. If stem cells from an adult are used to treat another unrelated person, they may trigger an immune response. The patient may need to take immunosuppressant drugs to stop their body rejecting the new cells. Scientists hope that embryonic stem cells will solve this problem. The body of a mother does not reject the embryo, so they hope that embryonic stem cells will not be rejected by the patient.

Some people feel that a great deal of money and time is being wasted on stem cell research that would be better spent on research into other areas of medicine. Yet in spite of all these concerns, there is a lot of investment into stem cell research as many scientists and doctors are convinced that stem cells have the potential to benefit many people.

At the moment, after years of relatively slow progress, hopes are high again that stem cells will change the future of medicine. Currently, in the UK, stem cell research is being carried out into potential therapies to treat:

- the spinal cord after injuries
- diabetes
- the heart after damage in a heart attack
- eyesight in the blind
- damaged bone and cartilage.

It is not known how many of these hopes will be fulfilled. Stem cell medicine has come a long way in the last 30 years. Who knows where it will be in another 30 years' time?

Figure 2 *Dream Alliance won the Welsh Grand National after revolutionary stem cell treatment on a badly damaged tendon. Stem cells were extracted from his bone marrow, cultured in the laboratory, and then injected into the damaged tendon, which healed perfectly. This treatment has been so successful in horses that trials in humans are now under way*

1 Describe *three* areas of medical research where the use of stem cells could provide valuable medical treatments. [3 marks]

2 Summarise the main arguments for and against the use of embryonic stem cells in medical research. [4 marks]

3 Explain how scientists are hoping to overcome the ethical objections to using embryonic stem cells in their research. [5 marks]

Key points

- Treatment with stem cells, from embryos or adult tissue, may be able to help with conditions such as diabetes.
- Most medical uses of stem cells are still experimental.
- The use of stem cells has some potential risks and some people have ethical or religious objections.

3.9 Preventing, treating, and curing diseases

Summary questions

1 Use the data on the global HIV/AIDS epidemic in one year in **Figure 1** and your knowledge of HIV/AIDS to answer the following questions.

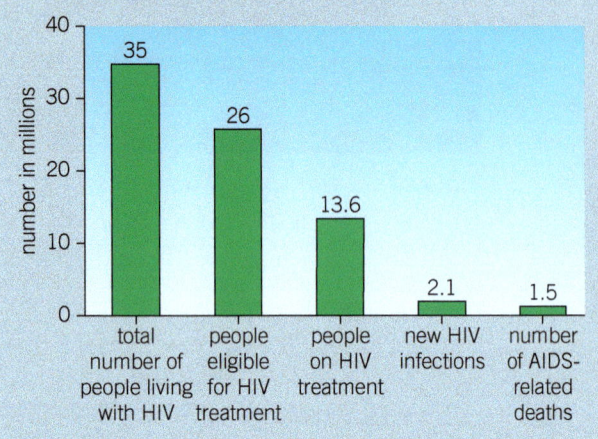

Figure 1

a What is the difference between HIV and AIDS? [2 marks]
b Approximately 70% of the people living with HIV/AIDS and 70% of the deaths from AIDS are in sub-Saharan Africa. Using data from **Figure 1**:
  i Calculate the approximate numbers of people living with HIV and dying of AIDS in sub-Saharan Africa in 2013. [4 marks]
  ii Explain why your answer is only approximate. [3 marks]
c i What percentage of the people suitable for treatment with antiretroviral therapy (ART) actually get treatment? [2 marks]
  ii Suggest reasons for this. [3 marks]
d i Give *three* ways of preventing the spread of HIV. [3 marks]
  ii Explain how each method works. [6 marks]

2 Vaccination uses your body's natural defence system to protect you against disease.
  a Describe how vaccination works. [4 marks]
  b Produce a flow chart to summarise the process of developing active immunity after:
    i a natural infection [4 marks]
    ii a vaccination. [4 marks]
  c There are vaccines for diseases such as diphtheria, polio, tetanus, and meningitis, but not for the common cold or tonsillitis. Suggest reasons for this. [2 marks]

3 Meningitis B and meningitis C are infections that can cause inflammation of the membranes around the brain and infection throughout the body (septicaemia). They are particularly serious in young children and teenagers, and can kill rapidly. Use the data on annual confirmed cases of meningococcal disease 1998–2010 in **Figure 2** to help you answer the questions below.

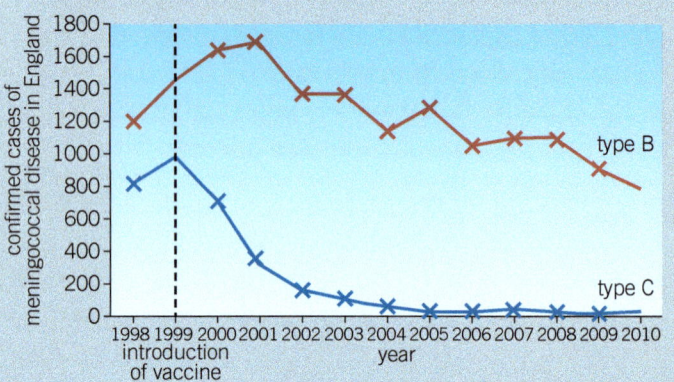

Figure 2

a How many cases of meningitis B and meningitis C were recorded in 1999? [2 marks]
b How many cases of meningitis B and meningitis C were recorded in 2005 and 2009? [2 marks]
c Suggest whether the introduction of the meningitis C vaccine in 1999 alone is responsible for the reduction in meningitis cases in England between 1998 and 2010. Explain your answer. [4 marks]
d Suggest *one* argument for and *one* argument against the introduction of a new vaccine against meningitis B. [2 marks]

4 a There are no medicines to cure measles, mumps, or rubella. What does this tell you about the pathogens that cause these diseases? [1 mark]
  b Suggest a medicine that might be used to make people feel more comfortable. [1 mark]
  c Doctors hope to get levels of MMR vaccination against measles, mumps, and rubella up to 95% of the population. Why is it important to get vaccination levels so high? [3 marks]

5 a Explain why new medicines need to be tested and trialled before doctors can use them to treat their patients. [5 marks]
  b Discuss why the development of a new medicine is so expensive. [4 marks]
  c Do you think it would ever be acceptable to use a new medicine before all the trials are completed? Explain the reasoning behind your answer. [5 marks]

3.9 Preventing, treating, and curing diseases

Practice questions

01 Medicines are used to prevent and treat diseases.

01.1 Match each medicine to its use.

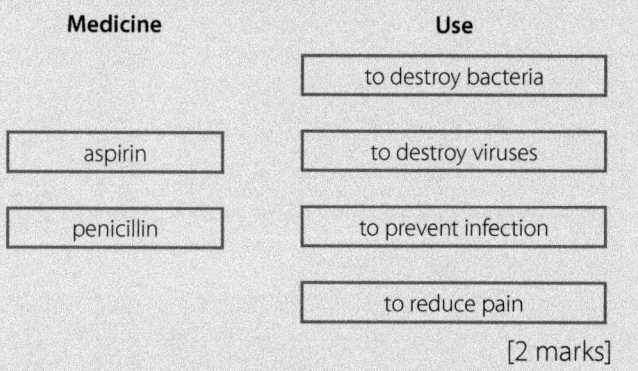

Medicine	Use
	to destroy bacteria
aspirin	to destroy viruses
penicillin	to prevent infection
	to reduce pain

[2 marks]

02 Whooping cough is a bacterial infection. Whooping cough can have serious side effects in young children.

02.1 Name **one** other bacterial infection. [1 mark]

02.2 Suggest how whooping cough bacteria enter the body. [1 mark]

02.3 Describe how the immune system responds to infection with the whooping cough bacteria. [3 marks]

02.4 **Figure 1** shows how the incidence of whooping cough has changed since 1940 and gives information about the whooping cough vaccine.

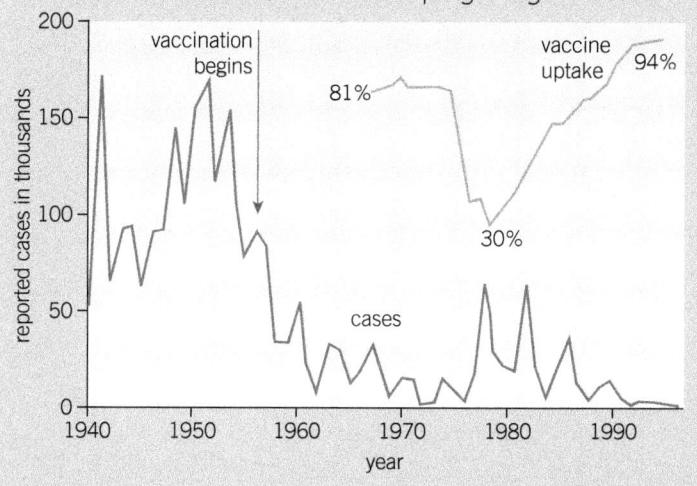

Figure 1

'Herd immunity' is when a large proportion of the population is immune to a pathogen and the spread of the pathogen is very much reduced. Some health professionals recommend that 95% of the population is vaccinated against whooping cough to ensure herd immunity.

Use data from **Figure 1** to explain why 95% vaccination is recommended. [2 marks]

02.5 In the 1970s the percentage of people vaccinated against whooping cough dropped steeply.

Suggest **one** reason why the vaccination rate dropped. [1 mark]

03 A child becomes unwell with measles and develops a rash.

A blood test shows that the concentration of white blood cells is higher than normal.

03.1 Explain how the immune system is working to destroy the measles virus in the child's body. [5 marks]

03.2 The measles vaccination causes a similar immune response to the one caused by the measles infection. However, the vaccination does not cause a rash.

Explain why the vaccination does not cause a rash. [3 marks]

04 Parkinson's disease is a disease that affects the brain. Over 125 000 people in the UK are estimated to be affected by Parkinson's disease.

Trials of a new drug to help treat the symptoms of Parkinson's disease began in 2016.

04.1 What would the new drug have been tested on before it was tested on patients? [2 marks]

04.2 The drug trial was a double-blind trial. Explain what is meant by a double-blind trial. [3 marks]

04.3 When the new drug is made available on prescription, patients will be monitored whilst they are using the new drug.

Give **two** reasons why patients are monitored. [2 marks]

04.4 Before the results of the study are published, they will need to be evaluated.

Who will need to evaluate the trial results? [1 mark]

Unit 3 in context

Pig-to-human transplants – a step too far?

Medical ethics involves applying an ethical code to the practice of medicine. An **ethical code** is a system of moral principles. Ethics is concerned with what is good for an individual and what is good for society. It sounds simple, but a quick look at what is happening in some areas of medical research shows that making ethical decisions isn't simple at all.

Sourcing tissues and organs

As you have learned, there are many ways in which body tissues and organs can become damaged or diseased. Sometimes the only hope for the person affected is to replace the tissue or organ, or to replace its function.

Since scientists first grew embryonic stem cells in the laboratory, there has been tremendous excitement and demand for stem cell technology to develop and provide cures for problems ranging from spinal injuries to heart disease and diabetes. There has also been controversy, with people determined to stop the research in its tracks to defend the rights of the early embryos used in the research. Researchers use spare embryos from fertility treatments, freely donated by the parents, to set up embryonic stem cell lines. These then continue in culture, sometimes for years, producing the embryonic stem cells needed for research and treatments. Here is a summary of the arguments put forward on both sides. Both sides feel that they are taking an ethical stance and have the moral high ground. What do you think?

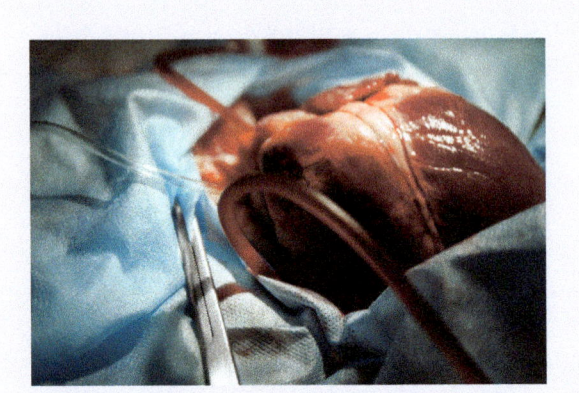

Figure 1 *A heart ready for transplant. Thousands of people across the world die every year waiting for an organ transplant – there simply aren't enough donor organs to go round. Stem cell technology is a long way from producing new hearts, kidneys, or livers. Organs from gene-edited donor pigs may be the way forward*

Table 1 *Arguments for and against using spare embryos from fertility treatments to produce embryonic stem cells for research and treatments*

Arguments for using spare embryos	Arguments against using spare embryos
For years, surplus embryos have been created in the process of fertility treatments and then destroyed if they are not used, and people do not appear to value human life any less as a result.	If stem cell therapies become routine, people will stop valuing human life.
If it is morally acceptable to use embryos for fertility treatment, in which they do not all survive, it can't be immoral to sacrifice a small number of embryos to set up the cell lines needed to cure devastating diseases.	Using embryos for stem cell research and treatments is a slippery slope that could lead to embryo farms, cloned babies, and fetuses used for spare parts.
The spare embryos will be destroyed anyway once the time limit for keeping them is over. It is surely better to use them in research that could benefit people rather than waste them.	Use of spare embryos for stem cell research and treatments could encourage society to tolerate the loss of a life to save a life.

The pig alternative

At one point people were very excited about the possibility of using tissues and organs grown in pigs for human transplants. The arrival of stem cell technology, along with a combination of technical hurdles, worries about disease, and ethical concerns, meant that work with pig donors almost stopped. But stem cell therapies have not arrived as quickly

3 Interactions with the environment

as was once hoped. What's more, gene-editing techniques mean scientists can modify the pig genome quickly and accurately. This will reduce the immune response in humans. They can then use the new, improved immunosuppressant drugs to help control any problems.

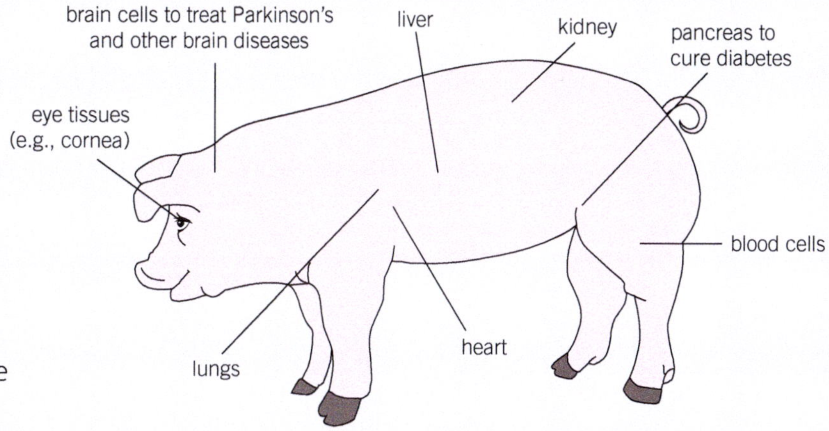

Pig hearts have already been transplanted into baboons that survived for over two years. Pig kidneys have functioned in a baboon for four months. Progress with pig tissues, rather than whole organs, is even more exciting. Tissues produce a much smaller immune response. In 2015 China approved the use of pig corneas, with all the pig cells removed, to replace human corneas affected by cataracts. Insulin-producing pig pancreas cells have been implanted into a number of patients. The cells are contained in a special capsule that protects them from the immune system. One patient had the implant for over nine years with no sign of either rejection or infection. He also had improved blood glucose control for some time.

Figure 2 *The main areas of a pig that are targeted by researchers for potential use in humans*

Scientists are trying a number of different techniques to prevent pig cells being rejected by human hosts. They include:

- Gene-editing pigs to knock out the antigens on pig cells that trigger a response in the human immune system,
- Producing pig cells with surface receptors that act as 'molecular sponges' to soak up the chemicals produced by human cells that trigger an attack by the immune system.
- Genetically modifying pig organs to generate antibodies against human immune cells. For example, transplanted liver cells would make antibodies to destroy the human immune system, but only around the transplanted organ.

Some companies are starting to build special farms on which to breed large numbers of disease-free genetically modified pigs for human medical use. There is still a long way to go with this research. It will probably meet as many objections as stem cell research has. However, for many years, people with diabetes injected insulin from dead pigs. Is it a step too far to let the pig cells make insulin inside the body in response to a normal diet? These living pig cells could remove the need for injections and the risk of diabetes-related tissue damage and death for good.

Similar implants are being used to contain modified human adult stem cells that also produce insulin. If the principle works, pancreatic cells produced from embryonic stem cells will also be encapsulated in this way. Which will work best – and which will people prefer?

1. What is the main problem with transplanted organs, whether the donor is human or animal? [4 marks]

2. **a** Give *three* reasons why people are excited about the use of stem cells in human medical research. [3 marks]
   b Discuss *two* of the ethical objections raised by some people to the use of embryonic stem cells in medical research. [5 marks]

3. **a** Give *three* advantages of using animals such as pigs as a source of organs and tissues for people. [3 marks]
   b Discuss the ethical arguments that might be raised for and against the use of pigs as a source of organs and tissues for people. [6 marks]

203

4 Explaining change

As you read this book, think how far the Earth has come since the first living organisms appeared over 3 billion years ago. The climate has at times been incredibly hot, and at other times incredibly cold. The combination of gases in the atmosphere has changed from being toxic to life to being rich in oxygen. Volcanoes, earthquakes, ice, sun, rain, and the mighty oceans have all helped to form the Earth. Now human activities seem to be affecting the Earth's atmosphere – and all the organisms that live on the Earth have to cope with the consequences.

Going back millions rather than billions of years, the Earth was ruled by dinosaurs. Plants similar to our modern ferns and mosses grew huge, and giant reptiles were the biggest herbivores as well as the top carnivores in the prehistoric ecosystem. In the 21st century, all that remains of life as it was then are the fossil remains and living relatives of the ancient organisms.

In this unit, you will be looking at some causes of environmental change, considering some of the ways in which people interact with their environment. You will explore how people affect the quality of both the air and the water around them. You will discover some of the secrets of ecology and the ways in which living things interact in their environment. Finally, you will learn some of the secrets of DNA, looking at human genetics, at how life has evolved over time, and at some of the latest technologies being used to change the genomes of the future.

Key questions

- Are people really causing global warming – and will it lead to climate change?
- How can water be made clean and safe to drink?
- How do the animals and plants in an ecosystem interact?
- How can humans have a positive impact on the environment?
- Why is everyone different?
- Is genetic engineering the key to feeding the world population?

Making connections

- Photosynthesis in plants is a key reaction in the carbon cycle. Look back to **Chapter 2.6** to remind yourself of what happens in photosynthesis, and how carbon dioxide levels and temperature affect the rate of the reaction.
- Organisms are involved in complex feeding relationships in ecosystems. You learnt about the chemistry of food and why animals all need food in **Chapter 2.5**.
- In **Chapter 3.8**, you learnt about different types of radiation, how radiation interacts with matter, and how it affects living cells. You will discover more about radiation when you look at the greenhouse effect and the impact of increasing levels of greenhouse gases in the atmosphere.
- Cell division by meiosis to form the gametes has a major effect on the genetic variation seen in living things, and in the way specific alleles are passed on from parents to their offspring. You looked at meiosis and formation of gametes in **Chapter 1.3**.

I already know...	I will learn...
the composition of the atmosphere	how the atmosphere of the Earth has evolved over time
the production of carbon dioxide by human activity and the impact on climate	to evaluate the evidence for climate change as a result of human activities and explore ways of mitigating the effects
the interdependence of organisms in an ecosystem	some of the factors that affect communities and the way in which animals and plants compete within an ecosystem
how organisms affect and are affected by their environment, including the accumulation of toxic materials	some positive human interactions within ecosystems (e.g., breeding programmes for endangered species and reducing deforestation) and their effects on biodiversity
that heredity is the process by which genetic information is transmitted from one generation to the next	how to describe single-gene crosses and to predict the outcome of different genetic crosses
that changes in the environment may leave individuals within a species, and some entire species, less well-adapted to compete successfully and reproduce, which in turn may lead to extinction.	that evolution is a change in the inherited characteristics of a population over time, which occurs through the natural selection of variants that give rise to phenotypes best suited to their environment.

Required practicals

Practical		Topic
11	Analysis and purification of water samples	4.10.12
12	Measuring population size and using sampling techniques to investigate the effect of a factor on the distribution of a species	4.11.6

4.10 The Earth's atmosphere

4.10.1 History of the Earth's atmosphere

Learning objectives
After this topic, you should know:
- a theory about how the Earth's atmosphere developed
- how to interpret evidence and evaluate different theories about the Earth's early atmosphere, given appropriate information.

Scientists think that the Earth was formed about 4.6 billion years ago. They think that, to begin with, it was a molten ball of rock and minerals. For its first billion years they believe that it was a very hot, turbulent place. The Earth's surface was probably covered with volcanoes belching hot ash and gases into the **atmosphere**.

The Earth's early atmosphere
There are several theories about the Earth's early atmosphere, although there is little direct evidence to draw on from billions of years ago. Scientists have reconstructed what they think the atmosphere might have been like, based on evidence from gas bubbles trapped in ancient rocks. They also use data gathered from the atmospheres of other planets and their moons in the solar system.

One theory suggests that volcanoes released carbon dioxide, CO_2, water vapour, H_2O, and nitrogen, N_2, and that these gases formed the early atmosphere. Water vapour in the atmosphere condensed as the Earth gradually cooled down, and fell as rain. Water collected in hollows in the crust as the rock solidified and the first oceans were formed. Another theory speculates that comets could also have brought water to the Earth. As icy comets rained down on the surface of the Earth, they melted, adding to its water supplies.

As the Earth began to stabilise, the atmosphere was probably mainly carbon dioxide. There could also have been some water vapour and nitrogen gas, and traces of methane, CH_4, and ammonia, NH_3. There would have been very little or no oxygen at that time. This resembles the atmospheres that are known to exist today on the planets Mars and Venus. Earth's nearest neighbours have atmospheres made up mainly of carbon dioxide with little or no oxygen.

After the initial violent years of the history of the Earth, the atmosphere remained quite stable. That is, until life first appeared on Earth.

Oxygen in the atmosphere
There are many theories as to how life was formed on Earth billions of years ago. Scientists think that life began about 3.4 billion years ago, when the first simple organisms, similar to bacteria, appeared. These could use the breakdown of chemicals as a source of energy.

Then, about 2.7 billion years ago, bacteria and other simple organisms, such as algae, evolved. Algae could use the energy from the Sun to make their own food by photosynthesis. This produced oxygen gas as a waste product. Over the next billion years or so, the level of oxygen rose steadily as the algae and bacteria thrived in the seas. More and more plants evolved and all of them were photosynthesising, removing carbon dioxide from the atmosphere, and making oxygen.

Figure 1 *Volcanoes moved chemicals from inside the Earth to the surface and into the newly forming atmosphere*

Figure 2 *The surface of one of Jupiter's moons, Io, with its active volcanoes releasing gases into its sparse atmosphere. This is likely to be what the Earth was like billions of years ago*

■ 4.10 The Earth's atmosphere

carbon dioxide + water $\xrightarrow{\text{(energy from sunlight)}}$ glucose + oxygen

$6CO_2 + 6H_2O \longrightarrow C_6H_{12}O_6 + 6O_2$

As plants evolved, they successfully colonised most of the surface of the Earth. The atmosphere became richer in oxygen. This made it possible for the first animal forms to evolve. These animals could not make their own food like the algae and plants could. They relied on the algae and plants for their food and on oxygen to respire.

Figure 3 *Some of the first photosynthesising bacteria probably lived in colonies, like these stromatolites in Shark Bay, Western Australia. They grew in water and released oxygen into the early atmosphere*

On the other hand, many of the earliest living microorganisms could not tolerate a high oxygen concentration, because they had evolved without it. They largely died out, as there were fewer places where they could survive.

1 Name and give the chemical formula of *five* gases that scientists speculate were found in the Earth's early atmosphere. Display your answer in a table. [5 marks]
2 Describe how the Earth's early atmosphere was probably formed during its first billion years of existence. [1 mark]
3 a Suggest why scientists believe there was no life on Earth for its first billion years. [1 mark]
  b Suggest *two* possible sources of the water that collected and formed our early oceans. [2 marks]
4 Explain how the level of oxygen in the Earth's atmosphere increased and why this was significant in the history of the Earth. Include any relevant chemical equations in your answer. [6 marks]
5 Explain why there is still debate and uncertainty amongst scientists as to the origins and composition of the Earth's early atmosphere. [5 marks]

Study tip

Remember that oxygen was not one of the gases in the Earth's original atmosphere. It was only made after the first simple organisms that could carry out photosynthesis had evolved.

Go further

Evaluating alternative theories

Scientists have found evidence from some of the oldest rocks on Earth that question assumptions that the early gases originated from volcanoes. Some scientists suggest that the mixture of gases could have been formed from solar debris, similar to comets, smashing into the Earth and vaporising around 500 million years after its formation.

Key points

- The Earth's early atmosphere was formed by volcanic activity.
- It probably consisted mainly of carbon dioxide. There may also have been nitrogen and water vapour, together with traces of methane and ammonia.
- As plants spread over the Earth, the level of oxygen in the atmosphere increased.

207

4.10.2 The Earth's evolving atmosphere

Learning objectives

After this topic, you should know:
- the main changes in the atmosphere over time and some of the possible causes of these changes
- the relative proportions of gases in the Earth's atmosphere now.

Synoptic link
To remind yourself about photosynthesis, look back at Topic 2.6.6.

Scientists think that the early atmosphere of the Earth contained a great deal of carbon dioxide. Yet the Earth's atmosphere today only has around 0.04% of this gas. So where has it all gone? The answer is mostly into living organisms and into materials formed from living organisms. As you saw in Topic 4.10.1, algae and plants decreased the percentage of carbon dioxide in the early atmosphere through photosynthesis.

Carbon locked into rock

Carbon dioxide, along with water, is taken in by plants and converted to glucose and oxygen during photosynthesis. The carbon in the glucose can then end up in new plant material. When animals eat the plants, some of this carbon can be transferred to the animal tissues, including their skeletons and shells.

Over millions of years, the skeletons and shells of huge numbers of these marine organisms built up at the bottom of vast oceans. There they became covered with layer upon layer of fine sediment. Under the pressure caused by being buried by all these layers of sediment, eventually the deposits formed sedimentary carbonate rocks such as limestone, a rock containing mainly calcium carbonate, $CaCO_3$.

Some of the remains of ancient living things were crushed by large-scale movements of the Earth and were heated within the Earth's crust over very long periods of time. They formed the fossil fuels coal, crude oil, and natural gas.

- Coal is classed as a sedimentary rock, and was formed from thick deposits of plant material, such as ancient trees and ferns. When the plants died in swamps, they were buried, in the absence of oxygen, and compressed over millions of years.
- Crude oil and natural gas were formed from the remains of plankton deposited in muds on the seabed. These remains were covered by sediments that became layers of rock when compressed over millions of years. The crude oil and natural gas formed is found trapped beneath these layers of rock.

In this way, much of the carbon from the old carbon dioxide-rich atmosphere became locked up within the Earth's crust in rocks and fossil fuels.

Carbon dioxide gas was also removed from the early atmosphere by dissolving in the water of the oceans. It reacted, for example, with metal oxides, and made insoluble carbonate compounds. These fell to the seabed as sediments and helped to form more carbonate rocks.

Over the past 200 million years, the level of carbon dioxide in the atmosphere has not changed much relative to the level it was when the Earth's atmosphere was mostly carbon dioxide. This is due to the natural cycle of carbon in which carbon moves between the oceans, rocks, and the atmosphere (see Topic 4.10.3).

Figure 1 *There is clear fossil evidence in carbonate rocks of the organisms that lived millions of years ago*

Shelly carbonates

Carry out a test to see if crushed samples of shells contain carbonates. Remember the reaction that all carbonates undergo with dilute acid. How will you test any gas given off?

- Record your findings.

Safety: Wear eye protection.

4.10 The Earth's atmosphere

Ammonia and methane

Volcanoes also produced nitrogen gas, which gradually built up in the early atmosphere, and there may have also been small proportions of methane and ammonia gases.

Any methane and ammonia found in the Earth's early atmosphere reacted with the oxygen formed by the evolving algae and plants:

$$CH_4 + 2O_2 \rightarrow CO_2 + 2H_2O$$

$$4NH_3 + 3O_2 \rightarrow 2N_2 + 6H_2O$$

This removed the methane and ammonia from the atmosphere. However, the levels of nitrogen gas, N_2, in the atmosphere could build up, as nitrogen is a very unreactive gas.

The atmosphere today

By 200 million years ago, the proportions of gases in the Earth's atmosphere had stabilised and were much the same as they are today.

Look at the percentage proportions of gases in the Earth's atmosphere today in the pie chart in Figure 2.

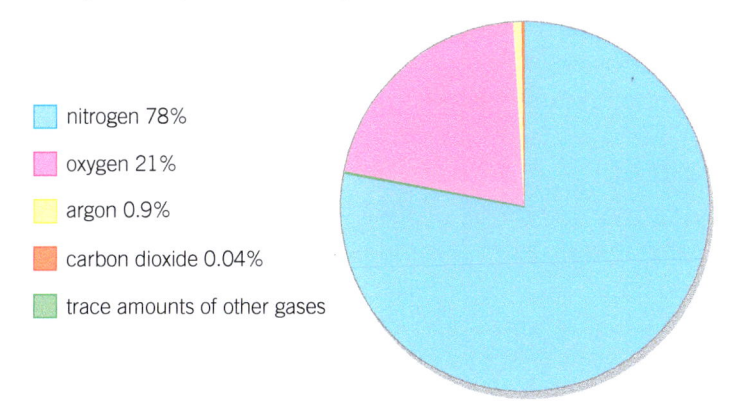

- nitrogen 78%
- oxygen 21%
- argon 0.9%
- carbon dioxide 0.04%
- trace amounts of other gases

Figure 2 *The relative proportions of nitrogen, oxygen, and other gases in the Earth's atmosphere. The Earth's atmosphere also contains water vapour, but the percentage in the atmosphere varies*

The noble gases are all found in air, with argon, Ar, the most abundant at about 0.9%. Neon, Ne, krypton, Kr, and xenon, Xe, together make up less than 0.1% of clean, dry air.

1 Copy and complete the table to show the percentage proportions of gases in the Earth's atmosphere today. [3 marks]

Nitrogen	Oxygen	Argon	Carbon dioxide	Other gases

2 Explain the origins of nitrogen gas in the Earth's early atmosphere and suggest why its percentage of the composition of air remains so high. [4 marks]

3 Explain how most of the carbon dioxide in the Earth's early atmosphere was removed to arrive at a level of around 0.04% in today's atmosphere. [4 marks]

Synoptic link

You will learn where the noble gases are situated in the periodic table in Topic 5.13.1 in the *Physical Sciences* book.

Key points

- Photosynthesis by algae and plants decreased the percentage of carbon dioxide in the Earth's early atmosphere. The formation of sedimentary rocks and fossil fuels that contain carbon also removed carbon dioxide from the atmosphere.
- Approximately four-fifths (about 80%) of the atmosphere today is nitrogen, and about one-fifth (about 20%) is oxygen.
- There are also small proportions of various other gases, including carbon dioxide, water vapour, and noble gases.

4.10.3 Material recycling

Learning objectives

After this topic, you should know:

- how materials cycle through the living and non-living elements of an ecosystem
- the role of microorganisms in the cycling of materials.

Synoptic links

You will learn more about the abiotic and biotic elements of an ecosystem in Chapter 4.11.

To remind yourself about the chemistry of food, look back at Topic 2.5.8.

You will learn more about feeding relationships and food chains in Topic 4.11.2.

Figure 1 *Plants like this English oak take carbon dioxide from the air and water from the soil so that they can photosynthesise. They use the products of photosynthesis combined with minerals from the soil to make other vital chemicals such as proteins*

Imagine a stable community of plants and animals in an ecosystem. The balance of the community depends on both the living or **biotic** components of the ecosystem and the non-living or **abiotic** components. The biotic components are the organisms in the ecosystem, including plants, animals, and microorganisms. The abiotic components include factors such as the properties of the soil, rainfall, and the amount of light available.

In a stable community, the processes that remove materials from the environment are balanced by the processes that return materials to the environment.

Plants as producers

Most life on Earth depends on photosynthesis taking place in producers such as green plants. These plants make carbohydrates from carbon dioxide in the air. Animals feed on the plants, and the carbon compounds are passed along a food chain. Photosynthetic organisms are the main producers of biomass for life on Earth. Both animals and plants respire, and this releases carbon dioxide back into the air.

The decay cycle

Living organisms constantly remove materials from the environment for growth and other processes. For example, plants take mineral ions from the soil all the time. These nutrients are passed on into animals through feeding relationships including food chains. If this were a one-way process, the resources of the Earth would have been exhausted long ago.

Fortunately, all the materials taken from the environment by plants are returned to the environment and recycled to provide the building blocks for future organisms. For example, many trees shed their leaves each year, and most animals produce droppings at least once a day. Animals and plants eventually die as well.

A group of organisms known as the **decomposers** break down the waste and the dead animals and plants. The chemicals that make up living organisms are made up mainly of carbon, oxygen, hydrogen, and nitrogen. These are the elements that need to be recycled to provide the building materials for all new life on Earth. The decay process means that the same materials are recycled over and over again. This often leads to very stable communities of organisms.

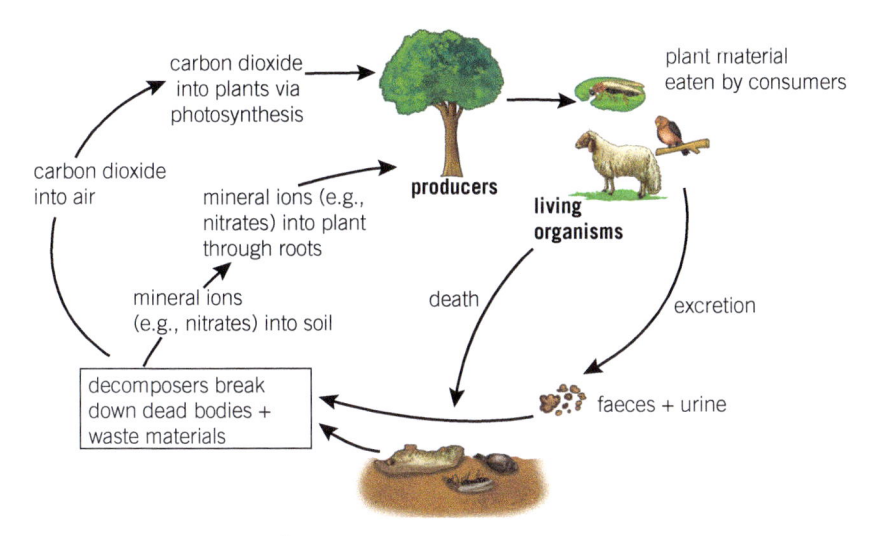

Figure 2 *The decay cycle*

Microorganisms and the recycling of materials

The decomposers are a group of microorganisms that include bacteria and fungi. They feed on waste droppings and dead organisms.

Detritus feeders, or detritivores, such as maggots and some types of worms and beetles, often start the process of decay. They eat dead animals and produce waste material. If you look carefully at Figure 3 you can see some of them in action.

The bacteria and fungi then digest everything – dead animals, plants, and detritus feeders, plus their waste. They use some of the nutrients to grow and reproduce and they release carbon dioxide, water, and mineral ions as waste products in the process. When things decay, they are actually being broken down and digested by microorganisms.

The decay of dead animals and plants by microorganisms releases substances that plants need to grow. Decay returns mineral ions to the soil, including nitrates that plants take up through their roots and use to make proteins and other chemicals in their cells. Decay also returns carbon to the atmosphere as carbon dioxide gas, which can be used by producers in photosynthesis.

The decomposers 'clean up' the environment, removing the bodies of all the dead organisms.

Figure 3 *This mole was broken down by decomposers over a period of several weeks and the material recycled into the environment*

1. **a** What is a decomposer? [2 marks]
   b Explain why decomposers are so important in a stable ecosystem. [3 marks]
2. Materials in an ecosystem are described as being recycled. Explain what this means. [6 marks]
3. Carbon and nitrogen are two of the key elements that are recycled in ecosystems. Discuss the importance of these two elements to living organisms and explain why it is so important that they are part of the decay cycle. [6 marks]

Key points

- Many different materials cycle through the abiotic and biotic components of an ecosystem.
- Photosynthetic organisms are the main producers of food and therefore biomass for life on Earth.
- Microorganisms play a key role in the cycling of materials through an ecosystem.
- Decay of dead animals and plants by microorganisms returns carbon to the atmosphere as carbon dioxide and recycles mineral ions to the soil.

4.10.4 The carbon cycle

Learning objectives

After this topic, you should know:
- what the carbon cycle is
- the processes that remove carbon dioxide from the atmosphere and return it again.

Every year about 166 gigatonnes of carbon are cycled through the living world. That's 166 000 000 000, which is 166×10^9 tonnes (or in standard form 1.66×10^{11} tonnes) – an awful lot of carbon! Why is carbon so important?

The amount of carbon on the Earth is fixed. Much of the carbon is locked up in stores referred to as **carbon sinks**. These sinks include fossil fuels, carbonate rocks such as limestone and chalk, and the carbon dioxide found in the air and dissolved in the water of rivers, lakes, and oceans.

Carbon atoms are also important in many of the molecules that make up the bodies of organisms. A relatively small amount of available carbon is cycled between living things and the environment (Figure 1) in a process known as the **carbon cycle** (Figure 2).

Figure 1 *Carbon is constantly cycled between living organisms and the physical environment*

Study tip
Make sure you can label the processes in a diagram of the carbon cycle.

Synoptic links
You will learn more about the abiotic and biotic components of an ecosystem in Chapter 4.11.

You will learn more about feeding relationships and food chains in Topic 4.11.2.

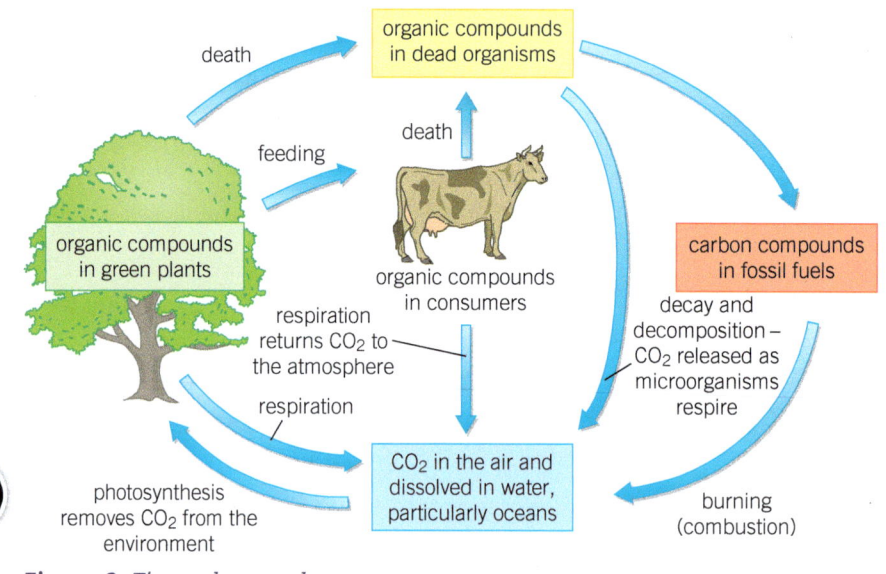

Figure 2 *The carbon cycle*

Photosynthesis
Green plants and algae remove carbon dioxide from the atmosphere for photosynthesis. They use the carbon from carbon dioxide to make carbohydrates, proteins, and fats. These make up the biomass of the plants and algae. The carbon is passed on through food chains to animals including primary, secondary, and tertiary consumers.

Respiration
Living organisms respire all the time. They use oxygen to break down glucose, transferring energy for their cells. Carbon dioxide, as well as water, is produced as a waste product. This is how carbon is returned to the atmosphere.

When plants, algae, and animals die, their bodies are broken down by the decomposers including blowflies, moulds, and bacteria that feed on the dead bodies. Carbon is released into the atmosphere as carbon dioxide as the decomposers respire. All of the carbon (in the form of carbon dioxide) released by the various living organisms is then available again. It is ready to be taken up by plants and algae in photosynthesis.

Figure 3 *Burning wood and fossil fuels to keep us warm, power our cars, or make our electricity, all releases 'locked-up' carbon in the form of carbon dioxide*

4.10 The Earth's atmosphere

Combustion

Wood from trees contains lots of carbon, locked into the molecules of the plant during photosynthesis over many years. Fossil fuels also contain lots of carbon, which was locked away by photosynthesising organisms millions of years ago.

When wood or fossil fuels are burnt (Figure 3), carbon dioxide is produced, so some of that carbon is released back into the atmosphere. Huge quantities of fossil fuels are burnt worldwide to power vehicles and to generate electricity. Wood is burnt to heat homes and (in many countries) to cook food.

Photosynthesis: carbon dioxide + water → glucose + oxygen
Respiration: glucose + oxygen → carbon dioxide + water
Combustion: fossil fuel or wood + oxygen → carbon dioxide + water

Industrial uses of limestone

Much limestone (calcium carbonate) was made from the shells of sea animals that died long ago. There are several industrial uses of limestone and most of them contribute to increased atmospheric carbon dioxide levels (Figure 4). When calcium carbonate is heated in lime kilns to produce lime (calcium oxide) for the building industry, carbon dioxide is a waste product. Some of this lime is used to make mortar for buildings and then the carbon dioxide is reabsorbed when the mortar sets. Limestone is also used in blast furnaces making pig iron and steel. Carbon dioxide is released as a waste product as the limestone is heated. Both of these industries add to global carbon dioxide emissions, although both are developing technologies to reduce the amount of carbon dioxide they release.

The future

For millions of years, the carbon cycle has regulated itself. However, as humans burn more fossil fuels, increasing amounts of carbon dioxide are released into the atmosphere. This is causing **global warming**. Scientists fear that the carbon cycle may not be able to maintain atmospheric carbon dioxide at a level that will support long-term human survival.

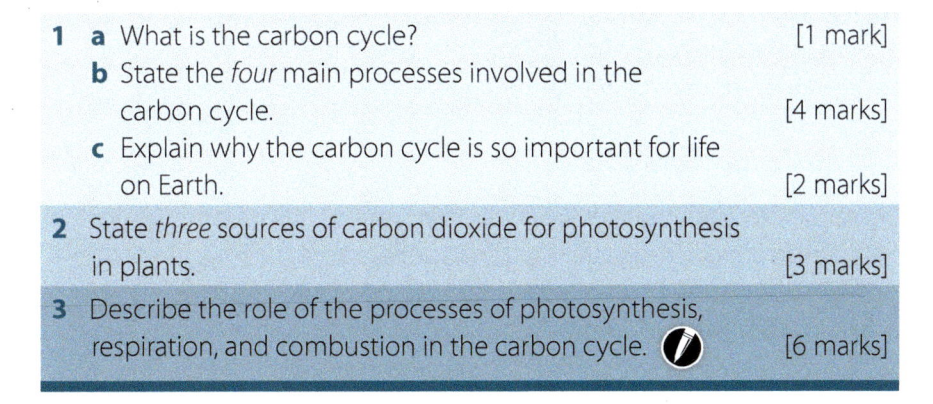

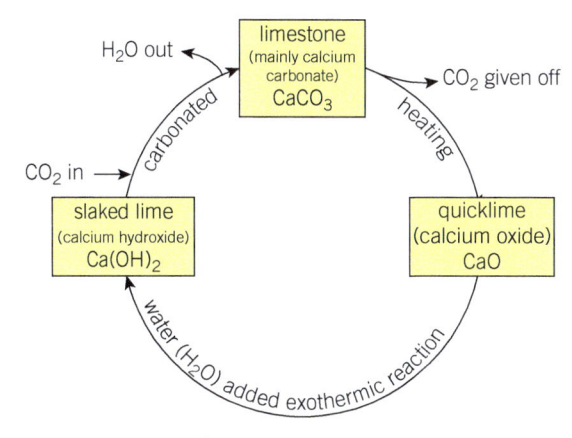

Figure 4 *The effect of the industrial uses of limestone on atmospheric and marine carbon dioxide*

Figure 5 *Marine organisms such a sea snails remove carbon dioxide from seawater to produce their calcium carbonate-rich shells*

Key points

- The element carbon is found as carbon dioxide in the atmosphere, dissolved in the water of the oceans, as calcium carbonate in seashells, in fossil fuels, in limestone rocks, and as molecules in living organisms.
- Carbon cycles through the environment in processes that include photosynthesis, respiration, combustion of fuels, and the industrial uses of limestone.

1 a What is the carbon cycle? [1 mark]
   b State the *four* main processes involved in the carbon cycle. [4 marks]
   c Explain why the carbon cycle is so important for life on Earth. [2 marks]
2 State *three* sources of carbon dioxide for photosynthesis in plants. [3 marks]
3 Describe the role of the processes of photosynthesis, respiration, and combustion in the carbon cycle. [6 marks]

213

4.10.5 The greenhouse effect

Learning objectives

After this topic, you should know:
- how the greenhouse effect works
- Ⓗ how different substances interact with radiation of different wavelengths.

You will have heard of the **greenhouse effect** and concerns (and some arguments) about global warming from reports in the media. However, these reports are sometimes biased or over-simplified, as they often seek out sensational headlines from scientific research without presenting the whole picture. Therefore, they can be misleading.

It is known that carbon dioxide, methane, and water vapour are the main **greenhouse gases** in the Earth's atmosphere, that is, gases that absorb energy radiated from its surface. Without carbon dioxide in the Earth's atmosphere, the average temperature on Earth would be about −19 °C, and life as it is now could never have evolved in liquid water. How do greenhouse gases warm up the Earth?

The Earth is heated by the Sun. Not all the energy reaching the Earth warms up our planet. Almost 30% is reflected back into space from the atmosphere and surface. The gases of the atmosphere let short-wavelength electromagnetic radiation pass through. The surface of the Earth cools down by emitting longer wavelength infrared radiation. However, greenhouse gases absorb this infrared radiation. The radiation stimulates the bonds in these molecules to vibrate, bend, and stretch more vigorously, raising their temperature. So some of the energy radiated from the surface of the Earth gets trapped in the atmosphere and the temperature rises. The higher the proportion of greenhouse gases in the air, the greater the increase in the temperature of the atmosphere.

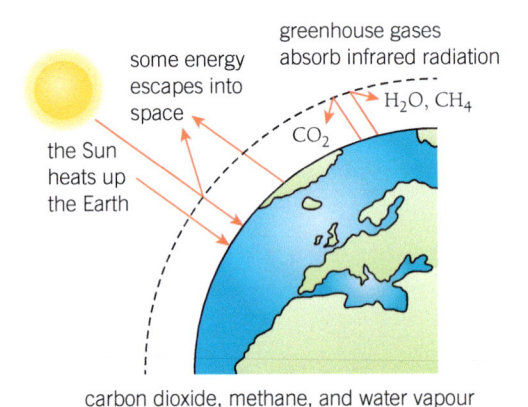

Figure 1 *The molecules of a greenhouse gas absorb the energy radiated by the Earth. This increases the store of energy of the gases in the atmosphere and warms the Earth. The Earth emits infrared radiation all the time. Whether the surface of the Earth warms or cools depends on the balance of incoming or outgoing radiation*

The increasing levels of greenhouse gases

Over the past century the amount of carbon dioxide released into the atmosphere has greatly increased. More fossil fuels than ever are used to make electricity, heat homes, and run cars. This has increased the amount of carbon dioxide produced enormously. Think about what happens when fossil fuels are burnt. Carbon has been locked up for hundreds of millions of years in fossil fuels. When used as a fuel it is released as carbon dioxide into the atmosphere. For example:

$$\text{propane} + \text{oxygen} \rightarrow \text{carbon dioxide} + \text{water}$$
$$C_3H_8 + 5O_2 \rightarrow 3CO_2 + 4H_2O$$

Methane gets into the atmosphere from swamps and rice fields. Another source of methane is emissions from the growing number of grazing cattle, and from their decomposing waste. The increasing human population produces more waste to dispose of in landfill sites, which are another source of methane gas.

There is no doubt amongst scientists that the levels of greenhouse gases in the atmosphere, especially carbon dioxide, are increasing. So you are experiencing an enhanced greenhouse effect, greater than the warming effect in pre-industrial times.

Go further

The levels of greenhouse gases in the atmosphere can be monitored using an instrumental technique called infrared spectroscopy. Infrared radiation stimulates the bonds in molecules of carbon dioxide and methane to vibrate more vigorously, absorbing some of the radiation, which can be detected and displayed on an infrared spectrum.

■ 4.10 The Earth's atmosphere

Figure 2 shows the data collected by scientists monitoring the proportion of carbon dioxide in the atmosphere at one location. The overall trend over the recent past has been ever-upwards.

The balance between the carbon dioxide produced and the carbon dioxide absorbed by carbon sinks (e.g., tropical rainforests and the oceans) is affected by human activity. As more trees are cut down for timber and to clear land (**deforestation**), the carbon dioxide removed from the air as the trees photosynthesise is reduced. Also, as the temperature rises, carbon dioxide get less and less soluble in water. This makes the oceans less effective as carbon sinks.

Higher

Interaction of electromagnetic waves and matter

We can look at the greenhouse effect in more detail by considering how different gases in the Earth's atmosphere interact with electromagnetic waves from the Sun. Some gases absorb electromagnetic waves, whilst some transmit or reflect these waves. This varies depending on the wavelength of the waves.

Look at the simple model of the greenhouse effect shown in Figure 1. You can see that some of the electromagnetic waves from the Sun do not enter the Earth's atmosphere. They are reflected back into space. However, visible light, short-wavelength infrared radiation, and radio waves penetrate the gases in the atmosphere and reach the surface of the Earth. The arrival of visible light is obvious as it reflects off surfaces and enables you to see the world around you. Most of the ultraviolet light from the Sun is absorbed by the ozone layer in the upper atmosphere, but some gets through and this causes your skin to tan.

The land (and, to a lesser extent, the oceans) is a good absorber of infrared radiation. In sunlight, the land warms up and emits infrared radiation at the same rate at which it absorbs it. The land emits much longer-wavelength infrared radiation than the Sun, as it is much cooler. However, because of its longer wavelength, the radiation emitted by the land is absorbed by the greenhouse gases in the Earth's atmosphere, transferring energy to the thermal energy store of the greenhouse gases and warming up the atmosphere.

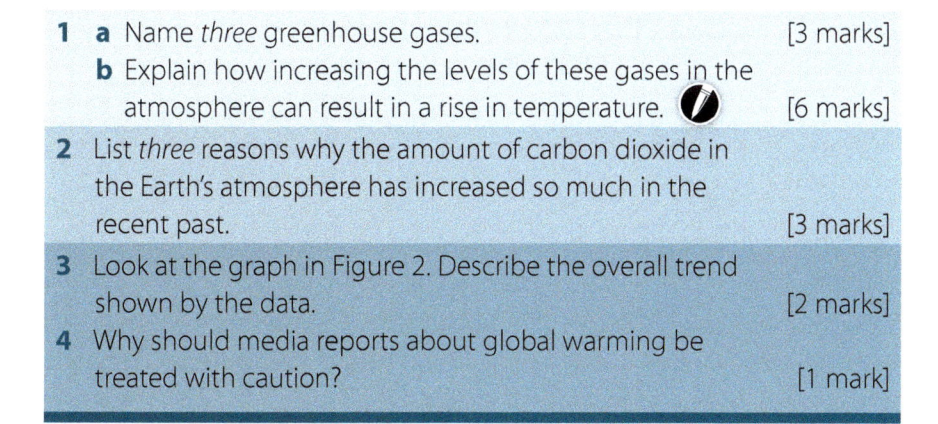

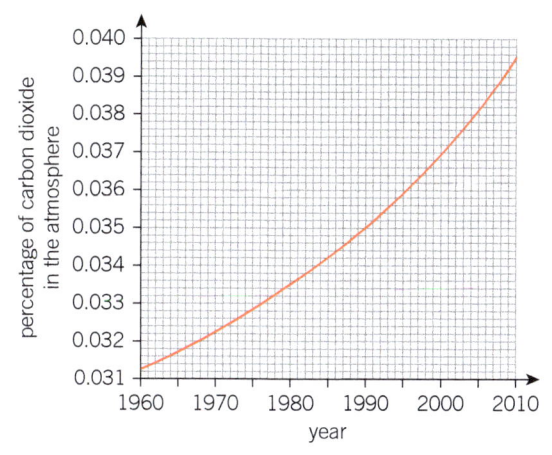

Figure 2 *The change in the level of carbon dioxide in the atmosphere over time is shown by this graph*

Synoptic link

To remind yourself about the spectrum of electromagnetic waves, look back at Topic 1.4.3.

---

1 **a** Name *three* greenhouse gases. [3 marks]
  b Explain how increasing the levels of these gases in the atmosphere can result in a rise in temperature. [6 marks]
2 List *three* reasons why the amount of carbon dioxide in the Earth's atmosphere has increased so much in the recent past. [3 marks]
3 Look at the graph in Figure 2. Describe the overall trend shown by the data. [2 marks]
4 Why should media reports about global warming be treated with caution? [1 mark]

Key points

- The amount of carbon dioxide in the Earth's atmosphere has risen in the recent past, largely due to the amount of fossil fuels now burnt.
- It is difficult to predict with complete certainty the effects on climate of rising levels of greenhouse gases on a global scale.
- However, the vast majority of peer-reviewed evidence agrees that increased proportions of greenhouse gases from human activities will increase average global temperatures.
- **H** Water vapour, carbon dioxide, and methane are greenhouse gases that increase the absorption of outgoing, long-wavelength radiation emitted as the Earth cools.

215

4.10.6 Analysing the evidence

Learning objectives

After this topic, you should know:

- how to evaluate evidence for human influences on climate change.

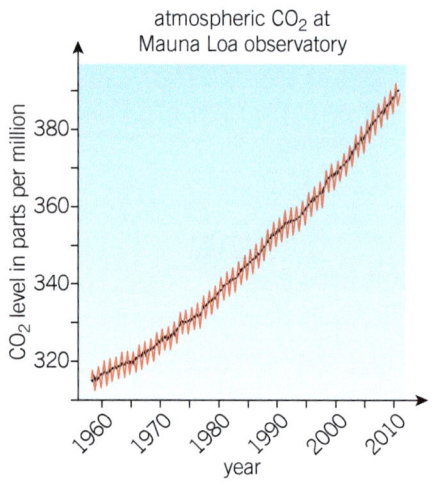

Figure 1 *The atmospheric carbon dioxide readings for this graph are taken monthly on a mountaintop in Hawaii. There is a clear upward trend that shows no signs of slowing down*

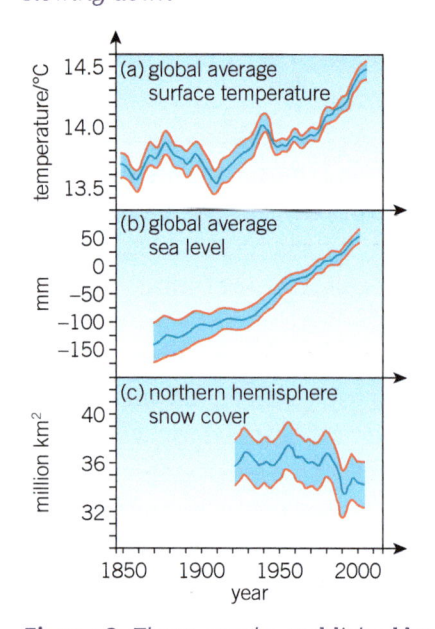

Figure 2 *These graphs, published by the IPCC (Intergovernmental Panel on Climate Change) show what appears to be a clear correlation between rising temperatures, melting snow, and rising sea levels. In each graph the blue line is the actual plot and the red lines show the uncertainty in the values*

There is a lot of debate about environmental issues such as global warming and climate change. The vast majority of scientists now think that the evidence shows that global warming is linked to human activities such as the burning of fossil fuels and deforestation, but not everyone agrees. It is very important to analyse and interpret data concerning environmental issues very carefully, and to evaluate the methods used to collect the data very carefully. In an area like this it is particularly important that any data used should be **repeatable**, **reproducible**, and **valid**.

Looking at evidence

There is hard scientific evidence for the build-up of greenhouse gases such as carbon dioxide in the atmosphere. For example, the monthly readings from the mountaintop Mauna Loa observatory in Hawaii provide a clear pattern of the changes in carbon dioxide levels over recent years (Figure 1). Scientists do not argue with this data. It is recorded in a simple, repeatable, reproducible and valid way.

However, there are many other questions to which there are not such clear-cut answers. For example, which of the observed changes in weather and climate are the result of natural variations, and which are the result of human activities? It is much more difficult to obtain repeatable and reproducible data to answer a question like this.

Some extreme weather patterns have certainly been recorded in recent years, yet throughout history there is evidence of other, equally violent, weather patterns. These occurred long before the heavy use of fossil fuels and extensive deforestation seen today. Also, weather is not the same as climate. Weather can change from day-to-day, but climate describes long-term patterns of weather over a long period of time in different areas of the world. It is evidence of climate change rather than freak weather that scientists are looking for – but the freak weather may itself be evidence of climate change!

Putting the evidence together

Climate change is shown by changes to patterns in the measurements made of such things as air temperature, sea temperature, rainfall, hours of sunshine, and wind speed. Scientists measure the daily temperatures in many different places. They also look at how the temperature of the Earth has changed over time, and how levels of carbon dioxide in the atmosphere have changed over centuries. They collect many different types of evidence. For example, they use cores of ice that are thousands of years old, the rings in the trunks of trees, and the types of pollen found in peat bogs.

In 2002, 500 billion tonnes of ice broke away from Antarctica and melted. Scientists have looked back at data from a number of sources to show that:

- the global surface temperature has been rising steadily
- the snow and ice cover in the northern hemisphere has been reducing
- sea levels have been rising (as a result of all the melting ice).

4.10 The Earth's atmosphere

Many of these changes can be related to increases in atmospheric carbon dioxide levels due to human activities – and there is growing evidence to suggest that there is a causal link between the two.

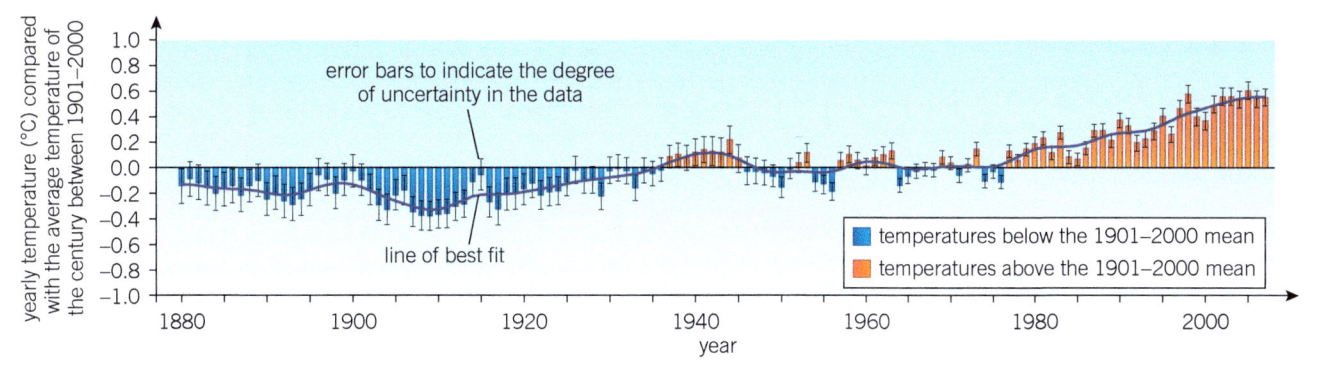

Figure 3 *This graph shows how global surface temperatures have varied from the 1901–2000 mean over 130 years. These data are widely regarded as very repeatable and reproducible*

How can scientists be sure?

There are clear uncertainties in the evidence base for the effect of human activities on climate change. Scientists analyse data on climate change using computer models based on the physics that describes the movements of mass and energy in the climate system. Computer models are only as good as the data put into them, which introduces uncertainty.

Many complex changes on Earth, such as volcanic eruptions, can affect the climate, as well as human interventions from burning fossil fuels and the limestone industry to deforestation and farming rice and cattle. Detailed data about the scale of these changes is not available from all the different countries of the world, which limits the accuracy of the models. Also, when scientists are predicting climate change, they have to make assumptions about future greenhouse gas emissions. This adds more uncertainties into the predictions.

Scientists continue to collect evidence. At the moment, most people and governments are convinced that lifestyles need to change, reliance on fossil fuels needs to be reduced, and rainforests need to be preserved in order to reduce the damage that climate change might cause.

> **1** It is important that data looking at the links between human behaviour and environmental changes should be repeatable, reproducible, and valid. Explain why. [4 marks]
>
> **2 a** Give a clear explanation of the difference between weather and climate. [2 marks]
>   **b** What is the difference between an apparent correlation between factors (such as carbon dioxide levels, human activities, global warming, and climate change) and one factor definitely causing an observed change? [4 marks]
>
> **3** Summarise the evidence shown in Figures 1, 2, and 3. Explain what the graphs appear to show and how these data might be used as evidence for human influences on global warming. What other data might you need to help confirm this conclusion? [6 marks]

Synoptic link

You can out more about line of best fit in Maths skills MS 2g.

Key points

- Human activities that involve burning fossil fuels have led to a large rise in the concentration of carbon dioxide in the air over the last 150 years.
- Over the same period of time the average temperature at the surface of the Earth has risen. The scientific consensus is that the rise in greenhouse gas concentrations has caused the rise in temperature.
- Climate describes the long-term patterns of weather in different parts of the world and climate change is shown by changes in patterns in air temperature, rainfall, sunshine, and wind speed.
- Scientists base predictions on computer models and on data collected in the field. They have to make assumptions about future greenhouse gas emissions. This means that there are uncertainties in the evidence base.

4.10.7 The impacts of climate change

Learning objectives

After this topic, you should know:
- some of the effects of increased levels of carbon dioxide and methane in the atmosphere.

Synoptic links

You will learn more about the impact of human actions and climate change on the distribution of animals and plants in Topic 4.11.10.

You will learn more about the genetic modification of crop plants in Topic 4.12.11.

Table 1 *Deadliest heatwaves*

Place	Year	Number of deaths
India	1998	2541
Europe	2003	71 310
Europe	2006	3418
Russia	2010	55 736
India	2015	2500+

Some scientists predict that global warming may mean that the Earth's average temperature could rise by as much as 5.8 °C by the year 2100. This would have a significant effect on weather patterns all over the world.

Consequences of global warming and climate change

People are worried about changing global climates. For example, in Europe it has been estimated that winters are already almost two weeks shorter than they were 40 years ago. Changing weather patterns all over the world will inevitably have wide-ranging consequences. Observed and predicted effects of global warming include:

- **Rising sea levels** as a result of melting ice sheets and expansion of the warmer oceans. This may cause the flooding of low-lying land and increased coastal erosion. Some islands could even disappear completely.

- **Loss of habitat.** For example, when low-lying areas are flooded by rising sea levels, habitats will be lost and so will the biodiversity of the area.

- **Increasingly common extreme weather events.** For example, more frequent and severe storms, or an increase in hurricane-force winds. In countries from the UK to Pakistan and India, massive floods have caused devastation to homes, businesses, and farms. Records show that this type of flooding is becoming more common and that floods are reaching higher levels than in the past (Figure 1). Extreme heatwaves are also becoming more common. The five deadliest heatwaves in history have all taken place since 1998 (Table 1).

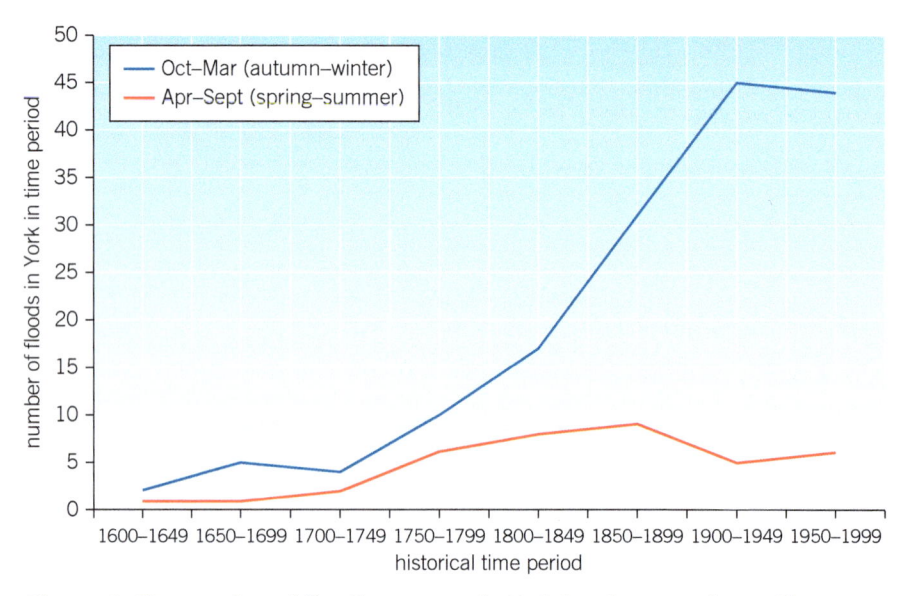

Figure 1 *The number of flooding events in York has increased steadily over the centuries. In 2015 areas of the city that had not been flooded before were underwater*

4.10 The Earth's atmosphere

- **Changes in the amount, timing, and distribution of rainfall.** Scientists have speculated that dry areas will get even drier and that monsoons in Asia will get heavier. Already areas as diverse as the Horn of Africa, the south–western areas of the United States, and Japan have experienced a lack of rainfall over a number of years. In Africa this has resulted in serious drought conditions in a number of countries (Figure 2).

- **Temperature and water stress for humans and wildlife.** For example, in many African countries such as Kenya and Sudan, temperatures are increasing as rainfall decreases (Figure 3). This is causing growing problems for both the human population and the plants and animals in these areas. The lack of water and high temperatures mean that crops fail, wildlife dies, and people starve. The combination of rising temperature and water stress can be fatal for plants and animals alike.

- **Changes in the distribution of plant and animal species.** As temperatures rise or fall and rainfall patterns change, conditions may become more favourable for some animals or plants. These species may be able to extend their range. Others may find that the change in conditions causes their range to shrink. Some will disappear completely from an area or a country and may become extinct. Rapid changes in the global climate will put ecosystems around the world under stress.

- **Changes in the food-producing capacity of different regions.** Farmers in areas such as California and many regions of Africa are struggling to grow food as conditions become hotter and drier. It seems reasonable to assume that as some places get less suited to growing crops, others will become more suited. However, as there is no existing experience of such dramatic rises in temperature over such short timescales, nobody can be sure yet of the likely effects in different regions. Worryingly, scientists predict that as the planet gets warmer, food production will fall. However, new technologies, including the genetic modification of plants, may enable us to develop crop plants that yield well in the new conditions.

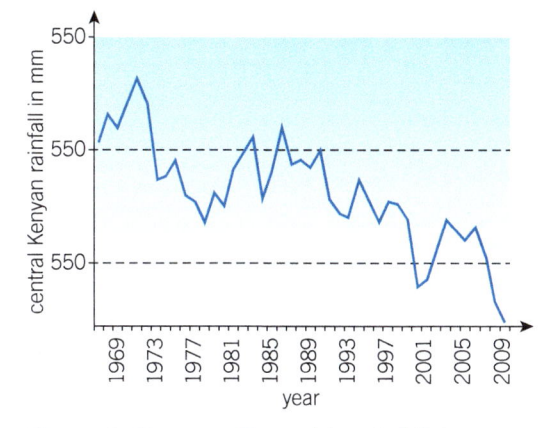

Figure 2 *The overall trend in rainfall in central Kenya over the last 40 years has been downwards*

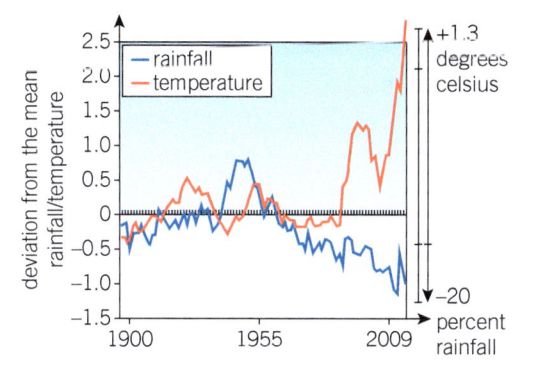

Figure 3 *Trends in rainfall and temperature in southern Sudan*

1 a Give *three* possible consequences of climate change. [3 marks]
  b Describe why these consequences are difficult to predict. [2 marks]
2 a Draw a table of the data on deaths as a result of heatwaves given in Table 1. Display the data in order of the severity of the heatwave. [4 marks]
  b Why is this data used to support the theory that climate change is a result of human activities? [3 marks]
3 a Using the graph in Figure 3, describe the changing conditions in Sudan. [4 marks]
  b Explain how these changes might be linked to rising carbon dioxide levels in the atmosphere. [4 marks]
  c Discuss how the changes seen in Figure 3 might affect the lives of the people, plants, and animals living in Sudan. [6 marks]

Key points

- Global warming and climate change are effects on the Earth's climate of increased levels of carbon dioxide and methane in the atmosphere.
- The possible consequences of global warming and climate change include:
  - rising sea levels
  - loss of habitat
  - more common extreme weather events
  - changes in rainfall
  - temperature and water stress for humans and wildlife
  - changes in the distribution of plant and animal species
  - changes in the food-producing capacity of different regions.

4.10.8 Mitigating climate change

Learning objectives
After this topic, you should know:
- how to mitigate the effects of climate change
- the scale, risk, and environmental considerations associated with mitigating the effects of climate change.

To tackle the problem of climate change, it is widely agreed that levels of greenhouse gases must be controlled and, if possible, reduced. There are a number of different steps people can take to try to **mitigate** (reduce) the effects of climate change. The **carbon footprint** of a product, service, or event is the total amount of carbon dioxide and other greenhouse gases emitted over its full life cycle. Individuals can reduce their carbon footprint – and so can companies, industries, and even whole countries. There are a number of ways in which people are trying to mitigate the effects of climate change.

Reducing greenhouse gas emissions
Using energy resources more efficiently
This can be achieved on both a large and a small scale. Most of the world's electricity is currently generated by burning fossil fuels, which releases carbon dioxide into the atmosphere. Central heating often burns gas, whilst air conditioning uses electricity. If companies and individuals reduce the amount of electricity and gas they use, the amount of carbon dioxide produced will be reduced. Changing to low-energy light bulbs, switching off lights and computers at the end of the day, and turning down the heating thermostat all help.

Better home insulation reduces the amount of heating required. Individuals can take steps to make their homes as energy-efficient as possible. On a national scale, energy-efficiency measures can be made compulsory for all new houses built.

Reducing the use of cars and planes (e.g., by walking or cycling instead of using cars and by holidaying more locally) will reduce carbon dioxide emissions. The development of more energy-efficient engines would reduce carbon dioxide levels in vehicle exhaust emissions.

Using renewable energy sources
If renewable energy resources such as wind, water, solar, or **biofuels** are used to generate electricity in place of fossil fuels, the carbon dioxide produced drops considerably. Biofuels are often made from plants that absorb carbon dioxide from the air during photosynthesis. This is returned to the atmosphere when the plants are burnt, making biofuel almost carbon-neutral. Nuclear power is another alternative means of electricity generation that releases substantially less carbon dioxide into the air than burning fossil fuels.

Reducing waste by recycling
Huge amounts of electricity are used in many different industrial processes. In addition, some of these processes (such as the use of blast furnaces) release carbon dioxide into the atmosphere. If resources such as paper, plastics, metals, and glass are recycled, the carbon footprint of the products made from them is substantially reduced.

> **Synoptic links**
>
> You will learn more about ways of reducing carbon dioxide and methane emissions, and mitigating the effects of climate change, in Topic 4.11.11.
>
> To find out about assessing the life cycle of a product in terms of its environmental impact, see Topic 8.24.14 in the *Physical Sciences* book.

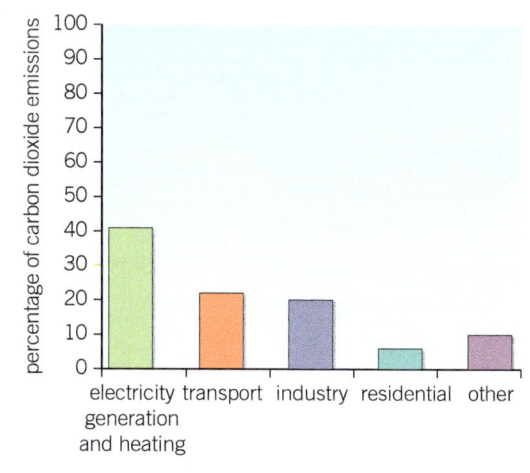

Figure 1 *The main sources of carbon dioxide emissions internationally. Reducing carbon dioxide emissions could have a major effect on global warming and climate change*

4.10 The Earth's atmosphere

Conserving forests
Forests act as large carbon sinks (see Topic 4.10.4). Over the last 50 years or so, huge areas of forests have been removed in a process called deforestation, in order to produce farmland for short-term use. If forests were conserved and trees replanted to replace the ones cut down, this would help mitigate climate change.

Managing carbon dioxide
One approach to reducing carbon dioxide levels in the atmosphere is to reduce the amount of the gas produced. Another is to find ways in which to capture, store, and remove the carbon dioxide once it has been produced. This can only be done on a large industrial scale. One solution is to collect the carbon dioxide produced in fossil fuel-burning power stations and industrial processes, compress it, and pump it deep underground to be absorbed into porous rocks. This could be done in old, redundant oil fields, coal mines, or salt extraction mines. The technique is called **carbon capture and storage (CCS)**. It is estimated that using CCS would increase the cost of producing electricity by about 10%, but it could reduce carbon emissions by up to 90%. However, the use of this technology is very limited as there are many technical difficulties.

Methane emissions also need to be controlled. There has been a huge increase in the numbers of cows raised for cheap beef, often on land made available by deforestation. There has also been a big increase in the amount of rice grown to feed people all over the world. Both cows and rice produce methane and are adding to greenhouse gas production. Reducing global demand for beef and developing strains of rice that do not produce methane are two possible solutions to the problem.

For any of these measures to be applied in a way that makes a real difference to the problem of climate change, there needs to be international agreement. It has taken a long time for many countries to accept the need to control carbon dioxide and methane emissions. In 2016, 196 countries of the United Nations signed up to the Paris Agreement on climate change. In the agreement, all countries pledged to work to limit the overall temperature rise to below 2 °C above pre-industrial levels, but are aiming to achieve a temperature rise of below 1.5 °C. The agreement comes into force in 2020.

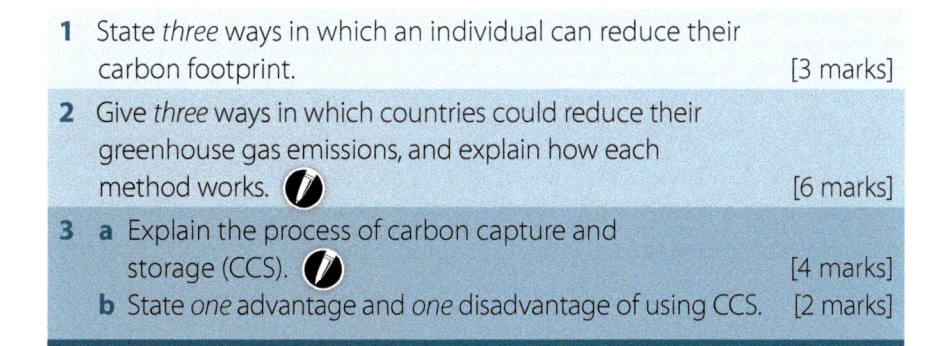

Figure 2 *In Costa Rica, conservationists are buying up land where rare cloud forests and rain forests have been destroyed, allowing the forest to regenerate slowly over time, taking carbon dioxide out of the atmosphere as it grows*

Synoptic links
You will learn much more about deforestation and its impact on the climate in Topic 4.11.9, and about positive ways in which forests can be restored in Topic 4.11.11.

You will find out more about methane production by cows and rice crops in Topic 4.11.10.

Key points
- Steps can be taken to mitigate the effects of climate change by reducing the overall rate at which greenhouse gases are added to the atmosphere. These include:
  - using energy resources more efficiently
  - using renewable energy sources
  - reducing waste by recycling
  - conserving and regenerating forests
  - developing techniques to capture and store carbon dioxide from power stations and industry.

---

1. State *three* ways in which an individual can reduce their carbon footprint. [3 marks]
2. Give *three* ways in which countries could reduce their greenhouse gas emissions, and explain how each method works. [6 marks]
3. **a** Explain the process of carbon capture and storage (CCS). [4 marks]
   b State *one* advantage and *one* disadvantage of using CCS. [2 marks]

221

4.10.9 Atmospheric pollutants

Learning objectives

After this topic, you should know:

- the main sources of air pollution
- the problems caused by increased amounts of pollutants in the air.

Pollution from fuels

All fossil fuels – oil, coal, and natural gas – produce carbon dioxide and water when they burn in plenty of air. Changing the conditions in which the hydrocarbon fuels are burnt can change the products that are made. As well as hydrocarbons, these fuels also contain other substances. The combustion of fossil fuels is a major source of atmospheric pollutants that can be harmful both to human health and to the environment. Both the hydrocarbon fuels and the impurities they contain contribute to the formation of these pollutants.

All fossil fuels contain at least some sulfur – especially the coal burnt in power stations and some of the diesel fuel burnt in ships and heavy vehicles. This reacts with oxygen when a fossil fuel is burnt and forms a gas called **sulfur dioxide**. This acidic gas is toxic and turns to sulfuric acid in moist air. This is bad for the environment, as it is a cause of **acid rain** that damages trees, as well as killing plant and animal life in rivers and lakes. Acid rain also attacks buildings, especially those made of limestone, and metal structures.

The sulfur impurities can be removed from a fuel *before* the fuel is burnt. This happens in petrol and diesel for cars, and in gas-fired power stations. In coal-fired power stations, sulfur dioxide can also be removed from the waste or 'flue' gases by reacting it with basic calcium oxide or calcium hydroxide.

When fuel burns in a car engine, even more pollution can be produced.

- When any fuel containing carbon is burned, it makes carbon dioxide. As discussed in Topic 4.10.8, carbon dioxide is the main greenhouse gas in the air.

- When there is not enough oxygen inside an engine, **incomplete combustion** occurs. Instead of all the carbon in the fuel turning into carbon dioxide, **carbon monoxide** gas, CO, is also formed. Carbon monoxide is a toxic gas. It is colourless and odourless, so you cannot tell that you are breathing it in. Your red blood cells pick up carbon monoxide and carry it around in your blood instead of oxygen. The carbon monoxide combines very strongly with haemoglobin in the blood. It takes up the sites on haemoglobin in the red blood cells that usually bond to oxygen. At low doses this puts a strain on the heart, because the blood cannot carry as much oxygen when some of the haemoglobin is bound to carbon monoxide. At higher doses a victim of carbon monoxide poisoning is starved of oxygen, gets drowsy, loses consciousness, and will die if not removed from the source of the gas.

- The high temperature inside an engine also allows the normally unreactive nitrogen gas in the air to react with oxygen. This reaction makes **nitrogen oxides** (Figure 1). Sulfur dioxide and nitrogen oxides cause respiratory problems in many people. For example, they can trigger asthma. Like sulfur dioxide, nitrogen oxides also cause acid rain.

Figure 1 *Motor vehicles cause air pollution. Modern engines are improving to meet governmental limits set for levels of different pollutants. However, there is evidence that the information on emissions published by some car manufacturers is unrealistically low. This is partly because their scientific tests are carried out in laboratories on roller tracks that do not resemble the conditions on real roads, where higher levels of pollutants (e.g., nitrogen oxides), are measured*

Figure 2 *A combination of many cars in a small area and the right weather conditions can cause smog to be formed. This is a mixture of **smoke** and **fog**, known as smog. Some of the yellowish brown colouration is caused by the presence of nitrogen dioxide gas,* NO_2

4.10 The Earth's atmosphere

- Diesel engines burn hydrocarbons with bigger molecules than those in petrol engines. When these large molecules react with oxygen in an engine, they do not always burn completely. Tiny, solid particles containing carbon and unburnt hydrocarbons are produced. These **particulates** get carried into the air. Particulates in the air are a health hazard. They can cause asthma and breathing problems. The smaller particulates are drawn deep into people's lungs and cause damage that can lead to heart disease and lung cancer.

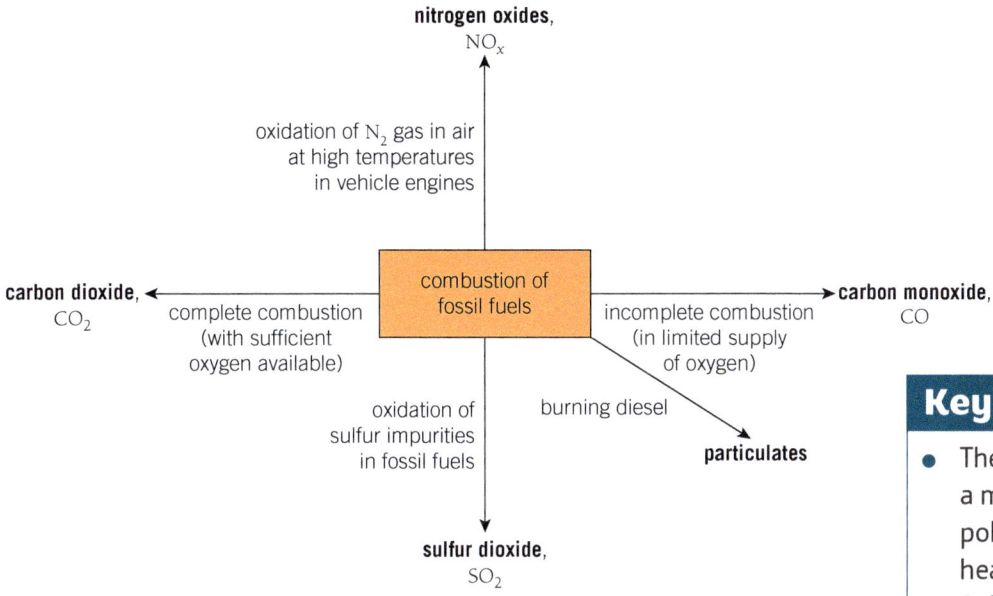

Figure 3 *A summary of the atmospheric pollutants produced when fossil fuels are burned under different conditions*

1. **a** What are the products of the complete combustion of a hydrocarbon, and which environmental problems do they cause? [3 marks]
   b When fossil fuels burn, which element present in impurities can produce sulfur dioxide? [1 mark]
2. **a** Which pollution problem does sulfur dioxide gas contribute to? [1 mark]
   b Which other non-metal oxides released from cars also cause this pollution problem? [1 mark]
3. How are the following substances produced when fuels burn in vehicles?
   a sulfur dioxide [1 mark]
   b nitrogen oxides [2 marks]
   c particulates [1 mark]
4. **a** Natural gas is mainly methane, CH_4. Write a balanced symbol equation for the complete combustion of methane, including state symbols, at the temperature in the flame. [3 marks]
   b When natural gas burns in a faulty gas heater, it can produce carbon monoxide (and water). Write a balanced symbol equation, including state symbols, to show this reaction. [3 marks]
   c Explain why carbon monoxide is so dangerous. [4 marks]

Key points

- The combustion of fossil fuels is a major source of atmospheric pollutants that can be harmful to health and to the environment.
- Sulfur impurities in fuels burn to form sulfur dioxide, which turns to sulfuric acid in moist air. Acid rain damages plants and buildings. It also harms living organisms in ponds, rivers, and lakes.
- Carbon monoxide, a toxic gas that combines with haemoglobin in the blood, is formed by the incomplete combustion of hydrocarbon fuels when there is not enough air. This can put a strain on the heart and at high doses it can kill.
- Particulates in the air include soot (carbon) from diesel engines and dust from roads and industry. The smaller particulates can go deep into people's lungs and cause damage that can lead to heart disease and cancer.
- At the high temperatures in engines, nitrogen from the air reacts with oxygen to form oxides of nitrogen. These cause breathing problems and can also cause acid rain.

4.10.10 The water cycle

Learning objectives

After this topic, you should know:
- the importance of water for life on Earth
- the processes of simple distillation
- the importance of the water cycle to living organisms.

Synoptic links

To remind yourself how water moves into and out of cells, look back at Chapter 1.3.

For more information on photosynthesis, look back at Chapter 2.6.

Water is probably the most important compound on our planet. Without it, life on Earth, both on land and in the seas, would not be possible.

- Water acts as the solvent for all the chemical reactions that take place in the cells of living organisms. The reactions take place in solution. It also helps to transport dissolved compounds into and out of cells in the processes of diffusion, osmosis, and active transport.
- Water itself is either a reactant or a product of the many biochemical changes that living organisms depend on. These include processes such as respiration (where H_2O is a product), photosynthesis (where H_2O is a reactant), and digestion (where H_2O can be either a reactant or a product).
- Rivers, lakes, and seas provide habitats for aquatic living organisms.

Simple distillation

When analytical chemists want pure water to add to an unknown sample before identifying it, they use distilled water. This water has no solids dissolved in it. Water is an excellent solvent as it can dissolve many substances. Therefore water sources in nature will be a mixture of water plus many other dissolved substances (called solutes). The mixture itself is called a solution. How can you make a sample of pure, distilled water from a solution?

Figure 1 shows the apparatus you can use for simple distillation.

Synoptic link

To revise the changes of state needed to explain distillation and the water cycle, look back at Topic 1.1.4.

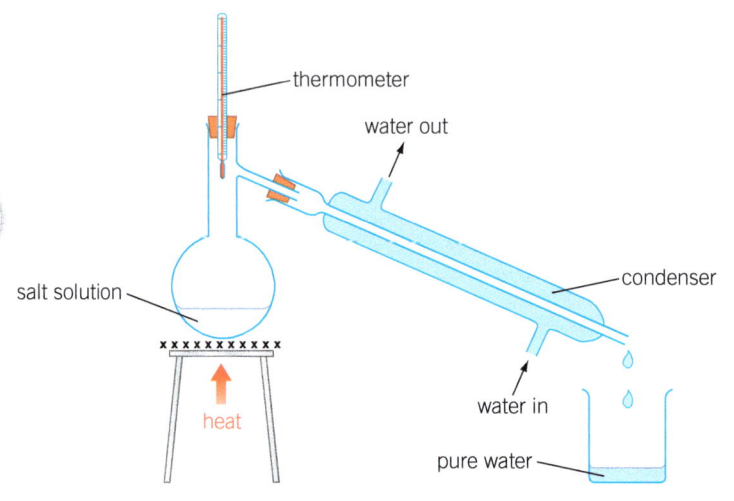

Figure 1 *Distilling pure water from salt solution*

Figure 2 *Seawater is distilled to make drinking water in a desalination plant*

In simple distillation, an aqueous solution is heated and boiled to evaporate the water. Anti-bumping granules can be added to the solution being heated to help it boil smoothly. The water vapour given off then enters a condenser. This is an outer glass tube with water flowing through it that acts as a cooling 'jacket' around the inner glass tube from the flask. Here the hot water vapour is cooled and condensed back into liquid water. The distilled water drips from the end of the condenser and is collected in a receiving vessel (Figure 1).

■ 4.10 The Earth's atmosphere

The water cycle

Water is vital for life. The water cycle provides fresh water for animals and plants on land before draining into the seas and oceans (Figure 3). Water evaporates constantly from the surface of the land and the rivers, lakes, and oceans of the world. It condenses as it rises into the cooler air and forms clouds where it is then precipitated onto the surface of the Earth as rain, snow, hail, or sleet. Water passes through the bodies of animals and plants, released during respiration in their lifetime, as well as when organisms decay. Animals also release water in urine, faeces, and sweat (in mammals), whilst plants release water into the atmosphere during transpiration. Every drop of water you drink has been through the bodies of many living organisms before you.

Study tip

The main stages of the water cycle are:
- condensation
- transpiration
- precipitation
- respiration.
- evaporation

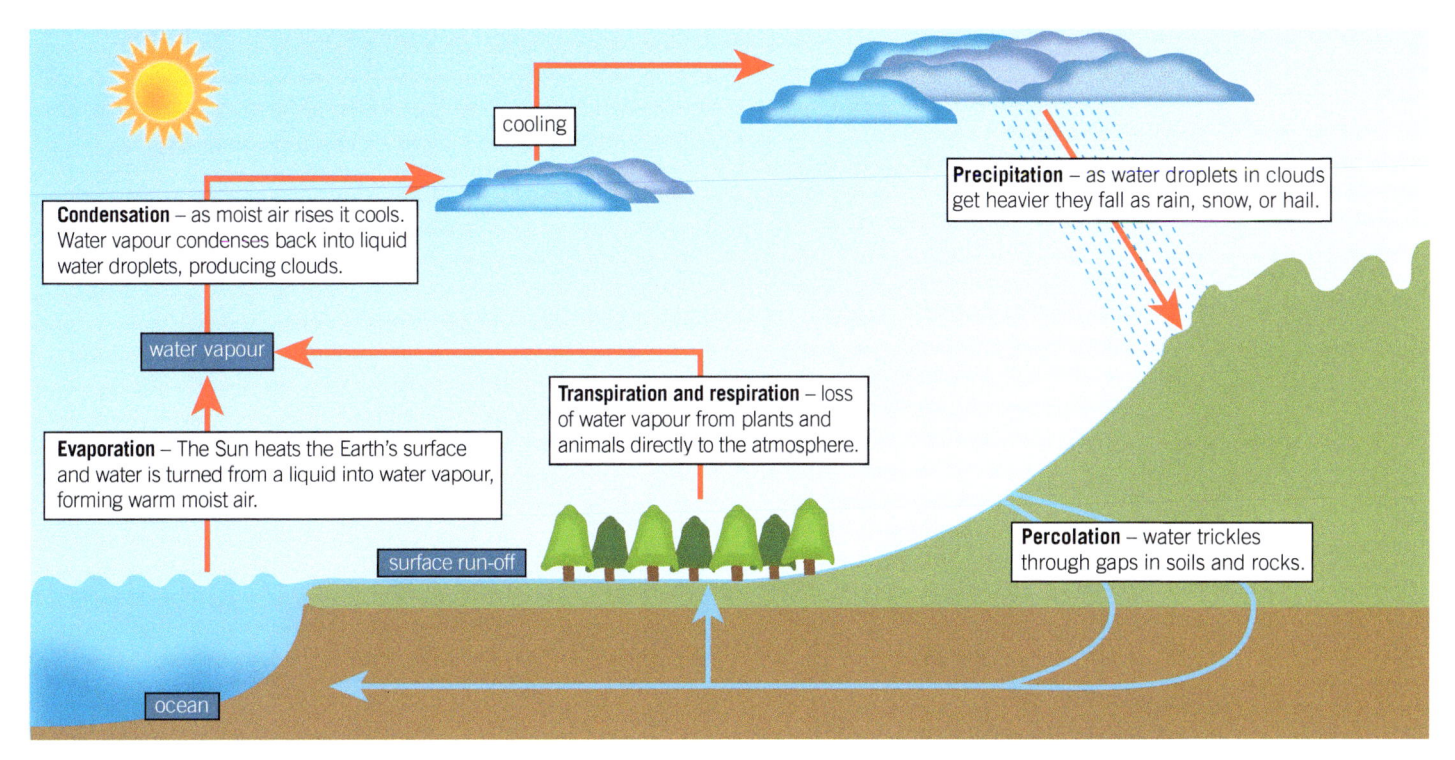

Figure 3 *The water cycle in nature*

Synoptic links

You learnt about the chemistry of respiration in Topic 2.5.1 and about transpiration in Topics 2.6.4 and 2.6.5.

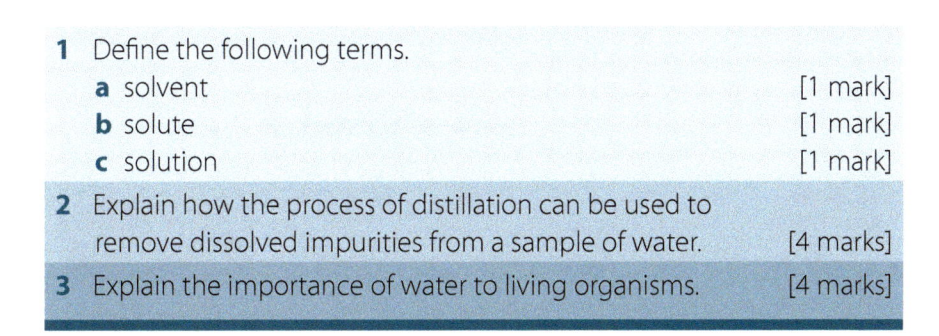

1 Define the following terms.
  a solvent [1 mark]
  b solute [1 mark]
  c solution [1 mark]
2 Explain how the process of distillation can be used to remove dissolved impurities from a sample of water. [4 marks]
3 Explain the importance of water to living organisms. [4 marks]

Key points

- Simple distillation is used to separate and collect a solvent from a solution (e.g., pure water from an aqueous solution of solutes).
- During distillation, water is boiled, and then water vapour is cooled and condensed as it passes through a condenser before collection as distilled water.
- The water cycle provides fresh water for plants and animals on land before draining into the seas. Water is continuously evaporated, condensed, and precipitated.

225

4.10.11 Potable water

Learning objectives

After this topic, you should know:

- the difference between potable water and pure water
- the differences in treatment of ground water and salty water
- how to carry out a simple distillation of salt solution and analyse water from different sources.

Water fit to drink

Water is a vital and useful resource. We use it for agriculture and in industry. It is an important raw material, as a solvent and as a coolant. Other uses of water are for washing and cleaning – and of course, for drinking. Providing people with water that is fit to drink, called **potable water**, is a major issue all over the world.

You will be familiar with the natural circulation of water around the planet from previous work studying the water cycle. In countries such as the UK, rainwater falls to the ground, replenishing supplies of fresh water in rivers and lakes. It also seeps down through soil and rocks to underground sources of water called aquifers. Fresh water can be obtained from these porous underground seams of rock by drilling a pipe down to form a water well.

The rainwater itself dissolves some gases from the air as it falls to the ground. Then, once in contact with solid land, it will dissolve soluble substances as it passes over them. Water from natural sources will always contain dissolved minerals (salts), as well as microorganisms from soil and decaying matter. The levels of both these impurities must be reduced to meet strict safety standards for drinking water.

The best sources of fresh water contain low levels of minerals and microbes to start with. When water is taken from rivers or from reservoirs made to

Figure 1 *About 97% of the water on Earth is found in its oceans and is not potable*

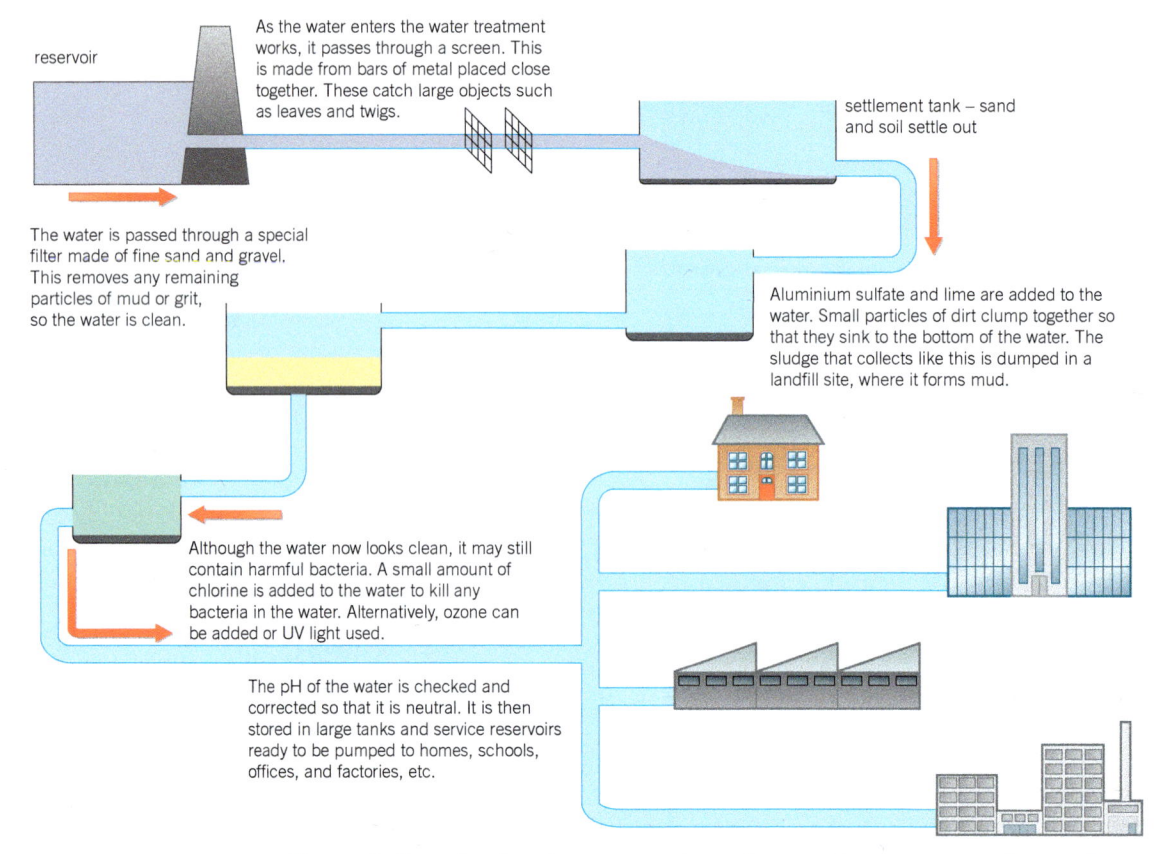

Figure 2 *From freshwater reservoir to end user – the treatment of water from a reservoir to make potable water*

4.10 The Earth's atmosphere

store fresh water, it has to be treated to make it safe to drink. This treatment involves techniques such as:

- passing the untreated water through filter beds made of sand and gravel to remove solid particles
- the addition of chlorine or ozone to sterilise the water by killing microorganisms or, without adding chemical sterilising agents, by passing ultraviolet light through the water.

Purifying salty water

In the UK, there is usually sufficient rain and natural supplies of fresh water to satisfy the needs of the population and industry. However, in countries with much drier climates and with few sources of natural fresh water, obtaining enough potable water can be difficult. Some of these places have to use sources of water that people in the UK would not consider. Water from any source, even seawater or salty water from marshes, can be made pure by distilling it. However, distillation is an expensive process. This is because of the energy costs involved in boiling large volumes of water, even though reduced pressure is used in a **desalination** plant. Under reduced pressure, water boils below 100 °C, saving on some of the energy costs. This process is called flash distillation.

Converting salty water to potable, useable water is called desalination. Desalination is used in the Middle East in some oil-rich nations, and on some islands with no natural sources of water apart from occasional rainwater. Besides distillation, a process called reverse osmosis can also be used to desalinate water. This uses membranes to separate the water and the salts dissolved in it. The membranes can remove 98% of dissolved salts from seawater. There is no heating involved, so it needs less energy than distillation. However, energy is still required to pressurise the water passing through, and corrosion of pumps by salty water is also a problem.

1 Water that looks colourless and clear may contain microorganisms. Give *three* ways in which the water could be made potable. [3 marks]

2 a How can you convert water from a natural source into pure water? [1 mark]
  b How can you test that the water is pure? [1 mark]
  c Why aren't anhydrous copper(II) sulfate or blue cobalt(II) chloride used to test the purity of water? [1 mark]

3 Explain why bottled water sold in the supermarket should not be described as 'pure' water. [3 mark]

4 a Why is a shortage of water a problem for some hot countries, even though they have large coastlines? [1 mark]
  b Define the term desalination. [1 mark]
  c i What is the main disadvantage of desalination using distillation? [1 mark]
    ii Name another process that can be used instead of distillation. [1 mark]

Analysis and purification of water samples

a Your teacher will give you a sample of salty water to test its pH, and another sample to desalinate by distillation (see Topic 4.10.10).

Using half the sample of distilled water collected, test for pure water by measuring its boiling point. Pure water boils at 100 °C.

Note that chemical tests for water (white anhydrous copper(II) sulfate turns blue or blue cobalt(II) chloride paper turns pink) only test for the presence of water. They do not tell you if the water is pure or not.

Using the other half of your distilled water sample, test its pH value. Record the results of your tests on salty water.

b Now, collect more water samples from different sources, find their pH, and determine whether or not they contain any dissolved solids.

- Record your results in a table.
- Explain how you would ensure that any samples collected are representative of that source.

Safety: Wear eye protection.

Key points

- Water is made fit to drink by passing it through filter beds to remove solids and adding chlorine, ozone, or by passing ultra-violet light through it (sterilising) to reduce microorganisms.
- Water can be purified by distillation, but this requires large amounts of energy, which makes it expensive.
- Reverse osmosis uses membranes to separate dissolved salts from salty water, but this method of desalination also needs energy to achieve the high pressures required.

4.10.12 Treating waste water

Learning objectives

After this topic, you should know:
- how waste water is made safe to release into the environment
- the relative ease of obtaining potable water from waste, ground and salt water.

Down the drain

Have you ever wondered what happens to all the waste that leaves our homes down the drains? Everything that drains from washing machines, dishwashers, sinks, baths, and toilets flows down pipes and enters the larger sewer pipes. All this, along with waste water from businesses and industry, is given the general name **sewage**. This, together with waste water from farming activities, has to be treated at sewage treatment plants to make it safe before it can be returned to the environment, usually into rivers or piped out to sea.

Sewage treatment

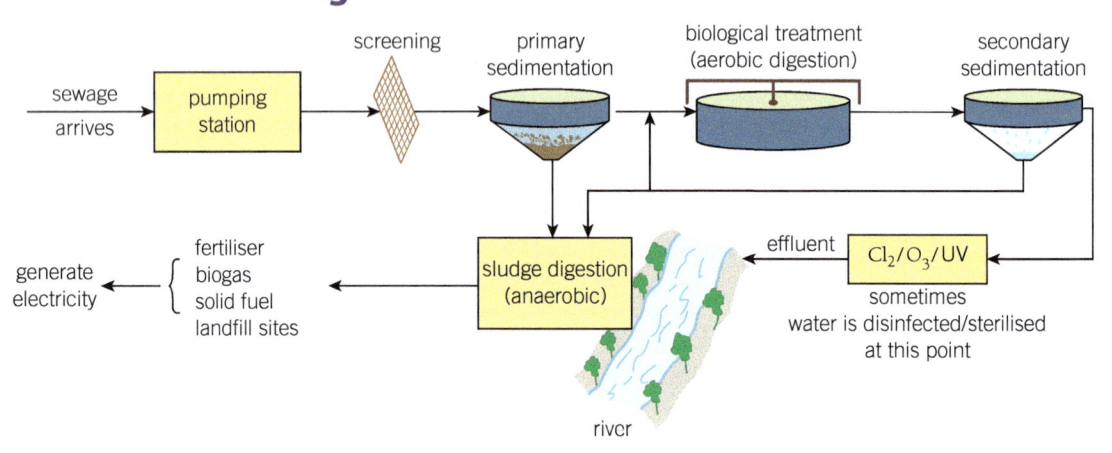

Figure 1 *The steps needed to make our waste water from urban and rural sources safe to return to the environment*

Sewage treatment involves a series of steps, which are described below and in Figure 1.

1. **Screening**

   Once the sewage arrives at the sewage treatment plant, the first step is to remove large solid objects and grit from the rest of the waste water. The sewage passes through a metal grid that traps the large objects.

2. **Primary treatment**

   In the first circular tank, the solid sediments are allowed to settle out from the mixture. Large paddles rotate, pushing the solids, called sludge, towards the centre of the tank. There the sludge is piped to a storage tank for further treatment.

   The watery liquid (effluent) above the sludge flows into the next tank. Although no solid matter is visible, this effluent still contains many potentially harmful microorganisms.

3. **Secondary treatment**

   In the second tank, useful bacteria feed on any remaining organic matter and harmful microorganisms still present, breaking them down aerobically (in the presence of oxygen). The tank is aerated

Figure 2 *A sewage treatment plant*

by bubbling air through the waste water. This can take from several hours to several days, depending on the quality of the waste water, the size of the tank, the rate of aeration, and the temperature.

4 Final treatment

In the last tank, the useful bacteria are allowed to settle out to the bottom of the tank as a sediment. The sediment is either recycled back into the secondary treatment tank or passed into the tank where the sludge is treated. At this point, the treated waste water is safe enough to be discharged back into rivers.

However, if the river is a particularly sensitive ecosystem, the water can be filtered one more time through a bed of sand. If necessary, the water can then be sterilised by ultraviolet light or by chlorine. However, the release of chlorine into rivers does cause concern, as toxic organic compounds of chlorine can be formed in the environment.

Treating the sewage sludge

The sludge separated off during the primary treatment of the sewage is not wasted. After further treatment, most can be dried and used as fertiliser on farmland to improve the soil or used as a source of renewable energy.

The sludge contains organic matter, including human waste, suspended solids, water, and dissolved compounds. It is digested anaerobically by microorganisms beneath the surface in the treatment tank.

This biological treatment can be carried out at a relatively high temperature of about 55 °C or a lower temperature of about 35 °C, which can take up to 30 days to complete. The higher temperature has the benefit of speeding up the breakdown of the organic matter, but energy has to be supplied to heat the sludge.

The breakdown products include biogas (a mixture of methane, carbon dioxide, and some hydrogen sulfide). Biogas can be burned and used to power the sewage treatment plant or provide electricity for the surrounding area. It can also be further cleaned to make methane, the main gas in natural gas, and piped into the gas supply.

Alternatively, the sludge can be dried out and turned into a crusty solid 'cake' that can be burnt to generate electricity (Figure 3).

Figure 3 *Dried sludge can be used as a renewable energy source, along with biogas and biomethane. All of these are made from sewage*

Study tip

When sewage sludge is dried it takes up a lot less space, so it becomes easier to transport it away from the sewage treatment plant.

Key points

- Waste water requires treatment at a sewage works before being released into the environment.
- Sewage treatment involves the removal of organic matter and harmful microorganisms and chemicals.
- The stages include screening to remove large solids and grit, sedimentation to produce sewage sludge, and aerobic biological treatment of the safe effluent released into environment.
- The sewage sludge is separated, broken down by anaerobic digestion, and dried. It can provide us with fertiliser and a source of renewable energy.

1 Draw a basic flow diagram listing the main steps used in a sewage treatment plant to make waste water safe to discharge into the environment. [4 marks]

2 **a** Describe what takes place in a primary treatment tank. [2 marks]
   b State *two* uses of sewage sludge. [2 marks]

3 Describe how the processes involving microorganisms in a secondary treatment tank and a sewage sludge tank differ. [2 marks]

4 Using the information here and in Topic 4.10.11, evaluate the use of waste water, salt water, and ground water from an aquifer as sources of potable water. [6 marks]

4.10 The Earth's atmosphere

Summary questions

1 The pie charts below show the atmosphere of a planet shortly after it was formed (**A**) and then millions of years later (**B**).

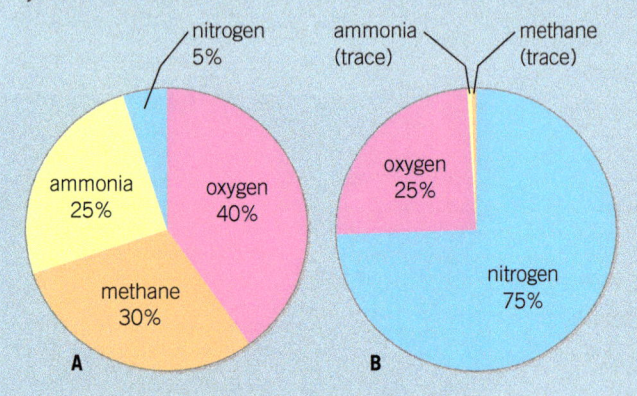

Figure 1

a Describe the changes in the planet's atmosphere over time. [2 marks]
b What might have caused the changes you described in **a**? [2 marks]

2 a i What gases are given off from fossil fuel power stations that can cause acid rain? [2 marks]
   ii Give *two* ways of stopping acidic gas from fossil fuel power stations getting into the atmosphere. [2 marks]
   iii Name the cause of acid rain, which comes from car engines, and how it arises. [2 marks]
  b State the main reason why levels of carbon dioxide in the Earth's atmosphere have increased so sharply over the past 100 years. [1 mark]

3 Gases that cause global warming are called greenhouse gases.
  a Write the formulae of *three* of these gases and explain how they cause the temperature of the Earth to rise. [6 marks]
  b Explain the effect of planting more trees on the levels of carbon dioxide in the Earth's atmosphere. [4 marks]
  c Discuss how you can help to reduce the levels of carbon dioxide in the air by changing your lifestyle. [4 marks]
  d Explain why a minority of scientists are not convinced that the global warming observed in recent years is a result of human pollution of the atmosphere. [2 marks]

4 a Name the processes **A–F** that are involved in the different stages of the carbon cycle. [6 marks]

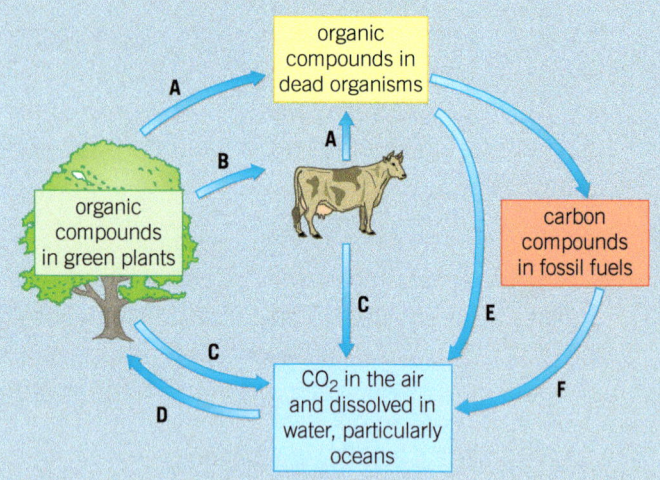

Figure 2 *The carbon cycle*

  b Describe how carbon dioxide is removed from the atmosphere in the carbon cycle. [2 marks]
  c Describe the *three* main processes by which carbon dioxide gets into and out of the atmosphere. [6 marks]
  d Give the *four* carbon sinks where most carbon is stored. [4 marks]
  e Explain why the carbon cycle is so important. [6 marks]

5 In some hot countries, getting sufficient fresh water is difficult. However, countries with large coastlines have plenty of seawater available. They can use desalination plants, such as the one in the photo below. These use a process called 'flash distillation' to turn the salty water into drinking water. Inside the desalination plant, seawater is boiled under reduced pressure, then the water vapour given off is cooled and condensed.
  a Why is the pressure reduced before boiling the seawater? How does this keep costs down? [2 marks]
  b An alternative process uses 'reverse osmosis' to remove the salts from seawater. This passes seawater through a membrane. The latest membranes can remove 98% of the salts from seawater.
    Why is reverse osmosis a better option than flash distillation for obtaining drinking water? [2 marks]

4.10 The Earth's atmosphere

Practice questions

01 Nitrous oxide is one of the three main greenhouse gases causing global warming.

01.1 Name the **two** other main greenhouse gases. [2 marks]

01.2 **Table 1** shows how emissions of nitrous oxides from road transport have changed from 1980 to 2009.

Table 1

Year	Estimated emissions of nitrous oxides in the UK in thousands of tonnes
1980	740
1985	820
1990	980
1995	900
2000	740
2005	570
2009	360

Use the data to copy and complete the graph in **Figure 1** to show how the nitrous oxide emissions from road transport have changed between 1980 and 2009.
The first and the last points have been done for you.

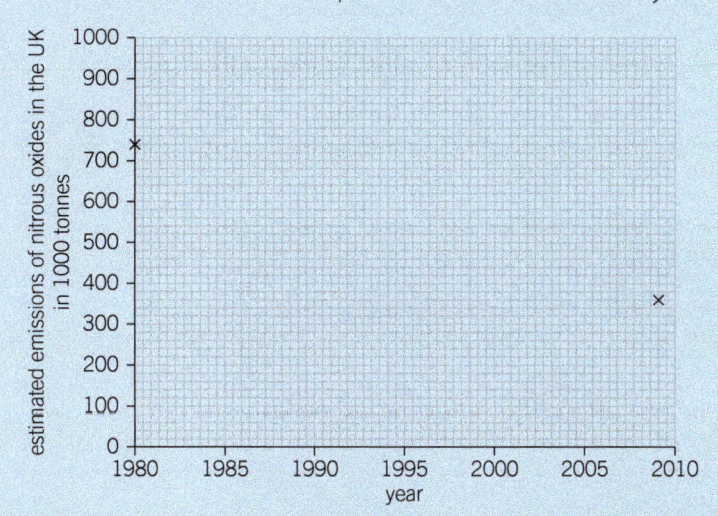

Figure 1
[2 marks]

01.3 Describe the pattern shown in the graph. [3 marks]

01.4 Select **one** possible reason for the decrease in nitrous oxide emissions from road transport in the last few years.
  A There has been a decrease in the use of cars from 1990.
  B All new cars have catalytic converters.
  C Nitrous oxide is no longer used in fuels.
  D Leaded fuel is not sold any more. [1 mark]

[AQA, 2013]

02 This question is about water.
Figure 2 shows different stages of the water cycle labelled **A**, **B**, **C**, **D**, and **E**.

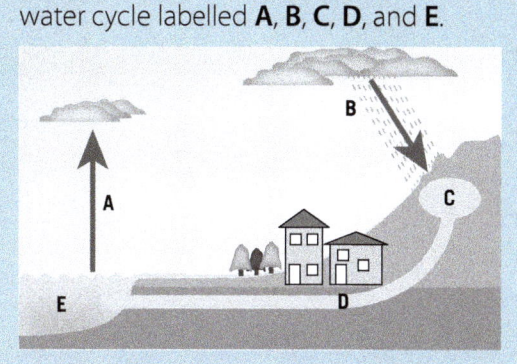

Figure 2

Use **Figure 2** and your own knowledge to answer the following questions.

02.1 Which stage shows the process of condensation? [1 mark]

02.2 Why is water at stage **E** not used as drinking water? [1 mark]

02.3 Water used for drinking is filtered and then treated with chlorine. Explain why. [2 marks]

03 Some scientists think that the Earth's early atmosphere was probably like that of Venus today. **Table 2** shows information about the atmosphere of Venus.

Table 2

Name of gas	Percentage composition of atmosphere
nitrogen	3.5
oxygen	trace
argon	trace
carbon dioxide	96.5
water	trace
Average surface temperature	460 °C

03.1 State **three** ways in which the atmosphere on Earth today is different to that on Venus. [3 marks]

03.2 The Earth's surface is covered in many oceans. The surface of Venus does not have oceans. Use the information in **Table 2** to suggest why Venus does not have oceans. [1 mark]

03.3 The Earth's atmosphere has changed since green plants first appeared on the Earth's surface. Explain how green plants and other organisms have changed the composition of the Earth's atmosphere. [4 marks]

Ecosystems and biodiversity

4.11.1 Organisation in ecosystems

Learning objectives

After this topic, you should know:
- what is meant by a stable community
- how organisms are adapted to the conditions in which they live
- the relationship between communities and ecosystems.

Organisms do not live in isolation. Any individual – even if one of a species that lives a solitary existence most of the time, such as a polar bear or a tiger – will be part of a population of organisms of the same species. Populations do not exist in isolation either – they live in complex **communities**. A community is made up of the populations of different species of animals and plants, protista, fungi, bacteria, and archaea that are all interdependent in a **habitat**. Within a community each species depends on other species for things including food, shelter, pollination (Figure 1), and seed dispersal (Figure 2).

Communities and ecosystems

An ecosystem is made up of a community of organisms interacting with the non-living or abiotic elements of their environment. The interactions of the living things make up the biotic elements of the ecosystem. All species live in ecosystems composed of complex communities of animals, plants, and other organisms that are dependent on each other and that are adapted to their particular conditions. The habitat of each organism is where it lives in an ecosystem. For example, on the plains in Africa, in the bark of a tree, or in a rock pool on a seashore.

The Sun is the original energy source for most ecosystems on Earth. Materials – including carbon, nitrogen, and water – are constantly being recycled through the living world in processes where microorganisms play a major part.

Synoptic link

To remind yourself of the recycling of materials within ecosystems, look back at Topic 4.10.3.

Figure 1 *Without the insects, birds, and mammals that pollinate them, many plants would not be able to reproduce*

Within any community the different animals and plants are often interdependent:
- Plants produce food by photosynthesis.
- Animals eat plants.
- Animals pollinate plants.

Figure 2 *Animals are often involved in seed dispersal – for example, animals will eat these berries and spread the seeds they contain in their faeces*

■ 4.11 Ecosystems and biodiversity

- Animals eat other animals.
- Animals use plant and animal materials to build nests and shelters.
- Plants need nutrients from animal droppings and decay.

Different animals and plants compete for various resources both within each species and with other species. Different communities exist close to each other and may overlap. It is important that you understand the relationships within and between communities. If one species is removed, or becomes very numerous, the whole community can be affected. This is called **interdependence**.

Stable communities

In some communities the environmental factors are relatively constant – they may change, but if they do it is in a regular pattern, such as the seasons of the year in the UK. In these stable environments, the species of living organisms may also be in balance. The number of species remains relatively constant, as does the population sizes of the different species, although they will vary slightly. These stable communities are very important. Examples include tropical rainforests (Figure 3), ancient oak woodlands (Figure 4), and mature coral reefs. These communities include a wide range of species – a single mature oak tree can house up to 1000 other species. Within limits, change can be tolerated and absorbed. For example, a falling tree allows light into the forest floor, so new seedlings can grow up. But when a large, stable community is lost, it cannot easily be replaced.

Figure 3 *Stable communities such as this tropical rainforest in Costa Rica take a very long time to form – and cannot easily be replaced*

Go further

It is important to understand the makeup of stable communities. This helps scientists to analyse the impact of their destruction and plan ways to conserve them. A mature oak tree is an example of a small, stable community. Over 1000 species can be dependent on the one tree.

Figure 4 *The communities of organisms in a bog are specialised to survive in wet, acidic conditions*

Key points

- An ecosystem is the interaction of a community of living organisms with the non-living (abiotic) parts of their environment.
- A habitat is where a particular organism lives in an ecosystem.
- A population is made up of all the organisms of the same species in a habitat.
- A community is made up of all the populations of different organisms that live in the same habitat.
- Organisms require materials from their surroundings and other living organisms to survive and reproduce.
- Within a community, each species depends on other species for food, shelter, pollination, seed dispersal, etc. If one species is removed the whole community can be affected. This is called interdependence.
- A stable community is one in which all the species and environmental factors are in balance so that population sizes remain fairly constant.

1 **a** Define a habitat. [1 mark]
  b Explain how an ecosystem differs from a community. [3 marks]
2 Give *five* examples of how animals and plants can interact in an ecosystem. [5 marks]
3 Describe an example of a stable community, and state why it is so important that it is stable. Your answer should include examples of at least *one* plant and *one* animal that live in this community. [6 marks]

233

4.11.2 Feeding relationships

Learning objectives

After this topic, you should know:
- the importance of photosynthesis in feeding relationships
- the main feeding relationships within a community
- how the numbers of predators and prey in a community are related.

Light from the Sun falls continually onto the surface of the Earth. It is the source of energy for most communities of living organisms. Green plants and algae absorb a small amount of this light for photosynthesis. During photosynthesis, glucose and oxygen are made. The glucose is then used to produce the range of chemicals that make up the cells of the plants and algae. This new material adds to the **biomass** of the organisms. Plants and algae are called **producers** because they produce most of the biomass for life on Earth.

Feeding relationships

The organisms within a community are connected by feeding relationships, and these relationships can be represented simply by food chains (Figure 1). Producers are at the beginning of all food chains because they produce glucose by photosynthesis. On land, the producers are almost always green plants. In the oceans, the main producers are the algae and tiny photosynthetic organisms called phytoplankton.

The animals that eat the producers are known as **primary consumers**. On land these are the herbivores, the plant-eating animals. They include animals ranging from sheep, hippos, and rabbits, to caterpillars, aphids, and an array of birds from parrots to hummingbirds. In the oceans, the primary consumers are often zooplankton, shrimps, crabs, sea urchins, and small fish.

Primary consumers are eaten by animals known as **secondary consumers**. These include carnivores such as lions, foxes, blue tits, eagles, and chameleons. In the oceans the secondary consumers include larger fish, turtles, and seals. Going up the food chain, secondary consumers may themselves be eaten by **tertiary consumers** – usually large carnivores such as polar bears, birds of prey, or tigers. Food chains are very simple models of the feeding relationships in a community (e.g., most organisms eat a variety of foods, not just a single species) but they are nevertheless useful in understanding how communities work.

producer → **primary consumer** → **secondary consumer** → **tertiary consumer**

phytoplankton → fish → seal → killer whale

Food chains are a great simplification of the feeding relationships within an ecosystem. Most primary consumers eat a wide range of different plants. Most carnivores have more than one prey animal (e.g., a fox will eat anything from worms

Figure 1 *Food chains can be used to represent feeding relationships within a community*

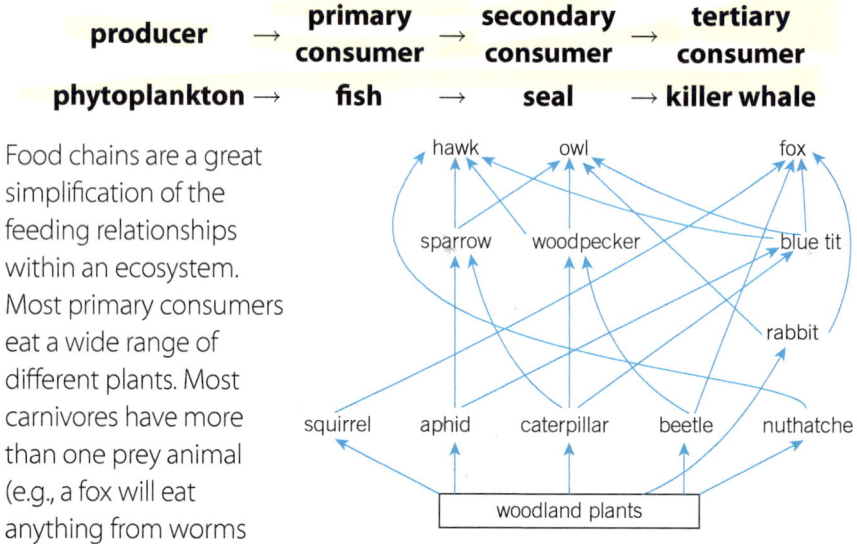

Figure 2 *A simplified woodland food web*

234

4.11 Ecosystems and biodiversity

and beetles to bird's eggs, rabbits, and lambs). These complex feeding relationships can be built up into models called food webs (Figure 2). Although a food web is still a simplification of the real situation, it gives us a better picture of the interdependence of species within an ecosystem in terms of food resources.

Predators and prey

Primary consumers eat plants or algae. This has its problems, because cellulose is very difficult to digest. Herbivores have to use a variety of methods to break down cellulose plant cell walls to get at the contents of the cells. Primary consumers have to find and eat enough plant material to provide them with the nutrients they need. The big advantage of eating plants is that they don't move around.

Secondary and tertiary consumers have a different problem. Their food is other animals, so it is high in protein and fat and relatively easy to digest. But animals move about. Before you can eat them you have to catch them. Consumers that eat other animals are known as **predators**. Consumers that are eaten are known as **prey**. Prey animals are often primary consumers but they may be secondary or even tertiary consumers in different food chains. Predators are always secondary consumers or above. In a stable community, the numbers of predators and prey rise and fall in linked cycles (Figure 3):

- If there is plenty of food available, the prey animals grow and reproduce successfully, so numbers increase.
- As prey animal numbers go up, there is plenty of food available for the predators, so predators can reproduce successfully and predator numbers increase.
- The high number of predators eat a larger proportion of the prey animals, so prey numbers fall.
- With fewer prey animals, there is less food for the predators, so they are less successful and predator numbers fall.
- With the reduction in predators, and the good food supply that results from fewer animals, prey numbers go up again and the cycle repeats itself.

---

1 a What is a producer? [1 mark]
b State why producers are the first organism in a food chain. [1 mark]

2 a Describe how food chains are a useful way to model feeding relationships in a community, and give *one* limitation. [3 marks]
b Explain why food webs can be a more useful model of feeding relationships in a community than food chains. [4 marks]

3 Use the graphs in Figure 3 to help you answer the following questions:
a Explain the way in which predator and prey numbers rise and fall in cycles in a stable community. [3 marks]
b Suggest reasons why the cycles of predator–prey populations do not always follow the expected pattern. [5 marks]

Synoptic link

You learnt about photosynthesis and how the products of photosynthesis are used to make the chemicals needed in cells in Topic 2.6.6.

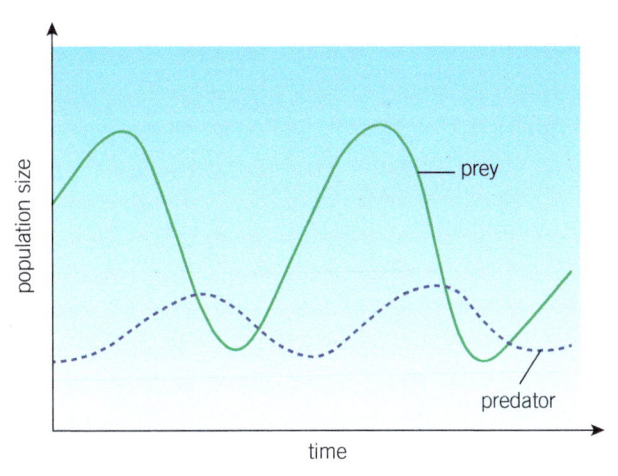

Figure 3 *The numbers of many different predator–prey populations show typical rises and falls*

Key points

- Photosynthetic organisms are the producers of biomass for life on Earth.
- Feeding relationships within a community can be represented by food chains. All food chains begin with a producer that synthesises new molecules. On land this is usually a green plant that makes glucose by photosynthesis.
- A food web can be used to represent the interdependence of species within an ecosystem in terms of food sources.
- Producers are eaten by primary consumers, which in turn may be eaten by secondary consumers and then tertiary consumers.
- Consumers that eat other animals are often predators and those that are eaten are prey. In a stable community the numbers of predators and prey rise and fall in cycles.

235

4.11.3 Factors affecting communities

Learning objectives
After this topic, you should know:
- some of the abiotic and biotic factors that affect communities.

To survive and breed successfully, organisms need to be well-adapted to the environment in which they live. For example, reindeer live in cold environments where most of the plants are small because low temperatures and light levels limit growth. They eat grass, moss, and lichen. Reindeer travel thousands of miles as they feed, because they cannot get enough food to survive in just one area. They travel in herds as protection against predators.

Abiotic factors affecting communities
Non-living factors that affect living organisms and communities include the following:

- **Light intensity:** light limits photosynthesis, so light intensity also affects the distribution of plants and animals. Some plants are adapted to living in low light levels, for example, they may have more chlorophyll or bigger leaves. Nettles growing in the shade of other bushes have leaves with a much bigger surface area than nettles growing in the open. However, most plants need plenty of light to grow well. The breeding cycles of many animal and plant species are linked to day length and light intensity.

- **Temperature:** temperature is a limiting factor on photosynthesis and therefore on growth in plants. In cold climates, temperature is always limiting. For example, the low Arctic temperatures mean that the plants are all small. This in turn affects the numbers of herbivores that can survive and limits the numbers of carnivores in the community (Figure 1).

- **Moisture levels:** if there is no water, there will be little or no life. As a rule, plants and animals are relatively rare in a desert as the availability of water is limited. However, after it rains, many plants grow, flower, and make seeds very quickly while the water is available (Figure 2). These plants are eaten by many animals that move into the area to take advantage of them.

- **Soil pH and mineral content:** the level of mineral ions, for example, nitrate ions, in the soil has a considerable impact on the distribution of plants. Carnivorous plants such as sundews thrive where nitrate levels are very low because they can trap and digest animal prey. The nitrates they need are provided when they break down the animal protein. Most other plants struggle to grow in areas with low levels of mineral ions. The pH of the soil also has a major effect on what can grow in it and on the rate of decay and therefore on the release of mineral ions back into the soil. A low (acidic) pH inhibits decay.

- **Wind intensity and direction:** in areas with strong prevailing winds, the shape of the trees and the whole landscape is affected by the wind. It also means that plants transpire fast.

Figure 1 *Snow leopards are one of the rarest big cats. They live in cold, high-altitude environments where there is very little prey for them to hunt*

Figure 2 *The flowering of the desert after rain*

- **Availability of oxygen:** the availability of oxygen has a huge impact on water-living organisms. Some invertebrates can survive in water with very low oxygen levels. However, most fish need a high level of dissolved oxygen. The proportion of oxygen in the air varies very little.
- **Availability of carbon dioxide:** the level of carbon dioxide acts as a limiting factor for photosynthesis and plant growth. It can also affect the distribution of organisms. For example, mosquitoes are attracted to their food animals by high carbon dioxide levels.

The abiotic factors that affect communities of organisms do not work in isolation. They interact to create unique environments where different animals and plants can live.

Biotic factors affecting communities

It isn't only abiotic factors that affect communities – biotic factors are very important too. The main biotic factors that affect living organisms and communities are:

- **Availability of food:** when there is plenty of food, organisms breed successfully. When food is in short supply, animals struggle to survive and often do not breed.
- **New pathogens or parasites:** when a new pathogen or parasite emerges, organisms have no resistance to the disease. A new pathogen can damage or even wipe out populations in a community.
- **New predators arriving:** organisms that have no defences against new predators may quickly be wiped out.
- **Interspecific competition (competition between species):** a new species may outcompete another to the point where numbers become too low for successful breeding. The grey squirrels that were introduced to Britain and outcompeted the native red squirrels are a good example (Figure 4). Another example is Japanese knotweed, which has become a very invasive plant pest.

Animals, plants, fungi, protista, bacteria, and archaea are all involved in constant struggles between members of the same species and between members of different species in their community for its resources. Their success in this competition makes the difference between life – including reproduction – and death.

Figure 3 *Mangroves are adapted to survive in waterlogged soil with low oxygen availability. The soil is covered regularly in salty seawater. Mangroves have adaptations to obtain extra oxygen from the air and to get rid of any excess salt*

Figure 4 *In the UK, red squirrels now only survive in areas such as Brownsea Island in Dorset, northern England, and Scotland where their competitors, the grey squirrels, have not reached*

Key points

- Abiotic factors that may affect communities of organisms include:
  - light intensity
  - temperature
  - moisture levels
  - soil pH and mineral content
  - wind intensity and direction
  - availability of oxygen for aquatic animals.
  - availability of carbon dioxide for plants
- Biotic factors that may affect communities of organisms include:
  - availability of food
  - new pathogens
  - new predators arriving
  - new competitors.

1 State the abiotic factors most likely to affect living organisms. [6 marks]

2 Explain how carnivorous plants survive in areas with very low levels of nitrate ions. [2 marks]

3 a Light intensity is an abiotic factor that affects the distribution of living organisms. State another factor that also does this. [1 mark]
  b Explain how light intensity and your chosen factor affect the distribution of living organisms. [4 marks]

4 Explain how a new predator can change the balance of organisms in a community, and ultimately the balance of living organisms in an entire habitat. [5 marks]

4.11.4 Competition in animals

Learning objectives

After this topic, you should know:
- why animals compete
- the factors that organisms are competing for in a habitat
- what makes an animal a successful competitor.

Each animal or plant lives with many other organisms. Some will be from the same species whilst others will be completely different. In any area there is only a limited amount of resources. As a result, living organisms have to compete for the things they need.

The best-adapted organisms are those most likely to win the **competition** for resources. They will be most likely to survive and produce healthy offspring. There is competition between members of different species for the same resources as well as competition between members of the same species. Animals often avoid direct competition with members of other species when they can. It is the competition between members of the same species that is most intense.

What do animals compete for?

Animals compete for many things, including:
- food
- territory
- mates.

Competition for food

Competition for food is very common. Herbivores sometimes feed on many types of plant, and sometimes on only one or two different sorts. Many different species of herbivores will all eat the same plants. Just think how many types of animals eat grass! The animals that eat a wide range of plants are most likely to be successful. If you are a picky eater, you risk dying out if anything happens to your only food source (Figure 1).

Figure 1 *Pandas only eat bamboo, so they are vulnerable to competition from other animals that eat bamboo as well as to anything that damages bamboo*

Competition is also common among carnivores. They compete for prey. Small mammals such as mice are eaten by animals such as foxes, owls, hawks, and domestic cats. The animal best adapted to finding and catching mice will be most successful. Carnivores have to compete with their own species for their prey as well as with different species. Some successful predators are adapted to have long legs for running fast and sharp eyes to spot prey. These features will be passed on to their offspring.

Prey animals compete with each other too – to be the one that *isn't* caught! Their adaptations help prevent them becoming a meal for a predator. Some animals contain poisons that make anything that eats them sick. Very often these animals also have warning colours so that predators learn which animals to avoid (Figure 2).

The introduction of a new herbivore can drastically reduce the amount of plant material available for other animals. For example, the introduction of rabbits into Australia led to the extinction of a number of common species that simply could not compete with the grass-eating and breeding abilities of the rabbits.

Figure 2 *The dramatic colours of these mullein moth caterpillars are a clear warning to predators to keep well away*

Competition for territory

For many animals, setting up and defending a territory is vital. A territory may simply be a place to build a nest, or it could be all the space needed for an animal to find food and reproduce. Most animals cannot reproduce successfully if they have no territory, so they will compete for the best spaces.

This helps to make sure that they will be able to find enough food for themselves and for their young. For example, for many small birds such as tits, the number of territories found in an area varies with the amount of food available. Many animals use urine or faeces to mark the boundaries of their territories.

Competition for a mate

Competition for mates can be fierce. In many species, the male animals put a lot of effort into impressing the females. The males compete in different ways to win the privilege of mating with a female.

In some species – such as deer, lions, and elephant seals – the males fight between themselves. The winner then gets to mate with several females.

Many male animals display themselves to females to get their attention. Some birds have spectacular adaptations to help them stand out. Male peacocks display extravagant tail feathers to warn off other males and attract females. Male lizards often display bright colours too (Figure 3).

What makes a successful competitor?

A successful competitor is an animal that is adapted to be better at finding food or a mate than the other members of its own species. It also needs to be better at finding food than the members of other local species. It must also be able to breed successfully.

Many animals are successful because they avoid competition with other species as much as possible. They feed in a way that no other local animals do, or they eat a type of food that other animals avoid. For example, many different animals can feed on one plant without direct competition. While caterpillars eat the leaves, greenfly drink the sap, butterflies suck the nectar from the flowers, and beetles feed on the pollen.

Figure 3 *The striking blue markings and dramatic crests of the male green basilisk lizard (Basiliscus plumifrons) in **a** are adaptations to attract a mate, as are the extravagant tail feathers of the male peacock in **b***

1 Animals that rely on a single type of food can easily become extinct. Explain why. [2 marks]

2 **a** Give *two* ways in which animals compete for mates. [2 marks]
   b Suggest the disadvantages of the methods chosen in **a**. [4 marks]

3 Suggest *two* adaptations you would expect to find in each of the following organisms and give *one* competitive advantage for each adaptation.
   a an animal that hunts small mammals such as mice [4 marks]
   b an animal that eats grass [4 marks]
   c an animal that is hunted by many different predators [4 marks]
   d an animal that feeds on the tender leaves at the top of trees. [4 marks]

Study tip

Learn to look closely at an animal and spot the adaptations that make it a successful competitor.

Key points

- Animals compete with each other for food, territories, and mates.
- Animals have adaptations that make them successful competitors.

4.11.5 Competition in plants

Learning objectives
After this topic, you should know:
- what plants compete for
- how plants compete
- adaptations that plants have to make them successful competitors.

Study tip
Plants compete for space, light, water, and mineral ions.

Animals compete for food, mates, and territory.

Plants compete fiercely with each other. They compete for:
- light for photosynthesis, to make food
- water for photosynthesis and for keeping their tissues rigid and supported
- nutrients (minerals) from the soil, to make all the chemicals they need in their cells
- space to grow, allowing their roots to take in water and nutrients and their leaves to capture light.

Why do plants compete?
As with animals, plants are in competition both with other species of plants and with their own species. Big, tall plants such as trees take up a lot of water and nutrients from the soil. They also reduce the amount of light reaching the plants beneath them. The plants around them need adaptations to help them survive.

When a plant sheds its seeds they might land nearby. In this case, the parent plant will be in direct competition with its own seedlings. As the parent plant is large and settled, it will take most of the water, mineral ions, and light. The parent plant will therefore deprive its own offspring of everything they need to grow successfully. The roots of some desert plants even produce a chemical that stops seeds from germinating, killing the competition before it even begins to grow!

Coping with competition
Plants that grow close to other species often have adaptations to help them avoid competition. Small plants found in woodlands often grow and flower very early in the year (Figure 1). This is when plenty of light gets through the bare branches of the trees. The dormant trees take very little water out of the soil. The leaves that were shed the previous autumn have rotted down to provide mineral ions in the soil. Plants such as wild daffodils, snowdrops, anemones, and bluebells are all adapted to take advantage of these things. They flower, make seeds, and die back again before the trees are in full leaf.

Another way in which plants successfully avoid competition is by having different types of roots. Some plants have shallow roots taking water and nutrients from near the surface of the soil, whilst other plants have long, deep roots that go far underground.

If one plant is growing in the shade of another, it may grow taller to reach the light. It may also grow leaves with a bigger surface area to take advantage of all the light it does get. Some plants have adaptations such as tendrils or suckers that allow them to climb up artificial structures or large trees to reach the light.

Figure 1 *Small woodland plants like these wild daffodils grow and flower early in the year, before their competitors even have leaves*

240

4.11 Ecosystems and biodiversity

Investigating competition in plants

Carry out an investigation to look at the effect of competition on plants. Set up two trays of seeds – one crowded and one spread out. Then monitor the height and wet mass (mass after watering) of the plants. Keep all of the conditions – light level, the amount of water and mineral ions available, and the temperature – exactly the same for both sets of plants. The differences in their growth will be the result of overcrowding and competition for resources in one of the groups.

The data in Figure 2 shows the growth of tree seedlings. You can get results in days rather than months by using cress seeds.

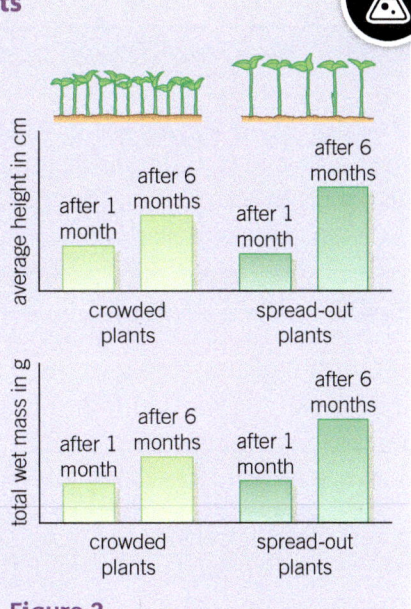

Figure 2

Spreading the seeds

To reproduce successfully, a plant has to avoid competition with its own seedlings for light, space, water, and mineral ions. Many plants use the wind to help them spread their seeds as far as possible. They produce fruits or seeds with special adaptations for flight to carry their seeds away (Figure 3). Plants also use explosive seed pods, animals, or even water to carry their seeds as far away as possible (Figure 4).

Figure 3 *The light seeds and fluffy parachutes of dandelions mean they are spread widely and compete very successfully*

Figure 4 *Coconuts will float for weeks or even months on ocean currents, which can carry them hundreds of miles from competition with their parents – or any other coconuts*

1. **a** Suggest *three* ways in which plants can overcome the problems of growing in the shade of another plant. [3 marks]
   b Explain how snowdrops and bluebells grow and flower successfully in spite of living under large trees in woodlands. [2 marks]
2. **a** Describe why so many plants have adaptations to make sure that their seeds are spread successfully. [2 marks]
   b Give *three* successful adaptations for spreading seeds. [3 marks]
3. The dandelion is a successful weed. Explain why its adaptations make it a better competitor than many other plants on a school field or a garden lawn. [6 marks]

Key points

- Plants often compete with each other for light, space, water, and mineral ions from the soil.
- Plants have many adaptations that make them good competitors.

241

4.11.6 Field investigations

Learning objectives

After this topic, you should know:
- how to measure the distribution of living things in their natural environment
- how finding the mean, median, and mode can help you understand your data.

Ecologists study the make-up of biological communities and ecosystems. They look at how abiotic and biotic factors affect the **abundance** and **distribution** of organisms. They also investigate the effect of changes in the environment on the organisms in a particular ecosystem. To do this, they must be able to measure how many organisms there are and how those organisms are distributed in the first place.

Quadrats

The simplest way to count the number of organisms is to use a sample area called a **quadrat**. You can use a square frame laid on the ground to outline your sample area. People refer to these frames as quadrats, too.

A quadrat with sides 0.5 m long gives you a 0.25 m^2 sample area. Quadrats are used to investigate the size of a population of plants. They can also be used for animals that move very slowly, such as snails or sea anemones.

You use the same-sized quadrat every time, and sample as many areas as you can. This makes your results as valid as possible. **Sample size** is very important. You must choose your sample areas *at random*. This ensures that your results reflect the true distribution of the organisms and that any conclusions you make will be valid.

There are a number of ways to make sure that the samples you take are random. For example, the person with the quadrat closes their eyes, spins round, opens their eyes, and walks 10 paces before dropping the quadrat. A random-number generator is a more scientific way of deciding where to drop your quadrat.

You need to take several random readings and then find the **mean** number of organisms per m^2. This technique is known as **quantitative sampling**. You can use quantitative sampling to compare the distribution of the same organism in different habitats. You can also use it to compare the variety of organisms in several different habitats.

Figure 1 *Measuring the number of plants in a particular quadrat*

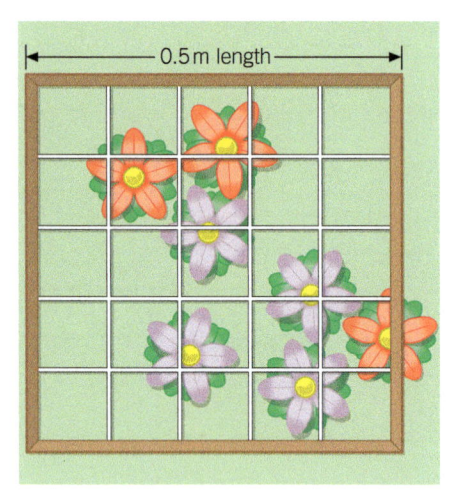

Figure 2 *It doesn't matter if organisms partly covered by a quadrat are counted as in or out, as long as you decide and do the same each time. In this diagram of a quadrat, you have six or seven plants per 0.25 m^2 (that's 24 or 28 plants per square metre), depending on the way you count*

Synoptic links

You can find out more about the maths you need for quantitative sampling in Maths skills MS 2b, 2d, and 2f.

Finding the range, the mean, the median, and the mode

A student takes 10 random 1 m^2 quadrat readings looking at the number of snails in a garden. The results are:

| 3 | 4 | 3 | 4 | 5 | 2 | 6 | 7 | 3 | 3 |

The **range** of the data is the range between the minimum and maximum values – in this case from **2–7 snails per m^2**.

To find the **mean** distribution of snails in the garden, add all the readings together and divide by 10 (the number of readings):

3 + 4 + 3 + 4 + 5 + 2 + 6 + 7 + 3 + 3 ÷ 10 = 40 ÷ 10 = **4 snails per m^2**

The **median** is the middle value when the numbers are put in order – in this case, the median is **3 snails per m^2**.

The **mode** is the most frequently occurring value – in this case, **3 snails per m^2**.

4.11 Ecosystems and biodiversity

Sampling is also used to measure changes in the distribution of organisms over time. You do this by repeating your measurements at regular time intervals and calculating the mean. Finding the **range** of distribution and the **median** and **mode** of your data can also give you useful information.

Counting along a transect

Sampling along a **transect** is another useful way of measuring the distribution of organisms. There are different types of transect. A line transect is most commonly used.

Transects are not random. You stretch a tape between two points, for example up a rocky shore, across a pathway, or down a hillside. This is often done where you suspect that a change is linked to a particular abiotic factor. You sample the organisms along that line at regular intervals using a quadrat. This shows you how the distribution of organisms changes along that line. You can also measure some of the physical factors, such as light levels and soil pH, that might affect the growth of plants along the transect.

> **Measuring population size and using sampling techniques to investigate the effect of a factor on the distribution of a species.**
>
> Once you have decided on the habitat you are going to investigate, you need to make a few more decisions before you start collecting your data:
> - Which species are you going to study? It has to be common but it may not be the most common – for example, your results on a school field might be more interesting if you look at the population size of daisies or dandelions rather than grass.
> - Which factor will you investigate? This could be an easily measured abiotic factor such as light levels or soil pH, or a biotic factor such as trampling, grazing, or competing organisms.
> - What will you do? You need to measure the population of your chosen organism throughout the habitat. Then take a transect across your habitat. Take regular quadrats along your transect to investigate any changes in both your environmental factor and the populations of your chosen organism.
>
> **Safety:** Follow health and safety instructions.

Study tip

You should know the difference between:
- mean (the sum of the values divided by the number of values)
- median (the middle value when all the values are listed in order of size)
- mode (the most frequently occurring value).

Study tip

Remember – you sample quadrats along a transect to see a change in species distribution in a line from A to B.

You sample quadrats on coordinates from a random number generator to count the number of a species in an area.

Figure 3 *Carrying out a transect of a rocky shore*

1 State the function of a quadrat. [1 mark]
2 a Describe how a quadrat is used to obtain quantitative data. [4 marks]
  b Explain why it is important for samples to be random. [2 marks]
  c In a series of 10 random 1 m² quadrats, a class found the following numbers of dandelions: 6, 3, 7, 8, 4, 6, 5, 7, 9, 8. Determine the mean density of dandelions per m² on the school field, the median value, and the mode from the data. [4 marks]
3 Explain the ways in which the information you get from quadrats and transects is similar and how it differs. [4 marks]

Key points

- A range of experimental methods using quadrats and transects is used by ecologists to determine the distribution and abundance of species in an ecosystem.

4.11.7 Biodiversity

Learning objectives

After this topic, you should know:

- what biodiversity is and why it is important.

Synoptic links

You will learn more about both negative and positive influences on biodiversity in Topics 4.11.9, 4.11.10, and 4.11.11.

You will learn more about genetic variation, adaptation, and evolution in Chapter 4.12.

Figure 1 *The number of available habitats has a major effect on the biodiversity of an ecosystem, as these images of volcanic rocks in Iceland and the English countryside clearly show*

Biodiversity is a widely used term both in biology and in the media. Maintaining biodiversity is widely regarded as a good thing. But what is biodiversity – and why is it so important?

Biodiversity and why it matters

Biodiversity is a measure of the variety of all the different species of organisms on Earth (global biodiversity) or within a particular ecosystem (local biodiversity).

In general, high biodiversity ensures the stability of ecosystems. It reduces the dependence of one species on another for food, shelter, and the maintenance of the physical environment.

As you have already seen, if there are relatively few species in an ecosystem and one is removed in some way, there is often a dramatic effect on other species. If there are lots of different types of organisms in an ecosystem (i.e., if there is high biodiversity) the loss or removal of one species has a limited effect because others take its place.

Habitats and biodiversity

The number of habitats available in an ecosystem affects biodiversity. Ecosystems that provide a large range of habitats tend to have great biodiversity. They are usually home to larger populations of a wider variety of species than ecosystems with relatively few habitats are.

In a hectare of a tropical rainforest you might find 450 different species of trees, compared with 5–10 species in a mature woodland in the UK. In turn, each species of tree acts as a habitat for hundreds or even thousands of other species of organisms. These include bacteria, lichens, and fungi, as well as an enormous range of invertebrate vertebrate species from amphibians and reptiles to birds and mammals.

The more species of tree there are in a forest, the more habitats there are and the greater the forest's biodiversity. Conversely, the sand dunes of a desert or a European beach offer relatively few habitats and so have low biodiversity.

Population size also matters. If there are many different species in a habitat, but the numbers of each population are very low, the biodiversity is fragile. Small populations are in much greater danger of dying out if an ecosystem is disrupted in some way than larger populations are. A larger population is more likely to have the genetic variation needed to make sure that at least some members of the population survive.

4.11 Ecosystems and biodiversity

Advantages of biodiversity

High levels of biodiversity are often important for the success and survival of an ecosystem. Reducing biodiversity threatens the existence of the ecosystem. Scientists now realise that the future of the human species on Earth also relies on us maintaining a good level of biodiversity. Ecosystems with high biodiversity help to provide the resources needed to sustain life – including human life.

Ecosystems with higher biodiversity offer economic benefits:

- High biodiversity sustains the resources needed for successful agriculture. For example, many crops (e.g., apples, tomatoes, cotton, and coffee) are pollinated by insects. Good biodiversity encourages many species of pollinating insects.
- High biodiversity sustains the resources needed for successful fishing, which is key to providing protein food for large parts of the world. Our seas and oceans should be kept clean and healthy. Then there will be plenty of habitats to support the fish we want to eat and all the forms of life needed to support their growth and breeding ability. The destruction of habitats such as coral reefs and mangroves reduces the biodiversity of the oceans and therefore affects the numbers of fish in the sea.
- High biodiversity sustains the resources needed for successful forestry. Healthy forests are needed to supply the timber used around the world, and healthy forests are biodiverse. This maintains pollinators and reduces the spread of disease.

Rainforests, with their enormous range of biodiversity, are under particular threat, as you will see in Topic 4.11.9. Yet the US National Cancer Institute has identified 3000 different plant species as potential sources of drugs against cancer – and 70% of these plants are found only in tropical rainforests. The discovery of new plants is also needed to source genes that may help current crop plants withstand the changes that are resulting from global warming. Rich biodiversity is important to give humans the best possible chance of success.

Scientists estimate that only around 10% of the different types of organisms currently living in the ecosystems of the Earth have been discovered so far. Unfortunately, many human activities are reducing biodiversity before the remaining species have even been identified. Humans have only relatively recently learnt to value biodiversity, and now need to work hard to try to halt the reduction of biodiversity before it is too late. People can make a difference at individual and local levels, but habitat protection is needed at global levels, too.

Figure 2 *Reducing biodiversity reduces the numbers of pollinators such as this bee pollinating a dog rose. Many of the fruit and vegetable crops we eat without thinking depend on a wide variety of insect pollinators*

1	Define biodiversity.	[2 marks]
2	Explain why an ecosystem with many habitats will usually have greater biodiversity than an ecosystem that is habitat-poor.	[4 marks]
3	Discuss the benefits to people of maintaining high levels of local and global biodiversity.	[6 marks]

Key points

- Biodiversity is greater in ecosystems that provide a bigger range of different habitats. These act as homes to larger populations of a bigger variety of organisms.
- Small populations are in greater danger of dying out if an ecosystem is disrupted in some way.
- Ecosystems with high levels of biodiversity help to provide the resources needed to sustain life, including human life.
- Ecosystems with higher biodiversity offer economic benefits by sustaining the resources needed for agriculture, fishing, and forestry.

4.11.8 Human factors affecting biodiversity

Learning objectives

After this topic, you should know:

- some of the effects of the growth in human population on the Earth and its resources.

> **Synoptic link**
>
> You learnt about air pollution in Topic 4.10.9, and about sewage treatment in Topic 4.10.12.

Humans have been on Earth for less than a million years, yet their activity has changed the balance of nature on the planet enormously. Several of the changes humans have made seem to be driving many other species to extinction. Some people worry that humans may even be threatening their own survival.

Human population growth

For many thousands of years, people lived on the Earth in quite small numbers. There were only a few hundred million people scattered all over the world, and the effects of human activities were usually small and local. Any changes could easily be absorbed by the environment where people lived. However, in the past 200 years or so, the human population has grown very quickly. In 2015 the human population passed 7 billion people, and it is still growing.

If the population of any other species of animal or plant suddenly increased like the human population has, nature would tend to restore the balance. Predators, lack of food, build-up of waste products, or diseases would reduce the population again. However, humans have discovered how to grow more food than could ever be gathered from the wild, can cure or prevent many killer diseases, and have no natural predators. This helps to explain why the human population has grown so fast.

People use the resources of the Earth – fossil fuels are used to generate electricity, for transport, and to make materials such as plastics; minerals from the rocks and soil are used to grow food. The more people there are, the more resources they use.

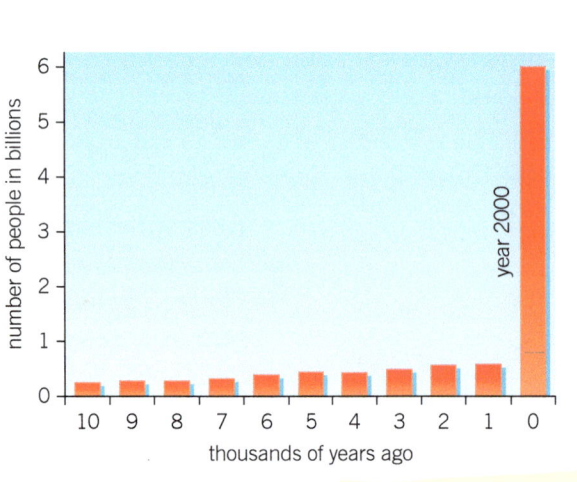

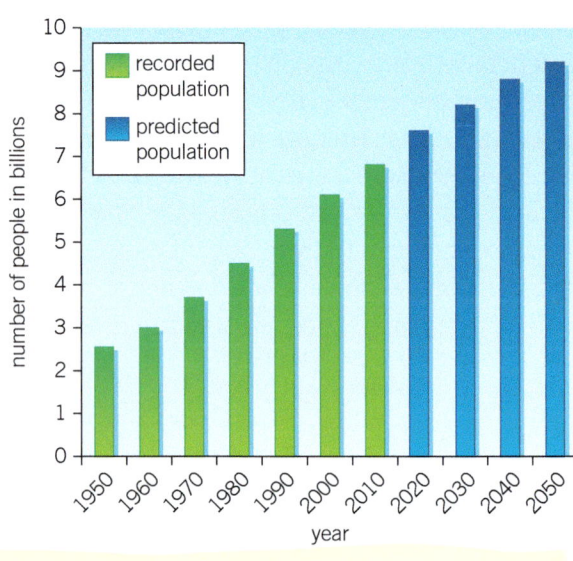

Figure 1 *Human population growth. Current UN predictions suggest that the world population will soar to 244 billion by 2150*

4.11 Ecosystems and biodiversity

The effect on land and resources
The increase in the human population has had an enormous effect on the environment. All of these people need land to live on.

- More and more land is used for building houses, shops, industrial sites, and roads. This destroys the habitats of other living organisms and reduces biodiversity.
- Billions of acres of land is used around the world for farming. Wherever people farm, the natural animal and plant populations are destroyed.
- Vast areas of land are quarried or mined to obtain rocks and metal ores, reducing the land available for other organisms.
- The waste produced by humans pollutes the environment and processing it takes up land, affecting biodiversity.

The huge human population drains the resources of the Earth. People are rapidly using up the Earth's finite reserves of metal ores and non-renewable energy resources such as crude oil and natural gas that. These resources cannot be replaced.

Figure 2 *Farmers grow the food we eat, but farming reduces biodiversity around the world*

Managing waste
Rapid growth in the human population, along with improvements in the standards of living in many places, means that increasingly large amounts of waste are produced. This includes human bodily waste and the rubbish from packaging, uneaten food, and disposable goods. The dumping of this waste is another way in which humans reduce the amount of land available for any other life apart from scavengers. There has also been an increase in manufacturing and industry to produce the goods people want. This in turn has led to increased **industrial waste**.

The waste produced by humans presents some very difficult problems. If it is not handled properly, it can cause serious pollution. Water may be polluted by sewage, by **fertilisers** from farms, and by toxic chemicals from industry. The air may be polluted with smoke and poisonous gases, such as sulfur dioxide. The land itself can be polluted with toxic chemicals from farming, such as pesticides and herbicides. It can also be contaminated with industrial waste, such as heavy metals. These chemicals can be washed from the land into waterways. If the ever-growing human population continues to affect the ecology of the Earth, reducing biodiversity, everyone will suffer the effects.

1   **a** Give *three* reasons why the human population has increased so rapidly over the past couple of hundred years. [3 marks]
    b Describe how people reduce the amount of land available for other animals and plants. [4 marks]
2   **a** Give *three* examples of resources that humans are using up. [3 marks]
    b List *five* examples of how the standard of living has improved over the past 100 years. [5 marks]
3   Explain in detail the different ways in which the ever-increasing human population is threatening biodiversity. [6 marks]

Key points
- Human interactions with local ecosystems can diminish or destroy biodiversity.
- Humans reduce the amount of land available for other animals and plants by building, quarrying, farming, and dumping waste.

4.11.9 Deforestation and peat destruction

Learning objectives

After this topic, you should know:
- what is meant by deforestation
- why loss of biodiversity matters
- the environmental effects of destroying peat bogs.

As the world population grows, humans need more land, more food, and more fuel. One way to deal with these increased demands has been to cut down huge areas of forests. The destruction of forests may have many long-term effects on the environment and ecology of the Earth.

The effects of deforestation

All around the world, especially in tropical areas, large-scale deforestation is taking place to obtain timber and to clear the land for farming (Figure 1). When the land is to be used for farming, the trees are often felled and burnt. This is known as 'slash-and-burn' clearance, where the wood is not used, it is just burnt. No trees are planted to replace those that are cut down.

The three main reasons for deforestation are:

1. to grow staple foods such as rice, or ingredients for making cheap food in the developed world, such as palm oil from oil palms
2. to rear more cattle, particularly for the beef market
3. to grow crops that can be used to make biofuels based on ethanol. These crops include sugarcane and maize, which are readily fermented.

The destruction of large areas of trees, whether in tropical areas or in cooler climates, has a number of negative effects. It increases the amount of carbon dioxide released into the atmosphere in two ways. Burning the trees leads to an increase in carbon dioxide levels from combustion. After deforestation, the dead vegetation decomposes and the microorganisms use up oxygen and release more carbon dioxide as they respire. Deforestation also reduces the rate at which carbon dioxide is removed from the atmosphere. Normally, trees and other plants use carbon dioxide in photosynthesis. They take it from the air and it gets locked up for years (sometimes for hundreds of years) in plant material such as wood. When we destroy trees, we lose a vital carbon dioxide sink. Dead trees don't take carbon dioxide out of the atmosphere. In fact, they add to carbon dioxide levels when they are burnt or when they decay.

Figure 1 *Deforestation and the changed use of the land show up clearly in this satellite image. The river shown is the Iguacu River, separating Brazil and Argentina. Above the river in Brazil you can see the green of the rainforest. Below the river in Argentina you can see fields, roads, and buildings*

Loss of biodiversity

Tropical rainforests contain more diversity of living organisms than any other land environment. When these forests are lost, biodiversity is reduced as many species of animals and plants may become extinct. Many of these species have not yet been identified or studied. Deforestation could be destroying sources of new medicines or food for the future.

For an animal such as the orangutan (Figure 2), which eats around 300 different plant species, losing the forest habitat is driving the species to extinction. This is just one of hundreds if not thousands of species of living organisms of all different types that are endangered by the loss of their rainforest habitat.

Figure 2 *The loss of biodiversity, from large mammals such as the orangutan to the smallest mosses or fungi, will potentially have far-reaching effects in the local ecosystems and for humans*

Deforestation is taking place at a tremendous rate. In Brazil alone, an area about a quarter of the size of England is lost each year (Figure 3). When the forests are cleared, they are often replaced by a monoculture (single species) such as oil palms. This process also greatly reduces biodiversity. The UK also used to be covered in forests, many of which were destroyed thousands of years ago. UK forests never had the range of biodiversity seen in tropical rainforests.

Peat bog destruction

Peat bogs are another resource that is being widely destroyed. Peat forms over thousands of years, originally in peat bogs. Over time the bogs may dry out to form peatlands. Peat is made of plant material that cannot decay completely because the conditions are very acidic and lack oxygen. Peatlands and peat bogs act as a massive carbon sink. They are also unique ecosystems, home to a wide range of plants, animals, and microorganisms that have evolved to grow and survive in the acidic conditions of a peat bog. These species include a number of carnivorous plants such as sundews, Venus fly traps, and pitcher plants (Figure 4). The UK and Ireland both have many peat bogs.

Peat is burnt as a fuel. It is also widely used by gardeners and horticulturists to improve the properties of the soil and provide an ideal environment for seed germination, helping to increase food production. When peat is burnt or used in gardens, carbon dioxide is released into the atmosphere and the carbon sink is lost.

Peat is formed very slowly and is now being destroyed faster than it is made. The destruction of peat bogs also means the destruction of the organisms that depend on them, and more loss of biodiversity.

Producing peat-free compost

In the UK, the government is trying to persuade gardeners to use alternative peat-free composts. This will reduce carbon dioxide emissions and conserve peat bogs and peatlands as habitats for biodiversity. Compost can be made from bark, garden waste, coconut husks, and other sources – the problem is persuading gardeners to use these alternatives.

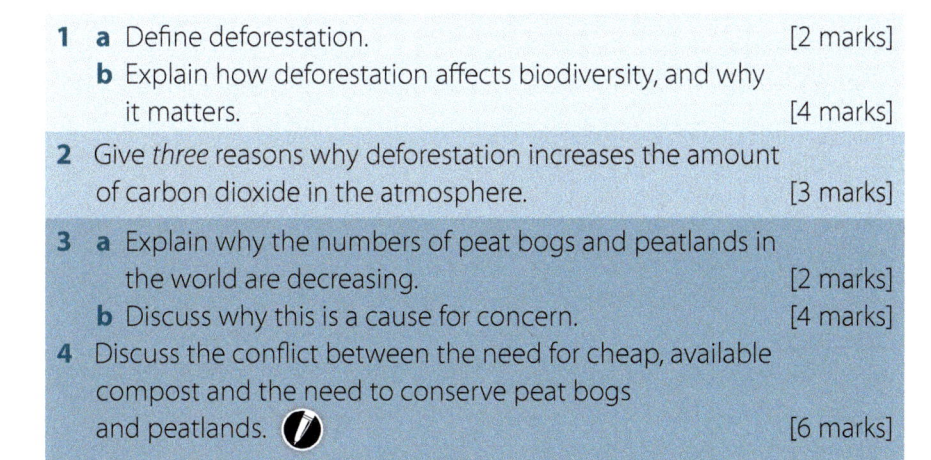

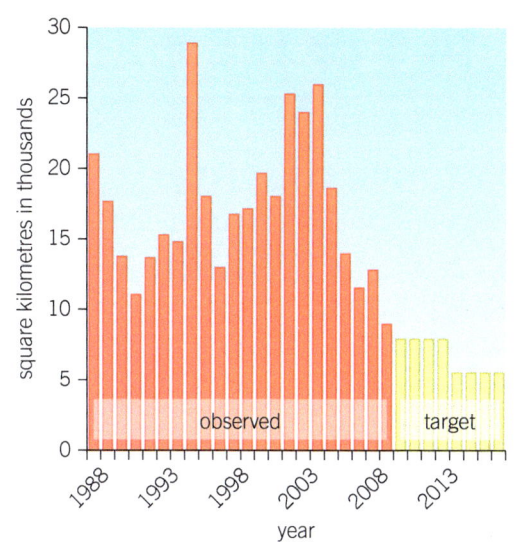

Figure 3 *The rate of deforestation is devastating. Even in the high-profile Brazilian Amazon, where deforestation rates are dropping, around 8–10 000 km² of tropical rainforest is being lost each year*

Figure 4 *These pitcher plants have evolved to grow on the acid soil of a peat bog. Insects fall into the body of the pitcher, where they are slowly digested*

1 a Define deforestation. [2 marks]
  b Explain how deforestation affects biodiversity, and why it matters. [4 marks]
2 Give *three* reasons why deforestation increases the amount of carbon dioxide in the atmosphere. [3 marks]
3 a Explain why the numbers of peat bogs and peatlands in the world are decreasing. [2 marks]
  b Discuss why this is a cause for concern. [4 marks]
4 Discuss the conflict between the need for cheap, available compost and the need to conserve peat bogs and peatlands. [6 marks]

Key points

- Large-scale deforestation in tropical areas has occurred to provide land for cattle and for rice fields and to grow crops for biofuels.
- The destruction of peat bogs and other areas of peat to produce garden compost reduces the area of this habitat and thus the biodiversity associated with it.
- Producing peat-free compost can protect peat ecosystems and biodiversity.

4.11.10 Land and water pollution

Learning objectives

After this topic, you should know:
- some negative human impacts on ecosystems from polluting the land
- some negative human impacts on ecosystems from polluting the water.

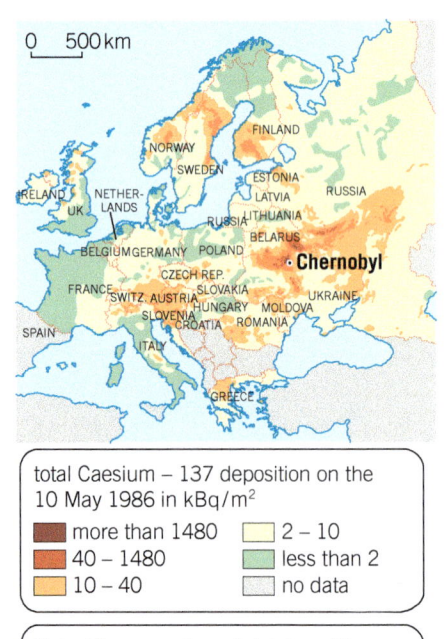

total Caesium – 137 deposition on the 10 May 1986 in kBq/m^2
- more than 1480
- 40 – 1480
- 10 – 40
- 2 – 10
- less than 2
- no data

Note: The map shows total deposition resulting from both the Chernobyl accident and nuclear weapon tests. However, at the level above 10 kBq/m^2, in most cases the effects of the Chernobyl accident are predominant.

Figure 1 *The accident at Chernobyl nuclear power plant polluted land a long way away – including areas of the UK*

Synoptic link
You learnt about the Chernobyl nuclear disaster in Topic 3.8.6.

As the human population grows, more waste is produced. If it is not handled properly, this waste may pollute the land, the water, or the air. Increased pollution kills plants and animals and reduces biodiversity in affected habitats. By polluting the land and the water, negative human interactions with ecosystems are increasing on both local and global scales. These interactions almost always reduce biodiversity in the ecosystems affected.

Polluting the land

People pollute the land in many different ways. The more people there are, the more sewage is produced. If human waste is not treated properly, the soil becomes polluted with unpleasant chemicals and gut parasites.

In the developed world, people produce huge amounts of household waste and hazardous (dangerous) industrial waste. The household waste goes into landfill sites, which take up a lot of room and destroy natural habitats. Toxic chemicals can spread from the waste into the soil. Toxic chemicals are also a problem in industrial waste. They can poison the soil for miles around.

Radioactive waste and nuclear accidents also cause problems. For example, after the Chernobyl nuclear accident in 1986, the soil was contaminated thousands of miles away from the original accident (Figure 1).

Land can also be polluted as a side effect of farming. Weeds compete with crop plants for light, water, and mineral ions. Animal and fungal pests attack crops and eat them. Farmers increasingly use chemicals to protect their crops. Weedkillers (or herbicides) kill weeds but leave the crop unharmed. Pesticides kill the insects that might attack and destroy the crop.

The problem is that these chemicals are poisons. When they are sprayed onto crops, they also get into the soil. Many of them have been designed to break down easily. Many other pesticides and herbicides are very selective, or are used in very low doses so that they do not affect other organisms. However, some – such as DDT – cause problems. They can be washed out into streams and rivers (see opposite). They can also become part of food chains when the toxins get into organisms that feed on the plants or live in the soil. The level of toxins in the animals that first take in the affected plant material is small, but sometimes it cannot be broken down in their bodies. So, at each stage along the food chain, more and more toxins build up in the organisms. This is known as bioaccumulation, and eventually it can lead to dangerous levels of poisons building up in the top predators (Figure 2).

Polluting the water

A growing human population means a growing need for food. Farmers add fertilisers to the soil to make sure it stays fertile year after year. The minerals in these fertilisers, particularly the nitrates, are easily washed from the soil into local streams, ponds, and rivers. Untreated sewage that is washed into waterways or pumped out into the sea also causes high levels of nitrates in the water. The nitrates and other mineral ions

4.11 Ecosystems and biodiversity

stimulate the growth of algae and water plants, which grow rapidly. Some plants die naturally. Others die because there is so much competition for light that they are unable to photosynthesise. There is a big increase in microorganisms feeding on the dead plants. These microorganisms use up a lot of oxygen during respiration.

This increase in decomposers leads to a fall in the levels of dissolved oxygen in the water. This means that there isn't enough oxygen to support some of the fish and other aerobic organisms living in it. They die and are decomposed by yet more microorganisms. This uses up even more oxygen. Eventually, the oxygen levels in the water fall so low that all aerobic aquatic animals die, and the pond or stream becomes 'dead'.

Toxic chemicals such as pesticides and herbicides or poisonous chemicals from landfill sites can also be washed into waterways. These chemicals can have the same bioaccumulation effect on aquatic food webs as they do on life on land. The largest carnivores die or fail to breed because of the build-up of toxic chemicals in their bodies (Figure 2). In many countries, including the UK, there are now strict controls on the use of chemicals on farms. The same restrictions apply to the treatment of sewage and to landfill sites, to help avoid these problems arising. Remember that most agricultural chemicals do much more good than harm, helping to produce enough food for everyone who needs it.

Figure 3 *This pond may look green and healthy, but all the animal life it once supported is dead as a result of increased competition for light and oxygen*

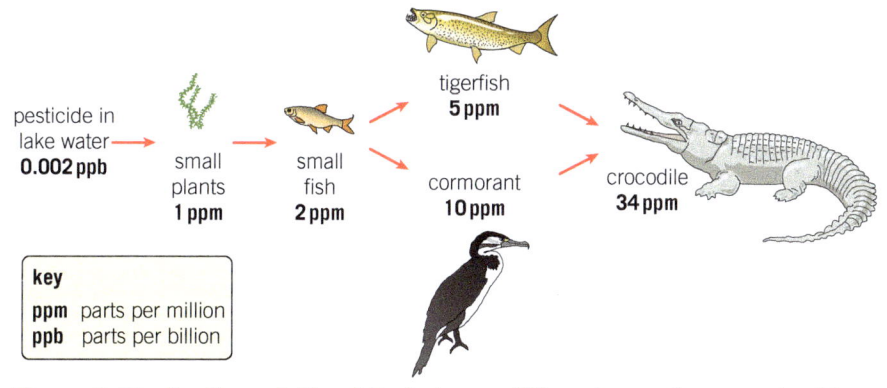

pesticide in lake water **0.002 ppb** → small plants **1 ppm** → small fish **2 ppm** → tigerfish **5 ppm** → crocodile **34 ppm**
cormorant **10 ppm**

key
ppm parts per million
ppb parts per billion

Figure 2 *The feeding relationships between different organisms can lead to dangerous levels of toxins building up in the top predators. The toxin shown here is the insecticide DDT*

1 **a** What is sewage? [1 mark]
  b Explain why is it important to dispose of sewage carefully. [5 marks]
  c What are bioindicators used for? [1 mark]
2 **a** Farming can cause pollution of the land. Describe the polluting effects farming can have on:
  i land [3 marks]
  ii water. [4 marks]
  b In the UK, a chemical called DDT was used up until the 1980s to kill insects. Large birds of prey and herons began to die and their bodies were found to have very high levels of DDT in them. Discuss how this might have happened and suggest why it took a long time for any link to be made. [6 marks]

Key points

- Unless waste and chemical materials are properly handled, more pollution will be caused.
- Pollution can occur on land, from landfill and from toxic chemicals such as pesticides and herbicides, which may also be washed from land into water.
- Pollution can occur in water from sewage, fertilisers, or toxic chemicals.
- Pollution kills plants and animals, which can reduce biodiversity.

4.11.11 Positive human impacts on ecosystems

Learning objectives

After this topic, you should know:
- how waste, deforestation, and global warming all have an impact on biodiversity
- some of the ways in which people are trying to reduce the impact of human activities on ecosystems and maintain biodiversity.

Synoptic link

You learnt about the production of peat-free compost to reduce peat bog destruction in Topic 4.11.9.

Figure 1 *Sand lizards are just one of six types of reptiles found on UK lowland heaths*

Figure 2 *Losing a single tree reduces biodiversity. For example, around 1000 different species live on an English oak, and just 19 trees studied in Panama supported 1200 species of beetles*

People are becoming more aware of the importance of biodiversity and of the many human threats to biodiversity around the world. Increasingly, scientists and concerned citizens are putting programmes in place to try to reduce these negative effects on ecosystems and biodiversity. People can help maintain biodiversity in many ways.

Breeding programmes for endangered species

Breeding programmes can restore an endangered species to a sustainable population, but it is difficult. Many rare animals and plants do not reproduce easily or fast and artificial breeding programmes must avoid inbreeding. Often the habitat that the organisms need to survive has also been lost. There are some high-profile international breeding programmes of animals such as the panda and Przewalski horses. Przewalski horses have been bred in zoos with the genetics of each animal carefully recorded. Herds of these horses now live wild again in a Mongolian national park. Many rare snails and amphibians now only exist in captive breeding programmes. They will only be released when their natural habitats are safe again.

Protection and regeneration of rare habitats

Many habitats have become increasingly rare, so the species of animals and plants adapted to living in them are increasingly under threat. People are protecting some of these rare habitats, sometimes enabling them to regenerate. This protects biodiversity, which may even increase again. Coral reefs, mangroves, and heathlands are all rare, threatened habitats that are now becoming protected. To protect coral reefs, carbon dioxide emissions and global warming must be tackled as raised temperatures and decreased pH levels are the major threats to these most biodiverse marine habitats. Mangroves are vital sites for young fish to develop in and are easily destroyed by too much or too little water or by changes in salinity (salt content).

Around 20% of all the lowland heaths in the world are in the UK, but this rare habitat has been disappearing fast. Now people are managing it to maintain its unique features and protect it from developers. They are even re-establishing lost heathland by removing trees, reversing drainage, and allowing ponies and cows to graze wild.

Reintroduction of field margins and hedgerows

In many agricultural areas farmers removed the hedgerows to produce huge fields in which to grow a single crop. This removed a wide variety of plants, birds, insects, and mammals – and in some places led to soil erosion and a reduction in soil fertility. Gradually farmers are replanting hedgerows and leaving wildflower margins round the edges of their fields, and the biodiversity of the countryside is increasing again.

4.11 Ecosystems and biodiversity

Reduction of deforestation and carbon dioxide emissions

Some governments are recognising the damage that deforestation and increasing carbon dioxide emissions are doing to the environment and to biodiversity, and are working hard to reduce the effect. At one point the rainforests in Costa Rica were being felled rapidly until the government recognised what was happening. Now the Costa Rican rainforests and cloud forests are largely protected. Farmland originally produced by felling forests is being bought and allowed to return to forest over time. Tourists pay to visit the amazing habitats and see the biodiversity for themselves.

Many governments are working with the transport and electricity generation industries to reduce carbon dioxide emissions (Figure 3). For example, the carbon dioxide emissions of new cars are falling steadily as a result of more efficient engines.

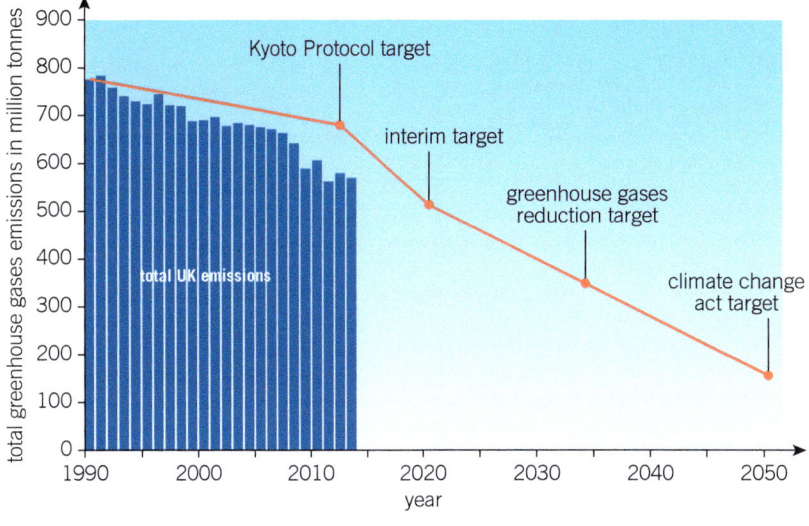

Figure 3 *Carbon dioxide emissions in the UK are falling as a result of the Kyoto Protocol (an agreement between many governments), the UK Climate Change Act 2008, and other legislation*

Recycling resources

Waste placed in landfill sites affects biodiversity by using land and producing pollution. Globally, many countries are working to recycle as much waste as possible – including paper, glass, plastics, and metal – rather than dumping it in landfill. There is also a drive to recycle organic waste as compost or in methane generators. It isn't just households that are recycling waste – companies from car manufacturers to brewers are doing the same thing. In 2012, General Motors recycled or reused 84% of their manufacturing waste. This saved 2.2 million tonnes of landfill and prevented 11 million tonnes of carbon dioxide emissions. Many governments have introduced taxes on putting material in landfill (Figure 4) – and as the tax has gone up, the amount of material put in landfill has gone down!

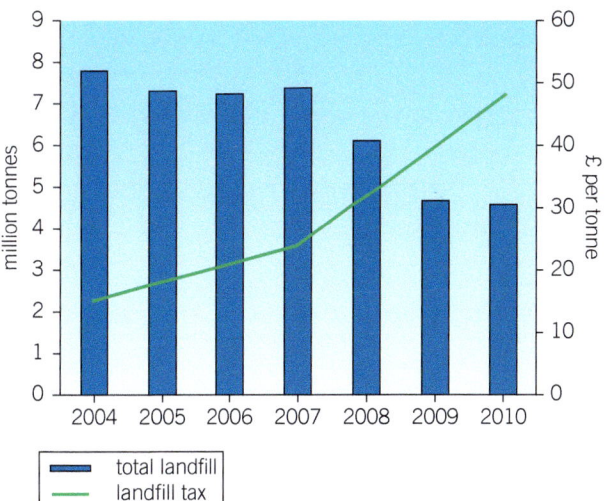

Figure 4 *Financial penalties can help to reduce landfill and protect biodiversity*

1. **a** Explain why it is important to maintain biodiversity. [3 marks]
   b Summarise the main ways in which people can help to maintain biodiversity. [5 marks]
   c Suggest an example of where there might be a conflict between maintaining biodiversity and human needs. [4 marks]

2. Using the data in Figure 3:
   a Describe the trend in carbon dioxide emissions in the UK since 1990. [1 mark]
   b Suggest how this data demonstrates the effect of governments on carbon emissions. [3 marks]
   c Discuss *three* examples of how a fall in carbon dioxide emissions globally might help to maintain biodiversity. [6 marks]

3. Using the data in Figure 4, suggest how taxes can be used to help reduce human damage to ecosystems and to biodiversity. [4 marks]

Key points

- Programmes designed to have a positive impact on ecosystems and biodiversity are now in place. These include:
  - breeding programmes for endangered species
  - reintroducing wider field margins and hedgerows to reduce monoculture
  - reducing deforestation
  - recycling resources.

253

4.11 Ecosystems and biodiversity

Summary questions

1   a   What is a community of organisms? [2 marks]
    b   Organisms within a community are interdependent. In the three communities listed below, explain *one* way in which some of the organisms are interdependent:
        i   an ancient oak woodland [2 marks]
        ii a desert [2 marks]
        iii a pond. [2 marks]
    c   Organisms within a community often compete with each other.
        i   Describe three ways in which organisms of the same species might compete against each other. [3 marks]
        ii Describe three ways in which organisms of different species might compete against each other. [3 marks]

2   Students carried out an investigation into the distribution of worm casts in different areas of the school grounds – heavily trampled areas of a path across the games field and a well-composted flower bed. They took nine 0.25 m² quadrat readings at random in each area. The results are in **Table 1**:

Table 1

Trampled area	Flower bed
4	6
3	7
7	5
4	8
5	9
2	9
2	6
0	9
4	4

    a   Why is it important that the quadrat samples are random? [2 marks]
    b   Describe a method students could use to ensure the quadrat samples are random. [2 marks]
    c   For a data set, state what is meant by:
        i   the mean [1 mark]
        ii the median [1 mark]
        iii the mode. [1 mark]
    d   Determine the mean, the median, and the mode of the results from the flower bed. [3 marks]
    e   What do the results suggest about the distribution of worms in an environment? [1 mark]

3   a   Explain why competition between animals of the same species is so much more intense than competition between different species. [1 mark]
    b   How does marking out and defending a territory help an animal to compete successfully? [2 marks]
    c   What are the advantages and disadvantages for males of having an elaborate courtship ritual and colouration compared with fighting over females? [5 marks]

4   a   Explain the difference between predators and prey animals. [2 marks]
    b   The graph in **Figure 1** shows a typical predator-prey relationship. Describe what is happening at the points labelled **A–D** on the graph. [4 marks]

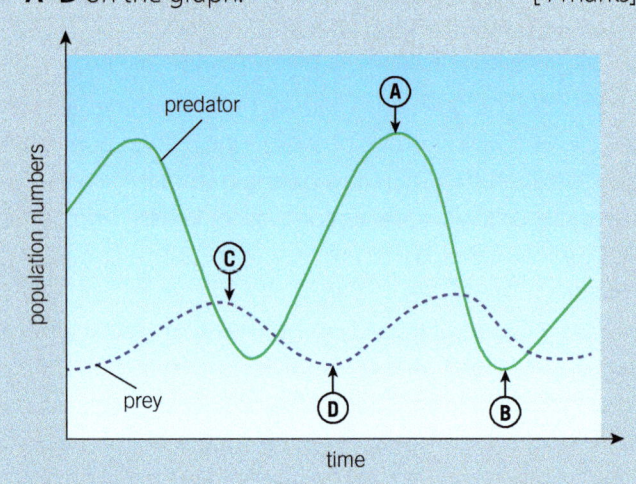

Figure 1

    c   **Figure 1** shows a theoretical model of the interaction between a predator and its prey. Suggest *two* reasons why observations from real communities might not look the same as this graph. [4 marks]

5   a   What is biodiversity? [2 marks]
    b   Explain why high levels of biodiversity are desirable in an ecosystem. [3 marks]
    c   How can the levels of biodiversity in different ecosystems affect people? [5 marks]
    d   i   Give *three* ways in which people can have a negative impact on an ecosystem, and explain how each might affect biodiversity. [6 marks]
        ii Give *three* ways in which people can have a positive impact on an ecosystem, and explain how each might affect biodiversity. [6 marks]

4.11 Ecosystems and biodiversity

Practice questions

01 There are different levels of organisation in ecosystems.
01.1 Define an ecosystem and a habitat. [2 marks]
01.2 Define a population and a community. [2 marks]
01.3 Give **two** resources that animals compete with each other for. [2 marks]
02 Bluebells are plants that grow under trees in woodlands.
A student used a 1 m² quadrat to estimate the number of bluebell plants growing in a woodland.
02.1 Describe how the student could have used the quadrat to estimate the number of bluebell plants in the woodland. [3 marks]
02.2 The woodland measured 150 m by 220 m. The mean number of bluebell plants in each 1 m² quadrat was 5.6.
Estimate the population of bluebell plants in the woodland. [2 marks]
02.3 Another student used transect lines to find out how the number of bluebell plants changes the further into a woodland the bluebell plants are found.
Table 1 shows the student's results.

Table 1

Distance into woodland in m	Percentage cover of bluebells			
	Transect 1	Transect 2	Transect 3	Mean cover
1	15	21	18	18
2	26	31	30	29
3	41	39	40	40
4	45	51	45	47
5	54	51	51	52
6	62	64	57	61
7	66	61	68	65
8	75	69	63	69
9	68	69	70	69
10	70	66	74	70

Draw a graph of the results in **Table 1**. You should only draw the mean cover results on the graph. [3 marks]
02.4 Describe the pattern of growth of bluebell plants in the woodland. [2 marks]
02.5 Suggest **two** abiotic factors that affect the growth of bluebells in a woodland. [2 marks]

03 A recent article stated:
Biodiversity across half of the world's landmass has fallen to potentially dangerous levels because the human race has continued to destroy habitats for land use.
03.1 Give **one** reason why higher biodiversity in an ecosystem is a benefit to humans. [1 mark]
03.2 **Table 2** shows data about the number of different plant species in two different fields. Each field is 100 m².

Table 2

Plant	Field A	Field B
buttercup	195	21
clover	348	0
daffodil	0	49
daisy	124	0
dandelion	167	0
plantain	205	930
wild garlic	26	0
Total number of plants		

The biodiversity index of an area can be calculated using the following equation.

$$\text{biodiversity index} = \frac{\text{number of different species}}{\text{total number of individuals}}$$

Use the biodiversity index equation and the information from **Table 2** to explain which field has higher biodiversity. [2 marks]
03.3 It is suggested that field **B** is more at risk of losing its biodiversity than field **A**. Suggest why. [2 marks]
03.4 Suggest **one** way in which the biodiversity in field **B** could be increased. [1 mark]

4.12 Inheritance, variation, and evolution

4.12.1 DNA and the genome

Learning objectives

After this topic, you should know:
- about DNA as the material of inheritance
- what a genome is
- some of the benefits of studying the human genome.

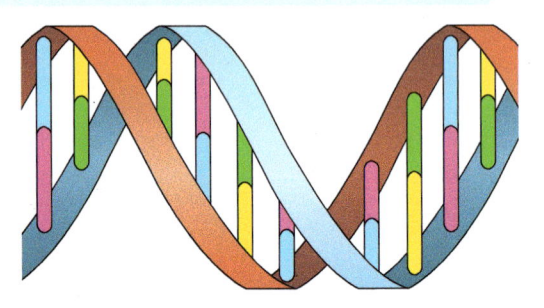

Figure 1 *A model of the DNA double helix*

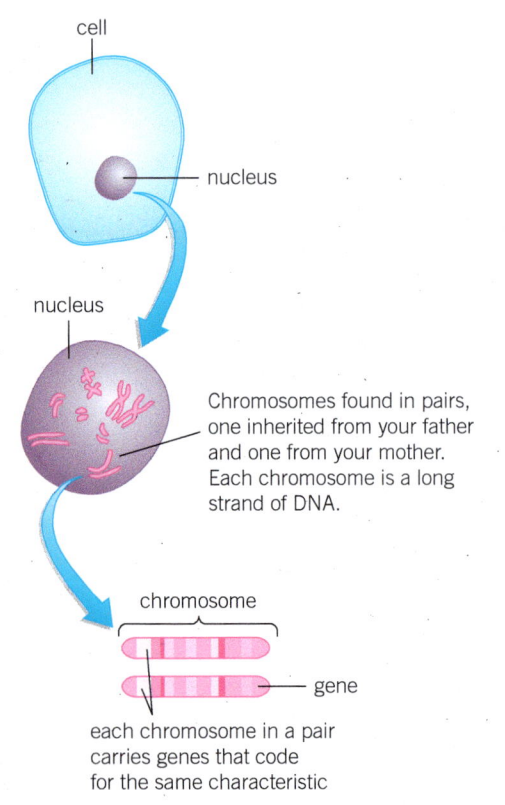

Figure 2 *The relationship between a cell, the nucleus, the chromosomes, and the genes*

Sexual reproduction involves the fusion (joining) of male and female gametes. These are the sperm and egg cells in animals. In sexual reproduction there is a combining of the genetic information from the two parents, which leads to variation in the offspring.

The formation of gametes involves meiosis, cell division that halves the number of chromosomes in the cells. You have 46 chromosomes in your normal body cells, arranged in 23 pairs. The gametes only contain 23 chromosomes each. You inherit half your chromosomes from your mother and half from your father when the gametes fuse to form a single fertilised egg cell containing 46 chromosomes.

DNA – the molecule of inheritance

Inside the nuclei of all your cells, your chromosomes are made up of long molecules of deoxyribonucleic acid (**DNA**). DNA is a polymer, a long molecule made up of many repeating units. These long strands of DNA twist and spiral to form a double helix structure (Figure 1).

Your genes are small sections of this DNA. This is where the genetic information – the coded information that determines inherited characteristics – is actually stored. Each of your chromosomes contains thousands of genes joined together (Figure 2). Each gene codes for a particular sequence of amino acids to make a specific protein. These proteins include the enzymes that control your cell chemistry. This is how the relationship between the genes and the whole organism builds up. The genes control the proteins, which control the make-up of the different specialised cells that form tissues. These tissues then form organs and organ systems that make up the whole body.

In 2003, scientists announced that they had managed to sequence the human genome. Working in teams all around the world, the Human Genome Project finished two years early, and under budget. This was because the technology used to chop up the DNA and read the chemical code had improved so fast during the life of the project (Figure 3). It was a scientific triumph – but why does it matter?

The human genome

The genome of an organism is the entire genetic material of the organism. That includes all of the chromosomes, and the genetic material found in the mitochondria as well. The human genome contains almost 21 000 genes that code for proteins. That sounds a lot until you discover that rice has 36 000 coding genes! We are not simpler than rice. The human genome has the ability to make many different proteins from the same gene by using it in different ways, or by switching part of a gene on or off.

4.12 Inheritance, variation, and evolution

Since the initial human genome was read, scientists have carried on with this work. They went on to sequence the genomes of 1000 people, and now they are busy with the current 100 000 Genomes Project. The aim is to find out as much as possible about human DNA.

It isn't just human genomes that are sequenced. Scientists are sequencing the genomes of hundreds of different **species** of organisms. They use similarities and differences in the genomes to help them work out the relationships between different types of organisms. This is changing the way in which living things are classified. Sequencing the genomes of bacteria and viruses allows us to identify the causes of disease very rapidly and to choose the correct treatment.

Why does the genome matter?

Understanding the human genome has taken years of work and billions of pounds – and there is still a great deal to find out. There are many reasons why scientists feel that all of this effort is worthwhile.

Understanding the human genome helps scientists to understand inherited disorders such as cystic fibrosis and sickle-cell disease. The more they can understand what goes wrong in these diseases, the more chance they have of overcoming them.

There are genes that are linked to an increased risk of developing many diseases, from heart disease to Type 2 diabetes. Understanding the human genome is playing a massive part in the search for genes linked to different types of diseases. The more we understand about the genome, the more likely we are to accurately predict the risk for each individual, so they can make lifestyle choices to help reduce the risk. Also, by analysing the genomes of cancer cells, scientists hope to get even better at choosing the best treatment for each person.

Understanding the human genome helps us to understand human evolution and history. People all over the world can be linked by patterns in their DNA, allowing scientists to trace human migration patterns from our ancient history. For example, most people have a small number of Neanderthal genes in their DNA, even though that branch of the human family died out around 40 000 years ago.

Figure 3 *Sequencing the first human genome took years. Machines like these mean it can now be done in days – soon it will take less than 24 hours*

Synoptic link

To remind yourself about meiosis and gamete formation, look back at Topic 1.3.10.

Key points

- The genome of an organism is the entire genetic material of that organism.
- The whole human genome has now been studied and this will have great importance for medicine in the future.
- The genetic material in the nucleus of a cell is composed of DNA. DNA is a polymer made up of two strands forming a double helix.
- A gene is a small section of DNA on a chromosome. Each gene codes for a particular sequence of amino acids, to make a specific protein.

1 a What is meiosis? [1 mark]
   b Explain why meiosis is important in gamete formation. [4 marks]
   c Explain how sexual reproduction introduces variation into the offspring. [4 marks]
2 a What was the Human Genome Project? [1 mark]
   b Give *three* ways in which the project was unusual. [3 marks]
   c Why do scientists continue to sequence:
      i   more human genomes? [4 marks]
      ii the genomes of other organisms? [3 marks]
3 Discuss the importance of understanding the human genome. [6 marks]

4.12.2 Inheritance in action

Learning objectives

After this topic, you should know:

- that different forms of genes, called alleles, can be either dominant or recessive
- how to predict the results of genetic crosses when a characteristic is controlled by a single gene
- how to interpret Punnett square diagrams
- Ⓗ how to construct Punnett square diagrams.

Study tip

Alleles are represented by letters of the alphabet. Capital and lower-case versions of the same letter are used. Always choose a letter that looks different as a capital and in lower case (e.g., B and b, A and a, N and n).

Figure 1 *You can tell the phenotype of these young mice by looking at them, but it is more difficult to be sure about their genotype*

Most of your characteristics, such as your eye colour and nose shape, are controlled by several different genes interacting. However, some characteristics, such as black or brown fur colour in mice, are controlled by a single gene. Some human characteristics, such as red–green colour blindness, are also controlled by single genes. The way in which single-gene features like these are passed from one generation to another follows some clear patterns. You can use them to predict what may be passed on. They are much easier to work with and understand than the majority of characteristics that result from multiple genes.

How inheritance works

The chromosomes you inherit carry your genetic information in the form of genes. Many of these genes have different forms, or **alleles** (sometimes called variants). Each allele codes for a different protein. The combination of alleles you inherit will determine your characteristics. You can make biological models that help you predict the outcome of any genetic cross.

Genetic terms

Some words are useful when you are working with biological models in genetics:

- **homozygote** – an individual with two identical alleles for a characteristic, for example, **BB** or **bb**
- **heterozygote** – an individual with different alleles for a characteristic, for example, **Bb**
- **genotype** – this describes the alleles present or the genetic make-up of an individual regarding a particular characteristic, for example, **Bb** or **bb**
- **phenotype** – this describes the physical appearance of an individual regarding a particular characteristic, for example, black fur or brown fur in a mouse (Figure 1).

Picture a gene as a position on a chromosome. An allele is the particular form of information in that position on an individual chromosome. For example, the gene for coat colour in mice may have the black (B) or the brown (b) allele in place. Because the mouse inherits one allele from each parent, the mouse will have two alleles controlling whether it is black or brown. The alleles present in an individual, known as the genotype, work at the level of the DNA molecules to control the proteins made. These proteins result in characteristics – such as coat colour or the presence of dimples – that are expressed as the phenotype of the organism.

Some alleles are expressed in the phenotype even when they are only present on one of the chromosomes. The phenotype coded for by these alleles is **dominant**, so the alleles for black coats in mice and dangly earlobes in people, for example, are always expressed if they are present. Use a capital letter to represent the alleles for dominant phenotypes,

4.12 Inheritance, variation, and evolution

for example, **B** for a black coat in mice. If a mouse inherits **BB** or **Bb** from its parents, it will have a black coat.

Some alleles only control the development of a characteristic if they are present on both chromosomes – in other words, when no dominant allele is present. These phenotypes are *recessive*, such as brown coats in mice and attached earlobes in people. Use a lower-case letter to represent recessive alleles, for example, **b** for a brown coat in mice, and they are only expressed if the organism is homozygous. A mouse would only have a brown coat if it inherited two recessive alleles, **bb**.

Genetic crosses

A genetic cross is when you consider the potential offspring that might result from two known parents. Remember that you need to look at both the possible genotypes and the possible phenotypes of the offspring.

Using genetic diagrams

You can model genetic crosses using a genetic diagram such as a Punnett square to predict the outcome of different genetic crosses (Figure 2). A genetic diagram gives you:

- the alleles for a characteristic carried by the parents (the genotype of the parents)
- the possible gametes that can be formed from these
- how these may combine to form the characteristic in their offspring. The possible genotypes of the offspring allow you to work out the possible phenotypes, too.

Inheriting different alleles can result in the development of quite different phenotypes. Genetic diagrams such as Punnett squares help to explain what is happening and predict what the possible offspring might be like. They give you the probability that a particular genotype or phenotype will be inherited in a given genetic cross.

1. **a** State what is meant by the term dominant allele. [1 mark]
   b State what is meant by the term recessive allele. [1 mark]
   c Describe the difference between being homozygous or heterozygous for a particular characteristic. [2 marks]

2. **H** Draw a Punnett square to show the possible offspring from a cross between two people who both have dangly earlobes and the genotype **Aa**, when **A** is the dominant allele for dangly earlobes and **a** is the recessive allele for attached earlobes. [5 marks]

3. **a** Explain how real genetic crosses may be used to help work out the genotype of a black mouse. [4 marks]
   b **H** Draw a Punnett square diagram for:
      i a homozygous black mouse crossed with a heterozygous black mouse. [5 marks]
      ii a heterozygous black mouse crossed with another heterozygous black mouse. [5 marks]

Phenotype: brown fur
Genotype: bb
Phenotype: black fur
Genotype: BB or Bb

Cross 1: bb × BB

Gametes	B	B
b	Bb	Bb
b	Bb	Bb

Offspring:
genotype: all Bb
phenotype: all black fur

Cross 2: bb × Bb

Gametes	B	b
b	Bb	bb
b	Bb	bb

Offspring:
genotype: 50% Bb, 50% bb
phenotype: 50% black fur, 50% brown fur

Figure 2 *Determining phenotype*

Key points

- Some characteristics (e.g., fur colour in mice and colour-blindness in people) are controlled by a single gene.
- Each gene may have different forms called alleles.
- The alleles present, or genotype, operate at a molecular level to develop characteristics that can be expressed as the phenotype.
- If the two alleles are the same, the individual is homozygous for that trait, but if the alleles are different they are heterozygous.
- A dominant allele is always expressed in the phenotype, even if only one copy is present. A recessive allele is only expressed if two copies are present.
- Most characteristics are the result of multiple genes interacting, rather than a single gene.

4.12.3 More about genetics

Learning objectives

After this topic, you should know:

- how to use proportion and ratios to express the outcome of a genetic cross
- how sex is inherited
- how to use family trees.

Genetic diagrams such as Punnett squares show you the predicted ratios of different phenotypes. They do not tell you the actual offspring, because every time gametes meet they are carrying a unique and random mixture of genes. You only see the expected ratios of phenotypes if you carry out lots of genetic crosses. This is why plants and animals that breed fast and produce lots of offspring are widely used to study genetics.

Direct proportion and simple ratios

Using Punnet squares, you can work out the proportion of the offspring of a genetic cross expected to have a particular genotype or phenotype. You can also work out the ratios of one genotype or phenotype to another.

Figure 1 shows two Punnett squares. One is of a genetic cross between two heterozygous black mice. The other shows the cross you looked at in Topic 4.12.2 between a heterozygous black mouse and a homozygous recessive brown mouse.

In Cross 1 you can look at both the genotype and the phenotype of the offspring. You can work out the proportions and the ratios between the different possible genetic combinations.

The proportions of the **genotypes** are:

$\frac{1}{4}$ or 25% homozygous dominant (BB)

$\frac{2}{4}$ or 50% heterozygous (Bb)

$\frac{1}{4}$ or 25% homozygous recessive (bb)

The possible genotypes appear in a ratio of 1 : 2 : 1 homozygous dominant : heterozygous : homozygous recessive.

The proportions of the **phenotypes** are:

$\frac{3}{4}$ or 75% dominant (black)

$\frac{1}{4}$ or 25% recessive (brown)

The possible phenotypes appear in a ratio of 3 : 1 dominant : recessive.

The proportions and ratios of the possible offspring will be the same for every heterozygous cross you look at.

- Look at Cross 2 between a heterozygous black mouse and a homozygous recessive brown mouse. Work out the proportions and ratios of the genotypes and phenotypes for this cross.

Cross 1: Bb × Bb

Gametes	B	b
B	BB	Bb
b	Bb	bb

Cross 2: bb × Bb

Gametes	B	b
b	Bb	bb
b	Bb	bb

Figure 1 *Genetic crosses*

■ 4.12 Inheritance, variation, and evolution

Sex determination

One feature of your phenotype is inherited not by a single gene or multiple genes but by a single pair of chromosomes. Humans have 23 pairs of chromosomes. In 22 cases, each chromosome in the pair is a similar shape. Each one has genes carrying information about the many different characteristics of your body. One pair of chromosomes is different. These are the **sex chromosomes**, which determine the sex of offspring.

- In human females the sex chromosomes are the same (XX).
- In human males the sex chromosomes are different (XY). The Y chromosome is very small and carries few genes other than those related to sexual characteristics.

When the cells undergo meiosis to form gametes, one sex chromosome goes into each gamete. This means that human egg cells contain an X chromosome. Half of the sperm also contain an X chromosome and the other half contain a Y chromosome. The inheritance of sex can be shown using a Punnett square (Figure 2).

XX × XY

Gametes	X	Y
X	XX	XY
X	XX	XY

Figure 2 *Using a Punnett square to determine sex inheritance*

Every pregnancy has a 50:50 chance of producing a boy and a 50:50 chance of producing a girl.

Family trees

You can trace genetic characteristics through a family by drawing a family tree (Figure 3). Family trees show males and females and can be useful for tracking inherited diseases, showing a family likeness, or showing the different alleles people have inherited. Family trees can be used to work out if an individual is likely to be homozygous or heterozygous for particular alleles.

1. State the sex chromosomes of:
   a human females [1 mark]   b human males. [1 mark]
2. Explain why the expected ratios in a genetic cross are only seen if there are large numbers of offspring. [2 marks]
3. A couple have three girls. They are expecting a fourth baby. Several people tell them that they are sure to have a boy this time.
   a Explain why people might think this is the case. [2 marks]
   b Explain why this statement is wrong. [3 marks]
4. a Ⓗ Draw a Punnett square to show the genetic cross between female tiger **A** and male tiger **B** at the top of the family tree in Figure 3. Use G for the dominant orange and g for the recessive white. [5 marks]
   b Give the proportion of the different genotypes and phenotypes in Figure 3, describe the ratios you would expect, and explain why they are not seen. [4 marks]

Study tip

In most genetic crosses, the letters represent alleles.

In sex determination, X and Y represent chromosomes.

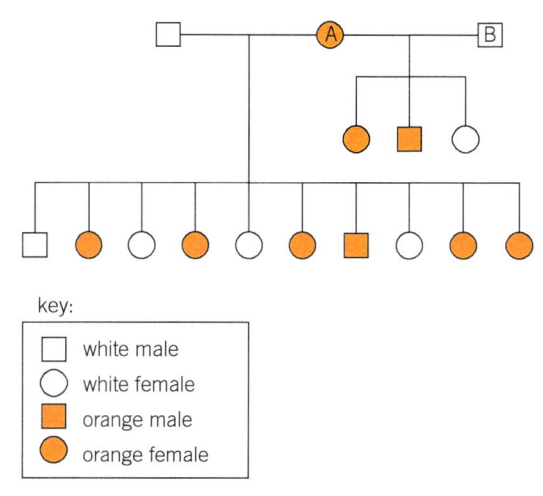

Figure 3 *A family tree to show the inheritance of orange or white coat colour in tigers*

key:
- □ white male
- ○ white female
- ■ orange male
- ● orange female

Key points

- Direct proportion and ratios can be used to express the outcome of a genetic cross.
- Punnett squares and family trees can be used to understand genetic inheritance.
- Ⓗ Punnett square diagrams can be constructed to predict the outcome of a monohybrid cross.
- Ordinary human body cells contain 23 pairs of chromosomes. 22 control general body characteristics only, but the sex chromosomes carry the genes that determine sex.
- In human females the sex chromosomes are the same (XX), whilst in males the sex chromosomes are different (XY).

4.12.4 Variation

Learning objectives

After this topic, you should know:

- what makes you different from the rest of your family
- why identical twins are not exactly the same in every way.

No one else in the world will have exactly the same fingerprints as you. Even identical twins have different fingerprints. What factors make you so different from other people?

Genetic causes

The basic characteristics of every individual are the result of the genes they have inherited from their parents. An apple tree seed will never grow into an oak tree. Every individual looks different, but there is usually less variation between family members than between members of the general population. Features such as eye colour, nose shape, your sex, and dimples are the result of genetic information inherited from your parents. The variation in them is due to genetic causes – but your genes are only part of the story.

Environmental causes

Some differences between you and other people are due entirely to the environment in which you live. For example, you may have a scar as a result of an accident or an operation. Such variation is environmental, not genetic. Genes play a major part in deciding how an organism will look, but the conditions in which it develops are important, too. Genetically identical plants can be grown under different conditions of light or with different mineral ions. The resulting plants do not look identical. Plants deprived of light, carbon dioxide, or mineral ions do not make as much food as plants with everything. The deprived plants are smaller and weaker as they have not been able to fulfil their genetic potential.

Combined causes of variation

Many of the differences between individuals of the same species are the result of both their genes and the environment. For example, you inherit your hair and skin colour from your parents. However, whatever your inherited skin colour, it will darken if you live in a sunny environment.

Your height and weight are also affected by both your genes and your environment. You may have a genetic tendency to be overweight, but if you never have enough to eat, you will be thin. Human height is an example of a characteristic determined by many genes, each with a number of different possible alleles. The different combination of alleles inherited for the height genes gives the genotype of each person for height. Your genotype determines around 80% of your final growth, but height is also affected by the environment. Factors such as your diet, both the type and the amount of food available when you are growing up, can also have an impact on your final height (Figure 2).

Investigating variation

It is quite easy to produce genetically identical plants to investigate variety. You can then put them in different situations to see how the environment affects their appearance. Scientists also use groups of animals that are genetically very similar to investigate variety.

Figure 1 *However much this Chihuahua (left) eats, it will never be as big as the Great Dane – it just isn't in its genes*

Study tip

Genes control the development of physical characteristics (phenotype).

Interactions of the genotype with the environment can affect the phenotype.

4.12 Inheritance, variation, and evolution

Human height is an example of a characteristic that is influenced both by genetics and by the environment. As Figure 2 shows, being male or female affects your height. Having parents with 'tall' or 'short' alleles for height will also affect your eventual height. However, factors such as the amount of food available when you are growing up will also have an impact on your height, whatever your genetic inheritance.

The only genetically identical humans are identical twins who come from the same fertilised egg. Scientists are very interested in finding out how similar identical twins are as adults. It would be unethical to separate identical twins just to investigate environmental effects. However, there are cases of identical twins who have been adopted by different families. Some scientists have researched these separated identical twins.

In one study, scientists compared four groups of adults:
- identical twins brought up together
- separated identical twins
- non-identical twins brought up together
- same sex, non-twin siblings brought up together.

The differences between the pairs were measured. A small difference means that the individuals in a pair are very alike. If there was a big difference between the identical twins, the scientists could see that their environment had had more effect than their genes (Table 1).

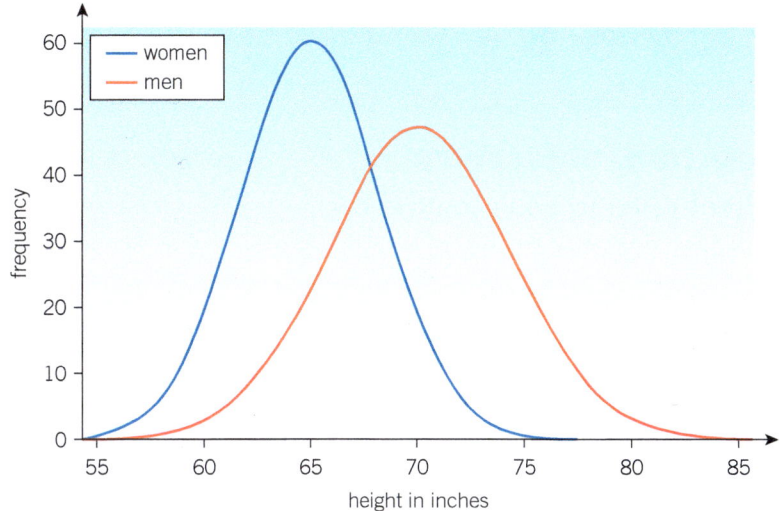

Figure 2 *Human height is strongly affected by genetics, but environmental factors are important, too*

Figure 3 *Whether identical twins are brought up together or apart, their behaviours are often very similar but never exactly identical as adults. This is because their different environments will have made some subtle differences*

Table 1 *Differences in pairs of adults*

Measured difference in:	Identical twins brought up together	Identical twins brought up apart	Non-identical twins brought up together	Non-twin siblings brought up together
Height in cm	1.7	1.8	4.4	4.5
Mass in kg	1.9	4.5	4.6	4.7
IQ points (average IQ is 100)	5.9	8.2	9.9	9.8

1 Both genes and the environment affect the appearance of individuals. Use the data in Figure 2 to help you give *one* example of:
  a how genes affect a person's appearance [1 mark]
  b how the environment affects a person's appearance. [1 mark]
2 a Suggest why identical twins that were reared together and identical twins that were reared separately were studied. [3 marks]
  b Using the data from Table 1, explain which human characteristic seems to be mostly controlled by genes and which seems to be most affected by the environment. [4 marks]
3 You are given 20 pots containing identical cloned seedlings, all of the same height and colour. Suggest how you might investigate the effect of temperature on the growth of these seedlings, compared with the impact of their genes. [6 marks]

Key points
- Variation is the differences in the characteristics of individuals in a population.
- Variation may be due to differences in the genes inherited (genetic causes), the conditions in which organisms develop (environmental causes), or a combination of both genes and the environment.

4.12.5 Evolution by natural selection

Learning objectives
After this topic, you should know:
- what mutation means
- how natural selection works
- how evolution occurs via natural selection.

Synoptic links
You learnt about meiosis and sexual reproduction in Topic 1.3.10.

For more about the competition between plants and animals in the natural world, look back at Topics 4.11.4 and 4.11.5.

You learnt about the effect of ionising radiation on cells in Topic 3.8.7.

Animals and plants are always in competition with other members of their own species. Organisms that gain an advantage are more likely to survive and breed. This is **natural selection**. By looking at what is happening at the level of the genes, you can understand how the process works.

Mutation and genetic variation
The individual organisms in any species may show a wide range of variation. This is partly because of differences in the genes they inherit that arise through meiosis and sexual reproduction. New variants – that is, changes in the genes themselves – arise as a result of **mutation**, a change in the DNA code.

Mutations can take place when the DNA is copied during cell division or when cells are affected by environmental factors such as ionising radiation. Those that take place when the gametes are formed may affect the phenotype of the offspring and introduce new variants into the genes of a species. In terms of survival, this is very important. A mutation of a gene can change the protein it codes for, or even prevent a particular protein being made in the cells. However, most mutations have no effect at all on the phenotype of the organism. Some *influence* the phenotype and a small number *determine* the phenotype. Of those, a few mutations are so harmful that the organism does not survive. Very rarely, a mutation produces an adaptation that makes an organism better-suited to its environment, or gives it an advantage if there is an environmental change.

Survival of the fittest and evolution
The theory of evolution by natural selection states that all species of living things have evolved from simple life forms that first developed more than 3 billion years ago. Evolution through natural selection produces changes in the inherited characteristics of a population over time that result in organisms that are well-suited to their environment. It may result in the formation of new species. The process can be summarised as follows:

- Individual organisms within a particular species may show a lot of genetic variation, which gives rise to a wide range of phenotypes.
- Individuals with characteristics most suited to the environment are more likely to survive to breed successfully (Figure 1).
- The alleles (variants) that have enabled these individuals to survive are then passed on to the next generation.

If two populations of one species become so different that they can no longer interbreed to produce fertile offspring, they have formed two new species.

Natural selection in action
When new variants arise from a mutation, there may be a relatively rapid change in a species. This is particularly true if the environment

Figure 1 *The natural world is often brutal. Only the best-adapted predators capture prey and survive to breed – and only the best-adapted prey animals escape to breed as well*

■ 4.12 Inheritance, variation, and evolution

changes. If the mutation gives the organism an advantage in the changed environment, making it more likely to survive and breed in the new conditions, the new allele will become common quite quickly.

Oyster problems

In 1915, the oyster fishermen in Malpeque Bay, Canada noticed a few diseased oysters among their healthy catch. By 1922, the oyster beds were almost empty. The oysters had been wiped out by a destructive new disease. Fortunately, a few of the oysters had a mutation that made them resistant to the disease. These were the only ones to survive and breed. The oyster beds filled up again, and by 1940 they were producing more oysters than ever (Figure 2). A new population of oysters had evolved. As a result of natural selection, almost every oyster in Malpeque Bay now carries an allele that makes it resistant to Malpeque disease. The disease is no longer a problem.

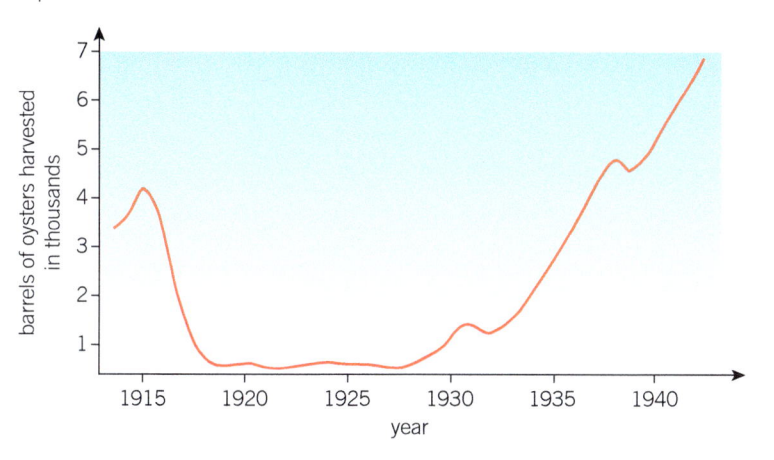

Figure 2 *The effect of disease and natural selection on oyster harvests*

Natural selection can bring about change very quickly. In bacteria, the genetic make-up of a population can change in days. The Malpeque Bay oysters took about 20 years. However, to produce an entire new species (rather than a different population) usually takes much longer. It has taken millions of years for the organisms present on Earth in the 21st century to evolve. Many of the different species that lived on Earth many millions of years ago no longer exist. The descendants of some of those species are the animals and plants you see around you.

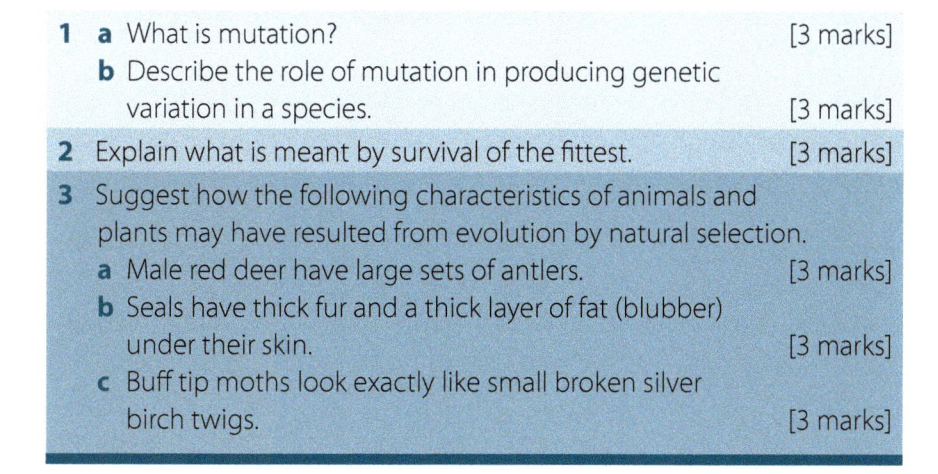

1   a   What is mutation? [3 marks]
    b   Describe the role of mutation in producing genetic variation in a species. [3 marks]
2   Explain what is meant by survival of the fittest. [3 marks]
3   Suggest how the following characteristics of animals and plants may have resulted from evolution by natural selection.
    a   Male red deer have large sets of antlers. [3 marks]
    b   Seals have thick fur and a thick layer of fat (blubber) under their skin. [3 marks]
    c   Buff tip moths look exactly like small broken silver birch twigs. [3 marks]

Synoptic links

You can find out about the evolution of antibiotic-resistant bacteria by natural selection in Topic 4.12.8.

Study tip

Remember the key steps in natural selection:

mutation of gene → advantage to survival → breed → pass on variant

Key points

- There is usually extensive genetic variation between a population of a species.
- All variations arise from mutations. Mutations are changes in the DNA code. This can alter the protein coded for by that gene or prevent the production of a protein.
- Mutations can happen when the DNA is copied during cell division or when cells are affected by environmental factors (e.g., ionising radiation).
- Most mutations have no effect on the phenotype, some *influence* the phenotype and a very few *determine* the phenotype.
- Evolution is a change in the inherited characteristics of a population over time through a process of natural selection that may result in the formation of new species.
- Evolution occurs through the natural selection of variants that give rise to phenotypes best-suited to their environment.

265

4.12.6 Evolution in action

Learning objectives
After this topic, you should know:
- how evolution takes place
- the role of isolation in evolution.

Planet Earth supports an amazing variety of life. Charles Darwin and his contemporary Alfred Wallace initially developed the scientific theory that explains the origins of all life on Earth – the theory of evolution by natural selection.

Principles of natural selection

The theory of evolution by natural selection was originally developed by Charles Darwin and published in 1859. It states that all the species of living things alive today have evolved from the first simple life forms. When Darwin suggested how evolution took place by natural selection, no one knew about genes. He simply observed that useful inherited characteristics were passed on.

In the 21st century scientists can apply modern knowledge of genetics, variants, and mutation to understand how the evolution of new species comes about. It follows the process of natural selection. The main principles of natural selection are:

- The individual organisms in a particular species tend to show a wide range of variation for each characteristic. This is as a result of sexual reproduction and of mutation.

- Reproduction always produces more offspring than the environment can support. The organisms that have inherited the characteristics most suited to their environment – the 'fittest' – are more likely to survive and breed successfully.

- When the surviving organisms breed, they pass on the variant that gives rise to the phenotype that has given them an advantage. This enables the organism to survive to the next generation.

Speciation

Any population will contain natural genetic variation. This means that it will contain a wide range of alleles controlling its characteristics that result from sexual reproduction and mutation. This is genetic variation. In each population, the alleles that are selected will control characteristics that help the organism to survive and breed successfully. This process is natural selection.

Sometimes, part of a population becomes isolated with new environmental conditions. Alleles for characteristics that enable organisms to survive and breed successfully in the new conditions will be selected. These are likely to be different from the alleles that gave success in the original environment. As a result of the selection of these different alleles, the characteristic features of the isolated organisms will change. Eventually, they change so much that they can no longer interbreed with the original organisms and a new species has evolved. This is known as **speciation**.

Figure 1 *Both the gaudy leaf frog (top) and the Golfo Dulce poison dart frog have evolved to live in rain forests. The Golfo Dulce poison dart frog has evolved even more specifically and is found only in certain areas of Costa Rica*

■ 4.12 Inheritance, variation, and evolution

How do populations become isolated?
The most common way in which populations become separated is by **geographical isolation**. This is when two populations become physically isolated by a geographical feature, for example a new mountain range, a new river, or an area of land becoming an island. Earthquakes can separate areas of land, and volcanoes can produce completely new islands. The formation of islands often leads to speciation. This is what has happened on the island of Borneo, on the Galápagos Islands, and in Australia. The species that have evolved to survive within these isolated environments are very vulnerable to climate change or habitat loss.

Sometimes organisms are separated by **environmental isolation**. This happens when the climate changes in one area where an organism lives, but not in other areas. For example, if the climate becomes warmer in one area, plants will flower at a different time of year. The breeding times of the plants and the animals linked with them will change and eventually new species will emerge.

Figure 2 *Both the marsupial koala and the eucalyptus tree it feeds on have evolved in geographical isolation in Australia*

Evolution and speciation is taking place all the time all over the world. For example, geographical isolation may involve very large areas such as Borneo or very small areas. Mount Bosavi is the crater of an extinct volcano in Papua New Guinea. It is only 4 km wide and the walls of the crater are 1 km high. The animals and plants trapped inside the crater have evolved in different ways to those outside it. During a three-week expedition in 2009, scientists discovered around 40 new species. These included plants, mammals, fish, birds, reptiles, amphibians, and insects. All of these species and plants are the result of selection in the specialised environment of the isolated crater. They include an enormous 82 cm-long rat that weighs 1.5 kg!

1 a Describe how populations can become isolated. [3 marks]
  b Explain why this isolation can lead to the evolution of new species. [5 marks]
2 Explain the difference between natural selection and evolution. [4 marks]
3 Islands often have their own endemic organisms – organisms that are found nowhere else in the world. Discuss how this can be used as evidence for the current model of speciation and evolution. [6 marks]

Study tip
The key elements of evolution (speciation) are:
- two groups of the same species become separated
- different natural selection takes place in each group
- eventually the groups become so different that they are no longer able to interbreed to produce fertile offspring.

Key points
- In evolution new species arise as a result of:
  - isolation (two populations of a species become isolated either geographically or environmentally)
  - genetic variation between populations
  - natural selection (operates to select the variants that give rise to the phenotypes best-suited to the environment of each of the two populations, which evolve in different ways to suit different conditions)
  - speciation (the populations become so different that successful interbreeding to produce fertile offspring is no longer possible).

267

4.12.7 Fossil evidence for evolution

Learning objectives

After this topic, you should know:
- how fossils are formed
- how fossils can provide evidence for evolution.

There is no record of the origins of life on Earth. It is a puzzle that can never be completely solved – no one was there to see it! Scientists don't even know exactly when life on Earth began. However, most think it was somewhere between 3 and 4 billion years ago.

Darwin's theory of evolution by natural selection is now widely accepted as the best explanation of the living world. The understanding of genetics and how characteristics are passed to offspring in the genes gives a clear mechanism for the process and helps to supply the supporting evidence needed. There are several other strong strands of evidence that also support the theory of evolution by natural selection.

What can you learn from fossils?

Some of the best evidence scientists have about the history of life on Earth comes from **fossils**. Fossils are the remains of organisms from millions of years ago that are found preserved in rocks, ice, and other places. For example, fossils have revealed the world of dinosaurs. These giant reptiles dominated the Earth at one stage and died out many millions of years before the evolution of the first human beings.

You have probably seen a fossil in a museum or on TV, or maybe you have even found one yourself. Fossils can be formed in a number of ways:

- When an animal or plant does not decay after it has died. This happens when one or more of the conditions needed for decay are not there. This may be because there is little or no oxygen present. It could be because poisonous gases kill off the bacteria that cause decay. Sometimes the temperature is too low for decay to take place. Then the animals and plants are preserved almost intact, for example, in ice (Figure 1) or peat. These fossils are rare, but they give a clear insight into what an animal looked like. They can also tell us what an animal had been eating or the colour of a long-extinct flower. Scientists can even extract the DNA and compare it with the DNA of modern organisms.

- Many fossils are formed when harder parts of the animal or plant are replaced by minerals as they decay and become part of the rock. This takes place over long periods. Mould fossils are formed when an impression of an organism is made in mud and then becomes fossilised, whilst cast fossils are made when a mould is filled in. Rock fossils are the most common form of fossils (Figure 2). One of the biggest herbivores found so far is *Argentinosaurus huinculensis*. It lived around 70 million years ago, was nearly 40 metres long and probably weighed about 80–100 tonnes! Among the largest carnivores was *Giganotosaurus*. It was about 14 metres long, with a brain the size of a banana and 20 cm-long serrated teeth. For comparison, the biggest living carnivorous lizard, the Komodo dragon, is about 3 metres long and weighs around 140 kg.

Using timescales

Timescales for the evolution of life are big:

a thousand years is 10^3 years

a million years is 10^6 years

a billion years is 10^9 years.

Figure 1 *This baby mammoth was preserved in ice for at least 10 000 years. Examining this kind of evidence helps scientists to check the accuracy of ideas based on fossil skeletons alone*

4.12 Inheritance, variation, and evolution

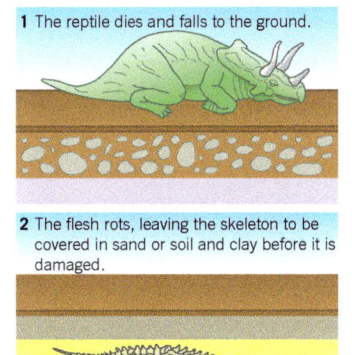

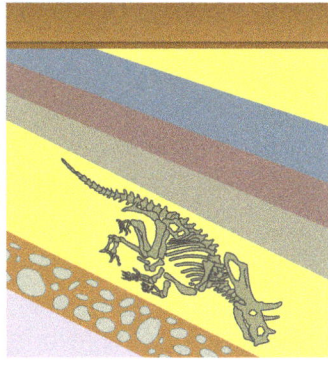

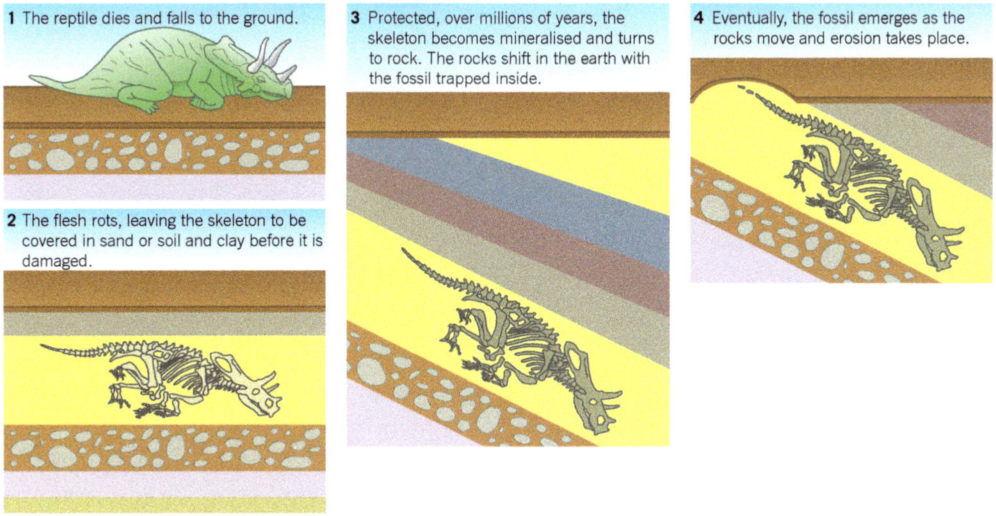

Figure 2 *It takes a very long time for fossils to form, but they provide us with invaluable evidence of how life on Earth has developed*

- Some of the fossils found are not of actual animals or plants, but are preserved traces they have left behind. Fossil footprints (Figure 3), burrows, rootlet traces (evidence of roots), and droppings are all formed. These help to build up a picture of life on Earth long ago.

An incomplete record
The fossil record is not complete for several reasons:

- Many of the very earliest forms of life were soft-bodied organisms. This means that they have left little fossil trace. The majority of any fossils that were formed in the earliest days will have been destroyed by geological activity including the formation of mountain ranges, continental movements, erosion, volcanoes, and earthquakes. This is why scientists cannot be absolutely certain about how life on Earth began.
- Most organisms that died did not become fossilised – the right conditions for fossil formation were rare.
- There are many fossils that are still to be found.

In spite of all these limitations, the fossils that have been found can still give you a snapshot of life millions of years ago.

Figure 3 *These footprints were found fossilised in volcanic ash. They were made by early humans and you can see clearly the adult prints and those of a child who walked along 3.6 million years ago*

1. There are several theories about how life on Earth began.
   a. Explain why it is impossible to know for sure how life on Earth began. [2 marks]
   b. Explain why fossils are such important evidence for the way life has developed. [3 marks]
2. a. What is the most common type of fossil? [1 mark]
   b. How long ago were many of these fossils formed? [1 mark]
   c. Summarise the main ways in which fossils are formed. [6 marks]
3. a. Describe how ice fossils are formed. [3 marks]
   b. Explain why ice fossils are so valuable to scientists. [4 marks]

Key points
- Fossils are the remains of organisms from millions of years ago that can be found in rocks, ice, and other places.
- Fossils may be formed in different ways including the absence of decay, parts replaced by minerals as they decay, and as preserved traces of organisms.
- Fossils give us information about organisms that lived millions of years ago.

4.12.8 More evidence for evolution

Learning objectives

After this topic, you should know:

- what fossils can reveal about how organisms have changed over time
- how the development of antibiotic resistance in bacteria can be used as evidence for evolution.

Using the fossil record

The fossil record helps scientists to understand how much organisms have changed since life developed on Earth. However, this understanding is often limited. Only small pieces of skeletons or little bits of shells have been found. Luckily, there is a very complete fossil record for a few animals, including the horse. These relatively complete fossil records can show you how some organisms have changed and developed over time (Figure 1). They can also help you to reconstruct the ecology, climate, and environment of millions of years ago.

Fossils also show you that not all animals have changed very much. For example, fossil sharks from millions of years ago look very like modern sharks. They evolved early into a form that was almost perfectly adapted for their environment and their way of life. Their environment has not changed much for millions of years, so sharks have also remained the same.

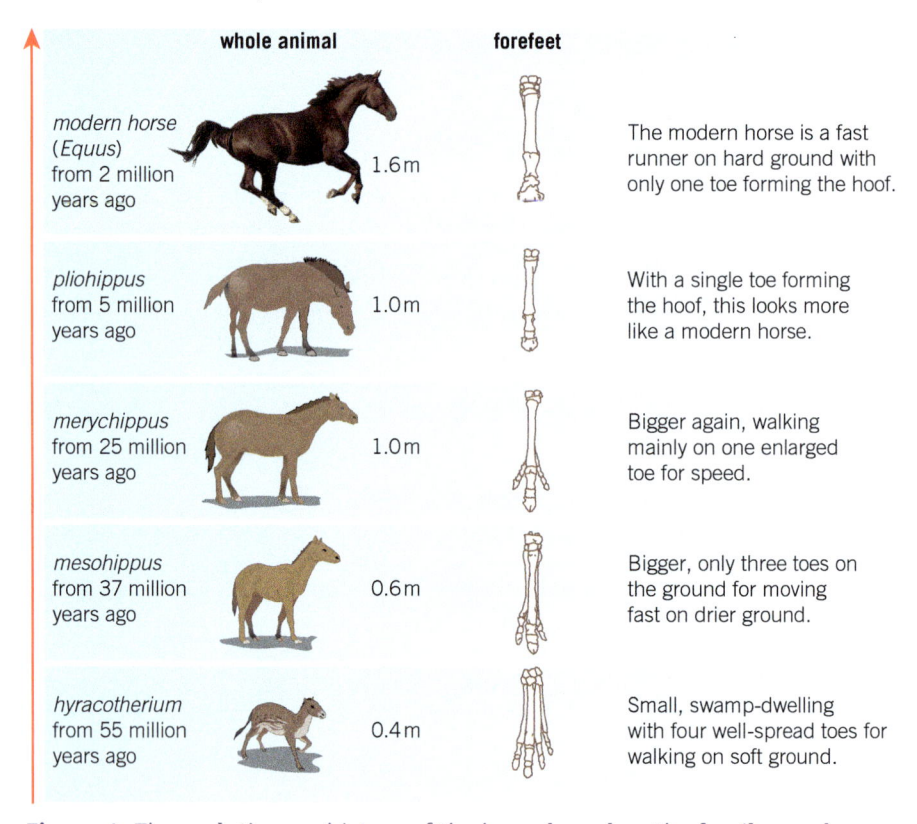

	whole animal		forefeet	
modern horse (*Equus*) from 2 million years ago		1.6 m		The modern horse is a fast runner on hard ground with only one toe forming the hoof.
pliohippus from 5 million years ago		1.0 m		With a single toe forming the hoof, this looks more like a modern horse.
merychippus from 25 million years ago		1.0 m		Bigger again, walking mainly on one enlarged toe for speed.
mesohippus from 37 million years ago		0.6 m		Bigger, only three toes on the ground for moving fast on drier ground.
hyracotherium from 55 million years ago		0.4 m		Small, swamp-dwelling with four well-spread toes for walking on soft ground.

Figure 1 *The evolutionary history of the horse based on the fossil record*

Antibiotic-resistant bacteria

If you are given an antibiotic and use it properly, the bacteria that have made you ill are killed off. However, some bacteria develop resistance to antibiotics. They have a natural mutation (change in their genetic material) that means they are not affected by the antibiotic. These mutations happen by chance and they produce new resistant strains of bacteria by natural selection (Figure 2). We can observe evolution taking place in bacteria because they reproduce at such a rapid rate.

4.12 Inheritance, variation, and evolution

Normally, an antibiotic kills the bacteria of a non-resistant strain. However, individual resistant bacteria survive and reproduce, so the population of resistant bacteria increases. Antibiotics are no longer active against this new strain of pathogen. As a result, the new strain spreads rapidly because there is no effective treatment. This is what has happened with bacteria such as MRSA (methicillin-resistant *Staphylococcus aureus* – Figure 3). More types of bacteria are becoming resistant to more antibiotics, making bacterial diseases more difficult to treat.

The evolution of antibiotic resistance in bacteria can be observed happening in a much shorter time than the evolution of a characteristic in plants and animals. This is because bacteria have such a fast reproduction time. In ideal conditions they can reproduce every 20 minutes. This means that many generations are seen in a very short space of time, which is very useful as evidence for how evolution takes place by the process of natural selection. The speed at which antibiotic resistance evolves does, however, have potentially serious consequences for human medicine and human health.

To prevent more resistant strains of bacteria appearing:

- It is important not to overuse antibiotics. For this reason, doctors no longer use antibiotics to treat non-serious infections such as mild throat or ear infections. Also, since antibiotics don't affect viruses, people should not request antibiotics to treat an illness that their doctor believes is caused by a virus.
- It is also important that patients finish their course of medicine every time. This is to make sure that all bacteria are killed by the antibiotic, so that no bacteria survive to mutate and form resistant strains.

Hopefully, steps like these will slow down the rate of development of resistant strains.

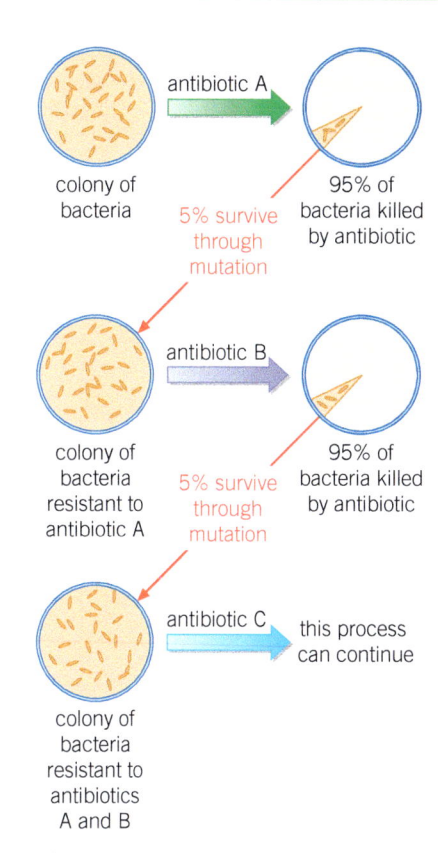

Figure 2 *Bacteria can develop resistance to many different antibiotics in a process of natural selection, as this simple model shows*

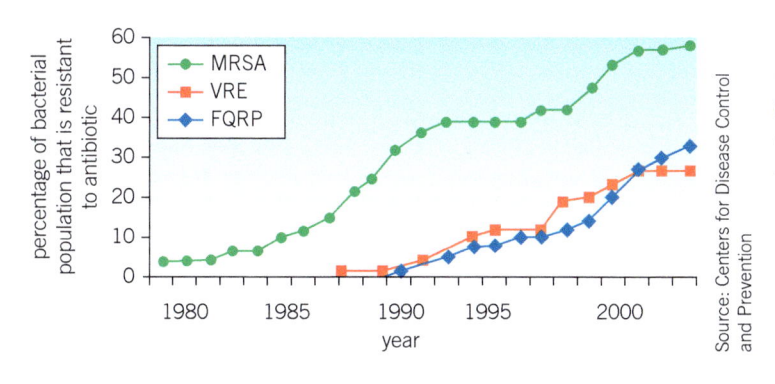

Figure 3 *Data from the US showing a steady increase in antibiotic-resistant strains of three common bacterial pathogens* – methicillin-resistant Staphylococcus aureus (MRSA), vancomycin-resistant Enterococci (VRE), and floroquinolone-resistant Pseudomonas aeruginosa (FQRP)

Key points

- You can learn from fossils how much or how little organisms have changed as life has developed on Earth.
- Bacteria that cause disease evolve by natural selection when exposed to antibiotics to give rise to antibiotic-resistant strains.
- The development of antibiotic resistance in bacteria is evidence of evolution occurring. It can be observed in a short time because bacteria reproduce very quickly.

1. Look at the evolution of the horse shown in Figure 1. Explain how the fossil evidence of the legs helps us to understand how hyracotherium and mesohippus lived and what they were like. [4 marks]
2. Describe how fossil evidence helps us to understand just how much organisms have changed, or not changed, over time. [4 marks]
3. a Make a flow chart to show how bacteria develop resistance to antibiotics. [6 marks]
   b Explain why bacteria are so useful as evidence for evolution. [3 marks]

271

4.12.9 Classification systems

Learning objectives

After this topic, you should know:
- the basic principles of classification
- the binomial naming system of genus and species
- how new technologies have changed classification.

Vanessa atalanta   *Plebejus argus*

Figure 1 *Organisms are identified by the differences between them. These two animals are both butterflies, but they belong to different species*

Classification is the organisation of living things into groups according to their similarities. Biologists classify organisms to make it easier to study them. Classification allows scientists to make sense of the living world. It also helps scientists to understand how the different groups of living things are related to each other. Perhaps most importantly, it enables scientists to recognise the biodiversity present in the world and gives them a common language in which to talk about it.

In studies of evolution, it is also essential to be able to identify and classify living organisms. This helps scientists to build up the relationships between different organisms, and to work out how they are related to organisms that are now extinct.

How are organisms classified?

Living things are classified by studying their similarities and differences. Classification as we know it really began in the 18th century with Carl Linnaeus, a Swedish botanist (plant biologist). He grouped organisms together depending on their structure and characteristics. Linnaeus made many careful observations of living things and used a hierarchical structure to classify them.

The way in which organisms are classified today is still based on the traditional Linnaean system, which is also known as the natural classification system. Linnaeus classified organisms into the following groups – kingdom, phylum, class, order, family, genus, and species.

Kingdoms

When Linnaeus first devised his classification system, the number of known types of living things was much smaller than it is today, so he suggested just two kingdoms, the animals and the plants. Kingdoms contain lots of organisms with many differences but a few important similarities. For example, all animals move their whole bodies about during at least part of their life cycle, and their cells do not have cellulose cell walls. On the other hand, plants do not move their whole bodies about and their cells have cellulose cell walls. Also, some plant cells contain chloroplasts full of chlorophyll for photosynthesis.

Now scientists know of many more organisms and they also know much more about them. Developments in microscopes have enabled scientists to compare the internal structures of cells. Developments in imaging techniques have given scientists much more evidence about the internal structures of many organisms.

Scientists also know a great deal more about the biochemistry of different organisms. It is even possible to analyse the DNA of different species and compare the genomes of organisms. As a result, new models of classification have been proposed. For example, at one stage, scientists

■ 4.12 Inheritance, variation, and evolution

suggested a five-kingdom model of classification. Now, most scientists accept a classification system with three domains and six kingdoms. Modern classification systems are largely based on theories of evolution that have been developed from the analysis of different DNA molecules.

At the moment, scientists out in the field still rely quite heavily on traditional observation to identify organisms. However, in future, portable equipment for analysing DNA quickly and cheaply will be part of every scientific expedition.

Naming living things

The huge variety of living organisms and the number of different languages spoken means that the same organism can have many different names around the world. This makes it impossible for one biologist to know what organism another is talking about!

The problem is solved because every organism has a scientific name given using a **binomial system** (again first put forward by Carl Linnaeus). Binomial means two names. The two names of an organism are in Latin and they give the **genus** and the species of the organism. Even in the time of Linnaeus, Latin was no longer spoken but was the language of scholars everywhere. This meant that no-one was offended because their language was not chosen, yet most people could understand the names.

Simple rules for writing scientific names

- The first name is the name of the genus to which the organism belongs. It is written with an initial capital letter.
- The second name is the name of a species to which the organism belongs. It is written with an initial lower-case initial letter.
- The two names are underlined when handwritten or are in italics when printed.

Table 1 *Examples of the scientific names of some common organisms*

Common name	Scientific name
Human being	*Homo sapiens*
Domestic cat	*Felis domesticus*
Blackthorn (sloe)	*Prunus spinosa*

Key points

- Traditionally, living things have been classified into groups depending on their structures and characteristics.
- The main groups of the traditional classification system are kingdom, phylum, class, order, family, genus, and species.
- Organisms are named by the binomial system of genus and species.
- As evidence of the internal structures of organisms became more developed due to improvements in microscopes, and the understanding of biochemical processes progressed, new models of classification were proposed.
- Modern classification systems are based on theories about evolution developed from analysis of differences in DNA molecules.

1 Define classification. [1 mark]
2 Describe what observations can be made to compare living organisms, and how modern technology has affected the way in which organisms are classified. [4 marks]
3 a Define a species. [2 marks]
  b Give *five* examples of species of living organisms, including at least *one* plant species and *not* including those given in Table 1. [5 marks]
4 a Define the binomial naming system. [2 marks]
  b Explain the importance of the binomial system for scientists around the world. [3 marks]

4.12.10 Selective breeding

Learning objectives

After this topic, you should know:
- what selective breeding is
- how selective breeding works
- the benefits and risks of selective breeding.

For centuries people have attempted to speed up evolution to obtain the characteristics they want in plants and animals. This happened long before any scientific idea of evolution was developed, and also long before the mechanisms of genetics were understood. From the earliest times, farmers bred from the plants that produced the biggest grain and the animals that produced the most milk. This resulted in plants that all had bigger grains and cows that all produced a lot of milk. This is called **selective breeding**.

How does selective breeding work?

You can change animals and plants by artificially selecting which members of a group you want to breed. Farmers and breeders select animals and plants from a mixed population that have particularly useful or desirable characteristics. They use these organisms as their breeding stock. They then select from the offspring and only breed again from the ones that show the desired characteristic. This continues over many generations until all of the offspring show the desired characteristic (Figure 2).

Figure 1 *Ancient images, like this one of agricultural work in Egypt, provide evidence that plants and animals have changed dramatically in appearance and nature from their wild ancestors as a result of selective breeding*

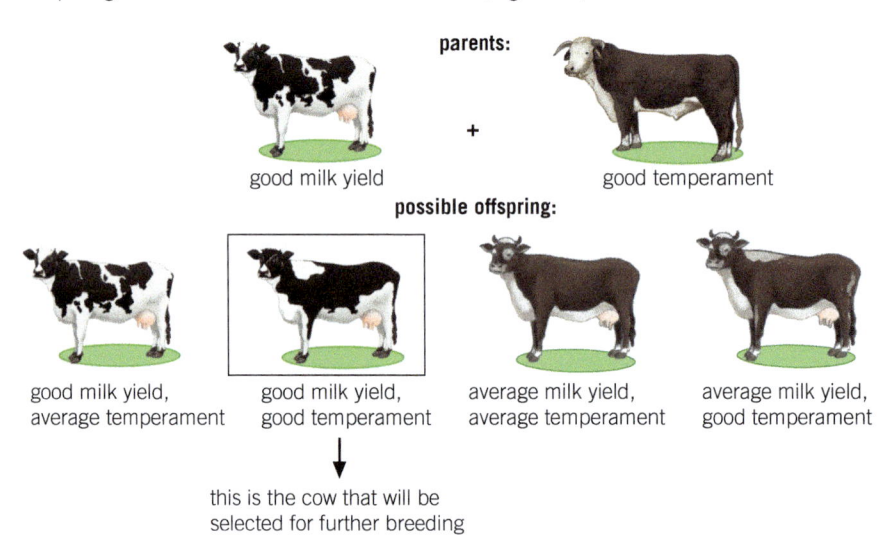

Figure 2 *Sometimes an animal or plant with one desirable trait will be cross-bred with organisms showing another desirable trait. Only the offspring showing both of the favoured features will be used for further breeding*

The process can be used to select for a whole range of features. Examples include:
- disease resistance in food crops or garden plants
- animals that produce more meat or milk
- domestic dogs and farm animals with a gentle nature
- large, unusual, brightly coloured or heavily scented flowers.

The results of centuries of selective breeding have been dramatic (Figure 3). Modern placid dairy cows that produce litres and litres of milk each day are very different to their aggressive, wild ancestors that produced enough milk

Figure 3 *The dog on the top is a long way from his ancestor, the wolf. Most pets are the result of years of selective breeding for largely cosmetic reasons*

for their single calf and little more. Modern fields of wheat with their large, heavy heads of grain show little resemblance to the wild grasses that were their ancestors. Genetic manipulation by selective breeding has resulted in animals and plants with strange combinations of genes that would probably never have occurred naturally. However, organisms that are either useful or simply enjoyable have been produced as a result.

Limitations of selective breeding

Selective breeding has been responsible for much of the agricultural progress that has been made over the centuries, but there is a major problem with it. Selective breeding greatly reduces the number of alleles in the population, because only individuals with the chosen alleles are allowed to breed. This not only reduces the variation between individuals, but also the variation in the alleles for a given characteristic. This is not a problem when conditions are stable. However, as soon as there is a problem – the climate changes or a new disease emerges – the lack of variation can mean that none of the animals or plants in the population can cope with this change. This can result in the population dying out. For example, bananas are all genetically very similar. The banana industry is at risk of being wiped out as a result of new aggressive diseases, because none of the plants are resistant to the pathogens.

There is also the problem of inbreeding. Some breeding populations have been so closely bred to achieve a particular appearance that animals are mated with close relatives. This results in very little variation in the population. Consequently, some breeds are particularly prone to certain diseases or inherited defects (Figure 4). For example, boxer dogs are at high risk of epilepsy, and King Charles spaniels have brains that are too big for their small skulls.

The pug is a small breed of dog with a flat face. Scientists at Imperial College, London discovered that the 10 000 pugs in the UK are very inbred. Not only do they struggle to breathe, but the genetic variation in their entire population is the equivalent of that of just 50 healthy dogs. Persian cats have similar problems, with breathing difficulties and watering eyes due to their very flat skulls. Some breeds of cow have problems giving birth because their calves are so big.

Figure 4 *Selective breeding for high milk yields, and a lot of inbreeding, means many dairy cattle have problems with their feet*

1 a Define selective breeding. [3 marks]
   b Explain why people have bred animals and plants selectively through the centuries. [4 marks]
2 a Explain why selective breeding reduces variation in the alleles of a breed of animals or plants. [3 marks]
   b Explain why variation is useful in a population. [3 marks]
   c Discuss the dangers of reducing the genetic variation in a population. [3 marks]
3 Explain, using an example, why inbreeding has caused health problems in some dog breeds. [6 marks]

Key points

- Selective breeding is a process by which humans breed plants and animals for desired characteristics (genetic traits).
- The genetic trait (characteristic) can be chosen for usefulness or appearance.
- Selective breeding involves choosing parents from a mixed population with the desired characteristic. They are bred together. From the offspring those with the desired characteristic are bred together. This continues over many generations until all the offspring show the desired characteristic.
- Selective breeding can lead to inbreeding, where some breeds are particularly prone to disease or inherited defects.

4.12.11 Genetic engineering

Learning objectives
After this topic, you should know:
- what genetic engineering is
- [H] how genes are transferred from one organism to another in genetic engineering to obtain a desired characteristic
- the potential benefits and problems associated with genetic engineering in agriculture and medicine.

Synoptic links
You learnt about bacteria in Topic 1.3.3, and about the use of insulin to treat diabetes in Topics 3.7.10 and 3.7.11.

Study tip
Don't confuse the vector used in genetic engineering with vectors as described in Topic 6.15.1 in the *Physical Sciences* book. The term 'vector' has different meanings in biology and in physics.

What is genetic engineering?
Genetic engineering involves modifying (changing) the genome of an organism. The gene for a desirable characteristic is cut out of one organism by enzymes and transferred to the genetic material in the cells of another organism that may, or may not, be of the same species. The gene is transferred using a **vector**, often a bacterial plasmid or a virus. This gives the genetically engineered organism a new, desirable characteristic. For example, plant crops have been genetically engineered to be resistant to certain diseases, or to produce bigger, better fruits.

Principles of genetic engineering
[Higher]

Genetic engineering involves changing the genetic material of an organism using the following process (Figure 1):

- Enzymes are used to isolate and cut out the required gene from an organism, for example, a person.
- The gene is then inserted into a vector (to carry it into the host cell) using more enzymes. The vector is usually a bacterial plasmid or a virus.
- The vector is then used to insert the gene into the required cells, which may be from bacteria, animals, fungi, or plants (Figure 1).
- Genes are transferred to the cells at an early stage of their development (in animals, the egg, or very early embryo). As the organism grows, it develops with the new, desired characteristics from the other organism. In plants, the desired genes are often inserted into meristem cells that are then used to produce identical clones of the genetically modified plant.

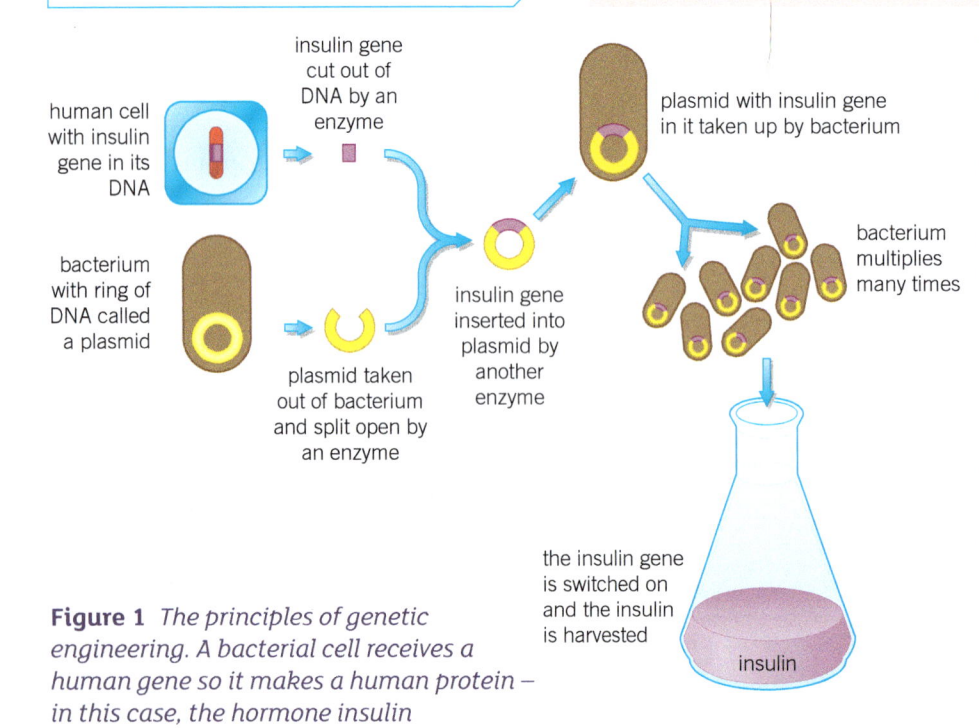

Transferring genes to animal and plant cells
Genetically engineered bacteria and fungi can be cultured on a large scale to make huge quantities of protein from other organisms, for example, human insulin and human growth hormone. There is, however, a limit to the proteins that bacteria can make. Scientists have now found that genes can be transferred to animal and plant cells as well as bacteria and fungi. New techniques are making genetic modification of a wide range of organisms easier all the time. For example, jellyfish genes have been used to produce crops that glow in the dark when they need watering. Examples of genetically modified

Figure 1 *The principles of genetic engineering. A bacterial cell receives a human gene so it makes a human protein – in this case, the hormone insulin*

276

4.12 Inheritance, variation, and evolution

animals include sheep that make complex human proteins in their milk, and mice that model human diseases, allowing scientists to learn more about both the diseases and possible treatments. However, it is with plants that most progress has been made.

Genetically modified crops

Crops that have had their genes modified by genetic engineering techniques are known as **genetically modified (GM)** crops. Genetically modified crops often show increased yields. For example, genetically modified crops include plants that are resistant to attack by insects because they have been modified to make their own pesticide. This means that more of the crops survive to provide food for people.

GM plants that are more resistant than usual to herbicides allow farmers to spray and kill weeds more effectively without damaging their crops. This increases the crop yield. Sometimes the genetic modification directly increases the size of the fruit or the nutritional value of the crop.

Increasing crop yields is extremely important in providing food security for the world's human population, which is growing all the time. For example:

- potatoes have been modified to make more starch and to be more resistant to several common pests
- soybeans have been modified to produce a healthier balance of fatty acids
- rice plants have been modified to withstand being completely covered in water for up to three weeks and still produce a good crop. Globally, 3.3 billion people rely on rice for their main food, and severe flooding in many rice-growing countries is becoming more common. This genetic modification could save millions of lives
- some GM grasses can absorb and break down explosive residues in the soil
- GM crops resistant to common diseases such as mosaic viruses and blights are being produced.

Sometimes GM crops contain genes from a completely different species, such as the jellyfish genes added to crop plants described earlier. Sometimes genetic modification simply speeds up normal selective breeding, by taking a gene from a closely related plant and inserting it into the genome, (e.g., flood-resistant rice). Many plant scientists hope that GM technologies will help to feed the world population. Perhaps GM plants can also remove more carbon dioxide from the atmosphere and solve the problems of global warming. As genetic engineering may also help to wipe out some human disorders, it is no wonder that scientists are excited by the technology.

Figure 2 *In many parts of the world, global warming is causing crop fields, such as those used for rice production, to flood. Flood-resistant GM rice offers hope to millions of people*

1 Explain what is meant by genetic engineering. [4 marks]
2 Give *three* examples of ways in which food crops have been genetically modified, and explain the advantage of each modification. [6 marks]
3 Ⓗ Draw a flow chart that explains the stages of transferring a gene for a shorter stem from one plant to another using a bacterial plasmid as a vector. [6 marks]

Key points

- Genetic engineering is a process that involves modifying the genome of an organism to introduce desirable characteristics.
- Genes can be transferred to the cells of animals and plants at an early stage of their development so that they develop desired characteristics. This is genetic engineering.
- Ⓗ In genetic engineering, genes from the chromosomes of humans and other organisms can be cut out using enzymes and transferred to the cells of bacteria and other organisms using a vector, which is usually a bacterial plasmid or a virus.
- Crops that have had their genes modified are known as genetically modified (GM) crops. GM crops often have improved resistance to insect attack or herbicides and generally produce a higher yield or increased nutritional content.

4.12.12 Ethics of genetic technologies

Learning objectives

After this topic, you should know:
- some of the concerns and uncertainties about new genetic technologies such as genetic engineering.

Go further

A new technique called gene editing has been developed. It makes it possible for scientists to make very precise changes in DNA itself. In 2016, UK researchers looked at the effect of using gene editing on very early human embryos. They were working on the cells that produce the placenta.

Synoptic link

You can remind yourself about genetic engineering in Topic 4.12.11.

Study tip

An ethical argument is one based on ethics. Ethics is a system of moral principles concerned with what is good for individuals and for society. People use ethics when they make decisions about how to live their lives. People make ethical judgements when they consider aspects of science such as genetic engineering.

One huge potential benefit of genetic engineering yet to be fully realised is its potential to cure inherited human disorders. Modern medical research is exploring ways of putting 'healthy' genes into affected cells using genetic modification, so that the cells work properly. Perhaps, in the future, the cells of an early embryo could be engineered so that the individual would develop into a healthy person unaffected by their inherited disorder. If these treatments become possible, many people would have new hope of a normal life for themselves or their children.

Gene therapy in humans has a long way to go. However, recently, scientists have had some very promising results whilst trying to find cures for diseases such as cystic fibrosis and a condition called macular degeneration that often results in blindness in older people.

The potential benefits of genetic engineering in agriculture and medicine are becoming more apparent all the time. There are, however, some concerns about using these new technologies before scientists fully understand any long-term impact they may have on individuals or on the environment.

Benefits of genetic engineering

People are already seeing many benefits from genetic engineering in medicine. Genetically engineered microorganisms can make the proteins humans need in large quantities and in a very pure form. For example, pure human insulin and human growth hormones are mass-produced using genetically engineered bacteria and fungi. Also, scientists can genetically modify mice so that they mimic human diseases. These mice are very useful in developing cures for conditions ranging from cancer to diabetes.

There are many advantages of genetic engineering in agriculture. These include:

- improved growth rates of plants and animals
- increased food value of crops, as genetically modified (GM) crops usually have much bigger yields than ordinary crops
- crops can be designed to grow well in dry, hot, or cold parts of the world
- crops can be engineered to produce plants that make their own pesticide or are resistant to the herbicides used to control weeds.

Short-stemmed GM crops, flood- and drought-resistant GM crops, and high-yielding, high-nutrition GM crops are already helping to solve the problems of world hunger. For example, almost 60% of the soybeans grown globally are GM strains.

4.12 Inheritance, variation, and evolution

Ever since genetically modified GM foods were first introduced, there has been controversy and discussion about them. For example, varieties of GM rice known as 'golden rice' and 'golden rice 2' have been developed (Figure 1). These varieties produce large amounts of vitamin A. Up to 500 000 children go blind each year as a result of lack of vitamin A in their diets. In theory, golden rice offers a solution to this problem but some people object to the way trials of the rice were run and to the cost of the product. As a result of this controversy, no golden rice is yet being grown in countries affected by vitamin A blindness.

Figure 1 *Yellow beta carotene is needed to make vitamin A in the body. The amount of beta carotene in golden rice and golden rice 2 is reflected in the depth of colour of the rice*

Concerns about genetic engineering

Genetic engineering is still a very new science, and no one can be sure what the long-term effects might be. For example, insects may become pesticide-resistant if they eat a constant diet of pesticide-forming plants.

Some people are concerned about the effect of eating GM food on human health. However, people eat a wide range of organisms with many different types of DNA every day as part of a normal diet. Our bodies have the enzymes needed to break down all sorts of DNA as part of normal digestion, so they should be able to deal with any extra genes.

Another concern is that genes from GM plants and animals might spread into the wildlife of the countryside. Some people are very anxious about the effect that these GM organisms might have on populations of wild flowers and insects. GM crops were often made infertile originally, which meant that farmers in poor countries had to buy new seed each year. Many people were unhappy with this practice. If these infertility genes spread into wild populations, this could cause major problems in the environment – although scientists are working hard to prevent this and there is little evidence so far of problems arising.

The majority of plant scientists believe that GM crops are the way forward and are probably the only way to solve the problem of feeding the world's expanding population and to cope with global warming.

Some of the main ethical objections to genetic engineering involve fears about human engineering. People may want to manipulate the genes of their future children to make sure that they are born healthy. There are also concerns that people might want to use this process to have 'designer' children with particular characteristics such as high intelligence or good looks. Genetic engineering raises issues for everyone to think about.

1. State *three* advantages of genetic engineering in agriculture. [3 marks]
2. One day genetic engineering may be used to cure human genetic disorders. Suggest how. [4 marks]
3. a Give a practical and an ethical argument for the use of genetic engineering. [4 marks]
   b Give a practical and an ethical argument against the use of genetic engineering. [4 marks]

Key points

- Modern medical research is exploring the possibility of genetic modification to overcome some inherited disorders.
- There are benefits and risks associated with genetic engineering in modern agriculture. These include the possible effect on wild flowers as a result of cross-pollination, and the possibility that insects might become resistant to pesticides.
- Some people have ethical objections to genetic engineering.

4.12 Inheritance, variation, and evolution

Summary questions

1 Amjid grew some purple-flowering pea plants from seeds he had bought at the garden centre. He planted them in his garden.
Here are his results:

Total seeds planted	247
Purple-flowered plants	242
White-flowered plants	1
Seeds not growing	4

  a Suggest the origin of the white-flowered plant. [3 marks]
  b Amjid was interested in these plants, so he collected the seed from some of the purple-flowered plants and used them in the garden the following year. He made a careful note of what happened.
Here are his results:

Total seeds planted	406
Purple-flowered plants	295
White-flowered plants	105
Seeds not growing	6

Amjid was slightly surprised. He did not expect to find that a third of his flowers would be white.
  (H) i The purple allele, P, is for the dominant phenotype and the allele for white flowers (p) is recessive. Draw a genetic diagram that explains Amjid's numbers of purple and white flowers. [5 marks]
  ii Compare the expected ratio of phenotypes suggested by the genetic diagram in b i with Amjid's actual results. [3 marks]
  c i Suggest another genetic cross that would confirm the genotype of the purple plants. [2 marks]
  (H) ii What results would you expect from this cross? [3 marks]

2 In 2003, two mules called Idaho Gem and Idaho Star were born in America. They were clones of a famous racing mule. They both seem very healthy. They were separated and sent to different stables to be reared and trained for racing. So far Idaho Gem has been more successful than his cloned brother, winning several races against ordinary racing mules. There is a third clone, Utah Pioneer, which has not been raced.
  a The mules are genetically identical. How do you explain the fact that Idaho Gem has beaten Idaho Star in several races? [2 marks]
  b Why do you think one of the clones is not being raced? [2 marks]
  c Scientists are carefully monitoring the clones' progress. Suggest the types of data scientists will need to collect to enable them to compare the three cloned animals as effectively as possible. [6 marks]
  d Many people are worried about using genetic engineering or cloning to produce racing animals, although they are happy with selective breeding that has been used for centuries. Suggest *two* possible concerns they might have. [4 marks]

3 a What is meant by the term GM crops? [2 marks]
  b Explain the main concerns of people about the use of GM crops around the world. [3 marks]
  c Most plant scientists believe GM technology will be the key to producing enough food to feed the world population. Explain how it can be used to achieve this aim. [6 marks]
  d One concern people have about GM crops is that they might cross-pollinate with wild plants. Scientists need to research how far pollen from a GM crop can travel to be able to answer these concerns.
Describe how a trial to investigate this might be set up. [6 marks]

4 a Define classification. [1 mark]
  b Explain two alternative ways of deciding how to classify an organism. [3 marks]
  c Discuss how ideas of classification have developed over time. [6 marks]

5 a What is a fossil? [2 marks]
  b Explain how rock fossils are formed. [3 marks]
  c Explain how ice fossils are formed. [2 marks]
  d Explain how fossils such as these can be used as evidence for the development of life on Earth. [6 marks]
  e Explain why fossils are of little use in helping us understand how life on Earth began. [3 marks]

6 a Describe how evolution takes place in terms of natural selection and speciation. [5 marks]
  b Explain the roles of isolation and genetic variation in the process of speciation. [6 marks]

4.12 Inheritance, variation, and evolution

Practice questions

01 Some characteristics are controlled by genes.

01.1 Corn colour is a genetically controlled characteristic. Each individual corn kernel is one offspring. Yellow kernels are caused by a recessive allele.
Figure 1 shows corn on the cob with some yellow corn kernels and some purple corn kernels.

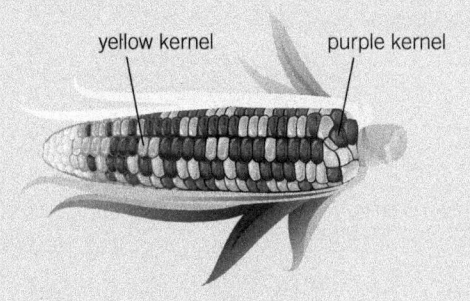

Figure 1

A student counted the number of yellow kernels and the number of purple kernels in a section of a corn cob. The results are shown in **Table 1**.

Table 1

Number of yellow corn	Number of purple corn
84	27

Calculate the ratio of yellow kernels to purple kernels. [1 mark]

01.2 ⓗ Based on the results in **Table 1** and the ratio of yellow kernels to purple kernels, draw a genetic diagram to show what the genotypes of the parents were.
Use the following symbols:
R = dominant allele
r = recessive allele [4 marks]

01.3 Describe the difference between a dominant allele and a recessive allele. [2 marks]

02 Land mines are a type of bomb. Bombs release very small amounts of chemicals that some animals can smell.
Bomb-sniffing rats have been selectively bred and used to find unexploded land mines. The rats are small and when the rats find a land mine, they scratch at the ground but do not cause the bombs to explode.

02.1 Describe how selective breeding could have been used to produce these bomb-sniffing rats. [4 marks]

02.2 Give **one** risk of selective breeding. [1 mark]

03 Read the information in the box opposite.

Insects can be both useful and harmful to crop plants.

Insects such as bees pollinate the flowers of some crop plants. Pollination is needed for successful sexual reproduction of crop plants.

Corn borers are insects that eat maize plants.

A toxin produced by the bacterium *Bacillus thuringiensis* kills insects.

Scientists grow *Bacillus thuringiensis* in large containers. The toxin is collected from the containers and is sprayed over maize crops to kill corn borers.

A company has developed genetically modified (GM) maize plants. GM maize plants contain a gene from *Bacillus thuringiensis*. This gene changes the GM maize plants so that they produce the toxin.

03.1 Describe how scientists can transfer the gene from *Bacillus thuringiensis* to maize plants. [3 marks]

03.2 Would you advise farmers to grow GM maize plants? Justify your answer by giving advantages and disadvantages of growing GM maize plants. Use the information from the box and your own knowledge to help you. [4 marks]
[AQA, 2015]

04 Human insulin is made using genetically modified bacteria. **Figure 2** shows the stages in modifying bacteria.

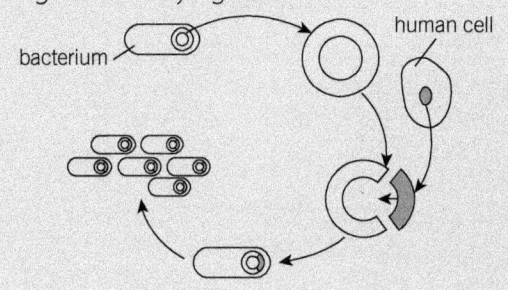

Figure 2

04.1 Describe how bacteria are modified to produce human insulin. [5 marks]

04.2 In a similar process, rye grass can be genetically engineered to have a high sugar content.
Some people might object to growing genetically engineered, high-sugar rye grass for feeding cattle. Suggest **two** reasons why. [2 marks]

281

Unit 4 in context

Gene technologies

Scientists are finding out more and more about DNA and genetics every day. The more they find out, the faster gene technologies are being developed. These involve scientists using knowledge of genetics and the genome to make life easier or better for people and for the environment. Some of these technologies have been around for a while but are no less amazing. Others are very new indeed.

DNA and crime

Unless you have an identical twin, your DNA will be unique to you. Other members of your family will have strong similarities in their DNA, but each individual has their own unique pattern. These unique patterns in your DNA can be used to identify you. A technique known as DNA profiling can be applied to make patterns from repeating sections of your DNA.

The DNA is broken down into small sections. A special process similar to chromatography is used to separate the sections. The sections are then stained. This gives a special image of repeating bars known as a DNA profile or DNA fingerprint (Figure 2).

These patterns are more similar between people who are related than between total strangers. They can be produced from very tiny samples of DNA from body fluids such as blood, saliva, and semen. The patterns of bars from one individual can be compared to the patterns from another. The likelihood of two identical samples coming from different people is millions to one. As a result, DNA fingerprinting is very useful in solving crimes. It can also be used to find the biological father of a child when there is doubt.

Originally the technique required a relatively big tissue sample to obtain enough DNA for the process to work. In recent years, another technique called PCR has enabled scientists to duplicate a DNA sample. Now it is possible to generate a DNA profile from a much smaller sample of material. As a result, detectives have been able to return to 'cold' cases and convict murderers and rapists years after they committed their crimes – criminals have been caught by DNA technology.

A DNA profile is not the same as a full genome sequence. In the future, as genome sequencing becomes faster and cheaper, we may be able to use it to identify criminals – leaving no room for doubt at all.

Genome sequencing saves lives

When the human genome was first sequenced, the process took years. Now the genome of a bacterium can be sequenced in hours and of a person in a couple of days. The technology is improving all the time, so the process is becoming faster, more repeatable and reproducible, and cheaper. Scientists and doctors are continuing to find new ways to use this amazing tool.

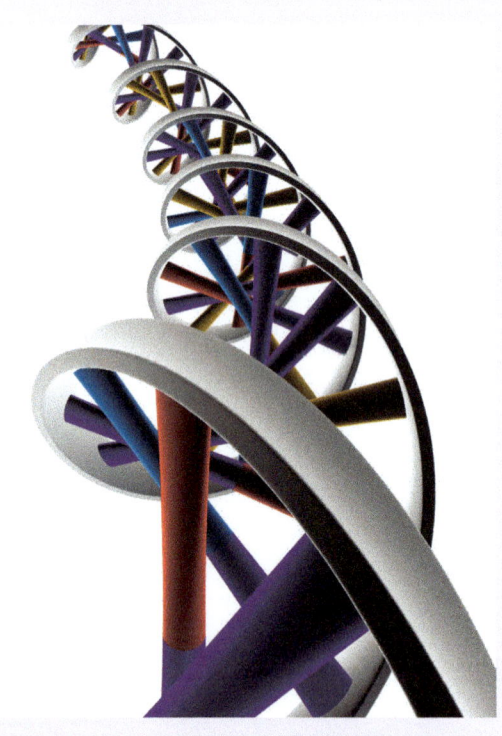

Figure 1 *DNA still holds many secrets, but scientists are getting closer to revealing the information stored within the twists of the double helix, shown here in a computer-generated model*

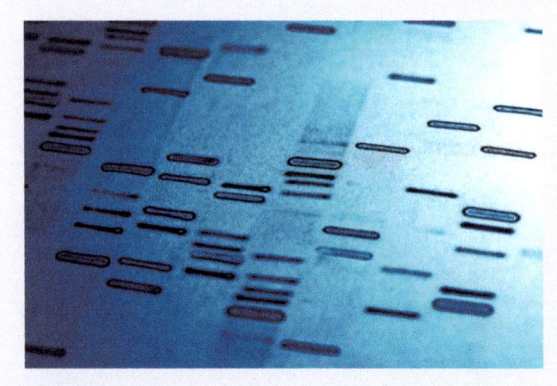

Figure 2 *The first time DNA fingerprinting was used to solve a crime, it identified Colin Pitchfork as the murderer of two teenage girls – and cleared an innocent man of the same crimes*

Case study 1

Doctors in a US hospital were in despair – a two-month-old baby boy was dying and they did not know why. His liver started to fail and everyone prepared for the worst. Then a research team tried a new superfast genome sequencing technique on the baby and his parents. It showed that he had inherited a rare mutation from both his parents linked to a disease in which the immune system is overactive and attacks the liver and spleen. Doctors gave the tiny baby drugs to reduce his immune response – and he is now at home and healthy.

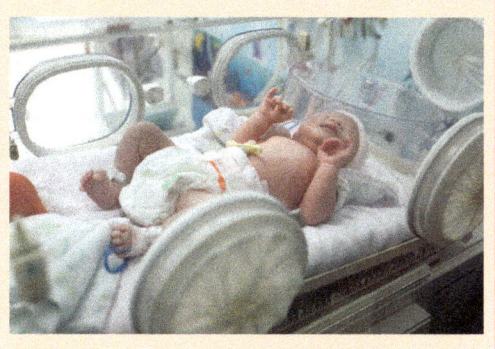

Figure 3 *Genome analysis will help doctors give more children a healthy future*

Every year thousands of newborn babies become very sick (and some die) with problems that their doctors cannot easily diagnose. New, fast genome sequencing of both babies and parents can help doctors to pinpoint the causes of many of these conditions. Often it helps them to treat them in the right way. Sometimes nothing can be done, but at least the cause of the problem is identified and that alone can be a comfort.

Case study 2

As you know, mutations in the DNA can cause cancer. There are many different types of cancers, and treating them can be difficult. A treatment often works for a time, and then becomes less effective.

Scientists at the Wellcome Genome Campus are doing some exciting work sequencing the genomes of both cancer patients and their tumours. They have discovered that while the genome of the patient remains constant, cancers don't stay still – they continue to mutate. This means that the cancer that doctors start treating is likely to mutate and become a different form of disease over time. This explains why cancers stop responding to treatment.

If doctors can analyse the cancer at intervals, they can spot new mutations and change the drugs used in treatment fast. Hopefully in the future this will make it possible to control and destroy tumours much more effectively and for much longer.

1 A known criminal is suspected of another crime. He has an identical twin who is completely innocent. Traditional fingerprinting can show which twin was involved, but DNA fingerprinting will be of no use at all. Explain why. [4 marks]

2 a Genome sequencing helped to save the life of the baby described in Case study 1. Explain why the baby was so ill when both of his parents were healthy. [3 marks]
  b **H** Choosing suitable letters for the alleles, draw a Punnett square to show how the baby inherited this rare disease. [5 marks]

3 The more scientists can learn about the genomes of people and pathogens, the more diseases they will be able to treat successfully. Discuss this statement. [6 marks]

Further practice questions

01 Table 1 shows information about different substances.

Table 1

Substance	Melting point in °C	Boiling point in °C	State of matter at 25 °C
chlorine	−101.5	−34.0	
sea water	−2.0	100.7	
sulfuric acid	10.3	337.0	
water	0.0	100.0	
zinc	419.5	907.0	

01.1 Copy and complete **Table 1** to show the state of matter for each substance at 25 °C. [2 marks]
01.2 Draw the particle model for a solid. [1 mark]
01.3 The density of copper is 8950 kg/m³. A student measured the mass of a block of copper. The mass of the block was 90.0 kg. Calculate the volume of the block. [2 marks]
01.4 The density of water is 1000 kg/m³. Explain why the density of copper is higher than the density of water. [3 marks]

02 **Figure 1** shows an animal cell.

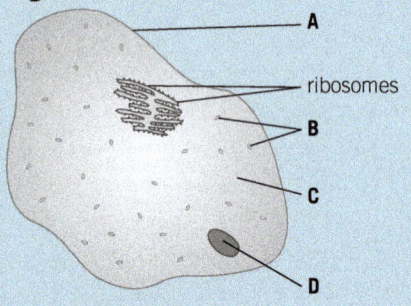

Figure 1

02.1 Which part (**A–D**) of the cell in **Figure 1** contains the DNA? [1 mark]
02.2 A scientist viewed DNA through an electron microscope. Explain why the scientist used an electron microscope. [2 marks]
02.3 (H) Chromosomes are made of DNA. Human body cells have 23 chromosomes. Rett syndrome is a rare sex-linked disorder. Most people with Rett syndrome are girls. A man and a woman have two boys and are expecting a third baby. Rett syndrome is a disorder that runs in the woman's family. The man and the woman think they are likely to have a girl because they already have two boys. Copy and complete the genetic diagram in **Figure 2** and give the probability of the man and woman having a girl.

Figure 2

[3 marks]

03 **Table 2** shows information about the particles that make up an atom.

Table 2

Name of particle	Relative mass	Charge
	1	
neutron		0
electron		

03.1 Copy and complete **Table 2**. [3 marks]
03.2 **Figure 3** shows information about carbon.

12
C
6

Figure 3

Use information in **Figure 3** to describe the structure of a carbon atom. [5 marks]
03.3 Carbon-13 is an isotope of carbon. How is an atom of carbon-13 different from the carbon shown in **Figure 3**? [1 mark]

04 Blood is made of different components. **Figure 4** shows the different components of blood.

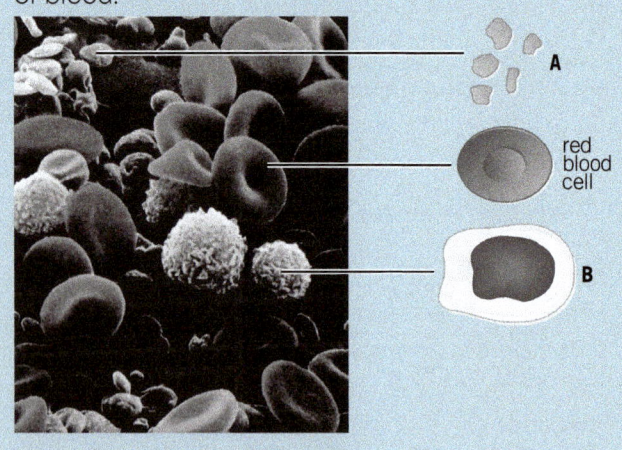

Figure 4

04.1 Name parts **A** and **B** in **Figure 4**. [2 marks]
04.2 Explain how the structure of a red blood cell is related to its function. [3 marks]

Further practice questions

04.3 The liquid part of the blood transports substances around the body.
Give **two** substances transported by the liquid part of the blood. [2 marks]

05 Radioactive sources emit ionising radiation. Ionising radiation is harmful as it can cause tumours to form within the body.

05.1 Describe the difference between benign and malignant tumours. [2 marks]

05.2 Describe how exposure to ionising radiation can lead to cancer. [2 marks]

05.3 Nuclear radiation can be used to treat brain tumours.
Explain how nuclear radiation can be used to treat brain tumours. [2 marks]

05.4 Chemotherapy is also used to treat cancer. Chemotherapy involves administering a poison into the patient.
The poison is absorbed by cancerous cells, where it causes cell damage.
Healthy cells within the body will also absorb some of the poison.
Suggest **two** advantages of using radiotherapy to treat cancer rather than chemotherapy. [2 marks]

06 Fertility can be controlled by a variety of hormonal and non-hormonal methods of contraception.
Table 3 shows some information about different methods of contraception.
Table 3

Type of contraception	Number of pregnancies per 100 women in one year
injection	6
implant	less than 1
diaphragm	12
not having sexual intercourse during ovulation	24
skin patch	9

06.1 Name **one** hormonal contraceptive method shown in **Table 3**. [1 mark]

06.2 Which type of contraception in **Table 3** is the most effective in preventing pregnancy? [1 mark]

06.3 Which type of contraception in **Table 3** would protect against sexually transmitted diseases? [1 mark]

07 A student conducts an experiment to determine the specific heat capacity of water.
The student sets up the apparatus as shown in **Figure 5**.

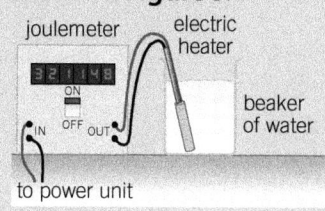

Figure 5

07.1 Name **two** other pieces of equipment that the student will need in order to determine the specific heat capacity of the water. [2 marks]

07.2 What readings should the student take in order to calculate the specific heat capacity of the water? [3 marks]

07.3 Write the equation that the student should use to determine the specific heat capacity of the water. [1 mark]

07.4 Using his results, the student calculated the specific heat capacity of the water correctly.
His value was 4700 J/kg°C.
The accepted value for the specific heat capacity of water is 4200 J/kg°C.
Suggest **three** reasons why the value calculated by the student was higher than the accepted value. [3 marks]

07.5 Suggest **two** improvements that the student could make to the experiment to get more accurate results.
Give a reason for each improvement. [4 marks]

07.6 Hot-water bottles are used to keep people warm in bed.
A new type of hot-water bottle is being produced that uses an alternative liquid to water.
The hot-water bottle is sealed and is heated in a microwave until it is warm.
The manufacturer has a choice of four liquids to use in the hot-water bottle.
Properties of the four liquids are shown in **Table 4**.

Further practice questions

Table 4

Liquid	Specific heat capacity in J/kg°C	Boiling point in °C
A	1790	130
B	4100	110
C	2512	225
D	4400	43

Which liquid, **A**, **B**, **C**, or **D**, would be best suited for use in the hot-water bottle? Explain your answer. [3 marks]

08 A group of students investigated the effect of five different concentrations of sugar on potato chips.

The students:
- cut five potato chips of the same size from one potato
- dried the outside of each chip
- recorded the starting mass of each chip
- placed one chip in each of the five concentrations of sugar solution
- removed the chips after 30 minutes and dried the outside of each potato chip
- recorded the final mass of each potato chip.

Figure 6 shows how the investigation was set up.

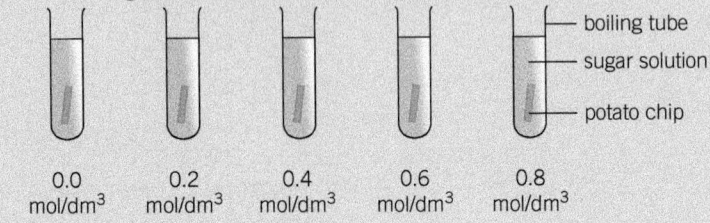

0.0 mol/dm³   0.2 mol/dm³   0.4 mol/dm³   0.6 mol/dm³   0.8 mol/dm³

Figure 6

08.1 Give **two** variables the students controlled in this investigation. [2 marks]

08.2 The teacher said the students should have carried out the experiment three times at each concentration.
Give **one** reason why. [1 mark]

08.3 **Table 5** shows the students' results.

Table 5

Sugar concentration in mol/dm³	Starting mass in g	Final mass in g	Percentage change in mass
0.0	1.13	1.35	19.5
0.2	1.03	1.10	6.8
0.4	1.19	1.10	−7.6
0.6	1.14	0.89	−21.9
0.8	1.05	0.70	

Calculate the percentage change in mass for the 0.8 mol/dm³ sugar concentration. [3 marks]

08.4 The data from **Table 5** is displayed in the graph in **Figure 7**.

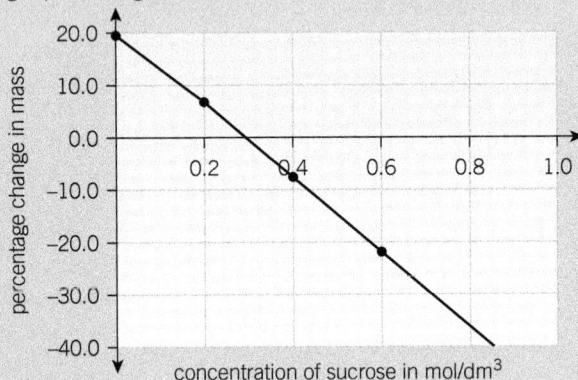

Figure 7

08.4 Use **Figure 7** to predict the concentration of sugar inside the potato cells. [1 mark]

08.5 Explain what happened to the potato chip in the 0.4 mol/dm³ sugar solution. [4 marks]

09 Chromatography can be used to study the composition of mixtures.

Figure 8 shows the results of chromatography on three samples of a chlorophyll.

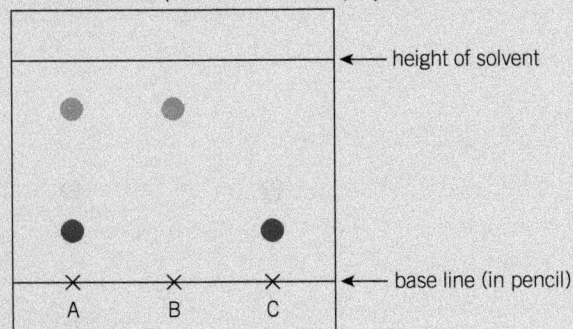

Figure 8

Which of the three samples, **A**, **B**, or **C**, is a pure sample?
Give a reason for your answer. [2 marks]

■ Further practice questions

10 Materials from living organisms are cycled through the ecosystem.
Explain how the materials in dead animals can become the new growth in a plant leaf. [6 marks]

11 The traces of radioactive substances in food and drink are due to tiny quantities of radioactive isotopes that occur in many natural substances.

11.1 Explain why radioactive isotopes are hazardous. [4 marks]

11.2 Smoke alarms contain a small amount of Americium-241 inside a sealed unit. Americium-241 emits alpha particles. Although the Americium-241 is hazardous, the risk of harm is low.
Explain how the Americium-241 can be both hazardous and low-risk. [2 marks]

12 Sodium lamps are often used in street lights.
Sodium lamps have an electric current that passes through vapourised sodium in the lamp. As a result, the sodium vapour becomes very hot and it emits light.
Describe how the sodium atoms emit light. [3 marks]

13 Match each key word to its definition.

Key word	Definition
	two alleles are different
gene	two alleles are the same
heterozygous	a small section of DNA on a chromosome
homozygous	all the genes present in an individual organism
phenotype	the observable appearance of an organism

[4 marks]

14 Evolution of bacteria happens in a much shorter time than evolution in other animals.
Explain how bacteria have evolved to become resistant to some antibiotics. [4 marks]

Maths skills for Synergy
MS 1 Arithmetic and numerical computation

Learning objectives

After this topic, you should know how to:
- recognise and use expressions in decimal form
- recognise and use expressions in standard form
- use ratios, fractions, and percentages
- make estimates of the results of simple calculations.

How big is a human cell? If one bacterium starts dividing, how many will there be in 24 hours? What is the probability that a child will inherit dimples from its parents?

Scientists use maths all the time – when collecting data, looking for patterns, and making conclusions. This chapter will support you in developing the key maths skills you need during your *GCSE Combined Science: Synergy* course. The rest of the book gives you many opportunities to practise using maths when it is needed in science.

1a Decimal form

There will always be a whole number of atoms in a molecule, and a whole number of protons, neutrons, or electrons in an atom.

When you make measurements in science the numbers may not be whole numbers, but numbers *in between* whole numbers. These are numbers in decimal form, for example, the height of a boy could be 177.8 cm, or the mass of a soil sample could be 25.5 g.

The value of each digit in a number is called its place value.

thousands	hundreds	tens	units	.	tenths	hundredths	thousandths
4	5	1	2	.	3	4	5

1b Standard form

Place value can help you to understand the size of a number, however some numbers in science are too large or too small to understand when they are written as ordinary numbers. Some numbers are very large, like the number of cells in your body. Other numbers are very small, such as the size of a bacterium or a virus.

Standard form is used to show very large or very small numbers more easily. In standard form, a number is written as $A \times 10^n$.

- A is a decimal number between 1 and 10 (but not including 10), for example 7.0.
- n is a whole number. The power of ten can be positive or negative, for example 10^6 or 10^{-6}.

Remember to add the unit if applicable, for example, a distance measurement could have the unit m (for metres).

This gives you a number in standard form, for example, 7.0×10^{-6} m. This is the diameter of a single human red blood cell.

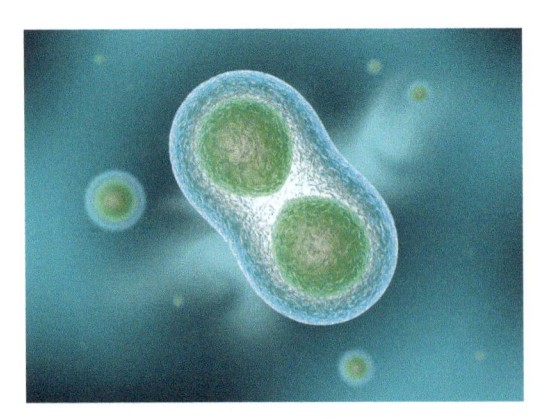

Figure 1 *Cells divide at different rates*

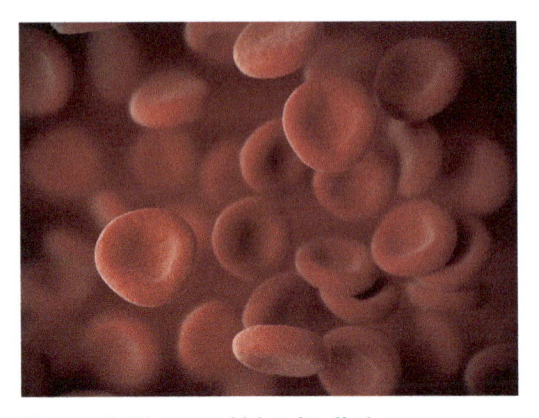

Figure 2 *These red blood cells have a diameter of approximately 7.0×10^{-6} m*

Table 1 explains how you convert numbers to standard form.

Table 1 *Converting numbers into standard form*

The number	The number in standard form	What you did to get to the decimal number	...so the power of ten is...	What the *sign* of the power of ten tells you
1000 m	1.0×10^3 m	You moved the decimal point three places to the *left* to get the decimal number	+3	The positive power shows the number is *greater* than one.
0.01 s	1.0×10^{-2} s	You moved the decimal point two places to the *right* to get the decimal number	−2	The negative power shows the number is *less* than one.

100 000 000 bacteria per cm³ of culture solution = 1.0×10^8 bacteria per cm³ of culture solution.

Multiplying numbers in standard form

You can use a scientific calculator for calculations using numbers written in standard form. You should work out which button you need to use on your own calculator (it could be `EE`, `EXP`, `10ˣ`, or `x10ˣ`).

> **Study tip**
> Check that you understand the power of ten, and the sign of the power.

> **Study tip**
> 1.0×10^8 m is the same as 10^8 m.

> **Worked example: Standard form**
>
> 1 mm³ of blood contains around 5 000 000 red blood cells (rbcs).
>
> How many red blood cells would there be in a standard blood donation of 470 cm³?
>
> **Solution**
>
> **Step 1:** 470 cm³ = 470 000 mm³
>
> Convert the numbers to standard form.
>
> 5 000 000 = 5×10^6 and 470 000 = 4.7×10^5
>
> **Step 2:** Calculate the total number of red blood cells in a blood donation.
>
> Total number of red blood cells = number of red blood cells/mm³ × mm³ blood
> = (5×10^6 rbcs/mm³) × (4.7×10^5 mm³ blood)
> = (5×4.7) × ($10^6 \times 10^5$) rbcs
> = 23.5×10^{11} rbcs
>
> In standard form = **2.35×10^{12}** red blood cells per blood donation

Figure 3 *You can use a scientific calculator to do calculations involving standard form*

MS 1 Arithmetic and numerical computation

1c Ratios, fractions, and percentages

Ratios

A **ratio** compares two quantities. A ratio of 2 : 20 of foxes to chickens means that for every two foxes, there are 20 chickens.

You can compare ratios by changing them to the form 1 : n or n : 1.

1 : n   Divide both numbers by the *first* number.
For every one fox there are ten chickens.

$$\div 2 \begin{pmatrix} 2:20 \\ 1:10 \end{pmatrix} \div 2$$

n : 1   Divide both numbers by the *second* number.
For every tenth of a fox there is one chicken (even though you can't really get 'a tenth of a fox').

$$\div 20 \begin{pmatrix} 2:20 \\ 0.1:1 \end{pmatrix} \div 20$$

You can describe the foxes in relation to the number of chickens using three different ratios, 2 : 20, 1 : 10, and 0.1 : 1. All these ratios are equivalent – they mean the same thing.

You can simplify a ratio so that both numbers are the lowest whole numbers possible.

> **Worked example: Simplifying ratios**
>
> In an investigation to look at the effect of pH on the rate of enzyme action, a student mixed 15 cm³ of acid with 90 cm³ of water. Calculate the simplest ratio of the volume of acid to the volume of water.
>
> **Solution**
> Step 1: Write down the ratio of acid : water.
> Step 2: Both 15 and 90 have a common factor, 5. $\div 5 \begin{pmatrix} 15:90 \\ 3:18 \end{pmatrix} \div 5$
> Divide both numbers by 5.
> Step 3: Both 3 and 18 have a common factor, 3. $\div 3 \begin{pmatrix} 3:18 \\ 1:6 \end{pmatrix} \div 3$
> Divide both numbers by 3.
>
> To get the simplest form of the ratio, you have divided by 15 (i.e., 3 × 5), which is the highest common factor of 15 and 90.

Synoptic link

To see examples of how scientists find ratios useful, see look at Topics 2.5.3, 4.12.2, and 4.12.3.

Fractions

A **fraction** is a part of a whole.

$\frac{1}{3}$ → The numerator tells you how many parts of the whole you have.
→ The denominator tells you how many equal parts the whole has been divided into.

To convert a fraction into a decimal, divide the numerator by the denominator.

$\frac{1}{3} = 1 \div 3 = 0.33333\ldots = 0.\dot{3}$ (the dot shows that the number 3 recurs, or repeats over and over again).

To convert a decimal to a fraction, use the place value of the digits to write the decimal as a fraction, then simplify. $0.045 = \frac{45}{1000} = \frac{9}{200}$

> **Worked example: Calculating the fraction of a quantity**
>
> A student has a 25 g sample of glucose. Calculate the mass of $\frac{2}{5}$ of this sample.
>
> **Solution**
> $\frac{2}{5}$ of 25 g = $\frac{2}{5}$ × 25 g
> Step 1: Divide the total mass of the sample by the denominator.
> $\frac{25 \text{ g}}{5} = 5 \text{ g}$
> Step 2: Multiply by the numerator.
> 5 g × 2 = **10 g**

■ Maths skills for Synergy

Percentages

A **percentage** is a number expressed as a fraction of 100.

$77\% = \frac{77}{100}$

Worked example: Calculating a percentage

In an area of 75 cm² on a rocky shore a student found that 27.3 cm² was covered by mussels. Calculate the percentage of the rock covered by mussels on this site.

Solution

$$\text{percentage of rock covered in mussels} = \left(\frac{\text{area covered in mussels}}{\text{area of sample}}\right) \times 100\%$$

$$= \frac{27.3 \text{ cm}^2}{75 \text{ cm}^2} \times 100\% = \mathbf{36.4\%}$$

Figure 4 *What is the percentage coverage of these mussels on a rocky shore?*

You may need to calculate a percentage of a quantity.

Worked example: Using a percentage to calculate a quantity

The biomass of the primary consumers in a food chain is 1500 kg. Only 11% of this biomass forms new material in the secondary consumers. Calculate the mass of material forming in new secondary consumers.

Solution

Step 1: Convert the percentage to a decimal.

$$11\% = \frac{11}{100} = 0.11$$

Step 2: Multiply the answer to **Step 1** by the total biomass in the primary consumers.

$$0.11 \times 1500 \text{ kg} = \mathbf{165 \text{ kg}}$$

You may need to calculate a percentage increase or decrease in a quantity from its original value.

Worked example: Calculating a percentage change

A student heats a 4.75 g sample of copper(II) carbonate and finds that its mass decreases to 3.04 g. Calculate the percentage change in mass.

Solution

Step 1: Calculate the decrease in mass.

$$4.75 \text{ g} - 3.04 \text{ g} = 1.71 \text{ g}$$

Step 2: Divide the decrease in mass by the original mass.

$$\frac{1.71 \text{ g}}{4.75 \text{ g}} = 0.36$$

Step 3: Convert the decimal to a percentage.

$$0.36 \times 100\% = \mathbf{36\%}$$

Remember that in this case the answer is a percentage *decrease*.

MS 1 Arithmetic and numerical computation

1d Estimating the result of a calculation

When you use your calculator to work out the answer to a calculation you can sometimes press the wrong button and get the wrong answer. The best way to make sure that your answer is correct is to estimate it in your head first.

> **Worked example: Estimating an answer**
> A photosynthesising plant produces gas at a constant rate of 0.34 mm^3/min. How much gas is produced after eight minutes?
>
> **Solution**
> Find 0.34 mm^3/min × 8 min. Estimate the answer and then calculate it.
>
> **Step 1:** Round each number up or down to get a whole-number multiple of 10.
> 0.34 mm^3/min is about 0.3 mm^3/min   8 min is about 10 min
>
> **Step 2:** Multiply the numbers in your head.
> 0.3 mm^3/min × 10 min = 3 mm^3
>
> **Step 3:** Do the calculation and check that it is close to your estimate.
> 0.34 mm^3/min × 8 min = **2.72 mm^3**
> This is quite close to your estimate of 3 mm^3, so it is probably correct.
>
> Notice that you could do other things with the numbers:
> 0.34 + 8 = 8.34 $\frac{0.34}{8}$ = 0.0425   8 − 0.34 = 7.66
>
> Not one of these numbers is close to 3. If you got any of these numbers you would know that you needed to repeat the calculation.

> **Study tip**
> When carrying out multiplications or divisions using standard form, you should add or subtract the powers of ten to work out roughly what you expect the answer to be. This will help you to avoid mistakes.

Sometimes the calculations involve more complicated equations, or standard form.

1. If the diameter of cell is 1.25×10^7 μm when viewed under an electron microscope at a magnification of ×500 000, what is the actual diameter of the cell? [1 mark]

2. **a** The concentration of a weak glucose solution was given as 0.000038 mol/dm^3. Express this concentration in standard form. [1 mark]

   b Bacteria in a fermenter produce human insulin at a rate of about 5×10^2 tonnes every year. If this rate is maintained, how many years will it take the bacteria to produce 1.25×10^4 tonnes? [1 mark]

3. **a** Students carried out several crosses between the same pair of black mice. Adding up all of the offspring they found that they had 17 brown mice and 51 black mice. What is the simplest ratio of these offspring? [1 mark]

   b In a sample of 350 wheat plants, students discovered that only 24% of them were healthy. The rest had been attacked by wheat rust or other pests. How many plants were diseased? [1 mark]

   c The approximate percentage of oxygen gas in the air is 20%. Express this percentage as a fraction. [1 mark]

MS 2 Handling data

2a Significant figures

Numbers are rounded when it is necessary to give an exact answer.

When rounding to significant figures, count from the first non-zero digit.

These masses each have three **significant figures (s.f.)**. The s.f. are underlined in each case.

$\underline{153}$ g   0.$\underline{153}$ g   0.00$\underline{153}$ g

Table 1 shows some more examples of measurements given to different numbers of s.f.

In general, you should give your answer to the same number of s.f. as the data in the question that has the lowest number of s.f.

Remember that rounding to s.f. is *not* the same as decimal places. When rounding to decimal places, count the number of digits that follow the decimal point.

Worked example: Significant figures
Calculate the rate of an enzyme-controlled reaction that gives off 25 cm³ of gas in 7.85 s.

Solution

Step 1: Write down what you know.

volume of gas given off = 25 cm³ (2 s.f.)   time = 7.85 s (3 s.f.)

You should give your answer to 2 s.f.

Step 2: Write down the equation that links the quantities you know and the quantity you want to find.

$$\text{mean rate of reaction (cm}^3\text{/s)} = \frac{\text{amount of product formed (cm}^3\text{)}}{\text{time } t \text{ (s)}}$$

Step 3: Substitute values into the equation.

$$\text{speed} = \frac{25 \text{ cm}^3}{7.85 \text{ s}}$$

= 3.184 713 375 cm³/s (too many s.f.)

= **3.2 cm³/s** (2 s.f.)

Learning objectives

After this topic, you should know how to:
- use an appropriate number of significant figures
- find arithmetic means
- construct and interpret frequency tables and bar charts
- make order of magnitude calculations.

Table 1 *The number of significant figures – the significant figures in each case are underlined*

Number	0.0$\underline{5}$ s	$\underline{5.1}$ nm	0.$\underline{775}$ g/s	$\underline{23.50}$ cm³
Number of significant figures	1	2	3	4

2b Arithmetic means

To calculate the **mean** of a series of values:

1 Add together all the values in the series to get a total.
2 Divide the total by the number of values in the data series.

You will often need to do this with your sets of repeat readings when conducting investigations. This helps you to obtain more accurate data from sets of repeat readings where you have some random measurement errors.

293

MS 2 Handling data

Figure 1 *What is the mean height of this group?*

Table 2 *A frequency table for the blood group of 25 people*

Blood group	Frequency
A	10
B	3
AB	1
O	11

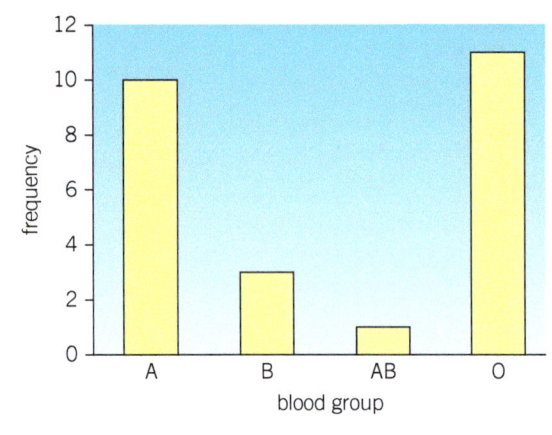

Figure 2 *Blood group O is the most common*

Study tip
Remember to leave a gap between each bar in a bar chart.

Table 3 *The frequency table for the pulse rate of 30 people*

Pulse rate in beats/min	Frequency
60–64	1
65–69	4
70–74	12
75–79	8
80–84	5
85–89	1

Worked example: Calculating a mean
A student wanted to measure the mean height of a group of five students.

Their results were as follows:

  162 cm   159 cm   169 cm   157 cm   163 cm

Calculate the mean height of the group.

Solution

Step 1: Add together the recorded values.

  162 cm + 159 cm + 169 cm + 157 cm + 163 cm = 810 cm

Step 2: Then divide by the number of recorded values (in this case, there are five students).

$$\frac{810}{5} = 162 \text{ cm (3 s.f.)}$$

The mean height of the group was **162 cm** (3 s.f.)

2c Frequency tables, bar charts, and histograms
Frequency tables and bar charts
The word data describes observations and measurements that are made during experiments or research.

Qualitative data is non-numerical data, such blood groups.

The frequency table (Table 2) shows the blood group of 25 people.

The height of the bars in the bar chart (Figure 2) represent the frequency of each category. Note the spaces between each bar.

You can also use bar charts to compare two or more independent variables.

Frequency tables and histograms
Quantitative data is numerical measurements.

Discrete data can only take exact values (usually collected by counting).

The frequency table (Table 3) shows the pulse rate of 30 people. The measurements are grouped into equal classes.

- make sure that the values in each class do not overlap
- aim for a sensible number of classes – usually no more than six.

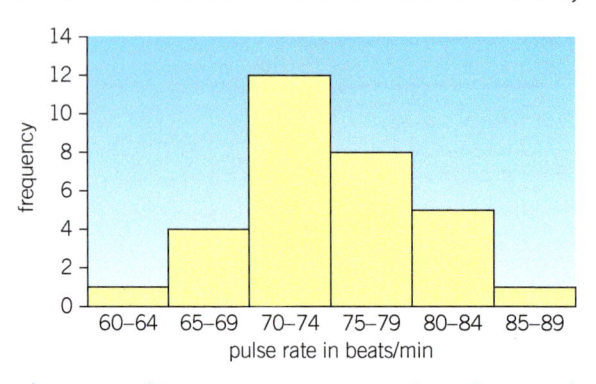

Figure 3 *A histogram to represent the pulse rate data*

294

■ Maths skills for Synergy

Continuous data can take any value (usually collected by measuring), such as mass, volume, or density.

Continuous data can also be displayed on a histogram. Look at the frequency table below (Table 4) and the histogram displaying the frequency data (Figure 4).

Table 4 *The frequency data for the heights of a type of plant in a field*

Height of plants, h in cm	Frequency
$0 \leq h < 10$	40
$10 \leq h < 20$	15
$20 \leq h < 30$	20
$30 \leq h < 40$	30
$40 \leq h < 50$	20

A histogram is similar to a bar chart, except that its classes and bars may have unequal widths.

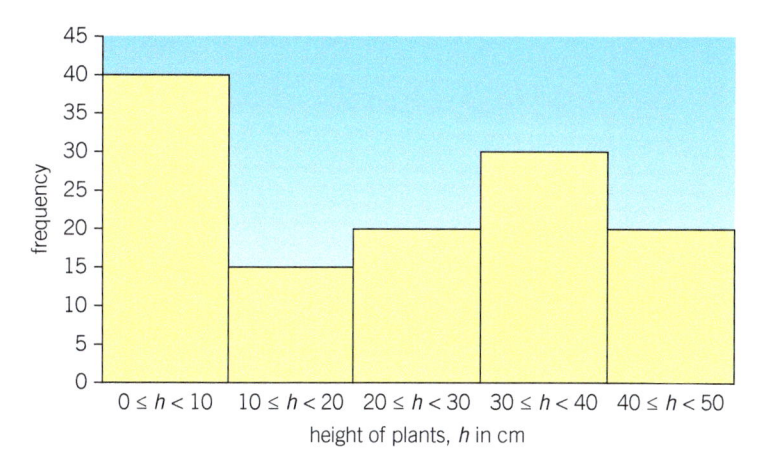

Figure 4 *A histogram to represent the plant height data*

You should be aware that in maths lessons you will meet a different type of histogram, in which:

- The frequency of each class is represented by the area of each bar, not the height of each bar.
- The vertical axis is labelled as the frequency *density*, not the frequency.
- The class widths are not equal.

Worked example: Calculating frequency density

A student investigated the heights of a type of plant in a small field.

Step 1: Calculate each class width.

Step 2: Use the formula frequency density = $\frac{\text{frequency}}{\text{class width}}$ to calculate the frequency density

Height of plants, h in cm	Frequency	Class width	Frequency density
$0 \leq h < 20$	40	$20 - 0 = 20$	$\frac{40}{20} = 2.0$
$20 \leq h < 30$	15	$30 - 20 = 10$	$\frac{15}{10} = 1.5$
$30 \leq h < 50$	20	$50 - 30 = 20$	$\frac{20}{20} = 1.0$
$50 \leq h < 60$	30	$60 - 50 = 10$	$\frac{30}{10} = 3.0$
$60 \leq h < 100$	20	$100 - 60 = 40$	$\frac{20}{40} = 0.5$

The frequency density data is displayed on a 'maths-style' histogram in Figure 5.

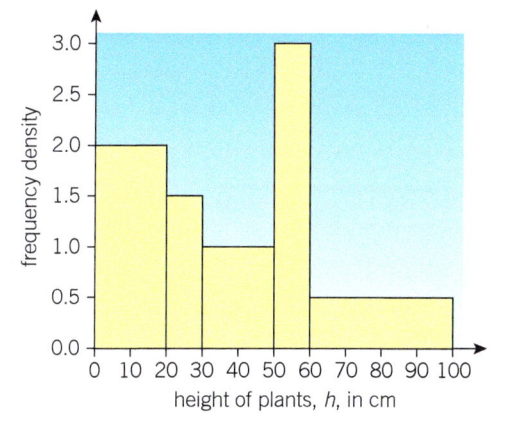

Figure 5 *The type of histogram used in maths to display frequency density*

295

MS 2 Handling data

Worked example: Estimating animal population size

Scientists used the capture-recapture technique to estimate the grey seal population in an area off the coast of Wales.

First sample: 50 seals

Second sample: 40 unmarked seals and 5 marked seals

Estimate the population size.

Solution
Step 1: Write out the formula.

$$\text{estimated population size} = \frac{\text{first sample size} \times \text{second sample size}}{\text{number of recaptured marked individuals}}$$

Step 2: Enter the data.

$$\text{estimated population size} = \frac{50 \times 45}{5}$$

Step 3: Work out the answer.

Estimated population size = **450 seals**

Figure 5 *Scientists use the capture-recapture technique to estimate the population of grey seals*

Synoptic link
You can find examples of how scientists use sampling techniques in Topic 4.11.6.

2d Sampling

Sampling means taking a smaller number of observations or measurements from a larger population or area. You can scale up the sample to make estimates about the larger area.

You may want to estimate the abundance (number) of selected organisms on your school field. The population of animals in an area can be estimated using the capture-recapture technique. This technique scales up the results from a small sample area to estimate a population. To do this:

1. Capture organisms from a sample area.
2. Mark individual organisms, then release back into the community.
3. At a later date, recapture organisms in the original sample area.
4. Record the number of marked and unmarked individuals.
5. Estimate the population size using the formula:
$$\text{estimated population size} = \frac{\text{first sample size} \times \text{second sample size}}{\text{number of recaptured marked individuals}}$$

Estimating plant populations from a sample
To work out the plant population in an area:

1. Mark a small area of land (1 m² is often ideal). Record the type and number of organisms in the area.
2. Take a number of samples of the area, and calculate the mean population for each organism present. The larger the number of samples taken, the more repeatable and reproducible your results.
3. To work out the total population of an organism use the formula:
estimated population size = mean population per unit area × total area

Worked example: Estimating plant population size

Students looked at five 1 m² areas of the school garden. They found that each area had two buttercup plants. Estimate the population of buttercup plants in the 60 m² school garden.

Solution
Step 1: Write out the formula.

estimated population size = mean population per unit area (/m²) × total area (m²)

Step 2: Enter the data.

estimated population size = 2/m² × 60 m²

Step 3: Work out the answer.

estimated population size = **120 buttercup plants**

2e Probability

The probability of an event occurring tells you how likely it is for the event to happen. A probability can be written as a percentage, a decimal, or a fraction.

Table 4 shows some probabilities you might come across when looking at genetic crosses.

Worked example: Calculating probability

A student did a survey of students with straight and curved thumbs in his class. 15 students had curved thumbs, and 10 students had straight thumbs. Calculate the probability that a student has curved thumbs.

Solution

Step 1: Calculate the total number of students sampled.

number of students sampled = 15 + 10 = 25

Step 2: Calculate the percentage of curved-thumbed students.

percentage of students with curved thumbs

$$= \frac{\text{number of students with curved thumbs} \times 100\%}{\text{total number of students}}$$

$$= \frac{15 \times 100\%}{25} = 60\%$$

The probability that a student in this class has curved thumbs is **60%**.

Table 4 *Probabilities in genetic crosses*

Probability	Fraction	Percentage
4 out of 4	$\frac{4}{4} = 1$	100%
3 out of 4	$\frac{3}{4}$	75%
2 out of 4	$\frac{2}{4} = \frac{1}{2}$	50%
1 out of 4	$\frac{1}{4}$	25%
0 out of 4	$\frac{0}{4} = 0$	0%

Synoptic link

You can find examples of these types of calculations in Topic 4.12.3.

2f Averages

When you collect data, it is sometimes useful to calculate an average. There are three ways in which you can calculate an average – the mean, the mode, and the median.

You saw how to calculate a mean in MS 2b.

How to calculate a median

When you put the values of a series in order from smallest to biggest, the middle value is called the **median**.

Figure 6 *Whether your thumb is curved or straight is controlled by a single gene*

Worked example: Calculating a median (odd number of values)

The thicknesses of seven oak leaves are shown below.

0.8 mm 1.2 mm 0.9 mm 0.9 mm 0.8 mm 1.2 mm 1.0 mm

Calculate the median thickness of the leaves.

Solution

Step 1: Place the values in order from smallest to largest.

0.8 mm 0.8 mm 0.9 mm 0.9 mm 1.0 mm 1.2 mm 1.2 mm

Step 2: Select the middle value – this is the median value.

median value = **0.9 mm**

If you have an even number of values, you select the middle pair of values and calculate their mean. This then becomes your median value.

How to calculate a mode

The **mode** is the value that occurs most often in a series of results. If there are two values that are equally common, the data is bimodal.

Figure 7 *What is the median height of these plants?*

MS 2 Handling data

> **Synoptic link**
> You can find examples of how scientists use these calculations in Topic 4.11.6.

> **Worked example: Calculating a mode**
> The masses of some invertebrates that fell into a pitfall trap are given below.
>
> 3.6g 4.2g 8.3g 6.5g 4.1g 4.2g 3.6g 4.2g 5.2g 3.2g 5.9g 3.2g
>
> Calculate the modal mass of the invertebrates collected.
>
> **Solution**
> **Step 1:** Place the values in order from smallest to largest.
>
> 3.2g 3.2g 3.6g 3.6g 4.1g 4.2g 4.2g 4.2g 5.2g 5.9g 6.5g 8.3g
>
> **Step 2:** Select the value that occurs the most often.
>
> mode = 4.2g

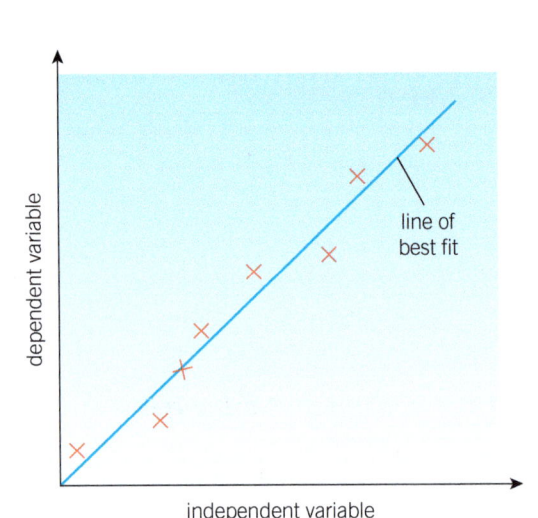

Figure 8 *A scatter graph*

> **Study tip**
> Use a transparent ruler to help you draw the line of best fit so that you can make sure that there are the same number of points on either side of the line.

2g Scatter diagrams and correlations

You may collect data and plot a scatter graph (see MS 4). You can add a line to show the trend of the data, called a line of best fit. The line of best fit is a line that goes through as many points as possible and has the same number of points above and below it.

If the gradient of the line of best fit is:

positive it means as the independent variable *increases* the dependent variable *increases*

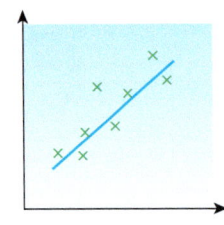

negative it means as the independent variable *increases* the dependent variable *decreases*

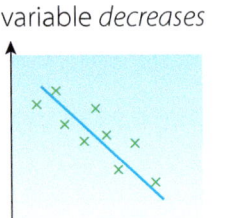

zero it means changing the independent variable has no effect on the dependent variable.

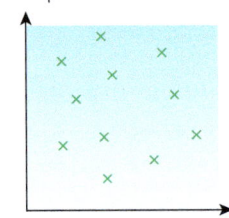

A relationship where there happens to be a link is called a correlational relationship, or **correlation**. You say that the relationship between the variables is positive, negative, or that there is no relationship.

For example:

- As you increase the light intensity, the rate of photosynthesis increases – a positive correlation.
- As the number of predators in a habitat increases, the number of prey decreases – a negative correlation.
- The colour of your hair has no effect on the likelihood that you will develop cancer – no relationship.

The presence of a relationship does not always mean that changing the independent variable *causes* the change in the dependent variable. In order to claim a causal relationship, you must use science to predict or explain *why* changing one variable affects the other.

Often there is a third factor that is common to both, which makes it look as if they are related. You could collect data for shark attacks and ice cream sales. A graph shows a positive correlation, but shark attacks do not make people buy ice cream. Both are more likely to happen in the summer.

2h Estimates and order of magnitude

Being able to make a rough estimate is helpful. It can help you to check that a calculation is correct by knowing roughly what you expect the answer to be. A simple estimate is an **order of magnitude** estimate, which is an estimate to the nearest power of 10.

For example, to the nearest power of 10, you are probably 1 m tall and can run at 10 m/s.

You, your desk, and your chair are all of the order of 1 m tall. The diameter of a molecule is of the order of 1×10^{-9} m, or 1 nanometre.

1. How many s.f. are the following numbers quoted to?
   a 13.0 [1 mark]   b 0.07 [1 mark]
   c 560 [1 mark]   d 10.13 [1 mark]
   e 0.999 [1 mark]   f 7×10^8 [1 mark]
   g 2.605×10^{-3} [1 mark]   h 1.01×10^{14} [1 mark]

2. A student was testing how rapidly the carbohydrase enzyme amylase breaks down a solution of starch, using the disappearance of the blue-black colour of an iodine indicator as the end point. They repeated the experiment three times and obtained the following results:
   1st test 180 s   2nd test 203 s   3rd test 175 s
   Calculate the mean time taken for the starch to be digested, giving your answer to the appropriate number of s.f. [2 marks]

3. A group of students tried some of Mendel's breeding experiments with peas. After crossing two pea plants that both had round peas, they found that they collected 275 round peas and 89 wrinkled peas.
   a What percentage of the peas were wrinkled? [2 marks]
   b If this cross is repeated, what is the probability that one of the offspring plants will produce round peas? [1 mark]

4. Students surveyed the number of snails in the school greenhouse using a capture-recapture technique. They captured 25 snails and marked their shells. A week later they captured 30 snails, and four of them had marks on their shells. Estimate the snail population of the greenhouse. [2 marks]

5. The heights of a class of students were recorded as follows:
   1.80 1.55 1.49 1.76 1.64 1.50 1.52 1.90 1.52 1.76
   1.58 1.58 1.70 1.76 1.64 1.80 1.64 1.70 1.50
   Calculate the mean, mode, and median of this data. [3 marks]

Worked example: Comparing orders of magnitude

If the size of a prokaryotic cell is of the order 1.2×10^{-6} m and eukaryotic cells are from around 1×10^{-5} m to 1×10^{-4}, estimate how the size of a prokaryotic cell compares to the size of:

a the smallest eukaryotic cell
b the largest eukaryotic cell
c to the nearest order of magnitude.

Solution

a Divide the size of the smallest eukaryotic cell by the size of the prokaryotic cells:

1×10^{-5} m $\div$ 1.2×10^{-6} m = approximately 10^1

So you can say that the prokaryotic cell is one order of magnitude (10^1) smaller than the smallest eukaryotic cells

b Divide the size of the largest eukaryotic cell by the size of the prokaryotic cells:

1×10^{-4} m $\div$ 1.2×10^{-6} m = approximately 10^2

c So you can say that the prokaryotic cell is two orders of magnitude (10^2) smaller than the largest eukaryotic cells.

Synoptic link

You can practise making orders of magnitude calculations in Topic 1.3.3.

MS 3 Algebra

Learning objectives

After this topic, you should know how to:

- understand and use the symbols: =, <, <<, >>, >, ∝, ~
- solve simple algebraic equations.

3a Mathematical symbols

You have used lots of different symbols in maths, such as +, −, ×, and ÷. There are other symbols that you might meet in science. These are shown in Table 1.

Table 1 *The symbols you will meet whilst studying science*

Symbol	Meaning	Example
=	is equal to	$2\,cm^3/s \times 2\,s = 4\,cm^3$
<	is less than	The mean height of a child in a family < the mean height of an adult in a family
<<	is very much less than	The diameter of a cell << the diameter of an apple
>>	is very much greater than	The number of cells in an adult human being >> the number of cells in a two-day-old embryo
>	is greater than	The number of producers in a food chain > the number of primary consumers
∝	is proportional to	The rate of an enzyme-controlled reaction ∝ the temperature
~	is approximately equal to	$272\,m \sim 300\,m$

3d Solving simple equations

Solving equations is an important maths skill. You will often have to use data from an experiment to calculate a variable. For example, if you know the length of an image of a cell, and the magnification of the image, you can calculate the actual length of the cell.

> **Worked example: Solving equations**
>
> Figure 1 shows a light micrograph of *Salmonella* bacteria. The magnification is ×1000. In the image, one of the bacteria has a length of 15 mm. What is the actual size of the bacterium?
>
> **Solution**
>
> **Step 1:** Substitute the values you have into the equation.
>
> $$\text{magnification} = \frac{\text{size of image}}{\text{size of real object}}$$
>
> $$1000 = \frac{15\,mm}{x}$$
>
> **Step 2:** Calculate the missing value.
>
> $$x = \frac{15\,mm}{1000} = 0.015\,mm$$

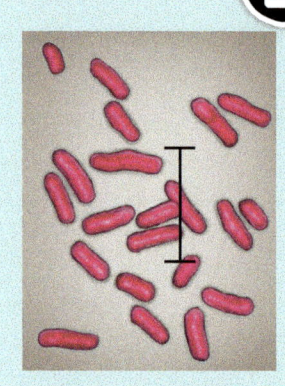

Figure 1 *Salmonella is a bacteria that is often a cause of food poisoning*

1. How would you read the following expressions as a sentence?
   a enzymes of the stomach work best in pH < 7 [1 mark]
   b rate of reaction ∝ the concentration of reactant A [1 mark]
   c $22\,cm^3 \sim 24\,cm^3$ [1 mark]
2. A student looked at a plant cell under a light microscope. The length of the cell was 20.0 mm. The magnification was ×100. What is the actual length of the plant cell? [1 mark]

MS 4 Data and graphs

During your *GCSE Combined Science: Synergy* course you will collect data in different types of experiments or investigations. The data will either be:

- from an experiment in which you have changed *one* independent variable (or you have allowed time to change) and measured the effect on a dependent variable
- from an investigation where you have collected data about *two* independent variables to see if they are related.

4a Collecting data by changing a variable

In many investigations you change one variable (the independent variable) and measure the effect on another variable (the dependent variable). In a fair test, the other variables are kept constant.

For example, you can vary the concentration of carbon dioxide (independent variable) and measure the effect on the rate of photosynthesis (dependent variable).

A scatter diagram lets you show the relationship between two numerical values.

- The **independent variable** is plotted on the horizontal axis – the *x*-axis.
- The **dependent variable** is plotted on the vertical axis – the *y*-axis.

The line of best fit is a line that goes roughly through the middle of all of the points on the scatter graph. The **line of best fit** is drawn so that the points are evenly distributed on either side of the line.

4b Graphs and equations

If you are changing one variable and measuring another, you are trying to find out about the relationship between them. A straight line graph tells you about the mathematical relationship between variables, but there are other things that you can calculate from a graph.

Straight line graphs

The equation of a straight line is $y = mx + c$, where m is the gradient and c is the point on the *y*-axis where the graph intercepts, called the *y*-intercept.

Straight line graphs that go through the origin (0,0) are special. For these graphs, y is directly proportional to x, and $y = mx$. If two quantities are directly proportional, as one quantity increases, the other quantity increases by the same proportion.

In science, plotting a graph usually means plotting the points and then drawing a line of best fit.

When you describe the relationship between two *physical* quantities, you should think about the reason why the graph might (or might not) go through (0,0).

Learning objectives

After this topic, you should know how to:

- translate information between graphical and numeric form
- explain that $y = mx + c$ represents a linear relationship
- plot two variables from experimental or other data
- determine the slope and intercept of a linear graph

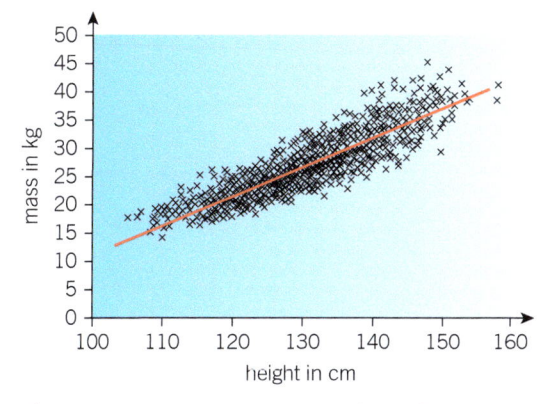

Figure 1 *A scatter graph with line of best fit showing the relationship between height and body mass*

Study tip

Look back at MS 2g to remind yourself about scatter graphs and correlations.

Study tip

m = the gradient of a straight line

c = the point where a straight line intercepts the *y*-axis

301

MS 4 Data and graphs

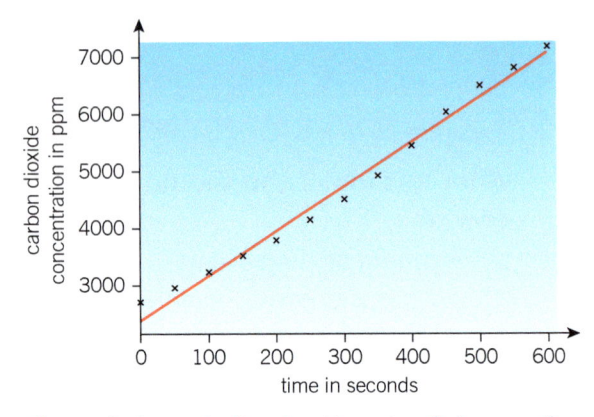

Figure 2 *A graph showing the rate of change of the volume of carbon dioxide produced by yeast during fermentation can tell you the reaction rate*

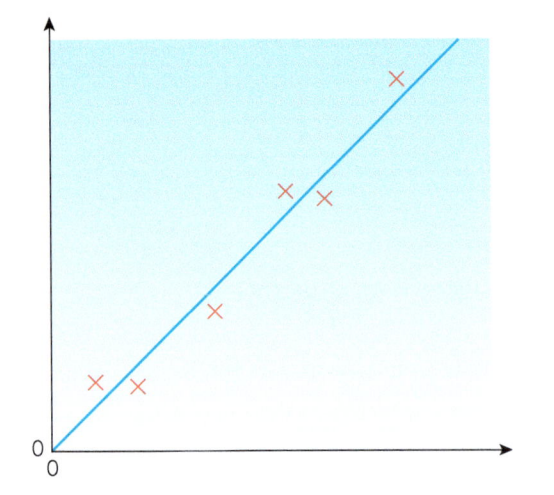

Figure 3 *A line of best fit that passes through the origin*

For example, if you are measuring the volume of a gas produced in a reaction over time, when the time = 0 s (at the start of the reaction), the volume of gas produced at that point will be obviously be 0 cm³.

However, if you are measuring the mass of reactants over time, in a reaction that gives off a gas, at time = 0 s, the y-intercept will not be zero but the starting mass of the reactants.

4c Plotting data

When you draw a graph you choose a scale for each axis.

- The scale on the *x*-axis should be *the same* all the way along the *x*-axis but it can be *different* to the scale on the *y*-axis.
- Similarly, the scale on the *y*-axis should be *the same* all the way along the *y*-axis but it can be *different* to the scale on the *x*-axis.
- Each axis should have a label and a unit, such as time in s.

4d Determining the gradient of a graph

The **gradient** of a straight line is calculated using the equation:

$$\text{gradient} = \frac{\text{change in } y}{\text{change in } x}$$

For all graphs where the quantity on the *x*-axis is time, the gradient will tell you the rate of change of the quantity on the *y*-axis with time.

When you are studying rates of reaction, you might need to calculate a gradient from a graph of either:

- the amount of a reactant as it decreases with time
- the amount of a product as it increases with time.

1. Sketch a line graph, labelling the *x* and *y* axes, that shows:
   a. A positive, constant gradient that passes through the origin (0,0). [1 mark]
   b. A negative gradient – the gradient decreases as *x* increases. [1 mark]

2. a. Write the general equation that describes a straight line on a graph, using the letters *y*, *x*, *m* and *c*. [1 mark]
   b. State what the letters *m* and *c* represent on the straight line graph. [1 mark]
   c. Write the general equation that describes a straight line on a graph that passes through the origin (0,0). [1 mark]

3. Calculate the gradient of the line of best fit in Figure 2. [1 mark]

MS 5 Geometry and trigonometry

5b Representing 3D objects

An important part of biology is visualising surface area to volume ratios in living organisms, and using simple models to explain the need for adaptations in exchange surfaces. It is helpful to be able to use 3D models of geometric shapes to demonstrate how these relationships work.

For biologists, the concept of surface area to volume ratio (SA:V) is very important when explaining, for example, factors that affect the rate of diffusion, the adaptations of exchange surfaces, and the adaptations of organisms for conserving water, warming up, and cooling down.

An important part of chemistry is visualising and representing the shapes and structures of elements and compounds. Throughout this book you will see 2D representations and models of the 3D shapes that make up all substances. Although you will not be expected to reproduce the the more complex structural diagrams, you should be able to interpret what given structures represent.

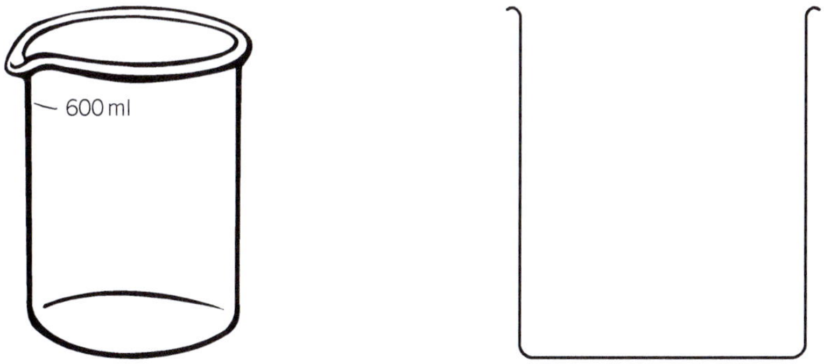

Learning objectives

After this topic, you should know how to:

- visualise and represent 2D and 3D forms including 2D representations of 3D objects
- calculate areas of rectangles, and surface areas and volumes of cubes.

Synoptic link

Examples of the use of surface area to volume ratio can be found in in Chapter 2.5.

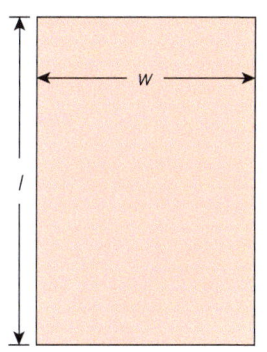

Figure 1 *When drawing experimental apparatus, a cross-section diagram is used instead of a diagram that shows the perspective*

5c Area, surface area, and volume
Surface area

You should remember the formulae for the area of rectangles and triangles.

- area of a rectangle = length, l × width, w (this also works for a square)
- area of a triangle = $\frac{1}{2}$ × base, b × height, h (this works for any triangle)

You can estimate the surface area of irregular shapes by counting squares on graph paper. This method is useful for estimating the area of a leaf, for example, if you trace the leaf onto graph paper.

The surface area of a 3D object is equal to the total surface area of all its faces. In a cuboid, the areas of any two opposite faces are equal. This allows you to calculate the surface area of the cuboid without having to draw a net.

area = lw

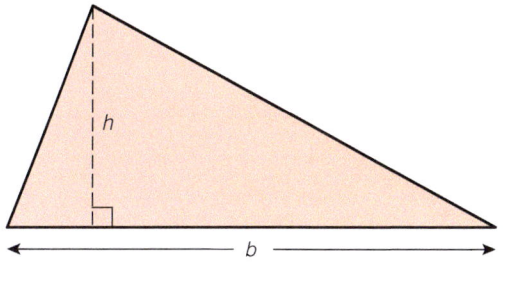

area = $\frac{1}{2}bh$

Figure 2 *Calculating the area of a rectangle and a triangle*

303

MS 5 Geometry and trigonometry

Figure 3 *What is the surface area of a grain of salt?*

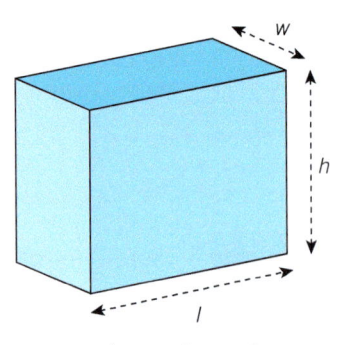

volume = $l \times w \times h$

Figure 4 *Calculating the volume of a cuboid*

Figure 5 *A 3D model of methane*

1 Look at the 3D model of methane, CH_4, in Figure 5.
   a Use the 3D model to draw a 2D ball and stick model of methane. [1 mark]
   b Draw a 3D model of methane. Find out and use the actual H – C – H bond angles in CH_4 in your answer. [2 marks]

2 A nanoparticle is made that has a cubic shape of side 20 nm.
   a Calculate the surface area of the nanoparticle cube, in nm^2. [1 mark]
   b Calculate the volume of the nanoparticle cube, in nm^3. [1 mark]
   c Calculate the surface area to volume ratio of the nanoparticle cube. The unit will be 'per nm' (/nm). [1 mark]

Worked example: Calculating the surface area of a grain of sodium chloride

A tiny grain of salt is a cuboid, measuring 15 µm × 20 µm × 80 µm. Calculate its surface area.

Solution

Step 1: Calculate the area of each face.

area of face 1 = 15 µm × 20 µm = 300 µm²
area of face 2 = 15 µm × 80 µm = 1200 µm²
area of face 3 = 20 µm × 80 µm = 1600 µm²

Step 2: Calculate the total area of the three different faces.

area = 300 µm² + 1200 µm² + 1600 µm² = 3100 µm²

Step 3: Multiply the answer to **Step 2** by 2 because the opposite sides of a cuboid have equal areas.

total surface area = 2 × 3100 µm² = **6200 µm²**

Volume

Use this expression to calculate the volume of a cuboid:

volume of cuboid = length, l × width, w × height, h

You can calculate the volume in different units depending on the units of length, width, and height.

Worked example: Volume of a cuboid

Calculate the volume of a ceramic block of length 15 cm, width 6 cm, and depth 1.5 cm, expressing your answer in cm^3 and m^3.

Solution

Step 1: Calculate the volume using the equation.

volume = length × width × height
= 15 cm × 6 cm × 1.5 cm
= 135 cm³
= **140 cm³** (2 s.f.)

Step 2: Convert the measurements to metres.

length = 0.15 m
width = 0.06 m
height = 0.015 m

Step 3: Use the equation to calculate the volume.

volume = length × width × height
= 0.15 m × 0.06 m × 0.015 m
= 0.000135 m³
= **1.35 × 10⁻⁴ m³** (3 s.f.)

Working scientifically for Synergy

WS 1 Development of scientific thinking

Science works for us all day, every day. Working as a scientist you will have knowledge of the world around you, particularly about the subject you are working with. You will observe the world around you. An enquiring mind will then lead you to start asking questions about what you have observed.

Observations and data are central to all scientific work. Collecting data is often the starting point for scientific enquiry. Scientific claims and theories are tested by checking their agreement with data. In this book you can find out about:

- how scientific methods and theories change over time (Topics 1.2.1, 1.3.1, 3.9.2, 4.12.7, 4.12.8, and Chapter 4.11)
- the models that help us to understand theories (Topics 1.3.4, 1.3.5, 1.3.6, 4.12.6, and Chapter 4.12)
- the limitations of science, and the personal, social, economic, ethical, and environmental issues that arise (Topics 3.9.9, 3.9.10, 3.9.11, 4.12.11, 4.12.12, 4.12.13, and Chapters 3.7 and 4.10)
- the importance of peer review in publishing scientific results (Topic 3.9.8, and Chapters 4.11 and 4.12)
- evaluating risks in practical work and in technological applications (Topics 3.8.6, 4.11.6, and Chapters 1.1, 3.9, and 4.11).

The rest of this section will help you to work scientifically when planning, carrying out, analysing, and evaluating your own investigations.

Figure 1 *All around you, every day, there are many observations you can make. Studying science can give you the understanding to explain and make predictions about some of what you observe*

WS 2 Experimental skills and strategies

Deciding on what to measure

Variables are quantities that change or can be changed. It helps to know about the following two types of variable when investigating many scientific questions:

- A **categoric variable** is one that is best described by a label, usually a word. For example, the fur colour of a mouse used in an experiment is a categoric variable.
- A **continuous variable** is one that you measure, so its value could be any number. For example, temperature, as measured by a thermometer or temperature sensor, is a continuous variable. Continuous variables have values (called quantities). These are found by taking measurements, and SI units such as grams (g), metres (m), and joules (J) should be used.

Making your data repeatable and reproducible

When you are designing an investigation you must make sure that you, and others, can trust the data that you plan to collect. You should ensure that each measurement is **repeatable**. You can do this by getting consistent sets

> **Study tip**
>
> **Deciding what to measure**
>
> There are more types of variable, but knowing about categoric and continuous variables will help you to make sense of scientific investigations. Understanding these variables will help you to decide for yourself how to plan fair tests and how to display your results. This in turn will improve your conclusions and evaluations.

Working scientifically for Synergy

of repeat measurements and taking their mean. You can also have more confidence in your data if similar results are obtained by different investigators using different equipment, making your measurements **reproducible**.

You must also make sure that you are measuring the actual thing that you want to measure. If you don't, your data can't be used to answer your original question. This seems very obvious, but it is not always easy to set up. You need to make sure that you have controlled as many other variables as you can. Then no-one can say that your investigation, and hence the data you collect and any conclusions drawn from the data, is not **valid**.

How might an independent variable be linked to a dependent variable?

- The **independent variable** is the one you choose to vary in your investigation.
- The **dependent variable** is used to judge the effect of varying the independent variable.

These variables may be linked together. If there is a pattern to be seen (e.g., as one thing gets bigger the other also gets bigger), it may be that:

- changing one has caused the other to change
- the two are related (there is a correlation between them), but one is not necessarily the cause of the other.

Starting an investigation

Scientists use observations to ask questions. You can only ask useful questions if you know something about the observed event. You will not have all of the answers, but you will know enough to start asking the correct questions.

When you are designing an investigation you have to observe carefully which variables are likely to have an effect.

An investigation starts with a question and is followed by a **prediction**, backed up by scientific reasoning. This forms a **hypothesis** that can be tested against the results of your investigation. You, as the scientist, predict that there is a **relationship** between two variables.

You should think about carrying out a preliminary investigation to find the most suitable range and interval for the independent variable.

Making your investigation safe

Remember that when you design your investigation, you must first:

- look for any potential **hazards**
- decide how you will reduce any **risk**.

You will need to write these down in your plan:

- write down your plan
- make a risk assessment
- make a prediction and hypothesis
- draw a blank table ready for the results.

> **Study tip**
>
> Observations, measurements, and predictions backed up by creative thinking and good scientific knowledge can lead to a hypothesis.

Figure 2 *Safety precautions should be appropriate for the risk. For example, Biuret reagent is corrosive, but you do not need to wear a full face mask. Instead, chemical and splash-proof eye protection should be worn, and care should be taken*

■ Working scientifically for Synergy

Different types of investigation

A **fair test** is one in which only the independent variable affects the dependent variable. All other variables are controlled and kept constant.

This is easy to set up in the laboratory, as long as no organisms are involved. Fair tests involving living things or fieldwork are almost impossible. Investigations in the environment and using living organisms involve complex variables that are changing constantly.

So how can you set up the fieldwork investigations? The best you can do is to make sure that all of the many variables change in much the same way, except for the one you are investigating. For example, if you are monitoring the effects of pollution on plants, they should all be experiencing the same weather, together – even if it is constantly changing (Figure 3).

If you are investigating two variables in a large population, you will need to do a survey. Again, it is impossible to control all of the variables. For example, imagine scientists investigating the effect of a new drug on diabetes. They would have to choose people of the same age and the same family history to test. Remember that the larger the sample size tested, the more valid the results will be.

Control groups are used in these investigations to try to make sure that you are measuring the variable that you intend to measure. When investigating the effects of a new drug, the control group will be given a placebo. The control group think they are taking a drug but the placebo does not contain the drug. This way you can control the variable of 'thinking that the drug is working', and separate out the effect of the actual drug.

Designing an investigation
Accuracy

Your investigation must provide **accurate** data. Accurate data is essential if your results are going to have any meaning.

How do you know if you have accurate data?

It is very difficult to be certain. **Accurate results are very close to the true value.** However, it is not always possible to know what the true value is.

Sometimes you can calculate a theoretical value and check it against the experimental evidence. Close agreement between these two values could indicate accurate data.

You can draw a graph of your results and see how close each result is to the line of best fit.

Try repeating your measurements and check the spread or range within sets of repeat data. Large differences in a repeated measurement suggest inaccuracy. Or try again with a different measuring instrument and see if you get the same readings.

Precision

Your investigation must provide data with sufficient **precision** (i.e., **close agreement within sets of repeat measurements**). If it doesn't, you will not be able to make a valid conclusion.

Figure 3 *Imagine investigating the effect pollution from a chemical factory has on nearby plants. You should choose a control group that is far away enough from the chemical plant to not be affected by the pollution, but close enough to be still experiencing similar environmental conditions*

> **Study tip**
>
> Trial runs will tell you a lot about how your investigation might work out. They should prompt you to ask yourself:
> - Do I have the correct conditions?
> - Have I chosen a sensible range?
> - Have I got sufficient readings that are close enough together? The minimum number of points to draw a line graph is generally taken as five.
> - Will I need to repeat my readings?

> **Study tip**
>
> Just because your results show precision it does not mean your results are accurate.
>
> Imagine carrying out an investigation into the energy value of a type of food. You get readings of the amount of energy transferred from the burning food to the surroundings that are all about the same. This means that your data will have precision, but it doesn't mean that they are necessarily accurate.

Working scientifically for Synergy

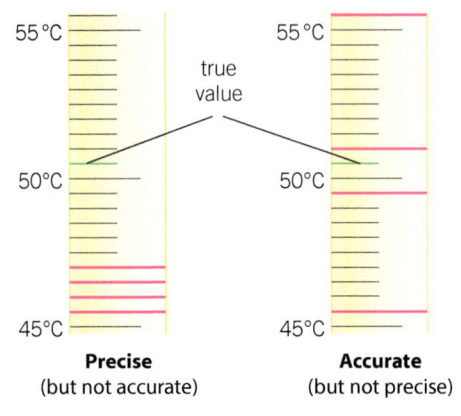

Figure 4 *The green line shows the true value and the pink lines show the readings measured by two different groups of students. Precise results are not necessarily accurate results*

Precision versus accuracy

Imagine measuring the temperature after a set time when a fuel is used to heat a fixed volume of water. Two students repeated this experiment four times each. Their results are marked on the thermometer scales in Figure 4:

- A **precise** set of results is grouped closely together.
- An accurate set of results will have a mean (average) close to the true value.

How do you get precise, repeatable data?

- You have to repeat your tests as often as necessary to improve repeatability.
- You have to repeat your tests in exactly the same way each time.
- You should use measuring instruments that have the appropriate scale divisions needed for a particular investigation. Smaller-scale divisions have better resolution.

Making measurements

There will always be some degree of uncertainty in any measurements made (WS 3). You cannot expect perfect results. When you choose an instrument you need to know that it will give you the accuracy that you want (i.e., it will give you a true reading). You also need to know how to use an instrument properly.

Some instruments have smaller scale divisions than others. Instruments that measure the same thing, such as mass, can have different resolutions. The resolution of an instrument refers to the smallest change in a value that can be detected (e.g., a ruler with centimetre increments compared to a ruler with millimetre increments). Choosing an instrument with an inappropriate resolution can cause you to miss important data or make silly conclusions.

But selecting measuring instruments with high resolution might not be appropriate in some cases where the degree of uncertainty in a measurement is high, for example, measuring reaction time using hand squeezes. (see Topic 2.5.10). In this case, a stopwatch measuring to one hundredths of a second is not going to improve the accuracy of the data collected (Figure 5).

Figure 5 *Despite the fact that a stopwatch has a high resolution, it is not always the most appropriate instrument to use for measuring time*

WS 3 Analysis and evaluation

Errors

Even when an instrument is used correctly, the results can still show differences. Errors of measurement are not necessarily mistakes but unavoidable differences between measured values and true values. Results will differ because of a **random error**. This can also be a result of poor measurements being made. It could also be due to not carrying out the method consistently in each test. Random errors are minimised by taking the mean of precise repeat readings and by looking out for any outliers (measurements that differ significantly from the others within a set of repeats) to check again or omit from calculations of the mean.

The error may be a systematic error. This means that the method or measurement was carried out consistently incorrectly, so that an error was being repeated. An example could be a balance that is not set at zero correctly. Systematic errors will be consistently above, or below, the accurate value.

Presenting data
Tables
Tables are really good for recording your results quickly and clearly as you are carrying out an investigation. You should design your table before you start your investigation.

The range of the data
Pick out the maximum and the minimum values and you have the **range**. You should always quote these two numbers when asked for a range. For example, the range is between the lowest value and the highest value in a set of data. **Don't forget to include the units**.

The mean of the data
Add up all the measurements and divide by how many there are. You can ignore outliers in a set of repeat readings when calculating the mean, if they are found to be the result of poor measurement.

Bar charts
If you have a categoric independent variable and a continuous dependent variable, you should use a **bar chart**.

Line graphs
If you have a continuous independent and a continuous dependent variable then use a **line graph**.

Scatter graphs
These are used in much the same way as a line graph, but you might not expect to be able to draw such a clear line of best fit. For example, to find out if the size of mussels is related to their distance from the low-tide line, you might draw a scatter graph of your results.

Using data to draw conclusions
Identifying patterns and relationships
Now that you have a bar chart or a line graph of your results, you can begin looking for patterns. You must have an open mind at this point.

Firstly, there could still be some anomalous results. You might not have picked these out earlier. How do you spot an anomaly? It must be a significant distance away from the pattern, not just within normal variation.

A line of best fit will help to identify any anomalies at this stage (Figure 7). Ask yourself – 'do the anomalies represent something important, or were they just a mistake?'

Secondly, remember that a line of best fit can be a straight line or it can be a curve – you have to decide based on your results.

Figure 6 *How you record your results will depend upon the type of measurements you are taking*

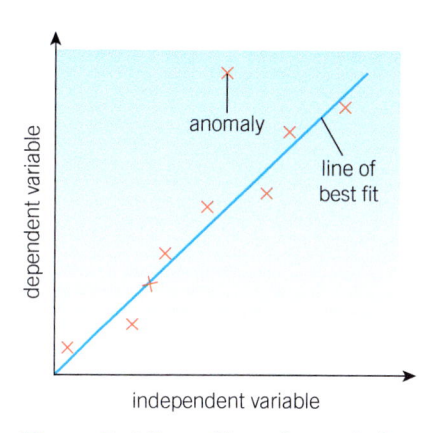

Figure 7 *A line of best fit can help to identify anomalies*

■ Working scientifically for Synergy

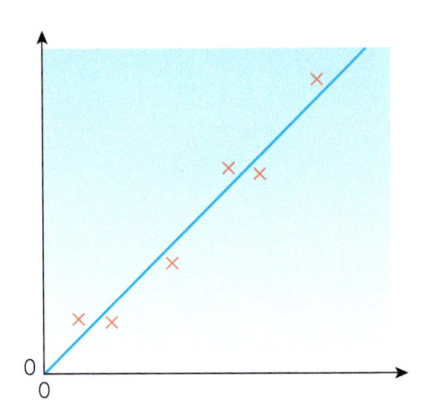

Figure 8 *When a straight line of best fit goes through the origin (0, 0) the relationship between the variables is directly proportional*

The line of best fit will also lead you into thinking about what the relationship is between your two variables. You need to consider whether the points you have plotted show a linear relationship. If so, you can draw a straight line of best fit on your graph (with as many points above the line as below it, producing a 'mean' line). Then consider if this line has a positive or negative gradient.

A **directly proportional** relationship is shown by a positive straight line that goes through the origin (0, 0) (Figure 8).

Your results might also show a curved line of best fit. These can be predictable, complex, or very complex. Carrying out more tests with a smaller interval near the area where a line changes its gradient will help to reduce the error in drawing the line (in this case a curve) of best fit.

Drawing conclusions

Your graphs are designed to show the relationship between your two chosen variables. You need to consider what that relationship means for your conclusion. You must also take into account the repeatability and the reproducibility of the data you are considering.

You must continue to have an open mind about your conclusion.

You will have made a prediction. This could be supported by your results, it might not be supported, or it could be partly supported. It might suggest some other hypothesis to you.

You must be willing to think carefully about your results. Remember that it is quite rare for a set of results to completely support a prediction or to be completely repeatable.

Look for possible links between variables, remembering that a positive relationship does not always mean a causal link between the two variables.

Your conclusion must go no further than the evidence that you have. Any patterns that you spot are only strictly valid in the range of values you tested. Further tests are needed to check whether the pattern continues beyond this range.

The purpose of the prediction was to test a hypothesis. The hypothesis can:

- be supported
- be refuted
- lead to another hypothesis.

You have to decide which it is, based on the evidence available.

Making estimates of uncertainty

You can use the range of a set of repeat measurements about their mean to estimate the degree of uncertainty in the data collected.

For example, in a test that looked at the effect of concentration on the rate of reaction between the enzyme catalase and hydrogen peroxide solution, a student got these results:

A given volume and concentration of hydrogen peroxide gave off 20 cm^3 of oxygen in 45 s (1st attempt), 49 s (2nd attempt), 44 s (3rd attempt), and 48 s (4th attempt).

The mean result = (45 + 49 + 44 + 48) ÷ 4 = 46.5 s

The range of the repeats is 44 s to 49 s = 5 s

So, a reasonable estimate of the uncertainty in the mean value would be half of the range.

In this case, you could say that the time taken was 46.5 s plus or minus 2.5 s, written as ± 2.5 s.

You can include a final column in your table of results to record the estimated uncertainty in your mean measurements.

The level of uncertainty can also be shown when plotting your results on a graph (Figure 9).

As well as this, there will be some uncertainty associated with readings from any measuring instrument. You can usually take this as:

- half the smallest scale division. For example, 0.5 mm on a metre ruler marked in millimetre divisions.
- half the last figure shown on the display (on a digital instrument). For example, on a balance reading to 0.01 g the uncertainty would be ± 0.005 g.

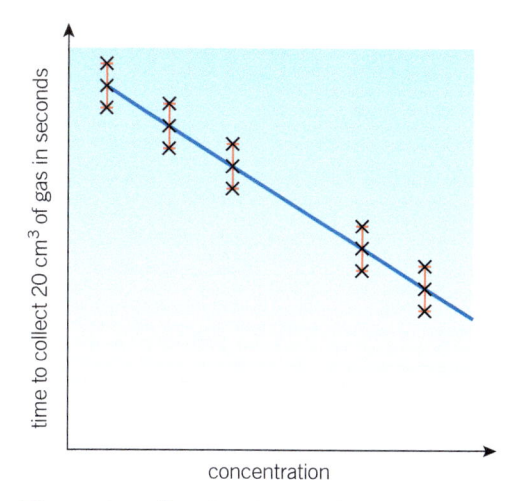

Figure 9 *Indicating levels of uncertainty. These are all the results of a group that chose five different concentrations to test and repeated each test three times. The spread of the repeat sets of results shown by plotting all readings on a graph gives a rough display of uncertainty*

Anomalous results

Anomalies (or outliers) are results that are clearly out of line compared with others. They are not those that are due to the natural variation that you get from any measurement. **Anomalous results** should be looked at carefully. There might be a very interesting reason why they are so different.

If anomalies can be identified while you are doing an investigation, it is best to repeat that part of the investigation. If you find that an anomaly is due to poor measurement, it should be ignored.

Evaluation

If you are still uncertain about a conclusion, it might be down to the repeatability, reproducibility, and uncertainty in your measurements. You could check reproducibility by: looking for other similar work on the Internet or from others in your class, or getting somebody else to redo your investigation using different equipment (this occurs in peer review of data presented in articles in scientific journals). You could also try an alternative method to see if it results in you reaching the same conclusion.

When suggesting improvement that could be made in your investigation, always give your reasoning.

Study tip

The method chosen for an investigation can only be evaluated as being valid if it actually collects data that can answer your original question. The data should be repeatable and reproducible, and the control variables should have been kept constant (or taken into account if they couldn't be directly manipulated).

Synoptic link

See the Maths skills section to learn how to use SI units, prefixes, and powers of ten for orders of magnitude, significant figures, and scientific quantities.

311

Glossary

abiotic non-living components of an ecosystem

abundance a measure of how common or rare a particular type of organism is in a given environment

accurate a measurement is considered accurate if it is judged to be close to the true value

acid rain rainwater in which acidic sulfur dioxide and nitrogen oxides have dissolved

active transport the movement of substances from a dilute solution to a more concentrated solution against a concentration gradient, requiring energy from respiration

activity the number of unstable atoms that decay per second in a radioactive source

adrenaline hormone that prepares the body for fight or flight

adult stem cells stem cells that are found in adults that can differentiate and form a limited number of cells

aerobic respiration an exothermic reaction in which glucose is broken down using oxygen to produce carbon dioxide and water and release energy for the cells

algae simple aquatic organisms (protista) that make their own food by photosynthesis

alleles different forms of the same gene sometimes referred to as variants

alpha radiation alpha particles, each composed of two protons and two neutrons, emitted by unstable nuclei

alveoli tiny air sacs in the lungs that increase the surface area for gaseous exchange

amino acids molecules made up of carbon, hydrogen, oxygen, and nitrogen that are the building blocks of proteins

amplitude the height of a wave crest or trough of a transverse wave from the rest position. For oscillating motion, the amplitude is the maximum distance moved by an oscillating object from its equilibrium position.

amylase enzyme that speeds up the digestion of starch into sugars

anaerobic respiration an exothermic reaction in which glucose is broken down in the absence of oxygen to produce lactic acid in animals and ethanol and carbon dioxide in plants and yeast. A small amount of energy is transferred for the cells.

anomalies results that do not match the pattern seen in the other data collected or that are well outside the range of other repeat readings (outliers)

anomalous results see **anomalies**

aorta the artery that leaves the heart from the left ventricle and carries oxygenated blood to the body

arteries blood vessels that carry blood away from the heart. They usually carry oxygenated blood and have a pulse.

artificial pacemaker electrical device used to correct irregularities in the heart rate

atmosphere the relatively thin layer of gases that surrounds the Earth

atomic number the number of protons (which equals the number of electrons) in an atom. It is sometimes called the proton number.

atria the upper chambers of the heart

background radiation radiation emanating from traces of radioactive substances in many natural substances

bacteria single-celled prokaryotic organisms

bar chart diagram in which numerical values of variables are represented by the height of rectangles of equal width

benign tumours growths of abnormal cells that are contained in one area, usually within a membrane, and do not invade other tissues

beta radiation beta particles that are high-energy electrons created in, and emitted from, unstable nuclei

binomial system system of naming organisms using two names

biodiversity a measure of the variety of all the different species of organisms on Earth

biofuels fuels made from animal or plant products

biomass the amount of biological material in an organism

biotic living components of an ecosystem

blood red liquid that circulates in the body, carrying oxygen to and carbon dioxide from the body tissues

blood vessels arteries, veins, and capillaries that carry blood around the body

boiling point temperature at which a pure substance boils or condenses, as measured at atmospheric pressure

bonds forces that hold atoms, molecules, or ions together

cancer the common name for a malignant tumour, formed as a result of changes in cells that lead to uncontrolled growth and division

capillaries the smallest blood vessels. They run between individual cells and have a wall that is only one cell thick.

carbohydrates molecules that contain only carbon, hydrogen, and oxygen. They provide the energy for the metabolism and are found in foods such as rice, potatoes, and bread.

carbon capture and storage (CCS) collection and storage of carbon dioxide emissions to prevent them from entering the atmosphere

carbon cycle the cycling of carbon through the living and non-living world

carbon footprint the total amount of carbon dioxide and other greenhouse gases emitted over the full life cycle of a product, service, or event

carbon monoxide clear, colourless, toxic gas given off in incomplete combustion of fuel

carbon sinks fossil fuels, forests, oceans, or other natural environments able to absorb carbon dioxide from the atmosphere

carcinogens agents that cause cancer or significantly increase the risk of developing cancer

carrier waves waves used to carry any type of signal

categoric variable has values that are labels, for example, types of material

causal mechanism something that explains how one factor influences another

cell cycle the three-stage process of cell division in a body cell that involves mitosis and results in the formation of two identical daughter cells

cell membrane the membrane around the contents of a cell that controls what moves in and out of the cell

cell wall the rigid structure around plant and algal cells. It is made of cellulose and strengthens the cell.

cellulose the complex carbohydrate that makes up plant and algal cell walls and gives them strength

central nervous system (CNS) the part of the nervous system where information is processed. It is made up of the brain and spinal cord.

charge-coupled device (CCD) an electronic device that creates an electronic signal from an optical image formed on the CCD's array of pixels

chemical properties the properties of a material that become apparent during or after a chemical reaction

Glossary

chlorophyll the green pigment contained in the chloroplasts

chloroplasts the organelles in which photosynthesis takes place

chromatography the process by which small amounts of dissolved substances are separated by running a solvent along a material such as absorbent paper

chromosomes thread-like structures of nucleic acids and protein found in the nucleus of most living cells, carrying genetic information in the form of genes

classification the organisation of living organisms into groups according to their similarities

clinical trials test potential new drugs on healthy and patient volunteers

cloning the production of identical offspring by asexual reproduction

combustion the process of burning something

communicable (infectious) diseases diseases caused by pathogens that can be passed from one organism to another

communities groups of interdependent living organisms in an ecosystem

competition the process by which living organisms compete with each other for limited resources such as food, light, or reproductive partners

compression squeezing together

concentrated describes a solution in which a solute (dissolved substance) is present in a high proportion relative to the solvent

concentration gradient the difference between two areas of concentration

continuous variable a quantity that can have any value as given by its measurement, for example, continuous variables include mass in g, volume in cm^3, temperature in °C, etc.

contraception methods of avoiding pregnancy by preventing an egg and a sperm from meeting or by preventing a fertilised egg from implanting in the uterus

contrast medium an X-ray absorbing substance used to fill a body organ so that the organ can be seen on a radiograph

coordination centres areas that receive and process information from receptors

coronary arteries the blood vessels that supply oxygenated blood to the heart muscle

correlation an apparent link or relationship between two factors

count rate the number of counts per second detected by a Geiger counter

cytoplasm the water-based gel in which the organelles of all living cells are suspended and most of the chemical reactions of life take place

decomposers microorganisms that break down waste products and dead bodies

deforestation cutting down trees to clear large areas of land

denatured the breakdown of the molecular structure of a protein so that it no longer functions

density mass per unit volume of a substance

dependent variable the variable for which the value is measured for each and every change in the independent variable (see **independent variable**)

desalination purification of seawater to obtain potable water

differentiate the process by which cells become specialised for a particular function

diffusion the spreading out of the particles of any substance in a solution, or particles in a gas, resulting in a net movement of particles from an area of higher concentration to an area of lower concentration down a concentration gradient

digested broken down into smaller, soluble molecules

dilute describes a solution in which a solute (dissolved substance) is present in a low proportion relative to the solvent

directly proportional a relationship that, when drawn on a line graph, shows a positive linear relationship that crosses through the origin

distribution where particular types of organisms are found within an environment

DNA (deoxyribonucleic acid) a large molecule that encodes genetic instructions for the development and functioning of living organisms and viruses

dominant a phenotype that will be apparent in the offspring even if only one of the alleles is inherited

donor a person who provides an organ for transplantation

drugs active ingredients in medicines

dual circulatory system the circulation of blood from the heart to the lungs is separate from the circulation of blood from the heart to the rest of the body

effectors areas (usually muscles or glands) that bring about responses in the body

electromagnetic waves electric and magnetic disturbances that transfer energy from one place to another

electron a tiny particle with a negative charge. Electrons orbit the nucleus of atoms or ions in shells.

electron microscope uses a beam of electrons to form high-resolution image of an object and can magnify objects up to around 200 000 times

electronic structure a set of numbers to show the arrangement of electrons in their shells (or energy levels)

electrostatic force the force between two charged objects due to their electric charge

embryonic stem cells stem cells from an early embryo that can differentiate to form the specialised cells of the body

endocrine system the glands that produce the hormones that control many aspects of the development and metabolism of the body, and the hormones they produce

endothermic reaction a reaction that requires a transfer of energy from the environment

energy levels specific energy values of electrons in an atom

environmental isolation isolation of a species resulting from an environmental change, for example, a change in climate

ethical code a system of moral principles

eukaryotic cells cells from eukaryotes that have a cell membrane, cytoplasm, and genetic material enclosed in a nucleus

exothermic reaction a reaction that transfers energy to the environment

fair test a test in which only the independent variable has been allowed to affect the dependent variable

fatty acids part of the structure of a lipid molecule

fertilisers substances added to soil or land to increase its fertility

follicle stimulating hormone (FSH) causes the eggs to mature in the ovary

formulations a mixture of substances prepared according to a formula

fossils the remains of organisms from millions of years ago that are found preserved in rocks, ice, and other places

fraction (maths) a numerical quantity that is not a whole number

313

Glossary

freezing point the temperature at which a pure substance changes from a liquid to a solid

frequency the number of wave crests passing a fixed point every second

gamma radiation electromagnetic radiation emitted from unstable nuclei in radioactive substances

gas the state of matter in which there are large volumes of space, on average, between particles. The particles move randomly at high speed.

gas exchange the diffusion of oxygen and carbon dioxide in opposite directions in the lungs

guard cells surround the stomata in the leaves of plants and control their opening and closing

genes units of inheritance carried on the chromosomes that code for the proteins needed to build new cells or new organisms

genetic modification the process by which scientists can manipulate and change the genotype of an organism

genetically modified (GM) an organism that has had its genome manipulated or changed through gene technology

genotype the genetic makeup of an individual for a particular characteristic, for example, hair or eye colour

genus the level of classification of organisms above species and below family

geographical isolation isolation of a species resulting from a geographical change, for example, formation of a new mountain range or island

global warming a gradual increase in the overall temperature of the Earth's surface, oceans, and atmosphere

glucagon hormone involved in the control of blood sugar levels

glucose a simple sugar

glycerol part of the structure of a lipid molecule

gradient the slope of a line on a graph. In a straight line graph it is m in the equation $y = mx + c$. To calculate m (or the gradient of a tangent drawn to a curve at any specific point), divide 'change in y' by 'change in x'.

greenhouse effect warming effect caused by increased greenhouse gases in the atmosphere absorbing the energy radiated by the Earth

greenhouse gases gases that contribute to the greenhouse effect, for example, carbon dioxide, methane, and water vapour

guard cells surround the stomata in the leaves of plants and control their opening and closing

habitat the natural home or environment of an animal, plant, or other organism

haemoglobin the red pigment that carries oxygen around the body in the red blood cells

half-life average time taken for the number of nuclei of a radioactive isotope (or mass of the isotope) in a sample to halve

hazards things that can cause harm, for example, an object, a property of a substance, or an activity

heart the organ that pumps blood around the body, forming part of the circulatory system

heterozygote individual with different alleles for a characteristic

homeostasis the regulation of the internal conditions of a cell or organism to maintain optimum conditions for function, in response to internal and external changes

homozygote individual with two identical alleles for a characteristic

hormones chemicals produced in one area of the body of an organism that have an effect on the functioning of another area of the body. In animals, hormones are produced in glands.

hypertonic (osmosis) a solution that is more concentrated than the cell contents

hypothesis a proposal intended to explain certain facts or observations

hypotonic (osmosis) a solution that is less concentrated than the cell contents

immunosuppressant drugs drugs to suppress the immune system

impulses electrical signals that travel fast through the nervous system

incomplete combustion when a fuel burns in insufficient oxygen, producing carbon monoxide as a toxic product

independent variable the variable for which values are changed or selected by the investigator

industrial waste waste material produced by industrial processes or activity

insulin hormone involved in the control of blood sugar levels

interdependence the network of relationships between different organisms within a community, for example each species depends on other species for food, shelter, pollination, seed dispersal, etc.

internal energy the energy of the particles of a substance due to their individual motion and positions

ionisation any process in which atoms become charged

ionising radiation radiation that causes ionisation in the medium through which it passes. Can be carcinogenic (cause cancer).

ions charged particles produced by the loss or gain of electrons

irradiated an object that has been exposed to ionising radiation

isotonic (osmosis) a solution that is the same concentration as the cell contents

isotopes atoms with the same number of protons and different numbers of neutrons

lactic acid the end product of anaerobic respiration in animal cells

latent heat the energy transferred to or from a substance when it changes its state

leukaemia disease in which the bone marrow no longer functions normally

level of hazard level of associated risk

light microscopes use a beam of light to form an image of an object and can magnify objects up to around 2000 times

limiting factors limit the rate of a reaction, for example, photosynthesis

line graph used when both variables are continuous. The line should normally be a line of best fit, and may be straight or a smooth curve.

line of best fit an 'average' line drawn through a set of points on a line graph

lipase enzymes that speed up the breakdown of lipids into fatty acids and glycerol

lipids include fats and oils and are found in foods such as butter, olive oil, and crisps. They are made of carbon, hydrogen, and oxygen.

liquid the state of matter in which particles are close together in a random arrangement. The particles are able to slip and slide over each other.

longitudinal wave wave in which the vibrations are parallel to the direction of energy transfer

malignant tumour cells invade neighbouring tissues and spread to different parts of the body in the blood where they form secondary tumours. They are also known as cancers.

Glossary

mass the quantity of matter in an object – a measure of the difficulty of changing the motion of an object (in kilograms, kg)

mass number the number of protons plus neutrons in the nucleus of an atom

mean the arithmetical average of a series of numbers

mechanical waves vibrations that travel through a substance

median the middle value in a list of numbers

medium a general word used in physics to describe a substance that can transmit waves

meiosis two-stage process of cell division that reduces the chromosome number of daughter cells. It is involved in making gametes for sexual reproduction.

melting point temperature at which a pure substance melts or freezes (solidifies)

meristem plant tissue made up of rapidly dividing plant cells that grow and differentiate into all the other cell types needed

microorganisms microscopic organisms, especially bacteria, viruses, or fungi

mitigate to lessen an effect

mitochondria sub-cellular structures that are the site of aerobic cellular respiration in a cell

mitosis part of the cell cycle where one set of new chromosomes is pulled to each end of the cell forming two identical nuclei during cell division

mobile phase the liquid (or gas) that passes through a solid (e.g., absorbent paper) carrying the components of a mixture being separated by chromatography

mode the number that occurs most often in a set of data

motor neurones carry impulses from the central nervous system to the effector organs

mutation a change in the genetic material of an organism

nanometres thousand-millionths of a metre

natural selection the process by which evolution takes place. Organisms produce more offspring than the environment can support. Only those that are most suited to their environment will survive to breed and pass on their useful characteristics to their offspring.

nerves bundles of hundreds or even thousands of neurones

neurones basic cells of the nervous system that carry minute electrical impulses around the body

neutrons dense, uncharged particles of the same mass as protons. The nucleus of an atom consists of protons and neutrons.

nitrogen oxides oxides of nitrogen released into the environment as a result of fuel combustion, especially nitric oxide and nitrogen dioxide

non-communicable diseases are not infectious and cannot be passed from one organism to another

nucleus (of an atom) the very small and dense central part of an atom that contains protons and neutrons

nucleus (of a cell) organelle found in many living cells containing the genetic information surrounded by the nuclear membrane

obesity the state of being grossly fat or overweight

oestrogen female sex hormone that controls the development of secondary sexual characteristics in girls at puberty, and the build-up and maintenance of the uterus lining during the menstrual cycle

osmosis the diffusion of water through a partially permeable membrane from an area with a high concentration of water (a dilute solution) to an area with a lower concentration of water (a concentrated solution) down a concentration gradient

ovaries female sex organs that produce eggs and sex hormones

ovulation the release of a mature egg (ovum) from the ovary

oxygen debt the extra oxygen that must be taken into the body after exercise has stopped to complete the aerobic respiration of lactic acid

partially permeable membranes membranes that allow only certain substances to pass through

particulates small solid particles given off by motor vehicles as a result of incomplete combustion of fuel

pasteurisation sterilisation by heating to a high temperature

pathogens microorganisms that cause disease

peer review evaluation of scientific research by others working in the same field

period the time taken for each wave to pass a fixed point

permanent vacuole space in the cytoplasm filled with cell sap

phagocytosis the ingestion of bacteria by phagocytes (white blood cells)

phenotype the physical appearance/biochemistry of an individual for a particular characteristic

phloem the living transport tissue in plants that carries dissolved food (sugars) around the plant

photosynthesis the process by which plants make food using carbon dioxide, water, and light

pituitary gland endocrine 'master gland' found in the brain that secretes a number of different hormones into the blood in response to different conditions to control other endocrine glands in the body

placebo a medicine that does not contain the active drug being tested, used in clinical trials of new medicines

plasma the clear, yellow, liquid part of the blood that carries dissolved substances and blood cells around the body

plasmolysis the state of plant cells when so much water is lost from the cell by osmosis that the vacuole and cytoplasm shrink and the cell membrane pulls away from the cell wall

platelets fragments of cells in the blood that play a vital role in the clotting mechanism of the blood

potable water water that is safe to drink

precise a precise measurement is one in which there is very little spread about the mean value. Precision depends only on the extent of random errors – it gives no indication of how close results are to the true (accurate) value.

precision a measure of how precise a measurement is

preclinical testing is carried out on a potential new medicine in a laboratory using cells, tissues, and live animals

predators animals that hunt and kill other animals

prediction a forecast or statement about the way in which something will happen in the future

prey animals that are hunted and killed by other animals (predators)

primary consumers animals that eat producers

producers organisms such as plants and algae that can make food from raw materials such as carbon dioxide and water

prokaryotic cells have a cytoplasm surrounded by a cell membrane, and a cell wall that does not contain cellulose. The genetic material is a DNA loop that

315

Glossary

is free in the cytoplasm and not enclosed by a nucleus. Sometimes there are one or more small rings of DNA called plasmids.

protease enzyme that speeds up the breakdown of proteins into amino acids

proteins molecules that contain carbon, hydrogen, oxygen, and nitrogen and are made of long chains of amino acids. They are used for building the cells and tissues of the body and to form enzymes.

protists single-celled, eukaryotic organisms that can live independently or can live inside other organisms

protons tiny, positively charged particles with an equal and opposite charge to that of an electron. The nucleus of an atom consists of protons and neutrons.

pulmonary artery carries deoxygenated blood from the heart to the lungs

pulmonary vein carries oxygenated blood from the lungs to the heart

quadrat sample area used for measuring the abundance and distribution of organisms in the field

quantitative sampling records the numbers of organisms rather than just the type

radiation dose in sieverts (Sv) is a measure of the risk of harm resulting from exposure of the body to ionising radiation

radioactive contamination is the presence of unwanted radioactive atoms on or in other materials or living organisms

random haphazard or unpredictable (e.g., the radioactive decay of an unstable atomic nucleus)

random error an error in measurement caused by factors that vary from one measurement to another

range the maximum and minimum values for the independent or dependent variables – important in ensuring that any patterns are detected

rarefaction stretched apart

reaction time the time it takes to respond to a stimulus

receptors cells that detect stimuli – changes in the internal or external environment

recessive a phenotype that will only be apparent in offspring if both of the alleles coding for that characteristic are inherited

recipient patient who receives an organ transplant from a donor

red blood cells biconcave cells that contain the red pigment haemoglobin and carry oxygen around the body in the blood

reflected thrown back at a boundary without passing through or being absorbed

reflection the change of direction of a light ray or wave at a boundary when the ray or wave stays in the incident medium

reflex arc bring about a reflex action. They involve a sense organ, sensory neurone, relay neurone, motor neurone, and effector

reflexes rapid automatic responses of the nervous system that do not involve conscious thought

refraction the change of direction of a light ray when it passes across a boundary between two transparent substances (including air)

relationship the link between the variables that were investigated

repeatable a measurement is repeatable if the original experimenter repeats the investigation using the same method and equipment and obtains the same or precise results

reproducible a measurement is reproducible if the investigation is repeated by another person, using different equipment and the same results are obtained

resolving power a measure of the ability to distinguish between two separate points that are very close together

R_f (retention factor) a measurement from chromatography – it is the distance a spot of substance has been carried above the baseline divided by the distance of the solvent front

ribosomes the site of protein synthesis in a cell

risk the likelihood of exposure to a hazard and the seriousness of any resulting harm

root hair cells specialised plant cells that increase available surface area for absorption of water and minerals from the soil

rose black spot a fungal disease of rose leaves

sample size the size of a sample in an investigation

secondary consumers animals that eat primary consumers

selective breeding speeds up natural selection by selecting animals or plants for breeding that have a required characteristic

sensory neurones neurones that carry impulses from the sensory organs to the central nervous system

sewage waste water from homes, businesses, and industry

sex chromosomes carry the information that determines the sex of an individual

sexually transmitted disease (STD) transmitted from an infected person to an uninfected person by unprotected sexual contact

shells areas in an atom, around its nucleus, where electrons are found

sieverts (Sv) unit of measure for radiation dose

simple sugars small carbohydrate units, for example, glucose

solid the state of matter in which closely packed particles are arranged in fixed positions. The particles vibrate but cannot move around.

specialised adapted to carry out a particular job

speciation the result of organisms changing so much through natural selection that they can no longer interbreed, forming a new species

species the smallest group of clearly identified organisms in Linnaeus's classification system, often described as a group of organisms that can breed together and produce fertile offspring

specific heat capacity energy needed to raise the temperature of 1 kg of a substance by 1 °C

specific latent heat of fusion energy needed to melt 1 kg of a substance with no change of temperature

specific latent heat of vaporisation energy needed to boil away 1 kg of a substance with no change of temperature

speed the speed of an object (metres per second) = distance moved by the object (metres) ÷ time taken to move the distance travelled (seconds)

statins drugs used to lower blood cholesterol levels

stationary phase the solid (or liquid supported on a solid) that the liquid (or gas) of the mobile phase passes through to separate the components of a mixture in chromatography

stem cells undifferentiated cells with the potential to form a wide variety of different cell types

stent a metal mesh placed in a blocked or partially blocked artery. They are used to open up the blood vessel by the inflation of a tiny balloon

Glossary

stimuli changes in the external or internal environment that can be detected by receptors

stomata openings in the leaves of plants, particularly on the underside and opened and closed by guard cells, allowing gases to enter and leave the leaf

sublimation the process by which some solid substances change directly into a vapour without melting

sulfur dioxide acidic gas formed when sulfur impurities released by the burning of fossil fuels react with oxygen during combustion. Causes acid rain.

symptoms physical or mental features indicating the presence of disease

synapses junctions between neurones

tertiary consumers carnivores that eat other carnivores (secondary consumers). They are usually found at the top of a food chain.

testosterone the main male sex hormone that controls the male secondary sexual characteristics at puberty and the production of sperm

thyroxine a hormone that controls the basal metabolic rate of the body

tobacco mosaic virus a virus that causes mosaic disease in plants

transect a measured line or area along which ecological measurements are made

translocation the movement of sugars from the leaves to the rest of the plant through the phloem

transmitted describes something that has passed through a substance rather than being absorbed by it

transpiration the loss of water vapour from the leaves of plants through the stomata when they are opened to allow gas exchange for photosynthesis. It involves evaporation from the surface of the cells and diffusion through the stomata.

transpiration stream the constant movement of water molecules through the xylem from the roots to the leaves

transplant the process by which a living tissue or organ is taken from a donor and implanted into a recipient

transverse wave a wave in which the vibration is perpendicular to the direction of energy transfer

tumour a mass of abnormally growing cells that forms when the cells do not respond to the normal mechanisms that control growth and when control of the cell cycle is lost

turgor the pressure inside a plant cell exerted by the cell contents pressing on the cell wall

Type 1 diabetes a disorder in which the pancreas fails to produce sufficient insulin

Type 2 diabetes disorder in which the body cells no longer respond to the insulin produced by the pancreas

urea the waste product formed by the breakdown of excess amino acids in the liver

urine fluid containing waste substances for removal from the body

vaccination process by which large numbers of humans and animals are protected against disease through the introduction of a small amount of a harmless form of a pathogen into the body to create immunity

vaccines dead or inactive pathogenic material used in vaccination to develop immunity to a disease in a healthy person

valid suitability of the investigative procedure to answer the question being asked

valves mechanisms within the veins to prevent the backflow of blood (valves open as blood flows through towards the heart, but close if blood starts to flow backwards)

variables physical, chemical, or biological quantities or characteristics

vector carries something from one place to another (e.g., a mosquito is a vector of malaria, a bacterial plasmid may act as a vector carrying a new gene into an organism in the process of genetic engineering)

veins blood vessels that carry blood away from the heart. They usually carry deoxygenated blood and have valves to prevent the backflow of blood.

vena cava the large vein that brings deoxygenated blood from the body into the heart

ventilated movement of air or water into and out of the gas exchange organ, for example, lungs or gills

ventricles chambers of the heart that contract to force blood out of the heart

viruses small pathogens that cause diseases in every type of living organism

volume the amount of space that a substance or object occupies

wave speed the distance travelled per second by a wave crest or trough

wavefront a line along the points on a wave that all have the same amplitude and direction of vibration at the same time (e.g., the crest of a water wave)

wavelength the distance from one wave crest to the next

white blood cells blood cells involved in the immune system of the body. They engulf pathogens and make antibodies and antitoxins.

white light visible light that includes all the colours of the spectrum

xylem the non-living transport tissue in plants that transports water from the roots to the leaves and shoots

zygote the single new cell formed by the fusion of gametes in sexual reproduction

Index

abiotic factors 236–237
absorption tests 170–171
accuracy 307–308
acid rain 222
active transport 44–45, 92
activity, radiation 168–169
adaptations
    exchange surfaces 81
    phloem 105
    photosynthesis 104
    xylem 104–105
adrenal glands/adrenaline 99, 101
adult stem cells 49, 198–199
aerobic digestion 228–229
aerobic respiration 76–77
agriculture 108–109, 118–119, 121, 128–129, 250–252
AIDS 182–183
alcohol consumption 140–141
algae 35
alleles 258–263, 264–267
alpha radiation 23, 72–73, 164–166, 170, 172
alveoli 81, 82, 89
amino acids 91, 93, 115
ammonia 209
amplitude 56, 58–59
amylase 93
anaerobic digestion 228–229
anaerobic respiration 78–79
angle of incidence 60–61
animal cells
    aerobic respiration 76–77
    anaerobic respiration 78–79
    differentiation 48–49
    osmosis 41
    structure 34
animals
    competition 238–239
    genetic modification 194–195, 202–203
    selective breeding 274–275
anomalies 311
antibiotic-resistant bacteria 270–271
antibiotics 190–191, 270–271
antibodies 187
antiseptics 180–181
antitoxins 187
aorta 86
arcs, reflexes 96–97
area 39, 303–304
arteries 84–86, 142–143
artificial hearts 145
artificial pacemakers 87
artificial selection 274–279
asexual reproduction 51, 178
atmosphere 206–231
    carbon cycle 212–213
    carbon dioxide 206–217
    composition 209
    decay cycle 210–211
    evolution 208–209
    greenhouse effect 214–217
    history 206–207
    oxygen 206–207, 209, 210

pollutants 222–223
potable water 226–227
recycling 210–213
sewage treatment 228–229
water cycle 224–225
atomic numbers 24, 26–27, 166–167
atoms
    electrons 22–23, 28–29, 66, 162–163, 166–167, 171
    radiation 162–167
    scientific models 22–23, 72–73
    sizes 26
    structure 22–31, 72–73
    sub-atomic particles 24–29, 72–73
atria 86
averages 111, 242, 293–294, 297–298, 309

background radiation 170, 172–173
bacteria 36–37, 67, 178–181, 190–191, 194, 211
    antibiotic resistance 270–271
    genetic modification 194, 276
bar charts 294–295, 309
benign tumours 174
beta radiation 164–167, 170–172
binary fission 178
binomial system 273
bioaccumulation 250–251
biodiversity 244–249, 252
biofuels 220
biosynthesis 115
biotic factors 237–241
blood 82–86, 148–151
blood vessels 84–86
boiling 4, 10–11, 16–19
bonds, strength 12
boundaries, refraction 61
brain damage 140
breathing 81–82, 88–89
breeding
    programs 252
    selective 274–275
bypass operations 142–143

Campylobacter 184
cancer 67–69, 171–175, 283
capillaries 84
carbohydrates 90, 93, 105
carbon 27, 208, 210–213
carbon capture and storage 221
carbon cycle 212–213
carbon dioxide 76–79, 89, 220–221, 237, 248–249
    atmospheric 206–217
    emissions 220, 253
    greenhouse effect 214–215
    photosynthesis 114, 116, 118–119
carbon footprints 220–221
carbon monoxide 136, 222–223
carbon sinks 212, 248–249
carcinogens 137, 141, 171–175
carrier waves 64–65
categoric variables 305

causal mechanisms 135
causes of cancer 174–175
cell cycle 46–47
cell membranes 34–35
cells 32–53
    active transport 44–45
    aerobic respiration 76–77
    anaerobic respiration 78–79
    animal 34, 41, 48–49, 76–79
    differentiation 48–49, 108–109
    diffusion 38–39, 80–81, 104
    division 46–51, 178
    eukaryotic 36–37, 46–51
    meiosis 50–51
    mitochondria 77
    mitosis 46–47
    osmosis 40–43, 104
    plants 34–35, 42–43, 76–77, 104–105, 108–109, 117, 122–124
    prokaryotic 36–37, 67, 178–181, 190–191, 194, 211, 270–271, 276
    sizes 37
    stem 48–49, 196–199
cellulose 35, 115
cell walls 35
central nervous system (CNS) 94–95
cervical cancer 175
changes of state 4–5, 10–11, 16–19
charge-coupled devices 68
chemical properties 27
chemotherapy 175
chlorophyll 35, 104, 114, 117, 122–124
chloroplasts 35
chromatography 122–125
chromosomes 34, 36, 46–47, 50–51, 256–257
classification systems 272–273
climate change 215–216, 218–219, 220–221, 248–249
clinical trials 192–193
cloning 108–109
clotting 83
combustion 213, 222–223
communicable (infectious) diseases 132, 178–191
    antibiotics 190–191, 270–271
    bacterial 184–185, 190–191
    defences 186–187
    pathogenesis 178–179
    prevention 180–181, 188–189
    spread 179
    vaccination 180–181, 188–189
    viruses 120, 174–175, 178–183
communications 64–65
communities 232, 236–241
companion cells 105
competition 237–241
complex carbohydrates 90
composition of the atmosphere 209
concentration gradients 38–39, 80–81, 88–89, 92
condensation 223–224
conservation of mass 11
consumers 234

Index

contamination 172–173, 250
continuous variables 305
contraception 156–157
contrast medium 68
control systems 146–151
coordination centres 147
coronary arteries 86
coronary heart disease 142–145
correlation 135, 298–299
count rates 168
crops 121, 128–129, 277–279
crude oil 208
cytoplasm 34–35, 41–43

data collection 301
data presentation 309
DDT 250–251
decay cycle 210–211
decimal form 288
decomposers 210–211
deforestation 215, 248–249, 253
denaturing 91
density 6–7
dependent variables 301, 306
desalination 227
detritivores 211
diabetes 139, 149–151, 196
diesel 223
diet 90–93, 138
differentiation 48–49, 108–109, 196–199
diffusion 38–39, 80–81, 104
digestive system 92–93, 186
direct proportion 260, 310
diseases 178–201
    antibiotics 190–191, 270–271
    causes 132
    communicable 132, 178–191
    genome sequencing 282–283
    human defences 186–187
    interactions 133
    medicines 190–199, 202–203
    non-communicable 132–145, 149–151, 174–175, 194–199
    pathogens 178–185
    plants 120–121, 128–129
    prevention 180–181
    risk factors 134
    stem cell medicine 196–199
    vaccination 180–181, 188–189
distillation 224
division
    meiosis 50–51
    mitosis 46–47, 108–109
DNA (deoxyribonucleic acid) 256
    bacteria 36
    eukaryotic cells 36, 46–51
    genome sequencing 282–283
    meiosis 50–51
    mutation 264
    profiling 282
dog breeding 274–275
dominant alleles 258–261
donors 144
doses of radiation 68–69, 172–173

double-blind trials 193
double circulation 85
Dutch elm disease 128–129

ecosystems 232–255
    abiotic factors 236–237
    biodiversity 244–249, 252
    biotic factors 237–241
    competition 238–241
    deforestation 248–249, 252
    feeding relationships 234–235
    field investigations 242–243
    habitats 218, 244, 252
    organisation 232–233
    positive impacts 252–253
effectors 94–97, 147
effluent 228–229
eggs 50–51, 98–99, 152–155, 158
electromagnetic waves 54–55, 58–69
    absorption 162–163
    communications 64–65
    energy 163
    gamma rays 66–67, 164–167, 170–172
    inverse square law 117
    matter interactions 215
    speed 58–59
electronic structure 28–29
electron microscopes 32
electrons 22–23, 28–29, 66, 162–163, 166–167, 171
electrostatic force 162
embryonic stem cells 48, 196–199
embryos 48
emission
    electromagnetic radiation 163
    radioactive 166–167
endangered species 248–249, 252
endocrine system 98–101
endothermic reactions 114
energy
    atoms 162–163
    changes of state 10–11
    ecosystems 232–233
    efficiency 220
    frequency 59, 163
    respiration 76–79
    specific heat capacity 14–15
    waves 56–57, 59, 66–67
energy levels of electrons 23, 28–29, 162–163
environment
    biodiversity 244–249
    climate change 248–249, 253
    deforestation 248–249, 252
    ecosystems 232–255
    transpiration 112
    variation 262–263
environmental isolation 267
enzymes 92–93
errors 308–309
estimation 111, 173, 292, 299, 310–311
ethics 198–199, 202–203, 278–279
eukaryotic cells 36–37, 46–51
evaporation 110–113, 223–224
evolution 264–271
exchange surfaces 80–81

exercise 138
exothermic reactions 76
extreme weather events 218

fair tests 307
family trees 261
farming 250–252
    cloning 108–109
    fungal diseases 121, 128–129
    GM crops 277–279
    greenhouses 118–119
    selective breeding 274–275
fatigue 78–79
fatty acids 90–91
feedback 100–101
feeding relationships 234–235
females 152–155
fertilisation 50–51, 158–159
fertilisers 247
fertility 153–159
field investigations 242–243
field margins 252
fingerprinting, DNA 282
fitness 79
flaccid cells 42
follicle stimulating hormone 98–99, 153–155
food
    chemistry 90–91
    digestion 92–93
    ecosystems 234–235, 237–238
    genetic engineering 277–279
    poisoning 184
forensics 282
forests 215, 221, 248–249, 253
formulations 190–191
fossil fuels 222–223
fossils 268–270
fractions 290
freezing 4
frequency 56, 59, 61, 163
frequency tables 294–295
freshwater 226–227
fungi 121, 128–129, 211
fusion, specific latent heat of 16

gametes 49, 50–51, 152–155, 158
gamma radiation 66–67, 164–167, 170–172
gases 4–5, 8–13
    atmosphere 206–217
    atmospheric composition 209
    internal energy 13
    pressure 8–9
gas exchange 39, 81, 82, 88–89
Geiger counters 164, 168–169
genes 34, 256–261, 264–267
genetically modified (GM) crops 277–279
genetic crosses 259
genetic engineering 194–195, 202–203, 276–279
genetics 256–283
    artificial selection 274–279
    classification systems 272–273
    DNA profiling 282
    evolution 264–267
    genome sequencing 282–283

319

Index

inheritance 258–261
natural selection 264–267
selective breeding 274–275
sex determination 261
speciation 266–267
variation 262–263, 270–271
genomes 256–257, 282–283
genome sequencing 282–283
genotypes 258–267, 282–283
genus 273
geographical isolation 267
geometry 303–304
glands 98–101
global warming 213–217
glucagon 148–149
glucose 44–45, 76–78, 98–99, 114–115, 148–151
glycerol 90–91
gonorrhoea 185
gradients of graphs 302
greenhouse effect/gases 214–217, 220–221
greenhouses 118–119
guard cells 110, 112
gut 92–93

habitats 218, 244, 252
haemoglobin 82
hair cells 104
half-life 168–169
hazards of radiation 172–173
health
    interactions 133
    lifestyle 132–141
    see also diseases
hearts 86–87, 137, 142–145
heat
    atoms 162
    changes of state 4–5
    greenhouse effect 214–217
    specific capacity 14–15
    specific latent 16–17
hedgerows 252
herbicides 250
herd immunity 189
heterozygotes 258–261
histograms 295
HIV 182–183
homeostasis 146–151
homozygotes 258–261
hormones 98–101, 139, 148–156, 196
horses 270
human papilloma virus 174–175
humans
    aerobic respiration 76–77
    anaerobic respiration 78–79
    biodiversity effects 246–249
    blood 82–89
    contraception 156–157
    diabetes 139, 149–151, 196
    digestion 92–93
    double circulation 85
    exchange surfaces 80–81
    hearts 86–87, 137, 142–145
    hormones 98–101, 139, 148–156, 196
    immunity 186–187

infertility treatment 158–159
menstrual cycle 152–155
nervous system 94–97
organs 81–82, 86–89, 92–93, 98–101, 150–155, 196
oxygen debt 78–79
puberty 152–153
reflexes 96–97
reproduction 152–159
transport systems 76–103
ventilation 81, 88–89
hydrogen 72
hygiene 180–181
hypertonic/hypotonic 40–43
hypothesis 306

ice, melting 16
immune system 187
immunity
    transplants 144–145
    vaccination 180–181, 188–189
immunosuppressant drugs 145
impacts of climate change 218–219
impulses 94–97
impurities 19
inbreeding 275
incomplete combustion 222
independent variables 301, 306
industrial waste 247
infectious diseases 132, 178–191
    see also communicable diseases
infrared radiation 62, 214–217
inheritance
    artificial selection 274–279
    DNA 256
    genetic engineering 276–279
    genomes 256–257
    mechanisms 258–261
    natural selection 264–267
    selective breeding 274–275
    sex determination 261
    speciation 266–267
    variation 262–264
insulin 98–99, 148–151, 196
intensity, inverse square law 117
internal energy 12–13
interspecific competition 237–241
intestines 92–93
intrauterine devices 157
inverse square law 117
investigations 306–311
in vitro fertilisation 158–159
ionisation 67, 171
ionising radiation 66–69, 134, 141, 171–173
irradiation 172
isolation 267
isotonic solutions 41, 42
isotopes 27, 165–169

kidneys 93, 99, 101
kinetic energy 8
kingdoms 272–273

lactic acid 78–79
landfill 253

land pollution 250
large intestine 92–93
latent heat 10–11, 16–17
lead 68
leaves 81, 104–105, 106–107, 110–113
leukaemia 196
levels of hazard 172–173
lifestyle 132–141, 179
light 58, 62, 117
    see also electromagnetic waves; waves
lignin 105
limestone 213
limiting factors 116, 118–119
line of best fit 298–299, 301–302, 309–310
line graphs 301–302, 309–310
lipases 93
lipids 90–91, 93, 115, 142–143
liquids 4–7, 10–13
livers 92–93, 140
longitudinal waves 54–55
lungs 81, 82, 88–89
luteinising hormone 153–155

magnification 32–33
male puberty 153
malignant tumours 174
Malpeque Bay, Canada 265
mass
    conservation 11
    numbers 24–27, 166–167
mathematical symbols 300
matter
    atomic structure 22–31, 72–73
    changes of state 4–5, 10–11, 16–19
    density 6–7
    electromagnetic wave interactions 60–61, 215
    internal energy 13
    kinetic theory 5, 8–9
    particle model 4–9, 12–13, 72–73
    purity 18–19
    specific heat capacity 14–15
    specific latent heat 16–17
    states of 4–21
    sub-atomic particles 22–29, 72–73
mean 111, 242, 293–294, 309
measles 182
measurement 308
mechanical waves 54–55
median 297
medicine
    cancer 67, 69
    coronary 142–145
    gamma rays 67
    genetic modification 194–195, 202–203
    stem cells 196–199
    testing and development 192–193
    X-rays 68–69
medium 54
meiosis 50–51
melting points 10–11, 16–19
membranes
    active transport 44–45
    cells 34–35

Index

diffusion 38–39, 80–81, 104
osmosis 40–43, 104
menopause 153
menstrual cycle 152–155
meristems 106, 108–109
metabolic rate 100–101
methane 209, 221
microorganisms
decay cycle 211
see also bacteria; fungi
microscopes 32–33
microwaves 58, 63, 64
mineral ions 44–45, 104, 105, 236, 250–251
mitigation of climate change 220–221
mitochondria 34–35, 77, 104–105
mitosis 46–47, 108–109
mixing, diffusion 38
mixtures 18–19, 122–125, 190–191
mobile phase 123–125
mobile phones 64–65
mode 297–298
modulation of carrier waves 65
molecule sizes 26
motor neurones 94–97
muscle fatigue 78–79
mutations 174, 264–267, 270–271

nanometres 26
natural selection 264–267
negative feedback 100–101
nerves 94–97, 196–197
nervous system 94–97
neurones 94–97
neutrons 23–27, 73, 165–167
nicotine 136
nitrates 250–251
nitrogen oxides 222–223
non-communicable diseases 132, 134–145, 174–175, 194–199
nuclear power 250
nuclei
atoms 23–27, 72–73, 165–167
cells 34–35, 46–47, 50

obesity 138–139
oestrogen 98–99, 152–156
oil, crude 208
optical fibres 65
order of magnitude 299
organisms, classification systems 272–273
organs
humans 81–82, 86–89, 92–93, 98–101, 150–155, 196
plants 106–107
stem cell medicine 196–199
transplants 144–145, 150–151
organ systems 85–86, 92–101, 107
oscillations 55, 65
osmosis 40–43, 104
ova 50–51, 152–155, 158
ovaries 98–99, 152–155
ovulation 152–155, 158
oxygen 82, 89, 237

atmospheric 206–207, 209, 210
debt 78–79
photosynthesis 114
oysters 265

pacemakers 87
pancreases 92–93, 99, 150–151, 196
parasites 237
partial reflection 60
particle model 4–9, 12–13, 72–73
particles
gases 8–9, 13
liquids 13
random motion 9
solids 12–13
sub-atomic 22–29, 72–73
particulates 223
pasteurisation 184
pathogens 178–185, 237, 270–271
peat bogs 249
peer review 173, 193
penetrating power 170–171
percentages 291
percolation 224
period of waves 56
permanent vacuoles 35, 42–43, 104
pesticides 250–251
pH, ecosystems 236
phagocytosis 187
phenotypes 258–259, 262–264
phloem 105–107
photosynthesis 35, 104, 114–119, 212
phylogeny 272–273
pig organs 195, 202–203
pituitary gland 98–101
plants
cells 34–35, 42–43, 76–77, 104–105, 108–109
cloning 108–109
competition 240–241
diseases 120–121, 128–129
genetic engineering 277–279
greenhouses 118–119
leaves 81, 104–105, 106–107, 110–113
meristems 106, 108–109
photosynthesis 114–119
as producers 210
roots 44–45, 104, 106–107
seed dispersal 241
tissues and organs 106–107
transpiration 110–113
transport 104–113, 120–121
plasma 82–83
plasmids 276
plasmolysis 42–43
platelets 83
plotting graphs 302
pollution 222–223, 250–251
populations 242–243, 246–247, 296
positive impacts on ecosystems 252–253
potometers 113
precipitation 219, 224
precision 307–308
preclinical testing 192
predators 235, 237

pregnancy 136, 141, 156–157, 158–159
pressure, gases 8–9
prey 235
primary consumers 234
probability 296–297
producers 234
progesterone 153–156
prokaryotic cells 36–37
properties of waves 56–57
proteases 93
proteins 91, 93
protons 23–27, 72–73, 166
puberty 152–153
pulmonary arteries/veins 86
Punnett squares 259–261
pure substances 18–19
purification 224, 226–227

quadrats 242–243
quantitative sampling 242–243
quarks 72–73

radiation/radioactivity 27, 66–69, 162–173
atoms 162–167
background 170, 172–173
discovery 164
doses 68–69, 172–173
half-life 168–169
hazards 172–173
ionising 67, 134, 141, 171–173
nuclear changes 166–167
nuclei 165–167
penetrating power 170–171
radiographs 68
radiotherapy 175
radio waves 58, 63–64
rainfall 219, 224
rainforests 248–249
randomness 9, 169
rates of
diffusion 38–39
photosynthesis 116–119
transpiration 112–113
ratios 260, 290
reaction times 95
receptors 94–97, 147
recessive alleles 259–261
recycling 210–213, 220, 253
red blood cells 82
reflection 60–61
reflexes 96–97
refraction 60–61
regeneration of
habitats 252
nerves 196–197
renewable energy 220
repeatable data 216, 305–306
reproducible data 216, 306
reproduction
asexual 51, 178
contraception
fertility trea
humans
sexu

resolving power 33
resources 247, 253
respiration 44, 76–79, 115, 212, 224
respiratory system 81–82, 88, 186
retention factors 125
ribosomes 34–35
risks
    diseases 134
    estimation 173
roots 44–45, 104, 106–107
rose black spot disease 121

Salmonella 184
sampling 111, 242–243, 296
scatter diagrams 298–299, 309
scattering of alpha particles 72–73
scientific naming 272–273
sea levels 218
secondary consumers 234
sedimentary rocks 208
seed dispersal 241
selective breeding 274–275
Semmelweis, Ignaz 180
sensory neurones 94–97
sewage treatment 228–229, 247
sex determination 261
sex hormones 98–99
sexually transmitted diseases 182–183, 185
sexual reproduction 50–51, 152–159
shells, electrons 23, 28–29, 162–163
sieve plates 105
sieverts 172–173
significant figures 293
simple sugars 90
sinks of carbon 212, 248–249
sizes
    atoms and molecules 26
    cells 37
    populations 242–243, 246–247
skin 186
small intestine 92–93
smog 222
smoke cells 9
smoking 136–137
solids 4–7, 10–13
solving equations 300–301
sound 54–55
speciation 266–267
specific heat capacity 14–15
specific latent heat 16–17
speed of waves 56–57, 58–59, 60
sperm 49, 50
spores 121
standard form 288–289
starch 115
states
    changes of 4–5, 10–11, 16–19
    of matter 4–21
statins 143
stationary phase 123–125
stem cells 48–49, 196–199
stems 106–107
stents 142–143

stimuli 147
stomach 92–93
stomata 81, 110, 112
storage heaters 15
straight line graphs 301–302, 309–310
sub-atomic particles 22–29, 72–73
    atomic structure 22–23, 72–73
    electrons 22–23, 28–29, 66, 162–163, 166–167
    elements 24–27
    isotopes 27
sublimation 4, 11
sugars 90, 93, 105
sulfur dioxide 222–223
surface area 39, 80–81, 303–304
synapses 96–97

temperature
    atoms 162
    diffusion 39
    gas pressure 8–9
    greenhouse effect 214–219
    photosynthesis 116
    specific heat capacity 14–15
    transpiration 112
territory 239
tertiary consumers 234
testes 98–99
testosterone 153
therapeutic cloning 198
thickness monitoring 170–171
thyroid gland 98–101
thyroxine 100–101
tissues of plants 106–107
tobacco mosaic virus 120
toxins 250–251
transects 243
translocation 105
transmission
    communications 64–65
    pathogens 179
    waves 60–61
transpiration 110–113, 224
transplants 144–145, 150–151, 195, 202–203
transport
    active 44–45, 92
    blood 82–89
    diffusion 38–39, 80–81, 104
    digestion 92–93
    diseases 120
    human body 76–103
    osmosis 40–43, 104
    plants 104–113, 120–121
transverse waves 55, 58–69
trees 128–129, 215, 221, 248–249, 253
trigonometry 303–304
tumours 67, 69, 174
turgor 35, 42–43

ultraviolet waves 66
uncertainty 310–311
urea 82, 93
uterus 152–155

vaccination 180–181, 188–189
vacuoles 35, 42–43, 104
valid data 216
valve replacement 142–143
vaporisation 4, 10–11, 16–19
variables 301, 305–307
variation
    inheritance 51, 262–264
    selective breeding 275
    speciation 266–267
vectors 276–277
veins 84–85
vena cava 86
ventilation 81–82, 88–89
viruses 120, 174–175, 178–183
visible light 58, 62
volume 6–7, 80–81, 304

waste
    landfill 253
    management 247
    water 228–229
water 11
    changes of state 11, 16–17
    climate change 219
    cycle 224–225
    distillation 224
    ecosystems 236
    osmosis 40–43, 104
    photosynthesis 114
    pollution 250–251
    potable 226–227
    purification 224, 226–227
    transpiration 110–113
    waste 228–229
wavefronts 60–61
wavelength 56–57, 61, 64
waves 54–71
    carrier 64–65
    electromagnetic 54–55, 58–69
    energy 66–67
    gamma rays 66–67, 164–167, 170–172
    inverse square law 117
    longitudinal 54–55
    properties 56–57
    reflection/refraction 60–61
    speed 56–57, 58–59, 60
    substances 60–61
    transverse 55, 58–69
    ultraviolet 66
    X-rays 66, 68–69
weight, disease 138–139
white blood cells 83
white light 62
wilting 42–43
working scientifically 305–311

X-rays 58, 66, 68–69
xylem 104–107

zygotes 196

Appendix: Physics equations

You should be able to remember and apply the following equations, using SI units, for your assessments.

Word equation	Symbol equation
wave speed = frequency × wavelength	$v = f\lambda$
density = $\dfrac{\text{mass}}{\text{volume}}$	$\rho = \dfrac{m}{V}$

You should be able to select and apply the following equations from the Physics equations sheet.

Word equation	Symbol equation
period = $\dfrac{1}{\text{frequency}}$	
thermal energy for a change of state = mass × specific latent heat	$E = mL$